SHARPEST

Volumes 1 & 2

**THE BIOGRAPHY OF
MARTIN SHARP AS TOLD TO LOWELL TARLING**

ETT IMPRINT
EXILE BAY

First published by ETT Imprint, Exile Bay 2021

SHARP (Volume 1) first published in 2016 by ETT Imprint

SHARPER (Volume 2) first published in 2017 by ETT Imprint

This book is copyright. Apart from any fair dealing for the purposes of private study, research, criticism or review, as permitted under the Copyright Act, no part may be reproduced by any process without written permission. Inquiries should be addressed to the publishers.

ETT IMPRINT
PO Box R1906
Royal Exchange NSW 1225
Australia

Copyright © Lowell Tarling 2016, 2017, 2021

ISBN 978-1-922473-68-4 (paper)
ISBN 978-1-922473-67-7 (ebook)

Design by Hanna Gotlieb and Tom Thompson

SHARP

Road to Abraxas

Part One: 1942-1979

THE BIOGRAPHY OF
MARTIN SHARP AS TOLD TO
LOWELL TARLING

ETT IMPRINT
EXILE BAY

Christ is more of an artist than the artists — he works in living spirit and flesh, he makes men instead of statues.

Vincent van Gogh
Letter to Emile Bernard, 27 June 1888

THANKS

The first and greatest thanks to Martin, whose cooperation and assistance made this book possible.

Secondly, I would like to thank my family: Amber, Joel and Zoë, and especially my wife Robbie who urged me to transcribe my taped interviews, pushed me to write this book, listened to every draft chapter and made innumerable editorial suggestions.

Thanks to Tom Thompson who made this production possible.

Thanks and gratitude to the following people, most of whom agreed to be interviewed on tape and many of whom contributed in other ways too:

Jim Anderson, Mic Conway, Melody Cooper, Peter Draffin, Roger Foley-Fogg, Susan Jensen, Sebastian Jorgensen, Marilyn Karet, Peter Kingston, Jeannie Lewis, Jon Lewis, Tim Lewis, Lex Marinos, Ted Markstein, Philippe Mora, Richard Neville, Michael Organ, Mal Ramage, Adrian Rawlins, Ian Reid, Peter Royles, Alexander (Sandy) Sharp, Roslyn Sharp, Russell Sharp, Garry Shead, Gary Shearston, Clayton Simms, Max Skeen, Tiny Tim, William Yang, Greg Weight.

And to all those who I have not mentioned by name, who spoke with me and emailed me, whose words and ideas I have used, my heartfelt thanks.

TABLE OF CONTENTS

1

1. The Little Prince 4
2. Art Father 17
3. Arty Wild Boys 30
4. OZ is a New Magazine 46
5. OZ Trial – London Calling 57
6. Fresher Cream 75
7. Art of Pop 93
8. Muybridge, Vincent & Tiny 107
9. Art About Art 121
10. Underground Meets the Underworld 133
11. The Yellow House 149
12. Yesterday's Papers 168
13. Counterculture Goes Mainstream 183
14. Out & About in Paris & London 198
15. Preparing for Tiny 207
16. Kold Komfort 223
17. Street of Dreams 233
18. Revenge of the Clowning Calaveras 246
Notes 260
Index 524

1.

THE LITTLE PRINCE

Finger painting, I remember doing that.
Miss Koulson was very good, my first art teacher.
MARTIN SHARP

Martin Ritchie Sharp was born in Sydney, 21 January 1942, the day of the first Japanese air strike on Rabaul, Papua & New Guinea. His first home was his Ritchie grandparents' place, Wirian, 3 Victoria Road Bellevue Hill.

For the duration of the war, Martin's father, Dr Henry Sharp had been assigned to the Medical Branch of the RAAF with the rank of Flight Lieutenant. At the time of Martin's birth, he was working on the RAAF Recruiting Train, which carried staff to deal with enlistments for the war effort. On hearing the joyous news, Henry hurried home the next day to welcome his newborn son. (1)

Within six months, Henry was shipped overseas where he joined the Spitfire Squadron 453, an Australian air control unit of the RAAF in England. (2) Martin said, 'He loved those years but the worst thing was having to examine the pilots and give them a health clearance. It's like writing a death warrant. The average age was 22 and he knew that 45 per cent of the time he'd never see them again.' (3)

That was Henry's life for the next three and a half years while his wife Joan (Jo) and son Martin were living an extremely comfortable life back home. Their only indication of World War 2 was the night of 31 May when three Japanese midget submarines entered Sydney Harbour and attempted to sink Allied warships. (4) Wirian has distant harbour views from the first floor verandah. Jo took baby Martin upstairs and watched the action like fireworks. She later told him the bombardments shook the house. Too young to comprehend those 'fireworks', Martin has a clearer memory of wartime double-decker buses painted in camouflage colours.

Martin spent his first three years in the company of his mother, grandparents Stuart and Vega Ritchie and their home-helps - cook, maid, gardener-chauffeur and Martin's 19-year old nanny Roma Leonard ('Nursy'). These were the most significant adults in Martin's early life. (5)

The Ritchie surname appears in both Martin's mother and his father's family. They are not connected. His mother's Ritchie line is Scottish, his father's is Irish. The Northern Irish Ritchies established in Bega NSW in the 1850s. Whereas from his mother's Scottish line, Martin's great-grandfather James Ritchie and brother, came to Australia with enough funds to start a tool-making business, making ploughs and farm equipment. The Ritchie Bros succeeded very quickly. In 1900 James Ritchie purchased a superb property called Telford, with absolute water frontage at the Royal National Park, Port Hacking.

After James' passing, his only son Stuart inherited everything and Stuart always improved massively on everything he touched. He transformed Telford into a grand residence and expanded Ritchie Bros into a major manufacturing and engineering firm. Located at Auburn, he built rails and carriages for NSW Rail. BHP was among Stuart's directorships (Commonwealth Steel Newcastle). It provided one-third of the Trans-Australia rail lines across the Nullabor and a quarter of the steel used to erect the Sydney Harbour Bridge.

After his marriage to Vega (Vee) Kopson, a Swedish-Australian, Stuart and Vee settled in 105 The Boulevarde Strathfield where Martin's mother

Joan (b. 1915) was raised and schooled at the local Meridan Girls College. Shortly before the Second World War, Stuart bought Wirian (3 Victoria Road, Bellevue Hill) located next door to Cranbrook School, which Martin and many Sharp relatives attended.

Says Martin, 'I'm not sure what Wirian means. The closest I've got is David Gulpilil - the wonderful actor - said it was the name of the tribe that lived around here. The house was built in 1920 and my grandparents and my mother moved here in 1937. I grew up there as a baby during the Second World War.' (6)

Henry returned from the war in 1945. Jo had married a doctor but a Flight-Lieutenant came home. Martin recalls, 'I remember the day he came back. I was about 3½. He was lying on the floor. He and my mother were loving and cooing while I was wondering, "Who's this guy? He's a bit fat. He's got hairy underarms…" (that sort of thing). Anyway, he was my Dad!

'When my father came back he didn't really connect with me. I think my mother knew him well but I didn't know who he was and in a strange way he never changed much from that person. He was always with adults and found it difficult dealing with children. He didn't like me as a baby. I don't get that feeling – he holds me up in a picture and sniffs my bottom. My mother said, "your father never liked children".

'My mother would've loved more children but she got sick. She got a staphylococcal throat. He came back from the war with something that infected her. So I think the war indirectly poisoned her health.' (7)

But the lounge parties continued – attended by socialites and sometimes celebrities. 'Cocktail parties were it,' says Martin. 'You never had such civilized, lovely people. The jabber of voices, the drinks, someone at the piano playing, it was a lovely thing but you'd never get the idea they'd been to a war and lost half their friends. You can imagine coming from the Battle of Britain to Bellevue Hill and trying to get back into civilian life!' (8)

On his return, Henry served in the RAAF section of Concord Hospital and later as Deputy Principal Medical Officer Eastern Area, NSW. In 1945-1946 he went away again, to serve as Principal Medical Officer in South Australia. His enlistment had committed him to a further 12 months after the end of the war.

Also back from the war was a group of artists who became known as the Merioola group. Merioola was a colonial mansion-cum-boarding house on Edgecliff Road Edgecliff, walking distance from Wirian. It was managed by Melbourne chatelaine Chica Lowe who encouraged artists, dancers, writers and theatre people to take up residence and form an artistic community. Artists included Donald Friend, Margaret Olley, Harry Tatlock Miller, Arthur Fleischmann and Justin O'Brien.

Jo knew Justin from the days when she had enrolled at the Julian Ashton Art School. She rekindled those art contacts while Henry was in South Australia. (9)

Henry came home proper in 1946 and stayed put, having served for the duration of the war plus the requisite 12 months. For the married couple, Grandfather Stuart purchased 25 Cranbrook Lane, Bellevue Hill, who moved in with 4-year old Martin. Henry returned to General Practice and started his academic work in dermatology, studying late in the room next to Martin's bedroom.

Martin recalls their family unit of three, plus maid and a nanny, 'When Dad came back there was a maid called Francis who he'd inherited from his Bega relatives. She was very old. My mother didn't like having her there. She couldn't eat her food. She used to spoon it into all the pewter jugs that were around, which was all right until the mould came out. Francis found the food had been dumped while my mother was getting thinner and thinner!'

Henry played his part in family life, enjoying cocktail parties and family get-togethers where Martin says, 'Henry loved playing piano badly, singing music hall and Gilbert & Sullivan songs'. He bought a beautiful

AWA walnut veneer radiogram to play his 78 records. He also made home movies and bought a sloop, Epacris.

Martin's paternal grandfather, Dr Walter Ramsay Sharp was a leader in his church community, an Alderman on the Vaucluse Council and an outstanding doctor. He died three years before Martin was born, leaving his wife Elizabeth Mary Alexander (known as Bessie) an independent income, three properties (including a Sharp holiday home in Bowral) two beautiful daughters and three handsome sons - all doctors - over whom she had a controlling hand. Martin recalls, 'She was in some ways quite severe'.

From Bessie's five children – Henry, Alan & Katherine (twins), Frank and Elizabeth – came 16 Sharp grandchildren. Bessie made a point of treating all her grandchildren equally. Still, Martin was proud to be the firstborn son of Gay's firstborn son. Conversely, on his Ritchie side Martin had no cousins. He was the only grandchild. This drew him to his Mother's side, especially in his childhood. Martin explains, 'I was the child of Jo my mother and I had to be.

'Although my mother tried very well to make me happy, I didn't grow up in a happy home. My father was very good at some things, we used to go to Port Hacking when things were going well.' (10)

Martin often spent his days going for walks with Jo around the suburb. They would regularly call on his grandparents at Wirian. Jo was always smartly dressed. (11)

Martin's earliest pieces include a letter 'To Mrs Sharp' and a 'Happy Easter' message. He wrote the following story: 'I am a wild bird and this is my story. I was born in a nest, in a tree near a church. My mother a pretty brown bird was soon able to fly. It was a joy to stand on the roof, to turn in the…'.

Another piece was based on his mother's sketch. It read: 'That morning as the ship left port a rainbow was seen in the sky an hour later. And it grew so dark that it soon lost sight of the coast. We had not even passed the cape before the storm struck us. It was so sudden.'

'My mother got me my first paints', said Martin. 'In fact she kept my first drawing. It's in a letter she sent to my father, Martin's First Drawing. He replied, "It's an animal. I don't know what sort though..." (a comment like that). I think all kids like to draw - as soon as you get a pencil and a bit of paper! I was always encouraged by my mother.' (12)

But for his parents' deteriorating relationship, Martin would have enjoyed an idyllic childhood. Instead, the fights, separations and ensuing divorce became a core of unhappiness that Martin would bear all his life.

Forever after he would idealise his parents' courtship: how they met in 1937 on a P&O liner traveling to London when Jo accompanied her parents to the coronation of King George VI. She - the beautiful wealthy heiress and Henry the dashing ship's doctor. Martin would treasure his mother's letters, describing the shipboard romance, the sites of London, and their theme song, 'that certain night', A Nightingale Sang in Berkeley Square. (13)

Sadly, Henry and Jo's marriage 'didn't get going after the war', said Martin. 'They worked very hard at it. I blame it on Hitler rather than anything else. To be a doctor is a very tough job. My mother was very supportive, she did everything she could'. (14)

He clarified, 'I think they were very keen on each other when they were young. Even the early marriage was good enough until Dad went away. I think they were comfortable. They both regret they didn't get married at that time but they waited. Then it all goes into letters. Until I read the letters, I never had any idea of how keen they were on each other. I can't imagine it from what I knew of them. I never saw them "in love" really. (I did actually, but only briefly).

'I think it was pretty tight after the war. They never quite got back those three years. I reckon it was difficult from then on. I can remember them fighting – shouting, shouting, and my mother saying, "Not in front of the child!" but it didn't stop. I can remember that sentence amidst all of this'. (15)

Both parents struggled to make the marriage work and Martin's grandfather was determined that it must. Henry, somewhat awkwardly played the fatherly role - swimming and fishing with Martin, sometimes reciting him poems but usually he was not around or not available. Henry worked all day in his medical practice and closed himself away at night, studying for his Diploma in Dermatological Medicine.

Martin's response was to retreat into himself or spend time with his mother and Ritchie grandparents. He enjoyed his first trip to the cinema with Jo to see Disney's Pinocchio. She had no difficulty being a loving mother and dutiful wife. She embroidered and made collages cut from magazines. Martin copied her. He made collages and drew pictures, many of which were treasured by his grandparents and found amongst their effects some 50 years later. Throughout his life, Martin appropriated images that go back to when he was as young as six years old. Boofhead and Ginger Meggs are childhood references.

Privately, Stuart drew occasional cartoons, so from an early age Martin was well aware of his grandparents' love of cartoonists like Phil May and Livingstone (Hop) Hopkins. (16)

Says Martin, 'There was a real love of cartoons in this family. My grandparents used to cut out Daily Mirror strips of Nancy and they'd make a little book. They loved cartoons. Boofhead was their favorite comic character. (17)

'I even learned to read with comics!' says Martin who, after an interest in Disney, graduated to Superman. When he was nine, DC Comics teamed Superman with Orson Welles in a 'the Martians are coming' edition. This puzzled Martin because 'a real person had entered into the comic strip world'. (18)

'My grandmother was a very good artist in a Pop sort of way. She used to make comic strips up for me – cut the Boofhead comics out of The Sun when it came out, bind them into a comic book. I liked tin soldiers as well. I used to have tin soldiers. I got so cross once, an arm fell off or something. He wouldn't stand up. I got cross and threw him and then his leg and head fell off, I got crosser still.'

Grandmother Vega amused Martin by making figurines out of wishbones. 'I wish I had some of those, they were beautiful,' said Martin. 'She used to make me little toys. Their legs would be the wishbone with little feet. She'd build the body around. They'd all be beautifully dressed and hand-painted, bride and groom, all sorts of funny characters'.

Martin also loved the mascot screwed on the front of his grandfather's 1930 Cadillac car, a squat silver policeman figure with a brown enamel face and a funny smile. Later in life Martin tried to locate it. He did not succeed.

Jo kept a novelty collection in a glass trinket cabinet that was full of little things she had collected or that Henry had sent back in his travels. Among them was a funny little mouse with red pants and big black ears. Martin didn't know who it was but, because of the colour and shape, it really caught his attention. Martin said, 'It was the most interesting in the whole cabinet - which was full of wonderful things. I think perhaps it was the plastic and the colour. That led to my interest in Mickey Mouse. (19)

'I first noticed Mickey Mouse among adult things that don't appeal to children, because your eye's too simple as far as recognising images is concerned. There were many other china bits there but the bit I loved most was this little figure of Mickey Mouse, which was probably off a charm bracelet. It was plastic - red, black and white, very bright. Everything else was crafted and beautifully done. This was real Pop. And I responded to it. I didn't know it was Mickey Mouse at the time. I didn't know Mickey Mouse from anyone. But I responded to that. I was always interested in Mickey Mouse.' (20)

There were songs too. Martin loved Bing Crosby's take on the Christmas story, a 78 record called The Small One sung from the point of view of the donkey. (21)

In 1949 Martin registered at Cranbrook for 'day school'. (22) Sometimes he was chauffeur-driven to school in the Cadillac. And although Martin describes himself as 'shy', day school seemed to be okay.

About that shyness, Martin said, 'I think the extrovert as a child depends on the relationship with the parents. And because it actually wasn't good, I think I was fairly introverted at that stage. It's like there's a piano in the house, but it doesn't get played.'

Painting class was one highlight. Martin's first art teacher was Miss Koulson who he describes as 'very good'. He says, 'There's a dinosaur painting from those days - a pterodactyl. Kids all paint dinosaurs at that age. Finger painting, I remember doing that'. (23)

On his father's desk back home, Martin noticed binoculars capable of seeing a much bigger world, and also a microscope capable of seeing one that was much smaller. Martin would peer into both while his father was away. 'I probably messed up his slides', he added.

'We used to have a verandah room next to my bedroom and in it was a microscope because my father used to study slides. There was also a huge pair of Japanese binoculars Uncle Frank had brought back from New Guinea, the "prize of conquest". So I was looking at the microcosm and the macrocosm'.

Martin was also using the binoculars to spy nude women at their windows. He was horrified when he spotted one. It was not the goddess for which he had hoped.

Said Martin, 'No one gave me any sex education except my mother and her friend. Her friend had a farm and they took us down to watch the horses having it off. I thought, "God, how embarrassing, do they realise we're watching?" And their cocks were that big...! That was my education into the birds & the bees.'

Roma (Nursy) was the first woman Martin saw nude. He said, 'when she was bathing, I could be there. It was completely natural and there was no thought about it because I'd never experienced it before. She wasn't seducing me, she was just natural – educating me. She was like Justin

(Justin O'Brien – later art teacher), one of those figures in my life – a metaphysical family'.

But when Henry made a pass at Nursy, she had to go. Martin found this out later in life but at the time he saw no reason why his favourite should have to leave.

In 1949, the Blake Prize was established as an incentive 'to raise the standard of religious art'. It was named after the artist and poet William Blake. (24) In 1951 Justin O'Brien, a Merioola artist, now Art Teacher at Cranbrook, was the inaugural winner of the Blake Prize for Religious Art, and Jo took Martin to see it. It was the first art exhibition he attended. He would never forget it.

Neither would Martin forget the Vincent Van Gogh reproduction of The Artist on the Road to Tarascon that Jo purchased to decorate Henry's consulting rooms after he attained his Diploma of Dermatological Medicine in 1952. With the help of Jo's parents, Henry set up rooms in Macquarie Street. He later moved to Wyoming (also in Macquarie Street) where his father Ramsay Sharp previously had rooms. Says Martin, 'My grandparents Ritchie were right behind the relationship. They backed him of course, the husband of their only daughter'.

Martin said, 'I remember them having a fight once when I was very small. She'd cornered him a bit in their suite. My father belted me once when I interrupted them. He belted me a few times. Anyway, she had him cornered in that room. And with those binoculars she'd see him rowing some girl out to his boat. He loved sailing. She said, "that bloody boat!" He'd escaped her again! He was a free spirit really.' (25)

Martin also remembers the Hornby Double-O train set given him by Grandmother Vega. He feels it was really bought as a celebration of Stuart's career. The adults played with it more than Martin did. To accommodate the train set, Henry built a shelving unit in Martin's bedroom. Henry loved model trains. He'd bring his friends into Martin's room to show it off. 'Suddenly I found my room taken over almost with this huge train set!' said Martin. 'When my parents were fighting I'd set the trains to have a head-on collision!' (26)

The Sharp family had a holiday house in Shepherd Street Bowral. In the late-40s/early-50s Uncle Frank, Aunt Edith (known as Dinks), Phillip, Erica, Russell and Rozzie lived there for a time. Martin and his mother stayed at the Bowral house with Uncle Frank and his family during an early break in the marriage.

He recalled, 'It was when the bogon moths moved. I can remember vividly because my mother hated moths. She had the lights on, they were battering themselves against her, she was screaming and she was a bit sad. She thought it was an attack. Perhaps I can recognize the sadness there. I remember walking with her and picking blackberries, it was nice. But I only went there once.' (27)

Telford on Port Hacking was the Ritchie retreat. In 2002, Martin wrote about it as if being there was amongst the happiest times in his late childhood. Telford – bought by Martin's great-grandfather in 1900. Improved to a point of magnificence by his grandfather. Visited sometimes every weekend by Martin, his parents and grandparents. Later, with his father less and less.

Martin wrote, 'I am a boy and I'm sitting with my mother Jo on the rocks, to the right of the boatshed at Telford. It is afternoon, my mother is telling me that when I'm older we will come to Port Hacking for holidays. I don't remember the journey there, with my mother and my father Henry, and grandfather Stuart, or the house. But I remember the rock pools, the waves, the afternoon sun and Jo's words. There are so many memories but this is where they start.

'My childhood and young teenage years in those holidays at Telford were shared most especially with Jan and Ian Skinner. I have a good photo of Jan Skinner, their mother Ida and their pup. I don't remember his name now but I do remember him eating all the frogs Jan, Ian and I collected as youthful naturalists.

'The main house at Telford was a beautiful house. It's seen many happy family days from my great-grandfather's time to the courtship and marriage of my grandparents, and my own parents.'

He goes on to describe himself as 'such a shy kid' who was befriended by the Skinner family, caretakers of the premises, living in the smaller residence on the acreage. With the children Jan and Ian, Martin shared games, jokes and cups of tea. Whereas there was a distance and a sadness in the big house, there was a warmth in the Skinner household.

Martin writes, 'There was love in your family and your home, and I became a part of that love. The silence between my parents is not something one understands at the time. Their marriage was beginning to fall apart. One feels it, not knowing what it is that is missing.

'As a child I took all the beauty and graciousness of Telford for granted, like the air one breathes.' (28)

Port Hacking is where Martin learned to love the blue groper fish, an image he later used in his pictures. 'It used to stop my heart when I saw it. It was so majestic – this fish – it was huge. I was always trying to catch it but it was never interested in anything I had to offer. It wouldn't flap away like it was scared, it was a very slow and elegant pace.'

Martin recalls a moment where Jan took his hand as they walked behind her father. Martin was slightly younger than Jan. They were following her Dad who was checking a bushfire. About having his hand held Martin says, 'It must have been the first time anyone had. I was so shy. I didn't hang onto it. She let it go. The whole walk I had my hand so close to hers but she never took it again.'

Ian, Jan and Martin discovered Pop Music together at Port Hacking by playing Bing Crosby, Al Jolson and novelty songs on Jo's 78 record player. Recorded by Kay Kyser and His Band, Three Little Fishies seemed to encapsulate their experience of learning to swim and learning to live, with encouragement from the Mother Fish.

Johnny Ray was popular too, especially with Jo. Other favourites included Guy Mitchell's 1950 hit The Roving Kind and Danny Kaye's punchy rendition of I've Got A Loverly Bunch Of Coconuts.

Much later in life, these memories came flooding back when Tiny Tim drew his repertoire from the same songbook, regularly including songs like I've Got A Loverly Bunch Of Coconuts in his marathons. (29)

Said Martin, 'When I first saw him at the Albert Hall I was sort of primed in that way.' (30)

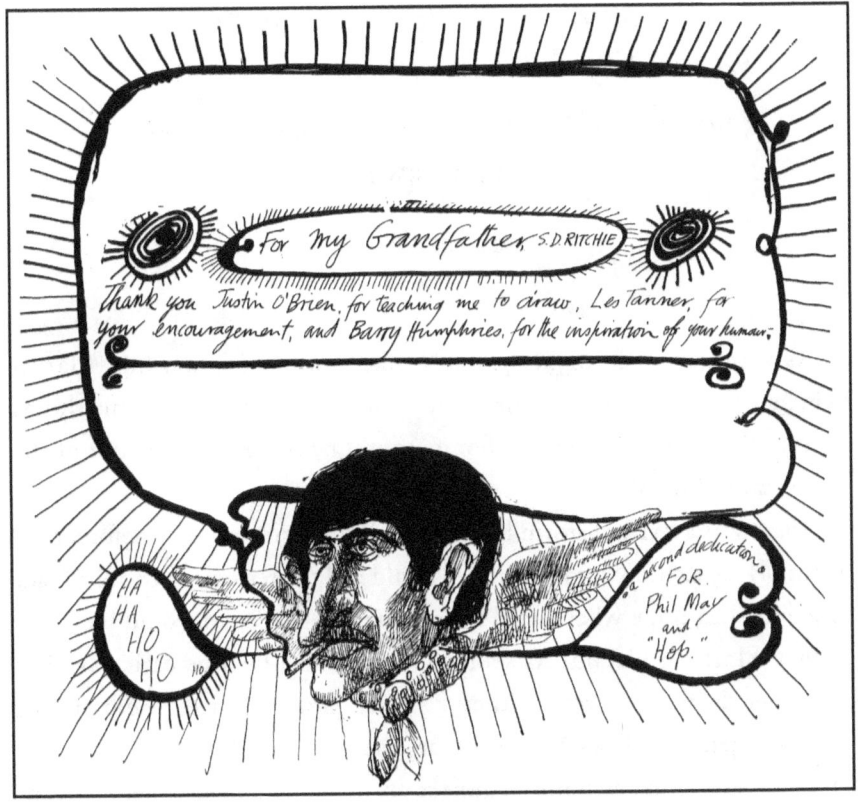

Title page of Martin Sharp Cartoons (Scripts 1966)

2.

ART FATHER

My parents took me out of Cranbrook because they didn't like those marks on my leg, hit by rulers, bruises and things like that.

TIM LEWIS

As a consequence of his parents' deteriorating relationship, Martin switched from dayboy to boarder at Cranbrook School. 'I think things were getting tight and tense at home, so it'd be better if I were out of the scene,' said Martin. (1)

There was a marital storm brewing and, if Martin was shy before, now he simply closed down. He recalls, 'I could feel the tension in the air: Dad, in the kitchen nook where we'd have breakfast. His head would be in the Sydney Morning Herald. As soon as he sat down he'd be eating behind the paper. It was as severe as that – silence. Stony silence. The marriage truly fell apart and I saw it years before the divorce'. (2)

Being aware of his family connection to the school in a general way, Martin was puzzled about specifics. He obviously knew his father Henry attended 1919-1927 as the second student to enroll. Honour Rolls were a constant reminder that Henry distinguished himself both academically and in sport. And Walter Ramsay Sharp – Martin's grandfather - was on the provisional committee that set up the school. With a sense of discovery Martin exclaimed, 'I'm in Cranbrook School for my father because his father was one of the founders!' (3)

Martin could not understand how his grandfather could be one of the actual founders without his name being listed? Staring at the Honour Roll, Martin could see the name Walter Ramsay Sh… almost scuffed off 'because it was the bottom one on the list'. Martin didn't comprehend the 'Ramsay' bit and he couldn't read 'Sharp'. He said, 'I wasn't sure if it was my grandfather because Ramsay Sharp wasn't a name that was used or even mentioned'. (4)

Walking distance from his parents' place and next door to his grandparents at Wirian, Martin became a boarder at the school. He was in for a rude shock. Australian high schools were cruel places in the 1950s. You couldn't get away from the brutality anywhere, not even at Cranbrook. Corporal punishment was not banned in New South Wales state schools until 1987 and not until 1995 in private schools. (5) Indeed it was encouraged in the 1950s. Everyone was familiar with the maxim, Spare the rod, spoil the child.

Attending the school from the age of eleven and a half to 17, Martin was caned 'plenty of times'. He said, 'I found it pretty tough. My housemaster told me that caning was good for a boy. They weren't allowed to kill you. That was about where they had to draw the line. I didn't even know where the bathroom was. I was too shy to ask anyone. So I wet my bed. The first night there. Can you imagine!' (6)

Juniors were subjected to ongoing victimisation, in and outside the classrooms and in the dorms. Martin got a couple of into scraps ('I wasn't that good a hitter'). He felt that fighting was 'institutionalised'. Boxing was in the sport curriculum ('bashing up your friends'). And, he added, 'there was a lot of bullying in the school hierarchy system. They're so cruel.' (7)

For most Australian schools of the time, the school hierarchy system meant all new boys, juniors and especially 'first formers' would be subjected to humiliating initiation rites. For the rest of the year they served as punching bags, and sometimes servants, to senior students. Next year everything would change, second formers were mostly left alone as a new bunch of first formers were subjected to the bullying – or what some call 'fagging'. On the other side of the Harbour Bridge, Martin's future friend, bespectacled Richard (Richie) Walsh was enduring similar experiences at Barker College. The rugby bullies dangled Richie from locker room clothes hooks and he was repeatedly caned. Said Martin, 'Richie had a rough time of school, because he was small. (8)

Martin was sexually assaulted in junior high. He bitterly recalled, 'The guy molested me when I was a first year junior'. Then, '…we worked out as a network that all the junior boys had been persecuted. So we got together and turned the tables on him, went to the teachers and said, "This guy's been molesting us…".' They may have spoken to him or chastised him but he was made prefect as soon as he got to the fifth. He was given official power!'

Five decades later, Martin was still angry. He blurt out these events on public radio, unconcerned that he may damage the school's reputation or that he might reveal too much of himself. He said, 'The ABC rang me up and said, "Have you got any memories of schooldays?" and I said, "As a matter of fact I have…I remember this guy used to bully us and molest us when I was at school…".' The interviewer cut in quickly and changed direction.

'They terrorised people!' Martin continued. 'You got used to having a rough time there, as par for the course. That's the system of those schools, training you to do the same in business when you get out. Thank God Justin (ie. Justin O'Brien) was there, I believe that was a miracle. There were some good teachers there, some terrific people'. (9)

In 1970, Martin lampooned the school motto in his Yellow House Catalog, featuring the Cranbrook School badge and reversing the school motto from 'To Be Rather Than To Seem To Be' to 'To Seem Rather Than Be'. He also quoted the William Blake poem, The Schoolboy.

But to go to school in a summer morn
O! it drives all joy away;

Under the cruel eye outworn,
The little ones spend the day
In sighing and dismay. (10)

Until he discovered the Art Room, Martin appeared to have no outstanding talent nor was he noticeably 'bad' at anything. He read a bit - not much, watched no television, enjoyed geography lessons, was useful at field sports and a reasonable swimmer. He was neither a champion rower like some cousins nor a champion footballer like his Dad. If Martin could be bothered with any ambition it might have been 'singer in a Rock band' - which wasn't in his consciousness at all until his senior years. (11)

Art was a compulsory subject that everyone studied at Cranbrook. It was also an extra-curriculum activity that students might pursue after school hours, like debating, dramatic society, cricket, football, swimming, rowing and a Scout group, only less structured. At first, Martin didn't know where the art room was located. 'No one ever told me and I never asked,' he said. He eventually found it and, instead of cosying up to Justin O'Brien, the art teacher – his mother's friend and winner of the 1951 Blake Prize that Martin had attended – initially Martin would not be coaxed in and just watched from outside. (12)

When Martin was in his second high school year, one of his future friends, Peter Kingston (Kingo) enrolled in form one. One imagines the two juniors in short pants passing each other in the corridors. Martin and Kingo shared the same art teacher and both used the art room as a sanctuary. Justin was a gay man. His art room provided safety from the sexual bullying instigated by heterosexual toughs. (13)

Justin had an informal approach to teaching, usually one-to-one, never didactic. Martin is grateful that Justin saw the importance of providing good paints and good brushes. 'Poster paints' Justin called them - water paints in jars. 'It was a dynamic art painting scene', said Martin, 'very different to the other classes. I didn't even think of it as a class. (14)

'Justin was wonderful. He was a human being to us. He wasn't the only teacher who was a human being I'm sure. But he taught by being a considerate and thoughtful person. Justin doesn't consider himself a practicing Christian but he was very religious as a younger man. He became gay late in life, when he was 36–37. He would have been chaste up til then. Virtually a priest I suppose. Then that side of him came out.

'He never gave me any trouble – never, ever, not once. So there is a lot between us because his morals are very good. I'd say Justin is definitely a Christian but he's out of the church because they won't accept him.'

In junior school Martin tried to make sense of the religious instruction. He said, 'I can remember absolutely distinctly - just gone to boarding school - and we're doing prayers - a sheet of paper, all beautifully printed. The first prayer said, O Lord, Our Father, forgive where we have erred and strayed, like lost sheep we have done those things which we ought not to have done and left undone those things we ought to have done, there is no help in us. I'm kneeling, reading this stuff. I'm just a kid and I don't know what they're talking about because I don't think I've done anything wrong!

'Now I can say, "Yes, I've done things wrong". Now I can say "I've erred...",' said Martin as a 52 year-old. 'I'm glad I learned the prayer but it seemed a very primitive way of instructing and wrong to inflict on children. It's the sin and guilt of adults. Kids are like they're still in the Garden of Eden, still connected to God.' (15)

Meanwhile Stuart Ritchie started thinking of his successor to the Ritchie Bros engineering operation. He had only two direct heirs, daughter Jo and grandson Martin. In those days it was unthinkable that a woman should hold the position of CEO, so Jo was out of the question. That question didn't even arise. Jo had no interest in running a huge engineering firm.

And - apart from being curious about the art room and getting himself into the second-15 football team – teenage Martin showed little interest in any career. Still, Stuart reflected on his grandson, in his mid-teens. One day he asked Martin to accompany him to look over the Newcastle plant. It was a non-event. Martin said, 'My grandfather took me up - only once - to see if I was interested. I wasn't fascinated by it. I was just horrified by the noise! He never said he'd train me to take it over nor did he expect me to.' (16)

In some ways, it was his father's side that was more career-conscious. Under the governance of grandmother Sharp, like their father Ramsay Sharp, their sons had become well-accepted group of charming doctors - Drs Henry, Alan and Frank Sharp – My Three Sons. Uncle Alan's work in vascular surgery was earning him huge accolades.

While some may have expected Martin - the son of a doctor's son - to be a medico, he felt no family pressure. Martin said, 'they didn't encourage me to become a doctor. They wanted me to become one but they never said, it's a beautiful thing making people well – or something like that - so there wasn't a lot of communication. There was no engagement about interesting me in medicine. I was not an intellectual so I was to them a bit dyslexic I think.' (17)

Without fail, the Sharp family celebrated every Christmas at Grandma Sharp's Vaucluse home and later at her Astor residence. Twelve cousins and their parents. On such occasions Martin mostly hung out with cousin David Massy-Greene (whose career as a pilot would earn him two world records in the late-80s). Martin (b. 1942) and David (b. 1943) were the 'older cousins'.

The main crop was Jane, Sandy, Phillip, Roger, Erica, Katie, Kate and Russell – followed by the 'littlies' - Andrew and Roslyn (Rozzie) both born in 1953. Four other cousins, Lizzy, Margie, Meme and Sally Millear lived in western Victoria and did not attend.

Martin describes the Sharps as 'very ho-ho-ho adults, very theatrical, laughing loudly, telling jokes.' He described Grandma Sharp's Family Christmas get-togethers as a 'strong family ritual, which demonstrated a strong family'.

While Grandma Sharp's daughters had enduring marriages - notwithstanding their wit, charm and success - her three sons were travelling a path that would some day break up each of their marriages. The children sometimes swapped scraps of information about their respective parents' antics. And Martin? He became plain surly when Grandma Sharp insisted that he and David should do Santa-duty and Martin should wear the whole damn costume.

The problem now with family get-togethers was that Jo and Henry's marriage was just a veneer. A decade of Henry's infidelities was an open secret. Said Martin, 'I believe he couldn't be true to her. She was always true to him, until a situation evolved where they accepted he had a mistress who was his secretary but he had many before. He even made a pass at my nanny!'

On weekends spent at home with his parents, Martin watched the marriage breaking down. Then Dorothy Muller, Henry's secretary, started calling around. To Jo's irritation, she and Henry worked tête-à-tête on the Woollahra Action Committee.

Some time later, Martin recalled a tradesman called Keith Hollingsworth spending more time than necessary talking to his mother. Martin describes him as a Beatnik Carpenter. (18)

Martin's parents separated in his mid-high school years.

'I was probably 15 or 16 when they separated,' said Martin. 'I remember my father saying, I've had enough, I'm getting out, that's what he said to me'. (19) Until he could find his own place, Henry moved into the Astor Hotel with his mother. He walked to work and spent his weekends sailing his sloop around Sydney Harbour, looking for a property appropriate to his new circumstances.

Martin's relationship with Henry was strained, probably because it was so strong with Jo. He received no sex education from his father. Said Martin, 'I didn't know how you get married. I thought you all got dressed up. No one said to me, you fall in love with this girl and get married to her. My father said to me, "if you get into trouble, let me know". Trouble he called it!' Stuart Ritchie did not fill in as Martin's absent father. 'He was a grandfather, not a father. He didn't give himself in that way.'

Martin found something of a replacement father in Justin, whose art room had evolved from a safety zone to a place of genuine interest. 'I wouldn't say Justin became a father figure,' said Martin, 'but he became an Art Father or something like that.'

Spending more and more time around Justin, Martin began painting a whole series of 'characters' evocative of real-imaginary characters - where did they come from? 'Maybe Justin,' said Martin. 'Maybe they came out of his unconscious or something?

'I would have covered just about every type imaginable. Roman emperors, racecourse people, gangsters, boxers, miners, conquistadors, the dentist, a beautiful picture of a tired boy holding up a Siamese cat - the only one I ever did of a kid.'

Martin would reproduce two of these pictures in his Yellow House Catalog - a piano player and a long-faced man holding a bird captioned, 'The saddest painting the lonely boy ever painted'. (20)

Another inspiration came from Sydney's Royal Easter Show. Artist, Arthur Barton was the acknowledged master of the Digger Cartoonist tradition. For 35 years Barton was affectionately known as the 'Rembrandt of Luna Park'. (21) He certainly captured Martin's attention.

Martin described Barton's impact, 'I loved the Easter Show. It was a mixture of everything. It was life itself. I loved those great rows of cattle, the big ring, thundering hooves of the trotting races. The Show was a passionate place. Jimmy Sharman - drum beating - and the boxers. All these fantastic archetypes - half-man/half-woman, the Pygmy Princess…so that was absolutely interesting.

'The Easter Show was where I saw some great poster artists at work – Arthur Barton was one of them, the painter from Luna Park. He had an assistant. They used to stand on a big scaffold at the Easter Show. A great wad of huge sheets of paper and two guys in white overalls and hats were up there, and they'd paint! I learned about lettering from watching them.

'They'd do these shapes, block it off into seven different squares, do a bit of a drawing, fill in few corners of the square and suddenly you'd have a Tarzan's Grip ad up there! It was like magic the way they'd paint so fast, or create these things, but there was suspense – they'd bring them up – they were very good. I always liked that sort of thing. You can see it in my character The Toff - that I painted when I was at school – the neon signs and the sense of Pop.' (22)

Enthused by the discovery of art, Martin entered a school drawing competition, which he won. Says Martin, 'The prize was so much $credit of art materials at the shop. It was strange - they didn't think I needed the prize, so they didn't give me the prize!' (23)

Being exhibited was even better than winning a drawing comp. Justin exhibited the best student pictures around the school corridors. But the pick were exhibited in the stairwell, positioned where every teacher and boy saw them as they walked up or down the stairs.

One day, Martin started painting an English Bobby. Martin explains, 'Somehow it turned into the toughest teacher in the school called Mr Bell – Cheery Bell, his nickname was. I did this painting of Cheery Bell with all the kids sitting at their desks. If you didn't bring your books you'd have to polish the bookshelves and I painted myself – or a boy equivalent to me – polishing the shelves in the background. No one had ever painted teachers before – real people.'

Justin hung Martin's cheeky portrait eye-height, halfway up the stairs. A crowd gathered 'jam-packed around the picture'. It caused quite a stir. 'I knew I was onto something,' said Martin, 'that's where one learned about the significance of exhibiting. First goal that one!' Far from being insulted, Cheery Bell felt flattered enough to want it. Negotiated through Justin, Cheery Bell got the picture and Martin got something else.

Cheery Bell was the English teacher who introduced the Bernard O'Dowd poem Australia to Martin's class. It remained with Martin for life. In 1988, Martin framed his OZ? Tapestry (commissioned for the State Library of New South Wales) with words from this poem, 'Last sea-thing dredged by sailor Time from Space…'. Martin said, 'He'd play the authoritarian to the boys, but he wasn't a shit, he was a very good teacher.' (24)

American singer, Johnny Ray's 1954 tour of Australia was the first live concert Martin attended. Johnny Ray – known as the Nabob of Sob - was his mother's 'heartthrob' at the time and Martin accompanied her to the show. Jo dressed as a Bobbysoxer and even wore an American sailor's cap to look the part. She simply loved Pop concerts, many held at the Sydney Stadium in Rushcutter's Bay, which (under promoter Lee Gordon) showcased acts like Ella Fitzgerald, Artie Shaw, Buddy Rich, Andrews Sisters, Louis Armstrong, Nat King Cole, Harry Belafonte…the list goes on and on through to the late-1960s.

Next, came Rock and Roll music, the rise of the teenager and a period that some social commentators have identified as a 'Youthquake'. From Coca-Cola, Levi jeans and 45 rpm singles, it came from several cultural fronts at the same time.

The film The Wild One starred Marlon Brando cast as the leader of a motorbike pack and Rebel Without a Cause starred James Dean in a constant state of teenage angst. Suddenly every male teenager wanted to dress like a grease monkey, which held no appeal for Martin, It was the music that attracted him. Not leather jackets and American World War 2 Army surplus clothing. 'At the time, I didn't see all those films we were supposed to have seen,' he explained.

Martin said, 'My early teens and Rock and Roll coincided. I was in Wirian upstairs. I was sick, I had a cold, I was listening to the radio. My grandmother must have been looking after me and I heard this weird sound come out of the radio. It was Elvis - Heartbreak Hotel. I remember the sensation in the house. Boy, did he make a huge impact, Elvis the Pelvis. Photos of him going wild. Incredible records. I had some of his - Rip It Up, Don't Be Cruel and Old Shep. See You Later Alligator - Bill Haley – fantastic graphics on this. I loved Rock Around The Clock. And Johnny O'Keefe became big. He was exciting. He had a great hit with Wild One.'

Martin's interest in British Rock started in 1958 with the release of He's Got The Whole World In His Hands by Laurie London, a 13-year old black kid from East London. 'I really love him singing, "He's got the whole world in his hunds". He sings hunds! Only rare things like Laurie London and Rock Island Line by Lonnie Donegan broke into the Australian pop charts. (Maybe Cliff Richard but I never had any interest in him.) Five years later the Beatles erupt out of Liverpool, break the domination of America on the popular music scene.' (25)

In his late-teens, Martin frequently accompanied his mother to concerts and shows. One was Water Ballet, created by American competitive swimmer and actor, Esther Williams. Held at the White City Tennis Courts in Rushcutters Bay, the organisers flooded one of the courts to enable this aquamusical featuring synchronised swimming and acrobatic divers. Meanwhile, at the Sydney Stadium, a short walking distance away, promoter Lee Gordon mounted his first Rock and Roll Show, featuring five big-name American acts.

Said Martin, 'I was watching Water Ballet. There were clowns, acrobatic swimmers and Esther Williams was the star of the show. It was "okay". And then I heard this incredible screaming and noise coming from the Sydney Stadium about 100 yards away. It was Bill Haley and the Comets. I wished I was there - not watching clowns diving off high-boards!'(26)

As he became more senior, Martin's school life had become "okay" too. The Cranbrook building boom was underway throughout the 1950s. The Cranbrook Memorial Hall was constructed during Martin's junior years and the purchase of Leura in Victoria Road from the Knox family provided additional accommodation for 60 boys in his senior years. The expansion brought the total number of students to 450, placing Cranbrook on the same level as other Associated Schools (private schools) in size. (27)

In his final year, the question for Martin was – where next? Clearly he had no interest in following in either grandfathers' footsteps. Martin didn't think he was good at anything but art. (28)

'At school I was an individual artist who was creating stuff. That was my most consistent period. I was a proper painter at school – (not that I knew at the time). But looking back on it I could see that I was. I was a painter and didn't even know it - then the rip hits the delta, you drop your load and you wonder? I went all over the place after that, but on purpose.' (29)

Vincent then came back into Martin's life. As an art prize, Justin awarded Martin Lust for Life, the fictionalized biography of Vincent van Gogh. The book was made into a film of the same name, starring Kirk Douglas as Vincent and Anthony Quinn as Gaughin. Released in 1956, it was a visual sensation. The book and the film, Martin loved both.

Martin said, 'I was very struck by Vincent's pictures as a child. I liked his style, it communicated to me. A film was made about his life called Lust for Life. I got that book as a prize in high school from Justin O'Brien and also another special prize from Justin, which was some paintings of his. I did a copy of one of Vincent's pictures - a still life which Justin gave me to copy.' (30)

Did Vincent make any actual impact on Martin's painting style? 'I think at school he did', said Martin. 'I also think I learned a bit from El Greco about how to shade a face.' (31)

Before leaving Cranbrook, Justin painted Martin's portrait as part of a series of young boys. Justin depicted Martin as a melancholy youth who seemed as world-weary as possible without losing one's innocence. During the sittings, Martin insisted on playing Rock and Roll music, an area where Justin's tastes didn't run. (32)

Martin repeated his final year at Cranbrook, 'an indignity intensified by his failure to be appointed prefect'. Like Martin, Richie Walsh was compelled to repeat his final year (Barker College) and 'was also deemed not to be prefect material.' (33)

Martin finished high school and Justin left for Europe within 12 months. He was replaced at Cranbrook by Peter (Charlie) Brown, who became friends with Martin and Jo. Charlie Brown would play a significant role in the formation of the Yellow House.

By the time he got around to leaving school, Martin had dropped the concentration camp rhetoric. 'I was quite happy in it by the time I left', he said. (35)

Where to next? Architecture was one possibility. Or maybe Justin was right - maybe Martin should go straight to Art School?

Extract from Martin Sharp CATALOG (Arcana 1971)

3.

ARTY WILD BOYS

Martin had a different attitude.
Money was no object. You can see how he grew up.
GARRY SHEAD

In 1960, Australia was governed by a conservative status quo. This was true of all levels of society – school, clubs, local councils, State governments, everything. The Prime Minister and Leader of the Liberal Party, Sir Robert Menzies, did his damnedest to out-Brit the Brits. He stood for stability, more of the same and remained untroubled by the Opposition Leader Arthur Calwell, who wore a shabby suit and never expected to win government. The Liberal Party had somehow convinced the whole country that all right-thinking Australians should vote Menzies. It went on for 17 years. Menzies came out with things like, 'I detest some of the wretches that get into universities. They are a collection of ratbags and larrikins!'

By the early-60s, the small farmlets that ringed Sydney were being bulldozed into dormitory suburbs - 3-bedroom homes that idealised what writer Afferbeck Lauder satirised as 'Gloria Soames: a spurban house of more than 14 squares, containing fridge, telly, wart wall carpets, pay-show and a kiddies' rumps room'. (1) Dull, that's what it was. The rise of the Australian middle class handed the PM a constituency of don't-rock-the-boat voters. You were weird if your parents didn't drive a Holden or a Ford Falcon. It's like the whole country was doing it in the missionary position with the lights off. 'Norman Normals' is how Martin would soon cartoon the male of this species – sometimes 'Alfs'. (2)

Nevertheless, there was a small subversive element and Australians enjoyed satire if they knew where to look. Comedian Barry Humphries fingered the spot as far back as 1958 with the release of his Wild Life in Suburbia EP record, featuring characters Mrs Edna Everage and Sandy Stone. It was successful enough to launch his stellar career. (3) Another well-accepted piece of satire was the novel (later the 1966 film) They're a Weird Mob, by John O'Grady - taking the pseudonym and point of view of Italian migrant 'Nino Culotta'. (4)

Australians espoused all things British and adopted all things American, right down to its comics, which came via Mad magazine - the funniest thing in the newsagency.

Clearly there were lots of jokes yet to be mined at the expense of the Norman Normals - True Blue Aussies who (in 1960 Australia) reckoned you wouldn't wanna be a Commie, Spag, Reffo, Kike, Poof, Pom, Wog, Ruski, Derro, teetotaler, 'JW', Abo or a woman. In 1960, there was much to protest about. The national referendum granting the vote to Indigenous Australians was seven years away and feminism was a decade away.

Teenagers had disposable income but that didn't give them a voice. 'Get a job', 'get a mortgage', 'respect your elders' - it was all that stuff in their ears. The post-War Baby Boom added four million to the population between 1946-1961. Teenagers sure had the numbers. Four million emerging voters whose input into society was being stonewalled. Right down to the acceptable length of a teenager's hair, everything had been figured out by their parents.

Everything was figured out. Even – or especially - the arts. Australian poetry was tightly controlled by two publications Poetry and Australian Poetry. If you couldn't impress them, you couldn't get in. There were few independent art galleries. In Sydney, the Art Gallery of New South Wales called 95% of the shots.

But what about Rock n Roll, that catalyst of social unrest? Not in this country. Pop Music television appearances were limited to Channel 9's Bandstand, hosted by the good-natured - 'square' - Brian Henderson. Male performers wore suits. Female performers dressed like debutantes. All media came from Sir Frank Packer, the ABC or some other power-group that excluded young people. Don't even mention independent ham radio stations. They were for geeks.

It was difficult to get a voice even via a simple thing like printing. The general public could only print two ways. (1) Silk-screening (for posters) and (2) duplicating machines, known as 'Gestetners', was how poets, propagandists and voluntary associations (churches, clubs, etc) self-published. (However, innovations to offset printing were well underway at the time.)

One thing that the media did right was to identify teenagers as a separate demographic. The discovery coincided with the rise of the advertising sector, which suddenly became sexy in the 50s when Madison Avenue NY discovered brand image. People with a non-specific creative talent often ended up in the advertising sector.

That's where social commentator Phillip Adams got his start, as well as entrepreneur John Singleton, photographer Greg Weight, artist Brett Whiteley and 'know all' (as Jenny Kee dubs him in her autobiography) Richard Neville. (5) About his brief time in advertising, Richard wrote, 'Adland taught me the basics of printing, layout and come-hither headlines'. (6)

In 1960, Martin followed Justin's advice and enrolled in the National Art School (East Sydney Tech). He remained in contact with his former art teacher, dropping in to see him from time to time until Justin left for Europe. Says Martin, 'Art school - that's where I met Jenny Kee and lots of great people – Peter Powditch, Geoff Doring and Peter 'Charlie' Brown. A good crowd of people, art students are'. (7)

Martin's life suddenly got a whole lot more exciting. He started dating Anou Kiisler, a student at Sydney Girls High School. He discovered Vadim's, a hangout for the Sydney Art intelligentsia. He also discovered Gauloises cigarettes, Double Bay clothes shops and interesting cars that he flagrantly mistreated. His friend, Garry Shead describes Art School Mart as 'extraordinarily witty - there would always be a little phrase. You'd be working it out – he was just so smart'. (8)

At this stage, Martin was really an artist by default. He said, 'I went to East Sydney Tech but I'd really stopped being a painter after school. I did a few pictures, not many. Maybe 3-4.' (9)

Art was one of several options, with the idea of studying architecture not totally buried. About his career path as 'artist' Martin said, 'I would have liked to have been other things as well. There was nothing else that I was any good at. I'd like to have been a singer. I admire people who can sing. That would have been something that was talked about. A couple of friends of mine were thinking of forming something when I was a teenager - something to take on Bandstand. Richard Neville was always dancing in the audience. He should have been performing!' (10)

Being a surfer was another crazy option. Sydney's Northern Beaches replaced Telford as Martin's weekend retreat. He enjoyed hanging out at Whale Beach and Newport. 'I would have loved to have become a surfer', he reminisced, 'I think they're magnificent. To watch them, courage and health – dancing on the edge of eternities - Infinity - just riding that wave. I might have sat on a board once or twice, but surfing evaded me. I probably wouldn't be sitting here if I'd been a surfer. I'd have gone in a whole new direction. I didn't get a surfboard - but I painted one once.' (11)

The Sydney Stadium at Rushcutters Bay was still a fascination. Martin described it as, 'the best venue I've been to. It was our Albert Hall, in a way. It should have been preserved!

'It was built for a prizefight with Jack Johnson and Tommy Burns. (Johnson was the Muhammad Ali of the 1910s.) A simple building. They eventually put a corrugated iron roof over it, the biggest in Australia. Concrete in two corners and then this big octagonal, corrugated iron flying saucer. The atmosphere was superb. The great neon sign with two boxers out the front. Gladiators.

'The stage revolved, so everyone could get a good look. It was very challenging to the performers – they had their backs to half the audience all the time. It was a strange way of doing it but it worked. Also their silhouettes cast these huge shadows against the back walls, people screaming and dancing – amazing! Police-shields to bring stars onto the stage, it was a sensationally exciting place.

'Lee Gordon put on a lot of shows there. Judy Garland sang there. I saw Johnny Cash there. (1959) It was exciting! I saw Peter, Paul & Mary there, what a fantastic show! Mary tossing her wild hair, oh boy, was she the belle of the ball! I've seen great shows there – Harry Belafonte, Louis Armstrong. I had a great Pop education I guess.

'It would seem to me that they would bring the whole Top 20 out in one show. I like Bobby Rydell (in a way)…Gene Pitney, Del Shannon – and Elvis of course was dominating from afar. You've got a second crop of Elvis would-bes - Frankie Avalon. Johnny Restivo was good, he had the Hippy Hippy Shake. Brenda Lee/Chubby Checker. Brenda Lee was the star of the bill but Chubby Checker stormed the show with The Twist. Everyone did the Twist. It still gets me moving!' (12)

Martin was also curious about the back room of the Royal George Hotel where a group of libertarian drinkers met. Known as the Sydney Push, the idea was the bastard child of Professor John Anderson, who occupied the Challis Chair of Philosophy at the University of Sydney 1927-1958. In his prime, Anderson questioned everything – aesthetics, literature, politics - and he outraged Sydney's clergy and conventionally minded citizens. (13) Rejection of conventional morality and authoritarianism was the common bond of the Sydney Push. They used phrases like 'non-utopian anarchism' and 'permanent protest' to describe their activities and theories. It was the kind of place where anyone silly enough to put up a proposition would get flattened.

At its core, the Sydney Push was dominated by a group of men like Darcy Waters, Roelof Smilde, cartoonist George Molnar and poet Harry Hooton. However, slap bang in the middle and often vehemently taking the floor, undaunted by her gender, was the outspoken and outrageous Germaine Greer. On the outer circle were people destined for greater things like Clive James, Paddy McGuinness, Mungo Macallum, Bob Gould and Margaret Elliott (Fink). (14)

Sometimes painter/art critic Robert Hughes would attend. Martin knew him from Vadim's. Sometimes Peter 'Charlie' Brown was there too. Curious, Martin would join the outer circle, smoke his Gauloises and sip pernod. Left-leaning anarchism wasn't exactly Martin's scene. He was more interested in the people. Had he been bothered with politics, Martin would have probably tilted to the right, like his family.

Not that his family offered reassurance. Henry had located a harbour property at Neutral Bay where he was building his future home for himself and Dorothy. And Wirian, once a haven, was a battlefield – with Jo and her father constantly fighting. As if the impending divorce wasn't bad enough, Jo had fallen in love with Keith Hollingsworth, which was completely déclassé. He was a tradesman for chrissakes! This was Lady Chatterley's Lover revisited!

Said Martin, 'Keith was about 10-15 years younger than my mother. Keith was not a posh person. He was a lower class person, an artisan. Because of her affair with Keith, my grandfather was distraught. Grandfather Ritchie said to her, "unless you break off your relationship with him...!" Whether that came from my grandfather or society's orders, I don't know. I don't think he would have done that because he adored my mother, she was his only child.

'She could have had anyone in Sydney if she wanted to play the game but she wasn't a person who played the game. They tried to court her, the divorced ones, the ones who thought she might be a loose woman, but she fell in love with this guy. She conceived with him!' (15)

Grandfather Stuart worked less and less until he retired. Says Martin, 'Then they sold up the Ritchie Bros engineering works. They demolished it for developers'.

Martin didn't want to be a managing director. He wasn't even sure that he wanted to be an artist. In 1960, the big names in Australian art were Sidney Nolan, Russell Drysdale, Albert Tucker and Arthur Boyd. Said Garry Shead, 'They were treated like gods. They were way out there. We didn't see them (I didn't anyway). You didn't criticize them. They were BIG painters.' (16)

Australian Modernism had been a battleground since the early 40s. Nobel prize winner, author Patrick White was the freshest thing on the menu, having won his second Miles Franklin Award. His 1957 novel Voss, with its Sidney Nolan cover, was studied in high schools. The Fair Dinkum School of Australian culture didn't like that. They believed the Bush Balladeers were the nation's best writers and the Heidelberg School were Australia's real artists.

Notwithstanding Melbourne's post-War bohemia (1937-1947), the Angry Penguins (1940s), the Heide group (1934-), the Ern Malley poetry scandal (1943), William Dobell's Archibald Prize controversy (1944) and success of Australian Modernism in London (1961 - Nolan, Boyd, Tucker amongst them), Australian art was as conservative as the rest of society the early 1960s.

No one wants to remember Addled Art, Sir Lionel Lindsay's 1946 book, which was essentially a rant. Lindsay writes, 'I am convinced that Modern Art (self styled) will die the death. I found that a three-colour photograph had been pasted on! The morality of this hoax, the mendacity without spendour, need not be discussed; beside it Picasso's pasting on of Le Journal is but a nursery pleasantry'. (17)

Lindsay was friends with Sir Robert Menzies - who as Prime Minister never shied from commenting on aspects of 'proper' Australian culture.

Then out of nowhere, London's Tate Gallery purchased a picture by former East Sydney Tech student, 22-year old Brett Whiteley. Titled

Untitled Red Painting he was the youngest artist in 90 years to be bought by the Tate. (18) Martin and Garry couldn't help notice Brett's international success - a young Aussie from Sydney's Lower North Shore! He lived up the road from Martin's Uncle Frank's family, in Longueville! If Brett Whiteley could, maybe other young Aussies could too!

Martin's lecturer John Olsen, was another success, in a modern vein. His one-person exhibition at the Terry Clune Gallery in October 1960 crowned him, according to writer Geoffrey Dutton, 'the most dynamic figure in the Sydney art world until 1963 when he went to Portugal…'. (19)

Despite these surges of interest, Martin's first year at art school had not proved the success for which his family had hoped. He had turned dilettantism into an art form. He was – I suppose – a 'face' - the student more interested in coffee shop conversations than attending lectures, the snappy dresser who splattered paint on clothes no one else could afford to buy. Said Martin, 'I liked dressing and finding interesting clothes. When you're a teenager you really do. It's such a language. I had a pink and black thin tie – very shiny.' (20) But no, Martin's first year at art school had not proved the cornerstone on which his parents hoped he might build a career.

In 1961, Martin quit art school and attended Sydney University to study Architecture, a nod to his drawing ability. In the same year, Richard Neville quit advertising and enrolled for an Arts course at the University of New South Wales and Richie Walsh switched from studying Arts-Law to Medicine at Sydney Uni.

Martin moved into St Paul's College, an all male residential college on campus. Like the Cranbrook School, there was a weighty Sharp heritage at Sydney Uni. Martin's grandfather, Dr Ramsay Sharp, left a bequest named after his parents (Martin's great-grandparents) the William Henry and Eliza-Alice Sharp Prize in operative surgery. Grandmother Bessie's brother, Dr Harold Ritchie, and Martin's father and uncles all graduated from medicine from Sydney Uni. This was Martin's new stamping ground, although his architectural course was not the focus of his attention, he was attracted by the drama society.

Needless to say, Martin's father had been there before him. Henry was co-originator of the Sydney University Revue in 1929. He performed on stage and wrote at least two plays – Mississippi Melody and Suppressed Desires. And now – in 1961 - Martin was creating posters for the Sydney University Revue. His art school reputation made him a natural choice. Martin's attendance coincided with the Golden Age of Sydney Uni drama: Clive James, John Gaden, Lyn Collingwood all took the stage at Sydney University in 1961.

Martin reels them off, 'There was some fantastic humour when I was there. Germaine Greer was the star of university, an absolutely riveting star of the stage. Great writers - Bob Ellis and people like this. I saw Bob Ellis acting in The Birthday Party as Petey – (by Pinter). Fantastic performance. Arthur Dignam - absolutely a star! John Bell putting on amazing plays. It was a very exciting period to be in touch with that crowd'.

Student Balls was another outlet for Martin's posters. Martin returned to art school after two university terms. He explained, 'I was meant to be doing architecture but I was hanging out with some artist friends from art school. I was living a double life really'. (21)

Art School is where Martin met Garry Shead, an art student with a mischievous turn of the pen. Schooled at Shore Grammar, Garry went to the North Sydney campus of the National Art School four days per week, the other day Garry would cross the bridge and attend the East Sydney campus. He met Martin through one of his teachers, David Strachan, who said, 'There's somebody you should meet…' and what a fortuitous meeting that turned out to be. 'I saw so much of him when we were at art school', said Garry, 'we became very good friends'. (22)

Garry hailed from the same North Shore locality as Richie Walsh and remembers noticing Richie way before he met him. Says Garry, 'I used to see him going to school (Barker) in his huge great boater, this little guy with a big suitcase. I didn't know who he was at that time. Only later on I realized it was him'.

Garry was full of ideas, one of which was Australia's first truly underground movie. In 1961, Garry started filming what became Ding A Ding Day at East Sydney Tech. It took five years to complete. Martin appeared in some early footage, on-and-off all the way through. Garry also attended Film Society screenings of the French New Wave cinema. This put him in contact with Albie Thoms and a whole new crowd.

Said Martin, 'Garry was doing poetic sort of stuff. He's always had a very romantic vision, a fantastic artist and a great filmmaker. He was the wave before the New Wave - the really New Wave! He had the nerve to get up and do it. He made very interesting films with nothing, just friends and nerve.' (23)

'Garry will be acknowledged as a great pioneer, being one of the first people who was onto it. A real innovator, very beautiful films. I had the good fortune to be in a couple of them, one - surprisingly - on the merry-go-round at Luna Park'. (24)

Garry was also cutting it as a cartoonist in the commercial world. August 1961 saw him filling in for Les Tanner as guest cartoonist in The Bulletin, followed by contributions to Sydney Morning Herald and the Sydney University paper Honi Soit. Martin followed suit. He recalls, 'I was sending cartoons to the Bulletin and they were getting published in the size of a postage stamp. Garry was getting these fantastic full pages! He was hot as a cartoonist - boy! Les Tanner was a wonderful cartoon editor of The Bulletin, he was a great friend of both of us'. (25)

In 1962 two exhibitions by a group known as the Subterranean Imitation Realists (also Annandale Imitation Realists) created quite a splash in the Sydney-Melbourne art world. It was the first group-Art salvo from the emerging generation. Cop this.

The works by Ross Crothall, Colin Lanceley and Mike Brown seemed to come from nowhere. Much of it was junkyard assemblage, with a nod to primitive art, Dada, the objet trouvé and urban larrikinism. Boyd,

Nolan and Tucker weren't even on their spectrum. This was an attack on Abstract Expressionism. The Subterranean Imitation Realists were pre-Pop. They anticipated Pop.

While drinking endless cups of coffee at Vadim's where - in the days of strict licensing laws - actor Kate Fitzpatrick served booze in coffee cups, Colin Lanceley recalls, 'We often played a game we called Aesthetic Chess which was played on table tops and involved placing and moving miscellaneous objects from our pockets to create visual tensions and patterns. We loved art and literature and we loved primitive art especially. We intensely disliked the kind of fifth-rate Abstract Expressionism which prevailed in Sydney at the time.' (26)

Martin and Garry knew - or knew of – this group as the previous batch of John Olsen's students from East Sydney Tech. In February 1962 the Subterranean Imitation Realists mounted their first exhibition at the Melbourne Museum of Modern Art and Design. Their second and final exhibition in May 1962 was held at the Rudy Komon Gallery, Sydney.

Martin describes the group, 'Colin Lanceley is a really fine artist who had a group who influenced me a lot. The Subterranean Imitation Realists used to do fantastic pictures, like Luna Park, Mug Lairs Picnic, all made of bottle tops. They painted a whole gallery out and hung their pictures in it, so their freedom was a terrific excitement to me. (27)

'The Subterranean Imitation Realists were a real inspiration because they'd taken over an art gallery and painted over it inside and outside, made a big mess of the place - painted a big car. They were three guys like a visual pop group. Talk about Pop Artists! They were an influence on me – more than Peter Blake or any of these overseas people.' (28)

What was known as Commem Day (University Commemoration Day) was a big thing in Sydney in the early 1960s. Parades through the city, floats, pranks. It was a day when everyone was tolerant of uni students' antics, like 'kidnapping' a celebrity – maybe a deejay, like Bandstand's Brian Henderson – and holding him/her to ransom (the money went to some cause). Another famous prank was when some students told a group of road workers that a bunch of uni students dressed as police were about to regale them. They then told the cops that a bunch of uni students were digging up the road as a prank. The students stood back and watched/enjoyed/photographed the confrontation.

Special editions of the university papers Tharunka and Honi Soit were sold by students up-and-down inner-city streets. Every railway station was manned. These were spoof papers – like a facsimile edition of the Sydney Morning Herald bearing the headline 'Sydney Harbour Bridge is falling down!' They usually featured a racey photograph of a female student baring slightly more flesh than readers were used to seeing in print. So once every year, clerks, shop assistants, schoolkids, factory workers - anyone near a train station, got treated to the students' take on things. The whole thing was a bit of a giggle. There was a good-natured acceptance of these uni pranks by the city at large.

In 1962, Richard Neville was made editor of the University of New South Wales' student publication Tharunka. At Sydney Uni, Richie Walsh and Peter Grose were the newly-sacked editors of Honi Soit. They were sacked for being too edgy and about to be reinstated.

Sydney Uni had a student publication, New South Wales Uni had one too, the Art School didn't. One night Garry had a dream that would lead to two courts cases and a heap of legal and artistic arguments for the next three years. Instead of cartooning for the Bulletin – why not do it for ourselves?

Said Garry, 'I woke up in the middle of the night with this idea for a newspaper – "sowing your wild oats" – and something arty to connect with it. I told Martin, "let's do a magazine for the Arts" and we got it together'. (29) Said Martin, 'I don't think Garry realizes how he inspired me in the early days – The Arty Wild Oat, which led to OZ magazine. Such a wonderful, gentle and humorous person!'(30)

The Arty Wild Oat was put together under the general editorship of Garry, assisted by Martin along with secretary Sue Wood, art editor John Firth-Smith, advertising Ernest Rushton, circulation Ian van Wieringen and production Robert J. Mayne. Its first issue was April 1962. (Copies may be viewed online.) (31)

Albie Thoms remembers it well, he writes, 'The Arty Wild Oat: its first issue featured an interview with Bob Hughes, who courted trouble by attacking the purchasing policy of the AGNSW, a trustee of which was the head of their school.

'Honi Soit now was edited by Richie Walsh and Peter Grose, with Mungo MacCallum as its theatre critic, Richard Brennan as film reviewer, and Penny McNicoll, the daughter of the editor of the Daily Telegraph, as news editor. She soon took up with Bob Ellis, who was writing long and usually long-winded features for the paper, including a somewhat envious one about Bruce Beresford's forthcoming film. For its cartoonists, the paper had the Architecture student, Geoff Atherden, later a leading television comedy writer, as well as occasional contributions from Martin Sharp'. (32)

So there were crossovers.

Tharunka editor, Richard Neville was curious. Martin remembers noticing him before meeting him. Martin says, 'I first met him when he was working for Tharunka. He came in to get some artwork for the advertising agency at a house in Neutral Bay. He came around to pick up a drawing and I thought he was rather strange - very straightly dressed yet he was a character. He clashed a bit with the bohemian house that he'd come into. I remember noticing him. We didn't communicate - I just noticed. But later on, of course, we became the greatest friends'. (33)

Richard Neville organized to meet Martin and Garry formally at the University of New South Wales Roundhouse in the third week of April 1962. It was a business meeting of sorts. Garry introduced himself, holding a copy of Arty Wild Oat and Martin lurked shyly in the shadows muttering, 'Art is pretentious'.

Over countless cappuccinos, Garry suggested collaboration between Arty Wild Oat and Tharunka and then Martin drove Richard home. On arrival, Martin asked Richard to pass him a tin opener. He jumped out of the car, sawed off the roof of his Triumph sedan, turned it into a convertible and – writes Richard, 'With a wave he was gone, taking a part of my heart with him'.

Next day they went spear fishing together. (34)

The second issue of Arty Wild Oat came out in July. Garry said, 'we did two issues. There was an interview with Norman Lindsay in the second one. I wrote to him and asked him to write something for our newspaper and he said, "Oh I'd love to - young people – I'll give my point of view on things…". That was the front main story of course. We did actually go and see him. Martin organized that. It wasn't that interesting. Norman Lindsay came out - then went inside to his little officey part of the house. I happened to follow him and he was actually doing his hair! We talked to him for about 20 minutes. He didn't invite us in.' (35)

Martin said, 'Garry Shead got Arty Wild Oat together and I worked on it with Ian van Wieringen, John Firth-Smith and a few others. Colin Lanceley wrote an article for it. We had an interview with Norman Lindsay. It was only a fold-over 4-sheeter - but it went quite well. It was like a student paper but it hadn't started from the Student's Representative Council (SRC), it started from some cartoonists.'

That was the point, Garry didn't ask anybody's permission to start The Arty Wild Oat, it was started by cartoonists. Although it came from the students, no student politics were involved and the editors couldn't be voted down. As it was not an official or semi-official organ of East Sydney Tech, its 7499 print-run seemed to invite an off-campus readership.

Said Garry, 'We did the Arty Wild Oat and we had students selling it. We distributed it to the art school, the University of New South Wales and the University of Sydney. That was where Richard Neville and Richard Walsh got the idea for doing OZ. We could create a newspaper from just throwing in our own money to make it, so that led to OZ. We had a journalist friend from school who organized the printing.' (36)

As well as Richard Neville, the art student 4-page flyer led to Martin and Garry meeting Richie Walsh. Martin said, 'This put us in contact with the editors of the universities Richard Neville and Richard Walsh, and their plan was to bring out a student newspaper - but on the streets.

'Commem Day spoof papers used to come out every year and they were sold to the public. This was an idea to do the same thing once a month, but amalgamate outside the actual university magazines and bring out our own magazine. Richard Neville and Richard Walsh were the experienced publishers. I was just there for the art and a bit of design'. (37)

And then Garry got suddenly taken out of the picture. In the 60s schools could discipline students for vagaries such as 'attitude', 'insubordination' or similar ill-defined transgressions. In the June issue of the Bulletin, Garry wrote an article with this opening paragraph, after which he was not readmitted to East Sydney Tech:

Teaching Artists How The Power Game Works. 'The benevolent attitude of the civil service toward its employees amounts to the stagnation that often accompanies senility. If some of the teachers who have been with the department 20 years or more were dismissed they would stand very little chance of keeping their heads above water. Therefore there is a moral obligation to keep them on to which there seems no immediate remedy...'. (38)

Said Garry, 'I was only at art school for two years 1961-62. I was a bit of an obnoxious kind of upstart, cocky. I wrote a piece for the Bulletin that was fairly critical of the art school teaching. Douglas Dundas was the head teacher there and he told me to come to the office and said, "Shead, I don't think you should bother coming back to art school next year".' (38)

Booted out of Art School – well, 'not readmitted' - Garry spent a long time out of work, wondering who on earth might want his talents? 'I wasn't allowed to go back so I had to get a job. For six months I was without a job. I didn't know where to start. I was in the laundry of my parents' place in Pymble at that time, writing, fiddling around and suddenly the mother of a friend of mine rang to say "there's a job at ABC Gore Hill, you should try for it as a scenic artist". So I went along and got the job'. Garry got a job as a set painter. He left home immediately. (39)

The ABC was an ideal environment for Garry, who need editing facilities to finish his film. It took until 1965 for him to complete it. (Ding a Ding Day has had several screenings over the years, including the Yellow House in 1970 and the Yellow House Retrospective at the Art Gallery of New South Wales in 1990.)

But before quitting art school and working at the ABC, there was telling moment when Garry showed Martin his latest cartoon for the Bulletin. It had three elements, the character, the gag and on the pavement the word Eternity.

Martin handed it back without comment.

Eternity.

'He took a good hard look at it', said Garry. (40)

'The first time I saw Eternity. I must have been about seven or eight, maybe a bit older,' said Martin. 'I was definitely on my own and I don't know when I was allowed out on my own. I was walking back from the Rose Bay Pier in Cranbrook Road. I saw it written on the pavement, on the left hand side of the road coming back around the second corner, and I wondered what it meant. I'd never seen anything written on the pavement before'. (41)

Extract from Martin Sharp CATALOG.

4.

OZ IS A NEW MAGAZINE

*After its lame beginning,
OZ became stronger with each issue.*

ALBIE THOMS

In 1957, publisher Lawrence Ferlinghetti and manager of the San Francisco City Lights bookstore, Shigeyoshi (Shig) Murao, were charged with disseminating obscene literature in the form of the Allen Ginsberg poem Howl. The poem contains references to illicit drugs and both heterosexual and homosexual sexual practices. In October of the same year, US Judge Clayton Horn ruled the poem not obscene. (1) This case was an early goal in a long-running generational war about censorship.

The team who would subsequently create OZ were in their early teens and may not have noticed the case at the time. They would later see the Howl trial as setting some sort of precedent for their own experience.

As an eighteen-year old, Martin definitely heard about the next literary scandal, the 1960 Lady Chatterley's Lover trial brought against Penguin Books under the British Obscene Publications Act. It was big news in certain circles, like the Sydney Push and amongst the next generation of writers. That the publishers escaped conviction by arguing it was a work of 'literary merit' created a legal precedent. (2)

Meanwhile, the Arty Wild Oat pushed a few boundaries, attracted lots of attention but after just two issues its small team was running out of puff. The publication needed much more content. It also needed to make the jump from art-stream to mainstream. Yet Arty Wild Oat certainly caught a mood, a target-readership and an attitude. The genie was out of the bottle. The two Richards knew it.

Editors, Richard Neville and Richie Walsh teamed up. Before Garry left art school and worked for the ABC, they organised a meeting with him and Martin, drank plenty of coffee and reached an agreement. Instead of issuing three separate publications - Tharunka, Honi Soit and Arty Wild Oat – they agreed to join forces and create one - with broader content and more pages. It would be political, sassy and funny.

The agreement led to a formal meeting held at Richard Neville's place. Not quite a Board Meeting, it was a type of party which welcomed friends as potential contributors. About 15 turned up. Richie brought cadet journalist Peter Grose and Richard gave a speech, while Martin and Garry formed a sub-group with Tharunka artists, Peter Kingston and Mick Glasheen and giggled at everything being said. (3)

Said Martin, 'Richard Neville called everyone over, had a party and everyone was excited by the idea of combining the papers and releasing a regular combined-talents university student paper on the streets. A rough memory of the times - Alex Popov…Michael Glasheen was cartooning, Peter Kingston for Tharunka, Richard Neville running full-page comics on the front. Writers: Gina Eviston, Robyn Cooper, Anou my girlfriend and Ann Kaiser a girlfriend of Richard's. That night OZ was born.

'Richard Walsh suggested the name, which I thought was silly at the time. I had my own idea - ASP for Australia's Satirical Paper. But OZ was perfect, of course. It's got a lot of angles to it: OZtralia, the Wizard of OZ. It's a paradoxical name – humorous, good-natured. It was just right actually. And so, there it was - OZ.' (4)

Meanwhile the coffee drinking sessions continued at Vadim's. Martin introduced Richard to Robert Hughes who was playing to a table of admirers as usual. Martin also introduced him to Sydney Uni arts student Louise Ferrier and Richard was dumbstruck. Richard wrote, 'Her beauty shriveled my savoir faire, her composure drove me nuts'. He babbled something about starting a magazine, tried to hold her interest until a bloke came to retrieve her. It was Peter Grose.

One night in late March, Martin and Richard drove all over the city plastering up posters that read, 'OZ is a new magazine'. Issue No 1 was released on April Fools Day 1963. It was launched on £50 working capital, 30 subscribers and no fulltime staff. A 12-month subscription cost £1 and the cover price was 1/6. Six thousand copies were distributed from an office in the Rocks area of Sydney found by Gina Eviston's father. It sold out by lunchtime, Richard ordered a reprint and described it as the happiest day of his life. (5)

The team comprised: editors - Richard Neville and Richie Walsh. Art Director - Martin Sharp. Artists - Garry Shead, Mick Glasheen and Peter Kingston. Staff - Anou Kiissler and Aggie Read. Melbourne editor - Paul Lawson. (6)

Summing up the spirit of OZ, social commentator Craig McGregor wrote, 'They know, to the faintest whiff of snobbery in a charity dinner, all about hypocrisy, pretense, cruelty, intolerance and authoritarianism of so much of Australian life. Like most young people they can't stand phonies and the smug self-satisfaction of many adults. They know absolutely what they are against, and it is a measure of their talent that their opposition finds bitter and memorable expression. But they are not sure what they are for.' (7)

There were 16 pages per month, mixing text and illustration. Necessity being the mother of invention, Martin was required to faithfully produce drawings on a regular basis each month. Not just cartoons, but also ads for Binkie's Burgers, Suzie Wong's Restaurant, Clune Galleries and the Gas Lash, an after hours speakeasy where his friends hung out.

Former Gas Lash manager, Ted Markstein described the place that so regularly bought the entire OZ back page for a Martin-drawn ad, 'A guy called Ron Murphy had a place called Binkie's, a late-night burger place on Elizabeth Street. The Gas Lash was next door. I ran it. It was a folk-singer joint. You couldn't get liquor in Sydney after 6.00 at night, so we ran it as a speakeasy and all society used to come down there.' (8)

Said Martin, 'It wasn't until I started drawing cartoons (which I've always been keen on anyway) for OZ magazine, that I was put into that position where I was working fast and spontaneously - a bit of collage, a bit of this, a bit of that and a bit of fast handwriting. John Olsen was one of my teachers. His spiky handwritten paintings were an influence, the vitality of his style.' (9)

Olsen broke away from East Sydney Tech and opened his own art school, The Rocks Art School. Cynthia Byrne (later married to Robert Klippel), Peter Powditch and Martin were part of Olsen's small class of six students. They left their East Sydney Tech courses and followed him there. In Cynthia's words, 'as if he were the Pied Piper'. It only lasted six months. (10)

Satire was busting out all over, Barry Humphries' monologues, the Mavis Bramston Show on TV. Canberra Times had a satirical column and the Phillip Street Theatre ran satirical revues. Even the Kings Cross Whisper claimed to be a satirical paper - all pushing boundaries in their own cheeky way.

Albie Thoms was certainly pushing boundaries at the Sydney University Dramatic Society with his Revue of the Absurd. Like everyone, he too was curious about OZ. Albie summed it up the first issue. 'My first response was that it seemed a bit roughshod and juvenile, with a crude collage on its cover depicting a man in a chastity belt, while an article inside lampooned sexual abstinence. Smugly, I found it all too unsophisticated and lacking in bite, and believed it vastly inferior to my own revue.' (11)

Censorship and free speech were issues of the time. Things were getting silly. American censorship required married couples in films to dress in neck-to-knee pyjamas and sleep in separate single beds. Nipples were airbrushed from magazine photos. Nudie magazines weren't nudie at all but usually dollybirds in underwear. Stocking tops were risqué. The Australian censors combed through each month's issue of US men's magazine Playboy seeking something that would enable it to be banned.

OZ 1 was exciting for readers and the editorial team. OZ probably felt invincible and enjoyed poking fun at right-wing establishment figures like radio commentator Eric Baume, modernist architect Harry Seidler, Queen Elizabeth II, Robert Menzies PM and Sydney's Social Top 20. Three more issues continued in this jocular vein before the law caught up with them.

The police contended that OZ 1 contained an article about chastity belts, which was deemed offensive, as well as an interview with an abortionist (an illegal practice at the time). Richie's father was so deeply shocked by the charges that he suffered a heart attack thought serious enough for the Walsh family solicitor to have the case adjourned until September.

In panic, the printers would not proceed with OZ 4. Now the OZ team had two problems - the printer and the law. Then Richie phoned Richard with a left-field idea - the Anglican Press. Of all things! Said Richard, 'Isn't it owned by the church?' Richie replied that its proprietor, Francis James, was a champion of free speech and a maverick.

Richard, Richie, Martin and Anou met Francis James on his premises. They came to an agreement and set a date for the press to roll. As they took their leave, the slightly world-weary proprietor shot out, 'You lot might think of yourselves as angry young men. Piffle! Young Walsh here will take to the establishment like a duck to water!' Richie didn't like that at all.

In an attempt to avoid a conviction, the OZ boys backed down. On a September Monday in 1963, at the Central Court of Petty Sessions, Richie's solicitor entered a plea of guilty on behalf of Richard, Richie and Peter Grose. The big shock came when Peter's solicitor told the court that his client was no more than a consultant, had completely disassociated himself from his two associates and on reflection, found OZ to be utterly worthless. The magistrate fined them £20 apiece and supporters of OZ hissed Peter as he walked out. (12) Peter Grose has since gone on to become a highly respected publisher.

Albie wasn't pleased with any of them for pleading guilty. He too had been picked up by the Police on a charge of obscenity relating to his Sydney Uni Revue of the Absurd. The charge related to the use of the word 'shite' and 'arseholes' in one of the songs in the Alfred Jarry play The Song of the Disembraining.

Albie writes, 'I was set back by the news that the editors of OZ had pleaded guilty to their obscenity charge, and wondered what bearing it might have on my own case, due to be heard the following month. When I next saw him, I castigated Richie Walsh for caving in, but he explained that he had been misled by his lawyer, who had recommended this course, believing that their convictions would not be recorded because they were first offenders.'

The lawyer reasoned that a conviction would not help Richie's future medical career nor Peter Grose's journalistic hopes. It would also mean Richard Neville probably could not travel to America. Richie explained to Albie that there was everything to be gained by avoiding conviction - which proved mistaken as they were convicted anyway.

At least Martin found it amusing. Writes Albie, 'The affair was gleefully mocked by Martin Sharp in Tharunka with a cartoon that showed Richard at first relishing the idea of a trial and the publicity it would bring, before putting on a suit to plead guilty'. (13)

In a subsequent issue, Richie saw to it that OZ took Albie's side in a piece titled 'Obscene or Absurd?' OZ particularly enjoyed the moment when the policeman said to Albie, 'Get me Alfred Jarry!' to which Albie replied, 'If you'd read your program you'd see he died in 1908!' The reprint, from the Sydney Push's Libertarian Broadsheet, also pointed out that it is 'probably a triumph for the freedom to be vulgar and in bad taste without being obscene'. (14)

This article led to Richie introducing Albie to the OZ crowd. Everyone seems to remember Richard Neville from their first meeting. Albie writes, 'He was a ball of energy, with sparkling eyes and an awkward way of standing, with his head held at an angle while he engaged you with a distinctive, toothy smile that Martin Sharp later made symbolic of OZ. Richard was most enthusiastic about my censorship victory, expressing genuine interest in my future plans, and invited me to contribute to his magazine, though I then had more pressing concerns.' (15)

OZ suited Martin. In his quiet way, he was an angry young man. He found himself in OZ. It gave him an artistic identity. Martin said, 'I went to art school and lost my style completely. It took OZ to pick it up again.' (16)

The OZ team had a thing about the parochial Aussie male. They called him 'Alf'. He was their equivalent of Barry Humphries' Sandy Stone character. Sometimes also known in OZ as 'Normal Normal', Alf is the typical owner of a 3-bedroom brick veneer house with a Holden to polish in the driveway. He's looking forward to a date with the wife at the RSL and a beer with the boys while watching Saturday football. 'Terrible drug that marijuana' complained a beer sodden Alf in Martin's OZ cartoon. (17)

This guy was almost everybody's father!

Like the two Richards, Martin was angry about the humiliations of his school life. Said Martin, 'Most satirists sat back pretty quietly at school and had a pretty rough time of it. That's certainly my case and certainly Richie Walsh's. Richard Neville is a bit more extrovert but he was still the brunt of a lot of pranks at school – so that was an interesting motive in OZ. It's the sort of rage that comes out quietly later.' (18)

For their heavy condemnation of his mother, Martin was also angry with his father's side of the family. Notwithstanding Henry's many infidelities, nor that Jo only took a lover after the marriage breakup, she was made to wear the blame for the impending divorce. Aunts Barbara and Edith (Dinks) were the only ones who gave her any family support. No doubt having married Drs Sharp themselves gave them certain insights.

Of the Sharp family, Martin said, 'The males did not talk to my mum. When it broke, which is a bit earlier than when they were divorced, it was pre Decree Nisi - no blame. "We won't put your name all over the papers if you don't make a fuss", which is what they were doing to my mother. It was terrible. And they were so bloody self-righteous about it. It was all bullshit!

'I guess my mother must have been considered a fallen woman. Society dropped her, not only the Sharps, except the wives of the Sharps who loved her, they used to come and see her – Dinks, Aunt Barb – but the Sharp family under the command of the hand that rocks the cradle…!' Martin was quoting the idiom 'the hand that rocks the cradle rules the world' which is how he regarded Grandmother Sharp's grip on her three influential sons. (19)

Martin had attitude, not uncommon among undergraduates in their early-20s. Martin was hanging with a crowd of young upstarts who were getting themselves a bit of a name around town as a precocious group of (probably) poseurs refusing to go along with the status quo. Art school friend Jenny Kee describes Martin and artist Peter Powditch as 'leaders of the pack' at art school. (20)

In this pre-Beatle era, surf culture was the thing in Sydney. Says Martin, 'The surfing-thing hit very big and some very exciting music came out of it. The whole sound was a terrific. I used to go to Surf City at Kings Cross – the Stomp was a great thing.' (21)

What Martin probably didn't know was that this was possibly his first brush with the Kings Cross underworld. Surf City was a former cinema owned by Lee Gordon and Abe Saffron that they converted into a disco called the Birdcage. After Lee Gordon left Australia it was leased to John Harrigan, or the Harrigan family, presumably by Abe Saffron himself. In fact Abe Saffron was involved in all the Sydney shows Martin talked about - Harry Belafonte, Chubby Checker, Bobby Rydell – the lot. (22)

Surf City featured surf music, Sydney's latest craze. Young men 'peroxided' their hair blond and, along with their surfie girlfriends, they pounded their feet on the dance floor, with their hands held behind their backs. Thoonk-thoonk. Following the bass lines. Thoonk-thoonk. That was known as the Surfer's Stomp.

The music might be 14-year old Patricia Amphlett (Little Pattie) singing her hit song Blonde-Headed Stompie Wompie Real Gone Surfer Guy. Or perhaps a new band called the Aztecs who started out at Surf City playing surf instrumentals. Around this time a singer called Billy Thorpe joined them and they completely changed that routine, becoming more like those Liverpool Mod bands that Australians were hearing about, like the Beatles whose first Australian release, Love Me Do was setting them apart from Gerry and the Pacemakers, Brian Poole and the Tremeloes and those other Pommie bands.

There were lots of Surfies around Surf City. They probably didn't even own a board! Meanwhile, Surfers – the real deal – were to be found at riding the waves, especially on the northern beaches. Sometimes Martin would leave his Paddington apartment/studio and spend Saturday afternoons with Richard, pretending to drink beer at the Newport Arms hotel (the 'Arms').

Though seldom venturing the surf themselves, Martin and Richard sometimes sat on the beach, watching the wave-riders. Martin got ideas for sketches from watching what beach people did. One Saturday afternoon he saw the full drama, wheelies, a punch up and a 'well-aimed chunder'. Richard recalls being with Martin when it happened, after which Martin raced to the OZ office where he wrote/drew the controversial cartoon, The Word Flashed Around the Arms, written in the first-person voice of the Ocker gatecrasher. (23)

On those northern beaches, Martin got to know surf-filmmaker Paul Witzig – a Sydney Uni guy - who Californian Bruce Brown hired to shoot Australian footage for his upcoming movie The Endless Summer. Witzig later worked as Brown's Down-Under liaison, screening Brown's films in New South Wales and Queensland.

Now with a track record as the poster artist of preference for student balls and art school events, Martin was asked to create a surf-themed poster for The Endless Summer, which he did. Not the famous pink, yellow and orange poster with the surfer carrying the board on his head. Another one. 'It wasn't very original', said Martin. (24)

Barry Humphries knew – or had met – Martin. Around this time he penned a poem, which he dedicated to him. The Old Pacific Sea is an odd one to associate with Martin, though it may have been inspired by Martin's The Word Flashed Around the Arms chunder-cartoon. It's the 'chunder in the old Pacific sea' song that Barry Crocker would sing in the 1972 film The Adventures of Barry McKenzie - by which time, whatever connection it may have had to Martin was surely lost. (25)

Their court case behind them and a surge of youthful energy before them, Martin, Richard and Richie at last agreed that OZ was on the right track. Richard was glowing in his mother's glory, having formally graduated as a Bachelor of Arts. Richie was doing well, studying medicine. Martin never stopped drawing. The circulation of OZ had doubled.

Albie writes, 'After its lame beginning, OZ had become stronger with each issue, featuring a Bob Hughes' caricature of God on the cover of the second, the send-up of the Bogle-Chandler murders on the third, and a satire on the Profumo Affair for number four. Each issue was crammed with small items ridiculing politicians, priests, and the pretensions of Sydney society, while Bob also lampooned the CND, Bob Ellis swiped at US politics, and Bruce Beresford offered criticism of contemporary cinema. They were supported by scratchy illustrations from the magazine's art director, Martin Sharp, together with cartoons by Garry Shead, Peter (Kingo) Kingston, and Mick Glasheen. Best of all were Martin's full-page monologues, combining small drawings with lots of written text, reversing the usual comic convention that limited words to slim panels and speech balloons.' (26)

The OZ team held a meeting after which they felt confident that they had ironed out whatever problems they had. Their readers were most forgiving. They seemed to understand that OZ was nobody's fulltime job and some of the team, Richie for example, actually studied while at university. Readers also sensed they were on the edge of something in a city where teenagers were growing longer hair and asserting their youth in all art forms. Agitprop theatre, underground film, Pop poetry and especially Pop music. Hairdressers were turning into celebrities. Fashion designers too. Clothes shops and record shops were where the teen dollar was being spent. Art galleries were suddenly interesting.

While parents were still arguing about the demerits of Abstract Expressionism, the art students were way beyond that. New York Pop artists Andy Warhol and Roy Lichtenstein were over-defining the images that the Abstract movement had lost. They painting down-to-earth subjects like comic books, money and tins of Campbell soup, taken straight from the commercial world. Said Martin, 'Pop Art was like a flavour. It was around. I was a bit younger than most of the Pop artists. I wouldn't say I was influenced, it was a flavour that was around'. (27)

Yes, things were going well for OZ, which they all agreed in their April meeting. Before the month was out, Martin, Richie and Richard each got a summons to appear at the Court of Petty Sessions for publishing an obscene magazine, OZ 6 – the one with the urinal cover.

'This time it's serious,' said Richard to his father. (28)

5.

OZ TRIAL
LONDON CALLING

*OZ was vulgar, abrasive, sometimes funny,
sometimes embarrassing, but good for Sydney.
It was certainly doing no harm to anyone when in 1964
the full ferocity of the old-style repressive laws of censorship
and criminal libel were unleashed on it.*

GEOFFREY DUTTON

To date, apart from brief forays by Barry Humphries into London's comedy circles, this Australian generation had yet to make its overseas impact. If they would not go to England, England first came to them.

In the time between entrepreneur Ken Brodziak's handshake agreement with manager Brian Epstein and the Beatles' arrival in Australia in June, the band transformed into an international phenomenon. Overnight, the £3000 Brodziak-Epstein deal seemed a pittance.

In March, Can't Buy Me Love, the band's sixth single was released and went straight to No 1. John's first book In His Own Write also came out that month and sold 50,000 copies on its first day. Also in March the John, Paul, George and Ringo started filming A Hard Day's Night.

Madame Tussaud's famous waxworks put their effigies on show. Everyone changed their hairstyles. Everyone changed their tastes. Even the Queen arked up. But Epstein would never renege on his bond. Shortly before the OZ trial – June 1964 - the Beatles were booked to play concerts in Adelaide, Melbourne and Sydney. (1)

With an eye on the Rolling Stones, Martin didn't think the Beatles actually called the shots. Rather, they spearheaded a movement with many players. He initially poked fun at them in OZ. Said Martin, 'I like to think I had long hair before the Beatles! Their hair was short! I think they cut it to become the Beatles!'

Until the Beatles tour, Martin was still looking to Australian bands for inspiration. Moving right along from former-hero Johnny O'Keefe, a Sydney-based band called the Missing Links was OZ magazine's pet rockers.

After name-checking 50s singers Laurie London and Tommy Steele, Martin explained, 'Not much had been coming out of London. It had been pretty silent at this stage. Suddenly England became interesting. The Beatles and the whole Liverpool Sound. Brian Poole the Tremeloes were great, Do you love me, now that I can dance…! The excitement of that scene! The Beatles had that fantastic Liverpool humour which really kicked in with similar Australian humour.'

So Martin had a change of heart - he liked them. No, loved them! He got completely caught up in the phenomenon and it had much to do with Greg Weight's ex-girlfriend, Jenny Kee, a proper livewire.

When the Beatles hit town, Jenny was in her second year at East Sydney Tech. Jenny and Martin knew each other from art school and also from Vadim's where Jenny recalls the OZ boys tête-á-tête, regularly scheming something up. She and her friend Vickii Maher had accompanied Martin and Richard to Luna Park shortly before the Beatles were due to arrive. They told the boys they were targeting the band and Martin thought he should tag along. Martin bought tickets for himself and his Mum to see the Beatles play the Sydney Stadium and he took Anou to see them arrive at their hotel, where Jenny and Vickii were sure to be.

The Beatles staying at the Sheraton Hotel, 40 Macleay Street Kings Cross, was the worst kept secret in town. Thousands of fans showed up. Thousands. Said Martin, 'I was a bit of a Stage Door Johnny in a way. I admired performers. I was always interested in meeting performers.' (2) He tried to smuggle Anou inside in a laundry basket, to no avail. It was impossible to get close. Yet Jenny and Vickii somehow cut through the pack.

Jenny and Vickii hung around the lifts, got to the 8th floor where they were greeted by a wall of bodyguards so they went back down. Then back up. Again they faced the wall of bodyguards, but this time Beatles' press secretary Derek Taylor was there too. Taylor beckoned them in and seconds later Jenny and Vickii were in John and Paul's suite. Later in the evening Jenny scored John Lennon. She wrote, 'He had his way with me and it was hot: a genuine emotional charge for us both'. (3)

Martin surmised some sort of agreement was reached that if Jenny came to London, John would take care of her – see that she got a job maybe? Something like that. Said Martin, 'There was this call for Jenny to get over there'. (4) Richard wrote, 'By morning she (Jenny) had decided to save up for a passage on a cruise ship to Carnaby Street.' (5)

What none of them yet knew was that Bob Whitaker, who was about to become a close friend, had received the same call. So impressed was Beatles manager Brian Epstein by Bob's photo-montage portraits of himself taken in Melbourne (two days before Sydney), that he appointed Whitaker as court photographer to the Beatles for the next two years. Bob's oeuvre is recorded in his book The Unseen Beatles. (6)

Said Martin, 'When they toured here Bob Whitaker did some portraits of Epstein and Epstein said they were fantastic. Rather imperial photos. And he got the job of being Epstein's personal photographer to the Beatles and went to London. So he was a contact.' (7)

Martin was about to find all this out when he and Anou accompanied Colin Lanceley to Melbourne to help hang his exhibition at South Yarra Gallery. Lanceley's first group show was organised by owners of the Heide Gallery, John and Sunday Reed, patron of so many artists. By 1964 the Subterranean Imitation Realists had split up and this was 25-year old Lanceley's second solo exhibition. (8)

Lanceley knew the Reeds and the Reeds knew everyone in the Melbourne arts circle, including Georges and Mirka Mora - who also knew everyone in the Melbourne arts. The Mora family spent many weekends at the Reed's gallery-home and at their beach house in Aspendale. Regular drop-in guests included artists Charles and Barbara Blackman, Fred Williams, John and Mary Perceval, Albert Tucker, Barrett Reid, Arthur Boyd, Sidney Nolan, Joy Hester, Asher Bilu.

In 1954 Georges (Gunter Morawski) founded the Mirka Café in Elizabeth Street, Melbourne, which exhibited Joy Hester's first major solo exhibition. Georges' wife Mirka was also a painter. And the eldest of their three sons, 15-year old Philippe, was already making short films. Artists dropped in, artists dropped out. Martin's visit to the Mora home may have been the first time he saw an all-family art environment at work and play. He was always interested in art/live-in environments.

The day Martin and Anou called on the Mora family, Martin's former art teacher, John Olsen, was present. Olsen and Georges got engrossed in conversation, leaving Martin and Anou to somehow talk Mirka into being photographed wearing a truly ghastly mask for the cover of August OZ. That is - the OZ in preparation - the one to hit the newsstands after/during the July court case. (9)

Photographer Robert (Bob) Whitaker was there too. That's how Martin met him. Mirka writes, 'Robert was wearing lovely tight shorts and I couldn't help seeing an air ticket popping out of his pocket as I was lusting over his tight, round bottom. Divine. He was so happy, he was going to London to photograph the Beatles, and Brian Epstein had given him the air ticket.' (10)

Said Martin, 'Bob Whitaker's mother is Australian. His father is English. I met him through the Mora family. I went down to Melbourne with Colin Lanceley to help him mount an exhibition. I met the Moras then and also got to know Philippe – a friendship developed.' (11)

Twenty-three year old Bob Whitaker was running his own photographic studio at the time. 'I soon became bored with fashion,' wrote Bob. One day, promoter/journalist/poet Adrian Rawlins phoned to announce that he'd got himself commissioned by Jewish News to interview Brian Epstein and he needed a photographer. Sure, said Whitaker.

The pair showed up at the Guest Lounge of Melbourne's Southern Cross Hotel. Epstein arrived 'immaculately dressed: well-pressed trousers, gingham shirt, smart shoes, silk socks an expensive watch and a gold bracelet'. Whitaker 'cautiously at first' took some shots then Epstein relaxed. At the end of the interview Eppy asked if he could see the pictures when developed.

In the developing room, Whitaker tricked them into photomontages, enshrouding Epstein's face with peacock feathers in one shot. Bob struggled through another mad crowd, handed an envelope to Epstein who promised to call when he'd had a good look. Eppy loved the shots. Which is how Epstein came to invite Whitaker to the UK as his Artistic Adviser. (12) Although he had only briefly met John, Paul, George and Ringo in Melbourne, in London Whitaker got to know them real well.

Shortly before the OZ trial, Australian's first national newspaper was launched in Canberra, Rupert Murdoch's The Australian. Working on the paper were a number of Honi Soi youngbloods, including David Solomon, Mungo MacCallum, Peter Grose and Martin, who supplemented the work of Bruce Petty by providing occasional cartoons.

In those days, Martin was doing a lot of b/w pen and ink work. He says, 'When I was about 22 I got a job when Petty went on holidays. For two weeks I worked in Canberra. They offered me a full-time job but I didn't want to live in Canberra. It was a good opportunity in way but it wasn't the way I wanted to go. One cartoon a week, I could handle.' (13)

At this time Martin was ensconced in a studio behind the Windsor Castle Hotel in Paddington Lane. He had a pet guinea pig, which unfortunately ate rat poison and died. He said, 'I'd left home and moved into a little studio in Paddington which I loved but then OZ broke and my mother said, 'you'd better come home'. (14)

The OZ trial, cast its long shadow on Martin's family life. While his grandfather Stuart seemed a little bit proud of Martin, his Sharp grandmother probably blamed Jo for her delinquent grandson. About her response to the trial Martin said, 'It was embarrassing. It must have been.'

Jo probably wanted Martin's company, that's why she invited him back. Apart from domestic help, she lived alone while Martin's father Henry was often gloriously sailing Sydney Harbour with his wife-to-be Dorothy, while his mother coped all blame. Even Stuart Ritchie turned his back on his daughter, appalled at the events that had led to the impending divorce. Martin overheard all this.

The Sharp side of the family was worse. Forsaking Jo's actual name, Grandmother Sharp had taken to referring to Martin's mother as 'Jezebel'. Remembering the music from his childhood Martin voiced the demonic sentiments, 'They were calling her Jezebel in their family discussions! That's what they described her as! Frankie Laine had a big hit called Jezebel - if ever the Devil was born, without a pair of horns, it was you Jezebel…! But she said to me, "I never regret marrying your father because otherwise I wouldn't have had YOU". And she always had a lot of young friends.' (15)

Jo started writing for OZ. The Social Top Twenty, 'An authentic survey of Sydney's most popular socialites, compiled by an independent OZ reporter…'. (16) That was Jo.

Said Martin, 'My mother was writing for OZ, we had the Social Top 20 in there. Richard Neville - they all really liked my mother. I envied her, because she had such charm. They'd go to her as soon as they arrived. So I was a bit jealous of my mother. She pinched my friends by the handful!

'And she ran that house as a hospitality place. She brought me up. Dad tried but he was too straight or something like that. She loved dancing, she was a bright young thing of the day, "laughing at danger…", said Martin, referencing the Noel Coward song Poor Little Rich Girl. 'But she really tried to be a perfect wife and perfect mother in every way she could.' (17)

Next, the Supreme Court of New South Wales. 'I was in trouble with OZ magazine,' Martin continued, 'my Ritchie grandparents were totally supportive because their dream was for me to be a cartoonist.' Martin was also proud of his father's support and he bragged to all his friends that Henry bought him an immaculate suit that he never wore to court. (18)

And so OZ went to trial and the publication became famous for being allegedly obscene, which was never its intent. OZ was not there to 'deprave and corrupt'. It was there to annoy. They saw themselves as satirists not pornographers! Said Martin, 'Youth always revolts against the leadership of age, I'm sure about that. I suppose we were satirists. I think that's the best description.' (19)

Richie Walsh agreed, 'In its heyday Australian OZ was probably more famous as an allegedly obscene publication than as the satirical magazine we aspired to be'. Walsh heads a long line of social commentators who can't see what the fuss was about. He wrote, 'Today that particular issue could be passed around among kids in a pre-school without causing alarm; but what was truly amazing was that the NSW Vice Squad, which took responsibility for pressing these charges, had found enough time to get affronted by our puny efforts: they devoted most of their daylight hours to organizing prostitution and illegal gaming houses for their mutual benefit!' (20)

Martin and the two Richards – the First Triumvirate - were charged under the Obscene and Indecent Publications Act. It was a criminal charge. If found guilty they could be sent to jail.

The prosecution argued that the cover illustration of Richard and two others fake-urinating into the Tom Bass sculpture-fountain on the front of the P&O building in Sydney was also morally dangerous. No disrespect to Tom Bass the artist was intended, it was a Richard Neville prank: a joke. That's all. (21)

Historian, Geoffrey Dutton, summed up the situation. He writes, 'OZ was vulgar, abrasive, sometimes very funny, sometimes embarrassing, but good for Sydney. It was certainly doing no harm to anyone when in 1964 the full ferocity of the old-style repressive laws of censorship and criminal libel was unleashed on it.' (22)

Social commentator Craig McGregor describes the anachronistic setting of the trial: 'No 1 court of the Court of Criminal Appeal, where the case was heard, continues the penal colony theme of the entire building: a grim, drab room of dark wood and masochistic benches, a huge stained-wood carving of the Royal Arms (Dieu et Mon Droit) at one end and high monastery pews at the other, the judges' bench set in the shadow of a massive overhanging canopy, and lowering over everything the portraits of red-robed past Chief Justices: John Nodes Dickinson, 1860-61, Sir Philip Whistler Street, 1925-134, Sir William Portus Cullen, 1910-1925...'. (23)

Nicely dressed, the three defendants and publisher Francis James took their places as the Crown opened with an argument about Martin's strip, 'The Word Flashed Around the Arms'. They sparred over colloquialisms like 'king birds', 'fairies' or somesuch.

Notwithstanding that the 1956 Howl trial and the 1960 Lady Chatterley's Lover trial had amply dealt with the word fuck in print, the prosecution pretended to be terribly shocked by Martin's 'Get Folked' caption. Martin's cartoon-satire on the folk singing revival was accused of being dangerous to public morality. John Olsen took the stand and said, 'It's just a colloquial term your Worship, no big deal'.

The trial generated so much attention that circulation of the next issue of OZ blew out to 40,000. Martin's OZ sketch of the trial was a judge dressed as a clown, the speech bubble captioned with a Judge Locke-ism, 'Young people, this is a court of law, not a circus'. (24) Judge Gerald Locke did not take kindly to being lampooned.

Right here, Martin and the two Richards earned their stripes as heroes of whatever youth culture was doing. The justice system turned them into folk heroes. In the face of a likely prison sentence, they were not backing off. It's a glimpse of the sheer confidence of a generation that was about to invade London in the form of Robert Hughes, Germaine Greer, Clive James and another 20 or so significant Aussies.

On 23 September 1964 Stipendiary Magistrate Mr GA Locke sentenced the two Richards to six months jail with hard labour and Martin to four. The company, OZ Publications Ink Ltd was fined £100 and printer Francis James was fined £50. In her sad diary, Jo penned, 'Mart had up for obscene article. Headlines in all the papers. You find out who all your friends are. You have very few.' (25)

Said Martin, 'We got sentenced by a very tough Catholic magistrate, who we did stir a bit as OZ was coming out. We published a few cartoons about him, which provoked him. I drew them. We were feeding the case back into the magazine as it was happening. The whole argument against OZ seemed absurd to us.'

Despite bringing a 'certain degree of fame', a glamorous trial and thrusting OZ forward in the battle against censorship, it sure took its toll. It seemed inconceivable that the sons of Colonel Neville, Dr Sharp, and a north shore Anglican stalwart would be incarcerated by the justice system. But the lads were 'taken down', handcuffed, fingerprinted, fed fish heads and given a taste of what a six months' sentence might feel like. Just overnight. Until Martin's father fronted the bail money.

The two Richards and Martin were released on bail, pending an appeal. Said Martin, 'My father was very good, he came to court every day and bailed me, Richard Walsh and Richard Neville out. He always said Richard Walsh never sent the bail money back. Richie Walsh doesn't remember that.' (26)

Writes Geoffrey Dutton, 'As soon as the OZ prosecution was announced, a defence appeal was launched by RF Brissenden, Clem Christesen of Meanjin, Max Harris and Rosemary Wighton of Australian Book Review, Professor Peter Herbst, Professor H Munro (of the Freedom to Read Association), Stephen Murray-Smith of Overland and James McAuley of Quadrant. Thus almost every editor of an intellectual journal in the country was supporting OZ, including Tom Fitzgerald who gave evidence as an expert witness at the trial. The defence was that there was literary and artistic merit, and that the publication was justified in that it would not deprave or corrupt. The expert witnesses included Dr Harry Heseltine, Professor May, Elwyn Lynn, Mungo MacCallum, John Olsen, the well-known headmistress of Abbotsleigh, Betty Archdale and Gordon Hawkins.' (27)

OZ had an excellent legal team. Organized by Richard's solicitor, Martin lists, 'Paul Landa, Neville Wran, Lionel Murphy, John Kerr… all Labor apart from Edward St John – who I thought was one of the best legal minds. I think they were looking for a civil liberties case. They were looking to test the defence that was used successfully by Penguin for Lady Chatterley's Lover in England, which was "artistic merit". I think it possibly opened the door that lead a lot of stuff that hasn't got any artistic merit at all.

'We were defended on the grounds of artistic merit. We won on appeal. A lot of great witnesses appeared for us, it was a bit of a cause.' But Martin wanted to get in the dock and speak for himself, which he says they were not 'allowed' to do. Looking back, he said, 'I thought that was pretty strange - and that's when you realise maybe something else is going on…!' (28)

Martin, Richard and Richie were front-page news – a dirty little rag, whatever. Said Martin, 'I'd been very quiet before OZ. OZ was the thing. I think it brought a certain degree of fame at a young age from an unusual angle. The court cases and the severity - particularly of the initial sentence - polarized the community.' (29)

Free, after what would not be his last taste of prison, Richard schlepped over to New Caledonia for a break. When he returned Richard wrote a feature about Sydney's illegal abortion clinics, widely believed to have been granted legal immunity by lucrative police protection rackets. Also, around this time, Australia sent a battalion to fight in the Vietnam War, giving OZ a strong political angle.

Martin went back to Melbourne for an art opening and also to help Mirka paint leaves and roses on the doors and windows of a restaurant she and Georges had recently purchased. (30)

While Martin was gone, Richard – who was in love with Louise – kept company with Anou. He writes, 'Two or three times a week, I rushed from my copywriter's desk to a five o'clock movie. Then it was a brisk walk to the OZ office to type out my Herald review. A lonely routine. When Anou tagged along, I was delighted. She was bright, flirtatious, original. Anou created her own outfits, sewing and trimming the gingham as I typed banalities. When Sharp went to Melbourne for an opening, all those hours in the back stalls took a toll on our self-control. The sex was hot, the guilt immense. My best mate's bird – how could I?' (31) Martin returned and for a while nothing was said.

Meanwhile, working for the ABC, Garry had the facilities to complete his seemingly never-ending project, Ding-A-Ding Day. The film includes historical footage covering the birth of OZ magazine. Said Garry, 'It took me years. When I got to the ABC I got access to editing equipment, which I learned and I finished the film in 1965. When Martin saw Ding A Ding Day - in the film there's a shot of Richard grabbing Anou and kissing her in the OZ office - and I think that shocked him.' (32)

Martin confronted Richard. Richard fessed up.

In his book, Hippie Hippie Shake Richard says, 'I confessed to my friend, who was rather piqued…for about two days. Then all was forgiven.' (33) Not quite. Friends recall Martin still fulminating about this incident 40 years later! Garry shrugged off the incident, 'That was the times – free love. People treated it very lightheartedly then.' (34)

After all he'd been through, maybe now was time for Martin to paint, which he had not really done since high school.

At this time, Greg Weight worked in an advertising agency. As an 18-year old, Greg was fascinated by the Sydney Push and sought them out after work. Folkies like Jeannie Lewis, Gary Shearston and Black Allen

Murawalla sang in the back room while the virtues of Philosophical Anarchism were being vigorously discussed out the front.

One night, at a Push session, Greg ran into the art teacher who replaced Justin at Cranbrook. Greg said, 'I was talking to Charlie Brown, bemoaning my fate of being trapped in the art department of an advertising agency and how I was more interested in the art world. Pop Art had emerged. It was an area that I was keen on and Charlie said, "Maybe you'd be the right person to meet Martin Sharp?"

'I was enthralled by that possibility because I'd been an ardent follower of OZ magazine. Charlie gave me his number. I rang up Martin and asked whether he needed any help. He agreed he needed as much help as he could possibly get because he was painting an exhibition. I became his studio assistant.

'I worked with him for about six months before he went to London. We got on really well. I sometimes did the over-painting, stuck silver leaf on paintings, painted frames, putting paper maché on a sculpture he was working on. It wasn't about creating museum art, it was about creating ideas. So the materials weren't Belgian linen and Matisse oil paints, it was whatever paint Martin felt inclined to use that had the right colour - straight out of the tube or straight out of the tin. There was a freedom in the making of things and the doing - so I really did learn a lot about just letting myself go creatively there.' (35)

Martin and Greg painted Martin's first exhibition, Art for Mart's Sake, to be held at Clune Galleries in March of the following year. In those days, Martin never thought to have Greg co-sign the pictures, as he did later when Tim Lewis played a similar role. Oil and lacquer, on paper mounted on board - pictures like Love Machine and Seventeen Minutes to Four are typical of the style. (36) The works resembled what Monty Python's Terry Gilliam would come up with five years later.

Said Martin, 'All those images were based on collages. I cut up old catalogues of dental equipment and made these collages out of them. I then had them blown up photographically and painted over them. That was 1965.' (37)

January 1965 marked the arrival of another pop sensation from England - the Rolling Stones.

Martin and Richard had gotten themselves invited to a party at Elizabeth Bay, held for the Stones. To Richard's surprise, Jenny Kee arrived at the party with Mick Jagger on one arm and Keith Richard on the other. 'Howdja do it?' spluttered Richard. (38)

Jenny writes it in her book, A Big Life. 'Janthia (Walsh) and I set out for the Chevron, where the Stones were staying. Although there were thousands of fans everywhere, plus police, plus bodyguards, the works, just as there had been for the Beatles, I must admit it didn't excite me nearly as much. We got ourselves invited to a publicity bash thrown on the roof of the hotel. I wore an exotic red floral silk kimono. Without any effort we were singled out by the Stones' manager, Andrew Loog Oldham, and asked to his room, where Janthia bathed herself in perfumes. She was paired off with Mick Jagger. I with Keith Richards, who was intense, silent and morose. I felt sorry for him. He didn't seem to be coping too well with his fame.' (39)

At the party, Richard chatted to Mick Jagger as much as he could and Martin connected too. However, before anyone could get too deep, Jenny and Janthia whisked their boys off to the Gas Lash – the speakeasy near Central Station that had added to its legend by recently being raided by the Vice Squad. Martin's convivial response to all this excitement was a cartoon in OZ, featuring a bare-breasted woman wearing sunglasses saying, 'I was rolled by the Stones'. Some say he drew Jenny, others reckon Janthia. (40)

To date, the Australian folk singing scene had been quite cultic. For Lefties only, it surfaced in the back rooms of pubs and often made heroes of unionists. The Basic Wage Dream by Don Henderson is a classic example. But there was something about Gary Shearston that set him apart from his older folkie peers - maybe his looks, his youth or his spirit. Gary was the only Folkie to appear on Brian Henderson's Bandstand, that's for sure.

Sydney radio stations began playing a track from his newest album Australian Broadside. The single Sydney Town was a Top 10 hit. The words included:

  Have you heard about OZ magazine
  Convicted on a charge of being obscene
  Seems you're not allowed to satirise
  If you tell the truth they call it lies. (41)

In April, Louise Ferrier sailed to London, which got Richard twitchy. He moved into investigative journalism and published The OZ Guide to Sydney's Underworld – with Martin's Dick Tracey cover. It listed a Top 20 of Sydney major criminals. The list deliberately left the No 1 spot blank but at No 2 Richard listed the name 'Len' who he, somewhat unwisely, described as a 'fizz-gig' (police informant).

Soon after the list was published, the fearsome Lenny McPherson called on Richard's house in Paddington. McPherson's primary concern was whether the OZ editors were part of a rival gang. They weren't. Just silly uni students. McPherson restrained himself from decking Richard for calling him a fizz.

The OZ Top 20 crim-list reportedly played a part in the death of Sydney felon Jacky Steele, who was shot in Woollahra in November 1965. Steele, who had been trying to take over protection rackets controlled by McPherson, had taunted McPherson that he was not No 1. OZ published extracts from the minutes of a confidential meeting of Sydney detectives held on 1 December 1965, leaked to the magazine by an underworld source. (42)

Less concerned about the underworld, Martin continued poking fun at establishment figures. Sydney's artistically-minded set were affronted that the NSW Minister for Public Works, Sir Davis Hughes, was high-jacking architect Jorn Utzon's original Opera House design. Hughes brought about Utzon's resignation and had the Opera House completed with designs that were inconsistent with the architect's original vision.

Martin drew a nasty-faced Hughes for OZ. He lampooned the Minister as the sinister face of Luna Park, his first drawing of a place that would constantly appear in subsequent prints, posters and paintings. (43)

Jo and Henry divorced in 1965.

Said Martin, 'My grandfather and my mother were fighting after the divorce. It caused a rift with them. My mother broke off the relationship (with Keith) and my grandfather didn't believe her. That caused a complete trauma. So he turned his back on his daughter. (44)

'It was a cataclysmic divorce. I stayed with my mother. She suffered terribly from the divorce – I know! And she was ripped off - I know! She had few loves in her life, she only had two. She fell in love with her doctor.' (45)

There was a lot of cross-pollination in Sydney's art-bohemia of the time. Musicians, actors, visual artists and writers worked in constant collaboration. Artists made films and filmmakers painted pictures. Along with David Perry, Aggy Read and John Clark, Albie Thoms set up an experimental collective, Ubu Films in Sydney. Albie loved Garry Shead's films. He wrote, 'I was amazed at the way Garry worked without a script, using his intuition and a feeling for location to determine what would take place.'

Garry invited Albie to help him with Broken Hearted, which he intended shooting in a day. It featured Martin playing the male lead, airily smoking Gauloises while his love interest was Judy Carroll, then John Firth-Smith's girlfriend and soon after, his wife. (46)

Another film group was run by Mick Glasheen, Johnny Allen and Peter Kingston. Mick Glasheen was one of the contributors to the UNSW revue where Roger Foley was running light shows. Roger and Albie developed a cooperative relationship because they needed each other's equipment. Said Roger, 'When Ubu were doing their lights shows they'd borrow their lights and film projectors from me and I'd borrow the films from them'. (47)

One of Roger's ideas was to use Martin's OZ magazine monologue cartoons in a UNSW university revue he had devised called First No Pinky, which is how he got to meet Martin. It was the Norman Normal sketch.

One enduring facet of the show is Martin's 'smile on a stick'. It was almost the logo for the show, appearing on the poster and also on the promotional brochure. That smile was the cover of OZ 25.

Next time Martin got involved with Roger (after his London years) Roger had evolved into lightmeister Ellis D Fogg.

Albie wrote, 'Some of our cast and crew were involved in that year's University revue, First No Pinky. Produced by Keith Johnson and Colin Anderson, it had sets by Martin Sharp, who also provided scripts based on his OZ contributions. One of Martin's evoked the ecstasy of the mystery-man writing Eternity on city pavements.' (48)

Shortly before leaving for London, in March, Martin held his first exhibition. Greg - the 'assistant' - was present. He said, 'It was at the old Clune Gallery (the gallery that became the Yellow House) and Martin was primed to do something because he was the darling enfant terrible in the Sydney set. His intention was to go to the UK and do something there but he wanted to leave with a bit of a celebration. That was the exhibition I worked on. Martin was absolutely engulfed by admirers and Anou clinging to his arm.

'It had nothing to do with me at the opening, but it was a lesson. You've got to be the artist, not bloody help the artist!' (49)

Said Martin, 'My first exhibition, I'll tell you about that – to Roma. I held my first exhibition for her unconsciously.' (50)

'I stopped working for OZ for a while and just needed to paint. I was doing very different work. It was quite Pop. I painted that exhibition at my mother's house.

'That's when I got into Dylan, Mr Tambourine Man, I loved that song. While the Beatles were singing about love, girls and that sort of stuff – fantastic stuff - they weren't as interesting lyrically. Dylan was amazing.

He was very impressive but one left the week before he had his concert here. I'd have loved to have seen that show at the Sydney Stadium!' (51)

'When I look at all the pictures I did just before I left for London I hadn't had a clue about dope or acid. I might have had a smoke by then but that didn't have a major influence. I was certainly doing psychedelic pictures, with titles from Dylan songs and things like that. But they weren't consciously psychedelic. Look at any time associated with smoking hashish and marijuana and you'll find that influence comes into art - like the Paris of the 1890s, the Surrealists, Baudelaire and all those people who smoked dope…'. (52)

Jo, of course, was immensely proud of her son. Henry was more standoffish. At the Sharp family gatherings that Martin now dreaded, Uncle Alan – the esteemed pioneer heart surgeon – took Martin aside and condescendingly explained the rudiments of art. And Henry affected a mixture of embarrassment and pride. Said Martin, 'I'm not saying my father didn't realise I was an artist. He'd come to my exhibitions but he'd come with two of his mates that I'd never met. They'd tell me, 'your father loves you' but it didn't feel like it to me!' (53)

Martin and Richard left for London in February 1966. Richie returned to his studies and continued to publish a reduced edition of Sydney OZ until 1969. He included regular contributions by Richard and Martin from London.

Shortly afterwards, Garry held his first solo exhibition at the Watters Gallery in Sydney. Called North Shore, titles like 'Wahroonga Lady in her Naked Lunch' were much more provocative than the actual pictures. Nevertheless, the police raided the gallery, Garry made the papers and surprisingly his pictures were not taken down.

And Greg got a job as photographic assistant to Alan Nye, one of the busiest fashion photographers in Sydney. Nye had his own studio in Yurong Street in East Sydney, constantly buzzing with beautiful models. It was the perfect place for a 19-year old to be.

Stuart Richie died in 1966 when Martin was in London. Said Martin, 'My grandmother said, "your grandfather died a brokenhearted man". I've got my grandfather's Will, he cut my mother off – just like that! Except, he left her an annuity. The excuse was to protect the Will from my father.' (54)

6.

FRESHER CREAM

*Martin held a farewell exhibition at the Clune Gallery:
cartoons, collages, popsicle-bright paintings.
Everything sold, even a portrait of me bopping
in a corduroy suit, the eternal groover.*

RICHARD NEVILLE

Barry Humphries was in London. Germaine Greer was in London. Louise Ferrier was in London. Robert Hughes was in London. Robert Whitaker was in London. Colin Lanceley was in London. Jenny Kee was in London. And more significantly for our two travelers – Martin and Richard - who needed somewhere sling their Army disposal rucksacks upon arrival, Richard's eldest sister Jill had established herself in central London.

In February 1966, Martin left Australia with quite a bang, as he'd hoped. The Clune Gallery exhibition was packed with admirers. It had been a bit of a risk, because although his OZ followers were used to Martin as a b/w cartoonist, he had not yet fully presented himself as a painter of pictures. Martin's Greg Weight-assisted collage-paintings gave every indication that a great career had been launched. Pictures from this series found their way into major galleries in time.

Based on his OZ artoons (or Sharp-toons), the NSW Uni review was running a different kind of Martin Sharp show - First No Pinky, produced/directed by Roger Foley. Martin attended its February launch shortly before leaving for London. Also in Sydney, Garry's film, Ding A Ding Day was shown at last, marking Martin's screen debut. But although Martin drew its OZ magazine ads, he did not catch the opening of Jim Sharman's production, On Stage OZ.

And a North Sydney publishing company, Scripts Pty Ltd, contracted Martin's first book for publication, Cartoons, A Selection from OZ, The Australian, The Sydney Morning Herald, Honi Soit, Tharunka, Etc. A 'best of' publication, this silver-coloured book featured Martin's Get Folked 'toon without controversy. (1)

Meanwhile, writer and Sydney Uni dropout literature student, Peter Draffin had written a novel Pop that had also been accepted by Scripts. (2) Said Peter, 'I'd seen a lot of Martin's drawings in OZ magazine and I knew he'd be a good person to illustrate my book, so I approached him and he liked it.' (3)

OZ and Pop were Martin's main drawing projects while tramping the hippie trail through Asia with Richard. Said Martin, 'I was drawing it on the trip and sending it back. Using Op Art a lot, Bridget Riley, wave pictures…'. (4)

Draffin recalled, '…that's what Martin did in cafés and stuff.' (5)

While Richard and Martin hiked the hippie trail, Richie kept OZ going in Australia. In the mail, he received a three-month burst from Martin, then a lessening contribution.

The cover for the March issue featured Martin's Boofhead, also inside - I Was Rolled by the Stones, The Australian Londoner/The London Australian (full page), plus an ad for On Stage OZ.

April: a full page strip called Two Innocents Abroad, the Adventures of Martin and Richard in cartoon format.

June: Two Innocents Abroad Pt 2 and another full-pager called Darling! depicting a grotesque Dame Edna Everage before Martin's trademark exclamation mark. (6)

With a no-pressure deadline, Martin had also been approached by publisher Ure Smith to illustrate Craig McGregor's People, Politics and Pop, a collection of McGregor's Sydney Morning Herald, Quadrant and Meanjin articles - a social history of these lively times. (7) Other than jokes about gauche tourists, few of Martin's on-the-road OZ-toons reflected his actual geographical location. (8)

In Peter Draffin's Pop, Martin sketches as if he is enjoying himself. The drawings follow the storyline, with pictures of the band, the party, filming and words like Pop and Wow that looked like black and white pre-psychedelic art.

In contrast, Martin's collage-illustrations for Craig McGregor's People, Politics and Pop, are autobiographical and sometimes angry. Private School deals with his impressions of Cranbrook, Three Gaoled Filthy Paper mocks the OZ trial, Martin even seems angry on behalf of Garry Shead's police bust - with bitter depictions of suburban love goddesses.

Completed in London, some of the images in McGregor's book are a type of 'trial run' for Martin and Bob Whitaker's Beatles Calendar and Martin's famous Dylan poster. (9)

In his book Hippie Hippie Shake, Richard gave his account of traveling Asia with Martin. It was a lovesick trip. Richard pined for Louise and Martin for Anou. In April OZ 27 Martin documents 'the adventures of the OZ overseas correspondents at the crossroads of the world – Singapore'. (10)

Martin and Richard traveled through Singapore, the Malay Peninsula, Bangkok, Cambodia, Laos, Burma, Calcutta and the Himalayas. Although the food didn't agree with him, Martin was deeply impressed by some places. He said, 'Richard Neville and myself went to Katmandu. It was certainly the loveliest place I'd visited in ages – the peacefulness of the people, water buffaloes, villages…the things that happened there – terrible wars were raged in such a lovely place.' (11)

It had now been a few months since Martin and Richard had seen the inside of a barber's shop. They were frequently pestered by locals wanting to know if they were the Rolling Stones? It's not difficult to imagine Richard sometimes saying yes. Martin and Richard experienced temples, saddhus, opium dens, cock fights and food that made Martin throw up.

Somewhere in Nepal they asked each other, as if for the first time, what each planned to do in London?

'I'll just wait for you,' Martin shrugged.

Richard admitted that he hadn't a clue what to do, to which Martin insightfully said, 'Do what you're good at - start a magazine'. (12)

Martin confirms, 'Richard didn't know what he'd do with himself in London, so I suggested he bring out OZ'. (13)

After climbing a Nepalese mountain in July, Richard returned to find Martin gone, leaving a note that read, 'See you in Swinging London'. Recovering from his friend's unforeseen exit, Richard wrote, 'A bit of a blow, yes, but I almost felt a sense of relief'. (14) Said Martin, 'Richard stayed in Nepal. I was a bit sick. I went on ahead of him.' (15)

Richard's eldest sister Jill Neville was amongst the early-60s wave of young Aussies to come to London. Between hanging out with the Sydney Push in the late-50s and working as a typist in Sydney's Daily Mirror, Jill saved the £80 'under 21' steamer fare to London. She arrived in 1960 and scored a job as an audio-typist at the BBC.

By 1966, Jill was living in Holland Park with her 6-year old daughter Judy, the child from a disastrous two-year marriage. Jill was witty, sassy and outspoken. She wore a fedora hat, had green fingernails and smoked through a Sally Bowles cigarette holder. Her visitors were the smart publishing and advertising set, plus newspaper and TV journalists. When Martin rapped on her door, she was tapping out her second novel. Her first, Fall Girl had recently hit the bookshops to great reviews. (16) Jill was indeed expecting Martin, though probably not in July and probably not without her brother.

Said Martin, 'Getting to London, one met a whole lot of other people who were rather similar to oneself – sensibility perhaps – maybe a lot to do with art school I suppose. Art students, terrific friendliness, no class barrier. This sense of a contained youth culture was completely different to adult culture. It had its own language, its own world, its own dreams. Very idealistic I think - as is natural with young people – the possibility of a peaceful world'. (17)

Richard arrived nearly two months later, in September, around the time Clune Galleries was holding an exhibition of OZ artwork in Sydney: Martin Sharp, Garry Shead, Peter Kingston, John Allen, Mike Glasheen, Mike Brown, Peter Fisher. It was another of Sydney's 'where is Martin Sharp?' moments. More or less broke, Richard banged on Jill's front door at night and read a note from Martin pinned to it, 'too late, it's swung'. Bang bang bang brought a yawning Martin to the door. Jill too. Richard found her kitchen stacked with Martin's pen and ink works. Richard was raring to reignite with Louise.

Knowing this, Martin played him a track from Dylan's new Blonde on Blonde double LP. The song was Visions of Johanna, which found 'Louise and her lover so entwined…'. Maybe Martin enjoyed seeing Richard squirming as the song progressed. (18) Martin would do this throughout his life: attribute a specific meaning to songs that the songwriter could never have foreseen.

Next morning, borrowing Jill's Mini-Minor, Martin drove Richard to find Louise. They set out for Biba's Boutique, a jungle of Art Nouveau where Jenny Kee worked. She might know where to track Louise. Jenny had reinvented herself as an up-to-the-minute dollybird Mod while Richard presented as a dusty hippie. Jenny wrote, 'He (Richard) came into the store on his first morning in London, fresh from an overland odyssey through Kathmandu and Kabul…a couple of paces behind him was Martin Sharp'. (19) All-round greeting, then yes, Jenny knew where Richard might find Louise. There was an affectionate moment in the backseat of the Mini when he did.

Once settled into London, money became more an issue for Richard than for Martin. In an attempt to get things moving, Jill took both of them to an advertising firm - her employers - with a view of finding them work. Maybe, their portfolio of b/w hand-drawn ads for Sydney's Gas Lash, Clune Galleries and Binkie Burgers wasn't up to their tastes. Either way, Richard still needed that $folding stuff, kinda desperately.

Martin, on the other hand, was living on a semi-independent income that enabled him to occasionally splash out. The UFO, the newest club in town, was where Martin got a close look at cutting edge underground bands. He said, 'The band that really impressed me most at that time was Pink Floyd. Seeing them at the UFO Club was a great scene. Syd Barrett was with them at that stage. I saw him perform light shows'. (20)

Syd Barrett - the guy who played slide guitar with a plastic school ruler! Pink Floyd – the band that played performance events rather than concerts! Martin was having a great time, while Richard wrote, 'mostly I was preoccupied, on the lookout for parties, pocket money and ways of making a splash'.

So Richard did what Richard does best. He simply talked. He got himself noticed pretty well immediately. When the Evening Standard phoned looking for 'that notorious satirist from Sydney' Richard talked himself up. He talked about the important revolutionary role OZ played in sweeping 50s-style Australia aside. He had an answer for everyone. When asked by the media what he was planning to do in London, Richard replied, 'Start OZ of course, the town needs a bomb under it!' The newspaper ran a pin-up shot of Louise (the OZ 'secretary') and described Richard as 'coolly ambitious'. Now that he'd boldly announced on a BBC live-to-air radio show that he was going to start OZ - Richard either had to do it or lose face. (21)

Leaving Jill's place, Martin scored temporary digs with Robert Hughes. Hughes had left Australia in 1964, living for a time in Italy before settling in London where he was doing very well indeed. At the time Martin stayed with him, Hughes was writing for The Daily Telegraph, The Spectator, The Times, The Observer and more. Soon, he would even write for OZ.

Hughes led to Martin re-connecting with Bob Whitaker. Martin moved in with him, but they were hastily on the hunt for better quarters.

Said Martin, 'Bob Whitaker was living out at Greenwich, which was a lovely area in the suburbs, but it was not quite what I was hoping for!'

The Kings Road Chelsea impressed Martin and Whitaker agreed. It was Whitaker, not Martin who found their first premises on the strip, opposite Picasso's coffee shop and handy to London's first 'psychedelic' boutique Granny Takes a Trip. The Kings Road was certainly the place to be - café society, Mod clothes, Psychedelia, colourful shop displays and a world of ideas walking past on the footpath. Designer Mary Quant was said to have shaped her pubic hair into a heart. She ran another famous Kings Road shop called Bazaar.

Martin recalled, 'Bob and I went to Kings Road one day and I thought, "This is fantastic!" Bob agreed - so he found a great place in Joubert Studios Kings Road. A little lady lived next door that we saw very rarely. That was Judy Garland, in the same little alley we were in. She was pretty wrecked. (22)

'It was a difficult-shaped place to live in, because you really only had front door, bathroom, kitchen, lovely glazed corridor and a huge studio – wood panels. I think it had been a display workshop for Joubert (ie. Amédée Joubert & Son) who was a great outfitter. There were samples of his work still lying around. It was a fantastic place for one person but it didn't quite work for two. Bob had the best room. He slept in the big studio, which was a cul-de-sac. I slept in a tent in the kitchen area. He'd found the studio, so it was fair enough. But it didn't give me a lot of privacy!' (23)

Chelsea is where Martin would spend his next three years. He admits it was conspicuously fashionable, though at the time he thought of it more as an artist's suburb. He said, 'Chelsea was always quite an artistic area – there are quite a lot of studios there and the Chelsea Arts Club. Oscar Wilde used to live there, Turner…!' (24)

Ah, Whitaker.

Coming from Melbourne in 1964, Whitaker located in London as part of the official Beatles crew. Whitaker photographed Beatlemania at its American peak. He was their official photographer at the concert at New York's Shea Stadium, attended by 55,000 fans, a world record attendance at the time. In May, while Martin and Richard were backpacking through Asia, Whitaker photographed the Beatles for the Revolver album, after which he toured with them in Germany and Japan.

Whitaker did the cover shot for the notorious Beatles' Yesterday and Today album. Known as the 'Butcher' cover, it features the four looking not so fab, in white smocks amongst decapitated dolls and raw meat. Sick of the usual publicity shots, John Lennon liked it and Paul defended it. Nevertheless in America and Canada, Whitaker's cover was condemned as being in extremely poor taste. It was withdrawn after some 60,000 were pressed. Licking his wounds from that setback, Whitaker showed Martin the Beatles' sanitised Revolver LP with his Butcher Cover replaced by a Klaus Voormann b/w sketch and a Bob Whitaker photo on the back.

About this time, Whitaker's tenure as Beatles photographer was being wrapped up. The band gave its last public performance in San Francisco on 29 August 1966 after which they would have no more need for an official photographer. Whitaker was down to taking happy snaps of George and Patti painting their house in psychedelic colours. In his book, The Unseen Beatles, he admits that both his career as a photographer and Martin's hopes as a Beatles cartoonist got only limited success.

It reads: 'With time on their hands they (Martin and Bob) worked several joint projects. They re-cycled some of Bob's Beatle photographs as poster ideas and humorous cartoons, though none of them were published. Their most ambitious and compelling scheme was for a Beatles calendar. It was never completed. Recalls Bob, "…because we gave up after spilling a bottle of Indian ink over one of the pictures"'. Twenty-five years later Bob published them in The Unseen Beatles. The calendar is b/w fun - Beatles cut-outs, captioned by Martin. (25)

Said Martin, 'I did a Calendar with Bob Whitaker's photographs and OZ lettering. I was full of confidence. Nothing came of it'. Martin dismisses meeting the Beatles as inconsequential. He said, 'I was just another guy they had to cope with'.

The indifferent reception to the Beatles Calendar was a setback. Martin came up with a better idea - he worked on a series of complex poster-images that people might stare at for ages after an acid trip. Psychedelic is how they were described.

Martin rejects that he may have initiated psychedelic poster art. He said, 'Oh no! I'm sure they were coming out in America. I think psychedelic posters came from San Francisco, Moscoso, Mouse, Bill Graham's Fillmore! They got all that Op Art vibration. So no, I didn't start it!' (26)

Psychedelic art grew out of Haight-Asbury's counter-cultural community. Leading proponents were San Francisco poster artists, Rick Griffin, Victor Moscoso and Stanley Mouse. Entrepreneur, Bill Graham used psychedelic artwork on the promotional posters for his concerts. The style was inspired by a blend of Art Nouveau, Victoriana, Dada and Pop Art. Sometimes the hippie artwork resembled what Aubrey Beardsley might have done with lurid colours. But it wasn't all about America. British artist Bridget Riley became hugely influential with Op Art that created optical illusions.

The first poster with which Martin greeted his England audience was the highly successful red and gold Mr Tambourine Man silk-screened 'Bob Dylan'. With the help of scissors, glue and his fabulous Finnish assistant Eija Vehka Aho, Martin created the image in Whitaker's studio using metallic foil, Indian ink and reflective paper. Martin confirmed, 'Yes, that was the first one'. (27)

Its impact grew slowly but grow it did. By the close of 1967 Martin's trippy Dylan poster was pinned up in teenage bedrooms, student dorms and hippie toilets from London to San Francisco and Sydney. Mr Tambourine Man has since been bootlegged, ripped off and even used as a cover of the Bob Dylan 1966 bootleg album. It was also the cover of OZ 7. Forty years later the Bob Dylan image was sold on merchandise (mouse mat, glasses case) by the Art Gallery of New South Wales for their 2014-15

Pop Into Popism exhibition in which Mr Tambourine Man was one of the gallery's six promo banners, waving in the Sydney breezes alongside Pop Art legends, Andy Warhol, David Hockney, Roy Lichtenstein, Keith Haring and Peter Blake.

Martin's next poster was the metallic Donovan, Sunshine Superman. Like the Dylan poster, it too was tremendously popular, with more Martin Sharp posters surely on the way. (28)

Martin explains his approach, 'The lettering are letters in one way, but they're shapes in another – the thing is to try and make the thing work as a visual whole - to convey information. I like the cheapness and the mass of posters, like Pop records.' (29)

Martin produced at least three other metallic-style posters in this 1966-67 period. He also did the OZ is a New Magazine cover for London OZ 1. About Martin's instant poster success, Richard adds, 'OZ associate, Peter Ledeboer, was so taken by my friend's visual flair that he set up a new company, Big O Posters, geared to produce and promote every piece of artwork created by Sharp'. (30) In 2015, it still reproduced Martin's art.

Richard and Louise cobbled together London OZ 1 at Jill's place. Jill was probably desperate for her brother to move out, as OZ was beginning to take over her premises, attracting a smattering of volunteers and callers, including former contributors to Sydney OZ. (31)

Said Martin, 'Richard is an excellent publisher, an excellent coordinator of people. Terrific psychology. Wonderful humour. He always smells a rat and turns it into something wonderful before it turns into a bigger rat!' (32)

London OZ 1 was launched 24 January (Jenny Kee's 20th birthday). Despite terrible reviews, it sold out, followed by OZ 2, which limped a bit. Another underground publication, IT (International Times) was launched only a few months before OZ so - although competitiveness wasn't cool in the hippie era - OZ had a direct competitor.

At this stage, OZ was a rebel without a big cause. The pro-marijuana cause soon came in February after Sgt Norman Pilcher and his Drug

Squad busted Mick Jagger and Keith Richards at Keith's country home, Redlands. That the police had a prepared warrant and an on-the-spot News of the World journalist showed all the signs of a set-up.

In June, Mick Jagger would be charged with possessing four pep pills and Keith Richards for allowing his premises to be used for the smoking of marijuana. Mick was sentenced to three months' imprisonment and Keith was given a year's sentence. Both were immediately imprisoned, but released on bail the next day pending appeal. In the four months leading to trial, the Legalise Pot campaigners cranked up their protests, with OZ magazine getting onboard and Martin creating his Legalise Cannabis poster. In the interim, Rolling Stones guitarist Brian Jones got busted too, again by Sgt Pilcher.

Building on the success of Martin's sell-out metallic Dylan poster, Big O printed and circulated Legalise Cannabis too, promoting what would be in July, a Legalise Pot Rally held in London's Hyde Park.

With OZ off and running, plus a market for his posters, Martin had two regular outlets for his art - except that this time around the OZ-cycle, improvements to offset printing techniques offered him colour. Brilliant colour. It had been a while since Martin had worked in full colour. Although they looked psychedelic, Martin's Dylan, Donovan and Legalise Pot posters were actually 2-colour printed on reflective paper.

The drab 1966 English winter saw Martin homesick for the Australian summer. With Pop at the printer, Draff left Sydney, intending to get to London sooner or later. In the interim, he encamped in a town called Formenterra, on the Balaeric island of Ibiza. Jenny Kee and friends had recently enjoyed Ibiza and returned to London prattling on about the sea the way Sydney-siders do and Londoners don't.

Lovesick and missing Anou, it was time for Martin to take a break from London's depressing weather. Time to visit the sun and Draff. Martin had never known – or didn't think he did – an author of 116 pages of continuous prose.

Said Martin, 'London was bleak. Certainly I was missing Australia. I was missing the beaches and thinking of summer and summer love – those sort of things. I didn't actually meet anyone under those circumstances, I was always thinking of Anou (who was my girlfriend). Peter Draffin was living on Formentera, Ibiza, the Balearic Isles, which are off the coast of Spain. There's a mysterious island just off the coast of Ibiza, which is meant to have been where the sirens sung to Ulysses.'

Martin penned the words: You thought the leaden winter would bring you down forever...(London)...so you rode upon a steamer...

Martin explained, 'I remember going to Formentera on a ferry - not a steamer - it was a small boat. They served cognac. The contrast of the sparkling water - the sun and the sea - to London in the winter, and how a summer love couldn't stand the hardness of the winter. And so you've got to make a choice – staying maybe in London or Australia? The difference between Bondi and the Serpentine!

'With tales of brave Ulysses, how his naked ears were tortured by the sirens sweetly singing... I probably have got more lyrics to that song than what I wrote originally. I wrote it to the tune of Suzanne – "Suzanne takes you down to her place by the river..." to me that was a very influential album by Judy Collins.

'Writing Tales of Brave Ulysses was a thrill to me. Very free and surreal imagery, like Whiter Shade of Pale and that great period of songwriting in the modern era. I was just getting a rhythm and the images came. I wrote some of it at Ibiza and some back in London. Or I may have written it all in Ibiza, (I'm not sure where I wrote it really.) The line the tiny purple fishes run laughing through your fingers - that was more Formentera than Ibiza, trying to catch those little fish. (33)

'I didn't know how to write rock lyrics because rock lyrics have their own special sound techniques. It's really a story-telling song about desire, summer and mythology.' (34)

Writing lyrics was not all Martin did while staying with Draff. Martin also drew up a 24-page book titled, Twice Upon a Time. Martin's may have intended it as his follow-up to Martin Sharp's Cartoons. He was more of a book/magazine illustrator at this stage, than a poster-artist.

Martin's introduction to this little book seems to offer itself to a broad impersonal readership, 'This book is written drawn, climb inside dear reader it is for no one else but you.'

Twice Upon a Time grapples with the cosmos. It is Intelligent Life in the Universe by Carl Sagan meets Vincent Van Gogh's Letters. From Carl Sagan, Martin quotes, 'The saucer myths represent a neat compromise between the need to believe in a traditional paternal God and the contemporary pressures to accept the pronouncements of science'.

And from Vincent, on the second-last page: 'How I wish you could see everything I see nowadays, there is so much beauty…' (turn page) '…before me. I can do nothing but pursue it'. Martin closes with a pen and ink sketch of Vincent on the road to Tarascon. (35)

Martin didn't approach a publisher with Twice Upon a Time but he thought enough of Tales of Brave Ulysses to share it with Suzie Cuthbert (later, Sue Weight). One evening, Suzie and friend Charlotte Martin called to see Whitaker. They were models. Charlotte from France, Suzie from Melbourne, (which is how she knew Whitaker). In the course of the evening, Martin showed Suzie his Tales of Brave Ulysses lyrics/poem. She thought they were great. (36)

Located in Margaret Street London, the Speakeasy Club was a late-night meeting place for record industry executives, artist agency execs and Rock stars who wanted to mix with other Rock stars. Jenny Kee worked at the bar. The Speakeasy is where Jenny caught up with John Lennon after their Sydney tryst. 'I don't suppose you remember me?' she shyly asked John, whose memory may have been sharper had he not been accompanied at the time by his wife Cynthia.

One night Jenny was serving drinks when Eric Clapton walked in with Charlotte on his arm. (37) Martin was certainly taken by Cream, having presented Richard with their first album Fresh Cream for his December birthday. Knowing this, Jenny phoned Martin to proclaim, 'You've got to come down here!'

Martin describes the scene, 'So I went to this club and there was this girl I knew called Charlotte Martin, a French model - very beautiful and quite tough - a very proud young thing - quite brusque with me. I saw her in the Speakeasy sitting with a couple of guys and I didn't know anyone else there, so I went and joined them. It was a Rock Muso's Club. I found out they were musicians and I said, "Oh, I just wrote a song!" One of the guys said, "I just wrote a tune". I said, "Here are the lyrics!" I wrote them down on a piece of paper, gave them to him, and in two weeks Eric turned up with a 45 record. He put that wonderful music to it. The lyrics would have got nowhere without him.' (38)

Martin has repeatedly told that story to interviewers. But Suzie Cuthbert was at that table too and Suzie seldom gets a mention. Suzie's former husband Greg Weight paints a fuller picture, 'Sue claims to have been partially responsible in encouraging Martin to give Eric Clapton - who she was friends with – Tales of Brave Ulysses - the lyrics. Now she is not one to tell lies. Suzie clearly says she was with Eric at a table at the Speakeasy. She'd read what Martin had written, and she encouraged him to give it to Eric.' (39)

Never a 'pop' star, Eric Clapton saw himself as a musician. He'd walked out of a successful band, the Yardbirds, because in his mind, they'd sold out with their pop song For Your Love, which peaked at No 3 on the UK charts.

Clapton next joined Britain's most credible blues outfit of the time, John Mayall's Blues Breakers. After recording the famous Blues Breakers album (often called the 'Beano' album because of the comic that Eric is reading on the cover shot), Eric left them to create what is acclaimed as the first 'supergroup', Cream. The band featured the best drummer - Ginger Baker, the best bassist - Jack Bruce and with Eric Clapton is God graffiti on a much-photographed wall in London – there were no doubts about Eric's credibility.

Cream was actually Ginger's idea. He asked Eric to join him. Eric agreed, providing Jack was on bass. Ginger and Jack argued incessantly ever since that pairing, which was uncomfortable in every way except musically.

The band's debut album, Fresh Cream peaked at No 6 on the UK charts and No 39 in America. It was a mixture of blues covers and compositions by Jack and Ginger. Lyrics were not this trio's long suit. Jack was roping in performance-poet/friend Pete Brown to infuse words into his brilliant riffs, leading to songs like Sunshine of Your Love and Strange Brew.

At this stage, Eric regarded songwriting as some kind of miraculous process. At a stretch, Eric reckoned he was good for about one composition per year and when Martin handed him the written-on serviette, this must have been the one!

In his autobiography Eric recounts, 'As it happened I had in my mind at that moment an idea inspired by a favourite song of mine by the Lovin' Spoonful called Summer in the City so I asked him to show me the words. He wrote them down on a napkin and gave them to me.' (40)

Commenting on the process, Martin said, 'Eric altered the words a little, just to fit them in, but he kept the whole idea of the song'. (41) 'To me it was like an entry into the world of popular song, joining the songwriters and meeting with the musicians on a level of working together.' (42)

What would become the Disraeli Gears LP was recorded at Atlantic Studios in New York, 11-15 May 1967. Atlantic Studio's kingpin, Ahmet Ertegun thought Cream had been signed to the label as a blues unit fronted by Clapton. Wasn't Cream all about Eric Clapton? Eric said no, Jack should sing most of the songs. That Eric claimed to be 'just the guitarist' didn't help. (43)

Ertegun didn't understand Eric's reticence. Neither did he follow the progressive – psychedelic - turn these Cream Blues were taking. But Ertegun had enough nous to hand the problem to someone who did get it, producer Felix Pappalardi. Pappalardi cut the group loose to do their thing. Sunshine of Your Love – okay. Strange Brew – yes. Eric refusing to sing Tales of Brave Ulysses – no problem. Jack improvised the vocals in one take over Eric's wah-wah. (44)

Wah-Wah?

Hearing the wah on Tales was a first for most people. 'What's that?' everyone asked, wondering about Eric's extraordinary guitar sound, mimicking both the human voice and ocean ripples.

The wah-wah effect had actually been around since the 1920s, used by trumpet and trombone players, but the first guitar wah pedal was created by Brad Plunkett at Warwick Electronics US in November 1966 and somehow Eric got one the day before laying down the song. (45)

Pete Townshend of the Who certainly felt Tales had upped the songwriting lyric stakes. In his autobiography he wrote, 'Jimi Hendrix was testing some of his first lyrical ideas at his shows. Eric's friend, the painter and designer Martin Sharp, was helping him write songs, and Martin's lyrics were very ambitious and poetic. Caught between two great emerging songwriting talents, I felt challenged to evolve.' (46)

Cream got Hippie-tinged while touring America. They grew their hair and started dressing in colourful paisley neck-shirts, scarves and jackets. Strange Brew/Tales of Brave Ulysses was rush-released as a 45 rpm single before the month was out.

Having received advanced copies, Eric decided to drop in on his co-writer to give him one. Not anticipating a Rock song, Martin was admiringly surprised. Eric too was another kind of surprised. While he had been in New York recording Disraeli Gears, Martin had moved into an attractive property known as The Pheasantry. Originally built around 1670 for Charles II's lover, showgirl Nell Gwynn, this pad had heaps more ambience than where Eric was living in some kind of apartment.

Sometimes described as an eccentric poseur with artistic connections, sometimes, a fast-talker with regal connections (ie. Lord Boothby). Or even a small-time crim with both cheeks carved into the 'Big Smile' by the hard men of the underworld, the Kray Twins. David Litvinoff (Litva) was really a procurer. The Procurer is the title of Lucien Freud's 1954 portrait of Litva.

Describing Litva, many people grope into the barrel of horrible words and select the worst one. Yet Martin and Eric describe him in glowing terms. Mick Jagger's Jumping Jack Flash was supposedly written about the guy.

Litvinoff could get anything – boys, heroin – whatever. His half-brother Emanuel Litvinoff is a well-respected Penguin novelist. (47) His other half-brother, Barnet Litvinoff, a respected historian. David was nothing like them. His gift was an ability to instantly sum up what anyone might want. When Litva met Martin, Martin was cooped up at Whitaker's place and he desperately wanted space. One day David Litvinoff and friend simply arrived at Whitaker's, right out of the blue. Walked in.

Said Martin, 'One day a couple of guys came through and there was this fast-talking older guy. They just walked in as if they owned the place and started rapping away - and that was David Litvinoff and some friend, Michael Rainey perhaps. Anyway I became friends with him and he said there was a studio going next door, a place called the Pheasantry - £14 a week, so I grabbed it. (48)

'The Pheasantry is where pheasants were raised for the Royal Table. It was a nice building, a bit of a grand entrance and a courtyard. It has a painting of Nell Gwynn on the outside. Also a minstrel's gallery but you had to have midget minstrels. It was a wonderful space. It was next door to a previous studio I shared with Robert Whitaker. There were three bedrooms, bathroom, kitchen, big studio room - that's pretty much it. It had a great atmosphere.' (49)

So when Eric dropped in to see Martin, he dropped into Nell Gwynn's Pheasantry - 152 King's Road Chelsea. At the time Eric was living at Regent's Park in what Martin describes as 'a rather straight sort of flat'. Apart from a sense of friendship that each sensed, Eric saw a fantastic bohemian studio and Martin saw an anchor tenant who would cover his share of the rent without fail, which had not (to date) been achieved by Martin's overnighters and drop-in friends. (50)

So Martin approached Eric with an idea, 'The Pheasantry was £14 a week to rent, I said, Would you like to...? He agreed to join us and moved in. That lead to doing the record covers, the discussions about Tiny and the friendship over the years.' (51)

Peter Draffin was passing through London and staying at the Pheasantry at the time. 'When Eric Clapton arrived I was moved out!' he laughs, adding by way of explanation, 'I was a complete nutter there!' (52)

OZ was finding its feet by July 1967 thanks to the strenuous assistance of Louise and friends. Sometime around OZ 3, Richard and Louise left Jill's place and moved into Notting Hill Gate - the 'thinking person's London' - where they paid half the rent that Martin paid at the Pheasantry.

Richard often called around. Martin recalls the jibes, 'Notting Hill Gate was a different sort of scene altogether, more intellectual, more committed. So, Richard was like: a bit superficial, Chelsea...! But I did find quite a bit of depth in it and a lot of great people'. (53) '

In August, Cream played their first headline venue in America at the Fillmore West in San Francisco. They stretched songs like Spoonful and I'm So Glad into drawn out musical jams, which suited their hippie trippy audience perfectly.

Things were now working out well for Martin - OZ, Big O posters, Cream. Wrote Richard, 'From his Chelsea studio, Sharp was beginning to personify the debonair King's Road glitterati. With his arty sense of style, late hours, prodigious talent and a timely inheritance from an aunt, the upper echelons of the pop/fashion elite drew him to their bosoms'. (54)

'I just wandered into it really', said Martin, 'it was only through cultural suction and time. Bob Whitaker helped a bit.' (55)

Prior to 1967, interaction between art and Pop music had been sporadic. Before the year was out it was de rigeur.

7.

ART OF POP

Martin was a very gentle man, with an insatiable appetite for life and new experiences.
ERIC CLAPTON

Pop Art really hit its straps in the early-60s. But in 1967, Art of Pop was nudging Pop Art to stage left.

The Beatles' sensational Sgt Pepper's Lonely Hearts Club Band album cover was one big reason. Created by British Pop artist Peter Blake - instead of by some Marketing Department - after Sgt Pepper's every frontline band strove for a 'concept' cover. Cream was already ahead of the pack. Disraeli Gears was well into production before anyone – not even Eric - knew anything about Sgt Peppers' cover art.

The commercial push for Art of Pop product came from the flowering of San Francisco's Hippie community and its cultural demands (ie. posters, t-shirts, comix and concept record covers). This would blossom mid-year into the Summer of Love. Martin's artwork anticipated it. Said Martin 'It was great to get to London and find a whole lot of people that were like oneself and they were extraordinarily welcoming, which was the mode of thought of the day - everyone was welcome. London was an immensely hospitable city.' (1)

Eric wrote in his 2007 autobiography, 'I had moved from Regent's Park to the King's Road Chelsea, to share a studio with Martin Sharp, with whom I had become good friends. Martin was a very gentle man, with an insatiable appetite for life and new experiences. At the same time he was very considerate and sensitive to others. An admirer of Max Ernst, who inspired a lot of his work, he was and still is a great painter.'

Martin was in the process of creating his Max – the Birdman – Ernst poster. Later he painted the image on canvas. It featured in the Mick Jagger/James Fox film Performance.

Eric picked up a brush too, painting his room in bright red and gilt, 'a reflection of the times'. (2) They became firm friends. 'Eric was my real connection with the whole scene,' said Martin, speaking about the world of Rock Music. 'I never knew how good he was really…' (3)

Eric became a regular customer of the King's Road fashion boutique, Granny Takes a Trip. He'd had a complete image makeover since his days as a straight-haired long-sideburned Bluesbreaker. He and his peers had moved with the times. Long hair had become a statement of personal freedom and a slap in the face to the old conservatives. Ginger's mad hair stuck out in all directions. Young people everywhere dressed in rainbow colours and grew moustaches, beards and long hair. Eric grew a mo. So did Martin, as painted in his Self Portrait of the time.

Apart from Eric's long absences from the Pheasantry, due to Cream's punishing touring schedule, Martin found living with a Rock star no different from living with anybody else. There was no bevy of teenage beauties hanging out the front and no one came in through the bathroom window. Eric walked King's Road unhindered. 'It was fairly easy-going really,' was Martin's comment about Eric's public fame. 'But King's Road was becoming incredibly fashionable – I guess it had always been so – there was this amalgam - people from every area of life. I think the tripping and the smoking helped. It was where I did my best work of the time.' (4)

As a flatmate, Martin describes Eric as, '…very quiet. He used to play a lot of acoustic guitar.' (5)

Meanwhile OZ magazine was finding its place in the market. 1967 was a boom year for underground publications, many of them running articles and pictures that deliberately provoked their parents' generation. Richard got right into that. London OZ was nothing like Sydney OZ, which Richie Walsh kept going (and which was never connected to the drug culture). The Art of Confrontation is where London OZ was increasing positioning itself.

It was Germaine who came up with the article 'In Bed With the English' in which she maintained that English men were no good in bed - a proposition she was willing to put to the test. (6) That was just one of a string of arresting articles that got OZ lots of attention.

Martin was a consistent contributor. Disengaged from the controversies surrounding Guide to Taking LSD, ads for sex products and deliberately provocative content, Martin said, 'I was just there for the art'. (7)

Everyone was busy at the Pheasantry. 'Obviously you can't be at a love-in if you're working hard,' said Martin. (8) 'I did the Donovan poster in the Pheasantry. I also did some OZ cartoons and things like that - quite a bit of OZ work. Bob (Whitaker) was helping with OZ as well.' (9)

Building on the success of Donovan - Sunshine Superman, Martin continued producing metallic posters for Big O, like, Max – the Birdman – Ernst, Sex! and Live Give Love – the latter credited to 'Martin Sharp and Michelangelo'. Printed with yellow ink on paper, Martin's Mr Tambourine Man was the cover of OZ 7 and was later sold independently as an OZ cover poster on newsprint.

Around this time Felix Dennis came to Richard and Louise's attention as a bit more than young OZ street seller. He could also sell ads, he was opinionated and he could write.

Felix wasn't Australian. He was the son of a part-time jazz pianist who ran a tobacconist's shop. Much later in life, when Felix had become one of the richest men in Britain, he credited OZ with teaching him entrepreneurial skills. (10) At this stage though, he was making a career-shift from hawking OZ along King's Road to hustling ads over the phone.

Released in May 1967 to great anticipation, the album Are You Experienced by the Jimi Hendrix Experience upped the Guitar Hero stakes for Eric. Hendrix was a black American guitarist who looked like no one else in London and sounded like no one else on stage. His fluidity on the instrument was astonishing. Coupled with his natural virtuosity, he was a left-handed guitarist who played an upside-down right-handed Fender Stratocaster guitar. It was impossible to copy his licks. Are You Experienced was only prevented from being No 1 by the Beatles' Sgt Pepper's album. Of Hendrix's arrival, Martin commented, 'There was this new gun in town. I guess there was a bit of pressure on Eric'. (11)

Martin found Hendrix absolutely compelling. In his Pheasantry studio he celebrated the musician with a Hendrix poster, sold by Big O in 1967 and reprinted in 1968. Based on a Linda Eastman photograph, Martin portrays Hendrix as a right-handed guitarist, a mistake that he corrected. Both versions have been equally well circulated over the years.

The mistake came about because Martin was working on Perspex, which is how the image came to be reversed. It also came about because Martin, who never played guitar, never really thought about the difference until it was pointed out.

Eric asked Martin to come up with a cover for Cream's Disraeli Gears. Collage had worked well for Martin in the past and Martin worked well with Bob Whitaker. So he asked Whitaker to take some shots of the band.

Cream had a series of gigs booked for Scotland. Whitaker decided to use the occasion for Martin's photo shoot. On the drive up, Eric, Ginger, Bob, Jack, and Jack's wife Janet, simply enjoyed themselves. Pointing everything out like a tour guide, Jack was especially proud of his Scottish heritage. They took two cars and pulled over at every opportunity to take in the majestic scenery.

Climbing the highest mountain in Britain, Ben Nevis (1344 metres), was Jack's idea. The plan was to shoot the cover shot from the top but, as the LSD took hold, other things happened instead. The band has seldom appeared so relaxed in each other's company. Then Cream got back to being Cream and toured Scotland, Whitaker returned to the Pheasantry and handed the prints to Martin. Martin got his scissors out and merged Whitaker's clipped-up photos into the collage that became the cover of Disraeli Gears. (12)

Quoting Whitaker's The Unseen Beatles, 'Bob supplied the portraits of the group for the day-glo montage. Bob's career in photography successfully expanded into many different areas, but this was his last brush with the world of pop music'. (13)

Over the years, this international award-winning cover has featured in the top echelons of most lists of Top 100 album covers. Martin had mixed feelings about it. 'I don't think it is a great record cover,' said Martin in 1993. (14) He learned to love Disraeli Gears and his later Wheels of Fire. Everybody else did. In 2005 he acknowledged it as his best-known image. He said, 'I am rather proud of them. I was trying to capture that electronic warmth of Cream, which I think I did capture particularly in Disraeli Gears.' (15)

Comparing the cover to other concept covers of the time, Dave Thompson, author of Cream - The World's First Supergroup, sums it up, 'A Martin Sharp collage that took a simple group portrait by fellow Pheasantry resident, photographer Bob Whitaker, and positively overwhelmed it with minute and fascinating details'. (16)

Angie Errico, author of Rock Album Covers, describes Disraeli Gears as, 'Attempting to transform the full kaleidoscopic vision of an acid trip into a one-dimensional album sleeve design defeated the imagination of most artists...This day-glo collage came as close as any design to visually expressing certain aspects of such chemically-induced experiences'. (17)

After printing the cover, the processing company returned the original artwork to Martin, and Martin gave it to Ginger. Ginger treasured it for 32 years. In 1999, while in the process of divorcing his third wife Karen (who had become a Mormon) Ginger explains, '...Karen held an auction to sell off a load of my stuff, including the award-winning artwork for the Disraeli Gears cover, given to me by Martin Sharp, and she kept all the money.' (18)

With Disraeli Gears awaiting release, Cream started planning their third album. That too required Martin to come up with another set of lyrics, plus album cover. Although a 3-piece on stage, the Cream-team now stretched to five, with Martin as their artist and performance-poet Pete Brown writing most of their best lyrics. And then came The Fool.

The Fool comprised Dutch designers, Simon (See-mon) and Marijke. They designed clothes and decorated pretty well anything, like John Lennon's piano, George Harrison's Mini Minor and the Apple Boutique (opened December 1967) on the corner of Baker and Paddington Streets. Martin introduced them to Ginger. Next thing, they were designing Ginger's clothes and then the Cream logo on his drumkit!

Ginger writes, 'Psychedelia was big during 1967 and its influence could be seen everywhere. Martin Sharp did the cover for Disraeli Gears and he introduced us to The Fool, Simon (Posthuma) and Marijke (Koger) and a third member Barry Finch. They were Dutch artists who made far-out furniture and did designs with psychedelic patterns. They made me trousers cut especially short to avoid getting entangled with the bass drum pedals and a purple velvet cloak with a rainbow lining…they also decorated my bass drum with the Cream logo.' (19)

It didn't end there. They also designed Eric's famed SG Gibson guitar and Jack's Fender Bass VI bass.

'I didn't see that Apple place,' said Martin. 'I didn't like those artists, so I never went to have a look at it. Simon and Marijke their names were – The Fool. They were real hustlers from Amsterdam, very clever but really on the make.' (20)

Cream's third album was planned as conceptually different to Disraeli Gears. It would be a double album, the second disc to be recorded live. Martin joined them in July-August, at IBC Studios in London where Cream laid down the first sessions for Wheels of Fire. It was the first time he'd been inside a recording studio. (21)

On 15 August 1967, Belgian surrealist artist René Magritte died.

While Eric was touring and recording in America, Martin designed a metallic-style poster for a 29 September gig at the UFO Club. Featured acts were: Dantalian's Chariot with Zoot Money and his Light Show, The Social Deviants, The Exploding Galaxy, Jeff Beck and Ten Years After. Martin's poster seemed to evoke Pink Floyd. He said, 'I never did one for Floyd. I'd have liked to, but the image I did for Dantalians Chariot was really Floyd's image.'

'Syd Barrett, was a real genius. I haven't found them as interesting since he left. Their leading light I'd say. Pink Floyd was his invention. And then when they got onto what he was on about they could then make it into a product and market it. They'd worked out the formula and they timed it right for commercial success. Without him they wouldn't even be a band, probably. He pulled them together and shaped it, kicked it off. That's what I feel.' (22)

Eric, Jack, Ginger and producer Felix Pappalardi continued their Wheels of Fire sessions at Atlantic Studios, New York City during a break in touring. It must have been an exhausting September and October for Eric. Back at the Pheasantry, his rent was regular as clockwork, paid by the Stigwood management group straight from Eric's Cream account.

Ginger sums up Cream's existence in 1967-68, 'In effect our tour had lasted for a whole year, with just brief breaks now and then in which we'd get a chance to go home'. (23)

Writes Eric, 'Our first American tour lasted seven weeks, culminating in a return to New York to play 12 nights at the Café Au Go Go and a couple at the Village Theatre, where we shared the bill with one of Martin Sharp's favourite artists, Tiny Tim.' (24) Well, he wasn't Martin's favourite artist yet. In fact, Eric was unlikely to have written about Tiny at all, had it not been for events that would follow in Martin's life, one year later.

Tiny Tim was born Herbert Khaury in 1932, which made him about 10 years older than his Rock Music peers. Born in New York, Herbie's father Butros was the son of a Lebanese Maronite Christian priest. Herbie's mother Tillie was the daughter of a Polish Rabbi. Butros voted Democrat, Tillie voted Republican. The arguments never stopped. Their only child Herbie found solace in the music of his 78 rpm records. He stayed in his bedroom and copied the voiceprints of the Swooner- Crooners.

Playing parties, talent quests and small clubs, Herbie's matinee idol image as Larry Love didn't get him anywhere. His out-dated repertoire of Swooner-Crooner numbers barely earned him anything throughout the Rock N Roll 50s. He appeared effeminate in white face make-up and cosmetics. Herbie's first paying gig came in 1959 at Hubert's Flea Circus on 42nd Street, where he appeared as the Human Canary in a freak show. He shared a bill with Estelline Pike the Sword Swallower, Lydia the Contortionist, the Elephant Lady and Destin the Magician who introduced him to his first proper manager, George King. Of his fellow performers, Tiny said in 1992, 'They were freaks of nature'. (25)

The 50s may have been tough, but the 60s welcomed him. George King gave Herbie a Mod look and re-named him Sir Timothy Thames. A New Yorker through and through, Herbie never quite got the British Mod accent. Soon he was back to his comfort zone, which was wearing perfumes and make-up and singing in the high voice. 'Okay,' said Mr King, 'you are now…Tiny Tim!'

From there, his legend grew although Eric had never heard of him when he supported Cream in September 1967. Neither had the audience. Tiny was a few months away from fame.

Spotted at Steve Paul's Scene by Peter Yarrow of Peter, Paul and Mary fame, Tiny Tim signed to the Reprise label and would soon burst onto the charts with one of the most identifiable songs ever, Tiptoe Through the Tulips. But right now, he was supporting Cream and facing a difficult audience because the gig was running so late that the audience from the second session was invading the first.

Someone in the audience chucked a padlock at Tiny's head. In his memoirs, promoter Bill Graham takes the credit for intercepting it. He writes, 'I went to see a Cream concert and the first show was supposed to start at eight and it started at nine-thirty. The audience for the second show came in and there was like nine thousand people in the place at the same time. Tiny Tim was on stage and somebody threw a lock that almost hit him in the face. I saw the thing in the air and I just reached up and grabbed it. That show was absolute chaos.' (26)

That's the first time Eric had anything to do with Tiny. Not that it mattered to him. Eric was more interested – and awed – by the opportunity to jam with the likes of BB King and the Butterfield Blues Band.

The 1967 American tour really consolidated Cream's success. Everything they touched turned to gold. Martin's cover art for Wheels of Fire was about to turn gold – with a silver studio album and a gold live album.

Martin said, 'Eric asked me to do a cover. He was probably touring while I was doing it. It was never meant to be gold. They did that to differentiate the two albums. It was originally a double album, which they later published as two single albums. I designed it as a foldout and that's the front of it. One picture is rectangular - so there's continuity between the folding cover and fluorescent-coloured middle. A bit like a couple of eyes made up – spots.' (27)

Eyes? Spots? Around this time, Martin also painted a picture called Abraxas. Sized like an LP cover, the similar explosion of colour suggests it may have been a Wheels of Fire contender? Likewise the Mighty Baby cover.

Disraeli Gears was released at the start of November to great acclaim. Said Martin, 'I think Cream devised the formula for 3-Rock musicians'. (28)

Martin penned the lyrics for Anyone For Tennis for the Sharp/Clapton contribution to the Wheels of Fire album. Eric wrote a tune but the track was left off the album. It didn't sound like Cream. There was no riff. 'It's about living in Chelsea,' said Martin. (29) Straight away that suggests it's never going to make it in America. Furthermore, it's full of in-jokes like, 'and the Bentley driving guru, is putting up his price…'

Said Martin, 'I remember going out with Eric and his Bentley. He'd got a Bentley and mate of his from school as the driver. They took it out for the first time and ran into another car. We had to walk home!' (30)

Briefly it appeared that Cream's two song writing teams might be Jack & Peter Brown and Eric & Martin. Martin said, 'I thought, "This is going to be it, I'm going to write songs!"' (31) How wrong he was. Martin only ever wrote two more. Do You Love Me? to be performed by Germaine in a film which was 12 months away. And one for Tiny Tim that Tiny never sang. (32)

Late-1967, young Philippe Mora came to London from Australia. Martin invited Philippe to stay at the Pheasantry. Philippe's Mum, Mirka describes Martin as 'kind to my son Philippe in London in 1967'. (33)

Philippe was a bargain. He had the effervescence of a 17-year old, yet was not fazed by famous company, having been brought up in an environment where Melbourne's best-known artists were houseguests.

Notwithstanding occasional Rock stars as drop-in guests, the Pheasantry was essentially an environment for creating visual art. Martin was always painting and there was usually a painter in the downstairs flat until Germaine came. Philippe hit the ground running. Totally broke, he painted frenetically, having no other means of income. He used house paint laced with insect repellent because hardware paint is the cheapest paint you can buy.

For OZ and Big O Posters, Martin produced the Plant A Flower Child poster, and for OZ 9 he submitted intergalactic images redolent of Twice Upon A Time.

OZ was hotting up. Prior to leaving Australia, Richie, Richard and Martin had railed against the Vietnam campaign. As Britain was not directly involved it did not become a frontline issue in London until the Tet Offensive, launched 30 January 1968. This was one of the largest military campaigns of the Vietnam War and gained world attention. It provoked another of Martin's famous OZ covers.

Richard explained, 'A photo from Saigon flashed around the world – the gun-to-the-temple execution of a Vietcong suspect. Sharp splattered this image with bright red ink, put it on our cover and penned the line The Great Society Blows Another Mind. Richie Walsh used it for Sydney OZ.' (34)

Around this time, Richie dropped in on London. Now a graduate with a degree in Medicine, Richie was a 'responsible citizen', married to Sue Phillips. On this visit, Richard was surprised that – probably for the first time in his life – Richie expressed a desire to take a drug. So, Richard whisked him off to the UFO Club, where Richie was stunned by light shows and music that didn't seem like music to him. Meanwhile, Martin scoured the trip dens of Chelsea but was unable to score. Thus concluded Richie Walsh's exploration into drug culture. (35)

In January 1968, Richard decided to take on Malcolm Muggeridge in OZ magazine. Muggeridge was widely considered as a 'sensible' social commentator by Christian conservatives. Richard took him on anyway. OZ was really hitting its straps now. Judged by its ads and lead articles, some thought it smutty, yet it attracted great contributors: leading New York Rock journalist Australian Lilian Roxon, cartoon artist Robert Crumb, Martin, Whitaker, Robert Hughes are just some in a long and brilliant list.

Hughes' The Art of Australia was published in 1966, the book in which he rashly claimed that the first 100 years of the colony produced no good artists at all. That opinion appeared to do his reputation no harm. As a critic, he was supposed to be nasty. His follow-up, Heaven and Hell in Western Art was in the typewriter. Around this time Hughes met Danne Emerson, whom he would soon marry.

In January-February 1968, Cream went back to America to record additional studio material for Wheels of Fire. During those Atlantic Studios sessions Eric recorded Anyone for Tennis on acoustic guitar. Very different from anything else on the album, it sounded more like a Kinks song. Anyone for Tennis never really gained traction until the 1983 release of The Very Best of Cream when it appeared as one of 12 songs alongside Tales of Brave Ulysses, Sunshine of Your Love, White Room and Strange Brew.

Although no one in Martin's circle particularly noticed, in February 1968, the album God Bless Tiny Tim was released. By June, it was high on the on the charts. The hit single from the album, Tiptoe Through the Tulips peaked at No 7 - none of which caught Martin's attention.

Between 7-10 March Cream played San Francisco's Fillmore West. The best takes of Crossroads, Spoonful, Traintime and Toad were used for the gold Wheels of Fire live disc.

In April, Richard and Louise spent 10 days in New York and returned with a string of American underground contacts for OZ magazine including Harvard acid guru Timothy Leary and Yippie countercultural warriors Jerry Rubin and Abbie Hoffman. Richard saw all publicity as good publicity. With Felix now in his ear, Richard was pushing and pushing, especially in New York.

Their New York connection was OZ writer Lilian Roxon, whom they had known from the Sydney Push. Roxon's writings became the foundation stone for serious Rock journalism. She was one of the leading lights of the social and musical scene that centred around a club frequented by the Andy Warhol set. Jimi Hendrix was there the night Lilian took Richard and Louise to Max's. Andy Warhol was at the next table. Richard plied him with samples of Martin's posters. 'Wow,' Andy remarked. (36)

Cream decided to break up in May, a process that would take a full six months. May was the month Anyone for Tennis was released as the B-Side of Ginger's song, Pressed Rat & Warthog. It only reached No 64 on US charts and No. 40 in Britain. Pressed Rat & Warthog showed that Ginger was no Flower Child.

Following the footsteps of his Cream lyric, Martin returned to the Balaeric Islands where he met up with - and broke up with - Anou. 'Do you think I stayed in Sydney too long?' she later questioned Richard. (37)

Martin also flashed in-and-out of Australia where he was not forgotten. Richie had kept his name alive in OZ. Draff's novel Pop had been on sale one year and Craig McGregor's People Politics & Pop was in the shops. In August 1967, Indigenous Australians were granted the right to vote. Well, that was news!

During Martin's London years, Garry and Martin had maintained contact. Said Garry, 'He was doing so well in London! He took off over there, whereas over here we were all struggling. He'd send me London OZs and I'd think Wow! Amazing! Martin would come back every year. Maybe twice – backwards-and-forwards. He couldn't decide if he wanted to live in Sydney or London'. (38)

These were low-key visits. Martin stayed with his mother, called on friends and visited Grandmother Vega, widowed and still living at Wirian. His parents' divorce was done. Henry was planning on marrying Dorothy the following year.

At this time, Garry's career at the ABC was drawing to a close. He was in a relationship with the famous American Civil Rights singer and activist, Odetta. They had met at a party in Paddington Sydney. Martin took Garry and Odetta to Telford, to reactivate old childhood memories.

Martin's mother lived in the Cranbrook Lane house. Said Martin, 'My mother wanted to come to London. I didn't want her to come. She wanted to come and see me but I was living such a different life, I suppose. She didn't come. She would have loved it of course.' (39)

Martin's Sharp grandmother, felt the opposite. Between her and Martin's uncles, there were no congratulations for Martin creating an award-winning album cover design and co-writing a hit song. Martin explained, 'It meant nothing to them. Their world – what mattered – is a respectable job, Royal Sydney Golf Club (which Grandma Sharp enrolled me in), St Paul's College (which she got me into) and Cranbrook School.' (40)

But there was an upcoming generation of younger Sharps, Martin's cousins, several of whom were very proud of Martin's achievements -

Sandy Sharp, Katie Sharp, Andrew Sharp, Russell Sharp and 15-year old Roslyn (Rozzie)…

In 1968 there was an explosion of Art in Pop. Every band wanted a concept album. Every gig required a psychedelic poster.

8.

MUYBRIDGE, VINCENT, MAGRITTE & TINY TIM

Brigitte Bardot called at the Pheasantry. Martin didn't let her in. He didn't believe it was Brigitte Bardot.

PHILIPPE MORA

The credibility of album cover artists ranked right up there with the bands. Matí Klarwein, Bob Seidemann and Robert Crumb stand out. British Pop artist Richard Hamilton designed the Beatles' White Album. Andy Warhol did the banana cover for the Velvet Underground's The Velvet Underground & Nico LP. And Hipgnosis launched a major design group on the strength of their cover art for Pink Floyd, starting with A Saucerful of Secrets. Alas, Album Cover Art was an art form with only about 15 years left in it, before the introduction of CDs shrank the images and 'packaging design' took over.

When hippie tribes reigned, bands from the West Coast of America became famous for their posters, like the Grateful Dead, Moby Grape and Jefferson Airplane. Young people taped them on bedroom walls, even ceilings, creating the perfect environment for listening to trippy music and burning joss sticks. Such posters were available from OZ magazine for 9/6. This was art everyone could afford.

Martin too did 'psychedelic' posters. That was the word used to describe his metallic Big O series. Using similar ideas as Disraeli Gears Martin did a Cream poster. Even though he loathed the image, what is done cannot be undone. It was off-and-running and has remained in circulation ever since. Devastated to see it reprinted as a postcard in 2005, Martin shredded it. 'It's the ugliest thing I've ever seen!' he exclaimed. (1)

More triumphantly - using a similar palette as his Hendrix - Martin did a blue-haired Mick Jagger cover for OZ 15. Behind Mick are little naked running men that were making regular appearances in Martin's 1967-1969 pictures. He found them in a 19th Century book of photographs of the human body, a favourite of art students.

Eaweard Muybridge (1830-1904) was an English photographer, important for his pioneering photographic studies of the human body in motion. His book, The Human Figure in Motion comprises still shots of naked people doing physical activities in a sequence. Like, 18 frames of a naked woman kicking front view – and nine frames of the same woman kicking side view. Or, 16 frames of a naked man batting at cricket. And, 11 frames of a naked running jumping man. (2) Muybridge recorded the time intervals between frames (ie. naked woman feeding a dog, time intervals .222 seconds. Martin gave this book a lot of thought. Ginger chose a painting from this period for his 1970 Ginger Baker's Airforce album, featuring eight frames of a naked running man. (3)

Michael Organ, Manager Repository Services from the University of Wollongong, has catalogued and dated Martin's posters from this period. About the Muybridge characters, he noted, 'A variant of this element of the cover (ie. OZ 15) featured in the design Sharp applied to the shopfront of The Sweet Shop in London during 1968, a clothing and design shop operated by Laura Jamieson.' (4)

Frequented by Twiggy, Jean Shrimpton and Keith Richards, the Sweet Shop sold silk velvet patchwork, appliqué cushions and wall hangings. The 'element' Michael Organ is writing about, is Martin's little naked running man.

Ever a keen book-buyer, Martin kept on reading Vincent's letters and contemplating the history of art. He enjoyed the democratic aspect of art books because, like posters, everyone could have a picture of – say, the Mona Lisa, Vincent's Chair or Man Ray's Lips. Martin explains, 'The images are freely available and I had quite a lot of art books'. (5) So Martin - who was equally comfortable with a pair of scissors as with a brush - starting cutting them up and realigning them, often placing the central image in an unexpected setting. At the Pheasantry, Martin began his earliest explorations into what would become Art Exhibition and Art Book.

Meanwhile, in San Francisco, the posters were certainly magnificent but harder to read. Not that it mattered, the gigs attracted huge audiences through word-of-mouth. However, some posters – for example, Moscoso complicated (and lost) the image as surely as the Abstract Expressionist painters before him. In contrast, Martin sought clarity, which he found in the art of René Magritte (1898-1967).

Said Martin, 'Magritte took over a lot. He put it really clearly because he had such a deadpan style of imagery. He could present any idea by juxtaposing images and combining them. It had a fantastic democracy. He had that style, something that everyone can understand. And people, whether they knew about art or not, had to accept it. It probably had a stronger effect on untutored minds than on the tutored (or equally so).

'If you look at Abstract Expressionism or Cubism, the general public was really thrown. These were really scientific explorations into the concept of Art. The public can't follow that image. They get lost in a maze of modern art. And the public got completely offended by the total loss of the image. Magritte put things so simply, mysteriously - images like anyone would paint - a sign-painter would paint! "Do me a man with a bowler hat" - you know?' (6)

From his childhood Martin reflected on Vincent van Gogh. The print, On the Road to Tarascon was in his father's surgery. And, the biographical novel, Lust for Life was awarded him by Justin. (7)

Vincent van Gogh only sold one picture in his life. He was financially supported by his brother Theo with whom he corresponded from August 1872-July 1890. After her husband's death, Theo's wife Johanna van Gogh-Bonger spent years compiling the collection of 844 letters written by Vincent, of which 663 were written to Theo. First published in 1914, (8) Martin had been reading those letters for quite a while. He quoted them in sketches going back to Formenterra, if not before.

Martin said, 'I was very moved by them. Van Gogh is definitely a saint of painters. He was extremely lonely and spent a lot of time writing. One of his greatest letters to his brother before he started painting was published in OZ, saying he felt he was worth something and that he had maybe 10 years in him, which was true to the year. (9)

'There was an exceptional relationship between the brothers. His brother provided him with the paint and canvasses and he did the pictures. Theo kept every letter that he wrote. So you've got an incredible parallel circumstance.' (10) Martin began cutting up Vincent's pictures and Magritte's pictures. He played around with them, setting them against each other in different combinations. Some, he kept.

There were changes afoot at the Pheasantry, Whitaker moved out and Germaine moved in. She was one of several friends who started writing books. Germaine moved into the downstairs flat and worked on her thesis, a document that would galvanise the feminist movement within two years - The Female Eunuch. Martin remembers her 'crying a lot'. (11) In Notting Hill Gate, Richard was compiling his first book Play Power for which Martin would do the cover. (12) And Robert Hughes was busy writing Heaven and Hell in Western Art. (13)

Martin now had a live-in girlfriend – Finnish beauty Eija Vehka Aho, who had so splendidly assisted with the circles of his Mr Tambourine Man poster. Charlotte Martin moved in with Eric.

But Eric had a lot weighing on his mind. The tensions within Cream were almost too much to bear. Wrote Eric, 'Our gigs became nothing more than an excuse for us to show off as individuals, and any sense of unity that we might have had when we started out seemed to have gone out of the window. We also suffered from an inability to get on. We would just run away from one another. We never socialized together, we never really shared ideas any more. We just got together on stage and played and then went our separate ways. In the end, that was the undoing of the music.' (14)

Exhaustion was another factor, it seemed the promoters were bleeding the band dry on a never-ending tour. Eric, Jack and Bruce took the line of least resistance. They kept going not because they wanted to or even needed to, the only reason Cream didn't disband was that it was easier not to. Dismantling one of the most successful bands of the decade meant the bean counters weren't happy. Nor the fans.

There were rumours aplenty that Cream was finished. Then they'd perform together and prove the journalists wrong. After a six-week tour of America, they made the official announcement: Cream's final concert was billed for November. In theory, Cream was still a unit when Philippe Mora joined the Pheasantry.

Said Martin, 'Philippe Mora arrived and then his girlfriend (Freya Matthews) moved in. It was good. There was enough room for us. Philippe and Eric got on really well, they were great friends I think'. (15)

As a painter, Philippe was pro-active. Maybe he kick-started Martin a bit, as after Philippe's arrival, Martin began to think about exhibiting, whereas Philippe thought about that as soon as he arrived. Martin burrowed through art books and eased back on OZ. Martin explained his sporadic contributions, 'Richard Neville got it together really, I was just there to help. I wasn't so keen, initially and then I got very keen on it for a while. Then I tapered off again. Virtually in the end I was doing nothing for it.' (16)

Better known as an actress (later director) than a gallery owner, Clytie Jessop was quite taken with Philippe's works and she invited him to exhibit in her gallery on The King's Road. Much to Philippe's surprise, the show was a great success. Eric was amongst the buyers.

Philippe wrote, 'Our Pheasantry scene was a kind of cultural catalyst and melting pot. RD Laing would drop in and say we were normal and everybody else was crazy.'

Philippe recalls Martin painting the psychedelic front door, Germaine writing downstairs, being encouraged by Pop Surrealist painter Eduardo Paolozzi and intimidated by curmudgeonly Francis Bacon. He also recalls the first draft of Jim's Sharman's Rocky Horror Show. Philippe wrote, 'When Jim got the original tape of the songs performed by Richard O'Brien he called me over to listen. I was unenthusiastic and thought it was corny – Frankenfurter! – but Jim insisted he could make it all work'. (17)

Through all the visitors, live-ins, drop-ins and all-night painting sessions, Martin and Whitaker found the time to make a short three and a half minute film centred around Germaine. It was screened at the 1969 Sydney Film Festival.

Said Martin, 'I made that little film with Germaine Greer called Darling Do You Love Me?. She was a brilliant performer.' (18)

'A writer called Anthony Hayden-Guest was there, photographer Bill King, Eduardo Paolozzi was in there somewhere, David Litvinoff and Tim Whitborne – who was a sort of painter - and they had some franchise on some prints of the Queen. Tim was a painter and I never actually saw the inside of his studio. That was a floor below.' (19) 'The Pheasantry was a bit like an evolving studio exhibition.' (20)

Around the time Cream's Wheels of Fire was released, Eric recalled David Litvinoff being in an excitable mood. He had scored the job of dialogue coach and technical adviser on the film Performance that was being shot in Chelsea by Donald Cammell and Nick Roeg.

Eric wrote, 'The particular expertise for which he had been hired was his knowledge of the underworld, as the movie, which was basically a star vehicle for Mick Jagger playing a faded-jaded rock idol, was set in the world of London gangsters. He was full of ideas about how he felt the story should develop, and every day he would come and see me to tell me about all the goings-on on set and to fill me in on whatever was going to be happening next day. One night he brought round the director Donald Cammell, who managed to stage a power cut in the flat, and then tried to grope my girlfriend Charlotte in the dark. A peculiar chap.' (21)

'I was sort of involved in Performance,' said Martin, 'I was on the edge of that - not really "involved". I asked my mother to send over a few of my high school pictures, some of the gangster ones. She did and they're in the film'. (22)

'I got on pretty well with Mick Jagger and James Fox. I met them during Performance. I also did some collages in it for Anita Pallenburg. They said, "Do you want the money or a credit?" I said, "I'll have the money" - £300 or something. It was useful at the time.' (23)

One picture in question is Martin's green/orange painting (not the poster) of Max – the Birdman – Ernst. The camera rests on it briefly around the 60-minute mark.

Friends now with Mick Jagger (or friendly, at least), Martin drew him for OZ. It was the first time Martin appropriated Hokusai's Wave in a picture. (24)

Cream wasn't the only band in the throes of breaking up. The Beatles had quit touring and had more time to spend in the studio. In August, September and October they recorded what would be known as the White Album. To date, John and Paul had dominated the Beatles' songwriting. They were so good! George was allowed one composition per album and poor Ringo had a total of two - Octopus's Garden and Don't Pass Me By - on 13 studio albums.

In September, at Abbey Road Studios, George spent a long night struggling with his latest composition, While My Guitar Gently Weeps. The crying guitar was the bit he couldn't get right. In the end, the Beatles scrapped it. Within three days George returned to the studio with Eric. Eric wasn't too sure about this because no one records on Beatles albums but the Beatles. 'Who cares?" George reassured, 'it's my song'. (25)

Wrote Eric, 'We did it in just one take and I thought it sounded fantastic; John and Paul were fairly non-committal but I knew George was happy. A couple of weeks later, George dropped by the Pheasantry and left me the acetates of the double album on which the song was going to appear.' (26)

Martin was seeing supermodel Donyale Luna at the time.

'Luna!' Martin stressed.

Six foot two inches tall, Donyale Luna had replaced Twiggy and Jean Shrimpton as the world's No 1 supermodel. Profiling her for The New York Times, journalist Judy Stone described her as, 'secretive, mysterious, contradictory, evasive, mercurial, and insistent upon her multiracial lineage - exotic, chameleon strands of Indigenous-Mexican, Indonesian, Irish, and, last but least escapable, African'. (27) Martin described her as the Priestess of Chaos. He said, 'I fell in love with the real thing for about a week. That was when chaos struck. It was the bust and everything'. (28)

In early September, Martin's OZ Norman Normal character sprang into unpleasant reality in the form of a cop, Sgt Norman Pilcher of the Drug Squad. Semolina Pilchard dripping from a dead dog's eye is how John Lennon described this guy in the song I Am the Walrus. (29) Semolina Pilchard had already nailed John Lennon, George Harrison, Mick Jagger, Keith Richards, Brian Jones and Donovan. Ginger called the Pheasantry to warn Eric that he had received an inside tip that Eric his was the next name on Pilcher's hit list of Rock stars.

Eric made a judicious exit to North London, where he stayed in a Robert Stigwood house until the heat was off. He didn't think to warn the others because he thought it was all about him. (30)

Martin related what happened next, 'The Drug Squad pressed the doorbell and said, "We've got parcel for you". We had about three flights of stairs and a buzzer for the door at the bottom, and there was a parcel from the Post Office. I got up for the door - having been got up very early and feeling a total wreck – and saw eight policemen standing there, some policewomen as well. They were, of course, looking for Eric - not for me.

'Philippe was there, his girlfriend was having a shower while all this was going on and they didn't know she was there. She's a frightfully nice girl from Melbourne and she came out unaware that Phillipe had been dragged out of bed in the nude and made to stand against the wall.

'Bob Seidemann (who did the 'girl with the aeroplane' cover for the Blind Faith album) was downstairs pressing the button trying to get in! I'm going, "Go away! Police! Run!" They dragged me away and gave me a cuff across the head. He pressed the buzzer again and I managed to get to it. He was so slow to catch on. Bob Seidemann started running and they arrested him. He ran out to King's Road. There's 5000 people out there and he's the only guy running!

'I was totally relaxed about the whole thing. They took me to Chelsea Police Station with Philippe and I just fell asleep because they got me up so early.' (31)

Martin was charged with possession of a small quantity of hashish. He wasn't too troubled by this, neither was his father when Martin wrote Henry, 'The court attitude to hash is becoming more and more reasonable, and the magistrates feel the police should be chasing real criminals and cease wasting time harassing me…us.' Martin's only real concern was that the story might hit the Sunday papers back home, causing more tension with the Sharps. (32)

Peeved that at his Sydney OZ trial, neither Richard, Richie nor himself were required to speak, Martin was not going to let this opportunity slip. Against the advice of his legal council, Martin spoke up. He said, 'I made an impassioned plea from the dock about understanding young people,' said Martin. (33) He also drafted a statement on the virtues of pot and its role in modern society, which he instructed his reluctant solicitor to read to the court. (34)

Martin explained the outcome, 'I got a suspended sentence, which I appealed against. I got a suspended fine or something. The Judge was very sympathetic and dismissed the case. Still, they made an awful blunder - they didn't come to get me.' (35)

Eric took it quite hard. He wrote, 'I felt terrible, because they busted Martin and Philippe, and I had not warned them, thinking that Pilcher would only be interested in me. I will never forgive myself for that'. (36)

Ginger relayed a second message from Pilcher, which was that if Eric got off his patch, he'd leave him alone. Wrote Eric, 'I felt quite ready to move, and as for the first time in my life I now had some money, I realised that I could use it to buy a house.' (37)

Ironically, and to everyone's satisfaction, four years later Pilcher was charged with conspiracy to pervert the course of justice after it was alleged he had committed perjury in a drug-related offence. In 1973 he was sentenced to four years imprisonment.

Eric now spent his time around the Pheasantry reading property magazines, like Country Life. Martin reckoned, 'because I thought music worked like drawing, I used to say dumb things like "Why don't you practice more often?"' (38)

Around this time, Richard reports Martin 'cooling on Rock'. Richard wrote, 'He recalled his boyhood. The long summer holidays at Port Hacking: swimming, fishing on the bay and listening to his mother's 78 rpm recording...the only time the rancour between his parents turned to romance.'

Collections of nostalgic songs of the 1930s and 1940s were being released as LP records. Martin snapped them up – Bing Crosby, Al Jolson, Ruth Etting. And a song by Al Bowlly being played from a shop along King's Road caught his attention, but he only heard it in snatches: Brother Can You Spare a Dime. (39) 'Al Bowlly!' said Martin, 'I discovered him in London.' (40)

Quitting at the top of their game, Eric at last embarked on Cream's final US tour in October. Having caught Tiny Tim's act at The Scene NY and noting Martin's fondness for songs of the 1930s and 40s, before leaving, Eric told Martin that Tiny would be performing at the Royal Albert Hall. 'You like a lot of old songs,' said Eric, 'you've got to go and see Tiny Tim, you're really going to love him'. (41) Years later, Eric confessed he never liked Tiny's singing. He said, 'His voice always frightened me'. (42)

Although the album God Bless Tiny Tim rode high on the charts and his falsetto rendition of Tiptoe Through the Tulips was getting lots of airplay, Martin hadn't heard it. He had only seen publicity pictures of Tiny and knew nothing else about him. As Richard said, Martin had cooled on Rock. He stopped listening to the radio and played records instead.

On 30 October 1968, Richard and Louise accompanied Martin and his date, model Hazel Ganpatsingh, to see Tiny Tim's concert, a sensational performance. Backed by the 30-piece National Concert Orchestra under the baton of producer Richard Perry, Tiny trilled like a Human Canary, got hunky like Elvis, flattened his voice like Sonny Bono and traversed the spectrum of popular song from Al Bowlly & Rudy Vallee to the Rolling Stones & Bob Dylan. He performed duets with himself, singing the female part of I Got You Babe with piercing effect. Surely this was the Douanier Rousseau of Pop! (43)

Martin said, ' I'd never heard Tiny sing until I saw him at the Albert Hall, that's why he blew me away because I thought, "Boy, this guy just knows...!" Brother Can You Spare Me A Dime was a song I'd heard just a snatch of on an Al Bowlly album, just two lines of it. I'd ask people, 'what's this song?' And then Tiny sang it at the Albert Hall and I was amazed. That's when I thought, 'I'd love to work with Tiny'. I thought I could do something for his staging or that whole Paper Moon world of popular songs. (44)

'When I saw Tiny at the Albert Hall and his total command of the whole language of popular song I thought: he is going to be in an absolutely unapproachable position. (45) I thought he would be the absolute heart of show business. Uncontactable. I didn't even try. I didn't even go backstage. And then I did get to listen to God Bless because Eric had a copy.' (46)

Before going to sleep that night, Martin wrote in his journal, 'First Impressions. Did you tiptoe through the tulips with Tiny Tim? To see his

London concert was a revelation. He is the "Spirit of Popular Music", an anthropologist, a mystic, the wise man disguised as a fool. He spans the whole of Pop with such grace and eloquence. He transcends the "campness" of his image and becomes a truly great entertainer (a compliment which cannot be paid to many of our contemporary pop "stars").

'I did see Tiny Tim backed by the London Philharmonic give, really GIVE, a performance that was great, not "groovy" not "gas man" but GREAT!!! He was generous and he loves music and he told me so in such an articulate, honest and open way that I felt the beauty. He sang me the songs that my grandparents were turned on by when they were my age, and he sang me the songs my parents loved, and he made me love them too – and he destroyed my prejudice and created the link between all music and showed me that it is one river of soul and sound and love and pain.' (47)

'It was in this ecstatic state that Sharp sought to take charge of the next OZ and make it entirely visual. Fine by me...' wrote Richard. (48) In the aftermath of Tiny Tim, Martin proposed that he and Philippe should compile a collage of images in the same way that Tiny had presented a collage of song. Continuity was maintained on the bottom third of each page by Eadweard Muybridge's little naked running men quoting or questioning Carl Sagan's propositions about the state of the universe and/or the meaning of life.

Borrowing freely from newspapers and images of people with physical deformities Martin and Philippe also collaged Lee Harvey Oswald, Salvadore Dalí, Vincent, Adam & Eve, Mick Jagger, President Nixon, Little Nemo, Pope Paul VI, Richard Neville, René Magritte, Miss United Kingdom, Queen Elizabeth II, the Duke of Edinburgh, Philippe Mora, Martin Sharp, John Lennon, Yoko Ono, Adolf Hitler, Siamese twins Chang and Eng Bunker, Crucified Christ, Tariq Ali, violent images of the Vietnam

War, a flashback to the OZ 1964 obscenity trial, Hokusai's Wave, a passing reference to 'Eternity' and a muscular Tiny Tim captioned with his song, The Icecaps Are Melting.

What was Magic Theatre OZ about? Was it the purposelessness of life or its quest? (49) Jenny Kee described Philippe as a 'powerhouse of creativity' and Magic Theatre OZ as 'one of the greatest works of the 60s'. Robert Hughes gave it the thumbs up too, describing it as, 'one of the richest banks of images that has ever appeared in a magazine'. (50)

Said Martin, 'It was expressing the experience of collage – running things backwards and forwards – playing with the form of the magazine. I did that with Philippe. I guess it was quite a good expression of the time, just absorbing all the material that was around. Tiny is in that, of course.' (51)

There is continuity between the back cover of Magic Theatre OZ and the front cover of next OZ. Martin's question mark was now a regular feature during this Exploration of Punctuation period, or what he later called Smartiples – visual puns. The front cover of OZ 17 featured a sideshot of Jenny and Louise nude, facing each other with Martin's red question mark as a backdrop. (52)

Using the same palette and energy, during this period Martin also did the cover for Richard's forthcoming book Play Power. (53) A contributor to OZ and a drop-in Pheasantry guest (when he was in the country), author of The Politics of Ecstasy, Acid guru Timothy Leary was enamoured by Martin's Abraxas picture. He requested it as the cover of the London edition of his book. (54) Martin wasn't particularly interested, but he said okay. Publisher, Paladin Granada, borrowed Martin's Abraxas and got a graphic artist to do the Sharp-like lettering. (55)

Abraxas wasn't Martin's only occult image. The previous year Martin had designed a set of 22 Tarot cards (the Major Arcana) for OZ. The Abraxas picture came from that same spirit, musings on Carl Jung's Seven Sermons to the Dead.

Film was a popular vehicle of the times. Martin got a taste for it working with Germaine and Whitaker. Philippe always had ideas. Now, the Rolling Stones were making their Rock And Roll Circus film, involving Eric in a band called The Dirty Mac (ie. John Lennon, Keith Richards, Mitch Mitchell and Eric). (56)

Back in Sydney there was Garry's film and Kingo's films. Albie Thoms was corresponding with Martin, recounting all his latest innovations. Albie's student, Bruce Beresford was living in London and Bruce knew Barry Humphries socially. They talked about government funding for Australian films. Film. Everyone was talking film.

There was movement at the Pheasantry. Eric's reading of Country Life magazine had paid off. A place called Hurtwood Edge was for sale for £30,000 and Eric was buying it.

Eric wrote, 'Next thing I knew, the deal was done and the house was mine. It was an extraordinary feeling. I'd never owned my own home. All my life, I'd been bumming around, from the first day I left Ripley, spending nights on stations or sleeping in the park, or staying on the couch at friends' houses, and then going back to Ripley. The most I'd had was a lease at the Pheasantry, and now I had Hurtwood…I moved in very quickly…'. (57)

He has owned it ever since

9.

ART ABOUT ART

Martin began to disappear after the Magic Theatre OZ, Richard was very happy to accept advice from Felix Dennis or me.

JIM ANDERSON

Scene: the Pheasantry – the flamboyant red oxide and white Louis XV façade and triumphal entrance: Eric Clapton moved out and Nigel Waymouth moved in.

One of the three proprietors of the Granny Takes a Trip boutique, Nigel was also a third of the graphic design and musical avant-garde partnership known as Hapsash and the Coloured Coat that designed posters, contributed to OZ and were described by writer, George Melly as 'Nouveau Art Nouveau'.

Said Martin, 'When Eric left I shared it with artist Nigel Waymouth. The Pheasantry was a great studio, I think one of my most creative studios. One tried to apply that lifestyle - the combination of music and art - to the Yellow House, it's pretty much the same feeling I think – different scales'. (1)

Ah, the Yellow House – partly conceptualized but unlikely to have been named at this stage. As he read the Letters, Vincent's dream of a studio of artists in the sunny south was beginning to resonate with Martin, who was itching to get back to Sydney. An all-art environment was an ambitious project. Martin was swapping ideas in his correspondence with Albie and conversations with Philippe.

'Philippe was doing a sensational series of paintings,' said Martin, 'he was only 17-18 or something. So sophisticated. Really great works. The opportunity was there at the Pheasantry, I guess. It was a good atmosphere – art and music. He was so young and he came from a very talented family.' (2)

Extending his interest in collage, after Magic Theatre OZ, Philippe got the idea to make a film from the off-cuts of Performance, the bin pickings of the film. Trouble In Molopolis was financed by the unlikely combination of Eric Clapton and an Australian artist living in London, Arthur Boyd. The drummer of an Aussie band in London, Tony Cahill of the Easybeats, handled the music with Arthur Boyd's son, Jamie. Robert Hughes lent his apartment as a location, Richard was PR man and Jenny Kee appeared as Shanghai Lil. (3)

Meanwhile, Cream was winding down. Commencing 4 October 1968, the band played its goodbye American concerts before returning home and bringing their last two years to a close at the Royal Albert Hall. The final concert was anti-climactic. Eric, Jack and Ginger left the stage without saying much to each other. They just wandered off. Ginger explained, 'When Cream died - it died. Short of murder, we couldn't solve a problem between us'. (4)

After the concert, the band's demeanour was called into question. Some said Eric was arrogant. Others reckoned he was depressed. Martin said he was self-effacing, 'Eric was incredibly modest. He'd didn't face the audience on stage at the Albert Hall. They're all up there and he's playing into the speakers with his back to the audience because he wasn't singing. Jack Bruce took over all the singing. Eric had lost his voice in a way, because there was beautiful singing on that first Cream album'. (5)

Eric was more candid, 'I'm an ego-manic with an inferiority complex. So I like attention and I don't like the attention.' (6)

Eric retreated to his Surrey estate. Charlotte partnered with Led Zeppelin guitar hero Jimmy Page, Eric took up with Alice Ormsby-Gore and what followed in the 70s were bleak years for Eric, battling his addictions.

Said Martin, 'Eric vanished. He went to live in the country back where he grew up. It's a terrible thing when popular music becomes an industry and puts so much pressure on people. At the Pheasantry we were smoking and maybe tripping a bit. I didn't know about any heroin. That happened afterwards, not at the Pheasantry - not that I had any knowledge of. But heroin has never been an interest of mine and never will be.' (7)

Jim Anderson arrived in England in 1963. A dropped-out lawyer and would-be writer, he met Richard Neville at the 1967 Legalise Pot Rally in Hyde Park but was not drawn into OZ until more than a year later. Jim worked with Richard on the book and shaped it into Play Power. He dropped into the Pheasantry one evening and met Martin and Philippe, drawing/collaging together at the time. That's how they met.

Sensing Martin's interest in OZ peaked with Magic Theatre, Richard was seeking other collaborators. OZ on its own was a big enough workload, to which he added the pressure of publisher Jonathon Cape's formidable book deadline. So Richard was pleased to involve Jim - his Play Power writer/researcher/editor - in OZ as well as Felix Dennis who had ideas for music reviews and – well – ideas for all sorts of things. Says Jim, 'Martin began to disappear after the Magic Theatre OZ, Richard was very happy to accept advice from Felix or me.' (8)

Jim's influence on the magazine became obvious in OZ 23, the Homosexual Issue resulted in Felix and him being hauled into Scotland Yard for a severe finger wagging. The warning was blithely ignored, leading to OZ 28 the infamous School Kids Issue and the subsequent Conspiracy and Obscenity Trial of 1971. (9)

Jim joined OZ and Martin went to Sydney. On this trip, 26-year old Martin was more businesslike and public. His visit coincided with the The Last OZ – the last Australian OZ. Richie was changing it into a political newssheet, the OZ Newsletter – 12 issues, $2.40. (10)

'OZ is dead', Richie headlined before signing out. He wrote, 'Australia has changed a good deal in the six years we have been in publication. We have passed from the arrogance of Menzies to the larrikinism of Gorton: from paternalism, through incompetence, to improvisation. The country has passed from a pathetic state of inferiority to a brutal kind of jingoism. We like the new mood and the new leadership no better than the old.' (11)

Martin was much chirpier. His Wheels of Fire-style OZ cover announced in tiny lettering, 'Sharp has returned…but not for long…ho ho ho'. Titled Martin Sharp: Expatriotism, his centrefold was a kangaroo evolving wings over nine stages then flying off overseas. Signed: 'Bye bye See Ya! Martin'. (12)

Despite responding cheekily to the subject of expatriatism, Martin was actually in the process of coming home for good. His peers were doing well in Australia and he was certainly impressed with cultural developments in his homeland. Ubu Films - Albie's film group - was at the forefront of underground film screenings. Ubu shows had become Happenings and Ellis D Fogg's Psychedelic Lightshows were as impressive as what was going on in Swinging London. The English underground press picked up on it. An article called 'The Sydney Scene' published in IT (International Times) wrote, 'Nothing much happens in Sydney, but Ubu is the major centre of what does happen'.

To welcome Martin back from London and filmmaker Aggy Read back from New York, an underground dance was staged at the Paddington Town Hall. It featured a new band, Tully. Writes Albie, 'What resulted from this combination was a psychedelic sound unlike anything heard in Sydney, mixing rock and jazz with the new electronic tones of a Moog synthesiser. The crowd of about a thousand stood awestruck as lights splashed over them and on to the surrounding walls, realising this was music to listen to rather than dance to, and Lightshows came into their own as a creative medium'. (13)

Over the next two years, Tully would regularly perform not-to-be-missed shows with compere Adrian Rawlins and light shows by Roger

Foley (Ellis D Fogg). Said Roger, 'The first concert where we used Tully was in the Roundhouse and that's what really blew me away because 1000 people came to the show and the Roundhouse shut the door – no more people – and another 1000 people were standing outside looking through the windows. The other thing that blew me away was all the people inside, instead of dancing to the light show and the bands, just sat down and watched them.' (14) Martin, like many others, saw a connection between what Tully was doing and what Pink Floyd had lost.

It was indeed a significant Sydney visit. Martin stayed with his mother, worked again with Richie Walsh, caught up with friends and family, checked out Greg Weight's photographic studio on South Dowling Street, found out what Garry Shead was doing, got to know Roger Foley a bit better, figured out Adrian Rawlins' role, met a young enthusiast - George Gittoes and, with the assistance of Peter 'Charlie' Brown, made arrangements for a Martin Sharp exhibition at Clune Galleries.

Family life had a few changes in store. Martin's father Henry married Dorothy Muller in 1969, meaning Martin now had a stepmother.

During this visit, Grandmother Sharp caught up with her errant grandson with his shoulder-length hair and velvet suits. Martin reeked of Swinging London. 'She was great', said Martin, 'I was doing the series of silkscreen lithographs. She took a keen interest. She wanted to see what I was doing. She saw the one with the cock and I was very embarrassed. Don't Leave Me Here Standing All Alone was its title. She said, "Oh! That's the engine that drives the train!" She was very frank.' (15)

The cock (Don't Leave Me Standing All Alone), the nipple (Boo Zoom), the exclamation mark (Exclamation), the egg (Float) and the question mark (Wot!) were part of Martin's series of archetypal symbols that he called Smartiples. Some he painted in Sydney, others in London, but – like Eadweard Muybridge's little naked running men - they provided a bank of simple images that he would constantly dip into in composing larger works.

Of this series, Carl Williams wrote in Apollo magazine, 'I see them as a counter-cultural version of Picasso's Demoiselles d'Avignon, an attempt by Sharp to go beyond what was expected of him, to stretch the psychedelic poster genre to breaking point and create a new visual language.' (16) Williams may be right. Martin was certainly simplifying what the Psychedelic poster artists were visually complicating.

Meanwhile, in the northern hemisphere where Martin was about to return, Tiny Tim had met Vicki Budinger at a signing session for his book Beautiful Thoughts. (17) Martin celebrated Miss Vicki in a full-page OZ magazine collage in which he quoted Tiny describing his perfect love, 'She is between 15 and 25 and is always with me. I guess I always need an audience and back in those very hard times when I first started to sing, I had to invent one. When I met my future wife I knew I had seen her before… she had come to me in a dream as a fairy princess. I fell in love with her. I shed a little tear and put it in an envelope to keep.' (18)

And Eric teamed up with former Spencer Davis Group multi-instrumentalist Stevie Winwood, Ginger Baker and the bass player from a band called Family, Ric Grech. They formed Blind Faith. Their first and only album (titled Blind Faith) was released in July, with the controversial Bob Seidemann cover of a bare-breasted pubescent girl holding a silver spaceship. The young girl was a London suburbanite, who posed with the consent of her parents and for a fee. ('An absolute genius work!' said Martin, 'It was the innocence…!') (19)

Steve Winwood has a different view. He said, 'I had nothing to do with it at all. It is what it is. If someone suggested that get put out today, I might have something to say about it'. (20)

Eric's contributions continued to be reticent. Not totally confident about song writing, Eric re-arranged the Buddy Holly song Well All Right and wrote one song, a hymn - the majestic and mysterious, In The Presence of the Lord. (21)

Tiny Tim's Second Album was released in January 1969. It did not duplicate the glory of the first. Martin had met Tiny fleetingly at the

Speakeasy Club, but in August 1969, when Tiny played Caesar's Palace in Luton (north of London), Tiny Tim's stars had tumbled to a point where he was at last accessible to his public.

Martin talked Louise and Richard to accompanying him to the venue. After the concert, all three went backstage. In his hand Martin carried a borrowed recording device and he taped everything Tiny said. Unfortunately Martin held the microphone too close and it came out quite blurred. After effusing about Tiny's genius, Martin asked Richard to 'get the gift'. Richard returned hauling an enormous picture from Martin's Exploration of Punctuation period. Said Martin, 'When I went to see Tiny at Caesar's Palace I took this lovely picture I'd done with an exclamation mark and gave it to him. It was a very nice picture.' (22)

Richard remembers it by its weight. He wrote about bearing the burden backstage, 'where it was presented to the astonished warbler'.

'Oh, what a shame, Mr Sharp,' said Tiny, 'It doesn't fit into my shopping bag'. (23)

Back at the Pheasantry, Nigel Waymouth kept painting and Philippe kept on working on his film. Philippe got the idea to paint on animation cells, where the finished image is on the reverse of the film/glass or Perspex. Philippe explained, 'You draw the image in a black line and then paint in the colour. Mart immediately picked up on this and expanded the concept by buying huge Perspex pieces and painting on them in the same process. Voila!' (24)

One day, while reading Jorge Luis Borges' memoirs, Martin came across a passage about Borges' meeting with the Spanish poet Federico Lorca. Mickey Mouse was discussed. Martin explained, 'Lorca could see Pop Art simply by understanding an image. He said, "Mickey Mouse is a symbol of America. I can read what's happening to America by studying Mickey Mouse". It's like an iridologist saying, "I can understand your health because I know what your eye is all about".' (25)

While Eric was living at the Pheasantry, Martin had done a picture of Mickey Mouse stepping out of a picture frame. He had also done a cut-back version of Vincent On The Road to Tarascon.

Perhaps Martin's parents were in his subconscious. Mickey Mouse - from Jo's trinket cabinet and Vincent's picture - from Henry's surgery?

Martin explained what happened next, 'I was doing a picture of Mickey Mouse. I was also doing a simplified version of Vincent On The Road To Tarascon and they were sitting next to each other. I had the sheet of Perspex 6 x 4 and I just put it over the two of them, traced it off and put them together. (26) 'Two girls were assisting me - Andonia and a friend. I've always liked to have some help in the studio, not always, but sometimes I do and they were a big help.' (27)

Martin was in the process of 'lifting' famous archetypal images. Fancy Our Meeting became strongly identified with Martin. Before the year was out, it would be transported to Sydney and exhibited in the Sharp Art Exhibition at Sydney's Clune Galleries. It was also a Big O poster, best explained by Michael Organ of the University of Wollongong. (28)

The juxtaposition of two familiar images in an unexpected setting led Martin to continue his experiments with art-on-art. He said, 'I'd been tracing out of art books. One of the first ones I did was Vincent Van Gogh's head coming out of the green chair and I thought, "Well, the purest thing is to actually cut up the image".' (29)

At the Pheasantry, Martin started creating his Artoons – published in 1972 as Art Book. (30) Snipping his way through art books of works by De Chirico, Magritte, Bonnard, Cezanne, Warhol, Degas, Holbein, Hamilton, Gaughin, Dalí, Arp, Duchamp, Vermeer, Ingres, Botticelli, Picasso, Signac, Goya, Whistler, Munch, Bacon, Man Ray, Monet, Piero Della Francesca, Mantegna, Matisse, Ernst, Seurat, Lichtenstein, Mondrian, Hokusai and especially Vincent, Martin laid the foundation for the Yellow House (1971), Art Book (1972) and Art Exhibition (1973). Some of these images – especially 'Matisse/Magritte' (known later as Pentecost) remained with Martin for life. (31)

Martin believes the very first example of appropriation is the picture painted by René Magritte in 1957. Said Martin, 'Magritte was an inspiration in the way that he would take a simple object and transpose it to another setting. In fact, he did use a figure from Primavera, in Ready-Made Bouquet – it's Botticelli's Primavera coming out of the back of a man with a bowler hat who is looking at a forest.

'I don't think I actually saw that before I started to do it, but looking at it now I see it as absolutely the first exploration of that area - using another art image in a Pop completely deadpan way. You're not altering it in any way, just a straight reproduction.' (32)

Although Martin's London years established his reputation as a great poster artist, lyricist, album cover designer and one of the OZ set, he found it tricky to exhibit his paintings. Other than Clytie Jessop's gallery and the Sigi Krauss' gallery, Martin describes his occasional exhibits as '…not in the sort of gallery I would have particularly liked to have exhibited in'. (33)

'I did try to get a few exhibitions going', he continued. 'Clytie Jessop was great. She used to show our work. She had a little gallery on Kings Road. Philippe had an exhibition there and I exhibited a few pieces there.

'And Sigi Krauss, where Michael Ramsden worked. Sigi opened this gallery in the West End and I had my collage show there Artoons. It became Art Book. That was just before I left. I suppose you can say about London - Performance – that movie – happened and I think things went a bit sour then. There was certainly a negative impulse from it - dramatic – exciting!' (34)

Certainly David Litvinoff got nervous. The Kray Brothers had been sentenced to jail some six months before the film, but not before noting that Litva had done too a good job as 'technical adviser' to the film. He was reputed to have betrayed underworld secrets. After Performance, Litva got jumpy and fled to the Philippines. Mr Jumping Jack Flash – god, he got mileage from that!

In March 1969 Martin had held his second solo exhibition Sharp Martin and his Silver Scissors at Sigi Krauss Gallery in Covent Garden, featuring collages based on famous works of art.

Then Martin attended two memorable concerts. The first, the 1969 Isle of Wight Festival held 29-31 August. The Festival attracted an audience of about 150,000 to see the Moody Blues, Bonzo Dog Band, Joe Cocker, Free, the Who and most of all Bob Dylan, who had not been seen since his near-fatal motorbike accident in July 1966.

Eric arrived the day before Dylan was to take the stage, so did John Lennon, Ringo Starr, Keith Richards and Charlie Watts. The sealed VIP area was reserved for Beatle wives and celebrities like Liz Taylor, Richard Burton, Jane Fonda, Roger Vadim, Syd Barrett, Donald Cammell and Elton John. Richard was in there somewhere. So was Jim. Towards the end of the concert, Martin got to the very the front of the stage.

'Front row!' said Jim, 'I was a few rows back. Richard was, maybe not the front row, but he was up there too. I went separately with a friend of mine, we did get quite close but it was an effort to get there. I didn't have any privileged sort-of situation.' (35)

Martin was so close that when Dylan sang his second-last song, Who's gonna throw that Minstrel Boy a dime...? he plucked a coin from his pocket, flicked it onto the stage and it went tink. Martin swore he could hear it on Dylan's 1970 album, Self Portrait.

Who's gonna throw that Minstrel Boy a dime...?

Tink.

'That's me!' Martin exclaimed. (36)

Richard remembers the concert too, he writes, 'Martin Sharp came tiptoeing through the slush, attired as a harlequin, "If only Tiny Tim was here," he said, "he's the one who can link up all the generations, a true minstrel of the age, ambiguous, multi-voiced, an immortal innocent, the most incredible songbird in captivity...". Yes Mart, yes. Ever since the night at the Albert Hall, this is how Sharp had been speaking'. (37)

The second-last concert Martin saw before coming back to Sydney was the Incredible Songbird himself at the London Palladium performing for Princess Margaret's Command Performance in November. Martin didn't make it backstage, though Princess Margaret did - after all, it was her concert. There's a famous photograph on Google Images of the Princess greeting Tiny Tim, singer Lou Christie and a rather uneasy David Bowie in the queue, awaiting his handshake. (38)

Martin came home before the year was out, though not before placarding Tiny's genius in Hippie Atrocities OZ No. 25 (December 1969). By this issue, the fresh influence of Felix and Jim was felt in both artwork and text. OZ 25 featured the Fabulous Furry Freak Brothers, Dylan's Great White Wonder bootleg LP, Elvis and Martin's two-page centre spread. It seemed like this was to be Martin's exit card before arguing with Richard about Tiny Tim and heading to Sydney. (39)

Jim Anderson recalls it this way, 'Richard was apologetic about handing over Martin's Tiny Tim b/w double spread for inclusion in OZ 25. He felt Martin had gone a little cuckoo and it would get OZ laughed at. It didn't worry new designer David Wills and me who were putting the issue together. David had already laid out his brilliant double spread on Elvis Presley, my favourite singer - before Bob Dylan and the Beatles turned up. Tiny Tim was just another welcome piece of magic for the hippie mix. Martin was lucky I did not hand-colour his b/w Tiny Tim masterpiece. David and I both thought about it.'(40)

Surrendering to Tiny Tim's unquestionable visual potential, Martin said, 'I used to try and talk people, Are you going to make a film about Tiny Tim? He's amazing!' Unable to stimulate interest Martin didn't give up. He said, 'So I did that cartoon in OZ, the double-page one…'. (41)

The one that proclaims a great talent has arrived. Hear ye, hear ye, the bluebird of happiness, the Prince of Song. Tiny Tim - The Spirit of Popular Music past, present and future, welcome to my dream.

Why did Martin return to Australia? He said, 'Artistic and romantic reasons. I didn't have the resources to live over there. You've got to be realistic. It wasn't like I was earning a lot of money. It was so easy to come back, some people leave it too long and they never come back. Luckily I managed to come back and bring back a lot of the stuff I'd been doing there, to do something interesting with it.' (42)

So goodbye London, and goodbye the 1960s.

'I still link into that period pretty strongly', said Martin in 1993. 'I think the 60s were a success - a big change, anyway. I'm still working with ideas I discovered then. I guess it's got a lot to do with smoking and thinking. To me, going to London was like going to university or something like that. Luckily meeting people and them being very open. They really were friendly times. Every door was open. It was the prime of one's youth as well. I'm just an interesting character who seemed to be somewhere at a certain time.

'I learned a lot but I couldn't have lived there. I wasn't together enough. I needed support. I just had a better chance of surviving here (Sydney). You can see how things work over there. If you're not born into it you'll never get it. I could have become a part of it I guess. I'm still remembered by some people as part of that 60s time - through OZ and stuff. (43)

About the time Martin was moving out, a lion called Christian was moving in.

Anthony (Ace) Bourke and John Rendall from Australia moved into the King's Road and bought a lion from the Harrods department store for 250 guineas.

A lion.

The three of them lived as flatmates. The lion called Christian became a King's Road celebrity. Then a book, a film, a youtube sensation, but more significantly for our purposes, this same Ace Bourke curated Martin's Martin Sharp – Sydney Artist exhibition at the Museum of Sydney in 2010. (44)

10.

UNDERGROUND MEETS UNDERWORLD

Martin asked me to photograph work that he'd brought back to Australia. I photographed them and he wanted to keep the ball rolling so we made prints, little frames. It was called The Incredible Shrinking Exhibition.

GREG WEIGHT

In the late-60s, Sydney's Kings Cross was Australia's Montmartre-cum-Greenwich Village. It had evolved into the place where the hippies met the hipsters.

Although tiny in size, Kings Cross is a densely populated locality. A short walk in any direction takes you to another suburb - Darlinghurst, Elizabeth Bay, Woolloomooloo. Or Potts Point - where Martin eventually located at 59 Macleay Street, a short Mini-Moke ride to Wirian and a short walk to almost every other happenin' thing in Sydney central. Jazz, poetry, Rock music, theatre, restaurants, the best coffee and the best tobacconist in town, all with a European – or cosmopolitan – beat.

Plus there is an Art history to the Cross. Poets Christopher Brennan lived thereabouts, Kenneth Slessor lived here. Artists, Sir William Dobell, Donald Friend, John Olsen and so on…

Kings Cross was a layered community. Depending on what you wanted - it wouldn't chase you but you could find it.

The Forbes Club was an illegal gambling joint frequented by Sydney socialites. Rev Ted Noffs ran the Wayside Chapel, a street church with a small events theatre. Atheist/anarchist John Webster from Speaker's Corner the Domain, carried his soapbox provocations into the broadly tolerant Wayside Chapel, where Noffs welcomed and debated him. Stripper Sandra Nelson made front-page news when she bared her breasts strolling Darlinghurst Road in mid-afternoon sunshine, wearing a Rudi Gernreich topless designer-dress – the very latest shocking thing from Europe.

The Piccolo Bar in Roslyn Street was another hangout. Run by Italian migrant Vittorio Bianchi since the 40s, it was, 'a meeting place for cabaret performers, prostitutes, hippies, punks, poets and nuns…denizens of the Cross', describes Roger Foley. (1)

Not far away was Clays Books, one of the few Sydney bookshops to stock books by the Beat writers. And that brought you up to the main strip where Owen Lloyd, the Bird Man of Kings Cross busked at the El Alamein Fountain, encircled by his enormous flock of budgies.

There was a smattering of hookers on this stretch, stoned but never whacked. Hare Krishnas chanted along the pavement. Buskers, spruikers and Jesus People too. Bouncers – big guys with folded arms – guarded the entrance of the Paradise Club, famous because of Sandra Nelson. And a row of motorbikes lined up outside the Pink Pussycat Strip Club. That's where a biker called Snake hung out, so named because he had a 6ft Diamond Python wrapped around his waist under his leather jacket. American troops in bars were a reminder of the continuing Vietnam War.

Sure it sounds rough, but unless someone did something incredibly stupid, like touching a stripper or something, people were rarely beaten up. Well, perhaps in the side streets but not too often on the main drag.

Located near the top of William Street, El Rocco was the most famous jazz venue in the country. Inside, TV people brushed shoulders with suburbanites, blue-collar workers, fake beatniks – anyone. When the Sydney production of Hair was staged at Kings Cross' Metro Theatre, the bandleader and percussionist was John Sangster from El Rocco. Tully, was the house band. And Albie Thoms ran the lights.

In the back streets of Kings Cross-Darlinghurst, John Bell and Ken Horler were seeking to locate their Nimrod theatre company. Ethereal poet Pip Proud wandered the streets in a cosmic haze. Kings Cross had it's own newspaper, the Kings Cross Whisper. Heck, this place even had its own witch. (Rosaleen Norton)

59 Macleay Street was the former Clune Gallery, run by Frank, Thelma and their son Terry Clune. The gallery had famously exhibited many breakthrough artists – such as John Olsen, Robert Klippel and a young Robert Hughes. It would become the Yellow House and continue to be a haven for artists. The Clune Gallery had been a major advertiser in early-60s Australian OZ, with Martin sketching their pen-and-ink ads. But the building was on the real estate market now.

This location was the closest Sydney had to the King's Road Chelsea, that's for sure. 'The Pheasantry was without a doubt the precursor to the Sydney Yellow House', wrote Philippe Mora, who lived with Martin when Martin was forming his earliest Yellow House ideas. (2)

In the late-60s there was a lot of talk about communal living. From the squatter movement to hippie collectives, London OZ was full of it.

In the summer of 1967, co-founder of OZ magazine's underground rival, International Times (IT) Jim Haynes, started an art-and lifestyle venture called the Arts Lab. Located in Drury Lane, Covent Garden, the programs were as freeform as the events – performance, dance, plays – 'happenings' they were then called, running late into the night. Legendary for a short time, the Arts Lab closed its doors in 1969, though not before inspiring some 50 other 'non-institutions' scattered around Britain. Martin knew about them, in the pages of OZ for starters. (3)

During his late-Pheasantry period, Martin had turned his attention to the subject of Art itself. Pre-eminent in his thinking were the works of René Magritte and the letters of Vincent Van Gogh in which Vincent idealised a 'studio in the south, in the sun'. That certainly couldn't happen in London.

Martin envisaged his Yellow House as a lot further south. (4) He said, 'I found London artistically challenging enough! The Yellow House was an idea that came out of London'. (5)

With a head full of Vincent, the Pheasantry and the Arts Lab (that he never mentioned) Martin began swapping ideas with underground filmmaker Albie Thoms and a keen young artist, George Gittoes. Martin had clear ideas about the general direction of the visual art on walls. And with a background in experimental theatre and film, Albie had ideas for the kind of happenings that could spring the place into life, especially at night.

Wrote Albie, 'I found it an engrossing idea, envisaging film screenings and music concerts among the paintings. So I agreed, promising to return after I had completed my engagement in Amsterdam'. (6) A sign of things to come? Albie's ongoing relationship with Martin would subsequently always be dotted with other film and theatre engagements.

Returning to Australia in April 1969, Martin took residency upstairs in the Clune Gallery along with 'protected tenants' ie. long term residents who could not be moved on until the property was sold. Meanwhile, Ian Reid, a young farmer from Captains Flat decided to buy the premises, therefore – in theory – everyone had to move out, leaving the premises vacant.

Pre-settlement, Ian arrived at his newly acquired property where he was unexpectedly greeted by Martin and two others. Ian had met Martin at the Pheasantry and on meeting him again agreed to allow 59 Macleay Street to continue as an exhibition space. Said Ian, 'I did it because it seemed like a good idea at the time and because I could. It became an early step in a journey of 1000 miles.

'I was a cattle farmer and came into some money. My lawyer said, "The Clunes Gallery and their property is for sale. Why don't you invest in real estate?" I said okay. I handed over a cheque, borrowed some, signed some papers and took a wander up Macleay Street to see my new premises. The atmosphere there was glum. I had purchased the property vacant possession but was greeted by Martin, Terry Clark and Charlie Brown and a lot of paintings in packing boxes. Having sold their property, the Clunes couldn't hold Martin's exhibition - so all that was up to me. And so the show began.' (7)

With the assistance of mutual friend Peter (Charlie) Brown, Martin presented Paint Your Own Gallery, an exhibition of his Pheasantry pictures along the lines of the cover for the newly released Ginger Baker Airforce LP record. For years afterwards, this is exactly what Martin's audience – fans – wanted from him. The egg. The toothy-smile. Eyeballs. Exclamation marks. Swirls. Little naked running men. Mickey Mouse meeting Vincent…but that was then. In 1970 the world was more serious than the hippie idealism had had preceded it.

With Australian forces directly involved in the Vietnam War, Sydney was extremely politically conscious. Martin did a b/w poster for the 1969 Vietnam Moratorium. Borrowed from the children's book Le Petit Prince, Martin appropriated Antoine de Saint-Exupéry's picture of the Little Prince which he captioned, 'We are them…they are us…Moratorium!' He created a sense of horror by replacing Saint-Exupéry's star with a skull. (8)

Held 3 May 1969, the University of New South Wales Vietnam Moratorium is where Martin first heard Jeannie Lewis sing. She could sing everything - folk, blues, jazz and opera.

Jeannie began her musical career in Sydney University revues in 1960. She sang with the Ray Price Jazz Quintet, was a semi-regular singer at the Sydney Baby Push (the name given to the second generation Push) and also at the Gas Lash. Jeannie was arrested in a demonstration in 1964 at Wynyard and helped convene the folk singers for a fundraising concert for the Freedom Ride, leading to civil rights for Indigenous Australians. At the 1969 Music for a Change Moratorium, Jeannie Lewis blew Martin away.

He said, 'I went to the Roundhouse at the University of New South Wales for a Moratorium - or something like that - and there was this incredible band with this wailing chick who was singing - like the best woman I'd ever heard sing. I thought, "Who is this? Where did this band come from? Is this what's been happening while I was away? This is as good as anything I've seen in the world!"' (9)

To organise the return of his paintings, it was back to London again briefly for Martin. In his absence, Philippe's subject matter had shifted to Degenerate Art. Subjects like meat (beef and pork chops) and religion (Jesus Christ). Steeped in 'artoons, Tiny Tim and anti-gallery art, Martin was initially unenthused.

Philippe struggled to get the visiting Martin involved, 'I had a hell of a time encouraging Martin to exhibit in a fine art gallery', Philippe wrote. 'For political reasons he shied away from it and preferred posters and cartoons ie. mass market and non elitist. I was in the same place but enjoyed galleries because of my background in galleries and parents but it all reached a climax for me with the Degenerate Art Show aka Crucifixion Show I curated with Sigi Krauss which included my anti-art Meat sculpture.

'I finally got Martin to contribute a painting in glass which was exhibited on the floor. I remember Mart at the Sigi Krauss gallery smashing the glass on his painting on the floor. Broken glass! Anyway, Mart enjoyed Sigi and the atmosphere. Sigi's Gallery was really the most avant garde place in London at the time. Stanley Kubrick came and used art from it in A Clockwork Orange – dancing Jesus figures and giant phallus.' (10)

There, Martin was exhibited alongside, 'Mora, Powell, Ramsden, Strawheim, Shamask, Philadelphia and other Neurotic Perverts'. (11) A member of the public took offence at the images and threw a brick through the gallery window. The idea of broken glass and broken windows captured Martin's interest. He made it a feature in his Incredible Shrinking Exhibition - photographs of his first show re-exhibited in small mirror-frames, which he worked on when he came back.

While Martin was gone, Tiny Tim played a 10-night stand in Sydney where he made a terrific impression at the Chevron Hilton, but Martin wasn't there. Ted Markstein was. He said, 'I saw Tiny Tim at the Silver

Spade at the Chevron. Half empty. Two hours. The most astonishingly versatile knowledgeable exponent of music I have ever seen in my life. Fucking fantastic. And the audience totally lacking comprehension as to what this master was illustrating to them about music!' (12)

Meanwhile, Greg Weight established his career as a photographer. From his South Dowling Street Redfern studio he did photo shoots for classy magazines, publicity and portfolio shots. Greg was regularly published in fashion magazines and the Sydney Morning Herald, which is where he surmises Martin may have spotted his name and remembered their old times together.

Said Greg, 'I'm working in my studio, the phone rings and it's Martin. He's back in Sydney. He came over. Very interested in the fact that I'd done photography. Asked me to photograph a lot of his paintings immediately. It was work that he'd brought back to Australia that he hadn't sold in the UK.

'I photographed them and he wanted to keep the ball rolling so we made prints of those. He made little frames (or had frames made). It was called The Incredible Shrinking Exhibition. The anticlimax that I'd felt at the end of our relationship when he went overseas was completely repaired by him coming back. I also realized that he hadn't forgotten what we'd done together. He wanted to reconnect.' (13) And so it has ever been with Martin and Greg.

Paint Your Own Gallery and The Incredible Shrinking Exhibition preceded the Yellow House. Most of the key players in what was to become the Yellow House attended – and were inspired by - that exhibition. The energy enticed a small team of key players. It was a rallying call of sorts. Roger Foley bought a picture. (14)

Questioned about his pre-Yellow House hopes, Martin replied, 'I wanted to create a place in which everyone could participate. I wanted to get something going, to give it a start, use it as a lubricant. I wanted to get paint, to be able to paint the whole place, to fulfil the fantasy perhaps and try to bring it into reality. A lot of people helped. There was a fantastic feeling, a magic atmosphere and a very high level of communication between the people who were there and the people who came into the place. It was expanding all the time'. (15)

Having generated a powerhouse of energy, Martin was well positioned to actualise Vincent's dream of an artist's community in the south, and Albie caught it from the start. Says artist Peter Kingston, 'It was Albie and Martin who started the Yellow House'. (16)

Albie already had his team. Filmmakers Aggy Read, Bruce Beresford and Peter Weir; film student Phillip Noyce; light artist Ellis D Fogg (Roger Foley); theatre director Jim Sharman and all those Contemporary Theatre Production Company, Theatre of Cruelty and Ubu Film people with whom he had done productions, projects and films.

Martin too had a team, though not as clearly defined. Around this time, George Gittoes, studying Arts at Sydney University, shared ideas with him as to how the Yellow House might proceed. (17) Richard (Dicky) Weight – Greg's older brother - was another cornerstone. He knew Martin from the National Art School and had applied to the Sydney City Council to paint the Sydney Harbour Bridge yellow. He painted the Yellow House yellow instead. (18)

Said Martin, 'As far as I knew this wasn't being done anywhere else at such a grass roots level. I brought back my London paintings. I had an exhibition all ready, which I'd done on my own, all arranged by the Holdsworth Gallery. A friend of mine, Peter 'Charlie' Brown was managing it. By the time I got back in the country he'd had a row with the lady running it and was no longer managing it. I was loyal to him, pulled out of that and I had to find somewhere else. What was to become The Yellow House was offered to me – but at that time it was just Sharp Art Exhibition. We started painting the walls to make it more interesting.

'I remember turning round to Terry Clark - my Maths Teacher at school - just a bit older than me - he was there helping, and his friend Charlie Brown who was a focal energy point. One night I can remember painting upstairs and some kids from Cranbrook turned up, lent a hand

and got into its spirit. They said, "Great atmosphere, boy this is fantastic - you can really do something here!" With this enthusiasm you can really make art work. There was an obvious need for people to express themselves. If you could just provide the context, then you could direct it. (19)

'I love exploring different mediums, so I'd take an idea from a collage-to- a-painting-to-a-cartoon or whatever. I was very open-minded as far as what medium I worked in. I find the commercial gallery scene pretty restrictive because really they're like boutiques – stores that sell art and have a different show every so often. Within that context you can put on a good exhibition and explore certain ideas, but you really don't have much freedom because it's too restrictive. So Paint Your Own Gallery, which later became the Incredible Shrinking Exhibition which became the Yellow House – got free of all that.' (20)

Martin organised both shows while living upstairs on the premises. At the very start, Martin lived almost alone, supported by a few companions, confidants and consorts. 'A few friends lived nearby. They started moving in as various people came and got involved with it. It was amazing to have a place that you could do what you like with. It was probably expected the building would be bought and pulled down, but it wasn't.' (21) Ian Reid comments, 'That was in some ways true. I'd bought the place because I could. I had no experience in real estate, I had no interest in real estate but somehow I found myself doing it, which is one of those things that you do in innocence.' (22)

Gradually the whole thing gained momentum, shunting – at this stage – to what would it would become within six months. Says Martin, 'It was a community of artists working together in the south.' (23)

Martin wasn't at 59 Macleay Street when Albie called to see him to lay ground plans. Dicky Weight was there and showed Albie the main gallery where he was painting the walls in the manner of Magritte's skies. But no, Martin wasn't present. He was at Palm Beach where he had rented a house to decamp. Albie roamed the empty rooms and found George Gittoes painting walls, ceiling – everything. Seeking Martin, Dicky pillioned

Albie (on Aggy Read's motor bike) to where Martin was staying with his secretary Bliss and a couple of assistants.

Brett and Wendy Whiteley were staying in a house nearby and invited everyone to dinner. Other guests included Peter Kingston, Mick Glasheen, and Peter Wright. (24)

Whenever he'd had enough of Yellow House preparations, Martin would head to Palm Beach, which can't have been totally relaxing. Whiteley's biographer writes of an irritating 'powerplay' between Brett and Wendy.

Add Martin's presence.

Since the Tate Gallery London established Brett's international reputation by buying his Untitled Red Painting in 1960, he and Wendy had done every cool thing there was to do. They had travelled the world, connected with Francis Bacon and lived in New York's Chelsea Hotel, a place where the cultural underworld hung out. Brett was the darling of the Sydney art set. Now - here was Martin, the homecoming king. Not just a friend but a rival also.

Seagull, the artist in a downstairs studio at the Whiteley's Palm Beach place said, 'Two camps would form, with Martin Sharp and his young friends at one end of the room indulging in a bit of grass, while the heavy mob – Brett, me and our friends – settled into serious drinking at the other'. (25) Serious drinking indeed. Jonny Lewis, who would later tag along with Martin, recalls drunken Brett and drunken Peter Wright coming to blows - the extraordinary thing being that 'Brett was fighting and painting at the same time!' (26)

From that time on, perhaps before, Brett always kept a challenger's eye on Martin's projects. From their angry co-efforts in the Yellow House to Brett's publication Another Way of Looking at Vincent Van Gogh (27) many felt Brett was constantly trying to outsmart Mart. It's something Martin strongly denies, 'I wasn't aware of any camps...!' (28)

At that initial Palm Beach visit, Albie recalls Martin showing no urgency about making things happen at the gallery, where the opening of the Incredible Shrinking Exhibition was scheduled for April Fools' Day 1971, less than a fortnight away.

Some, including Martin, speak of this exhibition as if it was the start of the Yellow House. It certainly attracted reviews, some hostile, which Martin snipped out of the newspapers and collaged in his Catalog – the collage and sketchbook that he was working on at night, in his comfortable apartment at the end of the building, overlooking Challis Avenue. The Catalog idea is a continuation of Magic Theatre OZ, only more personal. Less Robert Crumb and more Cranbrook.

Some journo wrote a review of Martin's exhibition: 'Sharp, with one eye a satirist and full of contempt for the young Bohemians he serves and exploits, confronts the viewer with repetitious vulgar lithographs in stark red and blue abounding in ghastly assemblages. In his homages to Van Gogh, his lack of comparable ability is crassly apparent and in their ways they are just as sickly as his pornography'.

Martin clipped that one for his Catalog and pasted it on an image of the Le Petit Prince blinded by a moonglow - the same Little Prince image as the Moratorium poster.

Another review: 'Martin, in his black velvet hat crammed down over his black locks – on his gnashing teeth smiling at the river of remarks – was supported by his velvet trousers and two-tone shoes, close to the echoes of his mind. Visit at your peril.' On this one, Martin pasted an Eadweard Muybridge naked male figure swinging a baseball bat. The hostile, over-stated, reviews kept Martin in laughs. (29)

Albie's 'review' is much closer to the spirit of the times: 'Martin's Incredible Shrinking Exhibition opened on April Fool's Day with Little Nell (Laura Campbell) tap-dancing in the Cloud Room to the sound of Bing Crosby singing Irving Berlin's 'Blue Skies'. It was a glittering occasion.' (30)

Little Nell was Martin's new girlfriend. She had appeared tap dancing behind Tiny Tim in the one-hour Channel 7 TV special A Special Tiny

Tim, filmed when Tiny toured the country in Martin's absence. (31) Martin spotted her tap dancing in a city arcade. Jonny Lewis filmed her.

Jon (Jonny) Lewis lived with his mother and brother Mark in Wylde Street Potts Point, a short walk from all this action. His friend, Bruce Goold knew of Martin's exhibition and he was up for crashing it. Of his sensational meeting with Martin, Jonny says, 'We wanted to crash it and crash it we did. That's where the paintings were knocked off…'. Yep, Jonny and Bruce stole two of Martin's pictures and inveigled them into the Women's loo. From there, to Jonny's mother's car and off they drove. Says Jonny, 'I started thinking, This is terrible, we shouldn't have done this!' So they backtracked, entered through the back gate, leaned the pictures against a tree in the garden and ran off.

Said Jonny, 'All we wanted was attention. Next day we thought we'd better go back and smooth things over. So we came back and there was Mal Ramage and Charlie Brown. So us two boys rolled up and I said, "We've got something to say. We're the guys who took the paintings, we're a bit sorry…". Charlie Brown said, "That's funny because we found them in the back yard". I remember a distinct smile came over Martin. I think they were all smiling. They thought we were good. So that was our entré and we started hanging around the place. And of course Martin wanted everyone to paint walls.'

In this way Jonny Lewis joined the pre-Yellow House collective and eventually moved in. According to him, he didn't actually contribute anything. 'I just absorbed it all, that's all I did'. Roger disagreed, 'Jonny helped everybody!' (32)

After this, preparations for the Yellow House began in earnest. Dicky helped Martin prepare the building. George started creating his Puppet Theatre room.

Came a time when it all became official, Albie went around assigning rooms. He took a top-floor room for himself. Peter Wright was next door. Colette St John moved in with him and assumed the role of cook. Musician Nic Lyon also moved in. And so on. Bliss also moved into a room on the top floor - next door to barrister and former Sydney University actor, Mal Ramage. Said Mal, 'I lived in the Yellow House for a period of time. I was the Straight Man in the Yellow House. I had to go and bail people out if they got into trouble and things like that. There used to be two mime characters, Julian (Jewellion) and his girlfriend Moth. And Julian got arrested one day. The Telegraph quoted me as saying that it was disgraceful that someone should be arrested just for making people laugh!' (33)

Thinking at first there would be no room for him, Jonny got genuinely excited when Albie crammed him in a tiny room in the mezzanine area, just big enough to throw a mattress on the floor. Having installed a parachute in his bedroom, Jonny reckoned, 'Everything was fantastic after that! This is where I got my education. I thought these people are great, these are the people I want to be with. I felt absolutely comfortable'. (34)

Others visited daily, with Peter Kingston (Kingo) opening a tearoom in the backyard so that visitors could sit and chat after experiencing the show. Kingo, who was one year behind Martin at Cranbrook School, got to know Martin when screening the film Who Lives in a Little House? at an architecture convention in the ballroom of the Hotel Australia. Martin just happened to be walking past, so Kingo said, 'Come and have a look at our film...!' The friendship went from there.

Said Kingo, 'Martin was at a crossroads, whether to go to New York and live there? Warhol and all those were very evident then in New York and Martin would have mixed in well there. But he chose to come back here and his life took a different turn. It would have been very different if he'd gone to New York. We're very glad he came back here because he got the Yellow House up-and-running with Ian Reid.' (35)

Dicky's brother Greg was also popping in-and-out, but this wasn't the Yellow House yet and Greg was yet to get fully involved.

Some spaces were totally vacant, except for Martin's large paintings left over from his previous show. He explained to Albie how these rooms could be converted into exhibition areas similar to the Cloud Room on the ground floor. Says Albie, 'where Magritte's puffy clouds on an azure sky were to provide the background for his next show'.

Martin and Albie discussed events, theatrical performances, film screenings and concerts. Albie immediately thought of London's Arts Lab – but 'getting it right'. He writes, 'Ours would be clean and colourful, in contrast to that place's dark and dusty spaces, a haven where we could celebrate the delights of living in Sunshine City'. In his book My Generation, Albie describes all his dealings with the Yellow House in this sort of detail.

Albie developed a program of activities to accompany Martin's exhibition: Filmmakers' Cinema on Thursday nights, soirées on Friday nights, screenings of old movies on Saturdays and cabaret on Sunday. Albie also wanted to establish an art school. He writes, 'As there was a didactic purpose to it all, preparing the audience for our further explorations, I suggested we call the enterprise the Ginger Meggs Memorial School of Arts, since it would be exploring Modernism from an essentially Australian perspective. Martin liked the idea...'. (36)

Jonny Lewis enrolled as the first student in the Ginger Meggs classes, which began with a Filmmaker's Cinema screening of Marinetti. This was followed in subsequent weeks by films by Garry Shead, Mick Glasheen and Peter Kingston.

Everything was taking shape and going to plan, so Martin scribbled a postcard to Richard Neville in London, 'What an incredible trip, a mind-blower – come and see Little Nell do the shimmy!' (37) But Richard was otherwise engaged.

Richard, Felix Dennis and Jim Anderson were fully pinned on an Obscenity charge. The date of the OZ trial was 22 June 1971, so they had plenty of time to prepare themselves and drum up publicity, which is unusual for a court case. The previous significant literary/obscenity charge had been the 1960 'not guilty' verdict for Lady Chatterley's Lover by DH Lawrence. It was contested and won, on 'literary merit', which put the OZ accused on thin ice, because a lot of people thought OZ had zero literary merit.

Dubbed the Schoolkids Issue, it wasn't FOR schoolkids. It was BY schoolkids. Get this difference to understand the trial.

Jim Anderson had been left in charge of OZ while Richard was in Greece or thereabouts. Jim foolishly – or brilliantly - depending on how you see it – let the schoolkids have their head. Unrepressed kiddie smut suddenly burst out of nowhere. Like, depicting Rupert Bear with a stiffy. For the first time ever, schoolkids had editorial control.

And the cover!

Says Martin, 'I wasn't involved in that issue. I certainly felt that it was a brilliant idea to give it to schoolchildren. It launched a new generation of kids. That's why it shocked so much, because kids spoke out and it just went like a bombshell, just the first time they'd ever been given the freedom of speech in the press!

'This Schoolkid's Issue was the sort of rage expressed exactly from the position they were in at the time. And the lawyer was John Mortimer, a famous playwright, and Geoffrey Robertson, a star of the law!

'So that was Richard's Production, that whole court case - sending out gilt-edged invitations inviting people to the OZ trial. His dress rehearsal case was in Sydney but his big show was defending himself at the Old Bailey.' (38)

By August 1971, the three accused were convicted of obscenity and given sentences ranging from 9-15 months, but released on appeal at which the trial judge (Judge Michael Argyle) was severely reprimanded for misdirecting the jury. Phew. All this was happening in London while Martin was 12,000 miles away.

And Jumping Jack Flash? Directly from Bali, Litva suddenly arrived.

David Litvinoff claimed to have upset London's East End underworld by revealing too much of their operations for the Mick Jagger film Performance. 'You're a big smiler,' said one of the Kray Bros, producing a carving knife and cutting a 'big smile' into Litva's cheeks, the scars of which he now bore. Although nobody quite knew how much to believe, Litva said he was a Talk Man for the Krays. That was his job. Litva called on problem-people, suggesting a quick resolution…'because the next guy to call is a whole lot bigger and won't be so patient'.

Although the Krays were in prison now, they still had their avengers on the prowl and - shit-scared - Litva came to Sydney (via Bali) to check Martin out. He frightened everybody. Says Roger, 'He absolutely terrified me'. (39). Says Greg, 'David could be very scary'. (40) Says Tim, 'He was a crazy man that one. Whoah!' (41)

Litva surfaced when Tim and Jonny were ambling past the Chevron Hotel. Martin parked his Mini-Moke and out leapt this firebrand dressed in shorts, sandals, Balinese shirt, dark glasses and smoking a 3-paper joint shamelessly on Macleay Street.

He walked straight up to Tim and Jonny and unleashed a torrent of words, 'Wut's these two gay boys doin walking down the street like this? You boys, going anywhere? Who do you think you are? I've seen people like you in the London streets…and anyway you can all go to fucken hell as far as I'm concerned!' Then, abruptly nice, 'Are you coming to the Yellow House boys?' (42)

Not that there was a Yellow House yet and not that he had even seen the premises, having come straight from the airport. 'That's what I mean about Litvinoff being mercurial', says Mal Ramage. 'I suppose he was a manipulator of people. I don't think he frightened me but I was wary of him, I was aware that he could turn very quickly. I think he had a great intellect actually.' (43)

Proprietor of the In Shoppe men's wear, Ted Markstein, lived opposite the Yellow House. Ted says, 'He was an evil bastard. They were mincemeat to someone like that. They were very naïve at the Yellow House. They had limited life experience. Maybe because they were young they lacked that natural self-protective suspicion.' (44)

Martin said, 'David came to the Yellow House. He was the main force, in a way – a terrific example.' (45)

11.

THE YELLOW HOUSE

*The Yellow House morphed out of Martin's exhibition.
It was a continuum. Nothing changed.*

IAN REID

Martin was running the pre-Yellow House by day. Albie was running it by night. Martin directed the walls. Albie directed the shows. Litva was added as a sort of manager-provocateur. His main jobs seemed to be putting out the garbage, sifting visitors and shaking up every proposition.

The 'Martin Sharp Gallery' at 59 Macleay Street was now shared.

Said Martin, 'The Yellow House was conceived as: the more artists involved...! And everyone was given a space they could work with. It was just totally starting off something, rolling and seeing how it went. Once I saw what happened I realised that's how you could do it. It was a big discovery that people are out there, willing to get involved and enjoying it'. (1)

At the outset, only a handful of name-artists were involved - Martin of course, and Brett. And - although few Sydneysiders had actually seen his films - Albie Thoms was a well-respected underground filmmaker. Those who cared to read the photographic credits in newspapers and fashion magazines would have noted the name Greg Weight. Posters plastered all over town told you about the Ellis D Fogg lightshows combined with

Tully concerts, where the ubiquitous performance-poet Adrian Rawlins took the role of slightly annoying compére.

Adrian was a Melbourne poet, performer, organiser, promoter and raconteur - probably best remembered simply as a 'character'. Adrian's art piece was himself. Performances were impromptu. He interviewed Brian Epstein when the Beatles came to Australia in 1964 and connected with Bob Dylan on his 1966 Australian tour, after which Adrian convinced himself that Dylan was a Christ, sacrificing himself. (2) Adrian (like the band Tully) was a follower of the silent guru, Meher Baba.

How did Sydney people get to hear all this was happening?

One medium that spread the word into suburbs was the ABC-TV program at 6.25. Each weeknight GTK (ie. Get To Know) was squeezed between the Six O'Clock News and the soapie Bellbird. From 1969-1974, GTK would broadcast a daily snippet of Pop-culture. It was usually a band, but sometimes art happenings, light show events, interviews with opinion-makers, etc. One evening the Burbs were treated to Adrian Rawlins laughing for five minutes. Just laughing.

During the 18 months since Martin had made 59 Macleay Street his domain, his lesser-known contributing artists were maturing fast. Under Martin's general umbrella and lessening influence, each was developing his/her own concepts. There was sufficient energy afoot to require art spaces (usually rooms) to be formally assigned by the newly formed Yellow House collective that gathered around the kitchen table. Their discussions took place against a constant background of recorded music since all rooms had been wired for sound by John Bee - a Kings Cross disco deejay. Tiny Tim was heard lots – as was Bob Dylan's Self Portrait LP - interspersed with vintage tracks from Al Bowlly and contemporary Rock.

Greg recalls, 'Everybody attended Yellow House meetings where laws were passed and secretaries took notes: Martin, Albie, George, Dick, me, Brett Whiteley occasionally. We were all talking about one thing and another thing and about where we were going to get the paint from when Brett got so bored with the conversation that he said, "Fuck man, you've got to jump on the kangaroo's back before it leaves the ground or else you're going to end up with a face full of dirt!" It rang home and we thought "Let's not talk about it, let's just do it". So Brett cracked it: "Dick get the paint, so-and-so do this, so-and-so do that, all meet here on Monday, we'll designate the rooms, get cracking and DO it!"' (3)

The artists treated the ceiling, walls, floors – everything – like an artist's canvas. What followed was feverish activity interspersed with evening theatre, film or musical events. 'Happenings' was an often-used word.

Some of the work had already been achieved, like Dick Weight's Cloud Room and Peter Wright's Spookyland, (so named by Arkie Whiteley). But most had to be created from scratch, like Martin's Fantomas Hall, Franklin Johnson's Stairway, Dick Weight's Tribute to Hokusai, the Infinity Room (Greg Weight and Julia Sale), Rembrandt to Magritte (Brett Whiteley and Martin's interior), the Magritte Room (Bruce Goold, Tim and Martin), the Bonzai Room (Brett Whiteley), George Gittoes' Puppet Theatre, Peter Wright's Ultra Violet and Kinetic Light Installation, the Capsule Room (Roger Foley) and the Yellow Room with a team comprising Martin, Peter Powditch, Philippe Mora, Peter Wright, Vivienne Pengally and Tim Lewis.

Says Roger, who lived close by, 'I used to constantly get called to come and repair the Capsule Room because people were bonking there all night. A lot of sex was going on in the Capsule Room. It was very comfy. All padded. Foam. We also had half-filled inner tubes underneath the floor so every time you moved it went down and somebody else would go up'. (4)

Germaine Greer's The Female Eunuch had only just been published, a book that would revolutionise everybody's thinking about women's issues, especially in this place. Many of the players knew Germaine from the Sydney University, the Sydney Push or even in London. (5)

Later, it would suit everyone to rewrite the history of the Yellow House as a non-sexist environment, though in reality, with few exceptions the art was left mainly to the 'boys'.

Says Adrian Rawlins, 'People were able to be in the Yellow House as either artists or appreciators if they wanted to be. The only criterion was their own genuine interest in what was actually going on. There were far too many runaway girls who were there because Martin had other ideas for them. In the back room there was a long refectory-type table and there would be Martin and 6-7 girls who painfully couldn't draw, patently had no visual perception whatsoever - but they were pretty, so they were there'. (6) Proprietor, Ian Reid describes Martin as, 'blessed with good looks, education, confidence, creativity, money and a magnetic personality'. (7) Female contribution was often secretarial and menial duties, or what may euphemistically be called 'assistants'.

Clearly Jeannie Lewis was not one of those. She was a major talent in her own right and Martin knew it. Martin had met Jeannie at the Roundhouse, University of New South Wales. He says, 'She was singing a song called Save the Country. It was so full of passion. It made me feel there's no need to go anywhere else when there are stars of the first magnitude here. I asked her to come and sing at the opening of the exhibition I had before the Yellow House'. (8)

Martin was so impressed that - if it can be said the Yellow House had a house band - Jeannie was it. She and her band regularly performed there every week and Martin paid them. At the end of the long and happy run, Martin thanked her and told her to take any painting she wanted. Jeannie chose the Vincent van Gogh, the one with the cartoon bubble and the words, 'I have a terrible lucidity when nature is so glorious…'. (9)

'But Jeannie,' Martin exclaimed, 'it's just a poster!'

'No it's not!' She replied. (10)

Greg Weight lived in his own South Dowling Street studio and regularly dropped in. Martin asked him to put a room in the Yellow House for the Spring (opening) Exhibition. Greg says, 'I'd gone to Cronulla and the sand dunes were, to my great delight, in pristine condition. Virgin. I shot a couple of rolls of film. When Martin invited me to be involved, I showed them to him and he said, "Let's make this a room, what will we call it?" There's nothing in the world more infinite than particles of sand so I ended up calling it the Infinity Room. That Infinity Room was also a suitable venue for one of Julia Sales' sculptures, which was a feathered chair and table - a total contradiction!' (11)

Greg's Infinity Room inspired Jonny Lewis to take up photography. First, he needed a camera, which he didn't have until Martin handed Jonny his paint-splattered Nikkormat before returning to London.

As a country boy, coming to terms with some of the events at the Yellow House wasn't straightforward for Ian Reid. An example was Jon Lewis' loop film of dolphins surfing. Says Ian, 'It was attractive - dolphins playing across the surface of an aquamarine wave before a golden beach. This was Art – but perhaps I couldn't recognize it as that at the time. Why the fuss? The point was that a young man had gone out, caught the magic of this scene on film and exhibited it. With hindsight it was a beginning for creative expression. It was a good and brave thing for him to have done.' (12)

The Stone Room was the first room to be completed. It was created by George, his mother Joyce Gittoes and Peter Kingston. Some saw it as the crown of their creation. Says regular visitor Ted Markstein, 'What blew me away was the creation in real life of the Magritte paintings, I thought that was fucking wonderful - the Stone Room!' (13) Says Jonny, 'The Stone Room that Kingo worked on day-after-day-after day, was extraordinary. There was nothing like it!' (14) In time, Greg's photo of the Stone Room became the cover of the catalog for the 1990 Yellow House Retrospective. (15)

Cinema nights continued, one was an amazing screening of George Greenough's Innermost Limits of Pure Fun. No one had ever shot footage inside the curl of a wave until Greenough figured out how to do it. Martin included a tribute to Greenough in the Stone Room in their version of Hokusai's Wave. He added a mirror ball on the tip of its spume, providing a fish-eye reflection of the installation, similar to Greenough's innovative technique. (16)

Says Mart, 'A number of people worked on it but the Stone Room was my idea. It was taken out of a Magritte painting which has a stone room with a table and all these items on the table. The door was open with a stone landscape. The difference is the Hokusai Wave in the doorway.' (17)

Hokusai's Wave created tension between Martin and Brett. Greg recalls, 'Brett Whiteley was back in town. Brett was intrigued by the Yellow House because he was really the star of the Sydney art world and now there was this other thing taking the spotlight, so he had to get close to it to find out what it was about.' (18)

Jonny remembers Martin and Brett working together on the Wave. Jonny describes their differences, 'Don't let Brett near oceans because he started turning the spray into ejaculate! Every night Martin would come and see this. He would paint over it and put back the Hokusai claw. Next day Brett would come over, look at it and say, "something's wrong here" and he'd paint the sperm back in. This went on for about a week.

'Bruce Goold, me, Brett and Martin were in the room when Martin threw a hammer across the room at Brett. Thankfully it missed. Brett was very shaken. We all were. I remember removing myself discreetly from the room and seeing Brett downstairs pacing up-and-down, smoking very nervously and saying, "He's lost it! He's lost the plot! He's gone! I tell you – he's lost it!"' (19)

To Brett, a master-painter, being over-painted was a real insult. To Martin, Brett was simply being a smartarse at the expense of the total concept. 'I think all the paintings in the building were directed by Martin' is how Roger Foley – Ellis D Fogg - sees it.

After the success of his show in Watters Gallery (an environment called WOOM credited to 'Ellis D Binns and Vivienne Fogg' – to indicate the close collaboration between artists Vivienne Binns and Ellis D Fogg), Albie said, 'Hey Foggy, you've got to come up here, we've got a room for you!' Martin already knew him from the First No Pinky 1966 show where Roger had brought Martin's cartoons the life on the stage.

'And that's when I built the Capsule Room in the Yellow House,' says Roger. 'I didn't live there, ever. I've always been an independent sort of fellow. It was certainly Martin's place, but it was Albie's too – because without Albie it wouldn't have been a "fun" place.' (20)

Sundays were set aside for multi-media music performances, starting with a Thirties Cabaret that Albie and Peter Wright put together. Borrowing tables and chairs from Juillet's restaurant next door, they converted the Cloud Room into a Thirties nightclub. With lights borrowed from Ellis D Fogg and a small stage set up at the end of the room, it featured Little Nell tap dancing to footage of Fats Waller performing Ain't Misbehaving. Actor Gillian Jones joined the performance too.

Writes Albie, 'It was a magical evening that hinted at the mixed-media explorations to come. During this Nell began tap dancing to the music, with the film projected over her. Bruce Goold joined in, wildly whirling around the tiny stage, before crashing into the sheet we were using as a screen, so that it fell over both of them. They continued to dance under it, and Albie projected the film onto the writhing result, creating a kind of kinetic Christo'. (21)

Another Sunday night, Adrian Rawlins read a spirited 21-minute rendition of the Allen Ginsberg poem Howl. Singer/guitarist Greg Quill performed with his band, Country Radio. And highly regarded bands Co-Caine and Sun made a musical contribution for the Yellow House crowd.

But most Sundays nights were lower keyed. Folksingers protested Vietnam. Nic played Japanese koto music. Or maybe Jewellion the Mime (Julian Greig) gave a performance. Martin spotted Jewellion dressed as Pierrot, performing with Jeannie somewhere. So he invited him to perform in the Yellow House. Jewellion moved in with his partner Moth, another clown. They camped in the corridor behind George's Puppet Theatre and busked daily on Bayswater Road. That's where Jewellion got busted and Mal Ramage had to barrister him out of trouble. Jewellion eventually found his way to France to study under Marcelle Marceau. There was a fundraiser. All the Yellow House people helped.

The musical line-up kept growing. Dubbed by Albie, the 'Dylan of the Domain', Peter Royles was a Kings Cross busker, usually located near the El Alamein Fountain.

Peter explained how he got involved, 'I hitchhiked to Sydney from Victoria in 1969. I came to Kings Cross and played guitar in the streets and coffee shops for a few years. I was playing the Domain's Speaker's Corner when David Litvinoff and Bruce Goold asked me to come and play the Yellow House, so I came along and became part of the music with Nic Lyon'. (22)

Peter pitched a tent in the roof and moved in, singing his Dylan songs and accompanying himself on twelve-string guitar and harmonica.

Meanwhile…

…in Eltham Melbourne, Marcus Skipper had formed a country blues band with his brother, classical guitarist Sebastian (Seb) Jorgensen who had returned from London. Seb was a bit of a legend. He'd won an international music award in Italy and shared the same bill as Jimi Hendrix at London's Festival Hall. Both Marcus and Seb were raised at the Montsalvat artist community near Eltham, founded by their father Justus Jorgensen. Ian Reid had visited that community and knew Seb. (23)

Writes Marcus, 'I was fronting a country blues band called Reuben Tice Memorial Band. Sebastian stole it and rebadged it the Oz Band, promising great things'.

The Incredible Oz Band declared their support for the editors of London OZ in their impending trial. Richard, Felix and Jim – the Second Triumvirate – were charged with Obscenity. And while Martin's former associates grappled with the law, the Yellow House crew continued its preparations.

In 1971 before Australia's 3rd Aquarius Festival was held in Canberra (the famous one was 1973, Nimbin NSW). The Incredible Oz Band took the Canberra stage by storm. Their performance was unstructured, confronting and loud. Marcus Skipper pulled down his trousers and dacked the drummer. Next, Adrian Rawlins joined the band for what Marcus described as, 'the longest, biggest, deepest, throatiest OM that ever stirred a solar plexus'.

Marcus continues, 'Adrian was made for the Theatre of the Absurd. He was going to bring style, poetry and charm to spruiking in Macleay Street. He joined our bunch of merry fellows and we bussed up to Sydney, into Kings Cross and the Yellow House. It was too small for our performance potential, so we broke up in bits. The rhythm section played the Magritte Room, the backup and singers went upstairs, Adrian worked the front door and hall and Seb shared the couch with Martin'. (24) Within 18 months Seb would be running the place.

The opening of the Yellow House was planned for Spring. In the interim, and with owner Ian Reid's tolerance, they moved into the next-door premises (No 61) that Ian also bought. Both houses would be joined by a hole knocked in the wall – featuring Lichtenstein's Whaam! and united into an artistic environment with Herman Hesse's Magic Theatre concept very much in mind – ie. price of entry – your mind'.

Money was a constant problem. To help keep the show on the road, Martin put up for sale his personal collection of works by 19th century cartoonist, Livingston Hopkins. Hop, as he was known, had been an influence on Martin from childhood. There were few buyers.

Away from it all, his own upstairs suite, in what Jonny calls Martin's 'salubrious' apartment, Martin was finalising his Catalog. Started in the pre-Yellow House period, this 32-page b/w American quarto-sized visual diary is a collage of his day-by-day gleanings and redolent of Magic Theatre OZ.

Pictures of/by Vincent, Tiny Tim, Robert Crumb, The Phantom, Von Mora, Munch's Scream, early high school Sharp, Magic Theatre Oz, the burning monk, Peanuts, OZ friends and little naked Muybridge figures skipping throughout the pages. Plus words, plenty of words - quoting Vincent, the press, his own diary notes, reviewers, Erich Fromm, an 11-year old boy and a passage about Abraxas. Enter The Little Prince. (25)

Just like the pictures, the writing was a smattering of wherever Martin's thinking was at when he picked up his pen, scissors and glue.

Said Martin, 'The Catalog - you could dive in anywhere, there were no rules as to what you read next. It's a great way of doing a book. I used other people's material. I didn't pay much attention to copyright. I started when we were getting the Yellow House together, while the 59 Macleay Street Exhibition was on. It was something I'd work on every night. I would cut up some quotes, stick them in, do a bit of embossing. It was that multi-level sort of thing'. (26)

The Yellow House was a buzz of activity as everyone involved themselves in preparations for the Spring Exhibition. Visitors chipped in and helped. Says Greg, 'There was this intense 3-4 months preparation, nobody was getting paid, you just had to get in there and do something, paint walls and do things. That concept surprisingly came off. The place just looked like a Christmas tree!' (27) Martin's mother Jo visited the place and said, 'Darling, it's getting more beautiful every day!' (28)

Now living at Lavender Bay, Brett, Wendy and Arkie Whiteley painted one of the rooms white and installed a miniature Moreton Bay fig in its centre, with photographs by Greg on the walls. Brett called it the Bonzai Room. David Litvinoff moved in with the Whiteleys and got pretty close to Brett. Says Jonny, 'Brett adored him. The eccentricity, it was so out there. I think that friendship was so intense that it possibly imploded.'(29)

Ted Markstein adds, 'David Litvinoff introduced Brett to smack. He told Brett that his pictures lacked "a sense of evil", which is not a good thing to tell someone of feeble mind - like Brett'. (30) The dark side of Litva is what that Martin and Eric Clapton never really saw, nor ever faced.

Painter, Antoinette Starkiewicz arrived from Melbourne. Sculptor, Tim Burns landed from Perth. The Sydney University Architecture students who were sent to do assignments on the place were co-opted into painting walls. Roger installed special effects lighting throughout the house. Sue Ellen cooked meals of brown rice and vegetables. Arthur Karvan, who had returned from a year in the US, was co-opted as financial manager and set about the impossible task of trying to raise funds.

Spray guns were brought in to paint the walls and sanders to polish the floors. Works from Martin's collection were added to the show. Among them were Scottish sculptor and artist Eduardo Paolozzi lithographs that Martin offered for sale at $200 apiece. Paintings by Peter Powditch, Philippe Mora and Michael Ramsden were hung. Visiting British fashion designer Zandra Rhodes helped Martin develop an all-white room where he displayed his Van Gogh-inspired drawings, Footsteps on the Road to the Yellow House.

The Ministry of Arts and Culture was a portfolio created in 1971 and Martin invited the new Minister to attend the opening of the Yellow House. He was arriving at 10.00pm. Driving everything to a last minute climax was becoming customary for Martin's openings and this one was no different.

The Yellow House was located next door to Juillet's restaurant, operated by French chef, Patric Juillet and his wife Chrissie Brett. Ian Reid helped kick-start this restaurant where, gangsters, socialites and artists ate at adjacent tables. Poet Allen Ginsberg ate there one evening in company with Brett Whiteley and other Yellow House people. A constant stream of pre-Yellow House and Yellow House stories are set in this restaurant. It was around the corner from their old haunt, Vadim's.

After staying up all night working on the Cloud Room, Infinity Room, Bonzai Room, Puppet Theatre, stairs and every other installation and mural, the exhausted crew staggered to Juillet's for a well-earned bowl of breakfast soup. They noted that the dawn western sky was filthy yellow. Before their last coffees those clouds broke and Macleay Street witnessed a dramatic hailstorm. Everything turned white in 10 minutes. Back at the Yellow House there was roof-drama. The Bucket Brigade galvanized into action while that staircase, so lovingly painted by Bruce Goold just a few hours before, needed major touch-ups. No sleep, now this.

They did it all, of course, with aplomb.

At 10.00pm the government car pulled up outside No 59. Someone from the Yellow House opened the car door and out stepped the Hon George Freudenstein, Minister for Arts and Culture. He walked to the front door to a small fanfare of music led by Nic Lyon on viola. Martin had placed a ribbon on the door, which the Hon snipped before entering. Once inside, there was wet paint everywhere. The combined fumes of the different paints they'd acquired free from the various paint companies hit the nostrils. Said Nic, 'It was pretty hard to walk in there. I don't remember what happened after that. I think we all went to bed. It was all a bit of a blur from then on.' (31)

Albie stayed awake. He recalls the night as a spectacular success, 'The Spring Exhibition at the Yellow House opened with an enormous party that brought Herman Hesse's Magic Theatre to life. As well as the artworks on the walls, Nic Lyon, Seb Jorgensen and Peter Royles provided live music. George Greenough's film was screened and George Gittoes performed a puppet play, while Jewellion's Pierrot glided from room to room. Other Yellow House residents appeared in fancy dress, hired from the Elizabethan Trust, with me choosing a Harlequin suit.

'Our massive installation quickly proved popular with the public, with parents bringing their children and people from the suburbs braving the demimonde of Kings Cross to see the show. It reversed the basic premise of Pop Art. Instead of turning popular imagery into fine art, we turned fine art images into popular art, exemplified by Martin's painting of Mickey Mouse meeting Van Gogh on the road to Tarascon.

'The critics' responses were varied, with the enthusiasts having reservations and the knockers outrightly dismissive. One described it as a "Mardi Gras of Jumping Jack Art" while another thought it "gay, crazy, and full of a mad sort of optimism…a festivity rather than an art exhibition". Another described it as "a continually disrupting and disorientating blend of the serious and unserious, the sophisticated and the slapstick, the vulgar and the nice", and one perceived that it "uses the past almost nostalgically for a statement about the present and the clichéd for an evocation of the new".

'Also damning was Ross Lansell in Nation, who claimed "serious artists have to discard such crutches as togetherness, pleasant though this immediately may be; they have to fight tooth and nail to forge their own various artistic identities, to take the creative process further than they can comfortably bear".'

In a letter to the magazine, Albie responded to Lansell's accusation that the artists were doing it in comfort. Albie wrote, 'we live without money, on one meal a day, with the roof over our heads uncertain, begging, borrowing and stealing materials for our art, ignoring legal restrictions that would have prevented us making it, and promulgating a lifestyle at variance with community standards'. (32)

Despite the newspaper critics, the vast audio-visual environment was attractive to television reporters. The ABC-TV show GTK filmed there on several occasions.

Jonny recalled one slightly edgy occasion, 'I remember Martin saying on GTK about the Yellow House, "It's the greatest conceptual art piece in the world." It was very arrogant of him in some ways – and he regrets it – and I'm thinking, "what does he mean?" I learned that it was Vincent's dream in the south. I still think that's extraordinary, that you would take the dream of one of the greatest artists in the world and recreate it as young people in the south, in the sun. That's fantastic!'

GTK sent a film crew to the opening. They caught up with Litva who was wearing a mask. 'He was fantastic,' says Jonny, 'because they asked "What's the Yellow House?" and Litva said, "There's 325 sexual deviants all living together here and we're making art." He's eating an apple while he's saying this. And I'm thinking, "I'm not a sexual deviant!" But it sounded good.' (33)

The Spring Exhibition continued to attract audiences, paying a dollar-a-head admission with an option on the Catalog for an extra 50c. Martin wrote on the cover 'It should be free'. They took turns on the door to collect the entrance fee, which some visitors objected to paying because the monitoring was inconsistent. One day it might cost $1, next day the doorkeeper had wandered off.

Clayton Simms, who worked at nearby Garden Island, was one visitor, straight off the street. He said, 'I didn't know what the fuck it was, I just thought, "These people want to live in a house with this great painted ceiling…" that's what I thought. It took a long time before I woke up that it was a gallery. I went there one Sunday night and suddenly someone asked me for money. I thought, 'That's it – it's a gallery!' (34) Ian Reid adds, 'I say bullshit – I think he got it right to start with! It was a house with a painted ceiling! If it was a gallery it would have been run like a gallery!' (35)

At the time, Martin poured out his dream to at least one interviewer. He said, 'The only thing we now lack is the people aren't with us. There will come a time when the people are with us. People may come in here who have never painted before. We'll just give them a brush or a musical instrument and they'll suddenly become interested. If this environment can become free enough to make them lose their inhibitions about being creative, and if everyone sang a song, or wrote poems, or drew a picture, or took a photograph, then each of these people would have found a way of understanding life – a way of looking at reality from a disciplined point of view. It's like looking through the lens of a camera, it opens you up'. (36)

The success of the exhibition surprised many but it was not built to last. When the property failed to sell at auction, Ian Reid decided it was time it paid its way with rents. On hearing this, Dicky was furious and Albie stormed out.

Albie writes, 'With Martin in agreement, and Arthur and Mal Ramage supporting him, Ian Reid came up with a proposal for the rental of its residential spaces to people prepared to pay a premium for the privilege of living there. Though I was grateful for the opportunity to have lived and worked in the place, I felt this was an attempt to profit from our labours, without any recompense and I said so at a meeting called in Arthur's apartment to discuss the plan. Martin responded that the Yellow House was his idea and that it was up to him to decide its future, which offended me deeply, since I, along with the others, had contributed so much to its final form. Furious, I stormed out, packed my bag and departed, leaving behind the environment that had taken over my life.' (37)

Said Ian, 'I didn't take on the responsibility of everybody's lives. If an expectation of dependence on me had developed in the Yellow House that was a mistake. It was a greater mistake to think that I had profited from their presence. What I did was provide the place where people could do things. I'll just say that if I asked the people to pay rent – well good on me! The party had to end some time. And if Albie says he stormed out, well – he stormed out. I was thinking, "This has gone far enough".

'Although it kept going with Jorgensen etc – I don't remember what the financial arrangement was (if there was one). That was okay, my life was going in a different direction at the time.' (38)

Ian was a responsible husband and father. He had married Martin's cousin Katie, who he met at the Yellow House.

For 'romantic reasons' (ie. Little Nell) Martin returned to London. Says Martin, 'I wanted to close the place, I didn't witness the last phase. George Gittoes said to shut it down. I felt it was getting too mad, so I shut it down. Sebastian wanted to keep it going.' (39)

Minus Martin, the remaining Yellow Housers took an around-the-kitchen-table vote, and Seb took on the leadership, management or whatever. The tenant proposal was not implemented. It was another eighteen months before the building was sold. In the interim, it was allowed to function as before, with younger artists replacing those who had left.

Albie's film and experimental theatre was replaced by music. Where films like Garry Shead's Ding A Ding Day were once screened, Seb was more interested in musicians. So was Nic Lyon.

Carrl Myriad and Janie Conway played there. Nikki Madden played there. Possibly every notable musician of the time played there. They'd go from playing PACT Folk – Sydney's primo music venue of the time - to the Yellow House. And if Seb or Nic thought they were passable musicians, they'd jam with them.

There were some magic moments. Mic Conway and the Captain Matchbox Whoopee Band played there. Seb asked them to. (They were only 12 months from their hit song My Canary Has Circles Under His

Eyes.) There were six band members plus partners. Mic Conway recalled British comedian Marty Feldman loving the band and hanging around for a day or so. (40) Others recall members of British psychedelic group, Pink Floyd, marvelling at the Stone Room and George Greenough's film. Some see traces of Greenough's influence in Pink Floyd's after-work.

Though the Yellow House continued to attract audiences, its open-to-the-public activities became fewer and less frequent. Some of the rooms were changed, not for the better. One of the original Yellow Housers was Roger Foley whose seniority made him 'responsible'. After Sebastian, he assumed the role of consultant.

Says Roger, 'Some of the young residents were very good artists but they were very young and innocent and could not look after the place. I lived just around the corner and I was happy to do that.

'These were people who lived their art form and were keeping the 60s spirit of peace and love alive. Most of Martin's Art was still in situ as Martin had walked out and gone to London, so Sebastian Jorgensen ran the House for a while, mostly as a live music venue which I continued to support as well as maintaining my Capsule Room environment in the house. One day Seb visited me and said he was returning to Melbourne and could not look after it anymore and gave me the keys to keep an eye on the place as my installation was also still there. I told him I did not want to manage the place but that I would be happy to advise and assist the residents from time to time.'

Roger continues, 'I sort-of became responsible. I had two rooms going, one was the Laser Infinity Room, which used a lot of mirrors and Perspex to create a sense of being in outer space. I'd drop in to see what was going on. "An electricity bill's come in Foggy, what are we going to do?" I said, "You've got to collect money at the door haven't you!"

'I was asked to add another room to fill in some empty space and built The Laser Infinity Room - a high tech take on Greg Weight's Infinity Room. David Ahearn organised a performance, an underground newspaper The Five Cent Joint found a home. Tim Burns was the only other member of the original group still involved, with his 'Road Smash' installation remaining on view.

'A very young Asco Sutinen (now Axel Sutinen) wanted to print a poster for what they were calling The Yellow House Chapter III and asked me if I wanted to be mentioned on it as Chester had asked me to build another environment - now called an 'installation'. I said "terrific" so he gave me a draft copy for me to add a credit about my contribution. There was no space left except on the side of the very busy psychedelic style poster so I quickly wrote a suggestion on the edge thinking that he would rearrange the text to fit it in. I was bemused and then pleased that he just printed it as it was with my writing on the side. Later, I realised that apart from Albie and Dick's Catalogue/Poster for the Spring Opening of both houses in September 1, 1971, and a couple of flyers from Martin and Albie, this was the only poster the House ever had.

'The group, now calling themselves 'Space Environment' included Christine Koltai and Phillip McKeon - now Phillip Arts - running touch and sensitivity classes, Chester Harris who had worked for London OZ - he illustrated Germaine Greer's essay on "Cunt Power" for the Female Energy OZ 29 July 1970 issue - and was now teaching art and continuing to draw extraordinarily graphic erotic works and selling them on the Macleay Street out the front. Also Ian Hartley and Asco Sutinen continued making new art.

'Later in Sydney I got a call from Chester saying there was an electricity bill they could not pay - it seemed no one was collecting the $1 entrance fee. I put together a small arts grant application to pay for a benefit concert at The Cell Block Theatre called Rock Ballet Fantasy, which included the world premier of Christine Koltai's ballet The Dolls, Albie Thoms films, Drum Majorettes, a Highland Pipe band, the Fogg Lightshow and the first public performance of my then girlfriend Gretel Pinniger as Madam Lash, with everyone contributing for free. We were all chuffed that Robert Helpmann came and praised the bizarre collection of performances, however our show did not draw a big enough audience and the electricity bill remained unpaid.

'Local kids started climbing over the fence late at night, stealing artwork including some of my light sculptures. And sadly, and unknown to me at the time, an embittered and inebriated ex-resident would return from time to time and smash artworks in an effort to close the place down.

'I felt like a bit of a Dad sometimes. Eventually people would come in off the street or over the fence at night and were stealing out of the rooms, Martin's pictures started to be smashed and vandals were attacking the place.' (41)

'It seemed as though the place would run down very quickly because of the lack of direction inherent in communal decision making - what we called the 'nice guy' problem - and also through this vandalism and lack of electricity. So I took it upon myself to inform the residents that unfortunately the place would have to close. I believe Ian Hartley rescued some of Martin's work that was still intact and took it to Wirian and closed the door. Some residents were very unhappy about this decision, the end of the dream, but they offered no solutions. I didn't know how to contact Ian Reid so I had to say, "Sorry, you people can't look after it properly, we're going to have to close". I left a message for Mal Ramage and sealed up the place best I could.'

'While collecting my own work I gathered more of Martin's stuff that was lying around damaged, including broken pieces of Abraxas that luckily all still fitted together - how did that get so broken I wondered? I took it all to Jo, Martin's mother who looked aghast at the state of it, put aside a few things and said if I liked it she would sell the rest to me. I offered her $500 for which she gave me a receipt. It seemed a very fair price to me as Martin had sold his Hendrix painting done in the same style as Abraxas to Jim Sharman for $500.' (42)

Over approximately a three-year period the Yellow House went through four phrases, each quite different from the others. All were under Ian Reid's protective ownership umbrella:

- 1970-1971 - pre-Yellow House exhibitions, all Martin.
- 1971-early/1972 - the period generally seen as the Golden Period, with artists under Martin's instruction by day, performers under Albie Thoms' baton by night. The house band was Jeannie Lewis et al, all under Arthur Karvan's general management.
- 1972 - musician Seb Jorgensen ran the place and an emphasis on music replaced the emphasis on film.
- 1972/early-1973 - young people moved in until Roger Foley closed the place for keeps.

The Yellow House Catalogue is one of the Yellow House's few in-house publications. It lists the following names as artists/contributors: 'Ian Reid,

Bliss, George Gittoes, Bruce Goold, Karen Hobby, Peter Kingston, Jon Lewis, Nic Lyon, Moth, Mal Ramage, Peter Royles, Sue-Ellen, Martin Sharp, Albie Thoms, Greg Weight, Peter Wright, Dick Weight, John Bee, Tim Burns, Bob Daley, Ellis D Fogg, Lyn Fuller, Franklin Johnston, Slavka Jovic, Arthur Karvan, Kaleidoscope, Tim Lewis, David Litvinoff, Aggy Read, Zandra Rhodes, Jim Sharman, Brian Thomson, Brett Whiteley, Wendy Whiteley, Julie Clarke and Trisha.' (43)

Maybe 1000 people painted, performed or helped in some way around the Yellow House. Maybe more.

Tim Lewis is among the unlisted artists. He was friends with Jonny Lewis, Bruce Goold and Dick Weight and lived with his parents at Double Bay. Tim says, 'I didn't finish East Sydney Tech because I went to the Yellow House instead. I certainly wasn't a prime player. I helped with Magritte Room.' Within a couple of years Tim would be working side-by-side with Martin, as Greg had done previously. (44)

Says Ted Markstein, who lived directly across the street, 'From my observation the Yellow House was absolutely incandescent for about seven months then it started to fall apart. Given the players, I'd say it was amazing it got seven months!' (45)

Ian Reid commented that he watched the Yellow House disintegrate, 'When Martin left, the creative energy and funding to pay the bills dried up. By the time the doors were closed it was 10 minutes past the hour. The properties were in a mess. It was costly to remediate and should have ended sooner.

'The role of patron isn't easy. While it's rewarding to support creativity, it's a failure to create dependence. At the end of the day, artists succeed if they have talent - and hopefully a "start" helps them along the way. With the wisdom of hindsight things might have happened differently but the Yellow House was a "happening". It provided the venue and I'm proud to have done so, it's become a part of our history and I have no regrets.' (46)

When the Yellow House was over, 57-61 Macleay Street became a boarding house until sold.

12.

YESTERDAY'S PAPERS

Sharp's grafts, looking simultaneously so familiar and extraordinary, help to recharge the originals.
GEORGE MELLY

Four years before, when London OZ launched its very first issue, the names usually associated with the publication were Martin, Richard and an under-acknowledged Louise Ferrier. Her leading role in OZ has seldom been fully credited. Some say that's because Louise is not a person to seek attention. Others say it's because women's contributions were consistently underplayed in those early pre-feminist days. In establishing OZ, Louise was involved in everything from business decisions to cover girl. She allowed the use of her premises and played the part of secretary as needed.

When Martin returned to London in 1972, Dr Germaine Greer's book The Female Eunuch had been around long enough to seep into cultural attitudes about women's rights. Published in October 1970 by MacGibbon & Kee, within its first six months the book was reprinted six times and translated into 11 languages. (1)

Greer reasoned that though women do not realise it, men subconsciously hate them and so women are taught by society to hate themselves. Groups who formerly saw themselves as politically correct were branded as guilty as the rest. Liberationist groups, participants in the Sexual Revolution, acid-eaters, American Beats, the Sydney Push, the Baby Push, Yellow House artists (designated a 'Men's Club' by participant Juno Gemes (2)), even the ideology-proud OZ editors, were shocked to read of themselves as having reenacted the sins of their fathers!

When Martin returned to London a different OZ trio was in the public consciousness, one that would famously always be associated with London OZ – charismatic gadabout Richard Neville, former OZ street-salesperson Felix Dennis and enthusiastic newcomer Jim Anderson. The three had created one helluva kerfuffle while Martin was gone.

Going back to January 1969 – OZ 17 – featured Jenny Kee and Louise's nude cover photo with Martin's Question Mark as background.

OZ 19 – Germaine cheekily unzipping Viv Stanshall's fly – ie. Viv from the Bonzo Dog Doo Dah Band. Thus far, with Richard peppering his endeavours with overseas trips, OZ editors Jim and Felix were traveling quite well.

Next, Hells Angels OZ, followed by OZ 22, an issue Jim Anderson would rather forget. Martin's Moon & Mickey Mouse cover restored confidence with readers in OZ 23 – 1969 the year of the Moon walk.

Then came Homosexual OZ with a cover photo of two of Jim's friends, a black guy and a white guy in a naked embrace - cock-to-cock as it were. OZ was right up with the times. Gay Liberation was on the move with spontaneous, violent demonstrations by the gay community at the Stonewall Hotel in Greenwich Village NY. Jim welcomed the subject, Felix didn't.

'Who's going to buy it Jim?' questioned Felix. Felix had cover-ideas of his own. He wanted to use Bob Seidemann's picture of a bare-breasted adolescent girl holding a silver airplane. It wasn't the Blind Faith album cover yet.

Says Jim, 'Felix fought really hard to have it on the cover. I had my first experience of coming up against the brick wall that was Felix Dennis. Felix did react very poorly. He banged my head against a brick wall. Felix was so strong – that's why he became a multi-millionaire in his wheelings and dealings with other people. You couldn't handle him.

'He gave way eventually so my cover was on – it sold out immediately. When the police realized what it was, they came around immediately and seized 25 copies of what we had left. Everything else was gone. Richard was away, he was always away…'. (3)

Although the OZ team didn't take it seriously, they were under police surveillance. Jim explains his casual approach, 'It was a warning but we were just treating it as a joke. We just did what we did at the time. We were part of the cultural upheaval, the anti-establishment feeling, the revolution. That's all it was. It was part of the territory. It was all around. We weren't more provocative than anybody else, we were just a bit more popular – we were distributed nationally – we were more dangerous in the eyes of the government.'

Then to Felix and Jim's dismay, two issues later in Women's Liberation OZ, Richard wrote, 'We are feeling old and boring at OZ…' and he asked schoolkids to contribute. Says Jim, 'Felix and I laughed when we saw that because we were not old and boring, we were the brand new boys at OZ full of enthusiasm and raring to go! When we were left alone, we exercised things to the max - I suppose - with our newly-found freedom – with Richard away. He was quite shocked with what happened with Schoolkids OZ!' (4) Richard Neville shocked. Now…that's a thought.

Next - Acid OZ, using Timothy Leary and an outrageous Robert Crumb cover with an acid-eater's eyes popping out of their sockets. Jim explained how this led to a big disagreement with Martin, 'For the Acid issue Martin sent us something from Sydney - which was a Mickey Mouse. In the Mickey Mouse frame was a blank space like a television screen with nothing in it. David Wills and I were looking at Martin's b/w illustration. I said, "David we can't have a black and white thing in a psychedelic issue, everything else is psychedelic, what can we do?"

'I said, "We can put in something in that blank space" and so I put in *Acid is good for you*. David and I did it together. Martin hated it. He never said anything to me directly but he really felt insulted by that. It seems that was the origin of a certain distance that always existed between Martin and me.' (5)

The next issue, OZ 28, May 1970, was the infamous Schoolkids Issue. Martin had nothing to do with it. Robert Hughes had an article in it. Thirteen months later – 23 June 1971 - Richard, Jim and Felix fronted the Old Bailey on charges of publishing obscene material and sending indecent material through the post. Nobody had ever been sent to jail for that before. What followed was the longest and most entertaining obscenity trial in history.

In support, John Lennon wrote the song God Save OZ. (6) Yoko wrote Do The OZ. Later came an off-Broadway production The Trials of OZ, a one-hour television film called The Trials of OZ, and a book by Tony Palmer also called The Trials of OZ. The trial cost British taxpayers £80,000. (7)

At the sentencing, there was something spiteful about Justice Michael Argyle's closing address, describing Felix as having limited ability and being a dupe of the other defendants. That insult cut Felix and probably motivated him to show his detractors he was second to none. The three accused were convicted of obscenity and given sentences ranging from nine to fifteen months imprisonment. They were released on appeal, at which the trial judge was severely reprimanded for misdirecting the jury.

All this happened while Martin had been running the Yellow House in Sydney.

Robert Hughes was appointed art critic for Time magazine in 1970 and had moved to New York. Eric had formed Derek & the Dominos, released a double album, retreated to Hurtwood Edge and sought privacy. Performance had been released to some sort of acclaim. Syd Barrett wasn't well. The Beatles had officially broken up. Philippe's film Trouble in Molopolis had been screened to positive reviews. Granny Takes a Trip had opened a branch in New York. And King's Road had made the shift from Bohemia to conspicuously fashionable. Said Martin, 'After the Pheasantry things started to go. Kings Road had a big tourist thing at that stage. You'd walk out in the street and they'd be taking snaps of local bohemians. You get a bit sick of it.' (8)

The whole scene had changed. Says Martin, 'King's Road Chelsea was still there but it was all over, disseminated, died or whatever.' (9)

Martin went in search of Little Nell, who had moved to England with her family. Nell got her toehold working the Portabello Road street markets. Her stall was next to Freddy Mercury's stall (later, singer of the band Queen). A couple of years had passed since Jim Sharman had shown Richard O'Brien's draft for the Rocky Horror Show to Philippe. What may have seemed like a corny idea back then was rapidly turning into a brilliant show in need of a tap dancer.

When Martin caught up with Nell in London, she was shaping up for the Rocky Horror role of Columbia in the West End stage show and – although nobody knew it yet – also the film. It was Nell's big break.

Actor Lex Marinos feels aspects of the Rocky Horror set design and costuming was more influenced by Martin than is generally acknowledged. Looking back, he said, 'I think Rocky Horror owes a lot to Martin, a lot of that imagery. It's brilliantly done but I can't help feeling Martin's influence was enormous on that show'. (10)

Little Nell's Mickey Mouse ears in the Toucha Toucha Touch Me sequence certainly seem like something Martin might have suggested. For a short time, almost everything Martin touched went a bit Mickey Mouse.

Those ears showed up again the following year when Martin designed the costumes for a stage show called Kaspar in which all characters wore Mickey Mouse ears.

Martin says, 'After the Yellow House I went back to London, with no money in my pocket, to see Nell. I had to get out of Sydney. I'd been writing to Nell a lot. I was in love with her, which - through the letters - was wonderful. I got there, we stayed a night in the Ritz and the money was gone.' (11)

Returning to his Kings Road haunts, Martin found people talking about other things, like Glam bands. Forget the glory days of Cream, Martin said, 'That scene had passed and another scene had taken over'. (12) King's Road was full of New Romantics who were evolving into Punks. A short walk from the Pheasantry up King's Road took you to No. 430 where Vivienne Westwood and partner Malcolm McLaren opened a boutique called Let It Rock. It would be better known in its next incarnation under the name SEX - selling bondage clothes as Punk streetwear. That's where Chrissie Hynde, later the singer of the band the Pretenders, would work as a shop assistant and where the Sex Pistols formed.

Martin stayed with friends, socialised and attempted to gather the possessions he had left after his previous stay. He said, 'I returned to London for romantic reasons but I was broke at the time and I really wasn't in a position to go anywhere. London was different, the people I knew were yesterday's papers and there was a new crowd in. I didn't have the Pheasantry anymore. I stayed with the Campbell sisters who were very kind to me. I worked for Big O Posters and did another exhibition'. (13)

He also ransacked small print galleries looking for affordable works, particularly by Magritte, which he found, purchased and brought back to Australia. He was also looking for Hokusai prints.

Martin's central project was continuing Art Book collage experiments that he had started at the Pheasantry. Martin felt as comfortable with scissors-and-paste as with a paintbrush. He was never shy about snipping pictures out of expensive art books if he had a worthy idea. Martin cut up pictures by Old and New Masters, reconfigured the images and glued 74 familiar fine art images in new and unexpected contexts. In time, art critics called his process 'Appropriation'.

In 1990 Martin admitted, 'I still don't know what Appropriation means, but I knew I was onto something with those collages and cutting up the art books. It was like I was going around looking for a parking spot and there's a spot in a crowded area – Oh, I'll just zip in there! It was as simple as that. It was real hard work but it was as simple as that'. (14)

At the time, they were a quiet success. The pictures were launched and celebrated at Sigi Krauss Gallery, Covent Garden. (15)

Jazz and Blues singer, critic, writer and lecturer, George Melly reviewed the show under the title Double Exposures. He wrote, 'Superficially, the fascination of the pictures comes from Sharp's skill at combining very unlikely images which manage to gel instantly and convincingly'. His conclusion gave Martin the thumbs up. 'I find these works more than simple aesthetic experiments. What most of his sources share originally is the fascination of icons, but modern icons tend through constant reproduction to lose their magic. Sharp's grafts, looking simultaneously so familiar and extraordinary, help to recharge the originals. His title is well chosen.' (16)

Publishers of Martin's Art Book, Mathews, Miller and Dunbar had made a name for themselves through their much-loved Art Deco-style book The English Sunrise. (17) That format explains the striking design of Martin's book, its simplicity, clarity and lots of white space. A significant difference is The English Sunrise is 8x8 where Art Book is 6x5. 'It's a wonderful book,' said Martin. 'I thought Art Book should be in that same small format. I think they should re-run it!' (18)

Martin described his process, 'Popular Song was a big part of it, collages about music and migration of images through painting through reproduction. It came at a moment when reproduction had moved far enough from the original images for us to be free with them. I started to cut up my art books, so Gauguin figures in van Gogh landscapes, Magritte figures in De Chirico landscapes. This inter-twining, as if the barriers had broken down between the individual world of painters and all the characters were inter-mingling in each other's pictures.' (19)

What to do about Tiny Tim was also constantly on Martin's mind. Tiny's second album had been less well received. (20)

Tiny's star had tumbled quite a bit since the Albert Hall Concert. He had enjoyed two huge moments only, 17 December 1969, his TV wedding to Miss Vicki's aired to an audience of 40 million people on the Johnny Carson Show. And he stole the show at the Isle of Wight Festival held 30

August 1970 before 600,000 people. The stadium was cramped, the sound appalling and the toilets disgusting. There were fights, broken fences, a prevailing sense of menace and lots of mud.

Joni Mitchell demanded respect. 'I'm an artist' she bleated to a barrage of cans. Jimi Hendrix had equipment problems, re-started, apologised, tried again and thanked the audience for their patience. Miles Davis found it pointless. Donovan and Ralph McTell felt the same. And then, like a ray of sunshine, out came Tiny Tim with his little ukulele, bassist and a light drummer.

In 2004 Q Magazine listed what followed as one of the Top 10 live performances in Rock history – Tiny Tim singing a medley built around Rule Brittania and There'll Always Be an England to an audience whose mood suddenly changed from mean to…singing along with Tiny Tim! Those were the only two great Tiny Tim moments since Martin had seen him in Luton.

On the other side of the ledger was the release of the high camp, low quality, bootleg LP titled Concert in Fairyland. It was a collection of studio demos - including On The Good Ship Lollipop and Animal Crackers - recorded back in 1962 way before he was famous.

The album lacked dignity. The cover art was crook. Tiny's fans thought it really was his third album. Was Tiny Tim some kind of joke? (21) A joke Tiny himself encouraged on his many television appearances, most prominently Rowan & Martin's Laugh-In. Sometimes he stole the show for all the wrong reasons but at the time, singing in the high voice and camping it up for a giggling public paid the bills, at least.

Tiny's management didn't seem to know what to make of him. Instead of giving him swooner-crooner songs that had worked so well in the past – unbelievably they followed the direction of that terrible bootleg and had Tiny sing On The Good Ship Lollipop, Oliphant the Elepant, Mickey the Monkey, I'm a Lonesome Little Raindrop and other puerile tunes. (22)

Turning Tiny Tim into a children's act was a silly idea. Tiny was more relaxed with cross-dressers than with children! None of this seemed to bother Martin. He saw beyond the joke. Martin had seen him at his glorious best and wanted to make a film starring Tiny Tim, who – despite ups-and-downs – was still one of the most famous faces in show business.

Martin said, 'I would have been always angling for it. The idea for the film came from the desire to work with Tiny ever since I saw him at the Albert Hall. When I saw him I thought he would become huge and I was looking forward to following his career. So I followed his career, but it started to vanish, I got worried about it, so I started to talk to film industry people.' (23)

Film was the medium of the time. Film and performance art had welded the Yellow House together in the evenings: Albie Thoms, Peter Weir, Garry Shead, Peter Kingston, Ellis D Fogg, and psychedelic surf filmmakers George Greenough and Paul Witzig. Also, while attending Armidale University, Martin's cousin Sandy (Alexander) Sharp co-wrote a script called Private Collection, a 1972 film featuring Pamela Stephenson, Grahame Bond, Noel Ferrier and Michael Caton. Sandy's brother Andrew (who had helped at the Yellow House) had been a child star playing the stage role of the Artful Dodger. Film was everywhere. Even Brett Whiteley shot film.

Meanwhile in London, Rocky Horror was on its way up. Bruce Beresford's The Adventures of Barry McKenzie was a big success. Having succeeded with his Trouble in Molopolis, Philippe Mora was working on his next film Swastika - controversially about Adolf Hitler's home life. Though banned in Germany, it would be released in 1973 to critical acclaim in the United States, England and France. Martin knew all this. And having worked on the edges of Performance, Martin had quite a few film industry contacts of his own.

Donald Cammell was Martin's first contact. Martin gave him a copy of his failed attempt to tape Tiny Tim. The tape was probably unlistenable and did nothing to capture Cammell's interest. But Sandy Lieberson, who founded the British production company Goodtimes Enterprises, saw a future in musical film starring the pop stars of the times. Lieberson was formulating plans for That'll Be The Day (1973 – David Essex and Ringo Starr) followed by Ken Russell's Lisztomania (1975 – Roger Daltrey). Lieberson was keen to hear Martin out, but Martin had no script, no contact with Tiny, just a general idea and a lot of enthusiasm.

Martin also approached Pete Townshend who was flush with the success of his Rock Opera Tommy. Townshend was sympathetic. He even offered the use of his home-studio facility. Martin explained, 'Pete Townshend has always had a very soft spot for Tiny. I think he felt guilty when they appeared together at the Scene in New York and Tiny had to follow the Who between major acts. Pete promised to introduce him with a big flourish but the boys in the band pushed Pete into another direction. He neglected it and he always remembered that as the time he let Tiny down.' (24)

As well as Art Book, Big O Posters, the last days of London OZ and discussions about filmmaking, Martin also looked up designer Zandra Rhodes, who had visited the Yellow House where their friendship began. She wrote, 'Martin Sharp, painter/cartoonist had his exhibition at the Yellow House and this was a great inspiration to me. He stayed with me in London, becoming a good friend'. (25)

Zandra invited Martin and Nell to model her first jumper for a Vogue magazine fashion shoot. Wearing pink, green, blue with bat sleeves and ducktails – Nell nibbled Martin's ear with Martin looking suitably sheepish in a striped top. (26)

Then from London to Paris, where Martin stayed with Matí and Sophie Klarwein, whom he had known since Pheasantry days. Matí's fame had grown through his album cover art. His Miles Davis double album cover, Bitches Brew and Santana's Abraxas were almost as famous as Disraeli Gears. Matí and Sophie also knew Salvadore Dalí.

While hanging out with people-who-knew-people (or at least knew where they lived) Martin decided to look up Man Ray who resided in Montparnasse. Martin admired Man Ray enormously. He had combined

Man Ray's 'lips' with an Edvard Munch bridge scene in Art Book. Martin didn't have a contact. It was a cold call.

In November of the previous year Man Ray had received massive acclaim in a monumental retrospective of 278 works at the Boymans-van Beuningen Museum in Rotterdam. The show was then to tour Paris, Denmark and finally, in triumph, to the Philadelphia Museum of Art. But at the last moment the Philadelphia Museum of Art changed its mind claiming it did not have the funds to bring the show to America. (26) Whether this was on his mind when he met Martin, we don't know, but it was a disappointing encounter.

Martin describes the meeting, 'Man Ray was with his wife, the model for many of his pictures. He was most upset that he'd never been given the accolades as a painter. I thought he held his own in photography alone. He took Magritte into the realm of photography. Beautiful simple images. I think he created some the greatest Surrealist images.

'That was what was bothering him. There was something that wasn't right as far as he was concerned - he hadn't been honoured. Complaining about Picasso getting so much money - something like that. It was a bit disappointing. I gave him an OZ magazine.' (28)

Martin's encounter with Salvadore Dalí was much more colourful.

With views of the Tuileries Garden, Le Meurice has been ranked among the most elegant hotels in the world. Each of the seven floors has a distinct style, with suites decorated in the style of Louis XVI and exquisite Italian marble bathrooms. Le Meurice was Salvadore and Gala Dalí's usual residence when staying Paris. They would arrive like royalty, with entourage, courtiers, performers, the works.

The Dalís were hosting the smart young people, the demi-mode, regulars from Dalí's Port Lligat studio/residence, transgender performer Amanda Lear, the Miles twins - who appeared in Performance as velvet-wearing Baudelarian figures carrying a Magritte painting, and the well-connected Spaniard Carlos Lozano. Sophie invited Martin to accompany her.

'Sophie was like a Matisse painting,' Martin describes. 'She was pure nostalgic Paris. Not many people in Paris had an idea of Pop Art but she did.' And so Martin came to meet the artist who counted The Great Masturbator (1929) amongst his Surrealist masterworks, 'Dalí was enthroned. This was his court. Incredible Spanish dancing, fantastic singing, flamenco guitars, stamping feet. And then it was upstairs to his room. It was the young and beautiful people - a sort of soirée going on. Sophie and I were about the oldest there.

'Dalí would come in, pair them off and send them into this room. Gradually pair-by-pair they were called into another room, and eventually all that was left was Sophie and I left outside. Then he came in again and took us to meet Gala. Gala was lying in bed. Both talked to us and then he showed us out.

'The next day we found out that he'd set up this orgy – extraordinary! All these people were involved in this orgy - about 20 people. There was this beautiful brother and sister from Morocco. One of these handsome Miles twins was fucking this guy's sister from Morocco. The brother dragged the Miles boy off and made love to his own sister. This was the quintessential thrill for Dalí – incest - this bizarre chemistry. He'd set the whole thing up. What an amazing memoir!' (29)

Martin walked the streets of Paris in his spare time, checking out art shops. He described one defining moment, 'I was very interested in Japanese prints. It was my hobby, I'd see if I could find any anywhere, because they were still rather cheap. In Rue de Banque I found this little shop that sold Japanese pictures. There was a big pile on the floor. I was looking through 200 of them. I was particularly interested in Hokusai. I recognised some by Hokusai, various other prints, and right at the bottom there was this fantastic picture, the best by far of the pile - which was full of excellent material. It was this abalone diver.

'Abalone divers are always women. They used to work from boats, dive down, cut the abalone off the rocks and come up again. And here's this most graceful Arabesque figure, a beautiful print. The shape of the hair reminded me of the curl of the stars in Starry Night. I thought, It looks like Utamaro. I asked her how much it was, it was 200 francs. I didn't have the money at the time but when I got the money I went back and picked up the print. I was very thrilled with it.

'I took it to more up-market Japanese print shop. I showed her this print and she said, Oh, this is by Hokusai! I couldn't believe this stroke of amazing luck finding a Hokusai - and one that I'd never seen before!

'I finished the mural, did one more in a shop somewhere, went back to London and took it to the Victoria & Albert Museum. Walking in with it wrapped up under my arm, people were reacting in a strange way to me as I was walking through the corridors, as if they sensed that I had a very rare picture under my arm.

'I wanted to get it identified. The guy in the Oriental Art section turned up a reference to it in a book called Decorative Arts Of Japan by an American woman published in about 1920. He said he knew the great English expert on Hokusai, Joseph Hillier. He said he'd check with him. (30)

'I went back some weeks later. He said he checked with this scholar and it might be a drawing after a painting by Hokusai or a print after a painting by Hokusai, but it wasn't a Hokusai. He offered me a small amount of money for it, which I refused. I brought it back to Australia.' (31)

Andy Warhol and his entourage came to Paris to film L'Amour around the same time as Martin discovered the picture he now dubbed The Lost Hokusai. 1974 had been a watershed year for Warhol. His outrageous 60s were shifting into his entrepreneurial 70s. Warhol's films had received both desultory and acclamatory reviews. He and his gang of assistants and hangers-on flitted between New York and Europe rounding up new rich patrons for portrait commissions. Martin was curious. Andy and Paul Morrissey were doing a film shoot in fashion designer, Karl Lagerfeld's apartment.

'Some Swedish girl was going to interview him,' said Martin, 'she took me along. He was making a film with Paul Morrissey - swept back hair, strong jaw, glasses. We went into this house. Joe Dellasandro and people were making the picture. In the central room of the house Andy Warhol was sitting knitting this dark green scarf, which was about 15 feet long.

'Very quiet and I thought very interesting. If he weren't there, nothing would be happening. He's the eye of the storm, sitting there calm, meditating. He provided the stillness so all the action could happen. I thought that was pretty impressive.' (32)

Martin returned to London, gathered his Magritte prints and the Art Book pictures, came to an arrangement with Big O Posters and wondered why his Tiny Tim film project was being greeted with indifference. As for OZ? He didn't quite drop OZ nor did he drop in. Editor Jim Anderson doesn't recall ever seeing him during this period, yet Martin continued to send occasional contributions.

One of Martin's most significant spreads came in OZ 43, A Letter From an Idle Fellow by Vincent to Theo in 1890. The letter affirms Vincent's belief that everything good comes from God and goes on to question one's métier or 'calling', from which Vincent sadly concluded that he was probably seen by society as 'an idle man of the worst type'. The article is illustrated with seven of Martin's pictures, including his Double Vincent collage, later to appear in Art Book. (33) Ten years to the day of writing this letter, Vincent van Gogh committed suicide.

Then, right out of the blue, came a commission that would affect Martin for life, 'I was down & out in London when I got an invitation to repaint the entrance to Luna Park, from Leon Fink!' (34)

In April 1969 the remaining six years of Luna Park's lease and contents had been sold for $750,000 to a consortium of business people called the World Trade Centre P/L, which included Leon Fink and partner Nathan Spatt. World Trade Centre P/L applied to construct a $50 million International Trade Centre on the Luna Park site. Approval was refused after which Leon Fink and Nathan Spatt formed Luna Park Holdings P/L, and they continued to run the place as an amusement park. In 1972 they announced a general program to upgrade the whole park. (35)

Leon's wife Margaret Fink had known Martin from early-60s university days when Martin had shyly checked out the Sydney Push where she, Margaret Elliott then, was a regular. Not as daunting as Germaine – but daunting.

'Leon Fink's wife Margaret knew me as an artist and cartoonist,' wrote Martin. She made the connection between Fairground Art and Pop Art and suggested that Martin would be the right artist to redesign the Face of Luna Park.

Martin took Leon's offer extremely seriously. He wrote, 'I approached it not as a sign painter or a person of the carnival, but as an intellectual artist. Like many people, I knew Luna Park as a permanent part of our landscape. I had never particularly liked it as a child but when I was a cartoonist for OZ magazine I did draw that smile as an image, which I also used in painting. (36)

'I suppose I could be described as a Pop Artist, drawing on the landscape of popular culture for imagery. Luna Park was very much that - the largest sculpted image of a face in Australia and entering through a huge mouth (certainly a Medieval image of the Gateway to Hell) one found a world of artistically primitive, but nonetheless powerful images, comic and grotesque.' (37)

13.

COUNTERCULTURE GOES MAINSTREAM

I left Australia in September 1967 and I didn't come back until 1971 and I was amazed in that brief period of time - 'Goodness me, something's happened!'

GARY SHEARSTON

After 23 years of Conservative rule, the close of 1972 saw the Australian Labor Party win government and the new Prime Minister Gough Whitlam speedily push through a raft of reforms that would radically change Australia's economic, legal and cultural landscape. Most urgently, the new Labor government abolished conscription and completed the process of disengagement in the Vietnam military campaign. The universities were no longer battlefields of protest.

Whitlam embarked on a wide-sweeping campaign of social reform that included healthcare, social security, education, Indigenous Affairs, Foreign Affairs, Women's issues, national symbols, environment, heritage and cultural affairs. The Family Law Act 1975, with its no-fault divorce, is one initiative that Martin would have welcomed a decade earlier, having witnessed the injustice that his mother was made to endure through the old system of lumping the blame on one party or the other. (1)

Change is what Martin came back to. A cheeky soapie called No 96 was a popular TV favourite, the critically acclaimed film Wake in Fright introduced brutal realism into Australian film and the Aboriginal Tent Embassy was erected in front of Parliament House (now Old Parliament House) to represent the political rights of Indigenous Australians.

Weirdly (for some) counter-culture had merged with the mainstream. Almost everyone under the age of 25 had smoked marijuana and skinny-dipped at least once. Young people didn't dress up - they dressed down. Bank clerks grew their hair and schoolteachers quit wearing ties.

On Australia Day 1972 the Sunbury Music Festival was held on a 620-acre farm outside Melbourne. Forty-five thousand hippies showed up. Adrian Rawlins was co-compere. Then a second antipodean Woodstock captured headlines when ten thousand alternative lifestylers converged on the little north NSW town of Nimbin for the 1973 Aquarius Festival. Many remained and set up communes. Now, back in the country – Richard and Louise were right on the spot. (2)

During Martin's absence, the Yellow House crowd had dispersed. Its legend had grown. A fully-fledged 'Yellow House person' was a highly credible thing to have been.

Greg had married Suzie Cuthbert – Suzie who introduced Martin to Eric Clapton and prompted Martin to scribble the lyrics to Tales of Brave Ulysses on a serviette. Bruce Goold concentrated on linocuts and woodblocks of Australian flora and fauna. George Gittoes experimented with holograms and computer-generated images. Garry Shead enjoyed artistic pilgrimages to Toyko, Paris and the United States. Roger Foley-Fogg could be spotted flashing around town in an open-topped car with girlfriend Madam Lash (Gretel Pinniger). Jonny Lewis was establishing his reputation as a photographer. Peter Royles headed north. Adrian Rawlins was emceeing major Rock festivals. Jeannie Lewis performed shows and joined the Music Board of the Australia Council of the Arts.. Nic Lyon was working in theatre and Arts Festivals. Jenny Kee opened the Flamingo Park fashion boutique in Sydney's fabulous Strand Arcade with designer-partner Linda Jackson. Brett Whiteley was a Sydney art legend. In a way they all were. And David Litvinoff was planning to return England. (3)

The Australian Council for the Arts, informally known as the Arts Council (established 1967), was strengthened under the Whitlam Government. Albie Thoms was a beneficiary of a $5000 grant from the Experimental Film and Television Fund to make Sunshine City a film to mark his return to Sydney from Europe. (4)

The strengthening of the arts in an official sense marked the demise of the arts in an unofficial sense. All those slightly chaotic inner-city amateur poetry readings, agitprop theatres and 'Happening' events were forced to either step up or close down.

The standout venue at this time was the Old Stables Theatre, a small, austere building more than one hundred years old, which had previously been a stable, taxi garage and gymnasium. There, actor/director John Bell, director Richard Wherrett and entrepreneur Ken Horler formed the Nimrod Theatre Company, which strove for excellent Australian content. Many of their connections linked to early-60s Sydney University revues.

Nimrod gained growing support from Australia Council - from $6500 in 1971 to $33,200 in 1973. (5) During that period attendances more than doubled from 18,763 to 44,550. (6) Using only the best playwrights and best actors, Nimrod gained a formidable reputation for staging quality Australian plays.

In his book, See How It Runs, writer Julian Meyrick sums it up, 'Throughout the course of its artistic life Nimrod flirted with pieces that evinced qualities opposed to its usual fare: productions that were dark (not light), interior (not exterior), spiritual (not social), difficult (not accessible), silent (not convivial).' (7)

Another change was Folk Music, which had carved itself a niche in the mainstream. From its beginnings as convict ballads and Labor songs sung in pubs, the movement had transformed into an articulate political voice. Artists like Jeannie Lewis, Margret Roadknight, Don and Marion Henderson, Michael Driscoll, Pat Drummond, Black Allen Murawalla,

Gary Shearston and John Ewbank were regulars at the old Corn Exchange building in Sussex Street named PACT House. Many of these singers had performed at the Yellow House. (PACT Folk moved to the YWCA Building in Liverpool Street in 1970.)

Jeannie was Martin's principal contact with this group - but there were others as well. 'Black Allen' Murawalla was the first Indigenous Australian that Martin got to know. ('Same for me,' said Jeannie, who had known him from the folk circuit, 'Black Allen was my first Aboriginal contact personally.') (8)

Gary Shearston was another folkie friend. With a poke at the Australian OZ trial, Gary had a 1965 hit with his song Sydney Town. Gary struck out for England and America in 1967 and came home to a very different country. Amazed by the difference Gary exclaimed, 'Goodness me, something's happened!' (9) Around this time Gary wrote the song Dingo, a song that Martin would see as fraught with symbolic meaning (10)

That's the kind of Sydney to which Martin returned thanks to Gough Whitlam, Australia Arts Council, Nimrod Theatre, PACT Folk, Germaine Greer, the OZ trials, the Aboriginal Tent Embassy and the nearly completed Sydney Opera House. Innovators like Albie Thoms, Garry Shead, Brett Whiteley, Greg Weight, Ellis D Fogg, Black Allen Murawalla, Jeannie Lewis, Seb Jorgensen, Dicky Weight, Philippe Mora, oh – such a long list. They all had a part to play in chipping down the Alfs and the Norman Normals. It's fair to say: OZ won.

Martin's parents were now eight years separated and divorced four. In an attempt to reconcile with his father, Martin chose to live with Henry and stepmother Dorothy for a time. He intended to paint his next exhibition – Art Exhibition – at their harbourfront place in Shellcove Road Neutral Bay. Dr Henry Sharp was now a Fellow of the Australian Medical Association with a string of honorariums, notably the Royal Alexandria Hospital for Children, Eastern Suburbs Hospital, Prince of Wales and Prince Henry Hospitals. He was a Macquarie Street dermatologist who explained his job to Martin as, 'You can't kill them and you can't cure them!'

Martin explains what happened when he moved in, 'I was going to live in the boatshed, have a studio there, do my exhibition there. I took over a few pictures that were important to me and put them up. I particularly liked a Peter Powditch one.

'My father came down and looked at them in a disparaging way and I felt, "I can't create here, this person doesn't respect that I'm hanging up my own pictures in a space I'm meant to be living in!" So I wasn't made welcome. As soon as he disapproved of those pictures I'd hung up I realised that his territorial imperative was so strong. I came back with Mum.

'I think when I held on for Wirian, (ie. heir apparent) that was the turning point because I didn't go to my father's side, I stayed with my mother's. He said to me that night, "That could cost you your patrimony!" – meaning - by hanging on to Wirian.' (11)

And so Martin went back to Jo. Back to Cranbrook Lane. Back to his playroom with the Hornby train set that he used to crash when his parents fought. Back to where he and Greg had painted the Art for Mart's Sake exhibition in 1964.

Martin used some of his Art Book collages as studies for the 10 pictures that he intended to return to their original medium as completed paintings. Over the next three months Tim Lewis assisted in what started out slowly, before peaking as all-night sessions. Said Martin, 'It must have been hard for Tim because the original designs were mine but we became a unit beyond ego in order to do a job.' (12)

Twenty-two year old Tim Lewis was a former Cranbrook student who was in Form One when Martin was completing his final year. He too was a product of Justin O'Brien's art classes. Tim learned to love Martin's art when he attended East Sydney Tech from where he soon found his way to the Yellow House. Said Tim, 'Jonny took me to the Yellow House. Martin was there. Martin said, Here's a paintbrush – go for it...'

That's how they met.

After the Yellow House, Tim moved to Double Bay and continued with his own paintings of geometric abstractions. Tim gave one of his pictures to a friend, Colette St John. Said Tim, 'Martin saw my painting and was blown away! He'd just returned from London where it was gloomy and cold. He came back to this blazing typical Australian summer and I'd done this painting, which had that intensity of that Sydney summer.

'Martin liked the painting and asked me to help him with his next exhibition - Art Exhibition. He was gathering people together to paint his book – Art Book. I think he had a concept of doing something like a Yellow House, getting a group of people together to help him paint but he only ended up with the two of us painting it - Richard Liney and another guy Victor Rubin - a good painter. They were only there at the beginning.' (13)

Tim worked on all the pictures. For the Matisse/Magritte picture (later repainted and re-titled Pentecost) Martin painted the room and Tim painted the bird. They both signed every picture.

Initially they stretched the canvases with help from drop-in friends. When that didn't work out, Tim introduced Martin to people who stretched canvases to a professional standard. Tim also introduced Martin to Liquitex paints, which Martin used for the rest of his life. (14) That Cadmium Yellow used in Film Script – the yellow that's half an inch thick – that's Liquitex. Naphthol Red Light, Bright Aqua Green and high viscosity Light Blue Permanent are all Liquitex - straight from the tube.

'That's where I got to know him,' Tim reflected. 'I was very young and naïve, and for me to be in this room with Martin - and then all of a sudden Richard Neville dropped in and got onto the typewriter. Brett Whiteley would pop in. He'd look at the paintings we were working on, "Oh wow man!" Then he would dart off. Jean Shrimpton popped in one day when we were painting. I was the young guy, starry-eyed and all that sort of stuff and here are my heroes!' (15)

One evening at the end of February Martin announced, 'We're going to a concert'. It was a Rolling Stones concert at the Sydney Showground. 'A really fab concert,' said Tim. 'Nikki James, Richard Cobden and I were in the Moke and we arrived at the top of William Street.

"Where are we going Martin?"

"We're going to a party for the Stones." Oh, okay.

'I thought we'd get out at the party. No, we go straight up to the penthouse - Nikki, Richard, Martin and myself. And then: "Is Mick there…?" – heavy bodyguard "…it's Martin Sharp…"

"Oh Martin – yeah – come in."

'There's Mick and Charlie. Mick was sitting there eating fish and chips. He welcomed us and asked nothing about the concert but about cheaper airfares and those sorts of mundane things.

'I had a packet of Drum. Mick said, "What is it? Dope?" I said, "No…" but Nikki James had just come back from India with a nice bit of hashish. So she packed a chillum and we had this really lovely conversation. Charlie asked us, "Does anyone want a Cold Duck?" (Cold Duck was the fizzy bubbly of the day.) So we had this amazing chillum with Mick and then all of a sudden – bang - it was over. We were downstairs at the party. Taking us to meet the Stones was an example of Martin being full of unsuspected surprises!' (16)

Then it was back to work.

Through Martin's studio Jo developed new friends, somewhat like the young bohemians she had known at Merioola, only wilder. Sometimes Tim stayed overnight. Brett swam nude in her pool, Colin Lanceley talked non-stop Art, former-Yellow House people were constantly dropping in. And, before his exit back to Britain, Jo also enjoyed the company of David Litvinoff.

Towards the end of March, Roger Foley-Fogg dropped by and filmed Martin and Tim at work. Roger's film shows two handsome young longhaired artists, smoking and deliberating over their 'takes' on Picasso's Demoiselles D'Avignon and de Chirico's Song of Love. Viewers also see Anne Kelly looking over the architectural plans for the face of Luna Park – Martin and Tim's next project. (17)

Jo sometimes cast her eye over Martin's paintings. Martin described her comments, 'My mother wouldn't have understood the metaphysics of

Reprise Of Giorgio De Chirico's Song Of Love, but she'd say to me, "Oh darling, that sky needs a bit more blue in it…" or something. She had a very good eye. It wasn't an intellectual eye but she was a Pop Art person and I was too - even though I was a Sharp'. (18)

Art Exhibition was held at Bonython Galleries in Paddington. 'Martin does like to work on tight deadlines', said Tim. 'I remember the opening, driving up in a Mini-Moke. Jo was in the Moke, Martin was in the Moke, Nikki James was in the Moke. We got to the opening. I saw all the people and I just freaked out. We hadn't slept for about three days. My head was on the Moon somewhere and I ran off. Someone chased after me and dragged me back to the exhibition.' (19)

Art Exhibition was well received. The National Gallery Canberra bought The Unexpected Answer (ie. Whaam), English model Jean Shrimpton bought a picture and someone else bought Botticelli/Picasso The Birth Of Venus. Commenting on the latter Martin said, 'That's been sold for quite a lot but it's worth it because the ideas behind that picture were ahead of the ball game. If you check Europe or America or anywhere I think they were on par and equal with what was happening there - but they didn't know that here at the time, they thought they were "amusing" ideas.

'Art Exhibition had some very valid ideas in the language of art which were paintings about paintings. But that was 1973 and years later it's become Appropriation – but it grew out of Magritte and Pop Art. Our environment was art books, so let's make pictures out of art books, cut them up and keep the images flowing through time – powerful images which already had resonance established – it was just a matter of having the nerve to play around with them, make new pictures and then paint them.

'After the Yellow House I couldn't look at an art gallery. It was very hard but I had to. The Yellow House exploded art galleries and to go back was a retrograde step as far as I was concerned, unless one can make a very esoteric comment using an art gallery as a theatrical setting for an idea encompassing the gallery – hence calling it Art Exhibition!' (20)

After seeing the exhibition, Nimrod director Richard Wherrett invited Martin to design costumes and sets for his production of Peter Handke's play Kaspar towards the end of the year.

But first, the Face of Luna Park.

Soon after Art Exhibition, Martin moved into the chauffeur's quarters of the two-storey Wirian garage. He set up his studio on the top floor, spent a week living downstairs and said, 'That's where I started – in that garage. I would have lived in the car if it had been there! It was very nice to sit in, as a kid'. (22)

Martin also acquired 'Bloke' - a red setter named after CJ Dennis' Sentimental Bloke and shifted into the corner room in the servants' quarters of the main house. A toehold.

Both Martin's grandmothers were sick. Grandmother Vega, Wirian's proprietor, was in a nursing home. Caretaker, Albert Peck was a legacy from Martin's grandfather. He checked the place, mowed the lawn and did maintenance duties. After a time, Tim followed Martin into the servants' quarters. And Richard and Sharon Liney moved in too. Tim explained, 'Martin was always funny about moving into the main house while his grandmother was alive'. (23)

Martin, Tim and Richard Liney started work on the Face of Luna Park in April, one week after Art Exhibition. The Sydney Opera House was to be formally opened by Queen Elizabeth II on 20 October 1973 but in the interim, the Opera House Committee had incensed Sydney's art community by their shabby treatment of the brilliant architect Jorn Utzon. Martin, Tim and Richard supported Utzon. (24)

The Face of Luna Park was, in a sense, a straightforward job. The main mission was to create a face in sync with Luna Park's previous five faces, especially the last one by Arthur Barton. Instead, Martin approached his task more 'scientifically'. While painting Art Exhibition with Tim, Martin took time out to study the mythological meaning of the Face of Glory.

A 9th-century Mahayana Buddhist Temple in Central Java was of special interest. Its name was Borobudur.

Martin said, 'Researching the history of the face, the earliest legends we could pick up were at Borobudur. We found out it was the Face of Glory, which is like the Luna Park face even in expression, guarding the Buddha. Inside Luna Park was a real Buddha, a real effigy in marble and gold leaf - not plaster and paint. It was the Real McCoy, surrounded by this court, which is the Endless River.

'So in Borobudur there's this Face of Glory guarding the Buddha and in Luna Park you've also got the Face guarding the Buddha.' (25)

But the main thing - for Martin, Richard and Tim - was to work with the Arthur Barton design. At this stage, Martin's personal involvement had less to do with the park itself and more to do with Arthur Barton's art, the artist he'd seen painting billboards at Sydney's Royal Easter Show in his teenage years. Martin said, 'After I got involved a lot of people thought it was the nostalgia that I got into. I can hardly remember Luna Park as a kid. I probably didn't like it that much as a kid - but later on in life, it became a passion. (26)

Arthur Barton was the Luna Park artist for a total of 35 years until he retired in 1970 due to failing eyesight. In 1968 he created the iconic Face with exuberant colours. Said Martin, 'Arthur Barton put the happy face on Luna Park. It was pretty sour looking before him. He was the best. He put a great big smile on its face. His works gives Luna Park its real spirit and if it wasn't there it wouldn't have been as exciting for us.' (27)

Luna Park would ever remain a central theme in Martin's art. This core group of artists and others who joined with them, would continue to venerate Barton's works and attempt to restore them years after their commission was fulfilled.

In his book Luna Park, Just for Fun, author Sam Marshall described the situation at Luna Park around the time of Martin's commission. He wrote, 'In 1972 the Park was opened for year-round operation, no longer having a three-month winter closure when rides were thoroughly overhauled and maintained. Time was closing in.

'A general program to upgrade the Park was started. Maintenance intensive rides such as the Spider and the Tumble Bug were removed. Plans for the Zipper, Hurricane and Astrospin were secured by Rod Earle and built in Australia at a cost of $90,000 each for introduction in December 1973. When these were installed at the front of the Park, the area resembled a parking lot for mobile rides. A lack of bridges accentuated this.

'Margaret Fink, then the wife of major shareholder Leon Fink, made the connection between Pop Art and Luna Park. Artists armed with paint and imagination were commissioned to revitalize the Park. Martin Sharp, having completed a colour scheme for the Dodgem Building, repainted the face with the assistance of Tim Lewis and Richard Liney who were also interested in Pop Art. They applied a zigzag motif topped by geometric clowns' heads and acrylic mirror to the towers. At a cost of $28,000, it was completed in June 1973 to coincide with the opening of the Sydney Opera House. Ha-Ha was painted on the tower bases. On the back of the face a mandala with a giant psychedelic eye was painted to keep an eye on the park.' (28)

Precarious and frequently stoned, Martin, Tim and Richard Liney sometimes painted from a high scaffold, with Tim scared of heights. Tim said, 'We started off painting the entrance. We had scaffolding up on the towers. The whole thing was scaffolded. Then Richard wanted to spray the lips with glitter – we did that. The mirrors on the towers were also Richard's – we did that too. Martin did the Ha-Ha. The Face itself was on a deadline. Again, no sleep for two nights before and all that of stuff, but we pulled it off!' (29)

Interviewed by Cleo magazine about Luna Park and Sydney Opera House, Martin said, 'They are Sydney's two great sculptures. We were working on the face when the Opera House opened.

'As we were not very happy with the way designer Jorn Utzon had been treated and his interior reinterpreted by other people, we widened the face's smile and painted Ha-Ha on the two flanking pillars. We made the entrance a cartoon laughing at the Opera House'. (30)

One crisp winter's morning in June a French tightrope walker - who was given this idea at Nimbin's Aquarius Festival - walked a high wire between Sydney Harbour Bridge's two northern pythons. It was an important moment for Martin, Tim and Richard who watched spellbound from below. Important because in the 1890s circus daredevil the Great Onzalo (aka Alfred Rowe) crossed Sydney Harbour on a tightrope where the Bridge now stands and Martin knew all about it.

'They built the Bridge over his footsteps,' Martin wrote about the Great Onzalo. 'In 1973 Philippe Petit on another tightrope strung between the northern pylons, formed the Cross high above Onzalo's path. That very moment two metal flake spray painters were increasing Luna Park's smile…Luna Park smiled when Philippe Petit crossed the wire.' (31)

Martin contributed to The Last Issue of London OZ published June 1973. He said goodbye to it all with a collage of Superman set against Vincent's Starry Night captioned with 'Please Clark – don't walk out on me! You're the only secret identity I've got!' An uncredited poem about death featured on the opposite page.

The last OZ also carried an ad for The Rocky Horror Show at the Kings Road Theatre. Little Nell's stars were beginning to sparkle. (32)

With the closure of OZ, Jim Anderson was immediately offered a contract with Harcourt Brace & Jovanovich to write an account of his 60s experience. Shaken by the OZ Trial, he sought anonymity instead. Jim's travels took him to Bolinas, a little town in California where he remained for years. (33)

Not at all shaken by the trial, Felix emerged with lots to prove. A dupe, indeed! From the ashes of OZ, Felix used his experience and contacts to lay the cornerstones of what would become Dennis Publishing, his publishing empire.

While all this was going on, the two Richards joined forces over a new publication, Living Daylights. Richard was editor and Richie the publisher. This offering was less counter-cultural and more cultural than their previous offerings. One of their great discoveries was cartoonist Michael Leunig.

Martin also contributed. One of his memorable cartoons was 'a land of sweeping plains' with Hal Gye's Sentimental Bloke sweeping the Central Desert. Another is Boofhead at the crossroads of life, puzzled by it all.

Not quite as whimsical, Martin also drew a dramatic Mickey Mouse with a death's head for Living Daylights. It intermingled with Martin's design theme for Richard Wherrett's coming Kaspar production at the Nimrod Theatre.

Said Martin, 'I did a drawing of Mickey Mouse with death's head - You Know Who I Am! It was a warning. It had Muscle Man in a Mickey Mouse costume with a death's head face. I did it intuitively - like you can feel death stalking. Richard Neville published it. But George Gittoes said I was wrong. He said it was an evil image and I shouldn't have brought it forth. I thought, there's one way of bringing it forth consciously - with a purpose - to give a warning!' (34)

Before the close of 1973 Martin became associated with Mickey Mouse like – say – Andy Warhol with Campbell's Soup. Fancy Our Meeting probably started it, Death Head Mickey seemed to confirm it, Kaspar would seal it and the Dream Museum collection enshrined Mickey as a permanent part of Martin's novelty collection.

Martin's novelty collection started when Martin purchased a little Mickey Mouse figure that he kept instead of giving it away. In his travels through London, Paris and Sydney, Martin was constantly popping into bric-a-brac shops looking for treasures. He said, 'I used to like buying them. I used to give them away as presents.' (35)

One day he found a heritage Mickey that he decided to keep. Placing it alongside several Mickey Mice from his childhood and several others, visiting friends kept giving them to Martin, which added to the growing collection, which Martin enjoyed. He also contemplated its sad side. Martin said, 'Kids always play with their toys, so the ones that you get are always the ones where the children haven't played with their toys. The children died or something like that.

'That led onto Kaspar. It was 1973, about the same time as I was doing cartoons for the Australian and Living Daylights, trying to get a flow between them so they interrelated.' (36)

About Kaspar, Martin said, 'It's one of the best things I've ever done.' Tim helped him paint the props. (37)

Kaspar was a play written by Austrian writer Peter Handke. It was about the Kaspar character acquiring language. Martin's poster featured a horrified Mickey, head on a stool, blocking his ears from the torrent of Ha Ha Ha Ha Ha Has. Cast members – who each played a variation of Kaspar – all wore Mickey Mouse ears.

Directed by Richard Wherrett, Martin's cousin Andrew was in the cast, along with Philip Sayer, Richard Cobden, Chris Haywood, Berys Marsh and Lex Marinos.

Lex writes, 'Kaspar came with an immense European reputation. Complex in style and lacking in narrative, it is loosely based on the true story of an autistic youth, Kaspar Hauser. Apart from the central role, there is a chorus of prompters, including Chris Haywood and myself, who present logical and illogical blocks of dialogue in a variety of tones and styles. It was funny, shocking and moving'. (38)

Lex further explains, 'It was quite an abstract play with one central Kaspar and other secondary Kaspers - who are the voices in his head, the voices outside of his head or whatever. We were all in formalwear, white clown face and Mickey Mouse ears. Martin's ideas, of course.

'It was a genius piece of design. It's not a big stage but Martin stripped the theatre back to the brick wall and started to paint the walls. It was a wonderful design to work in. All those swirling, wild brushstrokes emerged as a perfect metaphor for what was going on in Kaspar's mind.

'We were rehearsing and Martin would be on the stage painting. It was extraordinary seeing it take shape. One of the themes that he returned to continually in his work was Van Gogh's Crows Over the Cornfield. That tortured Van Gogh fantasy world was exactly right for the sort of mental anguish that the character was going through. One extraordinary day, Martin had the M-shaped or V-shaped crows flying. There's a line in the play where - at a point of seemingly awareness and recognition - Kaspar says, "Why are all these worms flying about?"

'We were rehearsing that scene while Martin was painting and he suddenly put a little squiggle into one of the crows and turned it into a black worm flying! It was just inspired. It was such a light-bulb moment where the set and the script came together!' (39)

There remained one big project before the year was out. Again with Tim's assistance, Martin painted a big (683 x 1024) portrait of Tiny, which was commissioned by Macquarie University. With a ukulele-playing Tiny Tim centerpiece, Martin painted Eternity in this major work. Martin shrugs off previous inclusions with 'I might have put it in some cartoons.'

At this stage Martin knew only what the press had written about Arthur Stace, the Eternity Man - that Stace was an alcoholic who had turned up at St Barnabas' Church Broadway in 1956, got impacted by a sermon and quit the booze. After this, he slipped out in the dead of night, most nights, and chalked the single word 'Eternity' on pavements from Martin Place to Parramatta. Martin wouldn't fill in the blanks about Mr Eternity's life until the publication of Keith Dunstan's book Ratbags in 1979. (40)

Said Martin, 'There are all sorts of images sourced in the big one of Tiny, just bringing together a whole lot of different worlds: Starry Night, Hokusai's wave, Tiny from his album cover, Eternity, Al Jolson, His Master's Voice dog, the Southern Cross, the Bluebird of Happiness, the landscape from the Little Prince (the most beautiful landscape on earth). The idea was to bring all those elements together and use the resonance of them as elements of making a new picture. That was done in 1973 - a big year of working with Tim Lewis and Richard Liney.' (41)

Tim added, 'The garage was lovely because there was a studio. That's where the Macquarie University's Tiny Tim was painted.' (42)

14.

OUT & ABOUT IN PARIS & LONDON

Mr Sharp saw me at the Albert Hall in 1968 in England. Later on when I came to Australia he followed me around.

TINY TIM

Martin had spent his past five years flagging Tiny Tim to all who would listen: filmmakers, visitors to the Yellow House, influential people and people who had no influence at all. On his 32nd birthday - 21 January 1974 - Martin went to see Tiny perform in a Worker's Club in Newcastle, north of Sydney.

Said Martin, 'By this stage I'd realised that I was going to have to do something about Tiny because he'd completely slipped from the top and was in the orbit where I could reach him.' (1)

They had previously met in London's Speakeasy club in 1968, which Martin recorded on a borrowed cassette player. He held the microphone too close and the sound was distorted. Richard and Louise were present at their second meeting in Luton where Martin again less-than-successfully attempted to tape the maestro. Determined to get it right this time, Martin purchased a state-of-the-art Marantz recorder, drove to Newcastle and unknowingly started his lifetime's work of recording everything Tiny said or did that was within his ambit.

Still one of the Top 5 most Famous Faces in the world, that famous face seemed like all Tiny had. He was facing a major career slump. Notwithstanding a Grammy nomination for his For All My Little Friends album, Tiny was dropped by Reprise Records and never again signed to a major label. He was also facing another kind of slump. When Martin met him, Tiny was just 48 hours away from heading back to New York where Miss Vicki would end their marriage.

It was a devastating collapse. Plucked from obscurity just six years before, Tiny had rocketed to stardom – the Top 10, best venues, best orchestras, best everything, plus the biggest celebrity wedding ever televised. Gradually it had all slipped away. Miss Vicki was slipping away too and taking their daughter Tulip with her. Not too many noticed that Tiny had reinvented himself as the New York-style defacto man, a religious one.

Martin described the circumstances of the Newcastle meeting, 'the grand stage was removed from him. The record deals were removed and he was exiled to the very outer suburbs of show business, which is where I saw him in 1974 in a Leagues Club. I wasn't feeling too fantastic at the time. I got a little tape recorder and dragged myself up there. He didn't really know me at that stage but I got a fantastic welcome'. (2)

Martin reintroduced himself in Tiny's dressing room, hit the recording button straight away and taped Tiny confidently and spontaneously. Martin explained, 'It seemed like a totally natural thing. That's what I was there for. It was like he was waiting for someone to come.' (3) 'I got to sing with him on the first song I recorded, "Miss you since you went away dear, miss you more than I can say." I just picked up the melody. I was like the audience meeting the singer again'. (4)

Martin presented Tiny with a copy of his newly published Art Book. Tiny flicked through the first few pages, then paused thoughtfully on the Hamilton image of a brown-hued negative of Bing Crosby against a surreal De Chirico street corner. Tiny exclaimed, 'Oh, it's Mr Crosby!'

Martin felt the connection had been made. He explained, 'about the same time as I was doing collages, Tiny was doing with songs what I was doing with images. That's why I clicked with him. I understood scientifically that he was really on an edge. And Tiny could get into Art Book, which was interesting because he doesn't know fine art.' (5)

Tiny reciprocated by signing a copy of Charles Dickens' A Christmas Carol to Martin, 'To my dear friend Mr Sharp, a pleasure meeting you, Tiny Tim 74'.

And so, from the dressing room to the stage. In those days, club audiences often treated Tiny's act with indifference – a curiosity more than a minstrel. Martin didn't care what the audience thought, starry-eyed from the warmth of their meeting Martin found Tiny equally impressive on stage. 'He was like a prophet', describes Martin, 'standing there, holding the microphone stand, doing Heaven Is My Home ad lib'. (6)

Before going their separate ways, Martin penned a note, which he handed to Tiny: Anything I can do to help, I really love what you're doing. As far as Martin was concerned, he'd made a promise and the note sealed the deal. 'It started from there I guess,' he explained. (7)

From now on, Martin's two great subjects were Tiny Tim and Luna Park. There were others too – Vincent, Mickey Mouse, the Southern Cross, the blue groper, the Little Prince, Boofhead, Hokusai's Wave, Indigenous Rights, crime, corruption and spirituality. Leaving the Luna Park assignment in the capable hands of Tim Lewis, Martin returned to London for seven months to fulfill two Zandra Rhodes commissions - set designs for her exhibition based on her 1971 and 1973 trips to Uluru, and a staircase mural in her house. (8)

What Martin found in London did not entice him to settle in. OZ magazine was long gone and everyone had moved on. Robert Hughes, Germaine, Richard and Louise – all gone. Eric was housed up in LA at 461 Ocean Boulevard, the name of his second solo album. And Philippe was in Europe screening his film Swastika at the Cannes Film Festival.

Pop Art was being written about in the past tense. Publisher, Thames & Hudson included Martin in the John Walker book, Art Since Pop. It was a compliment on one hand, but it was wrapping up an era with the other. The book featured Martin's vibrant Vincent collage, the original of which Martin had gifted to Jeannie. (9)

Plant a Flower Child was eight years ago. 'Peace & Love' were the watchwords of the previous generation. Kill a Hippie became a gag-line, a song and a board game. Punk Art reigned, not Pop Art. Artist Jamie Reid was about to cut a swathe with his image of a safety-pin-through-QE2's-nose for the Sex Pistols' God Save the Queen record. They mightn't like the connection but Punk artists owe two things to Martin: day-glo poster colours and - although Punks probably didn't go for silver scissors – it was still scissors and glue.

Martin painted Zandra's mural, re-read Jung's Synchronicity: An Acausal Connecting Principal (10) revisited The Hokusai Sketchbooks by James A Michener. (11) He also copped his first bout of kidney stones in London. At first, he didn't know what it was. These attacks would continue to dog him intermittently throughout his life.

Martin continued flagging the idea of a Tiny Tim movie to film and Pop people. Other than massive enthusiasm, at this stage, Martin wasn't offering them much more than three or four indecipherable tapes. 'I wouldn't say I was confident of their support', he said. (12)

He looked up Pete Townshend, a friend who had agreed to transfer the tapes from reel-to-reel to cassette in his home studio. 'There's some pretty good talks on them - as well as some preaching...', is how Martin described the content. 'Townshend did a lot to transfer early Tiny tapes in his studio. He probably has the mintest copies of the talking tapes and the first singing ones.' (13) These tapes have never surfaced, so who knows what Townshend thought of all this? Martin is fondly remembered in Townshend's autobiography. Tiny isn't mentioned. (14)

Sandy Lieberson knew Martin from Performance. He was working with Ringo Starr and David Essex on the film That'll Be The Day. Lieberson wasn't interested in Tiny but he got Martin a second commission. Said Martin 'I got a job in Paris through Sandy Lieberson to do a mural in his friend's house, I forget which Rue it was. The mural was Vincent on the Road to Tarascon with Starry Night in the background and it went down a 3-stepped stair. (It was quite a modern house.) I repeated the figure three times with the Starry Night in the background.'

Foraging through those Parisian bookshops, Martin found some film scripts, which he read and was struck by the idea of a remake of the 1927 film The Jazz Singer with Tiny taking Al Jolson's role, the son of a cantor who wanted to sing popular songs. (The idea was worthy enough for Neil Diamond to pick up on it in 1980 for his film of the same name.) The Jazz Singer was Martin's first idea for the Tiny Tim film. But it was the next idea that stuck.

Martin said, 'I started looking through scripts and came up with a Tin Pan Alley version of Orpheus and Eurydice. That became the feature film idea. I was getting the idea on the Metro in Paris.' (15) It surely would have made a wonderful animation (an animator like Eric Drooker). Tiny Tim aficionados would have loved it!

Martin's story opens in Luna Park where Orpheus (Tiny) is a singer and Eurydice is the magician's assistant. One day Orpheus begins to serenade her with I Got You Babe. A journalist hears his talent and organizes a concert at the Sydney Opera House. Later that night the journalist takes Eurydice to a nightclub where Mr Big is impressed by her performance. After being attracted to her, he introduces her to heroin. (Martin was increasingly aware of heroin casualties, both in London and in Australia.)

The Sydney Opera House Concert is a great success. Eurydice fails to take her bow. Mr Big rushes backstage to find that she has gone. The search for Eurydice is on. Orpheus joins the search. Time passes. Disguised as a street singer, one day Orpheus is surprised that someone – Mercury - throws Eurydice's button into his hat. He chases after Mercury who runs into a railway station. In lieu of a ticket Orpheus sings Brother Can You Spare a Dime and starts his downward journey led by the disappearing figure of Mercury.

His decent continues through the River Caves, until he finds himself directed towards the Ghost Train. Wildly he twirls his way through the

Hall of Mirrors to find himself in a huge empty theatre – the yet-to-be-renovated Floating Palais. On seeing him, the stage manager announces, 'You're on!' The pianist strikes up Begin the Beguine. Eurydice responds. The producer turns to Orpheus and says, 'You're on – but don't look at her, never look at her'.

Martin wrote, 'It is a terrible struggle but he forces his performance on. He stands at the footlights starring out at the audience…the comedy is ended. The curtains close, Eurydice rushes forward trying to embrace him. He rebuffs her. The curtains open for curtain call. Orpheus steps forward to tumultuous applause. The audience clamours for Eurydice. Orpheus turns toward the curtain, his hand raised to herald her. The curtains open. She steps from the darkness to a wild thrill of adulation.

'Orpheus, his eyes shining with love and pride cannot keep from glancing admiringly at her. Their eyes meet. Horrorstruck they are rooted to the spot. The curtain closes between them. Orpheus, downstage, rushes toward it but to no avail. Instead of pliant velvet he finds the curtain as hard and unyielding as stone.' (16)

Looking back, he said, 'The idea became real, the film we actually made, though in a documentary way.' (17)

About his state of mind at the time, Martin wrote, 'Confused by living between Sydney and London, trying to write a film script for Tiny Tim who had plummeted from World Fame to Obscurity, and who I considered then, and know now, as the most wonderful artist in the world. I saw him do a modern Orpheus and wrote accordingly.' (18)

While in London and Paris, Martin had left Tim 'holding the fort' (as Martin called it) at Wirian and Luna Park. Albert kept an eye on the Wirian and Tim worked on his own exhibition as well as the exterior colour schemes for the Floating Palais, Icy Mountains, Coney Island and Pirate Pete. Every day, with no driver's license, Tim drove from Bellevue Hill to Luna Park and back. No scaffolds necessary this time, he sat at a desk, worked off the architectural drawings and instructed tradespeople – invariably painters. (19)

Said Tim, ' I'd mock it all up, give it to the painters and they just painted it. Martin went to London leaving me with a Mini-Moke and Bloke - his red setter dog. By this time we'd moved into what used to be the servants quarters - Colette St John was there for a brief period of time. The rest of the house was curtained off because Martin's grandmother was in a nursing home. As she was still alive, I guess he thought, "I can't really move in – it's not appropriate …".

'When Martin was away for those months, the garage was my studio. I painted my Self Portrait show there. I got on very well with Jo. She liked me for some reason. But Martin had left me with this dog, which tended to wander, and this mad caretaker Albert. You never knew when Albert would show up. He maintained the place but he wasn't living there. He was living in Edgecliff.'

One day Bloke took off and never came back. Martin was in England at the time. Tim had to contact him and awkwardly explain that he'd lost him. Shortly before Martin's homecoming, Tim exhibited his Self Portrait at Coventry Galleries, which was well received. (20)

After seven months away, Martin moved back into Wirian. He also returned to work at Luna Park where the Carousel was the current focus of attention. The exterior colour schemes for the Floating Palais, Icy Mountains, Coney Island and Pirate Pete were now completed.

There had been lots of sadness in Martin's family while he was gone. His Grandmother Sharp had died. Uncle Frank also - father to cousins Phillip, Erica, Russell and Rozzie, whose mother, Aunt Edith had died two years before. Martin's mother – Jo – had deteriorating health (scoliosis).

Martin's Australian friends had moved on. 'We all had a lot of irons in the fire,' says Kingo. (21) Living Daylights was about to evolve into Richie Walsh's Nation Review. Richard Neville was courting his interviewer, music journalist Julie Clarke. Tim filmed them. Greg continued his trajectory as a highly sought magazine, art and fashion photographer. George was traveling the south coast of New South Wales surfing and producing a large series of photographs, drawings and paintings. Jonny was preparing his first exhibition for Bonython Galleries in Sydney. Albie was continuing with avant garde films. His understudies were launching their stellar careers – Bruce Beresford, Phillip Noyce and Peter Weir.

Attendance figures at the Nimrod Theatre had soared. Martin's previous poster for Kaspar was well received and knowing how much Martin loved Ginger Meggs, they asked him to design another poster, this one for Ken Horler's play, Ginge's Last Stand, the Nimrod Theatre's opening show for 1975. (22)

Roger Foley was evolving from Ellis D Fogg to 'Roger Foley-Fogg' or 'Mr Fogg'. Only the corporate world could provide the big budgets he required to operate as a light artist. Maggie Tabberer Associates scooped him up. She writes, 'We developed a close working relationship with an exciting new talent, Roger Foley, a lighting and sound whiz who worked under the name LSD Fogg (sic). Roger was wonderful.' (23) Roger and Maggie worked together for the next five years, at least.

And Jeannie was cutting a new album. It featured one of Jeannie's best-loved songs, the Graham Lowndes composition, Till Time Brings Change and a reprise of The Moon is a Harsh Mistress from Tears of Steel & the Clowning Calaveras. Martin offered to do the cover. She says, 'Once we knew each other, Martin was continually a source of inspiration. He and Greg did that cover.' (24) Titled Free Fall Through Featherless Flight it won Australia's 1974 Female Vocal Album of the Year.

In July, six teeth were mysteriously stolen from Martin's face of Luna Park. It was all over the news. No one knew what it was all about. 'That was a raiding party from Kogarah High School,' former student Garry Mallard confessed. He hoarded one of the teeth for eight years before taking it to the tip.

He said, 'It was one of those final year things where you had to nick something. Like, you had to nick like a chair from Central Station, or some famous thing from Hyde Park or a tram wheel from the Tram Museum. We used to make a book on it for charity – you'd take odds, have a party, get pissed and then different people say, "Okay, I'll get the tram wheel" or whatever. If they came back with it, the bet was won and you didn't make any profit. If they didn't come back with it, they lost and you'd make scads. The headmaster knew but he turned a blind eye to it. We were raising money for charity and they were all supposed to go back. It went up for auction at our school. I think they ended up getting $30 for each tooth.

'I didn't take the tooth - I only got the tooth. It didn't look like a tooth. They don't look like teeth close-up. I think it was made of ply. There might have been something about it on the news but I never noticed.' (25)

In August 1974 the Rembrandt of Luna Park, Arthur Barton died. Martin never met him. But Garry had, years before.

Said Garry, 'I'd gone to Luna Park and I came across the artist Arthur Barton. I got talking to him a little bit and I said, This stuff at Luna Park is equivalent to German Expressionist art and I wrote this bullshit article, which was published somewhere, Martin saw it and I think he was quite impressed by that. He got really involved with Arthur Barton's work and carried it on.' (26)

Fresh out of studying art at Caulfield Tech Melbourne, in September 1974, 21-year old Leigh Hobbs was asked to design the exterior colour scheme for the antique Carousel. It was his first commission. The horses were deteriorating and needed attention. All 43 horses were dipped in a bath of caustic soda to strip off the old paint, which the artists would later regret.

15.

PREPARING FOR TINY

There was $thousands to be paid in death duties. So to keep Wirian, Martin entered into an agreement with the Cranbrook School next door.

WILLIAM YANG

When Martin penned 'Anything I can do to help' and handed it to Tiny, Tiny probably didn't quite know what that meant. Neither – I guess - did Martin at that stage. Other than touting around a film script, there was no clear indication that Martin and Tiny would actually work together on any projects. It was little more than a manuscript and hope.

Martin had certainly been around films, recordings and concerts, but always on the sidelines. He didn't know much about direction, location shots, budgets and other complications involved in bringing a film project to fruition. Albie handled all that back at the Yellow House. And while Martin had contributed to Performance and Kaspar, they were really other people's projects.

While continuing his efforts with the Luna Park team, in February, Martin joined the production team of the film, Picnic at Hanging Rock, an Australian mystery drama film directed by Peter Weir, adapted from Joan Lindsay's 1967 novel of the same name. (1)

Said Martin, 'I tried to equip myself for working with Tiny - so I worked in film, I worked in theatre.' (2)

'I took a bit of a change of direction from all the things I enjoyed doing. Picnic At Hanging Rock was a big help. I knew I had to do something, so I tried to prepare myself as best I could by consciously learning. You open yourself up to seeing how it's done and that makes it easier when you have to do it yourself.' (3)

Martin's film credit was Artistic Adviser to the Director. He explained. 'It was to bring what I could to the film - ranging from a script suggestion to a set dressing. I offered what I could to Peter Weir and he took it or left it. He took a good deal of it and left a good deal of it. It was a wonderful experience. I knew people in the film industry but I never really worked closely with them. I'd known individuals but it was great to meet new people who understood and appreciated me, and I felt the same about them, comrades in Art.' (4)

The cast starred Anne-Louise Lambert, Helen Morse, Jackie Weaver, John Jarratt, Rachel Roberts, Vivean Gray, Dominic Guard and Garry McDonald. Garry McDonald was a former Cranbrook boy who was in the process of refining his Norman Gunston character for television. Another Cranbrookian was David Sanderson. Sanderson was working on the film's nature photography and was interested in assisting Martin with his Tiny Tim film, if and when it got going.

Martin's imprint on Picnic At Hanging Rock is slight but present for those who look closely. For example, Martin's Lost Hokusai print hangs on the wall in the headmistress' office. And around the 75-minute mark 'Sara Waybourne' looks through her scrapbook before going to sleep. The scrapbook is filled with Martin's Victoriana-styled collages. Martin also took it upon himself to unpick the symbolic language behind words - the girls' names for example – Irma, Marian and Miranda. The first four letters of each name are the same. 'Three parts of the one whole,' Martin concluded. (5)

Picnic At Hanging Rock was being played against a backdrop of major drama concerning the Wirian estate to which Martin was heir apparent. As well as the house finances, there were constant upheavals. Tim was planning to travel overseas, Sharon moved in with Richard, Martin's cousin Andrew joined them. Victoria Cobden was Martin's new girlfriend - Richard Cobden's sister – plus there was a string of blow-ins. Every relationship drama was being played out before a household audience. Even so, Martin refused to move into his grandparents' quarters while Grandmother Vega was alive.

Caretaker Albert Peck had no such qualms. He moved in while she was still in hospital.

Martin's grandparents had separate upstairs bedrooms. Stuart had the large adjoining room to Vega's palatial bedroom. They shared a common bathroom even though Vega's room also had a private bathroom. Albert moved into Stuart's room. He had his own kitchenette.

Albert knew the nuts and bolts of running Wirian from years of experience whereas Martin could barely cook a meal. Puzzled by his maintenance man's intentions, Martin questioned, 'How long was Albert intending to stay? I don't know. Whether he was staying the length he was meant to stay or whether he was intending to spend his life here? I don't really know. He lived a very separate existence. We didn't use that part of the house at all, so he was living in that whole half of the house. I really respected his space.' (6)

Former Wirian resident, photographer William Yang, explained the conundrum, 'Albert Peck was a tie-over from the old world. He was a retainer from Martin's grandmother. There was an unspoken agreement between Albert and Martin that he came into the house. Albert in return – I was told – looked after Wirian. Albert was a servant in a way. He did the garden, mowed the lawns, took out the garbage, did the repairs. He did all the odd jobs. He even had the key to the place. Martin did not have the key to the place. Martin had to call.' (7)

Finally, Martin's Grandmother Vega died, leaving Martin, and to a lesser extent Jo, as her beneficiaries. Albert had the run of half the house – curtained off – while Martin still lived out of a bedroom in the servants' quarters. The number of residents and overnighters was building. All bedrooms were full, so Kathy Lette and Gabrielle Carey, known as the Salami Sisters, lived under Martin's dining room table for a while. That's where they slept until they moved back to the suburbs and wrote Puberty Blues. Before heading overseas Tim said, 'A lot of people have lived at Wirian at some stage. It was a very exciting time.' (8)

But Martin needed more space to accomplish his projects. The pictures were getting bigger. He was working on a canvas titled Miss Australia and planning another huge Tiny Tim canvas. About dossing down in the servant's quarters, Martin said, 'There was six of us. I couldn't sleep up there anymore. It took a big emotional step to go through to that part of Wirian. Albert wasn't encouraging it at all. He liked the seclusion I'm sure, whereas I wanted him to move a bit further away.'

Martin was referring to the northwest corner of the house where beyond his grandparents' bedrooms was Jo's former bedroom (with its beautiful bay window) and Martin's former nursery. Either would have made an ideal bedroom, but Albert was staying put.

Martin continued, 'I thought, Albert could have the nursery room and the bathroom. A unit - put a door on it. I tried a few times but he thought that room was too hot. As soon as anything is sharp you have to get your way back into it one way or another, and I certainly had to get my way back into this. I hadn't really run a house before, so there was a sort of pressure.' (9)

Albert appeared to have no friends outside Wirian though he had a sister somewhere. For occasional breaks, he went on fishing trips on the Shoalhaven River. As well being 10-15 years older than Martin and friends, Albert was unlike everyone else around the place. He wore short-sleeved polyester shirts, fawn-coloured trousers and pullovers in winter. William

Yang described his appearance as 'totally ordinary', except that Albert loved leather coats. He also admired Adolf Hitler for his Final Solution to the Jewish question and said so openly, which freaked everybody out.

Not only did Martin have to struggle with the internal politics of Wirian, he was also worrying about the Tiny Tim film, Luna Park and the biggest drama of all – death duties – which was like a slow train coming.

William explained, 'There was debate then whether Martin would in fact keep Wirian because there was $thousands to be paid in death duties. So to keep Wirian, Martin entered into an agreement with the Cranbrook School next door. He sold the garage, the tennis court and his circular drive to the school. That was one of the crises.' (10)

Another was the news of David Litvinoff's suicide death in England in April. 'He was a fantastic man. I miss him,' said Martin. Others were not so generous, blaming him for Brett's growing heroin addiction.

Martin reminisced, 'It was great that David came out to Australia. When he went back to London the scene had gone. He liked boys I suppose. He was staying out in the country with a youngish interior decorator who asked him to move on. It was a delicate situation. He rang up a few people, gave a few hints, gave away some nice shirts and everything he had, went to a chemist asked for some pills, took them and that was it. David had no recognisable place in society – something he could earn a living from - he was a sort of court jester, I suppose.' (11)

His friendship with Rock stars had provided Litva with an outstanding collection of tapes. He sold his extraordinary library of reel-to-reel tapes. They finished up in Martin's care, including Bob Dylan's legendary 'Judas' May 1966 concert - a sought after bootleg recording in its day, (12) Brian Jones' Joujouka Music years before its release. Cocksucker Blues by the Rolling Stones – at one stage considered for the soundtrack of Performance. Nobody else had those, not then. Fortunately Martin had a big house. Over the years, residents, drop-ins and passers-through would simply 'leave' stuff at Wirian. Maybe clothes, paintings, books, personal effects, chairs and sometimes - as gifts - figurines.

Martin's Dream Museum grew out of his novelty collection. Sensing the delights of a toy museum, Martin and Richard Liney were discussing the concept perhaps for Luna Park. They occasionally bought figurines that caught their eye. These were added to Martin's childhood toys and accumulation of Mickey Mice, which quickly grew into a small collection.

Said Martin, 'Richard and I had similar taste about Tiny Tim, Luna Park, novelties and popular Art. He's someone I could share these ideas with. We founded the Dream Museum together. We thought that Luna Park should have been snap-frozen. We were entranced by its crumbling plaster dreams. We tried to see an economical way of using the "junk" that had survived there for the past years and adding to it a world of novelties, comic characters and childhood memories. We funded the Dream Museum initially then Luna Park started to put a bit in.

'There's a state of existence which can be described as noveltihood. Certain people from the comic world achieve great success as a comic character and certain human beings become honoured with noveltihood like Prince Charles and Lady Diana, Muhammad Ali, Ginger Meggs, Pinocchio, Jesus, Alice in Wonderland, Popeye, Jiminy Cricket, Sad Sack...you get that interesting world. Where else - in a strange way - would Jesus and Alice in Wonderland meet? And Mickey Mouse and Ginger Meggs...?' (13)

Peeking into bric-a-brac shops and auction rooms, one day Martin spotted a half-peeled tangerine that he took to be somebody's leftover lunch. Martin was surprised it was a legitimate carved object. When it came up for auction Martin bid on it and bought it.

Returning to Wirian, Martin played the song Hello Hello from a bootleg Tiny Tim cassette. The words were, '...would you like some of my tangerine?' which Martin heard as an invocation from Tiny. Visitors may recall seeing that little tangerine object on his desk, table or sideboard all his life, seldom more than a couple of metres away from wherever he was working.

Back at the Park, the main projects were the Carousel and the Games Pavilion. Tim had gone and Peter Kingston (Kingo) had joined. Martin, Richard and Kingo worked together on the Pirate Pete murals. Leigh Hobbs stripped the statues of the Big Boys back to chicken wire and rebuilt them as American tourists, Larry and Lizzie Luna. Jonny Lewis set up a darkroom underneath Wirian where he restored a caché of historical Luna Park photographs. At the start of the year, Jonny's father, Tom Lewis, was sworn in as Liberal Premier for NSW, a position he held for approximately 12 months. In this period, Luna Park was effectively under his jurisdiction. Things might have been okay if it had stayed that way.

The Luna Park lease, held by Leon Fink and Nathan Spatt, was due to expire in October 1975. In the interim the tenancy shifted to a week-to-week basis while new lease documents were being drawn up. All major renovations were temporarily suspended and all development ideas postponed.

Nathan Spatt's son Maurice was appointed general manager and he had ideas of his own, like a restaurant in the shape of an ice cream cone designed by architect Harry Seidler. There were plenty of ideas around, including the one they all dreaded - turning Luna Park into a casino, but none could proceed because everything hung on the all-important lease. Plenty of investment dollars had already been spent. The total cost of the Carousel renovation had been $100,000. The Zipper, the Hurricane and Astrospin had been $90,000 each. (14) Martin's Face cost $28,000 and was fantastic! (15)

The combined artists' efforts were welcomed by the public and by the old timers who had worked at the Park. One day, admiring the work, former manager Ted Hopkins gave the artists his approval, adding, 'If I had a chance there is only one thing I'd like to re-do – the Ghost Train'. (16) The artists were thinking the same way.

A Ghost Train theme is what Jeannie asked of Martin for the set design of Tears of Steel & the Clowning Calaveras, her multi media, double-LP production featuring song, theatre and dance. It was the first show at the new Seymour Centre, a multi-purpose performing venue within the University of Sydney precinct. (17)

Jeannie had been deeply impressed by Kaspar because it centred on a boy who had lost the power of speech. Twelve months before, Jeannie's father had a stroke and suffered the same disability. He never spoke 'language' again. Jeannie dedicated Tears of Steel & the Clowning Calaveras to him.

At the start of the year Jeannie saw the film The Battle of Chile in which she heard the singer Àngel Parra whom she had met in Cuba in 1967. When Jeannie heard him singing she started to weep. In her personal notes Jeannie penned, 'This personal connection to 11 September 1973 added to my commitment-to/compassion-with the people in Chile and those who arrived here courtesy of the Whitlam govt. In the cinema tears surged up and then I got SO angry.' (18)

Soon after, friend/singer Margret Roadknight gave Jeannie a book of Palbo Neruda poems in which Jeannie found the poem that inspired Tears of Steel.

I learned life from your death,
My eyes had begun to mourn
When I discovered within me
Not tears, but undying arms.
Wait for them! Wait for me!

'It's on the album,' said Jeannie. 'Mexico has been a big influence in my life since I was three.' (19)

She described the show, 'There were eight performers, three were singers (who had to do other things), and two dancers and two actors – Lex Marinos and Nicholas Lathouris. Death is very visible in Mexican culture. We hide it and they don't. The calaveras are the skulls. The skeletons represent politicians or different characters in Mexican life and they are "calaveras". It was in two parts. The first part was about people who I saw as martyrs-performers. The costumes for the first half were clown costumes except mine. I wore red because I was the human presence.

'The second half was Tears of Steel which lyrically consisted of the Neruda poem, two poems of mine, a poem of Denis Kevans - all set to music by Michael Carlos. In that half there's an indigenous mask which is half life/half death. The other actors had half their face painted as a skull and I was the normal!

'The piece that Martin did as the backdrop is his interpretation of that life/death mask and that came together across the back of the stage at the end of the second half. Martin was in there painting it at the last minute, technicians going hysterical.

'Martin had done a small painting of that image to go on the back cover of the Tears of Steel LP. I went over to Wirian to pick up the artwork to take to EMI. Martin had torn it into pieces because he said, "Jeannie the death side is too strong". (Years later he framed the pieces in a yellow heart shape frame and gave it to me.) ' (20)

The clown costumes for the show were borrowed by Martin from Luna Park and faithfully returned after the show. Plus, Martin added, 'there was a real piece of the Ghost Train on the stage!' (21) 'I have no idea where,' Jeannie replied. (22)

Said Martin, 'Jeannie is very in touch with things that are happening in the unconscious of the community. She has the power to bring these things through. Not a seer - more of a medium.' (23)

In his notes Martin wrote, 'Because of the Luna Park/Ghost Train connection - humorous horror - Jeannie wanted me to design the show to illustrate her ideas. I provided some clown costumes and masks from Luna Park for the Bravo Pour le Clown song.

'The most ambitious song was The Crucifixion by Phil Ochs, the soon-to-commit-suicide singer songwriter. To illustrate this song, Jeannie wanted the huge sliding panels to come together each side bearing half the skull and half a smiling face. She was still learning to sing the long and difficult song at dress rehearsal and I had left the painting of the Death/Life face to the last minute, hoping she wouldn't insist. I challenged her over the song and its gruesome imagery, but true to herself at all cost, she persisted. The face was done in a heart-shape and became one of the most powerful moments in the show. It was a song I never really understood until the night of the Ghost Train Fire. (24)

'Doing that was so hard - two of those images - Jeannie's record cover. When I did it for the show it was just like a heart-shape, half as a smiling red face, and the other half was a skull and they came together in two big panels behind Jeannie at a certain point of the song. They came together (bang!) like that. Abraxas. So the images are coming through – me, as one who is sensitive to it, and Jeannie - through something unconscious or whatever workings of inspiration.'

One of the cast, Lex Marinos summed up Martin's contribution, 'What was extraordinary was Martin's ability to take stuff and make us see it differently. I was very impressed. Perfect design.' (26)

For a break, Martin and Jonny went on a road trip to Surfer's Paradise and looked up Peter Royles – the Yellow House answer to Bob Dylan - who was working at the Captain's Table restaurant. 'They came and swam with the dolphins', wrote Peter. (27)

At Luna Park the main projects were the Games Pavillion, Pirate Pete, Coney Island and the Orchestral Mural. Richard Liney started restoration of the Floating Palais in January 1976. (28)

Author of Luna Park, Just for Fun, Sam Marshall wrote, 'One third of the Carousel framework was remade, and a new floor and surrounding picket fence were built. Artist Garry Shead painted the wide fascia around the Carousel with postcard scenes.' (29)

Married with a three-year old daughter Gria, Garry and his wife Meryl lived at Lavender Bay where Brett, Kingo and artist John Firth-Smith lived as well. Garry was painting his own canvasses by night and working in a charcuterie (that he would soon own) by day. Martin invited Garry to join the team. His first job was the restoration of Pirate Pete alongside Kingo, Richard and himself. Shortly afterwards Garry was asked to paint the Carousel. Arthur Barton never saw these efforts, reflects Garry, 'that was past his time.

'Martin got me the job - and I really needed a job. He got me to do Pirate Pete with Kingo. I was living at Lavender Bay. I rowed over in the morning, parked the boat and went to work. Martin was working on Pirate Pete as well and I learned so much from him. He was so good with the graphic way he painted. I picked up lots of techniques.'

Everyone involved at the artistic level was handpicked by Martin. 'Martin got the team together,' explained Garry, 'because Fink & Spatt didn't know who to ask for'. (30)

Kingo reflected on the sequence of events, 'Leon Fink bought the rights to demolish the park and then found he couldn't demolish it. He got Martin in and Martin got me in. They certainly weren't interested in paying us much. We were just glad to be there, glad to get some sort of wage. So we're grateful to Leon for that.

'We had full reign of the place over the art side. We tried to save all the Arthur Barton artworks and stabilize the place. I worked on Pirate Pete's Sea Battle, Coney Island, we were trying to tidy up the River Caves and eventually the Ghost Train - we hoped - but the whole thing overtook us.' (31)

In May 1976 Neville Wran was elected Premier of New South Wales. He surprised everyone by not automatically granting another five-year lease. Why the hesitation? Not only was management on a week-by-week tenancy, but staff, tradespeople and artists. 'We were all on it. It could have ended at any time,' said Kingo. (32)

Week-by-week. Every time the document crossed Wran's desk, he put it aside. Week-by-week. The place was starting to run down.

In his notes Martin wrote, 'In 1976 while working at Luna Park, I walked into the deserted Ghost Train building, exploring its twisted black corridors. It took nerves of steel to step into the nightmare tunnels of Hell's Railway armed only with a torch, its pale beam picking out the leering faces of the demons and grotesque laughing skeletons. It was very spooky in there, just me and them.

'I came across a small black cupboard door. It prised open. The torchlight revealed, not a forgotten skeleton, but a glittering track of water, and in a distant grotto, with saxophone raised stood Mickey Mouse, the plaster Pablo of this Magic Theatre. By chance I had discovered the door that links the Ghost Train to the River Caves.' (33)

Meanwhile, death duties were being negotiated on the Wirian estate and Martin had to ensure Jo was okay. Said Martin, 'My mother had laughter, she'd keep going, she couldn't stop herself. It was almost like having a humour fit. So she didn't lose her happiness. All my friends became her friends. They'll all go to see her – the younger generation. She was someone they could talk to.'

As soon as a strategy for death duties was in place, Martin figured he could raise money by mortgaging Wirian. This placed Martin in a position where he realized he might actually have the money to fund the Tiny Tim film himself. He said, 'As soon as I found out I met Mr Morris who was my grandfather's solicitor who didn't understand art. It was a difficult difference but - through Boofhead and things - it's all connected.' (34)

'I found out I could get a mortgage, so I did.' (35)

Wirian with a mortgage over it! Never! Albert was horrified!

Martin was ready for Tiny when he arrived mid-year 1976 for his third Australian tour. In June/July 1976 Tiny played small clubs to a mixed reception. He was booed at an Essendon Hotel in Melbourne but welcomed at Wirian. Martin even had a film script ready. (36)

Tiny had been through quite a bit since their last meeting. He had been evicted from the apartment in Brooklyn where he had lived with Miss Vicki and their daughter little Miss Tulip. Tiny's father had now passed and he rather shamefully moved back in with his mother, back to his childhood home in Washington Heights – avoiding neighbours - before fleeing to Florida.

Then Tiny Tim got his first biographer. Despite years in the public spotlight, no one really knew Tiny's full background until writer Harry Stein tracked him down. Stein's book filled in the early days, where Tiny was born, school, family, first crush, Hubert's Flea Circus, Steve Paul's Scene. Playboy Press published Tiny's first biography. (37) It was generally well received even though stories about the Honey Method and the like seemed unnecessary.

The source? Tiny himself.

Tiny explained, 'Why do I tell them about my showers and everything? Show business is not a private life. If I wanted a private life then I should have been anything but in show business. If I'm a stockbroker or if I'm working in a business, I have a good right to say, What I do in my private life with Miss Vicki, or whoever I'm with, I'm sorry I can't tell you. It's a public business. I also tell them these things because fans want to know what you're doing and who you're doing it with. This is the precise gossip business.

'When I took on myself these things, I said All right, it is a public relations business. Fans want to know. The public wants to know about the star. The public wants to know intimate lives - and the paper is not there to praise the star. The paper is there to get circulated readers. So Tiny Tim, Nice Guy Does Good Show – that's not what they want to hear. They want to hear the other side - Ahh, he can't be like that! That's what they want to hear.' (38)

Unimpressed by Stein's bio, Martin wrote, 'Harry Stein is typical of those who have been drawn by the strange power of entertainers and yet been unable to come to terms with Tiny's real genius, which exists not in the realm of his personal behaviour, fascinating as this may be, but in the area of his greatest magic, his vocal virtuosity. He was fascinated by the man but he never listened to the singer.' (39)

And so Tiny came to Wirian and Martin got to host the Leonardo da Vinci of Popular Song, the Eternal Troubadour, the Chameleon, in the Wirian kitchen. Martin said, 'People talk of great artists – Vincent van Gogh comes immediately to mind. Another one is Tiny – equal magnitudes, different mediums'. (40)

Strumming his ukulele, Tiny harangued against fornication and birth control, while confessing his love for actress Miss Cybill Shepherd and Wirianette Miss Sue Cameron. Tiny proclaimed, 'The early times just in Australia alone were Miss Cameron - Sue Cameron in 1976 in Mr Martin Sharp's house - one wonderful moment's time! (41)

Martin's fascination with Tiny was non-negotiable and Martin taped everything to cassette. Tiny responded in full voice, preached and shared many of his love-fantasies on tape. They also discussed an idea of recording a multi-volume History Of Popular Song (Musical History Tour) starting with Volume One – Henry Burr, through Russ Columbo, Irving Kaufman, Rudy Vallee, Bing Crosby and into the modern period.

However, the main achievement of this Australian tour was that the first footage was shot. Said Martin, 'We shot our first film in 1976. The film started with Tiny arriving at the airport and then in the kitchen here. I don't think we got the sound for it. The Marathon idea was mooted then. He felt the idea of a medley would be best because it was his most popular. He was 100% sure because at all the clubs the people loved this kind of music, which was his ad lib marathon. He said, "Take my word for it." So I said, "Okay."

'And then I was watching Mohammad Ali fight against that Japanese wrestler, Inoki, who looked like a Marvel superhero. It was a big showbiz fight: Ali vs the toughest wrestler in the world.' (42)

The fight between American boxer Muhammad Ali and Japanese professional wrestler Antonio Inoki was held in Tokyo on 26 June 1976. At the time, Ali was the reigning WBC/WBA Heavyweight Champion. Inoki was staging exhibition fights against champions of various martial arts, in an attempt to show that pro wrestling was the dominant fighting discipline.

'Incredible fight,' said Martin. 'A real Barnum-Bailey feel to it, a top showbiz concoction: the two great strongmen, in their own styles, fighting one another. Ali came out with gloves, the wrestler without them, and for 20 rounds he lay down and fought Ali with his feet. I don't think Ali even scored a punch. Everyone thought it was a fake fight, but I thought it was the most exciting fight I've ever seen in my life!

'I watched that fight and thought, that's the idea to make that medley. A Marathon - challenge the world. This is the showcase. So I sent a telegram to Tiny, we talked about it and he mentioned the idea to his manager Joe Cappy, who loved it, and so it was developed from that.' (43)

They talked about the film straight away. Martin mentioned Al Jolson's The Jazz Singer, an idea Tiny liked. From there, they moved to Orpheus and Eurydice and a non-stop singing marathon. Said Martin. 'I added that we have to make it like that fight between Mohammad Ali and Inoki. The idea of the World Non-Stop Singing Record came up. Tiny thought it was a good idea.'

These early discussions were taped at Wirian and at the Southern Cross Hotel Edgecliff where Tiny was staying. Said Martin, 'One was trying to develop the shape of the marathon in the pure historical context so that it went from the first song to the last. He wasn't committed to doing something as formal as that.' (44)

Verbal agreement had been reached. Tiny went off to his next gig in Jamaica, talked it through with his manager and fired back a telegram that read, 'Dear Mr Sharp Mr Joe Cappy is very enthused and very interested in doing your idea of the one hour song marathon all that's required is the following three round trip first class airplane tickets to Australia three paid for rooms in a first class hotel and weekly allowances for me and the financial settlement feel free to call him if you can come up with this sincerely and thanks again for everything Tiny Tim.' (45)

While Luna Park was going wrong, Tiny Tim was going right. Martin applied to the Film Commission for grant, writing an impassioned letter that did not remotely conform to their bureaucratic conventions.

Calling the film project The Lyre Bird – Tiny Tim, Martin wrote, 'I agree that any project involving Tiny Tim may seem quite eccentric, and often I have been considered quite eccentric myself for thinking him more than a "put on" that most people take him for. Nonetheless, nothing can ever persuade me that he is less than a genius.' (46)

To celebrate or announce his success with Tiny, Martin painted what might be called the 'first draft' of a painting called Song of Songs in 1976 and retitled Film Script in 2004 after 28 years of overpainting. (47)

Martin exhibited the earliest version of this picture in his 1976 Hogarth exhibition. That's how he met Willy de la Vega from Argentina whose brother had married Martin's mother's friend.

They met because Willy got roped into carrying Martin's 136 x 319 cm picture into the gallery, after which Willy became terribly enthusiastic about Tiny. He said, 'Martin had an exhibition at the Hogarth Galleries and we came to Wirian to pick him up and that's when I met him. We had to carry the painting to the exhibition while Martin was still painting it.' (48)

Years later, Willy was with Martin on the night of the murder at Wirian.

16.

KOLD KOMFORT

I would keep Martin company while he was working. He was always working on a lot of things at once so there would be preparations for shows, paintings he was working on, various collections, stuff to do with the house, etc, etc, plus endless visitors, interviewers and collaborators.

SUSAN JENSEN

Martin painted less but he wrote more. He started a daily journal/sketch book and he began writing letters, lots of letters, to people in authority – the Premier, for example, mostly about the deteriorating state of Luna Park. He also wrote two magazine articles for Quadrant and two love poems to the Park, penned with the ardour of a teenage romancer.

I care so much about you that my feelings are beyond intellect.

You – Park – are in my blood.

I have explored every inch of your dusty corridors... (1)

Martin also leant towards the Christian faith, there are quiet references throughout his pictures. Did this start with Vincent's Letters? Carl Jung? Arthur Stace? Tiny Tim? Victoria Cobden? Or was this religious fascination ignited when researching the symbolic meaning of the Face of Glory with Tim?

The early-mid 70s has been touted by the media as a hedonistic time, famous for things like LSD, public nudity and free love. There was another side as well. Although conventional churches would never admit it, it was a religious period. Young people rejected organised religions in droves and sparkled with a new type of fervour. Artists and musicians generally weren't atheists. They celebrated gods, gurus and Gaia. Atheists were people with Science degrees.

George Harrison and Donovan favoured Maharishi Mahesh Yogi. We've Been Told Jesus Is Coming Soon was a track on Eric's new album. Tully became a Meher Baba band. Pete Townshend was a Meher Baba devotee. New Zealand band Home displayed Guru Maharaji banners on their stage.

One day, Yellow House itinerant Jesus Adam called on Wirian. Martin describes what occurred, 'We were in the kitchen - he came to stay out of the blue with his wife and baby. And he said, Sometimes I can "do" things - bring through another world - I can do it with a light bulb sometimes and he gestured to the light bulb. I wasn't stoned or anything, this was 11.00am – and his face changed into the Man of Constant Sorrows, like the description in Psalms. He was very moving – directing it at me. Then his eyes brimmed with tears. He was very kind - in agony but still loving. And he said: You're to be a messenger, what I have to say to you can't be said in words – something like that - and then he dragged me back to normality.

'He only stayed a few days. I chased him out in the end'. (2)

What the media called 'cults' were in their heyday. You couldn't avoid the Hara Krishna Temple chanting its mantra all over town. The Children of God marshaled the streets. Muktananda, Bubba Free John, Bhagwan Shree Rajneesh, Krishnamurti, AC Bhaktivedanta Swami Prabhupada and Sun Myung Moon sprang into public consciousness.

Jenny Kee embraced Buddhism. Adrian Rawlins got into Meher Baba. Richard Neville started meditating. And Martin had his own guru – Tiny Tim.

Martin combined Tiny's face with the word Eternity for the cover of the January 1977 issue of the socio-political Quadrant magazine. The issue also featured a full page b/w of Tiny, taken from one of Martin's pictures in London OZ. It was a collage of a collage. (3)

Said Martin, 'I cover a lot of my feelings about Tiny at that time in that article. Eventually it was the feeling that I couldn't convince anyone to do anything with Tiny. Margaret Fink was thinking of making a film with him.' (4)

Margaret Fink's concept was nothing like Martin's. Hers was a comedy to be called The Projectionist, 'but it didn't come through', said Martin. (5) So he ran the idea past Peter Weir who was working on The Last Wave. He seemed more interested in making a film about 'Martin's obsession with Tiny Tim' than about Tiny Tim. Martin also approached Jim Sharman though he didn't expect any real interest. And Philippe was in the country producing his memorable Mad Dog Morgan feature film, starring Dennis Hopper, who was as uncontrollable in real life as the character he was playing. (6)

Martin continued over-painting Song of Songs. It was an evolving picture. Words and images changed continually over the next 35 years. At this early stage the two core images featured Tiny and the Opera House. (7)

For their second show of the year, Nimrod Theatre commissioned a third poster from Martin, this one for Garry McDonald's Young Mo, about the comedian Roy Rene/Mo Mccackie. Martin's poster could not have been more stripped back - no time, no date, not the name of the show, no '…written by Steve Spears', none of that. Just Mo's face and one word – 'Nimrod'. It became the theatre's official logo, on letterheads and mastheads. You could even buy it on a keyring.

Susan Jensen shared an apartment with Jeannie whom she helped with the show Tears of Steel & the Clowning Calaveras. Susan - who never lived in Wirian – was introduced and became one of Martin's main assistants. She writes, 'I would keep him company while he was working on various things and be an extra pair of hands for him, doing whatever needed doing at the time'. (8)

As usual there were lots of ongoing posters, pictures and projects. One of which was the Haymarket poster, with Vincent's Starry Starry Night sky emblazoned with the word Eternity. Susan noted this as a significant spiritual statement, 'The Haymarket poster is an important bringing together of two special spiritual and artistic threads.

'I don't recall seeing the combination of the starry night and Eternity before this. I can almost hear the click in Martin's mind. Martin often noted the parallels between Tiny and Vincent, different gifts but the same link between creativity and spirituality expressed in a uniquely different way. Victoria (Cobden) was one of the first people we all knew who became a truly believing Christian so it was a significant event.' (9)

Sensing that Luna Park was a disaster waiting to happen, Martin and Tim painted the Luna Park towers sinking beneath Hokusai's Wave. Sourced from a collage by Richard Liney, Martin gave it the Biblical title Babylon the Great is Fallen (Revelation 18 v 2). He worked on it for years. (10)

Against a puce-yellow sky a dark form lurks. Redolent of Hokusai's 'great wave' back cover of the back cover of Mick Jagger OZ 15, is it a beast? A shadow? A premonition? Says Tim, 'The brown shape was painted in by Martin several years after I stopped painting the picture.' (11)

Much later in life, Martin's carer and friend Angelica Tremblay, wrote about this picture, 'Martin had many artists, friends and different people working over the years using brown and different coloured pencil drawings in different parts of the work and I was one of them. He never finished the work.' (12)

The formal real estate transaction between Cranbrook School and Wirian began in 1977. When the school finalized its land purchase, they took the garage, tennis court and the circular drive. As for the Cadillac? Martin simply drove it around instead of the Moke. One other task yet remained: cataloging Grandmother's goods. (13)

In the next Quadrant, Martin followed his previous Tiny Tim article with his thoughts on Luna Park. Photos of Martin was the 8-page centerpiece of the February issue. An article by Elwyn Lynn summed up Martin's career thus far and a b/w photographic study by Bernard Cumming shows Martin painting Mo. (14)

Another photograph has Martin sitting at a table in the room that would later become his studio. Visitors and friends know the room well. Martin referred to it as his Studio. They called it his Inner Sanctum. It brimmed with whatever Martin was working on at the time. In this picture, the room is surprisingly sparse.

For Quadrant Martin wrote, 'I love Luna Park, and sometimes I feel Luna Park loves me, but it has been an arduous romance'. Sometimes pure Pop, Martin name-checked, 'Ginger Meggs, Mickey Mouse, Little Nemo, Krazy Kat, The Sentimental Bloke, Tiger Tim, The Phantom, Dr Strange, Captain Marvel, Grock, Santa Claus, Dame Edna, Norman Gunston, Snugglepot and Cuddlepie, Charlie Chaplin, Houdini, Mandrake, Mr Jiggs, Mo, Popeye, Punch and Judy, Boofhead…and all the others'.

He also expressed concerns, 'Luna Park is in a state of flux. Great treasures of popular art are vanishing, it needs an eager army to answer their calls for help'. The article pushed for Luna Park as a Dream Museum, an art gallery to Pop. (15)

Still that lease remained unsigned.

The artists became unsettled. They saw the rides deteriorating before their eyes. They had actually been asked to stop working on some of them and were switched to working on the Mid-Way instead – where a Souvenir Shop (Magic Shop) was introduced. Martin wrote a stream of letters. He said, 'I have a book full with Dear Leon just trying to express how important it was, and how I really felt that - with all my heart - about the place'. Martin wrote to Leon, 'It's no use at this point describing in detail the vast amount of decay that needs rebuilding at Luna Park…'. (16)

Peter Kingston and Garry Shead felt the same and attended meetings with the leaseholders to this effect. Kingo's personal notes reflect the management's indifference to the artists' concerns. He writes of a meeting with Leon Fink (with Nathan Morris and Garry Shead also present). Kingo states that the previous Saturday night some friends had noticed a couple of loose planks on the Coney Island end of the Big Dipper. He quotes Leon's response, 'If we listened everything we heard - followed every rumour - we'd have a fulltime maintenance staff!'

Kingo's meeting with Maurice Spatt fared no better. He wrote, 'Maurice goes – rather proudly, even smugly, no responsible authority approaches us. On our present lease we are a law to ourselves. Amazement expressed by us. Kingo: We must make it safe anyway.' (17)

Was this simply bravado on the manager's part? Underpinning their confident front, the lease document remained unsigned and the week-by-week tenancy must surely have sapped all business confidence.

While all this was going on at the Park, Tiny agreed to tour Australia the following year and Martin scrambled for money to film him. Martin had been haranguing Leon about the condition of the Big Dipper, now he needed a loan. Leon obliged, taking as collateral Martin's Lost Hokusai.

Said Martin, 'I gave it to him as collateral against $3000. I was whinging to him about the Big Dipper and I accepted a cheque from him knowing that I didn't really believe him when he said: I'll do everything possible on the Big Dipper because I didn't want to lose the chance of making the film. That's a confession I've told no one before but I'm telling you now. I felt that was a moment where I should have stuck to my guns, but I was fairly broke and I suppose he almost paid me to keep quiet - when I think about the mechanics of it in that way. So one makes terrible mistakes.

'Leon didn't quite rise to the occasion. He didn't think Luna Park was the most important thing that he owned - but it was you see. He ran a whole lot of other things at the same time and maybe he was too immersed in his other businesses to say, I'll give Luna Park the attention that it needs. I believe at the certain times during the course of events, we personally - by our actions - allowed that fire to occur.

'I thought someone would be killed on the Big Dipper - that was my intuition and that's why I stressed it. I was onto the Big Dipper but I never picked the Ghost Train.' (18)

Still the lease remained unsigned.

So much to do, Martin needed an assistant. Susan Jensen recommended Melody Cooper. Susan writes, 'Martin needed someone to be his right hand person assisting him with all sorts of work relating to both his art and the house. Melody trained in production/set design/costuming at NIDA and was working part time with Linda Jackson at Flamingo Park. I thought she would be the perfect person to help Martin because she has such a variety of really amazing skills.' (19)

Flamingo Park! Another success. Located in Sydney's Victorian-style Strand Arcade, Jenny Kee partnered with designer Linda Jackson and built a creative, attractive and flamboyant business. Martin bought a Flamingo Park dress and presented it to Little Nell's youngest sister, Cressida Campbell, who joined the other artists at Luna Park.

Melody Cooper's arrival at Wirian sparked another room-reshuffle. She moved into the accommodation under the garage until the Cranbrook School asserted its property rights. Melody then settled into Martin's former bedroom in the servant's quarters when he took over his Grandmother's upstairs rooms. Melody also had a downstairs room for her studio, which Martin shared.

Affirming his right to the property was difficult for Martin, not encouraged by Albert. About moving into his Grandmother's grand bedroom Martin says, 'There was a bit of inhibition I suppose - about the house and things like that'. (20)

Richard Neville moved into the nursery room in the northwest corner of the house. 'Richard did his courting at Wirian,' said Martin. (21) Richard was commissioned to write a book about serial killer, charismatic and dangerous Charles Sobhraj, who preyed on western backpackers. This was an unexpected turn coming from someone who had romanticized the Hippie Trail in OZ magazines – he now monstered it. (22)

Richard's co-author was Julie Clarke. She had known Martin since Yellow House days. Julie's name (spelt 'Juli') appears on The Yellow House poster, which is the closest 'official' listing anyone has of the artists who were involved. (23) Tim explained, 'Martin knew Julie before Richard and it was through Martin that Richard met her'. (24) Julie moved in with Richard.

All this coming and going didn't suit Albert who made his likes and dislikes no secret. Richard's friendship with Martin was too entrenched for Albert to call it into question but with Julie it was different. Albert let it be known that he disliked Julie Clarke. Her ABC job didn't help.

Albert liked people who dedicated themselves to the house, people who fixed and cleaned things. Plus he didn't like people wasting electricity. Like, Sharon Liney putting only one pair of knickers through the tumble dryer! To make his point, Albert stretched Sharon's knickers over a giant tin and placed it in the kitchen for all to see. (25)

Describing the caretaker-general, William Yang said, 'You were answerable to Albert. He sort-of ran the place. If you didn't keep the kitchen tidy, Albert would be down on you. If you knocked chips off the wall, Albert would be around. If you scratched the floor, Albert would be onto you. There were a whole lot of little rules that Albert made. He was like the groundsman.' (26)

But Albert did get along with Melody. 'Albert was the glue that held Wirian together', she wrote, 'he made sure the utilities were paid and the rent was collected from the various bodies'. One of her first jobs was to assist Albert in getting Martin's grandmother's things ready for sale, 'so he could pay the death duties and keep Wirian'. (27)

The garage, the driveway, grandmother's effects, all sold — why stop there? Why not sell the lot. When Cleo magazine interviewed Martin for their August issue, they wrote, 'For Sale signs at Wirian, people tug the iron tolling bell and ask to be shown around the house. Martin has an undated ticket to Orlando Florida. He hopes that once in the States he will be able to make a film with Tiny.' (28)

In those days, Wirian did not totally centre on Martin's projects (as it did later). Everyone was busy. Some – like Julie – came-and-went and had their own careers. Richard and Julie also had a book to write about Charles Sobhraj. Susan Jensen worked for Cameron Management, a Double Bay-based agency for models, actors and photographers. Back from overseas, technology-minded Tim was working with video and computers. He interviewed Richard with Julie as his producer. And Jonny created a downstairs darkroom where he was occupied reprinting the Ted Hopkins photographic negatives found at Luna Park. In fact, the whole crew was still loosely engaged at Luna Park.

Martin's fourth poster for the Nimrod Theatre was designed for the cabaret-style show Kold Komfort Kaffee. It must have been quite an opening night as - despite a capacity audience - 'no profit had been made, as all the money was used on food and champagne'. (29)

Knowing that the Premier was expected to attend, Martin went to the Nimrod specifically to engage Neville Wran on the subject of the Luna Park lease and its onerous week-by-week tenancy. Being on friendly terms with Wran's wife Jill Hickson, Martin felt this connection might grant him a sympathetic ear from the Premier.

Said Martin, 'It was the last night of Kold Komfort Kaffee. I went especially to see him. I said, "I'm really worried about Luna Park".

'And Wran said, "I've got nothing against Leon Fink, but while he's got that partner I'll never give him the lease - because he can't say things like that about me. I'm human. I bleed!' This is what he said. I thought it must have been something about his wife or something...?' (30)

And then the problem was revealed. The disagreement stemmed from a gathering at the up-market Pruniers In The Park restaurant in Woollahra some 12 months previously. Someone overheard Nathan Spatt talking about Neville Wran in a derogatory manner but there is some question as to whether Spatt said something insulting about the Premier's new wife, Jill Hickson, or whether he was ridiculing Wran's Socialist roots, citing the Premier's 'hypocritical' attitude to the pilot's strike at the time and restlessness of the union movement in general.

'I'm human, I bleed…' what could that mean? Martin asked Spatt about the meaning of his conversation with the Premier.

'What did you say that could have offended him?" said Martin. 'And he said, "I was only saying what was said in the papers - about him being a scab for flying to Norfolk Island with Abeles (ie. Sir Peter Abeles) and breaking the plane strike.'

A scab.

Martin continued, 'I went to Leon and said, "He's not going to do anything until you get rid of Spatt".

'And Leon said, "I can't get rid of him, so that's that!"

'So the terms were stated. Wran said, "Unless you get rid of Spatt - no lease". And Leon said, "No go".' (31)

Cold comfort indeed.

17.

STREET OF DREAMS PRODUCTIONS

We worked pretty full on for Mart on Street of Dreams and the World Non-Stop Singing Record. Printing posters and t-shirts, making props, painting sets, doing make up and hair for Tiny...

MELODY COOPER

In November 1978 Regency Entertainment brought Tiny to Australia for a tour of Leagues Clubs, shopping centres and other inconsequential venues.

Martin extended the visa and booked Tiny for two concerts plus recording sessions from the close of 1978 to 13 January 1979. Most crucial was the legal agreement with Tiny's management. Without this, prearranged concert plans, studio bookings and the film could fold overnight. Fortunately, there were green lights everywhere.

The 125 x 330 cm Song of Songs picture was to be Martin's 'statement' for the year, yet he still found time to create posters for friends. Actors John Gaden and Kate Fitzpatrick go way back to Sydney University days with Martin. Towards the close of 1978 they played the lead roles in the Paris Theatre Company play Visions. Martin's black and red poster wrapped their faces in a fiery heart with the words Paris and Visions ablaze, like Fitzpatrick's lips.

Martin also did a poster for another play starring John Gaden, Patrick White's play Signal Driver. He sketched a bit too as he always did, in his address book, on scraps of paper or whatever was around.

As well as the marathon, Martin also had ideas for a more intimate Tiny Tim show, which – of course – required an accompanying poster. His Song of Songs Tiny Tim face seemed perfect to replicate, so he re-sketched that. And the Kirk Gallery in Cleveland Street Sydney seemed an ideal venue, providing an opportunity to work with old friends.

Just like the old days – an Ellis D Fogg (Roger Foley) light show!

With the Kirk Concert pencilled in, Martin sketched a new poster, and drafted the words: Martin Sharp and Roger Foley's Magic Theatre proudly present Ellis D Fogg's 10th Anniversary Laser Show starring The Eternal Troubadour Tiny Tim and Dream Theatre of Song at the Kirk 422 Cleveland. (1) Alas, the Australian tour management had another booking for Tiny that night. The Kirk was cancelled.

Roger shrugs it off, 'Tiny couldn't be in Sydney for it. Can't remember why. We were all very disappointed'. (2)

Ellis D Fogg was used to putting on shows. That's what Albie, Seb and he did in the Yellow House. Martin took charge of the walls while they directed the stage. Martin never directed anything. Now, with everything under his baton, Martin was painfully aware that he was moving into areas in which he had little or no experience. Of this Tiny Tim tour Martin confessed, 'He (Tiny) was working with very primitive tools - someone like me who knows nothing about recording!' (3)

How do you organise a recording session?

What does musical copyright mean?

Where do you hire a PA system?

What is the role of a musical director?

Simply finding a venue was tricky enough.

Martin needed all the help he could get and he got it. Melody was his faithful assistant and cousin Russell Sharp set Martin's Street of Dreams

Productions onto a business footing. Russell also assisted Martin with the logistics of producing the LP record that became titled Chameleon.

Said Russell, 'I incorporated Street of Dreams and we also created the Chameleon record covers'. (4)

Plans were constantly changing. The Festival of Sydney became involved: A Century of Song in One Smash Hit - 50-minutes of non-stop singing was to be staged at Sydney Opera House. But the Festival of Sydney didn't pick up the option, so that was on-then-off too.

The Song of Songs picture changed with every new twist, and there were many. Words changed, the image of the venue changed. 'I was changing it from the Opera House to one of the theatres,' said Martin. 'Eventually we settled on Luna Park.' (5) (Later, Luna Park would become the Moon.)

The Regent? The State? Paddo Town Hall? These venues were all considered and others too. Luna Park surfaced as the best idea. It made sense. Tim, Garry, Kingo, Jonny, Cressida, Michael Ramsden, Lee Hobbs, all worked there. The artists knew the administration and they were friends with Leon and Margaret Fink.

Richard Liney had spent his past two years restoring the Floating Palais, a 1935 concrete barge surmounted with an elegant timber pavilion. Martin saw its potential, 'We were trying to get all sorts of different venues. I'd been working at Luna Park and Richard Liney had just restored the Palais beautifully, so the venue was probably at its tiptop best and we hired it.' (6)

'I always had the desire to bring Tiny and Luna Park together. I thought my role in it was to give him a bigger setting and to give the opportunity for him to do what he most wanted to do. I was trusting him absolutely, artistically.' (7)

Martin's assistant Melody was extremely versatile. She needed to be! One day she might be sewing costumes - the next, placing business calls. Lots of others helped too – some were paid, others simply willing hands – like, Richard Wherrett from the Nimrod, Ted Robinson from Clowning

Calaveras plus a production crew, film crew, musicians, hired hands and many more. Especially Nathan Waks.

Jeannie had known Nathan since 1970, when (aged 19) he was Principal Cellist in the Sydney Symphony Orchestra. It was she who introduced Martin to Nathan after one of her shows. (8) In 1978, Nathan was Founding Director and Artistic Adviser to the Australian Chamber Orchestra and best known for his performances with the popular Sydney String Quartet. So we can safely assume that Martin wasn't just being modest when he gave all credit to Nathan for Martin's Tiny Tim shows and recordings.

Meanwhile, Street of Dreams Productions, operating from Wirian, had to cater for everything right down to mundane stuff like the ticketing and booking recording sessions… none of which could go ahead unless the contractual agreements with Tiny's management went smoothly.

They did.

On 4 December 1978, Tiny and his management signed an agreement with Martin's Street of Dreams Productions for Tiny to act (playing himself) in a movie produced by Martin. The film was to be 'a portrait of Tiny' set around a marathon-medley.

Tiny was still keen on a Musical History Tour. Describing his concept of how the marathon should be, Tiny told Martin, 'I would like to put on a non-stop continuous dance singalong medley. Firstly you would have old numbers like Babyface and Four Leaf Clover and then complete Rock songs from the late-40s - of course the Blacks always had it with the Rhythm and Blues - and then up to the White 50s, up to Soul and the 60s, and up to the current time.' Martin taped the discussion.

'This way several things happen: firstly you take what the public liked on stage and put it on record. In fact, the medley has already been proven successful on stage. I find my key thing in the medley are the styles of Harry Richmond, Henry Burr, Bill Murray and the other great artists shown to their best advantage. Secondly, it's never been done before in such a way. Thirdly, it goes on forever, they can dance to it without stopping and they can sing to it. And if this works, then the doors are open because it's no more the Tiptoe image alone!' (9)

Martin was enthused, 'A Marathon - challenge the world! This is the showcase, the backbone of the film. On one level the film is an athletic event - it's also the showcase for talent, singing ability, memory and composition. Tiny had to do the thing off the top of his head and endure! It's a musical tour de force!' (10)

Sydney was just the start. Certain that Tiny would be a sensation, Martin had even bigger plans. He told the Sydney press that the Century of Song marathon concert could pave the way for a lavish production at New York's Madison Square Garden! (11)

Comes a time for everyone to relax. From the handily located Cosmopolitan Double Bay hotel where he was staying, Tiny made frequent visits to Wirian where he sat around the kitchen table, strummed his uke, sang, talked, preached, didn't eat in public, fixated on 'Miss Ingrid' and engaged Richard, Albert and anyone who came through the door in fervent discussions.

Melody's friend - William Yang (who had arrived from Queensland) - photographed Tiny. Les Bean was there. Les – formerly known as Angel Lust - had shifted her devotion from the band Devo to Tiny Tim. Michael Barker was there too. He was a photography student doing an assignment about Martin. And Adrian Rawlins assumed the role of compère. 'Tiny's favourite announcer internationally,' explained Martin, who kept the tape recorder running throughout all this and had a film crew in the room while this was all going on, 'which didn't really come out', he said. (12).

With the show definitely on the road, Martin reworked his Ellis D Fogg/Kirk Gallery image into a new poster, more like a handbill - the b/w World Non-Stop Singing Record - Tiny Tim and the Time Machine, Song of Songs – Eternity. Staged to celebrate the centenary of Thomas Alva Edison's invention of the phonograph, the venue was not named on the handbill because it was printed before that was confirmed. (13)

Then they all got even busier. Les Bean sourced some interesting fabric, which Melody sewed into costumes. Melody said, 'I made costumes for him. The Blue Bird of Happiness Suit, the Mickey Mouse costume and ears, the white satin Pierrot. We worked pretty full-on for Mart on Street of Dreams and the World Non-Stop Singing Record. Printing posters and t-shirts, making props, painting sets. Doing make-up and hair for Tiny (an ordeal I will never forget, getting all Tiny's hair under a Mickey Mouse cap...!) (14)

Nathan called in. He was formally introduced as Tiny's musical director. Tiny established rapport with Nathan and got on particularly well with pianist Marvin Lewis, whose repertoire favoured old time tunes. Stand up and sing for your father an old time tune…! Tiny and Marvin became a type of duo within the seven-piece band comprising Dave Ellis (bass), Dave Donovan (guitar), Tony Ansell (keyboards), Geoff Oakes (sax), John Harding (violin), Doug Gallagher (drums) Marvin and Nathan.

A rehearsal was held at the Floating Palais. Martin described, 'We went down to the Palais to have a rehearsal. Tiny did songs like Lonely Troubadour, San Francisco and a few other songs that weren't in the marathon. He said, "You can do all the rehearsing in the world but if it's not right on the night if there's a spirit of negativity there!" So he was not one to rehearse.' (15)

In mid-December Tiny played the Nimrod Theatre to a packed house. (16) He performed against Martin's set for the previous show, Kold Komfort Kaffee, which had not yet been changed over to a pre-World War 1 set for a play about comedian Stan Laurel's relationship with an Australian singer and dancer.

Martin described Kold Komfort Kaffee as perfect for Tiny. Regrettably, he was not permitted to film the show. 'It was a terrific concert,' Martin said, 'My father was there with Dorothy, his wife'. (17)

Nathan booked EMI Studio 301, the best studio in Sydney, for the second week in January 1979. He also added Peter Haslem (trombone), Eric 'Boof' Thompson (trumpet), Mike Kenny (electric piano) and esteemed actor, David Gulpilil (didgeridoo and click sticks) to the forenamed musicians. Martin was credited as the producer.

Alistair (Al) Jones from the Slim Dusty Band was also present in the studio 'nimbly advising' – as Martin penned on the record credits. Of his own role, Martin explained, 'Nothing made me feel qualified to produce. Tiny said, "You can be my record producer". I said, "I can't produce records!" but he said – I've got it on tape somewhere – "You know enough about my music and I reckon you can". So he just appointed me.' (18)

'The Chameleon sessions was Tiny and Nathan Waks, and me being an absolute fan and saying, "Go for it!" and I probably suggested a few of the songs. He was very happy to do them. I just tried to serve, assisting the artists to do their best.' (19)

Martin described the session as starting with 'about 15 takes' to 'break the musicians in'. He said, 'there's probably some struggle that goes on between performer and musician - they've got to feel each other out.' The first song, Brother Can You Spare A Dime? was recorded in two takes. 'I think it's great', said Martin, 'although Tiny said he liked the Crosby version better'.

The Great Pretender was shaping up as the name of the album until William Yang's louche cover photograph of Tiny begged the title Chameleon.

The inclusion of the Great Pretender track was actually one of Martin's suggestions. Meekly he said, 'I think I actually suggested Tiny sing The Great Pretender. Sometimes if you suggest them, he'll do one. But he really knows what he wants. I just catch it and get it down as well as I can - for the world, I guess.'

Other songs recorded for the album were: Street of Dreams, Tipperary, Deep Night, The Song Without a Name, The Hukilau, My Song, My Way, Staying Alive, St Louis Blues, Dancing in the Street and the Mickey Mouse Club March - which should have been released as a single. 'Tiny said that too,' said Martin, 'It should have been!' (20) (St Louis Blues and Dancing in the Street remained unreleased until 2006.)

The song Country Queen also appeared on Chameleon, a track that was previously recorded and Martin acquired the rights. Martin explained, 'Country Queen was recorded in Nashville on the day that Elvis Presley died. I think it got out as a 45 and hadn't done anything on True Records. Tiny gave us the tapes to use on the album. That song is the only one we didn't record, so it's not us.

'They were spontaneous recordings. There were no arrangements written. Nathan really produced that record. I was the financial producer and getting the people together. So it was a pretty ad lib situation and not the sort of circumstances I would really like to put Tiny in. I think Tiny should have the best equipment at his command and any musician he wants. He speaks through his songs. That's his highest form of communication'. (21)

The following week Tiny returned to the studio with Marvin Lewis on piano and they recorded the 11 tracks that make up the piano-based Wonderful World of Romance album. They recorded an 'unplugged' style album 'direct to disc' with Marvin and Tiny having a jolly good time together, running through old time favourites - She's a New Kind of Old-Fashioned Girl, songs like that. This record was pressed, inserted in a plain white cover and mostly given away to friends. (22)

Chameleon had a more commercial motive. Martin pressed 800 and called it 'an audition record'. But it was much better than that. It certainly ranks among Tiny's best.

One stage show, two LP records and shooting film made for a huge fortnight. As if that was not demanding enough, the marathon was booked for the Floating Palais, 12 January 1979.

But first, Training Camp.

Martin announced the Non-Stop Singing Marathon as an athletic event on par with Japanese wrestler Inoki and boxer Muhammad Ali. Wirian became Training Camp Central. The walls of the room (later known as the Film Editing Room) were tricked up with the yellow curls of Vincent van Gogh's Starry Starry Night sky and Tiny made himself available to the press. Transsexual, Miss Natasha turned up too, all of which was successfully filmed.

Said Martin, 'We had a training camp for him right here on the balcony. Tiny was singing songs, playing ping-pong with his ukulele and it was billed as the World Professional Non-Stop Singing Record Training Camp. We got some good film of that. And then we had a press conference here in the house. Various people asked questions about him and his ideas. He called the marathon an athletic justification.'

'Have you been training this morning?' asked one journalist.

'No,' Tiny replied, 'I've been training for the last eight years!' (23)

Evening came, Tiny returned to his hotel, Martin cleaned the house and prepared for the marathon the following day where he and Tiny crossed the harbour by boat - all filmed. Said Martin, 'The Nimrod provided a boat for us, so there was a good esprit de corps I think.'

Martin described what happened next, 'Dressing room, tune up, the band's there. The crowd starts drifting in – not a lot of people at first but it starts to build up. We had a special costume for Tiny.

'Before the show he ordered a big box of mangoes. He'd always give me anything that was left over so I thought, "I'll get a few mangoes from this" - but he'd eaten them. That was his secret ingredient I think, to give him strength to do the show, he'd eaten this whole box of mangoes!' (24)

The band had arrived, the same line-up as for the Chameleon sessions. Tim Lewis and Richard Liney helped with stage sets. (25) Film crews set up in three vantage points, so nothing was lost if one should stall. Hayden Keenan and George Gittoes were geared for action. Sydney Morning Herald photographer Robert Macfarlane was camera-ready for tomorrow's papers. Roger assisted with lights. Leon Fink was discreetly overseeing. Garry and Ted Markstein watched all this from John Firth-Smith's boat in the harbour. (Ted was about to start a couple of months helping Garry, painting at the Park.) (26)

Tiny splashed a puff of face powder on his cheeks and John McDonald, the ringmaster from Ringling Brothers Circus walked to the mike and announced the opening act - Jeannie Lewis!

After two years out of the country, Jeannie was surprised to come home to a request from Martin. She said, 'I'd only just got back and they had the Non-Stop Singing Record. Martin asked me to come and sing at Luna Park dressed as Pierrette! (Melody may have made that.)' (27)

Martin proudly announced, 'Jeannie Lewis opened the show. She sang some beautiful songs, The Artist's Life, King Kong and one other song. She was dressed as a Pierrette.' (28)

Jeannie was followed by Adrian Rawlins, 'Ladies and gentlemen, guys and gals, welcome to the setting of the world non-stop professional singing record. Would you welcome to the stage America's Ambassador of Song, the Eternal Troubadour, the Human Lyrebird, the Superman of Song, MR TINY TIM!' (29)

Dressed in his comic strip suit, Tiny emerged stage-left, blowing kisses, carrying his shopping bag and trying not to trip over the leads on the way to the microphone.

Said Martin, 'He started off with the first song ever written for the phonograph - My name is Mr Phonograph, I'm not so very old, my father's name is Edison and I'm worth my weight in gold. A great start then he just launched off into this non-stop marathon. Often I had the feeling he was trying to lose the hounds that were after him. The musicians were the hounds trying to catch the fox. He was trying to shake them off. He'd try to find songs they didn't know.

'He knew his material of course and Marvin Lewis knew his material very well. Tiny would sing in blocks of songs. He'd construct this marathon out of these various blocks.' (30)

Jeannie, who joined the audience after performing her set, was astounded. She described what she saw, 'I looked up and there was this band of amazing musicians, some I'd worked with. Amazing musicians! I thought – only they would be able to follow Tiny! I mean, for Nathan who had to produce it! I don't know how he did it because Tiny would just drop bars, go into the next bit and do something else…! I just don't know how they followed him – but anyway, they did! He'd drop bars everywhere - he'd be going into the next song - but they were with him.' (31)

Red shirt, red lights, red hair, red stage. Red was the dominant colour of the comic strip suit, the colour of much of the Palais' sets and décor, and as if that wasn't all red enough, there was a filter on the lights, making Tiny's mop of normally burgundy-dyed hair positively glow.

Without a pause Tiny launched into the up-tempo Goody Goody. Some began to dance but before they could settle into the song it switched to It's A Good Day then Don't Sit Under The Apple Tree (With Anyone Else But Me). The pace slowed, Shine On Harvest Moon. Pennies From Heaven. Faster - Coming In On A Wing And A Prayer, Don't Fence Me In followed by the first song of the night where Tiny used his famous falsetto - Cool Water.

Swanee, For Me And My Gal, I Want A Girl Like The Girl That Married Dear Old Dad then a few songs which seem to relate to his estranged wife Miss Vicki – I Wonder Who's Kissing Her Now, After The Ball and Just One More Chance. Strong audience response, many waltzed, leading to Just A Gigolo, which Tiny sang in firm – not fey - voice. The pace quickened, Accentuate The Positives, followed by The Chattanooga Choo Choo a real tongue twister, which Tiny sang real fast. Everyone got on the dance floor for It's Gonna Be A Great Day.

Through all of this, Tiny never missed a lyric, never played his uke and rarely used the high voice. One minute the audience was swaying, next dancing. They came to a standstill for Mame, an Al Jolson song they might have heard their Grandma sing.

Praise The Lord And Pass The Ammunition, Give Me That Ole Time Religion, Bad Moon Rising, Blue Suede Shoes, I Don't Want To Set The World On Fire. Tiny was peaking.

He slowed the mood for the swaying rhythm of He's Got The Whole World In His Hands during which a bell was heard at the two hour mark.

The audience went wild, Tiny blew kisses and squeezed 'thank you, thank you' between phrases of the song.

'I rang the bell,' said Martin. 'The line was, "Every time I look at the holy book I want to tremble, when I read about where the carpenter clears the temple, but the buyers and the sellers..." - and that's where the bell went - are no different fellas to what you and I profess to be'. A fantastic moment, his artistic endeavour and his religious faith coinciding.' (32)

Michael Row The Boat Ashore came next. Tiny was clear of the two-hour mark. He had achieved what he set out to do and the record was set. Huge applause.

Singing from an interminably long lyric sheet Tiny chose as his encore a power rendition of Staying Alive – an endurance test in itself – 'stayin' alive! stayin' alive...!' The audience of 300 were partying hard, cheering, clapping.

After two hours, 15 minutes and seven seconds Tiny stepped back from the mic, which passed to Adrian Rawlins who proclaimed, 'I think we've witnessed a historic event – the new World Heavyweight Singing Champion, the one and only – Tiny Tim!'

'Thank you, thank you,' responded Tiny, leaving the stage. 'And God bless you all.' (33)

'We filmed it of course,' said Martin. 'Hayden Keenan helped with sound. Martha was helping with the camera. George Gittoes shooting through a prism up the front. Russell Boyd was shooting one of the cameras. Mike Edols was doing another and Tom Cowan too. Wonderful cinematographers – masters. To get the whole show down on three cameras is very different to video. The cueing system was designed by Bill Hicks. So the whole show was captured. Elizabeth Knight was working on the film. She was a great help. She'd been in the Paris Theatre Company. She was the producer really for that concert.' (34)

After the marathon, Tiny chatted to Victoria Cobden backstage then came out to do some more filming dressed in the Pierrot made by Melody.

Martin said 'The crowd had left. It was really just the film crew there and a few other people who were hanging around. We were all very happy with the concert and the filming. The night was a great success. Tiny came back dressed as Pierrot and sang Lonely Troubadour. It was a very touching song. He was very inspired by Miss Ingrid at the time. She was right up the back of the Floating Ballroom and he was singing Lonely Troubadour to her.' (35)

After Tiny, the band and everyone else had packed up and gone, Roger and his assistant needed to double-back to pick up the lights.

With an eerie resemblance to the Sentimental Bloke character that Martin appropriated for his Land of Sweeping Plains cartoon, Roger watched Martin sweeping the dance floor all by himself – he was the last to leave.

Martin was so happy that he didn't want the night to ever end. (36)

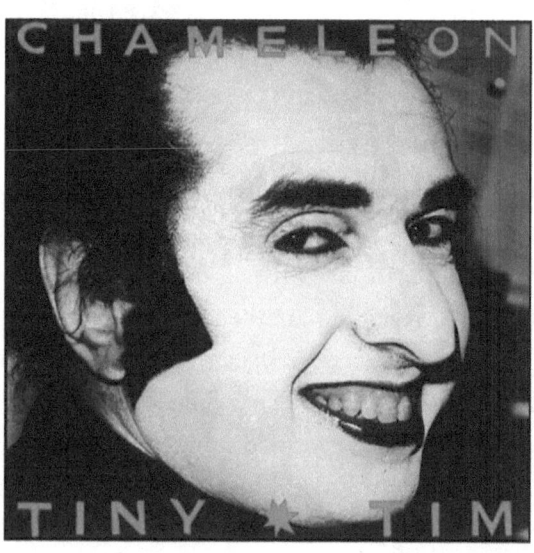

18.

REVENGE OF THE CLOWNING CALAVERAS

The piece Martin did as the Clowning Calaveras backdrop is his interpretation of that life/death mask. He had done a small painting of that to go on the back cover of the Tears of Steel LP. Martin tore it into pieces because he said, 'Jeannie, the death side is too strong'.

JEANNIE LEWIS

Melody Cooper and Steven Teather lived at Wirian now. William Yang had moved in and Martin was on the edge of selling the place. He was hiring out Wirian as a film set. For example, some indoor scenes for Fatty Finn were shot in Wirian.

Film companies negotiated with Albert, not Martin. He only chimed in to enquire about how to proceed with his own film, which was being worked on only a room away from where they were filming. (1)

Martin invited lots of film people to check out his footage of the Non-Stop Singing Marathon, but they all had different opinions - Haydn Keenan, Chris Cordeaux, David Lowrie, Marilyn Karet, Michael Norton.

Since glory days of painting the Face of Luna Park, Premier Wran still refused to sign that bloody lease and the artists' morale was at a trickle. The week-by-week tenancy meant the artists didn't know whether they'd even be back next week and management certainly didn't have the confidence to make an investment in – safety, for example.

Kingo had already forcefully expressed himself, Garry too. Martin was constantly writing to Leon Fink, Nathan Spatt and Nathan's son Maurice (now manager). The Big Dipper was their main concern.

And then came a blast from the past. Martin said, 'I was on the edge of selling Wirian when Dr Pepper, a mad disc jockey and singer from Melbourne came up and gave me a trip and took me to Luna Park. I hadn't had a trip for 10 years and suddenly we decided to take the ferry to Luna Park.'

Dr Pepper goes back to Yellow House days. David Pepperall started Australia's first import Rock record shop and had been a musician, bookseller, record retailer and writer for Daily Planet, Go-Set, Nation Review, Rolling Stone, Digger and Juke. That night, he took back Martin to Luna Park.

At the Circular Quay turnstile Martin and the Doctor were greeted by two enormous people, a man and a woman, 'weighing 25 stone each!' Astonished, Martin said, 'You're going to Luna Park and Lizzie and Larry Luna sell you the ticket. You're in the Magic Theatre. These weren't hallucinations, they were genuine.'

In his pocket Martin was carrying a cassette recorder with a Tiny Tim tape inside. He continued, 'I've got Tiny Tim on a cassette and I'm trying to take it over to Luna Park. This is to meld Tiny and the place together so that I can make the film there. And they said, "You'd better leave Tiny with us (or your recorder) because you don't know what's it's like over there tonight". It was a matter of trust, they were the Guardians at the Gate. I said, "Ok I'll leave it with you, I'll pick it up on the way back - you listen to it!". They said, "Ok" so that felt right because I could tell that they knew somehow that we were on a voyage of seeking reality there. We rode across on the ferry.

'Walking down the mid-way in the Park I saw monsters, werewolves, Draculas and vampires. They were people who'd bought masks that go right over their heads. Thirteen dollars they were selling for. Thirteen. These people were walking through the Park that never had this heavy degree of image. I thought, "The place is being taken over by monsters!" It always had a more fun imagery.

'Where are they all coming from - these monsters? All sorts of terrible things like skeleton horses, grotesques, plastic shit and the terrible end of Psychedelic Art. I tracked this bad vibe to this Magic Shop, painted black. I knew one of the nicest girls who used to work at that shop. I was surprised - I expected to see some witch selling this stuff!

'Anyway the night went on. We went for three rides around the River Caves, just kept rowing. It was amazing, just like a Buddhist shrine. I don't know if we went on the Ghost Train, I can't remember.' (2)

UNESCO had proclaimed 1979 as the International Year of the Child. It was said to be the brainchild of Canon Joseph Moermann, Secretary-General of the International Catholic Child Bureau in Geneva - but Martin disputed that. He reckoned it was the concept of a Sydney woman. That's what Canon James Whild told him when they discussed the matter. Martin said, 'I think it was a warning - the Year of the Child. I could have been making more of a fuss. I was not being as critical as I should have, because I wanted to make the film.' (3)

Martin was also clipping cartoons that he felt related to Luna Park. One, signed Tenat TTO had a pregnant Neville Wran with the Harbour Bridge, the Opera House, Luna Casino in the background and a harbour full of sharks. Also a Jenny Coopes cartoon, 'Mr and Mrs Sin go to Luna Park'. Another, located in hell, which wasn't consciously meant to be Luna Park – but it is, if you choose to see it that way - the words above the portal read: Abandon Hope All Ye Who Enter Here. (4)

Eerily, what Martin, Kingo and the others feared most - and virtually predicted - happened. 'On 16 April 1979, 13 people were injured on the Big Dipper when a steel runner came loose and halted a Dipper carriage,' reported Sam Marshall, author of Luna Park Just for Fun, 'The following carriage rammed into the rear, injuring its occupants. A warning had been served.' (5)

'It was the first time the Big Dipper had a smash,' said Martin, 'A lot of the old people then tried to shut down the place because they knew this was it. They knew it was a real warning. They were in touch with the place, the Carneys. Only when they feel safe enough will Carnies settle in a spot and build there instead of moving on. The funfair is a carnival that's settled down. But no, the Park stayed open.

'Tiny was like the Angel Gabriel marking the turf. Coming up to the two hours he starts going into, "Every time I look into the Holy Book it makes me tremble…!" The big statement that he made is "…the money-changers in the Temple." And Luna Park was the Temple in this instance, a holy place but a funfair at the same time. The Big Dipper happened, they didn't do anything. Once the Big Dipper smashed and they didn't close it down, you'd then say that they became culpable.

'As an artist I can occasionally remember the images leading up. There was an intention towards doing up the Ghost Train. There was meant to be a new Ghost Train done by Bruce Petty. Then the struggle for the real estate became so intense.

'Everything was done on the cheap. They had the oldest fire extinguisher, the oldest fire sprinklers. It was meant to look like a funfair, but not meant to succeed like a funfair. That was the whole business principle behind it. So they could say, We can't run a funfair. We've tried hard for five years. We've put everything into it. Were running at a loss. We're honourable. We want to put up our casino on the spot! The Big Dipper smash was a warning. I'm not particularly blaming anyone for it. They kept refusing to give Leon the lease.' (6)

Thursday 7 June, Martin received the first cut of the film. After looking at it Martin said, 'the whole film had a pretty weird feel to it'. (7)

Next day Australian Playboy published a Gahan Wilson cartoon with a face just like Luna Park and two kids asking, 'How come there's no exit?'

This cartoon was drawn from America. (8)

On Saturday 9 June Garry was working on the Carousel until nightfall. He said, 'I happened to walk through the Ghost Train (it was about

5.00 before I went home) and I was amazed how much rubbish there was – stuff thrown out, paper, crap, and I thought, Jeez this is dangerous!' (9)

The evening was calm and warm. The moon was touching full. Around 8.00 Martin walked into the editing room and switched on the Moviola. The screen was frozen on an image of Tiny pointing straight at the viewer and looking severe. Martin wondered what it meant?

'It means I've got to edit the film myself,' he concluded. 'The Moviola can be on every day and you don't take notice of the picture. I interpreted it as, You've got to edit the film yourself which was all I could think of - because I was worried about other people cutting it wrong.' (10)

Then it happened.

Sam Marshall writes, 'On Cracker Night, 9 June 1979, no trains were running due to a rail strike. The Big Dipper was still being repaired. The Ghost Train was the only train operating in Sydney that night. A minimum of three attendants were usually needed to operate the Ghost Train – an operator, a ticket collector and a third person who patrolled the interior for any mischief. On this night, there were only two staff, leaving the interior unpatrolled and vulnerable. What was not supposed to happen happened. A fire broke out and quickly spread in the timber building with its bitumen-covered roof. There were no sprinklers and water pressure was low.' (11)

Martin was in the editing room, cutting Tiny in his Pierrot costume into the film. 'Tiny drew my attention to the fact that something amazing was going on,' said Martin. (12)

'I was anxious when I picked up the film splicer for the first time. I struggled to splice the two pieces of film together. I made one join then the next seemed to spring out of my hands, uncoiling into a perplexity tangle. I made the first cut about the time Luna Park was going up in flames. The phone rang. I left the Moviola with the half completed edit and ran to the next room.' (13)

It was Arkie Whiteley, she said, 'Luna Park's on fire!' Arkie was looking out the window from their place at Lavender Bay with Luna Park directly in front of her. Martin wasn't quick to understand because Arkie's voiceprint sounded like a friend - Mandy Wright.

Mandy Wright.

Said Martin, 'The doorbell rang - it was Mandy and Peter Wright. "We've just come from the Whiteley's and we thought we'd call in". (That's how Arkie picked up her voiceprint.)'

Martin replied, 'Arkie just rang. Luna Park's on fire.'

Peter said, 'We've just left Lavender Bay, it looked like fire. I said to Mandy I've never seen the Park look so bright. The lights were blazing like a huge surge of power going through the place!'

Martin freaked, 'I've got to go over!'

He sped there, thinking through the problems they'd had with management and letters he'd never sent. Martin had mixed feelings at first, 'Initially I thought the fire might be a good thing'.

He felt the fire might be enough to get the park back onto a safer and more artistic footing.

Martin said, 'As I arrived out of the tunnel onto the Cahill Expressway the impact was immediate. The whole centre of the Park seemed to be an inferno with flames gushing into the still sky. I thought, The whole place is going up! (14)

'The whole sky was orange, like a huge bush fire surging out of the middle of Luna Park. You could see it as soon as you got anywhere near the Bridge.' (15)

'By the time I'd reached the Park, through the crowds and blocked traffic, the fire had subsided considerably and the damage was not as vast as the flames had indicated. The superstructure of the Big Dipper was still burning and then the fire was just smouldering. I worked my way round to the entrance.' (16)

Walking into the Park, Martin ran into the leader of the Muktananda crowd, 'Quite a powerful figure, he reminds me of a Crowleyish sort of figure. I'd met him a few times before. He was the first person I knew when I got there. And a beautiful girl called Willow - Tiptoe by the willow tree. When I first met her, I gave her a possum. She was on the merry-go-round at Luna Park. Then I went over to her place and he arrived. It was kinda like a competition. He talked about his film and I talked about mine. He won her and became her boyfriend. The next time I see him it's at the fire at Luna Park! (17)

'It appeared no one was hurt,' Martin continued, 'I sighed with relief, at least this will get some action and prise the dead hand of the management off the place, I thought. Some of the Park may have been lost, but the ludicrous conflict between management and the Premier would be brought into the open and the Park would be saved.

'It was a fire in the Ghost Train. They got everyone out. I saw a gap in the crowd around the gate and pushed through - the security guard's back was turned - I got past him, stepping over fire hoses, drawn onwards. "Hey you! Where are you going?" I hesitated and turned back, "I work here" (Why didn't I have my badge!) "No one's allowed in mate – outside!" I felt if anyone was allowed in, it should be me. I joined the crowd outside the gate, found my way to the car and went home.' (18)

Back at Wirian, Martin rang Kingo who was at Palm Beach. Kingo didn't believe what Martin was telling him. So Martin rang Richard. Martin and he returned to the Park. As they drove, the announcement came over the radio - four dead in the Luna Park Ghost Train blaze... more bodies expected.

'It's over,' Martin said to Richard, 'That's the end. All our dreams for Luna Park had gone up in the Ghost Train blaze!'

Said Martin, 'Richard and I stood outside the entrance and talked with some reporters who had come late to the scene. We saw Maurice Spatt, the new manager being interviewed. We should have gone over and spoken with him but we both hung back. We went home. It was impossible to sleep. We listened to the grim reports on the news and I played Jeannie Lewis' record Clowning Calaveras.' (19)

Said Martin, 'This is all prophecy about Luna Park!' (20)

'It was Jeannie as an artist singing - but it was also Luna Park. No one else could have made that connection. I was involved in both Luna Park and Jeannie Lewis. This concert was three years before the fire. Clowning Calaveras is based on the Festival of the Dead in Mexico where they make death sweets, skulls made of sugar and they dress up in masks. It's like a Ghost Train Festival, if you like. And Jeannie wanted it to be like the Ghost Train, with that sort of imagery. That was the sort of imagery I related to anyway, it was Pop Art.

'There was a real piece of the Ghost Train on the stage – paper skulls, luminous skeletons all around the walls. The image she wanted me to create which I did for the show (but I couldn't do it for her record cover) was that double-faced life/death heart-shaped Abraxas - skull on one side and a loving face on the other. The two came together with two huge sliding walls.'

Horrified by news broadcasts and shocked by what he had witnessed, Martin played the first track,

Glitter and be gay, that's the part I play, forced to bend my soul, to a sordid role...

He explained, 'Luna Park has been a pawn in a political game.

Rising Of The Tide is the second track:

Where does it lead to this madness
  the waste of time - pace of time ahead...
Full moon keeps rising on the city,
  The sun it keeps moving on the other side,
  Am I to rule for quite a while longer,
  Before we see the rising of the tide...
(Martin: 'The icecaps are melting the tide is rushing in...!')
The law that rules the land is getting harder.
No one seems to know just how it started...
'...like the fire.'
Once again a child had to be the victim...

'...the kids in the fire.'

These songs followed by The Crucifixion, written by Phil Ochs - the late great American singer-songwriter who hanged himself in 1976. Martin said, 'Before Jeannie recorded the song there was just his version of it. I knew it related but I didn't know how.

'When I played it on the night of the Ghost Train fire, after having been to Luna Park, suddenly I understood the song. I knew the lyrics had meaning because of exactly what we'd just seen. It's got very specific lines about fire, sacrifice of children, it's also about Christ. It all came through so strongly. I think I was weeping in horror and amazement.

'The next day I found out that the man who'd been killed in the fire was named John Godson – God Son - so the song called The Crucifixion was about the death of the Son of God. Suddenly it went bang!' (21)

The TV news was terrible. The charred rumble revealed the bodies of six children and one adult: John Godson and his sons Damian and Craig and Waverley College students Jonathon Billings, Richard Carroll, Michael Johnson and Seamus Rahilly.

'That's another image that bears thinking on, the image of John Godson with his two children, one on each side. The other boys were like the four Apostles - four boys from Waverley College - who'd come from Mass. And then you found out that the Public Relations guy who worked at Luna Park at the time had been the Priest. He actually said, "I knew those boys, I baptised them". He left the Priesthood. So they're strangely following him.' (22)

Martin played The Moon's A Harsh Mistress. There was a big moon on the night of the fire. Kingo had already picked the essence of the song. Before the fire, Martin received a note from Kingo saying, 'Play The Moon's A Harsh Mistress to Leon Fink!'

'The moon's a harsh mistress, the moon can be so cold' said Martin. 'Our dreams about the park and the vision we could see for it. There was such goodwill there - a treasure of the past. So that song we related to'. (23)

'For anyone who's young death is particularly mysterious - in a way that's the point of it. It is sacrifice - showing that we walk on thin rails and outside is the hurricane of destruction. It's the place of Golgotha, the place of the skull - the Ghost Train - you get a Pop-Art parallel. And then you get these whole events that are caused by plotting, not caring for kids, carelessness, living a human life, the way of the world. It was the Year of the Child.

'When Tim and I were researching the history of the face, I read this legend. The earliest ones we could pick up were at Borobudur, the temple in Bali, a Buddhist temple that has Hindu images guarding it. You enter through this mouth-like doorway. We found out it was the Face of Glory.

'An earthly King wanted Krishna's wife – God's wife or whatever - and he sent the heaviest guy that he had - called the Seizer to seize things. The Seizer goes along to Krishna and announces that the other fellow wanted his wife and Krishna creates this creature to opposes the Seizer. (I get characters like Neville Wran - because Neville Wran is an atheist) - and the Seizer threatens Krishna. So Krishna creates a beast, which is Hunger Incarnate. The Seizer sees that he is about to be devoured by this creature and he pleads for mercy and - being the way of gods - Krishna grants mercy.

'But he's created Hunger Incarnate which wants to devour. It pleads for mercy to satisfy its hunger. Krishna - with a stroke of genius - says, "Eat yourself". And it starts from the tail and eats everything up to the face and Krishna says, "For this act of sacrifice you shall forever be known as the Face of Glory and shall guard my Temple".

'In Borobudur the image is the Face of Glory, which is like the Luna Park face even in expression, guarding the Buddha. You see, inside Luna Park there was a real Buddha, a real effigy of the Buddha in marble and gold leaf, surrounded by this court, which is like the Endless River. I see it as a conquest of Buddha by dark forces. The Face has always had an unconscious manifestation - being the Face of Sydney - the largest face visible in the city. Also it's a Horned God. Through the two towers, it has a Satanic element in its look. Like Abraxas – comedy/tragedy.

'One line that freaked my mother out – "Abraxas is - the mother's love for the son is the son's horror of the mother". Unreal reality. Illusion becoming reality, the beauty of a lion the instant it strikes down its victim, the saint and betrayer, the curse of God - of good and evil. Beyond the comprehension of man. If you do try to understand it, it drives you mad. Fear of it is wisdom.

'Luna Park was in the city of Sydney, in fact an unconscious presence that sat on the Endless River. The River Caves went round and round and you flowed down the river eventually past the Buddha. He hadn't been picked consciously for that reason. It was unconscious or naïve art, a folk art gesture of truth. But in the actual image-reality, there was Buddha, and in a strange way, worshipped by unknowing people.

'So unconsciously, it was most probably the most important Buddhist shrine in Australia as far as its set-up was concerned. That was replaced with an act of horror and chaos, dark forces manifested. Does that apply to the world? I think it does. He came in fire you see, "I come in fire".

'It happened where man poked fun at death, the Ghost Train, (you went in and came out alive). So where the fire started, the imitation fire turns into a real fire - with the help of someone pouring petrol and a match on it or it happens in its own right. So it was certainly ready to catch fire. But I do feel that it was helped by characters who were caught up in the whole suction of the event. Sydney was on tenderhooks, as Sydney gets when there's a train strike. People are meeting a whole lot of new people at bus stops, hitching and a whole different thing happens.

'The only train running that day in Sydney was the Ghost Train. It's terrible because it's true. It is hard to get onto, something of another world, but it's crucial to our world to understand it. The whole concept of the Ghost Train is to confuse you. Unpredictable, tricks, illusion. The people going through the Ghost Train saw what had been an imitation fire. So people accepted the beginnings of the fire as an illusion - part of the ride.

'They get burned where man mocks death, in the year dedicated to children. It was a message to Sydney and I think it's made me stronger as a Christian but I'm still pretty bad. I still wouldn't even classify myself as being one - even having so much information. Tiny has always steered me in that direction but also the events at Luna Park.

'I could understand them a bit and then suddenly to just become clear - that there was a poetic language working to say "this is a crucifixion, Golgotha, death by fire". I think all these things are the archetype manifesting itself that was realised in Christ. It doesn't cut out the Egyptian gods that preceded it, it's just the wave that broke eventually on the beach.

'The archetypes are all present in this, the sacrifice of the seven, also Pentecost, the pouring out of the Spirit. It had the dark side but what was revealed by the deaths was the light side. Abraxas if you like. The dark face and the light face. What appeared to be horrendous and chaotic had its beauty, which would sustain the parents at least - especially the Christians.

'Abraxas - God and the Devil in their counterpoint. Darkness/Light. The tide going in and out at the same time. Terrible Abraxas. To look upon Abraxas is blindness. To know it is sickness. To worship it is death. To fear it is wisdom. To assist it not is redemption. I don't know what it means. I've never been able to work that out. It's not for man to know Abraxas. When you're locked up in it, I suppose it destroys you. Abraxas is the Sun, but at the same time the terrible sucking gorge or the void.' (24)

Kingo summed it up, 'Martin never stopped feeling guilty about the Ghost Train fire'. (25)

'I couldn't cope with it,' said Martin, 'the passions of romance and things that make it a hand-to-hand situation. Desire and spirituality.' (26)

That night Martin created a belief system that would be reflected in all his future works and everything that happened next.

Said Susan Jensen, 'The fire was definitely the crisis point for Martin. All those threads that were coming together over time suddenly merged into a complete picture of spiritual reality.' (27)

Martin pulled out some photographs that Michael Barker had recorded of the Ghost Train ride. Examining one of the pictures he said, 'This would appear to be seven clocks which are related to the seven deaths in the Ghost Train. And then on closer inspection, I realized there was another clock that was hidden by a man who was doing some carpentry. I remember feeling uneasy because I thought, "Oh God, I thought it was seven, now it's someone else".

'There was a further one when the North Sydney Swimming Pool had been emptied. When I looked through to the end of the pool I saw there were eight crosses and behind them was Luna Park. I hoped there'd just be seven'.

Martin now expected an eighth death.

Martin fully expected it to be Kingo or himself. He said, 'Kingo and I were very tense – who's going to go?' (28)

NOTES

CHAPTER 1

(1) Martin Sharp, interview 11 April 1993.

(2) See Wikipedia, 'Spitfire Squadron 453'.

(3) Martin Sharp, interview 3 March 2011.

(4) See Wikipedia, 'Japanese submarines attack on Sydney Harbour'.

(5) Martin Sharp, interview 11 April 1993.

(6) Martin Sharp, interview 19 March 2005.

(7) Martin Sharp, interview 12 February 2011.

(8) Martin Sharp, interview 12 February 2011.

(9) Margaret Olley, Margaret Olley, Far From a Still Life, Meg Stewart, pp. 113-115, 139-140, 151-154, Random House, 2005. Also, Wikipedia, 'Merioola and the Sydney Charm School'.

(10) Martin Sharp, interview 12 February 2011.

(11) Martin Sharp, interview 11 April 1993.

(12) Martin Sharp, interview 23 April 1987.

(13) A Nightingale Sang in Berkeley Square was a hit song for Vera Lynn in 1939. It would become Henry and Jo's 'song' when they were apart. They may have read into the lyrics references to their own courtship – Berkeley Square, Mayfair and a London moon. See also interview with Martin Sharp, 5 April 2011.

(14) Martin Sharp, interview 12 February 2011.

(15) Martin Sharp, interview 11 April 1993.

(16) Martin Sharp, interview 11 April 1993.

(17) Boofhead is a comic strip by Robert Bruce Clarke which first appeared in the Sydney Daily Mirror in May 1941, continuing until 1970. Also Martin Sharp, interview 5 July 1984.

(18) Martin Sharp, interview 16 October 2003.

(19) Martin Sharp, interview 23 April 1987.

(20) Martin Sharp, interview 5 July 1984.
(21) Martin Sharp, interview 16 October 2003.
(22) AC Child, Cranbrook – The First Fifty Years (1918-1968), Waite & Bull, 1968.
(23) Martin Sharp, interview 11 April 1993.
(24) See Wikipedia, 'Blake Prize for Religious Art'.
(25) Martin Sharp, interview 12 February 2011.
(26) Martin Sharp, interview 5 April 2011.
(27) Martin Sharp, interview 12 February 2011.
(28) Martin Sharp, Memories of Telford, a special interest publication, 2002.
(29) Martin Sharp, interview 6 May 2002.
(30) Martin Sharp, interview 1 February 1983.

CHAPTER 2

(1) Martin Sharp, interview 11 April 1993. Also, AC Child, Cranbrook – The First Fifty Years (1918-1968), Waite & Bull, 1968.

(2) Martin Sharp, interview 12 February 2011. See also former student Tim Lewis, interview 2 June 2014. Because of the brutality Tim's parents removed him from Cranbrook School and enrolled him elsewhere. He says, 'I got caned and all that sort of thing. My parents took me away from Cranbrook because they didn't like those marks on my leg, hit by rulers and bruises and things like that'.

(3) Martin Sharp, interview 12 February 2011.
(4) Martin Sharp, interview Martin 5 April 2011.
(5) Times Educational Supplement, London, 10 January 1986.
(6) Martin Sharp, interview 18 January 1994.
(7) Martin Sharp, interview 11 April 1993.

(8) Richard Neville, Hippie Hippie Shake, p. 49, Wm Heinemann Australia 1995. Also, Martin Sharp interview 17 April 2002.

(9) Martin Sharp, interview 18 January 1994. Martin did not name the perpetrator but added angrily, 'He's got a family, he's got kids in the school now – or he has had – I'd have a word with him if I saw him again!'

(10) Martin Sharp, Catalog, p. 4, 5, 36. Reid Books, 1971.
(11) Martin Sharp, interview 6 September 1982.
(12) Martin Sharp, interview 11 April 1993.
(13) Peter Kingston, interview 28 October 2014.
(14) Martin Sharp, interview 11 April 1993.
(15) Martin Sharp, interview 18 January 1994.
(16) Martin Sharp, interview 5 April 2011.
(17) Martin Sharp, interview 12 February 2011.
(18) Martin Sharp, interview 12 February 2011.
(19) Martin Sharp, interview 11 April 1993.
(20) Martin Sharp, interview 11 April 1993. And, Catalog, p. 4, 5. Reid Books, 1971.

(21) Sydney Morning Herald, Arts and Entertainment, 15 August 2005.
(22) Martin Sharp, interview 16 October 2003.
(23) Martin Sharp, interview 11 April 1993.
(24) Martin Sharp, interview 16 October 2003.
(25) Martin Sharp, interview 31 July 2003.
(26) Martin Sharp, interview 16 October 2003.
(27) AC Child, Cranbrook – The First Fifty Years (1918-1968), Waite & Bull, 1968.
(28) Martin Sharp, interview 29 December 1990.
(29) Martin Sharp, interview 6 September 1982.
(30) Martin Sharp, interview, 6 September 1982. The picture is titled After 'Still Life' by Van Gogh (1957), synthetic polymer paint, water colour on paper.
(31) Martin Sharp, interview 29 December 1990.
(32) Martin Sharp, interview 11 April 1993.
(33) Richard Neville, Hippie Hippie Shake, pp. 19, 49. Wm Heinemann Australia 1995.
(34) Martin Sharp, interview 18 January 1994.

CHAPTER 3

(1) Martin Sharp, Cartoons, p. 8. Scripts Pty Ltd, 1966.
(2) Afferbeck Lauder, Let Stalk Strine, p. 20, Ure Smith, 1965.
(3) Barry Humphries, Wild Life in Suburbia, an EP (extended play) recording on the Score label, 1958.
(4) Nino Culotta (John O'Grady), They're A Weird Mob, Ure Smith, 1957.
(5) Jenny Kee, A Big Life, p. 30, Penguin 2006.
(6) Richard Neville, Hippie Hippie Shake, p. 8. William Heinemann, 1995.
(7) Martin Sharp, interview 16 October 2003.
(8) Garry Shead, interview 13 February 2015.
(9) Martin Sharp, interview 29 December 1990.
(10) Martin Sharp, interview 6 September 1982. A photo of Richard Neville poised to hit Bandstand's dance floor - see Hippie Hippie Shake, p. 121. William Heinemann, 1995.
(11) Martin Sharp, interview 16 October 2003.
(12) Martin Sharp, interview 16 October 2003.
(13) Brian Kennedy, A Passion to Oppose, John Anderson, Philosopher, Melbourne University Press 1995.
(14) Anne Coombs, Sex and Anarchy, The Life and Death of the Sydney Push, Penguin Books 1996.
(15) Martin Sharp, interview 12 February 2011.
(16) Garry Shead, interview 13 February 2015.
(17) Lionel Lindsay, Addled Art, p. 15, 37. Hollis & Carter London, 1946.
(18) Margot Hilton and Graeme Blundell, Whiteley, An Unauthorised Life, p. 46 Pan MacMillan, 1996.
(19) Geoffrey Dutton, The Innovators, p. 190 MacMillan 1986.

(20) Martin Sharp, interview 16 October 2003.

(21) Martin Sharp, interview 6 September 1982.

(22) Garry Shead, interview 13 February 2015. Also, Richard Walsh, The Australian 3 December 2013

(23) Martin Sharp, interview 29 December 1990.

(24) Martin Sharp, interview 6 September 1982.

(25) Martin Sharp, interview 29 December 1990.

(26) Colin Lanceley, Colin Lanceley, p. 19, Craftsman House 1987.

(27) Martin Sharp, interview 6 September 1982.

(28) Martin Sharp, interview 29 December 1990.

(29) Garry Shead, interview 13 February 2015.

(30) Martin Sharp, interview 29 December 1990.

(31) See Arty Wild Oat, University of Wollongong Research Online. ro.uow.edu.au (digital collection)

(32) Albie Thoms, My Generation, p. 100.

(33) Martin Sharp, interview 23 April 1987.

(34) Richard Neville, Hippie Hippie Shake, p. 19. William Heinemann, 1995.

(34) Garry Shead, interview 13 February 2015.

(35) Martin Sharp, interview 6 September 1982.

(36) Garry Shead, interview 13 February 2015.

(37) Martin Sharp, interview

(38) Garry Shead, The Bulletin, 30 June 1962.

(39) Garry Shead, interview 13 February 2015.

(40) Garry Shead, interview 13 February 2015.

(41) Martin Sharp, interview 5 January 1991.

CHAPTER 4

(1) The People of California (plaintiff) V Lawrence Ferlinghetti. The defendant is charged with a violation of Section 311.3 of the Penal Code of the State of California.

(2) DH Lawrence, Lady Chatterley's Lover. The Penguin second edition, published in 1961, contains a publisher's dedication, which reads: 'For having published this book, Penguin Books were prosecuted under the Obscene Publications Act, 1959 at the Old Bailey in London from 20 October to 2 November 1960. This edition is therefore dedicated to the twelve jurors, three women and nine men, who returned a verdict of "not guilty" and thus made D. H. Lawrence's last novel available for the first time to the public in the United Kingdom'.

(3) Richard Neville, Hippie Hippie Shake, p. 23-27, William Heinemann 1995.

(4) Martin Sharp, interview 6 September 1982.

(5) Richard Neville, Hippie Hippie Shake, p. 27, William Heinemann 1995. Oz Magazine, p. 13, August 1963.

(6) OZ Magazine, p. 11, September 1963.

(7) Craig McGregor, People, Politics and Pop, p. 83-84, Ure Smith, 1968.

(8) Ted Markstein, interview, 1 January 2015.
(9) Martin Sharp, interview 29 December 1990.
(10) Darlene Bungey, John Olsen, An Artist's Life, p 179, ABC Books, 2014.
(11) Albie Thoms, My Generation,
(12) Richard Neville, Hippie Hippie Shake, p. 29-30, William Heinemann 1995.
(13) Albie Thoms, My Generation, p. 153.
(14) OZ magazine, 'Obscene or Absurd?' p 12, Xmas and New Year Issue, 1963/64.
(15) Albie Thoms, My Generation, p. 155 and thereabouts
(16) Martin Sharp, interview 29 December 1990.
(17) Martin Sharp, Cartoons, p. 30, Scripts Pty Ltd 1966.
(18) Martin Sharp, interview 6 September 1982.
(19) Martin Sharp, interview 12 February 2011.
(20) Jenny Kee, A Big Life, p. 27, Penguin Lantern, 2006.
(21) Martin Sharp, interview 16 October 2003.
(22) Duncan McNab, The Usual Suspect, the Life of Abe Saffron, p. 84, McMillan 2005.
(23) Richard Neville, Hippie Hippie Shake, p. 36-37, William Heinemann 1995.
(24) Martin Sharp, interview 22 October 2003.
(25) Barry Humphries, Neglected Poems and Other Creatures, p. 49. Angus & Robertson, 1991.
(26) Albie Thoms, My Generation, p.146.
(27) Martin Sharp, interview 29 December 1990.
(28) Richard Neville, Hippie Hippie Shake, p. 35, William Heinemann 1995.

CHAPTER 5

(1) Glenn A Baker The Beatles Down Under…Wild & Woolley 1982.
(2) Martin Sharp, interview 16 October 2003.
(3) Jenny Kee, A Big Life, p. 34-38, Penguin Lantern, 2006.
(4) Martin Sharp, interview 31 July 2003.
(5) Richard Neville, Hippie Hippie Shake, p. 39, William Heinemann 1995.
(6) Bob Whitaker, The Unseen Beatles, Conran Octopus 1991.
(7) Martin Sharp, interview 31 July 2003.
(8) Colin Lanceley, Colin Lanceley, p. 10, Craftsman House 1987.
(9) Cover OZ magazine, No 12 August 1964. Mirka Mora acknowledges this in Wicked But Virtuous, My Life, p. 140-141, Viking, 2000.
(10) Mirka Mora, Wicked But Virtuous, My Life, p. 58, Viking, 2000.
(11) Martin Sharp, interview 31 July 2003.
(12) Bob Whitaker, The Unseen Beatles, p. 7-9, Conran Octopus 1991.
(13) Martin Sharp, interview 5 July 1984.
(14) Martin Sharp, interview 12 February 2011.
(15) Martin Sharp, interview 12 February 2011.
(16) OZ magazine, 'Social Top Twenty' p. 14, Xmas and New Year Issue, 1963/64.
(17) Martin Sharp, interview 5 April 2011.

(18) Martin Sharp, interview 12 February 2011 and 11 April 2011.
(19) Martin Sharp, interview 17 April 2002.
(20) Richard Walsh, The Australian, article 'Wizards of satire put OZ on the map'. 25 March 2013.
(21) Martin Sharp, interview 8 November 2006.
(22) Geoffrey Dutton, The Innovators, p. 225-227, Macmillan 1986.
(23) Craig McGregor, People, Politics and Pop, p. 85-86, Ure Smith, 1968.
(24) Martin Sharp, Cartoons, p. 2, Scripts Pty Ltd 1966.
(25) Martin Sharp, interview 11 April 1993.
(26) Martin Sharp, interview 17 April 2002
(27) Geoffrey Dutton, The Innovators, p. 225-227, Macmillan 1986.
(28) Martin Sharp, interview 17 April 2002
(29) Martin Sharp, interview 6 September 1982.
(30) Mirka Mora, Wicked But Virtuous, My Life, p. 58, Viking, 2000.
(31) Richard Neville, Hippie Hippie Shake, p. 54, William Heinemann 1995.
(32) Garry Shead, interview 13 February 2015.
(33) Richard Neville, Hippie Hippie Shake, p. 54, William Heinemann 1995.
(34) Roger Foley email 16 November 2014, Garry Shead interview 13 February 2015 and my diary notes.
(35) Greg Weight, interview 24 November 2014.
(36) The Everlasting World of Martin Sharp, p. 11, Ivan Dougherty Gallery, 2006.
(37) Martin Sharp, interview 5 January 1991.
(38) Richard Neville, Hippie Hippie Shake, p. 51, William Heinemann 1995.
(39) Jenny Kee, A Big Life, p. 43, Penguin Lantern, 2006.
(40) Martin Sharp, Cartoons, p. 30, Scripts Pty Ltd 1966.
(41) Gary Shearston, 'Sydney Town', An Anthology of Gary Shearston, 2007.
(42) Wikipedia, see OZ magazine.
(43) Martin Sharp, Cartoons, p. 22, Scripts Pty Ltd 1966.
(44) Martin Sharp, interview 11 April 1993.
(45) Martin Sharp, interview 12 February 2011.
(46) Albie Thoms, My Generation, p. 249.
(47) Roger Foley, radio interview with Sally Baillieu (undated, probably 2013).
(48) Albie Thoms, My Generation, p. 249.
(49) Greg Weight, interview 24 November 2014.
(50) Martin Sharp, interview 12 February 2011.
(51) Martin Sharp, interview, 16 October 2003.
(52) Martin Sharp, interview 5 July 1984.
(53) Martin Sharp, interview 12 February 2011.
(54) Martin Sharp, interview 12 February 2011.

CHAPTER 6

(1) Martin Sharp, Cartoons, Scripts Pty Ltd, 1966.

(2) Peter Draffin, Pop, 116 pages, Scripts Pty Ltd, 1967.
(3) Peter Draffin, interview 20 March 2015.
(4) Martin Sharp, interview 22 October 2003.
(5) Peter Draffin, interview 20 March 2015.
(6) OZ Magazine, No 26 (cover) and p. 3, 4, 7, 12, 15, 16, OZ 27 p. 6, OZ 28 p.19.
(7) Craig McGregor, People, Politics and Pop, Ure Smith, 1968.
(8) Martin Sharp, interview 22 October 2003.
(9) Craig McGregor, People, Politics and Pop, Ure Smith, 1968.
See 'Private School' p. 187, 'Three Gaoled Filthy Paper' p. 87, Suburban love goddesses, p. 19, 47, 'Excuse I', p. 35. Beatles collage p. 72 and 'Bobby Dylan' p. 161.
(10) OZ Magazine, No 26 April issue.
(11) Martin Sharp, interview 11 April 1993.
(12) Richard Neville, Hippie Hippie Shake, p. 58-64, William Heinemann 1995.
(13) Martin Sharp, interview 16 October 2003.
(14) Richard Neville, Hippie Hippie Shake, p. 62, William Heinemann 1995.
(15) Martin Sharp, interview 11 April 1993.
(16) Jill Neville, Obituary, The Independent, 12 June 1997.
(17) Martin Sharp, interview 19 March 2005.
(18) Richard Neville, Hippie Hippie Shake, p. 65, William Heinemann 1995.
(19) Jenny Kee, A Big Life, p. 64, Penguin Lantern, 2006.
(20) Martin Sharp, interview 19 March 2005.
(21) Richard Neville, Hippie Hippie Shake, p. 68-69, William Heinemann 1995.
(22) Martin Sharp, interview 11 April 1993.
(23) Martin Sharp, interview 16 October 2003.
(24) Martin Sharp, interview 22 October 2003.
(25) Bob Whitaker, The Unseen Beatles, Conran Octopus 1991.
(26) Martin Sharp, interview 5 July 1984.
(27) Martin Sharp, interview 22 October 2003.
(28) Martin Sharp, interview 16 October 2003.
(29) Martin Sharp, interview 6 September 1982.
(30) Richard Neville, Hippie Hippie Shake, p. 82, William Heinemann 1995.
(31) Richard Neville, Hippie Hippie Shake, p. 77, William Heinemann 1995.
(32) Martin Sharp, interview 6 September 1982.
(33) Martin Sharp, interview 16 October 2003.
(34) Martin Sharp, interview 6 September 1982.
(35) Martin Sharp, Twice Upon a Time, photocopy signed by Martin and held in the author's collection. He wrote, 'Drawn on the Baleric Isle of Formenterra Spain in the late 60s whilst stayed with Peter Draffin.' Martin – 12.6.1985.
(36) Martin Sharp, interview 31 July 2003.
(37) Jenny Kee, A Big Life, p. 67, Penguin Lantern, 2006.
(38) Martin Sharp, interview 6 September 1982.
(39) Greg Weight, interview 24 November 2014.

(40) Eric Clapton, The Autobiography, p. 90, Century London, 2007.
(41) Martin Sharp, interview 5 July 1984.
(42) Martin Sharp, interview 16 January 1991.
(43) Jack Bruce, Composing Himself, p. 97, Jawbone Press.
(44) Dave Thompson, Cream, The World's First Supergroup, pp. 150-154, Virgin 2005.
(45) Wah Wah Pedal, see Wikipedia.
(46) Pete Townshend, Who I Am, p. 108, Harper Collins 2012.
(47) Emanuel Litvinoff, Journey Through a Small Planet, 138 pages, Penguin, 1972.
(48) Martin Sharp, interview 16 October 2003.
(49) Martin Sharp, interview 19 March 2005.
(50) Martin Sharp, interview 6 September 1982.
(51) Martin Sharp, interview 19 March 2005.
(52) Peter Draffin, interview 20 March 2015.
(53) Martin Sharp, interview 16 October 2003.
(54) Richard Neville, Hippie Hippie Shake, p. 72, William Heinemann 1995.

CHAPTER 7

(1) Martin Sharp, interview 16 October 2003.
(2) Eric Clapton, The Autobiography, p. 92, Century London, 2007.
(3) Martin Sharp, interview 5 July 1984.
(4) Martin Sharp, interview 16 October 2003.
(5) Martin Sharp, interview 5 July 1984.
(6) Christine Wallace, Greer – Untamed Shrew, p. 134, Macmillan 1997.
(7) Martin Sharp, interview 23 April 1987.
(8) Martin Sharp, interview 19 March 2005.
(9) Martin Sharp, interview 16 October 2003.
(10) Marsha Rowe, 'Felix Dennis Obituary', The Guardian, 23 June 2014.
(11) Martin Sharp, interview 5 July 1984.
(12) Jack Bruce, Composing Himself, p. 101-102, Jawbone Press.
(13) Bob Whitaker, The Unseen Beatles, p. 151, Conran Octopus 1991.
(14) Martin Sharp, interview 11 April 1993.
(15) Martin Sharp, interview 19 March 2005.
(16) Dave Thompson, Cream, The World's First Supergroup, pp. 187, Virgin 2005.
(17) Angie Errico, author of Rock Album Covers, p. 33, Octopus 1979.
(18) Ginger Baker, Hellraiser, p. 272, John Blake Publishing 2010.
(19) Ginger Baker, Hellraiser, p. 110, John Blake Publishing 2010.
(20) Martin Sharp, interview 11 April 1993.
(21) Martin Sharp, interview 1 February 1983.
(22) Martin Sharp, interview 5 July 1984.
(23) Ginger Baker, Hellraiser, p. 110, John Blake Publishing 2010.
(24) Eric Clapton, The Autobiography, p. 97, Century London, 2007.

(25) Tiny Tim, interview 4 October 1991.

(26) Bill Graham, My Life Inside Rock and Out, p. 226-227, online.

(27) Martin Sharp, interview 22 October 2003.

(28) Martin Sharp, interview 6 September 1982.

(29) Martin Sharp, interview 5 January 1991.

(30) Martin Sharp, interview 5 July 1984. Note: up until early-1967 Cream's road manager was Eric's friend Ben Palmer. See Jack Bruce p. 102.

(31) Martin Sharp, interview 6 September 1982.

(32) Martin Sharp, interview 19 March 2005.

(33) Mirka Mora, Wicked But Virtuous, My Life, p. 99, Viking, 2000.

(34) Richard Neville, Hippie Hippie Shake, p. 105, William Heinemann 1995.

(35) Richard Neville, Hippie Hippie Shake, p. 106, William Heinemann 1995.

(36) Richard Neville, Hippie Hippie Shake, p. 108, William Heinemann 1995.

(37) Richard Neville, Hippie Hippie Shake, p. 114-115, William Heinemann 1995.

(38) Garry Shead, interview 13 February 2015.

(39) Martin Sharp, interview 5 April 2011.

(40) Martin Sharp, interview 12 February 2011.

CHAPTER 8

(1) Lowell Tarling, diary notes.

(2) Eadweard Muybridge, The Human Figure in Motion, Bonanza Books NY, 1989. Also, Martin Sharp interviews, 5 January 1991 and 22 October 2003.

(3) Ginger Baker's Airforce, record album, released 1970.

(4) Michael Organ, Sixties Sharp - the pop & psychedelic art of Martin Sharp, online.

(5) Martin Sharp, interview 6 September 1982.

(6) Martin Sharp, interview 5 July 1984.

(7) Irving Stone, Lust for Life, Grosset & Dunlap, 1934.

(8) The Complete Letters of Vincent van Gogh, in 3 volumes, Thames & Hudson, 1958, 1978, 1988, 1999.

(9) A Letter from a Idle Fellow, OZ 43 July/August 1973.

(10) Martin Sharp, interview 6 September 1982.

(11) Martin Sharp, Cleo August 1977.

(12) Richard Neville, Playpower, 360 p, Jonathon Cape, 1970.

(13) Robert Hughes, Heaven and Hell in Western Art, Weidenfeld & Nicolson, 1968.

(14) Eric Clapton, The Autobiography, p. 103, Century London, 2007.

(15) Martin Sharp, interview 16 October 2003.

(16) Martin Sharp, interview 6 September 1982.

(17) Philippe Mora, Art Monthly, p. 9-10, Dec 2002-Feb 2003.

(18) Darling Do You Love Me? A film by Martin & Bob Whitaker, assisted by Harry Youlden and Alisdair Burke. Starring Germaine Greer.

(19) Martin Sharp, interview 16 October 2003.

(20) Martin Sharp, interview 11 April 1993.
(21) Eric Clapton, The Autobiography, p. 104, Century London, 2007.
(22) Martin Sharp, interview 5 January 1991.
(23) Martin Sharp, interview 5 July 1984.
(24) Martin Sharp, interview 16 January 1991. Also OZ 15 September 1968, back cover.
(25) Mark Lewisohn, The Complete Beatles Recording Sessions, p. 153-154, Hamlyn 1988.
(26) Eric Clapton, The Autobiography, p. 105, Century London, 2007.
(27) Judy Stone, The New York Times, 19 May 1968, see article ' Luna, Who Dreamed of Being Snow White'.
(28) Martin Sharp, interview 5 July 1984.
(29) John Lennon, I Am the Walrus (Lennon-McCartney) 1967.
(30) Eric Clapton, The Autobiography, p. 107, Century London, 2007.
(31) Martin Sharp, interview 5 July 1984.
(32) Richard Neville, Hippie Hippie Shake, p. 125, William Heinemann 1995.
(33) Martin Sharp, interview 5 July 1984.
(34) Richard Neville, Hippie Hippie Shake, p. 125, William Heinemann 1995.
(35) Martin Sharp, interview 5 July 1984.
(36) Eric Clapton, The Autobiography, p. 107, Century London, 2007.
(37) Eric Clapton, The Autobiography, p. 108, Century London, 2007.
(38) Martin Sharp, interview 5 July 1984.
(39) Richard Neville, Hippie Hippie Shake, p. 126, William Heinemann 1995.
(40) Martin Sharp, interview 16 October 2003.
(41) Martin Sharp, interview 6 September 1982.
(42) Lowell Tarling, diary notes.
(43) Tiny Tim, Live at the Royal Albert Hall, released by Rhino, 2000.
(44) Martin Sharp, interview 31 July 2003.
(45) Martin Sharp, interview 16 October 2003.
(46) Martin Sharp, interview 31 July 2003. Martin later changed 'unapproachable' to 'beyond approach' (27 May 2005).
(47) Martin Sharp, 30 October 1968 Diary, diary notes.
(48) Richard Neville, Hippie Hippie Shake, p. 126, William Heinemann 1995.
(49) OZ Magic Theatre, No 16, November 1968.
(50) Jenny Kee, A Big Life, p. 93, Penguin Lantern, 2006. Robert Hughes, University of Wollongong: ro.uow.edu.au/cgi/viewcontent.cgi?article=1015&context=ozlondon
(51) Martin Sharp, interview 16 October 2003.
(52) OZ magazine No 17.
(53) Richard Neville, Play Power, p. 361, Jonathon Cape, 1970.
(54) Timothy Leary, The Politics of Ecstasy, p. 301, Paladin 1970. The original painting was exhibited at the Yellow House in the early 1970s. With Martin's approval, a restored print was made in 2012 by Roger Foley.
(55) Martin Sharp, OZ No 4 June 1967. For the complete Tarot, see Michael Organ, sharp-tarot.blogspot.com.au. Also Martin Sharp, interview 22 October 2003.

(56) The Rolling Stones, Rock And Roll Circus released 1996.

(57) Eric Clapton, The Autobiography, p. 109, Century London, 2007.

CHAPTER 9

(1) Martin Sharp, interview 19 March 2005.

(2) Martin Sharp, interview 16 October 2003.

(3) Philippe Mora, film Trouble in Molopolis written by Philippe and Peter Smalley premiered at the Paris Pullman Chelsea in 1970 in aid of the OZ legal fund.

(4) Ginger Baker, Blind Faith CD Deluxe Edition, liner notes, p. 5.

(5) Martin Sharp, interview 5 July 1984.

(6) Eric Clapton, interview 20 June 2013 with Tom Kovats (youtube).

(7) Martin Sharp, interview 19 March 2005.

(8) Jim Anderson, interview 12 May 2015.

(9) Jim Anderson, Lampoon, p. 8-12, 2011.

(10) Martin Sharp, interview 6 September 1982.

(11) OZ – The Last Issue, Australian OZ p. 2.

(12) OZ – The Last Issue, Australian OZ cover and pp. 8-9.

(13) Albie Thoms, My Generation, p. 343.

(14) Roger Foley, interview 11 February 2014.

(15) Martin Sharp, interview 12 February 2011.

(16) Carl Williams, 'Alternative OZ', Apollo Magazine, 20 September 2013.

(17) Tiny Tim, Beautiful Thoughts, 1969 JP Torcher.

(18) Martin Sharp, print.

(19) Martin Sharp interview 5 July 1984.

(20) Steve Winwood, Atlanta Journal, 'Steve Winwood talks Clapton, Traffic and EDM', 1 May 2015.

(21) Blind Faith CD.

(22) Martin Sharp, interview 16 October 2003.

(23) Richard Neville, Hippie Hippie Shake, p. 171, William Heinemann 1995.

(24) Philippe Mora, email 22 May 2015.

(25) Martin Sharp, interview 5 July 1984.

(26) Martin Sharp, interview 5 July 1984.

(27) Martin Sharp interview, 16 October 2003.

(28) Michael Organ, Sixties Sharp - the pop & psychedelic art of Martin Sharp, online.

(29) Martin Sharp, interview 6 September 1982.

(30) Martin Sharp, interview 16 October 2003.

(31) Martin Sharp, Art Book, p. 31, Mathews Miller Dunbar, London 1972.

(32) Martin Sharp, interview 5 July 1984.

(33) Martin Sharp, interview 11 April 1993.

(34) Martin Sharp, interview 16 October 2003. See also Paul Buck, Performance, A biography of the classic sixties film, Omnibus Press 2012.

(35) Jim Anderson, interview 12 May 2015.

(36) Lowell Tarling, diary notes. Also, Martin Sharp, interview 16 October 2003.

(37) Richard Neville, Hippie Hippie Shake, p. 162, William Heinemann 1995.

(38) Martin Sharp, interview 16 May 1995.

(39) OZ magazine 25, Hippies Atrocities, p. 19-20.

(40) Jim Anderson, email to Lowell Tarling 18 May 2015.

(41) Martin Sharp, interview 31 July 2003.

(42) Martin Sharp, interview 11 April 1993.

(43) Martin Sharp, interview 11 April 1993.

(44) Anthony Bourke and John Rendell, A Lion Called Christian, 180 pp, Bantam Press London, 1971, expanded and updated 2009.

CHAPTER 10

(1) Roger Foley, email dated 4 February 2015.

(2) Philippe Mora, email to Lowell Tarling, 15 October 2014.

(3) John Hewison, Too Much, Art and Society in the Sixties, p.164-181.

(4) Martin Sharp, interview 29 December 1990. Martin says it was he who thought of the Yellow House name, 'I was obviously reading Vincent's letters of the time'.

(5) Martin Sharp, interview 11 April 1993.

(6) Albie Thoms, My Generation, p. 435.

(7) Ian Reid, interview 13 February 2016.

(8) Antoine de Saint-Exupéry, The Little Prince p. 82, Harcourt Inc, 1941. Martin Sharp poster, 1969, authorized by the Arts Vietnam Committee.

(9) Martin Sharp, interview 7 November 1983.

(10) Philippe Mora, emails 22-23 May 2015.

(11) Poster, Crucifixion Exhibition, an exhibition of Degenerate Art, Sigi Krauss Gallery, 23 April-21 May 1970.

(12) Ted Markstein, interview 1 January 2015. Ted lived opposite the Yellow House, at Selsden apartments. He often visited the Yellow House between 1970-1973. Ted ran the fabulous In-Shoppe, Sydney's answer London's Carnaby Street. See The In-Shoppe Drop-Out, POL magazine, 1974. Guest editor: Richard Neville. Interviewer: Louise Ferrier.

(13) Greg Weight, interview 24 November 2014.

(14) Roger Foley, interview 11 February 2014.

(15) Martin Sharp, interview 'just before the opening of the Yellow House', 1971. See also Hazel de Berg interview, 9 June 1970.

(16) Peter Kingston, interview 28 October 2014.

(17) George Gittoes, email 5 July 2014.

(18) Greg Weight, interview 24 November 2014

(19) Martin Sharp, interview 28 October 1984.

(20) Martin Sharp, interview 29 December 1990.

(21) Martin Sharp, interview 16 October 2003.

(22) Ian Reid, interview 13 February 2016.
(23) Martin Sharp, interview 29 December 1990.
(24) Albie Thoms, My Generation, p. 441-451, Media Publishing Ltd, 2012.
(25) Margot Hilton & Graeme Blundell, Whiteley – An Unauthorised Life, p. 92-93.
(26) Johnny Lewis, see Lowell Tarling's diary notes, 21 May 2015.
(27) Brett Whiteley, Another Way of Looking at Vincent Van Gogh, Richard Griffin Publisher, 1983.
(28) Margot Hilton & Graeme Blundell, Whiteley – An Unauthorised Life, p. 92.
(29) Martin Sharp, Catalog, Reid Books, 1971.
(30) Albie Thoms, My Generation, p. 441-451.
(31) Justin Martell with Alanna Wray McDonald, Eternal Troubadour, the Improbable Life of Tiny Tim, p. 210, Jawbone Press 2016.
(32) Jon Lewis and Roger Foley, interview 26 July 2014.
(33) Mal Ramage, interview 8 February 2016.
(34) Jon Lewis and Roger Foley, interview 26 July 2014.
(35) Peter Kingston, interview 28 October 2014.
(36) Albie Thoms, My Generation, p. 441-451, Media Publishing Ltd, 2012.
(37) Richard Neville, Hippy Hippy Shake, William Heinemann Australia, p. 270. For a blow-by-blow description of the London Oz trial, see The Trials of Oz by Tony Palmer, Blond & Briggs, 1971.
(38) Martin Sharp, interview 6 September 1982.
(39) Roger Foley, interview 11 February 2014.
(40) Greg Weight, interview 24 November 2014.
(41) Tim Lewis, interview 2 June 2014.
(42) Jon Lewis and Roger Foley, interview 26 July 2014.
(43) Mal Ramage, interview 8 February 2016.
(44) Ted Markstein, interview, 1 January 2015.
(45) Martin Sharp, interview 14 November 1984.

CHAPTER 11

(1) Martin Sharp, interview 28 October 1984.
(2) Anthony Scaduto, Bob Dylan, Abacus, 1972, p.236, 239. Also, Clinton Heylin, Dylan: Behind the Shades, Viking Penguin, 1991, p. 161.
(3) Greg Weight, interview 24 November 2014.
(4) Roger Foley, interview 26 July 2014.
(5) Germaine Greer, The Female Eunuch, Granada Publishing, 1970.
(6) Adrian Rawlins, interview on film by Roger Foley, at the Yellow House Retrospective, 1990.
(7) Ian Reid, interview 13 February 2016.
(8) Martin Sharp, interview 7 November 1983.
(9) John A Walker, Art Into Pop, see Illustrations 54, Thames and Hudson, 1975.
(10) Jeannie Lewis, interview 7 May 2015.

(11) Greg Weight, interview 24 November 2014.

(12) Ian Reid, interview 13 February 2016.

(13) Ted Markstein, interview 1 January 2015.

(14) Jon Lewis, interview 26 July 2014.

(15) The Yellow House 1970-1972, published by Art Gallery of New South Wales, 1990.

(16) Albie Thoms, My Generation, p. 441-451.

(17) Martin Sharp, interview 14 November 1984. Peter Kingston disputes that the Stone Room was Martin's idea. He says, 'I was sort-of stuck in the Stone Room, which is really my idea...' interview, 28 October 2014.

(18) Greg Weight, interview 24 November 2014.

(19) Jon Lewis, interview 26 July 2014.

(20) Roger Foley, interview 26 July 2014.

(21) Albie Thoms, My Generation, p. 441-451.

(22) Peter Royles, email to Lowell Tarling, 5 January 2015.

(23) Betty Roland, The Eye of the Beholder, Hale & Ironmonger 1984. 'An insider's portrait of the establishment of Monsalvat, Eltham Victoria, under the magnetic influence of painter Justus Jorgensen' – cover lines.

(24) Marcus Skipper, email 21 June 2014.

(25) Martin Sharp, interview 16 January 1991, referencing Le Petit Prince by Antoine de Saint-Exupéry.

(26) Martin Sharp, interview 5 January 1991

(27) Greg Weight, interview 24 November 2014.

(28) Jo Sharp, interview with Martin Sharp, 5 April 2011.

(29) Jon Lewis, interview 26 July 2014.

(30) Ted Markstein, interview 1 January 2015. Ian Reid is amongst several to say they never saw David Litvinoff have anything to do with smack. However, most people (Ian and Mal Ramage amongst them) reckon that when it came to Litvinoff stories, you never knew what was fictionalized and what was true. The Bali story? The Kray Brothers hanging him from a window ledge? The 'big smile'? Maybe he made it all up.

(31) Nic Lyon, interview 16 August 2015.

(32) Albie Thoms, My Generation, p. 441-451.

(33) Jon Lewis, interview 26 July 2014.

(34) Clayton Simms, interview 23 October 2014.

(35) Ian Reid, interview 13 February 2016.

(36) Martin Sharp, taped interview 1971.

(37) Albie Thoms, My Generation, p. 441-451.

(38) Ian Reid, interview 123 February 2016.

(39) Martin Sharp, interview 16 October 2003.

(40) Mic Conway, interview 24 January 2015.

(41) Roger Foley, email 6 February 2015 and interview 11 February 2014.

(42) Roger Foley, Notes on the Yellow House, 2015.

(43) The Yellow House, a mimeographed A3 newsletter-style publication re-printed by Roger Foley with the encouragement of Albie Thoms 2013.

(44) Tim Lewis, interview 2 June 2014.

(45) Ted Markstein, interview 1 January 2015.

(46) Ian Reid, interview 13 February 2016. Also, 27 February 2116.

CHAPTER 12

(1) Germaine Greer, The Female Eunuch, 354pp, MacGibbon & Kee, 1970.

(2) Juno Gemes, Facebook 2014.

(3) Jim Anderson interview, 12 May 2015.

(4) Jim Anderson interview, 12 May 2015.

(5) Jim Anderson interview, 12 May 2015.

(6) John Lennon, Wonsaponatime CD, track 8. Jim Anderson, Michael Ramsden and a chorus of others were on the original recording, all eliminated by Phil Specter who only used John Lennon's guide vocal in the final recording.

(7) Geoffrey Robertson wrote both the stage show and the film script. The most comprehensive book on OZ is Tony Palmer, The Trials of OZ, 275 pp, Blond & Briggs 1971. See also, Nigel Fountain, Underground – the London Alternative Press 1966-1974, pp. 231, Routledge, 1988. And Jonathon Green, Days in the Life – Voices from the English Underground 1961-1971, pp. 468, Heinemann, 1988.

(8) Martin Sharp, interview 16 January 1991.

(9) Martin Sharp, interview 5 April 2011.

(10) Lex Marinos, interview 25 May 2015.

(11) Martin Sharp interview, 5 April 2011.

(12) Martin Sharp, interview 11 April 1993.

(13) Martin Sharp, interview 16 October 2003.

(14) Martin Sharp, interview 29 December 1990.

(15) Martin Sharp, Art Book, 40 pp, Mathews Miller & Dunbar, 1972.

(16) George Melly, Double Exposures, I have the cutting, not its reference.

(17) Brian Rice & Tony Evans, The English Sunrise, 80pp, Mathews Miller & Dunbar, 1972. Reprinted in 1987 by Chatto & Windus.

(18) Martin Sharp, interviews 6 September 1982 and 16 January 1991.

(19) Martin Sharp, interview 19 March 2005.

(20) Tiny Tim, Tiny Tim's Second Album released January 1969.

(21) Tiny Tim, Concert in Fairyland released August 1969.

(22) Tiny Tim, For All My Little Friends released 1969.

(23) Martin Sharp, interview 13 April 1983.

(24) Martin Sharp, interview 13 April 1983.

(25) Zandra Rhodes and Anne Knight, The Art of Zandra Rhodes, Jonathon Cape, 1984.

(26) Georgina Howell, In Vogue, Sixty years of celebrities and fashion from British Vogue, p. 327, Penguin Books 1975.

(27) Neil Baldwin, Man Ray – American Artist, p. 351, Da Capo Press 2001.

(28) Martin Sharp, interview 5 July 1984.

(29) Martin Sharp, interview 5 July 1984.

(30) J Hillier, Hokusai, Phaidon Press, 1955.

(31) Martin Sharp, interview 16 January 1991.

(32) Martin Sharp, interview 29 Dec 1990.

(33) OZ magazine 43, July/August, p. 4-6. Also Martin Sharp, Art Book, p. 2, Mathews Miller Dunbar, London 1972.

(34) Martin Sharp, Letter to Monseigneur, 13 June 1986.

(35) Sam Marshall, Luna Park – Just for Fun, p. 105-106, Luna Park Reserve Trust, 1995.

(36) Martin Sharp, Cartoons, p. 22, Scripts Pty Ltd 1966.

(37) Martin Sharp, Letter to Monseigneur, 13 June 1986.

CHAPTER 13

(1) Doug Aiton & Terry Lane, The First Century, p. 103-106, Information Australia 2000.

(2) Roger Foley film, The Aquarius Festival, Nimbin 1973, restored by Fogg Productions 2014.

(3) See David Litvinoff, Wikipedia.

(4) Albie Thoms, My Generation, p. 415-441.

(5) Julian Meyrick, See How It Runs, Nimrod and the New Wave, p. 226-227, Currency Press, 2002.

(6) Julian Meyrick, See How It Runs, Nimrod and the New Wave, p. 277, Currency Press, 2002.

(7) Julian Meyrick, See How It Runs, Nimrod and the New Wave, p. 75, Currency Press, 2002.

(8) Jeannie Lewis, interview 7 May 2015.

(9) Gary Shearston, interview 1 November 2001.

(10) Gary Shearston, Dingo, recorded in London in 1974 on the album of the same name.

(11) Martin Sharp, interview 5 April 2005.

(12) Martin Sharp, Cleo magazine, August 1977.

(13) Tim Lewis, interview 2 June 2014.

(14) Tim Lewis, interview 2 June 2014. Martin also told me this, in my diary notes.

(15) Tim Lewis, interview 2 June 2014.

(16) Tim Lewis, interview 2 June 2014.

(17) Roger Foley film, Martin Sharp Prepares, 21st March 1973, restored by Fogg Productions 2014.

(18) Martin Sharp, interview 12 February 2011

(19) Tim Lewis, interview 2 June 2014.

(20) Martin Sharp, interview 29 December 1990.

(21) Tim Lewis, interview 2 June 2014. Also 19 May 2015 (Facebook message).

(22) Martin Sharp, interview 16 October 2003.

(23) Tim Lewis, notes on telephone conversation 5 June 2015.

(24) See Wikipedia, Sydney Opera House. Utzon was not invited to the ceremony, nor was his name mentioned.

(25) Martin Sharp, interview 3 March 1984.
(26) Martin Sharp, interview 16 October 2003
(27) Martin Sharp, interview 7 November 1983.
(28) Sam Marshall, Luna Park – Just for Fun, p. 106, Luna Park Reserve Trust, 1995.
(29) Tim Lewis, interview 2 June 2014.
(30) Martin Sharp, Cleo magazine, August 1977.
(31) Martin Sharp, 'Notes from the River Caves', Quadrant, February 1977.
(32) OZ – The Last Issue, No 48, Winter 1973.
(33) Jim Anderson, Lampoon, p. 20-21, Dennis Publishing, 2011.
(34) Martin Sharp, interview 5 July 1984.
(35) Martin Sharp, interview 5 July 1984.
(36) Martin Sharp, interview 5 July 1984.
(37) Martin Sharp, Cleo magazine, August 1977.
(38) Lex Marinos, Blood and Circuses, An Irresponsible Memoir, p.92, Allen & Unwin, 2014.
(39) Lex Marinos, interview 25 May 2015.
(40) Keith Dunstan, Ratbags, Golden Press 1979.
(41) Martin Sharp, interview 5 January 1991.
(42) Tim Lewis, interview 2 June 2014.

CHAPTER 14

(1) Martin Sharp, interview 16 October 2003
(2) Martin Sharp, interview 24 January 1997
(3) Martin Sharp, interview 1 February 1983.
(4) Martin Sharp, interview 24 January 1997.
(5) Martin Sharp, interview 6 September 1982.
(6) Martin Sharp, interview 27 May 2005.
(7) Martin Sharp, interview 11 February 1983.
(8) Zandra Rhodes and Anne Knight, The Art of Zandra Rhodes, p. 123, Jonathan Cape 1984.
(9) John A Walker, Art Since Pop, Illustration 54, Thames and Hudson, 1975.
(10) Carl Jung, Synchronicity – An Acausal Connecting Principle. Routledge and Kegan Paul, 1972.
(11) James A Michener, The Hokusai Sketchbooks, Charles E. Tuttle, 1959.
(12) Martin Sharp, interview 27 May 2005.
(13) Martin Sharp, interview 16 October 2003.
(14) Pete Townshend, Who I Am, p. 108, Harper Collins, 2012.
(15) Martin Sharp, interview 13 April 1983.
(16) Martin Sharp, Street of Dreams film script, the first draft.
(17) Martin Sharp, interview 13 April 1983.
(18) Martin Sharp undated letter to Monseigeur.
(19) Tim Lewis, notes on telephone conversation 5 June 2015.
(20) Tim Lewis, interview 2 June 2014.

(21) Peter Kingston, interview 28 October 2014.

(22) Julian Meyrick, See How it Runs, Nimrod and the New Wave, p. 232, Currency Press. 40,550 attendees in 1973, 72,478 in 1974.

(23) Maggie Tabberer, Maggie, Allen & Unwin, 1998.

(24) Jeannie Lewis, interview 7 May 2015. Also see Free Fall Through Featherless Flight CD.

(25) Garry Mallard, interview 9 November 1983.

(26) Garry Shead, interview 13 February 2015.

CHAPTER 15

(1) Picnic at Hanging Rock, a film by Peter Weir premiered in August 1975.

(2) Martin Sharp, interview, 16 October 2003.

(3) Martin Sharp, interview 5 January 1991.

(4) Martin Sharp, interview 13 April 1983.

(5) Martin Sharp, Cleo magazine, August 1977.

(6) Martin Sharp, interview 5 August 1983.

(7) William Yang, interview 5 August 1983.

(8) Tim Lewis, interview 2 June 2014.

(9) Martin Sharp, interview 5 August 1983.

(10) William Yang, interview 5 August 1983.

(11) Martin Sharp, interview 14 November 1984

(12) Bob Dylan, The Bootleg Series Vol 4, known as the 'Albert Hall' concert, it was recorded in Manchester 17 May 1966. It became commercially available in 1998.

(13) Martin Sharp, interview 5 January 1991.

(14) Sam Marshall, Luna Park, Just for Fun, pp. 106-110, Luna Park Reserve Trust 1995.

(15) Martin Sharp, Luna Park Timeline, a private document.

(16) Ted Hopkins, Report on Luna Park, p. 27, 1980.

(17) Martin Sharp, interview 3 March 1984.

(18) Jeannie Lewis, Tears of Steel & the Clowning Calaveras, see liner notes, 1976.

(19) Jeannie Lewis, email 8 May 2015.

(20) Jeannie Lewis, interview 7 May 2015.

(21) Martin Sharp, interview 7 November 1983.

(22) Jeannie Lewis, interview 7 May 2015.

(23) Martin Sharp, interview 3 March 1984.

(24) Martin Sharp, Luna Park notes on Clowning Calaveras retyped in 1983.

(25) Martin Sharp, interview 3 March 1984.

(26) Lex Marinos, interview 25 May 2015.

(26) Peter Kingston, interview 28 October 2014.

(27) Peter Royles, email 6 February 2015.

(28) Report on Luna Park, p. 27, 37, 39, 42, 43. Published 1980.

(29) Sam Marshall, Luna Park, Just for Fun, p. 110, Luna Park Reserve Trust 1995.

(30) Garry Shead, interview 13 February 2015.

(31) Peter Kingston, interview 28 October 2014.
(32) Peter Kingston, interview 28 October 2014.
(33) Martin Sharp, undated notes (retyped by me in 1983).
(34) Martin Sharp, interview 5 April 2005.
(35) Martin Sharp, interview 16 October 2003.
(36) Martin Sharp, interview 27 May 2005.
(37) Harry Stein, Tiny Tim, Playboy Press, 1976.
(38) Tiny Tim, interview 4 April 1992.
(39) Martin Sharp, 'The Real Tiny Tim', Quadrant, January 1977.
(40) Martin Sharp, interview 6 September 1982.
(41) Tiny Tim, interview 4 October 1991.
(42) Martin Sharp, interview 13 April 1983.
(43) Martin Sharp, interview 13 April 1983.
(44) Martin Sharp, interview 29 November 2004.
(45) Tiny Tim, telegram to Martin Sharp, 16 July 1976.
(46) Martin Sharp, The Lyre Bird – Tiny Tim, application to the Film Commission 1976.
(47) Kym Bonython, Modern Australian Painting 1975-1980, p. 66, Martin Sharp, Song of Songs – Festival of Sydney 1978, Rigby, 1980. And, The Everlasting World of Martin Sharp, p. 24, Ivan Dougherty Gallery 2006.
(48) Willy de la Vega, interview 27 April 1992.

CHAPTER 16

(1) Martin Sharp, two poems – in the author's collection.
(2) Martin Sharp, interview 7 July 1984.
(3) Martin Sharp, cover and article 'The Real Tiny Tim', Quadrant, January 1977. Also Martin Sharp, interview 27 May 2005.
(4) Martin Sharp, interview 16 October 2003.
(5) Martin Sharp, interview 29 November 2004.
(6) Martin Sharp, interview 27 May 2005. Philippe Mora's Mad Dog Morgan, starring Dennis Hopper and Jack Thompson (1976) is available on DVD.
(7) Kym Bonython, Modern Australian Painting 1975-1980, p. 66, Rigby Ltd 1980. This depiction shows Martin's picture as it was in 1978, before the over-painting. Titled Song of Songs – Festival of Sydney, it later became known as Film Script.
(8) Susan Jensen, email 4 July 2015.
(9) Susan Jensen, email 11 July 2015.
(10) The Everlasting World of Martin Sharp, p. 27, Ivan Dougherty Gallery, 2006.
(11) Tim Lewis, Facebook 13 December 2014.

(12) Angelica Tremblay, Facebook 30 December 2014.
(13) Martin Sharp, personal notes, Sharp Papers Vol 3 (held by the author).
(14) Elwyn Lynn, 'Those Silver Scissors', Quadrant, February 1977.
(15) Martin Sharp, 'Notes from the River Caves', Quadrant, February 1977.
(16) Martin Sharp, interview 29 January 1985.
(17) Peter Kingston, notes held in Martin Sharp's papers. Tape: 29 January 1985.
(18) Martin Sharp, interview 29 January 1985.
(19) Susan Jensen, email 4 July 2115.
(20) Martin Sharp, interview 5 August 1983.
(21) Martin Sharp, author's diary notes.
(22) Richard Neville and Julie Clarke, The Life and Crimes of Charles Sobhraj, 352 pp, Jonathon Cape Ltd, 1979.
(23) The Yellow House, a mimeographed A3 newsletter-style publication re-printed by Roger Foley with the encouragement of Albie Thoms 2013.
(24) Tim Lewis, interview 2 June 2014.
(25) Melody Cooper, email 5 July 2015.
(26) William Yang, interview 5 August 1983.
(27) Melody Cooper, email 5 July 2015.
(28) Cleo magazine, August 1977.
(29) Julian Meyrick, See How it Runs, Nimrod and the New Wave, p. 141, Currency Press.
(30) Martin Sharp, interview 3 March 1984.
(31) Martin Sharp, interview 3 March 1984.

CHAPTER 17

(1) Martin Sharp, photocopy of sketch, in the author's collection.
(2) Roger Foley-Fogg, Facebook message, 20 May 2115.
(3) Martin Sharp, interview 2 February 1983.
(4) Russell Sharp, interview 6 June 2015.
(5) Martin Sharp, interview 29 November 2004.
(6) Martin Sharp, interview 13 April 1983.
(7) Martin Sharp, interview 29 November 2004.
(8) Martin Sharp, interview 16 October 2003.
(9) Tiny Tim, talking to Martin Sharp at the Cosmopolitan Motor Inn, Sydney 4 December 1978. Tiny is reading the contract aloud and discussing it.
(10) Martin Sharp, interview 13 April 1983.
(11) Martin Sharp, Sydney Morning Herald, 8 January 1978.
(12) Martin Sharp, interview 29 November 2004.
(13) Martin Sharp, poster Tiny, produced as a postcard by Lamella Sydney, 1981.
(14) Melody Cooper, email 5 July 2015.
(15) Martin Sharp, interview 29 November 2004.
(16) Julian Meyrick, See How it Runs, Nimrod and the New Wave, p. 273, Currency Press.

(17) Martin Sharp, interview 29 November 2004.
(18) Martin Sharp, interview 1 February 1983.
(19) Martin Sharp, interview 24 January 1997.
(20) Martin Sharp, interview 5 July 1984.
(21) Martin Sharp, interview 1 February 1983.
(22) Wonderful World of Romance, Custom Records, a facility of Studio 301.
(23) Tiny Tim, film Street of Dreams.
(24) Martin Sharp, interview 29 November 2004.
(25) Tim Lewis, Facebook message, 1 July 2015.
(26) Ted Markstein, Facebook message, 23 June 2115. 'It was for the 360 degree projection attraction in Luna Park. April-May 1979. I did two 8' x 4' panels.'
(27) Jeannie Lewis, interview 7 May 2115.
(28) Martin Sharp, interview 29 November 2004.
(29) Tiny Tim, film Street of Dreams.
(30) Martin Sharp, interview 29 November 2004.
(31) Jeannie Lewis, interview 7 May 2115.
(32) Martin Sharp, interview 29 November 2004.
(33) Tiny Tim, film Street of Dreams.
(34) Martin Sharp, interview 29 November 2004.
(35) Martin Sharp, interview 29 November 2004.
(36) Roger Foley-Fogg, author's diary notes 2114.

CHAPTER 18

(1) William Yang, interview 5 August 1983.
(2) Martin Sharp, interview 3 March 1984.
(3) Martin Sharp, interview 3 March 1984.
(4) Undated photocopies are in the author's collection, original clippings at Wirian.
(5) Sam Marshall, Luna Park, Just for Fun, pp. 112, Luna Park Reserve Trust 1995.
(6) Martin Sharp, interview 3 March 1984.
(7) Martin Sharp, interview 13 April 1983.
(8) Australian Playboy, June 1979. Undated photocopy in the author's collection.
(9) Garry Shead, interview 13 February 2015.
(10) Martin Sharp, interview 3 March 1984.
(11) Sam Marshall, Luna Park, Just for Fun, pp. 112-113, Luna Park Reserve Trust 1995.
(12) Martin Sharp, interview 3 March 1984.
(13) Martin Sharp, notes on Luna Park that I rekeyed for him 1982/83.
(14) Martin Sharp, notes on Luna Park that I rekeyed for him 1982/83.
(15) Martin Sharp, interview 3 March 1984.
(16) Martin Sharp, notes on Luna Park that I rekeyed for him 1982/83.
(17) Martin Sharp, interview 3 March 1984.
(18) Martin Sharp, notes on Luna Park that I rekeyed for him 1982/83.

(19) Martin Sharp, notes on Luna Park that I rekeyed for him 1982/83.
(20) Martin Sharp, interview 11 December 1983.
(21) Martin Sharp, interview 7 November 1983.
(22) Martin Sharp, interview 3 March 1984.
(23) Martin Sharp, interview 7 November 1983.
(24) Martin Sharp, interview 3 March 1984.
(25) Peter Kingston, interview 28 October 2014.
(26) Martin Sharp, interview 7 November 1983.
(27) Susan Jensen, email 11 July 2015.
(28) Martin Sharp, interview 7 March 1984.

(Top)Martin at Wirian (courtesy David Newland); (Lower) At Wirian - Martin, Toto Renshaw, Peter Royles, Lowell Tarling (photograph by William Yang).

Jim Anderson, Felix Dennis and Richard Neville "admire" the Schoolkid's issue of London OZ 28.

(Top) Albie Thoms, Martin Sharp and Richard Neville (photograph by Jon Lewis); (Lower) OZ Schoolgirls "team".

Martin Sharp outside Luna Park on 31 May 1981 (photograph by Peter Adams).

(Top) 11 May 1983, Richard Neville and his wife, a very pregnant Julie Clarke visit Martin at Wirian. (Lower) Richard is standing in front of the Vincent Collage that Martin was working on at the time.

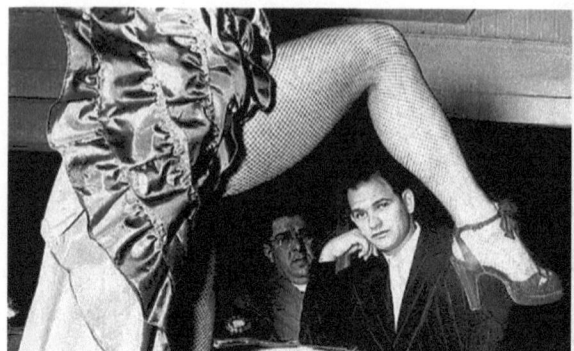

(Top) Abe Saffron, posing at his own hotel Rooservelt in 1951; (Lower) Abe Saffron with the Luna Smile.

(Top) The Yellow House by Joel Tarling; (Lower) Pee Wee Wilson of The Delltones with Tiny Tim.

Martin Sharp in the early stages of painting Tiny Tim's Non-Stop Singing Record (courtesy David Pepperell).

(Top) Yensoon, Wirian 1983; (Lower) William Yang in the kitchen at Wirian, 1983.

Martin Sharp with Lowell Tarling, with the Tiny Tim film variants above them (photograph by Peter Jensen).

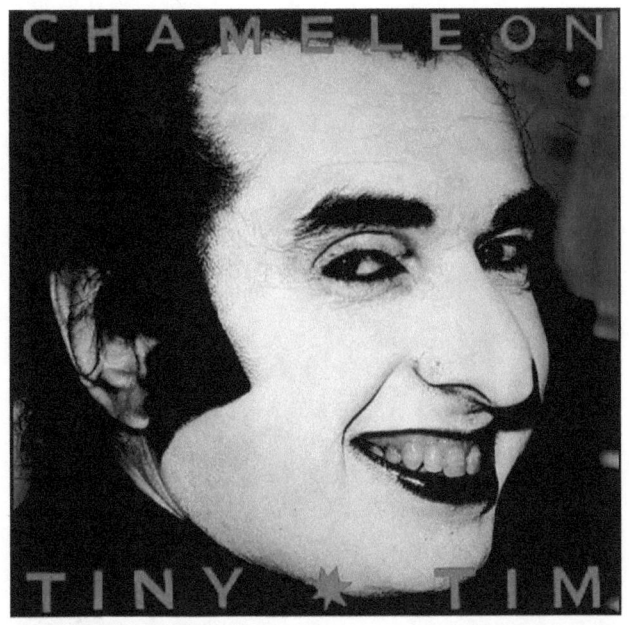

(Top) Tiny Tim's Chameleon, using a photograph by William Yang; (Lower) Martin Sharp with Tiny Tim in Sharp's Kold Komfort Kaffe setting (photograph by David Pepperell)

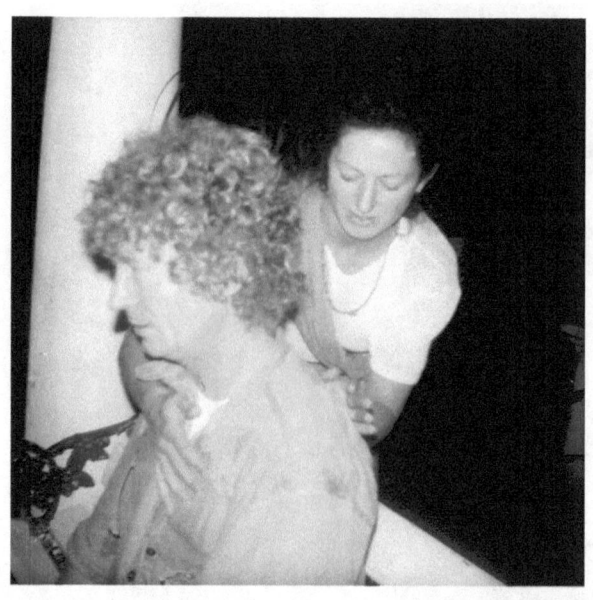

(Top); 12 November 1984. A party is held at Wirian for Eric Clapton, who was touring Australia. Brett Whiteley receives a head massage from Narelle Perroux. (Lower) Harold the Kangaroo Thornton with Toto Renshaw (photo by Joel Tarling).

(Top) Lowell and Martin in the hallway at Wirian. (Lower) Lowell with Garry Shead, both squatting for the camera, with Michael Glasheen and Judit Shead chatting in the background.

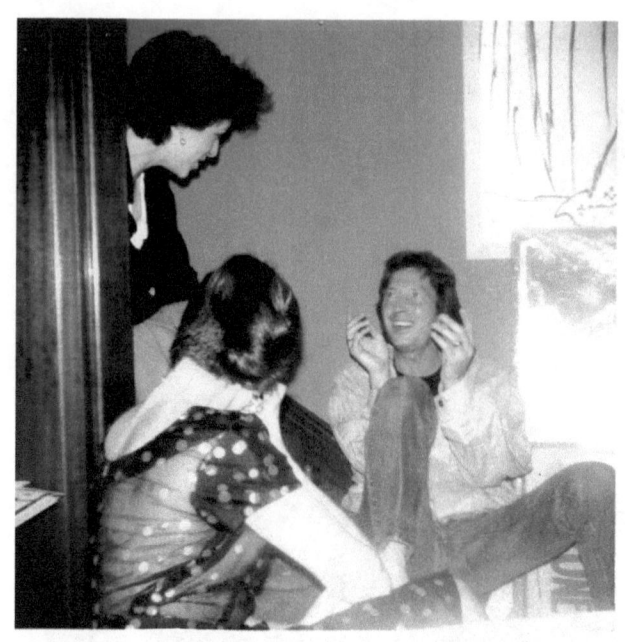

(Top) Eric Clapton, Wirian 1983; (Lower) Tiny Tim with Alistair Jones, Wirian 1984 (photographs by Lowell Tarling).

(Top) Jon Lewis at Wirian, 1983; (Lower) Les Bean and pooch.

Martin Sharp at work on the Luna Park face.

(Top) Ted Hopkins, innovator at Luna Park, with Martin Sharp (photograph by Jon Lewis); (Lower) Luna Park fire in full blaze.

*Martin Sharp at the Luna Park exhibition 1984
(photograph by Jon Lewis).*

(Top) Joel Tarling (left) with Martin at the Sydney Opera House Walkway Paint-In, March 1986; (Lower) Martin at Wirian, 1985 (photograph by William Yang).

Martin Sharp with Lowell Tarling and Les Bean at Wirian 1985 (courtesy William Yang).

Jenny Godson with Martin Sharp's paintings of her family (photograph by Peter Royles)

Arthur Stace (above) and homage to Arthur Stace and Martin Sharp by Ignatious Jones (below).

(Top) Martin (ABC special); (Lower) Martin working on his portrait of David Gulpilil.

(Top) Martin with Jon Lewis at Jon's opening 2012; (Lower) Martin, as photographed by Jon Lewis 2012.

SHARPER

Bringing It All Back Home

Part Two: 1980-2013

THE BIOGRAPHY OF
MARTIN SHARP AS TOLD TO
LOWELL TARLING

ETT IMPRINT
EXILE BAY

Synchronicity is an ever present reality

for those who have eyes to see.

Carl Jung

TABLE OF CONTENTS
2

1.	The Funfair & the Nightmare	312
2.	Wirian	323
3.	Hokusai, Elvis and the Dingo	333
4.	Unpicking the Code	343
5.	Devil in the Detail	352
6.	Tidying Up	363
7.	The Brighton Cut	374
8.	This is Not the Yellow House	383
9.	Courage My Friend	394
10.	Tiny Tiptoes Off-Stage	406
11.	Gospel According to Martin	417
12.	Greatest Editor	428
13.	Telford, Travel and the Tiny Tim Show	437
14.	Changing Dimension	447
15.	Hippie Hippie Shock	459
16.	Poverty Delux	470
17.	Stayin' Alive	482
18.	Why Martin Matters	493
Notes		498
Bibliography		520
Index		524

1.
THE FUNFAIR AND THE NIGHTMARE

I heard bikies talking about kerosene and matches in the Ghost Train.
Because of their attitude I gathered that they had lit the fire.
Leslie Dowd

Luna Park was closed immediately after the fire and a Federal Inquest was held into its cause. Coroner Kevin Anderson resolved nothing in declaring, 'The cause of the fire cannot conclusively be stated', adding somewhat gratuitously, 'a statement made to Police soon after the fire indicated that it had been deliberately started, that statement had been shown to be false and mischievous'. [1] False and mischievous! *He doth protest too much* - is what Martin reckoned.

Witness Tina Shakeshaft testified that she overheard someone in a group say, 'You shouldn't have done that' followed by talk of kerosene and matches. (2) Her companion, Trevor Dinsmore backed her account. [3] By-stander Robert Baikie said, 'I heard someone mention a jet of flame. I thought, well, how on earth can an electrical fire start a jet of flame?' [4] And Leslie Dowd added, 'I heard one or two bikies talking about kerosene and matches in the Ghost Train…because of their attitude I gathered that they had lit the fire'. [5]

The Park owners were found not guilty of criminal negligence and so – to general relief – they avoided criminal prosecution but didn't get off unscathed. The Inquest publicly criticised their 'reluctance' to implement full and proper fire precaution measures. [6] Management took it hard. As the sorry tale seeped out, many people felt guilty. Leon Fink 'did a lot of weeping,' said Martin, adding, 'He did confess to me one night that he felt one eighth responsible'. [7] Summing up the artists' feelings Peter Kingston (Kingo) admitted, 'We were all culpable'. [8] Martin also carried that weight, 'There are some who are consciously responsible but a lot of people are unconsciously responsible. We (the artists) made it look safe.' [9]

Martin came to believe the fire was the collective negligence of the entire City of Sydney. But the cause, Martin believed, was a deliberate criminal act. He was convinced that Abe Saffron had hired a bikie gang to torch the park to make way for future developments. Said Martin, 'Juanita Nielson disappeared from the Carousel Club at the Cross - that was the connecting bond between her and Abe Saffron. (Plus you get the same fairground imagery – the Carousel, right?) He's also the secret figure behind Luna Park'. [10]

Abraham (Abe) Gilbert Saffron was third generation Australian Russian-Jewish stock, born in inner-Sydney Annandale (1919). He attended Fort Street High School. His mother wanted him to study medicine but Abe was too street-smart for that. By the age of 8 he was dealing in cigarettes, selling them to his father's card-playing kitchen-table friends. Abe quit school at 15 to pursue a career in the family drapery business Saffron & Sons. His extra-curricular business activities got him into trouble.

Shortly before World War 2 Abe was caught being a runner for an SP bookie. His second brush with the law came in 1940 when he was caught selling six 'hot' car radios. Author Duncan McNab wrote, 'The magistrate took a rather dim view of his enterprises and gave him six months' imprisonment for shock value, then suspended the sentence on the proviso that Abe was of good behaviour. He went back to the family business.'

In January 1942 (a fortnight before Martin was born) Abe started two-years service as an enlisted soldier. After his discharge, Abe signed up for a stint in the merchant navy where he ran into an old friend, Hilton Kincaid who treated wartime rationing like six years of opportunity. Caught with 60 bottles of whisky, Kincaid was suspended from duty for three months and not deemed an appropriate person to hold a Hotelier's License. This is why he needed Abe to partner his future operations after they both left the navy in July 1944.

These were the days of the '6 o'clock swill' where all pubs were legally required to close at 6.00pm, so there was a lively market for sly grog. Abe Saffron & Hilton Kincaid's first pub was in Kurri Kurri, then Hotel Newcastle, West End Hotel Balmain, Gladstone Hotel Darlinghurst, also pubs in Bankstown, Mortdale, North Sydney and the Civic, corner of Goulburn and Pitt Streets Sydney. Every deal was a partnership, sometimes involving Abe's brother Henry. These acquisitions gave them the leverage to buy the Roosevelt nightclub in Orwell Street Kings Cross, in 1947, the jewel in their crown.

The Roosevelt was the toast of Sydney society and the second home of American commissioned officers. It was a top glamour spot for senior police with their demoiselles and sometimes their wives. The Roosevelt comprised restaurant facilities, singers, musicians, dancers, baccarat, sly grog, burlesque and (later) topless showgirls who – like London's better known *Windmill Theatre* – were permitted to bare their breasts if they didn't move, like a tableaux. Women wore evening gowns and gloves. Men wore suits and silk ties. Abe gave plenty of money to charities, treated his staff like family and was regarded as one of the outstanding young men of Sydney's business community.

However, in 1951 Abe was required to give evidence at a Royal Commission into the amount of alcohol being consumed outside the legal trading hours. The proceedings exposed Abe's network of silent partnerships, revealing that he owned many more slices of the pie than anybody had previously thought. Five years later the press trashed his reputation. For someone who eschewed publicity, Abe must have found the hypocrisy disturbing – (Protestant revenge on an up-jumped Jew?). The Vice Squad raided his Macleay Street office and found a feather duster, an electric vibrator, (deemed 'obscene'), a copy of Marquis de Sade's *120 Days of Sodom* (on the banned list) and other paraphernalia - like a camera. It was an exciting court case being the only way Sydney-siders ever saw words like 'sodomy', 'vibrator' and 'penis-like fertility symbol' in print. The case was eventually dropped but Saffron emerged with a sleazy reputation. The Roosevelt and other Saffron establishments suffered a downturn. [11]

Towards the close of the 50s Abe teamed up with another old friend, entertainment entrepreneur Lee Gordon, an American living in Australia. Lee had contacts and Abe had collateral. They brought Frank Sinatra to Sydney, which made them plenty of money. Author Duncan McNab, surmises that meeting Sinatra in Las Vegas may have been Abe's first brush with organised crime. The success of the Sinatra show spurred them to bring out Top 40 acts that Martin and his art school friends faithfully attended at Sydney Stadium: Nat King Cole, Harry Belafonte Johnny Cash, Crash Craddock, Chubby Checker, Bobby Rydell,. Roy Orbison - 'everybody'. [12]

By the 1960s, Abe had interests along the Dirty Half Mile between El Alamein Fountain to the Coca Cola sign at the Darlinghurst Road and William Street intersection. Clubs included the Pink Panther, Persian Room, Venus Room, Crazy Horse, Les Girls and the Pink Pussycat. By now Abe was acquainted with heavies like Lennie McPherson, Big Jim Anderson, Last Card Louie and the Black Prince.

Family was one thing – business another. Abe's wife Doreen persuaded her husband to purchase a smart 3-storey residence in Hopetown Avenue Vaucluse, which became the Saffron family home. In 1969 Abe moved office from 44 Macleay Street (across the road from Clune Gallery) to Lodge 44, 44 New South Head Road. About the time Abe moved out of Macleay Street, Martin and the Yellow House team moved in. The Yellow House was almost opposite Abe's former Macleay Street office.

The police certainly noticed the Yellow House. Sex and drugs were associated with the premises, so they dropped in hoping for a payoff. They had no idea what Hippies were about and were disappointed to find an art place not a bordello. Roger Foley (Ellis D Fogg) recalled, 'I was there when the police came around.

They knew there were a lot of women in the Yellow House. They thought it was some kind of brothel. They never actually asked for money but implied that something could be arranged. There was a lot of sex going on in the place - but it was free. That's when they lost interest.' [13]

Roger's girlfriend performed at Sandra Nelson's club (not a Saffron club). Gretel Pinniger, known as Madam Lash, took part in a televised discussion panel in which she openly spoke about corruption in the Kings Cross Vice Squad. According to her biographer, Abe wanted her rubbed out! Fortunately for Gretel, one of her suitors Lennie McPherson stepped in and calmed the waters. [14]

Like all Yellow House residents, Jonny Lewis had to deal with underworld characters whose aggression might turn on a whim. Jonny described one encounter, 'Peter Wright and I were in the bar at *Juillet's*. Jimmy Sweeten was there. He pulled a gun out, put it in my tummy and clicked the chambers click-click-click-click. I was that stoned I don't think I responded the way he wanted me to - I just ordered my drink.' [15]

David Litvinoff had genuine underworld connections, as he did in London. Sometimes he bought heroin and kept it secret. The Yellow House tribe were acid-eaters and stoners, they had no interest in smack. As the 70s progressed, Martin would see *'the needle and the damage done'* when heroin ravaged some of his closest friends and associates, so he grew to hate the stuff.

By the mid-70s Abe's business arrangements had become increasingly complex. Although his name doesn't appear on the documents, he had a piece of the action in most fringe entertainment venues on that Dirty Half Mile. One example - in 1977 Togima Leasing P/L acquired a lease where Kings Cross Station now stands. The Saffron name was absent even though Togima was a Saffron corporate entity. The premises were retail sex downstairs and gambling upstairs. Although his name is not on the documents, in like manner, Saffron certainly had a business interest in Luna Park, especially in the gaming machines. [16]

Martin continued, 'Anyway - skip 18 months or so – I'm at Wirian, cutting the film, Haydn Keenan's working with me and some friends of his came over who were drunk and mandied. A really heavy-looking chick had black hair and a white face. She was beautiful in a sinister way and very out of it. She gets bored with the film, comes out and says, "I used to work at the Park". I said, "Oh, really?" She said, "I used to work in the Magic Shop". And I said, "Oh?" (*Bang-Bang-Click-Click*.) She said, "Yeah, Abe got me the job there. He runs it with two Sydney businessmen". So Abe was involved back then! Abe had the Magic Shop and all these bloody spooky monster images were radiating out. That was the beachhead he took the place from.' [17]

Martin embarked on an intense study of spiritual significators pointing to aspects of the Luna Park story. Police and Inquest statements were just the beginning. Martin kept press clippings, photographs, extracts from occult encyclopedias, metaphysical indicators, symbolic evidence and Biblical verification.

Examples: (1) the name 'God-son', (2) $13 price tags at the Magic Shop, (3) the Pope on a train to Auschwitz for the first time ever, (4) Bob Dylan recording his *Slow Train Coming* album, and (5) Saffron's Jewish connection, 'Behold, I will make them of the synagogue of Satan, who say they are Jews and are not' Revelation 3:9. Martin made a point of following the imagery – masks, skeletons, clocks – and if couldn't figure what it all meant, he was damn sure it meant something!

Tenders for the use of the park site were called on 31 July 1979. These were hastily withdrawn and responsibility shunted from the Department of Lands and Services to the Premier's Department. That switch meant that as prime real estate, Luna Park could be bulldozed and turned into a casino, a World Trade Centre, high-rise apartments or anything else. This sparked an urgent call to action. Martin, Kingo, Richard Liney and Tim Lewis started an affirmative action group known as *Friends of Luna Park*. Towards the close of 1979 they staged three exhibitions of toys and memorabilia as part of their strategy for generating wider public concern.

When State Government regrouped for discussion, it decided to stay with a theme park concept - modernised where necessary - in line with what was happening to such parks all over the world. The government called for a second round of tenders. After considering them all, it concluded that none satisfactorily met the requirement to provide amenities similar to those available before. A third round of tenders was called in March 1980.

One of the Friends of Luna Park, Sam Marshall, witnessed the next development. He wrote, 'Realising the gravity of the situation, the artists who made up Friends of Luna Park were joined by people of all backgrounds, professions, ages and municipalities to preserve Luna Park.

While the tenders were being considered, Friends of Luna Park staged a "Save Luna Park Day" on 28 June 1980. Support for the traditional Luna Park was demonstrated by a protest march from the Opera House over the Bridge to the Face where a free concert appropriately headlined by rock group Mental As Anything included a play by Bundenna school children – "Luna's Longest Laugh". Friends of Luna Park was concerned that one of the world's last traditional amusement parks would become a casino or an American-style theme park. At the rally it was announced that, at the Friends request, the National Trust had classified the face and towers as items of national heritage, and given the rest of the Park a "recorded" classification.' [18]

As well as contributing artwork and other resources, Martin arranged for these events to be filmed and spliced into his film about Tiny. He thanked Friends of Luna Park in his film credits.

Following their success, Friends of Luna Park held a well-attended public meeting in the Lower Sydney Town Hall in mid-July. Three months later the Department of Public Works commissioned the group to prepare a formal report – known as *The Luna Park Report* - in which they would make recommendations for the individual rides and the future of the whole park. For the next five years, a bound copy of this A3-document had a permanent place somewhere on the long table in Martin's Inner Sanctum studio. [19]

On 23 September 1980 the lease was granted to Australian Amusements Associates (later known as Harbourside Amusements). Harbourside Amusement Park Pty Ltd comprised: Sir Arthur George, brothers Harold and Colman Goldstein, Brian Treasure, Michael Edgley – all co-directors, and David Baffsky as solicitor. [20]

'It looked like a very solid sort of thing,' said Martin. 'The public get given what looks like a strong show business team. Suddenly it falls apart, Edgley drops out.' [21] Leaving, Brian Treasure who had a business connection with Saffron, Harold and Colman (Col) Goldstein his first cousins once removed, David Baffsky was Saffron's lawyer. And a Saffron-controlled company Arcadia Amusements & Vending hired its machines to Harbourside Amusements.

Martin said, 'I go along to a party. I see Marcia (Premier Wran's first wife). She says, "What's happening at Luna Park?" I say, "Col Goldstein has got it". She says, "Col Goldstein! Abe's always wanted that". I can't believe it! She said, "Abe's always wanted the Park!" Col Goldstein is Abe Saffron's cousin! And the whole thing went snap - one step further into place.' [22]

In a taped statement made to Russell Sharp, Maurice Spatt confirmed what was said, 'The winners of the tender have screwed the government. You know who you are dealing with? Abe Saffron. You know who's behind this? Sir Arthur George, Col Goldstein and his brother, and it's Abe Saffron. Hal Goldstein told someone who I know very well, who told me to my face that Abe Saffron is in it with them. That's who you are dealing with. They want the place to peddle drugs to the children, they don't give a fuck about Luna Park'. [23]

Sam Marshall summarised the next development. He wrote, 'On a rainy 31 May and 1 June 1981, an auction was held within Luna Park to sell anything detachable. Larry Freels, a collector from San Francisco, paid $140,000 for the Carousel and $20,000 for the Gebruder organ. The carousel animals were shipped back to America…Friends of Luna Park bought the Barrels of Fun, Turkey Trot and Joy Wheel for $9200 to keep them in the Park. In these two days, Luna Park, including the name, was dismembered and scattered about Sydney'. [24]

Many of the original rides, placards, games, effects and murals were auctioned off by Geoff K Gray Auctioneer. [25] With a view of some day bringing it all back, the Friends of Luna Park bought as much as they could. After the auction, Martin and friends followed a truck to the tip, grabbed what was salvageable and stashed in Wirian for safekeeping. Visitors were now greeted at the front door with a display of vintage fairground art.

Said Martin, 'After the fire came the auction. We saved some Arthur Barton's paintings from being thrown out and others we recommended be saved – which they were. We brought some over here and we've been restoring them. I wasn't strong enough to hold it all. You can only hold so much. Some were too damaged and old.' [26]

'The Mystic East had a real Buddha - a real religious figure in a world of plaster and fantasy - as part of that fantasy. Sitting on an endless river - Buddha, beautiful, marble, it was the heaviest thing in the Park. It was sold at the Auction, sitting with a number on its wrist and bought by this guy from Sunshine Advertising Agency. They had to pillage the place to get this enormous marble statue. They needed cranes to get it out. It was taken on the back of the truck, chained like a prisoner. Its expression of course was bliss. It was like a lynchpin in the place. After it went, they should have destroyed the Park.' [27]

Demolition began two days after the auction. Along with the Big Dipper and Davy Jones Locker, the River Caves were bulldozed. The Wild Cat and the Carousel were dismantled and removed. Kingo said, 'There was a lot of art at Luna Park, which disgracefully got sold at the auction. It should have all been "not for sale". A lot of it got dispersed, such as the Buddha. The whole of the River Caves was taken as landfill.' [28]

Friends of Luna Park - Martin, Kingo and others - compiled the bulk of the text for *The Luna Park Report*. From his Developing Room underneath Wirian, Jonny reconstructed old photographs taken by the Park's former electrical engineer, manager and (later) owner, Ted Hopkins. Jonny says, 'All those photos in the Report, they were Hoppy's photographs. What I did was "liberate" all the old negatives from the Luna darkroom - and I'd print them.' [29]

Around this time, photography student Michael Barker called on Martin. Said Martin, 'Michael comes around and says, "I'm interested in your work, I'm doing a project on you, I'd like to come to Luna Park". I was very impressed with his demeanour, enthusiasm, personality and everything. I said, "I can only let a certain number of people in and the place is full up".

'But Jonny Lewis dropped out of being the photographer so I asked Michael to replace him and he agreed, he was thrilled. I feel in a way it was fated, that I was destined to meet him somehow. Luna Park was very heavy to go into at that time. It was dark and rainy, the place looked like a misery. We hadn't been in since the fire. I did wonder whether it was too heavy for Michael, but he seemed such a fantastically optimistic person, enthusiastic, tremendously helpful and he took some absolutely fantastic pictures. He was a lovely young guy very balanced, very together.

'We were preparing the *Report*. I'd always had the feeling that there were to be eight people to die in relationship with the fire, before that thing had passed its passage. The tension was incredible – someone – something - has got to go. We just had to ride it out somehow.'

Martin had three strong premonitions. The first was Greg's photograph of the Ghost Train exterior where seven clocks are apparent but an eighth clock was hidden by a carpenter (or someone like that). Martin's second premonition was a photograph of the North Sydney Olympic Pool, with the Luna Park Face in the background. It revealed eight 'crosses' marking the eight lanes. The third was the arrival of a sacred blue kingfisher – symbol of peace and prosperity - that would later appear in Martin's *Tapestry* (1990) and other pictures. Michael Barker was in an upstairs building in the Park when a blue kingfisher flew onto the paving then onto his finger, as Michael showed Martin. A blue kingfisher in the city of Sydney was a rare sight indeed. A wild bird, hopping on Michael's finger and remaining there was truly extraordinary!

Martin continued, 'the Report was finished and Michael went back to art school. We then got the proof copy and Michael came over to look at it. He asked if he could take a photograph of himself standing on the Big Dipper looking towards the Harbour Bridge then he headed off to a class party at Paddington Town Hall.

'It was a full Moon, Kiss was giving a concert in town. (I mentioned the Kiss concert because the crowd was a strange manifestation of the Ghost Train thing.) Michael was riding his motorcycle home from the end-of- year party where he had completed the second-last year of his photography course. He was driving along Tara Street and came up to the Ocean Street intersection. A car ran into the back of him, pushed him into a stream of traffic, he was hit by a car and killed. We dedicated the Report to him.' [30]

Michael Barker died on 21 November 1980, aged 21. Martin expressed deep sorrow to the Barker family. In response, Michael's brother John started calling on Wirian. He became involved in filming Luna Park, which Martin found incredibly courageous. Their mother wrote Martin a long letter of thanks. Martin treasured it. [31]

Most of Martin's friends date his conversion to Christianity to the time of the Ghost Train fire. There were other influences too. 'Vicki Cobden got religion in a pretty bad way', said former Yellow House resident, Mal Ramage. 'Vicki Cobden was important in the matrix of Martin's behavior.' [32]

Vicki wasn't the only one. Susan Jensen too, 'I became a Christian in 1981 and clearly remember a conversation with Mart soon after when he said to me "I wish I had your faith". I said, "you can, it's just a choice like any other choice". I think he already did believe at the time - the fire was his spiritual wake up call. I agreed with Martin that the fire was arson and the work of the Devil. I hope it was comforting to him to know that not just I, but others also, recognised that real evil was clearly active in that event and we didn't think Martin was overreacting or imagining things.' [33]

Former owner of the Yellow House building Ian Reid, who married Martin's cousin Kate, occasionally called on Martin. Unimpressed by his religious direction, he said, 'I studied with different eastern masters and that became my orientation. Martin was his own authority and was immersed in the Bible, Christianity, revelations and magical thinking which I didn't want any part of.' [34]

Martin actually dated his interest in Christianity five years earlier, back to 1974 when watching Tiny on stage in a Newcastle Leagues Club, 'like a prophet' ad-libbing *Heaven Is My Home*. (35) Much later in life, sensing his unworthiness, Martin said, 'I still wouldn't call myself a Christian' although Richard Neville certainly did. In one of his newspaper columns he announced, 'Martin is a Christian. He has been known to pace up and down his old family mansion reading out favourite verses from the New Testament to startled young girls'. (36)

Martin's concern was the fate of Luna Park, which connected with his thoughts on collective guilt, action and redemption. When uncertain how to proceed he said, 'I got my instructions for Luna Park from an eight-year old girl playing ping-pong on the terrace. Kids can be totally freaked out by fire. If they didn't want the Park any more, I could understand that. It was up to them because they were the ones who'd been sacrificed. If the kids didn't want it, what was the point? I wanted to find out. The people who were running the Park didn't run it in the right way - they didn't clear the soul of the place. Tiny sang, "Every time I look into the Holy Book I want to tremble, when I read about the part where the carpenter cleared the temple..." and Luna Park was the temple. "And the buyers and the sellers are no different fellas than what I profess to be" that was when Tiny marked the turf!' (37) And Michael Barker with the iridescent blue kingfisher on his finger was 'like a young St Francis'. (38) Such references were being peppered throughout Martin's works, especially the film.

In May 1981, Martin hired Michael Edols and crew to film Tiny in his home town. The New York footage starts with a trip down memory lane, sites from Tiny's old neighbourhood. His mother Tillie, showed the film crew Tiny's bedroom with 'Jesus Saves' in his youthful scrawl still visible on the peeling wall.

Notwithstanding his strict Christian ethic ('you can look but you mustn't touch') one evening, Tiny told Edols to bring his film crew to his hotel room. There they found an alcohol-affected Tiny in the company of Pleasure Aims, a performer from *Melody Burlesque*. For the benefit of the camera, Tiny declared the wonders of champagne and Ms Aims bared her breasts. (39)

Back in Australia, Martin included the Pleasure Aims segment in the film, which he screened for Tiny's management when he visited New York later in the year. 'They were horrified!' said Martin. (40)

Adding to this, Martin spliced News footage of the Ghost Train fire with songs from the marathon. Some was quite subtle, Tiny blowing a kiss became the Judas Kiss in the Garden of Gethsemane, ('...and if I kiss you in the garden...'). Martin explained this at length to all his assistants. (41)

There were also practical aspects to consider, and complications concerning song copyrights, each needing to be cleared by their respective estates. That was one of Marilyn's jobs – first to locate, then contact, representatives of each estate and come to a financial agreement for inclusion of their song in the marathon, which spanned 139 songs. Martin explained, 'A song that is crucial might cost $50,000 for 30 seconds and not $150 like most of them'.

Cutting and pasting on his editing machine, created a film that seemed more like a collage rather than a tightly scripted plot. Martin had hopes of success, 'People will be forever trying to make a cult film – or another Rocky Horror. You can't manipulate or predict things like that. People will see the film on Tiny and they'll go see it again and again. They'll sing along with it, they'll really get into it!' [42]

Briefly, there was some talk of releasing the entire Marathon in cassette format [43] but other Tiny Tim music – tighter projects - took priority. The first was a 45rpm single to commemorate Luna Park. Tiny sang the 1930 Rudy Vallee song, Wind in the Willows, on one side, the other was their own Luna Park Song. Martin got Al Jones and his friend Mic Conway to write and perform it. Al had a solid background in Pop/Rock/Country music. Being a member of Slim Dusty's Travellin' Band, 10 of Al's songs had appeared on various Slim Dusty LPs. And Mic had co-written hits for the Captain Matchbox Whoopee Band. Coming from a Vaudeville/jug band background, Mic had always admired Tiny. 'When I was at school, a lot of people worshipped Sgt Pepper. Well, Tiny Tim's God Bless LP was my Sgt Pepper!' Mic affirmed. [44] Al and Mic co-wrote the *The Luna Park Song* though Al recorded the song without Mic because he was on tour. Street of Dreams Production released the two sides as a 45rpm single. Martin's cover artwork was in the same vein as his *Friends of Luna Park* letterhead and the *Save Luna Park* poster.

Martin did lots of other work too. He wasn't painting much on canvas but he was certainly creating posters. He did one for another kind of OZ – *Circus* OZ. In 1978 the Soapbox Circus and New Ensemble Circus amalgamated to create Circus OZ with Mic as front man. Martin also designed the Al Jones Late Show poster for the Stables Theatre where Al worked with actor Lex Marinos. [45] He also did the poster for Jeannie Lewis' cabaret show. She said, 'At the end of 1979 we did *Krazy 4 You*. Martin did the poster for that. And then I did *Piaf*.' [46]

Martin also created several other black and white (or black, white and red) posters in this period - for the Patrick White play *Signal Driver* and the Louis Nowra play *Visions*. Also - Finks Circus, Circus Animals (for Cold Chisel), as well as the prints, *Ignatz Paints His World* and *Ginger Meggs in Japan*, the later of which – in time – Martin and Tim would repaint together on canvas. Another new piece was *Couples*, (bought by Patrick White) a collage worked with scissors and glue. [47]

While Martin was busy being prolific, his Face of Luna Park was being re-faced. A cast was taken so a replica could be made. In mid-1981 the largest piece of Pop Art in the Southern Hemisphere was defaced, dismantled and dumped on the ground in front of the Park's twin towers, awaiting a couple of surfboard makers to make a fiberglass mould.

Writes Sam Marshall, 'Surfboard makers Darryl Holmes and Stephen Johnson grappled with the difficult task of working with facial features on such a huge scale.

They repaired the face then made a fibreglass mould and demolished the original face. The mould was reinforced and reinstated but it was a poor copy of Martin Sharp's clown face with a lumpy forehead, bloodshot eyeballs and pupils that were at the centre of the eye opening – the position of the eye when terrified.' [48]

2.
WIRIAN

Wirian is an internal Yellow House rather than an external one.
Martin Sharp

Pre-AIDs Sydney 1980s: Taylor Square, Imperial Hotel, Kinselas, Sylvia and the Synthetics, Jimmy & the Boys, Mad Max, Brett Whiteley's *Lavender Bay* series, Hogarth Gallery, *Billy Blue* magazine, Wild & Woolley, Patrick White & Manoly Lascaris, the 4th Sydney Festival, Oxford Street shops, The Rocks, Nimrod Theatre, Australian Film Commission, Lord Dudley Hotel, Regular Records, Singo, the Madam Lash shop 'Gay Birds', Vittorio Bianchi's Piccolo Bar, Double J Radio, the Elton John tour, the Gay Mardi Gras after-party, amyl nitrate, Flamingo Park. Sex joints, soirees and excess.

Martin entered the 80s with a partly shot film, an inheritance not properly under his control, a rickety love life and the cause of the Ghost Train fire an unsolved mystery. Although the media still portrayed him as one of the naughty wizards of OZ magazine, he wanted to be remembered for other things. He wasn't all about Artoons and OZ. Although Martin didn't paint much, he created posters, edited film, produced records, organized Tiny Tim concerts and deciphered religious and quasi-religious imagery gleaned from the general media. He videotaped pertinent news stories and collated press clippings into A4 plastic folders, which he referenced for synchronicity and symbolism. 'I'm just trying to make dilettantism into an art,' he quipped. [1]

In fad-conscious Sydney, the new kid on the Art block was Ken Done. Done walked out of corporate life as Creative Director at the influential J Walter Thompson advertising agency. He started his own business selling hand-painted Sydney

Harbour t-shirts from his house in Ridge Street North Sydney and quickly became Sydney's most accessible artist. He held his first exhibition in 1980 at Holdsworth Gallery. Soon after, he and his wife Judy opened a shop in The Rocks and sold fabrics, designs and prints. He produced postcards, magazine covers, t-shirts, posters, sheets, pillowcases, calendars, books and even paintings. Done's blatant commercialism annoyed fine art critics but he didn't care. Done Art had tourist appeal. Sydneysiders wanted Ken Done sheets and Martin Sharp posters. Done's exuberant beachscapes were inescapable as t-shirts and Martin was commissioned to create the 1981 City of Sydney festival poster.

'I always accepted that I was selling something,' said Ken, 'some artists pretend they don't but there are no artists who don't want to sell their work. I work on that principle'. [2]

Martin's colleagues were no longer the frontline provocateurs they were in the 60s. By the 80s, each of the OZ Trio (for different reasons) loathed the unprincipled hedonism that they were credited having unleashed. Martin had always been kinda cosmic. Richie Walsh had always been kind of sensible. Richard Neville was the puzzle. Along with Germaine Greer, he had been a judge at Amsterdam's art and pornfest, the 1970 Wet Dream Film Festival - how could this same Richard loathe the New Hedonism? Well, he did. They all did.

Now married, Richie Walsh edited and managed *Nation Review* until its sale in 1979. He then moved into the corporate side of publishing. Whenever he and Richard got together they bounced ideas, puns and jokes off each other. The two Richards were a great two-person act when they shared the media 'I talk without full stops' is how Richie Walsh described himself. [3] And of course, Richard Neville was a self-confessed motor-mouth dating back to university days.

Writer and journalist Julie Clarke knew Martin from the Yellow House and he introduced her to Richard. Richard and Julie became a couple and co-authored an unlikely biography, *The Life and Crimes of Charles Sobhraj*. Many were shocked that the Eternal Groover who had idealised the counterculture, would give any credence to a Hippie killer. That Richard found the experience harrowing was a bit of a relief. [4]

Richard and Julie married in December 1980 and bought a property in Blackheath NSW. He took on the improbable role of presenter on Channel Nine's *Mike Walsh Show*, a sort-of TV Housewives Choice. Core material was whatever was faddish in popular culture: Hippies, Yuppies, Greenies, eco-tourists, mystics, lifestylers, the New Age, the lot. This laid the groundwork for Richard's next incarnation as a Futurist. [5]

Richard and Julie's 45-acre *Happy Daze* property was 4k out of Blackheath on the fork of Pulpit Rock and Hat Hill Road. (Jenny Kee would soon buy 5-acres also on Hat Hill Road.) Richard and Julie both had family connections in the upper Blue Mountains. Richard's grandparents owned *Upalong*, a fine house in Mount Victoria beyond Katoomba. And Julie's brother Rolley lived in Mount

Victoria and was a handy carpenter. Over the years the out-of-the-way location of Happy Daze provided a haven for Sallie-Anne Huckstepp, Martin and even – at one stage – Salmon Rushdie.

With the Rolley's assistance and Richard's nephew Michael Braund, Richard and Julie added two studios, improved the gardens and extended the house to maximise their breathtaking views of the Grose Valley. In time, they made Happy Daze spacious and attractive. Before Richard and Julie fixed it up, it was a derelict party house where young people gathered on weekends to drop acid and party. It didn't even have electricity. Having fantasised about buying it himself, local resident, Max Skeen recalled the selling price being $50,000 ('A lot of money back then') but added, 'Richard bought it cheaper than that'. [6]

Back in Bellevue Hill, Wirian housed Russell Sharp, Martin's cousin and personal assistant. Also at Wirian were society photographer - William Yang, slightly world-weary jack-of-all-musical-trades - Al Jones, assistant film editor and advisor - Marilyn Karet who a guest described as 'the only Wirian-person who was patently sane'. Albert Peck ran the house. There were many other assistants, helpers and advisers too, including Nathan Waks, Paul Healy, Chris Cordeaux, Sally Fitzgerald, Peter Kingston and sometimes drop-in guests who no one had ever heard of - like 'Robert' the Jehovah's Witness who rapped on the front door and was surprised to be invited inside for coffee and a welcome discussion about the Apocalypse. He gave Martin a Watchtower magazine that Martin kept on display for ages, next to the cardboard figures of Charles & Di waving.

In the 14-year interim since Martin and Richard went to London most of the OZ and Yellow House people had traveled overseas too. Some never came back. Germaine Greer and Barry Humphries remained in England. Robert Hughes and Little Nell moved to in New York and Jim Anderson vanished to Bolinas California where he stayed for years. Jim flashed back to Sydney in 1981, held a show at Hogarth Gallery, caught up with a few friends including Martin and Richard, who he met in a pub in Paddington. Jim then returned to Bolinas where he re-mained until the mid-90s. [7]

After the success of his film about bushranger *Mad Dog Morgan,* Philippe Mora moved to Los Angeles where, in 1980, he married Pamela and laid the groundwork for his next film, *The Beast Within*. Philippe's painting *Da Corner* was permanently parked in the Wirian hall beside remnants of Luna Park. It was among the first things visitors saw when they walked in. [8]

The old team was well and truly scattered. Garry Shead was in Budapest where he had met his future wife, artist Judit Englert. Brett Whiteley and his family lived in Fiji before returning to Lavender Bay where Kingo and John Firth-Smith also lived. Mick Glasheen moved to Sydney's northern beaches. John Bell journeyed from Northern Australia to Papua New Guinea. George Gittoes and Gabrielle Dalton moved south to Bundeena. Tim Lewis, Albie Thoms and Jonny Lewis traveled extensively throughout America, Europe, Asia and the Middle East. Greg and Sue Weight bought an acreage near Glenorie, 44k north-west of Sydney and Roger Foley-Fogg stayed in Sydney and worked with designer Maggie Tabberer. [9]

Martin was still childless but the first wave of children was born to many of his friends: Arkie Whiteley, Claudia Karvan, Christabel Draffin, Tilly Lewis, Gria Shead, Naomi Gittoes, Alex Weight, Osha and Minyo Weight. In their own way they were all fascinated by the Dream Museum and its toys. Little Sky McCreadie from next door was another regular.

Amber Tarling was one of the Dream Museum kids. 'That Dream Museum!' she reminisced. 'There were certain things you couldn't touch. There was a respect, there was an order and we always had to pack it up after playing. George Gittoes' daughter said to me that Martin was like an uncle. It's a shame he didn't have children. He would have been a great Dad.' Her sister Zoë's childhood perspective was, 'Martin's home was focused on creative play - drawing or painting.' [10]

Over the years, Wirian inspired lots of kids. Martin welcomed student projects and happily cooperated. Mart's art was the subject of many school activities. Roger's daughter Electra did her Year 9 assignment about one of Martin's paintings. [11]

Wirian was gradually becoming an extension of Martin's fascinations. Almost every scene that follows will happen somewhere in Wirian. When Tiny came to Australia, he always spent a lot of time at Martin's house. The Anglican Archbishop of Sydney visited Wirian. The Governor of New South Wales did too. Princess Eugenie showed up in beachwear. Bob Geldof, Russell Crowe, Keith Haring, Peter Allen, Jimmy Barnes, Reg Mombassa, Jack Thompson, David Gulpilil, Zandra Rhodes, Eric Clapton, Marianne Faithfull, Lin Utzon and many other distinguished guests have dropped in over the years, as did Tiny Tim's cousin Hal and his wife Sherry. [12]

Martin's pictures and posters were all created on the premises, either in the hall, the Dream Museum, his bedroom studio and his Inner Sanctum. Some, like the restoration of Arthur Barton's 1935 *The Building of Loona Park* (4.25 x 3.5 m), demanded the kind of space only a big hallway could provide. The size of Wirian made all this possible.

From a family residence, under Martin's governance, Wirian slowly but irrevocably evolved into an artist's studio and storage space. Wirian is prime Sydney real estate in up-market Bellevue Hill across the road from the Fairfax mansion and next door to the Cranbrook School. Built for the wife of a grazier in 1923, Stuart and Vee Ritchie bought it in 1937. [13] Designed by Halligan & Wilton architects, Wirian has a *porte cochère*, formal lounge room, smoking room, ballroom, butler's pantry, four majestic upstairs bedrooms, servants' bedrooms, two (later three) upstairs bathrooms, an upstairs bow window with leadlight glazing, a room under the house where boarders have lived over the years and a kitchen with its still-working Kooka stove. Before Martin settled his probate debt by selling part of the land to Cranbrook School, Wirian also had a garage with chauffeur's accommodation, tennis court and turning circle-cum-parking area at the end of the driveway on the Cranbrook side of the property. (14)

Wirian had a history of hosting grand social events, that Stuart and Vega Ritchie continued. While Martin's father and uncles endured the horrors of World War II overseas, their womenfolk were attending lovely soireés, dances and cocktail parties in Wirian's grand rooms. Guests included industrialists, celebrities, Governors-General and many other illustrious guests. Martin and his mother lived there for the first four years of his life. They moved into their own house in Cranbrook Lane after his father was demobilised from the Army.

Martin inherited Wirian when he was in his mid-30s. It took a while, but he eventually moved into his grandmother's quarters. Her enclosed bedroom verandah became Martin's second studio (the first being the grand dining room which Martin's guests dubbed the Inner Sanctum).

Martin did not nest easily in the mid-70s, he was too used to moving around. He came-and-went between Sydney, London, Paris and New York usually leaving Tim Lewis back home to 'hold the fort' (as Martin called it).

He encountered Andy Warhol in New York. In the 60s, Warhol's New York City studio, The Factory, was a model for open-door art houses. By the end of the decade, things got too crazy. Valerie Solanas shot Warhol on behalf of the Society for Cutting Up Men (SCUM), of which she was president, secretary and its total membership. The shooting had a profound effect on Warhol. He retained his most trusted art-workers, shut the door on the rest and entered his entrepreneurial phase.

Martin recalled Warhol's calm manner of handling public pressure, 'I was in New York visiting Tiny and Nell took me to an opening of an exhibition,' Martin recalled. 'It was all going on inside and he was sitting outside on a little table being very quiet, just taking photographs of people every now and then. He was being so polite, being very kind to everyone who came up to him - and he had a lot of people. I noticed he was making an incredible effort and he was actually shaking a little bit under the table.

'There was something about his poise and I said, "Do you go to church?" He said, "Yes I go to Mass every Sunday". I thought that was incredibly interesting. I didn't know why I asked that particular question, just that he was being so kind to people. He was giving himself to an extreme degree and I could see under the table, at a considerable cost to himself.' (15)

But Martin had no idea how to run a grand residence. He turned Wirian into part museum and part artists' colony then mortgaged it to finance his film. (16) Artists and musicians came and went. In his absence, Tim Lewis and Richard and Sharon Liney were great at fanning Wirian's bohemian vibe. Then Martin came back and it became Tim's turn to go overseas so Martin and Richard Liney created the 1978 Dream Museum Exhibition for the Art Gallery of New South

Wales. Shortly afterwards, the Lineys left, which left a vacancy in the guardianship of Wirian.

Martin invited his grandfather's former servant/gardener to move in and Albert Peck monitored everything. He charged each tenant $25pw rent and ensconced himself in Martin's grandfather's upstairs bedroom.

Said Martin, 'I thought it went really well for a number of years. I liked him. I thought he was teaching me how to run the place. He was quite good with money. There was a bit of a crisis though...' [17]

The new Wirianites (not all at the same time) were Melody Cooper, Stephen Teather, Susan Jensen, Richard Neville, Julie Clarke, William Yang, Victoria Cobden, Al Jones, Victor Rubin, Marilyn Karet and Cressida Campbell. [18]

The house was beginning to shape into Martin's personality. The dining room became his Inner Sanctum studio, the ballroom became the Dream Museum, the Smoking Room became the film editing room and every room was a smoking room. There was a blur of people coming by day and staying overnight or a bit longer - like Salami Sisters, Kathy Lette and Gabrielle Carey. Lette wrote about it: 'We lived under Martin Sharp's dining room table for a while. Martin had a huge empty mansion, full of ghosts, but he was only supposed to live in the back bit, the servant's quarters under a weird will; then as he got older he could move into other areas. The house was full of artists and musicians.' [19]

Informed that Sallie-Anne Huckstepp was on the run from the underworld, Richard rescued her and housed her in the privacy of *Happy Daze* in Blackheath. After a time, he asked Martin if he could move her into Wirian. Martin said okay. Sallie-Anne arrived spaced out on Mandrax and slurring her words. She lived there but had little to do with Martin who told her biographer John Dale, 'She had a broken leg when she came, she was on crutches, Richard told me she'd had a miscarriage. It wasn't a blessing to have her but there was enough room. She had a little daughter. Some guy used to come and visit her, quite a tough guy on a very expensive motorbike.' [20]

Photographer, William Yang moved in too. He said, 'In September 1979 I had hepatitis, so I decided I'd come from Brisbane to Sydney in the Spring. Melody and Steven were the two lodgers and Albert was a retainer. Richard and Julie lived there. It's a large house and people find their own way, where they fit it. Nothing is defined. It's totally intuitive. Albert assumed that Martin was incapable of looking after his own finances. He paid all the bills, collected the rent and had all the keys, so he had a considerable position of power in this place. If you wanted to gain admission to this place you had to be screened by Albert. If Albert didn't like you he could make life hell. He spent a lifetime tyranising the lodgers. Albert put a price on everything. People would borrow objects but with Albert there was always a fee. Albert regarded Martin as profligate with money. And for an ordered mind it was almost an unbearable situation for Albert to be in, to look after the books - yet Martin would spend money like he usually did.' [21]

Albert had the territorial imperative over the house. To prohibit houseguests from watching 'too much' television, he kept the TV set in his room. As punishment for being untidy, Albert confiscated all cigarettes and alcohol lying around from the previous night. These he stashed in his room and – like the 8-year old Abe Saffron - sold them back to visitors when they ran out. Friends urged Martin to get rid of Albert but he wouldn't. Then, it came to a head. Said Martin, 'That whole thing had a very strong rich metaphysic to it. There was a big Luna Park meeting and Peter Royles came from the bush and stayed.' [22]

Late one evening, while sitting around chatting, Richard Neville said, 'I'd like a drink'. Albert replied, 'I've got some scotch'. So Richard bought himself a nip or three. Next day Richard was talking and let slip the sentence, 'Albert sold me whisky' which caught Martin's attention because he felt the whisky was the property of Toto Renshaw, another visitor. So Martin fronted Albert, 'Did you see any whisky?' And Albert said no. 'It was the wrong answer for Martin,' said William, 'that was the beginning of the end.' [23]

'I thought Toto would come back for his whisky,' Martin explained, 'Everything was in a state of flux. I was with Cress (Cressida Campbell) at the time and I'd given up smoking, so I was putting myself through quite a bit. Melody asked to have a party and use the end room. The last thing I needed was a party around the place. I was totally cloistered in my room, keeping very quiet. There was a lot of ping-pong being played on the balcony and I was trying to be peaceful. I couldn't get to sleep.

'I came downstairs and told Melody and Steve it was time to move along. Certainly there was a loss of temper, that's for sure. Sometimes I've gone right off and thrown things everywhere. Sometimes just one thing - well aimed. It only happens under rare circumstances. Paranoia builds up and everything you've been holding back comes out. You've lost communication with people. I felt I'd been pushed into a situation where you just explode. I didn't want things to happen the way they did.' [24]

Melody helped Albert move out. She and Stephen left as well. Says Melody, 'Albert left at the same time that Stephen and I left. Mart had given up smoking, told no one he was doing it, but gave permission for me to have a party. It was for the end of a season of a play I had done at Sydney Uni for Rex Cramphorn. During the party, where we of course were smoking joints, Mart lost the plot and threw us all out. He apologised the next day and wanted us to stay but the damage had been done. Stephen and I helped Albert take all his stuff to his sister's house, and I never saw Albert again.' [25] Albert's demise left another vacancy. William explains, 'The physical world doesn't touch Martin much and so there's always a role here for the physical protector of the house.' [26]

Admitted to the bar in 1977, Anthony (Toto) Renshaw was a barrister working from Clive Evatt's Wardell Chambers and - like Jonny Lewis – he was the son of a former Premier of New South Wales. Although his father Jack Renshaw was a

Labor premier, Toto had upper class affectations. He was a first-rate Go player, collected samurai swords, drank Johnny Walker scotch, played Japanese Gagaku music, thought nothing of calling people 'fools' to their faces if necessary and dressed awfully well. Some people found him frightening.

Said Martin, 'It was just after the second mortgage had been taken out, the second hump of the Tiny film. A friend of Andrew Sharp, my cousin, brought Toto around. I was pretty amazed by Toto. I was pretty wary of him as well. I saw the performer in him immediately and his fantastic brain (not really being used in the right way somehow). His clothes, the look, the pose, the whole thing was like Old Wirian, as it would have been in my grandfather's days. Toto knew the city as a commercial centre with a hierarchy in a sort-of sense. He knew some of people from the other side - Arthur George, the Masonic stuff and the behind-the-scenes political maneuvering. It was the time of the Luna Park business and Toto brought the whole of that world into visibility.' [27]

For a brief time, Toto might have moved in to take up Albert's former role. Cousin Russell Sharp took that role instead. Russell was the younger son of Dr Frank Sharp. After an idyllic childhood, his mother died in 1972. His father died two years later. His childhood home in Longueville was sold and 25-year old Russell was shaken to the core. He tried working in sales, selling cookware, water reticulation systems and real estate but he didn't enjoy the work. One day he ran into Martin at the Piccolo Bar in Kings Cross. Martin suggested he move into Wirian. Russell agreed and fell straight into the role of getting Martin's affairs in order. Russell put the film and recording company *Street of Dreams Productions* onto a business footing. Also - working with Don McGregor (of McGregor Screenprints) - an attempt was made to sell Martin's posters commercially. Melody explained, 'Russell helped with posters and the business side of the Noive & Voive record label.' [28]

Russell said, 'I moved in after Albert had moved out. I was just a gofer. I did what I could. I organized quite a lot of posters, especially the ones done by Mambo and the McGregor Prints. The Nimrod posters - I sold those, I remember at the time Martin took possession of a lot of them and he was selling them. Some were $300. Then we did a whole series of other posters. Stephen (Lawson) printed an edition of about 100 and I sold them, it was a 3-way split.' [29]

Back from overseas, Roslyn Sharp made a point of visiting Wirian. Over the years she got involved with Martin more and more, but at this stage Russell was her main concern. She said, 'I'd go there mainly to see Russell. After our parents died, Russell suffered a lot and Martin was very kind to him.' [30]

'I was there for two and a half years,' said Russell. 'I was devoted. Cressida Campbell was there for a little while. She was going out with Martin. Willy (William Yang) was there. Jonny Lewis had his studio there. Alistair was there. We had *Noive and Voive* Records. That was our little record label. I incorporated *Street of Dreams* and we also created the *Chameleon* record covers.' [31]

Returning to Australia in 1980, Tiny – now with mulberry-coloured hair - completed the remaining tracks for the Chameleon LP. They were Deep Night, Song Without A Name, My Song, Dietetic Baby and Tiny Bubbles (the last two were not included on the release). St Louis Blues and Dancing in the Street were held over until 2006. They also reworked Stayin' Alive with Australian actor/musician David Gulpilil on didgeridoo (which somehow got lost in the mix when released to LP). Added to these were the masters for a song titled Country Queen recorded by Tiny on the day of Elvis' death in 1977 but not released. It was added to the LP record. Eight hundred copies of the album were released. Martin gave most of them away to friends. The few that were sold did little to recoup costs. [32]

When it came to Arts Grants, the 1970s was a most generous decade, especially for someone as established as Martin. Financial support may have been forthcoming had 'Tiny Tim' not been associated with Martin's project. After some negotiations, the Australian Film Commission (AFC) agreed to support the project with a small grant. Martin was surprised, 'Haydn Keenan helped a lot. When we showed the first compilation I didn't expect them to be interested.' [33]

Other than that $20,000 contribution from AFC, Martin carried all the production costs that he had hoped to share. In order to finish the film, produce records and keep running concerts, Martin re-mortgaged Wirian. Tiny must have been pleased to know that from this time onwards, and for the rest of his life, somewhere in the Antipodes was a small outpost constantly working on his music, taped conversations, film and visual images, the first-fruits of which proved excellent.

Artistically, things were going well for Martin and his ragtag crew, but privately there was some sadness. Martin had a very candid and close relationship with his mother. They shared things that most young people keep secret from parents. Martin discussed all aspects of his love life with his Mum, including pregnancy terminations. For all his achievements, Martin only had to do one more thing to impress her - father a child.

Said William Yang to Martin, 'Jo said to me "There's only one wish I ever wanted".

'And that is what?' he replied.

'The child – the child isn't it?'

Said Martin, 'I guess so, yes.' [34]

Martin's girlfriends were generally okay about the tight mother/son bond but unimpressed with Tiny's commentary on their relationship. In his lengthy phone conversations with Martin, Tiny expressed strict views on birth control and abortion, which Martin seemed to accept. 'I don't believe in birth control. I don't believe in rhythm. I don't believe in abortions,' Tiny effused, 'I believe according to the Scriptures man's duty is to be fruitful and multiply!' Was Tiny over-moralising as a form of satire? Martin didn't think so. [35]

Faced with another pregnancy termination, Martin fell to pieces, 'Tiny showed me the wrongness of it. I felt the real physical and spiritual effect of the whole thing. I was always disappointed. Things were going awfully wrong. I'd taken an awful lot of risks I guess. At that time I was really self-aware. I don't know if that was prayer or whatever but I was on the edge of hysteria. Sobbing. It was the worst sort of agony I've had.' [36]

Martin had a mini-breakdown. In an act of contrition, he burned off his hair. [37]

3.
HOKUSAI, ELVIS AND THAT DINGO

Two guys are looked upon as having the same talent, going back 10 years – Brett Whiteley and Martin Sharp. Brett Whiteley is an independently wealthy man. Martin Sharp is independently bloody unwealthy, unhealthy and his paintings are very hard to buy.
John Singleton

Martin was trying to get organised. He had a stack of A4 folders into which he filed news stories. The latest was that Harbourside Amusement planned to reopen Luna Park at the end of April (1982). In another group of folders, Martin stored Tiny Tim clippings from the 60s to the present. He kept historical pieces like 'The Great Crooners' Tiny's 1969 *Playboy* magazine article, Miss Vicki's 1975 nudie spread in *Oui* magazine - up to the latest from the Sydney Morning Herald's *TV Guide*: 'Don't be fooled by the unusual appearance of Tiny Tim, underneath is a very talented man'. Plus the sheet music for *Tiptoe Through the Tulips* and whatever the American press was writing about Tiny. Martin kept adding to those folders until they needed shelves. Then he added to the shelves until they needed a room. The room was the original Butler's pantry, easy access from the Inner Sanctum.

There, assistants catalogued Martin's taped conversations with Tiny, which comprised a library of 200 cassettes that kept growing. Tiny often phoned Martin from anywhere in America, sometimes anywhere in the world, and they'd talk for an hour or more, which resulted in at least one more tape to label, date and file. Martin said, 'Tiny is a difficult person to understand. I've been given a particular insight, especially by seeing the Albert Hall concert, so there was never any need to convince myself. I need re-convincing every now and then, which the tapes help do because I listen to them. I've got some friends who've hated Tiny. Some people I've been very close to haven't understood the interest. It puts a lot of pressure on those particular relationships because it means the best part of oneself one cannot share with them. People say, why don't you do more cartoons? Why don't you do some paintings? A lot of people are more sentimental about me returning to those areas. Maybe I'll do some again. I see no difference between doing a poster, a painting or a Tiny Tim show. I don't discriminate between what the medium is, I'm only following the spirit of the thing in understanding as best I can how to respond.' [1]

With a push from Russell and following the successful process of the Al Jones/Mic Conway *Luna Park Song* single, Street of Dreams Productions released Tiny's *Chameleon* and *Wonderful World of Romance* LPs.

Then a Nimrod Theatre employee found a stack of Martin's original Nimrod posters stashed under a staircase: Kaspar (1973), Ginge's Last Stand (1975), Young Mo (1977), Kold Komfort Kaffee (1978), Sideshow in Burlesco (1979) and Venetian Twins (1979). Street of Dreams Productions (ie. Russell) bought the lot for re-sale. The timing coincided with Nimrod commissioning Martin to mark the 10th anniversary of the theatre with another poster. Russell arranged for a new edition of 1000 to be produced on better quality paper and sold in sets of seven as a fundraiser for the theatre. Martin's Nimrod Series generated a lot of interest. The Mo poster was made into a keyring and Nimrod 10 became made a badge. [2]

Other poster commissions followed, not all as successfully. Against his better judgment, the Nuclear Disarmament Party talked Martin into doing their poster. Despite their best persuasive efforts, in the end they wouldn't use his 'Drop the Bomb' motif. 'That's the whole point,' Martin exclaimed, 'Nobody would drop the bomb!'

One evening Martin ran into former Labor PM Gough Whitlam at a party. In chatting, Gough told Martin that his antecedent, William Sharp (1844-1929) was a great Labor man. Martin hadn't given Great-Grandfather Sharp much thought. He was feeling slightly estranged from his father's side at the time. Said Martin, 'I found out my great-grandfather was the Labor Member for Redfern, Gough told me that. My family never told me that, never! They were all Liberals.' [3] Seizing the moment, Whitlam asked Martin for a poster for the International Socialist Congress. Martin explained, 'I normally don't do posters for the Socialist Congress but when Gough Whitlam rings up you don't really say no, do you? (Well… sometimes I do.)' [4]

So Martin did the poster and – like the Nuclear Disarmament Party - they didn't use it. The problem was that Martin expressed what he wanted to express, which was not necessarily in sync with the person doing the asking. Over the years, Martin's (later) assistant Dave Rowe saw him struggle with many commissions, 'With Circus OZ he was comfortable. He'd name his figure and they were happy. If it was someone like Cold Chisel, he was happy. He'd name the figure and do the poster. But when it was an outside source - Martin wasn't any good at deals.' [5]

Martin said, 'The ingredients they gave me were the fist clutching the rose, the Australian flag and the world in crisis. So I ask – "name me a time in history when it hasn't been in crisis?" In the end, the Socialist Congress' sub-committee declined to use the poster. I don't mind if people don't like it but I wish they hadn't asked me in the first place because all I did was give them what I thought was a good poster. That's why I don't like dealing with committees. Usually when I do a poster I say: if you want a poster sometime, let me know. Gough was a bit embarrassed, I don't think he was quite embarrassed enough!' [6]

Yes, Martin disliked committees but enjoyed creating posters for Circus OZ, Cold Chisel and friends. He'd volunteer his services, as he did for Mic and Jim Conway's *Vaude Villains* show and Jeannie Lewis' new *So You Want Blood* show that accompanied her new album of the same name. Jeannie was also involved in a fund raising concert at Paddington Town Hall, the *Apmira Art Sale for Land Rights* held at the same venue. Martin did their poster too.

In 1983, the State Government of New South Wales was moving towards passing the Aboriginal Land Rights Act in line with other States. 'Apmira' is the Arunta word for 'land'. Jeannie had been involved in the Land Rights movement since the early-60s. Gary Shearston too. He set Kath Walker's (Oodgeroo Noonuccal) *Aboriginal Charter of Rights* poem to music and wrote the song *Dingo*, which Martin began listening to intently because it linked to current news events. [7]

Martin revisited the guilt he felt over losing the Abalone Diver print. He was convinced it was a 'lost' Hokusai print of his daughter diving for abalone. Martin worried about it, wrote about it, and went over and over it in his mind. He checked with foremost Hokusai scholar Joseph Hillier, who concluded it was not bona fide. He didn't convince Martin. A woman who ran a Japanese shop in Double Bay told Martin that she knew some experts on Japanese master painters and Martin let her take it to Japan. He said, 'I got a letter from the woman saying, "Bad news, I've lost it at the airport." I was completely shattered because (a) I'd lost something very valuable and (b) because it was probably one of Hokusai's last and major works as a print. I felt I'd let him down – I had discovered it and I'd lost it.'

Uneasy about the loss, Martin wanted to preserve the image, it was the least he could do. Martin and printmaker Kristin Coburn recreated a print from a photograph taken by William. Martin and Kristin reproduced it faithfully, without commentary. 'I was so ashamed for having lost it,' said Martin, 'this way, I could at least to keep it alive.' [8]

Ever one to write letters, Martin corresponded off-and-on with the producer of Tiny's hit albums God Bless Tiny Tim and Tiny Tim's Second Album. Richard Perry had gone on to produce some seriously big names, like Ray Charles, Ringo Starr, Captain Beefheart, Rod Stewart, Pointer Sisters and many others. Perry had a soft spot for Tiny, whose first album literally launched his career. He appreciated Martin's efforts and - as musical director of the brilliant 1968 concert at the Royal Albert Hall - Perry held the original 4-track master tapes of the night. He copied them to cassette for Martin who now shared his Damascus Road epiphany with friends. The shattering version of I Got You Babe usually quelled any detractors. [9]

Known for his biographies of Lenny Bruce and Elvis Presley, Martin read Albert Goldman's sympathetic treatment of Tiny in his biography of Lenny Bruce. Goldman reckoned that Tiny had a unique understanding of the language of popular song. In 1968 he wrote, '…a dream theater that echoes beguilingly with all the voices of Tiny Tim. To say that these are the most perfect impersonations of old singers ever heard would hardly do justice to the art that has re-embodied these entertainers in electronic avatars, summoning them up out of the past to caper again before a strobe-lit oleo.'

Martin was miffed that someone as insightful as Goldman could be so hard on Elvis. In his final concert, Martin was awed by Elvis' rendition of My Way whereas Goldman found it embarrassing. How could a perceptive writer like Goldman not see what Martin saw? [10]

So Martin wrote him and included a cassette copy of Tiny's Royal Albert Hall concert. Although he failed to change his mind about Elvis, Martin reactivated Goldman's interest in Tiny. Goldman wrote back, 'Dear Martin Sharp, I appreciate your suggestions for Elvis though I must confess that I am not as impressed by the evidence of what used to be called "second sight" as you are. Elvis had been singing My Way, an absurdly inappropriate song, for some time prior to the last show. I suspect his problem with the words owes more to what is called a mental block than a sign of deathly weakness. I forbear to go further'. [11]

About Tiny he enthused, 'I had never heard him with a big orchestra in a large hall. Tiny Tim remains a unique and remarkable performer with an astounding sense of the history of popular song'. In return he sent Martin a signed copy of his book, Ladies and Gentleman Lenny Bruce!! with references to Tiny underscored. [12]

Negotiations were underway to bring Tiny back to Australia in September. Notwithstanding that he had completely run out of money, Martin decided that this time Tiny should play the best available venue in town – the Concert Hall at Sydney Opera House.

Martin worked on the poster with enthusiasm, shaping Tiny's face into the vaulted Opera House roof with the Harbour Bridge with Luna Park aglow in the background. Red, white, yellow, light blue and dark blue. Martin believed this poster was as memorable as anything he'd ever done. When asked, 'What do you think will be remembered of Martin Sharp?' he pointed to the Tiny Tim/Sydney Opera House screen print and said, 'That one – certainly!' [13]

Tiny's September tour set the template for all future ones. An entrepreneur (this time Peter Conyngham) brought Tiny out. He checked the Eternal Troubadour and his manager into the Cosmopolitan Hotel not far from Wirian and booked him into shopping centres, RSL Clubs and other ordinary venues. Sometimes it was tough going. 'Tiny Tim for tiny prices!' yelled a Grace Brothers spruiker, 'Underpants reduced to only 99c while Tiny Tim is in the store!' [14] After the completion of those tedious bread-and-butter commitments, Martin kept Tiny in the country, took over the costs, ran a concert at a prominent venue and whisked Tiny into recording studios. All subsequent visits to Australia would follow this pattern.

In August, Tiny arrived at Sydney's Mascot Airport accompanied by his US manager Bill Hollander. Representing Martin's interests, Russell was Australian tour manager. One of the first things Tiny did was to sit with Martin and look at footage of the film, which he enjoyed. Tiny teased the press. 'It took Mr Sharp years to get it together, editing. He's got so much film. He took the film to New York. There were some scenes with...er ...you know...er...naked women in it.' [15]

He spent the next day discussing various booking arrangements with Conyngham, then back with Martin for recording and concert ideas. Tiny appeared at a Beauty Show at the Chevron Hotel, performed the Bexley North RSL Club, performed at the Campbelltown RSL Club, did radio interviews with Jonathon Coleman, John Singleton and Lex Marinos. He then met Mic and Jim Conway with whom he would be performing at the Paddington Town Hall. The following day, Tiny did an interview with Roger Crosthwaite from the Daily Telegraph followed by the interview with Southern Flyer - which is how I met him - on the deck, in the sunshine, at the Cosmopolitan Hotel Double Bay. [16]

The 1982 tour comprised a series of club gigs, press interviews and department store appearances, not all well attended. Martin took it all on the chin. He described one venue, 'Six people at Sylvania Heights. There's this huge empty room, they've stayed away in droves! And Tiny did another powerhouse performance. He said, "Whenever there's more than two, it's a show" (a reiteration of Matthew 18:20 - "Whenever two or three are gathered together in my name...") and an amazing show I guess. They're all joking at first and digging each other in the ribs. He'll wear them out. He'll wear out all their resistance until they're up there on the floor dancing. He'll amaze them and they won't even remember it because they won't even want to say he was amazing!' [17]

The Opera House Concert was the big one. It was the place to be if you were in town that Saturday night. The sea of faces comprised Yellow House people, creatives, friends, fashionplates and the kind of people spotted in the Sun-Herald's social pages. Adrian Rawlins came up from Melbourne to compere. Tiny's appearance sure made an impression in a bespoke suit made by Pitt Street tailor, Tony Bechini with fabric designed by Martin. Tiny's shoes were held together with gaffa tape and he carried a shopping bag. Under the musical direction of Nathan Waks, he sang old songs, new songs and songs from his Chameleon album, opening with Martin's favourite *Street Of Dreams*. Martin saw beyond the literal lyric and said, 'He gives it a different meaning'. [18]

Attendance was good but the concert didn't come close to breaking even. The Concert Hall seated 2500 and was probably half full. With no money in the Street of Dreams account the venue still had to be paid for and miraculously – yes, miraculously! - a royalty cheque for Martin's lyrics to *Tales of Brave Ulysses* arrived in the nick of time. Martin usually prompted the music publisher for payment but not this time. Martin wrote to Eric Clapton to thank him. 'This is the first time they've ever sent them spontaneously. It is what paid for the concert at the Opera House'. [19]

Two days later, Martin and Tiny got together at EMI Studio 201 and recorded four new songs: *The Bible My Mother Left For Me*, *Keeping My Troubles To Myself*, *The Last Mile Of The Way* and Tiny's own composition *Forever Miss Dixie*. The four songs read like a mini-summary of Tiny's career, especially the lyric, 'You only liked me best when I was playing the jester...' in *Keeping My Troubles To Myself*. Martin was overjoyed with the recordings, 'Religiously Tiny is the most powerful person I've met. It was unexpected because it was initially a musical interest. And then another side emerged.' [20]

The highlight of the following weekend was a concert at the Paddington Town Hall with the Conway Brothers band as Tiny's support act and backing. Mic was quite awed, 'I didn't know what to expect. There was no rehearsal. We had Peter Dean-Butcher playing t-chest bass, Jim Parnell on guitar (he was very very good), me and Jim. The guitarist had to follow whatever key Tiny was in and whatever he was doing. So they did - and we did. I'm not a good enough musician to follow someone just like that. I didn't know what was going to come next. I ended up playing washboard because I had no idea where he was going. We had no idea what was going to happen. We were in a state of shock.' [21]

Four days after the Paddo concert, Martin, Tiny and his entourage dined with radio personality John Singleton (Singo) at Eliza's Restaurant Woollahra. Singo teased Tiny about his religious beliefs and goaded Martin about his commitment. Martin taped the interaction and played it to visitors and friends.

Singo told Tiny, 'There's only two guys who are looked upon as having the same talent - going back 10 years – Brett Whiteley and Martin Sharp. Brett Whiteley is an independently wealth man. Martin Sharp is independently bloody unwealthy, unhealthy and his paintings are very hard to buy. And when he does them, he won't sell them. Do you suggest God's going to say, "Brett Whiteley at least you gave your talent a go and Mr Sharp you just kept it to yourself" or "Mr Sharp – well at least you're a nice bloke and because you have lack of respect for everyone you've met – you wouldn't give them your paintings because they weren't worthy of them! – well Mr Sharp, you're a good person and Mr Whiteley – you're a dickhead?"'

Tiny replied, 'What's most important in what you've just said is how the grace of God will judge Mr Singleton not how he will judge Mr Sharp.'

'Well that's my worry isn't it,' Singo replied, giving up. [22]

Still enthused by Richard Perry's recording of Tiny's Royal Albert Hall concert, Martin played it to all who called in – and there were many when Tiny was in town. Chris Cordeaux came back, Nico became a regular and Victor Rubin moved into Wirian and played the role of gatekeeper way too efficiently. Tiny liked visitors. He enjoyed the fuss. He made himself accessible and posed for the camera. William Yang snapped away, as did others. One of the classic shots was Roslyn Sharp's photo of Tiny in his stage clothes, strumming his uke while lying in Martin's ensuite bath. [23]

Having chalked up another successful Australian tour, Tiny planned to return the following year. The completion date of the film was a minor sticking point. Tiny told the press, 'The film should be out in maybe another year'. [24] The footage, which was once all about Tiny, was now also about Luna Park. But Tiny trusted Martin. They did a joint-interview with ABC Radio and the presenter described Martin's film as an 'open ended project which will go on indefinitely'. Martin blamed lack of financial resources, 'The film will be finished when its ready, but it's very unlikely that it will receive the support of tax schemes and film commissions and things like this because it's a bit too unusual, so it takes longer to make these things without that sort of advantage'. [25]

Tiny returned to New York and broke-up with his current love, Miss Dixie within 24 hours of arriving home. Home was now the Olcott Hotel, West 72nd Street on New York's Upper West Side, next to the famous Dakota Hotel where *Rosemary's Baby* was filmed and John Lennon was shot. [26] Tiny spent the next three months playing bars, clubs and vaudeville shows after which he signed a multi-city deal with Americana Hotels. Around this time Tiny met James 'Big Bucks' Burnett (known as 'Bucks') from Dallas Texas. Bucks would enjoy a productive relationship with Tiny and he got to know Martin as well. [27]

Tiny's American fans were surprised by the *Chameleon* album and frustrated that they couldn't buy it. Select tracks were popular with some independent FM radio stations, some were fascinated by Tiny's new image but the Post-Punk generation looked to acts like Boy George, Madonna, INXS, Prince and Michael Jackson. Even Martin was beginning to pay Michael Jackson lots of attention after the release of his *Thriller* film clip, loaded with occult imagery.

In an attempt to generate some funds, Martin held an exhibition at Hogarth Gallery Paddington. It was billed as 'Some Posters, A Few Prints and a Couple of Drawings'. Again, the room was packed with well wishers, many of whom hoped Martin would stop spending time and money on the film and get back to the type of cartoons and paintings that had consolidated his reputation during those halcyon 60s days.

The show was directed by Sally Burrows and Elizabeth Evatt, wife of well-known defamation lawyer, Clive Evatt. Saffron was one of his clients – 'absolutely dedicated to defending his good reputation'. [28] Clive's older brother was Herbert Vere Evatt – the judge, parliamentarian, writer and President of the United Nations General Assembly (1948-49). The Evatts owned Hogarth Gallery. They also owned 'Leurella', a big family home in the Blue Mountains. Clive inherited it from his father, Clive Evatt Snr. Located in Leura NSW it resembled Wirian with a tree-change.

The Evatts were curious about Martin's Dream Museum, which had not succeeded in finding a permanent space at Luna Park. In fact, between 1979-1982 there was no Luna Park. Clive commissioned Kingo to design a maquette for a Pop Art representation of Boofhead. Kingo's concept was passed to a tradeperson from Lithgow who cut out and installed a massive Boofhead in the Evatts' bush amphitheatre across the road from Leurella on the edge of an escarpment with breathtaking views of the Jamison Valley. Some locals thought the 12ft Boofhead statue ruined the landscape; others thought it was funny. Kingo explained, 'Clive Evatt commissioned me to do a sculpture on the front of Leurella. Somehow I never got to do it. Clive commissioned someone else – probably much cheaper. He would have shown them the small maquette which I cut out in 3D. It was a combined effort – Clive wanting to put something there and my idea of the fourth explorer - Blaxland, Wentworth, Lawson and Boofhead. I think they've done a jolly good job, by the way. Whoever did it - I'm really pleased the way it all came together.' [29]

This set a Pop Art theme, which blended well with the Toy Museum inside and the reclaimed railway signage in the gardens. Gradually, Leurella expanded into being the biggest toy museum in the southern hemisphere, displaying the best 20th Century toys – Tintin, Boofhead, Alice, The Mad Hatter, Barbie, Noddy, dolls, toy trains, etc. Undoubtedly inspired by Martin and Richard Liney's original Dream Museum, every time they went overseas, the Evatts brought something back to add to the collection. Clive and Elizabeth were serious art collectors too. Their collection included works by Brett Whiteley, Arthur Boyd, Tim Storrier, Jeffrey Smart and other A-listers. They had kept in close contact with the progress of the Yellow House artists over the years.

Back in Bellevue Hill, Martin ran out of money again. He wanted to pick up the master tapes for *Last Mile of the Way* from EMI but he owed them money. He was wondering how to solve this, when he met 'this rather strange woman' while walked to the Double Bay shops. She said, 'Hello, you're Martin Sharp'. Later she rang up, 'Can I do anything for you?' Martin said, 'As a matter of fact I'm a bit short of money…'. She lent him the money. Martin got his master tapes but he'd also acquired Mad Robyn. The mission now was to turn those tapes into vinyl before Tiny's next tour.

Then she called around. 'You're looking hungry,' she said and cooked boiled carrots, mashed carrots, food Martin didn't want to eat. Robyn Giffen was her name. Martin described her, 'a pathetic person who'd had a nervous breakdown and appeared like a shambling eccentric. When I was here on my own, she changed, she started stalking me around the table and asking me very weird questions. She was certainly getting strong and there was this act she was putting on, incredible to see, but it was impervious to penetration. I was half holding onto reality by tidying up and she was trying to break me from it. She started to stare at me and I felt myself going under hypnosis. It was like a snake charmer and I was going out. I admit I was weak at the time, I was terribly exhausted, the place was a wreck, everyone was overworked, the show had happened, the record had been done. Whatever it was – it was like she turned from this pathetic crone into this most powerful witch and evil force. I grabbed an old cross my grandfather had: "I know who you are, get behind me!" It broke the attack, she just cringed, she just frizzled up. She ended up in a mental hospital – broken up with her husband.' [30]

Then Russell decided it was time for him to move out. He said, 'I couldn't stay there forever, I couldn't make a living out of it. I had to start my own life.' [31] Roslyn Sharp expanded, 'Russell hitchhiked up to Cape Tribulation in Northern Queensland and gave all his possessions away before he left. I think he was extremely traumatised when my mother died, then our father dying, then our grandmother dying and Longueville being sold. He didn't know what to do with his life. He looked up to Martin a lot and Martin was kind to him, but some of the other people in the house were horrible.' [32] Russell eventually moved into a flat in Forbes Street where he lived for six years. He then moved to a place in Glebe from which he started a florist business, *Just For Love*. He made a good fist of the business and won some corporate clients.

*

Martin kept watching – studying – the News. In October 1982 Lindy Chamberlain was found guilty of the murder of her daughter Azaria and jailed in Darwin's Berrimah Prison. It was an outrage! The whole country was split down the middle saying she was guilty or not guilty. The Free Lindy campaign found a voice on talkback radio and public hearings. Martin gave the case lots of attention. 'She's been made the Joan of Arc,' he said, 'I challenge you to do your worst. I'm not going to change my story one inch! This stuff needs a scholastic mind – especially Luna Park. I don't know the mathematics of it, I've only got the intuition. I'm learning a bit of the other. It is a crucible situation, there's so many possibilities'.

Martin gave the Azaria case it's own set of A4 files, He taped the radio programs, videotaped the television broadcasts and collected a stack of newspaper billboards. He believed the Azaria case had similar resonances to Picnic at Hanging Rock and the Ghost Train Fire. [33]

The history of the case: on 17 August 1980, 9-week old Azaria Chamberlain was taken from a tent at Ayers Rock (soon to be Uluru) by a dingo. The first Coronial Inquest held in Alice Springs, under Coroner Denis Barrett found a dingo took Azaria and that no member of the Chamberlain family was responsible for her disappearance. Those who understood the case saw it as a good result, though it did make the Northern Territory police look slack.

In November 1981 the Northern Territory Supreme Court quashed the first inquest and ordered a new one hiring the services of so-called forensic experts. Towards the end of 1982 Lindy, heavily pregnant, was found guilty of first-degree murder and sentenced to life imprisonment. Her husband, Seventh-day Adventist minister Michael, was declared an accessory and received an 18-month suspended sentence. Public opinion was strongly divided, even amongst Martin's friends. Sandy Gutman (aka Austen Tayshus) lampooned the case and included lots of Chamberlain jokes in his repertoire, like 'Azaria Chamberlain please make your way to the St John's Ambulance tent, your mother is waiting'. Ho ho ho.

Martin felt otherwise. He believed the treatment of the Chamberlain family showed deep flaws in the Australian consciousness. It showed immense prejudice towards women, contempt for the testimony of Aboriginal trackers and antipathy towards the Seventh-day Adventist (SDA) faith - an antipathy that Martin did not share possibly because in Victoria Cobden's hour of need, SDAs Noni Hedges and Peter & Anita Simmonds had been kind to her. Victoria Cobden was an outspoken defender of Lindy. [34]

Martin began collecting Azaria billboards. Martin had always been fascinated by billboards, like when Elvis died in 1977. Going back to 1966, there's a dozen billboards depicted on page 40 of his *Cartoons* book [35] and Martin had a stack of them, some of which he glued onto a huge backing board and turned into a collage. He did it for Elvis. And for Vincent he collaged postcards, pictures and clippings. Martin wasn't painting much but he was creating canvases and having them framed to exhibition standard.

One of the few pictures that he did start was a Luna Park clown face (Snow Job). He spent the next fifteen years nearly obliterating it with huge textured blobs of white paint (snow) reflecting his increasing frustrations with the bureaucracy.

4.
UNPICKING THE CODE

How many Martin Sharps would it take to change a light bulb?
None, he'd have it classified by the National Trust and he'd leave it there.
Al Jones

By reading imagery as others read words, Martin was convinced he was onto something. 'It's like an iridologist saying, "I understand what's going on because I know what your eye is about".' [1] It was his 'contribution'.

Martin often felt weighed down with too many ideas, too many worries and not enough resources, 'I've got to turn all this into art – or bring it through – or at least "get" it'. [2] Martin was strident when Tiny was in Sydney. 'I'm making the film so people can see him as I've seen him,' Martin enthused. 'I have a fair idea of how good I am as an artist and my interest is to such a degree in Tiny Tim that I wouldn't be making a mistake about it.' [3] Five months later he languished, 'Sometimes the spirit is there, sometimes it's not. I suppose getting tired and rundown makes problems appear insurmountable'. Pointing to the stack of 250 cassettes of Tiny's phone conversations, Martin added, 'Maybe the best thing I've ever done is these tapes. Tiny said that to me once. So maybe it's going to just be the tapes and they'll be a curiosity - or something - later on.' [4]

Tiny was due back in August. Once announced, the tour became Martin's priority. Psyching up was a natural part of the process. Playing *Keeping My Troubles To Myself* at full belt was part of that. The four songs on this outsized 45rpm record are: *The Bible My Mother Left For Me, Forever Miss Dixie, Keeping My Troubles to Myself* and *The Last Mile of the Way*. The cover featured nothing other than a black and white profile shot of Tiny looking pensive, taken by William Yang.

Martin liked the image so much that he appropriated it for his Kinselas poster announcing Tiny's late-night concerts in September. (5)

Martin would constantly play that record. He would stand close to his punchy little Aiwa speakers, turn the volume to max, close his eyes and bow his head in an attitude of prayer, as the music spilled from his Inner Sanctum into the hall, anteroom and film editing room. Guests were often overwhelmed. Knock knock. Martin sometimes opened the front door, shyly sucking a cigarette with a whirlwind of music pounding in his Inner Sanctum. Or maybe Les Bean did the opening, her clothes painted Jackson Pollock-style. 'Ooo hellooo' she would say, 'he's in there'. Follow the music.

The entry hall was still full of fairground art and objects that appear to have been placed there for some forgotten reason. An 8ft tapestry of Tiny dressed as Pierrot, standing in the Luna Park dominated the back entrance wall. Clown heads. An upright piano. Philippe Mora's *Da Corner* painting, constantly moved around but never hung. For a time, a sex doll lay forlorn beside the front door. Someone brought it around and Martin left it where it was put. It was in desperate need of air. To the left Arthur Barton's *Loona Park* picture was being restored. To the right, the Inner Sanctum - where anything could be happening – gales of laughter, bursts of song or 'Eets beaootiful Marteen' - Willy de la Vega, effusing about Martin's 7ft x 5ft *Vincent Collage*.

Affectionately dubbed 'the Inner Sanctum' by friends and inmates, there was nothing 'inner' about it. Calling it 'Martin's Studio' might have been more accurate. It's where he spent most of his time. There was lots of bric-a-brac in this room: a Billy Tea poster, a plastic Michelin Man, his mother's painting, a Mickey Mouse telephone, Japanese prints, In-Out trays, a photo of his father in stagewear, records by Tiny, Jeannie Lewis or W C Fields, an outsized Goofy doll, a cardboard Prince Charles and Lady Di waving, a Peter Kingston chess set, a tangerine object, a coffee table book titled *Fairground Art* and several other beautiful books.

Scattered about the surface of the outsized former dining table (under which the Salami Sisters had lived) were bills, half-written letters, sketches, paint splattered coffee cups, news clippings, pictures, cut-outs, invitations, scissors, crayons – lots of stuff, including an African hand-held thumb piano known as a kalimba, the only musical instrument Martin ever played. The control panel was Martin's address/phone book, covered with doodles and as handy to him as the ashtray.

Martin was such a hospitable host that some guests felt puzzled at their reception. Scots College English Master, Peter Jensen could not grasp why this famous Australian artist would stop whatever he was doing in order to accommodate a mere drop-in like him. 'What did I do to deserve all this?' a glazed-eyed Peter asked after Martin played him a tape in which Tiny explained what he'd do if he were Pope.

Visitors might include Richard Neville accompanied by a very pregnant Julie Clarke, or Adrian Rawlins, or Margaret Fink - or a surprise guest like Joe P Rick out of the band Jimmy & the Boys. A couple of Cold Chisels called in too, wanting Martin to do the poster for their show 'An Evening with the Circus Animals'. Bill Lucas, an architect dressed in shorts and a short-cut silver jacket, dropped in and spun out. Cousins Roslyn Sharp and Katie Reid visited and danced. Russell showed up with state-of-the-art video equipment. Extras from *Mad Max 2* sat in the Inner Sanctum and didn't say much. Eventually a core group formed around Peter Royles and Toto Renshaw who called in drunk pretty regularly – two heavy drinkers with an audience of – say - six non-drinkers including Martin who was taping everything they said and did.

For a time it seemed Peter and Toto visited for the express purpose of creating spontaneous drama. Martin understood people's needs to perform, especially those who had been denied the conventional stage. He called it the 'Magic Theatre'. He'd seen it all before when a tramp named John Ivor Golding walked straight off the street into the Pheasantry - rapping - just hyper-babble - before leaving as quickly as he came after ensuring he did something shocking. Martin recalls, 'Bags and overcoats stuffed with newspapers. Harold Pinter got one of his characters from this guy.' [6]

One night Peter Royles smashed Martin's framed Picasso/Signac collage (the *Art Book* picture). Everyone was alarmed. What happens now? Toto threw Peter out. Martin brought him back. William was cheeky enough to photograph the pair, though at those sessions you wouldn't see Al or Marilyn for dust. Next night, Toto went head-to-head with Peter again. It was a 'from the uttermost to the guttermost' routine, each exaggerating their social differences. At one point, Toto tried to intimidate Peter, threatening to 'turn the head upon the neck'. In a blink, Peter clipped him. 'You got nothing!' Peter mocked.

'Do it again!' Toto exploded, 'Do it again! Do it again!' He kept repeating 'do it again'. Toto produced mace, 'You have stirred me up! You are an amateur!'

Martin intervened, 'I hope you would never use mace, knives or even a fist in this house, Toto'.

Peter switched the mood, 'Put some music on Martin, instead of this bullshit'. Martin played Elvis singing How Great Thou Art at ear-splitting volume. He was awed, 'I'd say Elvis is religious to the point where – well, you can hear by the way he sings his spiritual songs. That was his last concert.' [7]

Later, that same night, the subject of how Martin might fund the film came up and the possible sale of Wirian was mooted. Peter suggested a price of $1.5 million. Martin had other ideas, 'I don't think it's time at the moment'. Martin tabled his immediate financial requirementss, which were $400,000 to pay his debt plus $100,000 to keep the film going. He was on thin ice but the assets were still manageable. Martin never kept his financial problems secret, the possible sale of the house crept into the background of many conversations. [8]

Afterwards, Martin described Toto and Peter as 'archetypal figures'. Like Tiny and Les, Peter's drive to perform was beyond money and applause. If he didn't have gigs, he busked. If he had nowhere to busk he turned up at Wirian and played to Martin and guests whether they wanted him to or not. He performed drunk or sober, always with gritty passion. Songs like Don McLean's *Vincent*, Bob Dylan's *Just Like Tom Thumb Blues* and his own compositions. Session players and professional musicians were sometimes appalled when Peter was in full voice with Martin actually taping him. Admitting that Peter can be 'incredibly annoying' Martin added that he and Peter had 'a very close bond'. It was Peter, not those pro-musicians, who Martin wanted to record in a studio.

Martin was showing the film one night and Peter suddenly remembered what he'd heard that very night, 'I overheard guys talking at the Cross about how they burned down Luna Park and I never realized they weren't bullshitting until the next day when I read the papers.' This startled Martin, 'You've known that for years and you've never told me?' Peter explained that it wasn't until the film moved him to a certain degree that everything came flooding back. [9]

Martin taped Peter's account, had the tape transcribed and added it to other witness statements about the Ghost Train Fire. Never questioning that Peter might have been drunk or surreal, Martin took Peter's statement at face value and gave it to the Police. It read, 'I overheard a mob of bikies talking about the night and what they had done. I heard them say they went to the Ghost Train. One of them was talking about using lighter fluid to light the fire. They were all very drunk and seemed to know a lot about what happened. It wasn't until I read about the fire in the papers the next day that I realised what had happened myself.' [10]

Martin's new girlfriend, Yensoon Tsai came out of nowhere. Someone suggested she was married, that her married name was Robinson and she was part-owner of a fish and chips shop in New Zealand. William disliked their disbelief, which he found disrespectful. In his book *Sydney Diary* William describes Yensoon like this: 'She was from Taiwan. Her father was a classics scholar and a taoist priest who had raised and educated her in the ancient Chinese way.' [11]

Yensoon designed her own traditional Chinese costumes. She read palms, boiled up herbal remedies, quoted the *Tao Te Ching*, cast the i-Ching and evoked the spirit of an oracle. Martin liked her dish of fried duck. He said, 'There's always been a Chinese sympathy in this house. My grandmother used to have some Chinese help and some of the others too. There are a lot of fans here. Gifts and things. A sort of spirit was here from a few Chinese things. Then Willy (William Yang) came. [12]

'Yensoon has been very kind taking me to see Dr Ling an old Chinese physician who uses herbs to treat my kidney stones. He's a dear man, sitting in the back of a Chinatown grocery. They get on very well. Both are pleased they have met another Chinese who understands Taoism.' [13]

Cruising talkback radio stations late one night Martin taped a track, *Elvis Calling from Heaven*. The voice certainly sounded like Elvis or a damn good impersonator. For a time, Martin played it to visitors. One night, while playing the track, Martin was so overwhelmed by the spirit of Elvis that he prostrated himself before the speaker system. 'Did you feel that?' he said afterwards, finding his feet. 'I was thrown down!'

The following night, hopeful of recreating the same spiritual force, Martin played *Elvis Calling from Heaven* to Richard and Julie. The Elvis voice concluded: 'Ah hope you realise ah am with God now, he is my Manager, ah even have a Golden Guitar…'. When Richard's convulsions of laughter failed to dissolve Martin's reverential attitude, Richard snapped, 'Very touching, it makes me want to go to Hell!' Martin was sadly disappointed.

The following night Sociology lecturer, Robert Wolfgramm called in from Melbourne. Martin had enjoyed Robert's gospel music, particularly his *Refugee* LP. Robert did not crack up laughing when Martin played *Elvis Calling from Heaven*. 'What is it?' Robert questioned. Martin thought it might be Elvis communicating from Heaven. Robert was non-committal, which Martin took as agreement. As Robert was Fijian by birth, Martin showed him his great-grandfather William Kopson's late-19th century 'Fiji Diary'. Kopson was Martin's grandmother Vega's father. At the age of 20, Kopson left Sweden to seek his fortune and Fiji was part of his adventure. 'An *Illywacker* sort of character' is how Martin described him. He knew very little about his Kopson antecedent and summed him up with, 'he was probably seafaring – he made oars'. [14] Robert was fascinated by the authenticity of the 1870s document. In turn, he played Martin some demo tracks from his forthcoming gospel album, *Persecution Games*.

The Delltones too had an album in the pipeline - *Bop Til Ya Drop* - and Chief Delltone, Peewee Wilson, fancied a Martin Sharp cover, photographs by Jonny Lewis and liner notes by Tom Thompson. Martin had seen them perform at the Sydney Stadium in the late-50s, backing Johnny O'Keefe and playing their own set. The Dellies certainly knew their Elvis catalogue and Martin thought they were ideal to join with Tiny on *Are You Lonesome Tonight* at the late night show at Kinselas. Martin and Peewee had no difficulty reaching an agreement: the Delltones performing with Tiny and Martin doing their album cover. Martin's cover was lurid pink ultra hip 50s-style, which perfectly matched the songs.

Then the Cranbrook School asserted its construction rights, which meant guests could no longer park in the Wirian driveway. Everyone, except Martin, now parked outside the gates in Victoria Road, with Martin using the reduced car space to rest his $1800 Peugeot that had long died.

Martin created a new poster for model, Maureen Turquoise's fashion show at Sydney Textile Museum Mosman. It was one of the last posters he did using the services of McGregor Screenprints. For the next 15 years or so he used Stephen Lawson, a former Cranbrook student. (Tim Lewis was one year below him.) Unlike Martin and Kingo, Stephen had never got along with art teacher Justin O'Brien. 'For some reason Justin and I didn't click,' Stephen said, 'Justin put me off art entirely. He corrected and changed everything I did. But when Peter Brown came along, I got on famously with Peter.'

Stephen had a printmaking business in Kent Street Sydney. In the early 70s, Stephen and his girlfriend Lucinda Strauss, painted the rear stairs of the Yellow House. A decade later, Stephen and Martin reconnected. Stephen explained, 'Richard Liney had a place down the road called the Architecture Gallery. He brought Martin into my studio. Martin rang up one day and asked would I do it? The first one was *Tiny Tim Kinselas*. That was a street poster. That *Kinselas* poster is MG litho paper. I used to always prefer printing on the rough side because that made the look and feel of the print better. Martin quite liked it but when we did the Fine Art Limited Editions they were Art Paper, which is 100% cotton.' (15)

Producer, Hayden Keenan had done a lot of work with Martin on *Street of Dreams*. His film *Goin' Down* had its premier screening in Sydney. Martin didn't attend although he was interested in the film because it was about the hardcore goings on in the shared house where Roslyn lived in Potts Point. In the interim, Roslyn had lived in London and New Orleans. She worked as a radiographer and had a strong interest in photography. (16)

Then Tiny arrived.

Eight fans gather at the airport to welcome him, accompanied by his manager, Neil Hollander, who talked with a New Yorker's drawl. When Tiny got through the gate, Martin shyly presented him with the *Keeping My Troubles To Myself* record, after which they were locked tête a tête. Astonished travelers stared in disbelief as Tiny casually ambled through Sydney's international terminal at 9.30am.

Martin arranged a meet-and-greet function on the same day. Tiny and Mr Hollander were expected at Wirian at 2.00. Guests started trickling in at 1.00 - guests with showbiz and art connections dressed for the occasion, nibbling whatever Les Bean offered from a tray as she ballerina-ed her passage around the room. At five-to-two there was a knock. It was Peter Royles drunk. Seconds later Tiny arrived in the same doorway. Seizing the moment, Peter drew him away, 'I wanna show you something Tiny' and he whisked the Eternal Troubadour into the Dream Museum and shut the door leaving guests, and even Mr Hollander, wondering where Tiny went.

Five minutes passed. Another five. Then KER-RASH! The door to the Dream Museum burst open and out bounced Peter on one leg, holding his shin and saying fuck rather a lot. Tiny was in a flap because he couldn't handle the sight of blood. What happened? It was all about Peter showing Tiny his new Fender Twin amp, which he picked up then dropped on his shin. It was a deep graze. Martin and Les sorted it out - Tiny was escorted around the room meeting the Delltones, radio presenters, ABC people, journos and Yensoon, who made a quiet impression. (17) Les left a different kind of impression. Some thought her crazy - but what would they know? Les took on quite a lot of the 'responsible' stuff around the house, including cleaning. Also, she didn't drink, allowing no other explanation for her Dada performance routines than her will to do them.

Les had a private schooling where she excelled at horse riding and ballet. She would have been an excellent ballerina but she had the wrong sort of figure. In Wirian, she frequently pranced from room to room doing *petit saut* and *petit pas*. That was normal. To add to the performance, Les played several musical instruments by randomly plucking or banging them. Every week she would perform at talent shows in Paddington's gay clubs. Every week she'd come last. Tiny accepted her as part of the general ambiance. Mr Hollander hated her. [18]

One memorable night, Les swanned into the Wentworthville RSL Club, past security in her painted clothes. She hit the dance floor as Tiny was breaking into *Babyface*. Les swirled into her quazi-ballet routine and others joined her. With Tiny in full flight, people started dancing, cavorting, having fun. Horrified, Mr Hollander called security, had Les ejected, took out an AVO against her and threatened to cancel the Kinselas shows should Les be admitted. 'I don't want that woman within 50 metres of Tiny!' he exploded. Although he liked her, Tiny was too browbeaten by Hollander to intervene. [19]

The following night Tiny played the Castanet Club's Funny Festival in Newcastle, north of Sydney. Mr Hollander didn't attend, Les did. She danced, gyrated and did her crazed ballerina routine when the band - the Castanet Connection – broke into exciting but disorderly version of *Rock Around the Clock* with Tiny in full cry. A helluva moment! After the show, Les was literally mobbed by admirers. After Tiny - she was certainly the star that night.

Martin wasn't there but he arranged for the Castanet show to be taped. He studied the tape and fixed on Tiny's take on the Men At Work song *Down Under*. 'Did you hear that?' said Martin, focusing on the lyric, 'you better run you better take cover'. He interpreted this as a Jeremiad on the city of Sydney for its unwillingness to remediate the situation at Luna Park. Martin believed an admission of corporate guilt and a memorial to the victims would make a solid start. Luna Park was always in Martin's thoughts but with Tiny in town, Tiny was the immediate focus. Down Under, eh? [20]

After the in-store appearances, clubs and ordinary bookings, Martin always organized at least one 'Art' gig for every tour, inviting friends, cousins, artists and non-RSL type people to attend. Redolent of the *Chameleon* album and *Wonderful World of Romance,* Tiny's four late-night concerts at Kinselas (11.00pm-1.00am) were like charming 1940s nights. Naturally enough, there were crazy moments too.

Photographers went wild when the Delltones joined Tiny on *Are You Lonesome Tonight*. So did Peter Royles. He scrambled onto the stage yelling 'Tiny! Tiny!' This was way too much for one audience member, who grabbed Peter by the neck and down they went. *Do you gaze at your doorstep and picture me…crash…*two tables down, eight drink-splattered guests, broken glass underfoot. This was surely a bridge too far? Les was among those who berated Peter afterwards: 'Martin is paying for all this and you do THAT!' Several friends advised Martin to kick Peter out for keeps. But Martin appreciated that the arrival of an international star can cause a surge of energy to which some people are drawn. Instead of banning Peter, Martin booked him as Tiny's support act on the following night. Peter played out the interval, absolutely sober. [21]

Back home, Martin introduced Tiny to his mother who lived in an apartment in Elizabeth Bay. She was charmed. Returning to the film editing room, he showed Tiny the rushes of the film, which included lots of footage of the Ghost Train Fire. This seemed okay with Tiny. The completion date was the only niggle. Ever keen to get Tiny into a studio, Martin arranged for him to record the raunchy AC/DC song *Highway to Hell*. The name Denny Burgess came up as a muso who could coordinate the session. Denny (and brother Col) had a strong Rock CV - going back to the Throb, the Masters Apprentices and even AC/DC. Martin contacted Denny and asked him to put together Tiny's backing band, which he did, assuming the recording would run more-or-less like other Rock sessions. However, the first thing Denny saw when he walked into the Sun Studios (near Central) was Yensoon in full traditional Chinese attire, 'She didn't say a thing the whole time we were there'. It took him aback. 'Hmm…this is going to be different,' Denny reflected. [22]

Denny continued, 'We learned *Highway to Hell* but it was changed around. We realized we had to follow Tiny. We couldn't play a set thing because he'd change it each time. It was incredibly interesting - I came out of there going, "This guy is amazing" because he was so different - different attitude to recording, different way of doing things.' [23]

As well as recording and performing, Tiny was on a constant round of media interviews. One of the most successful was with actor Kate Fitzpatrick who concluded, 'He should be declared a National Treasure by the US Government'. After the interview she whisked him off to the Botanical Gardens where Tiny was photographed singing *Tiptoe Through the Tulips* amongst the poppies. [24]

Through all this activity, it's difficult to believe Tiny found time to take a break but when he did – usually late at night - he would sit around Wirian's kitchen table with Martin and maybe Al, William, Marilyn, Jonny, Yensoon, Fergus, Anne-Louise, Nico, Peter, Les Bean…whoever was in the house at the time. He'd strum his little uke, sing a bit and talk about his latest Miss.

Tiny's last appearance before heading home was Ringling Circus in the southern Sydney suburb of Revesby. The idea was to film Tiny in a cage with a lion. But Tiny was afraid of everything – mice, cockroaches – he was even afraid of Jane, Martin's somnolent corgi. Tiny showed up at the Circus with Martin and Yensoon, he greeted the film crew, saw the lion and froze. (This was one mangy and submissive lion!) Tiny agreed to enter the cage if the lion tamer came in too. It really was a non-event and the Australian press got a pretty lame story, but that's not how it came across in America. Unexpectedly, the American media picked up on the 'Tiny in the Lion's Den' story. When he got back to New York, Tiny's agent announced that he had 18 months of appearances at the Great American Circus. Tiny was required to perform a 10-minute medley after the trained bear and before the elephants. [25]

The 10th Anniversary celebrations of the Sydney Opera House were held after Tiny had gone. Martin's poster was sold (in two editions) from the Opera House gift shop and he was invited to attend the Cocktail party for 400 friends of the House at which Jill Wran, wife of the State Premier, was Guest of Honour. To celebrate the occasion on 20 October, ABC Radio broadcasted a day-long series of programs about the history and personalities of Sydney Opera House. The Sydney Symphony Orchestra played and there was a cocktail party in the evening where Lin Utzon, daughter of Jorn Utzon, the architect of the masterpiece, delivered an impressive address that Martin described as 'magnificent'. Lin was a ceramicist whose work was being exhibited in David Jones Gallery Sydney at the time. She became one of Martin's most valued friendships. Like Martin, Lin had been a student of East Sydney Tech (National Art School). Her ceramic works were exhibited all over the world - Copenhagen, New York, Oslo, Beijing. Whenever she came to Sydney, she always came to Wirian.

Towards the close of the year, Martin started preparing an exhibition, to be held in 12 months time at Ivan Dougherty Gallery Paddington. Martin collaged news clippings, cartoons and billboards about Luna Park, intending to mask his message for receptive eyes only. His canvases began to clutter up with words, like his Vincent Collage. Anyone who took the time to read everything would have the entire Ghost Train saga in detail from Martin's perspective – which would have taken hours. Through a labyrinth of eastern and western mysticism Martin was seeking answers. He revisited Jeannie Lewis' *Clowning Calaveros*. 'Once again a child had to be the victim'.

'The kids in the fire…' said Martin '…and Azaria Chamberlain.' [26]

Martin was also contemplating the song *Dingo* by Gary Shearston. Martin picked a prophetic voice in Gary's Dingo song of 10 years ago – 'Run dingo run'. In the early-to-mid 60s Gary had been instrumental in shaping an authentic Australian voice in folk music. He moved in London and wrote the novel *Balkenna* and had a Top 10 hit with the Cole Porter song, *I Get A Kick Out of You*. Peter Paul and Mary recorded his song *Sometime Lovin'*. Gary returned to Australia, studied for the Anglican priesthood and kept recording new material, which Martin enjoyed. [27]

Martin sketched a dingo in the jaws of the happy/sad face of Luna Park when he drew the cover for Robert Wolfgramm's new Gospel album, *Persecution Games*. [28]

5.
DEVIL IN THE DETAIL

Martin's paintings are like symphonies - like music.
And music is the greatest art that humankind has invented.
Roger Foley

Martin started the year creating three '1984' posters, two for 'Sydney Festival '84' [1] and a cover/poster for the January POL magazine. [2] Having designed more than 15 posters over the past two years [3] Martin was moving away from that form of expression. Using Stephen Lawson's services, Martin transitioned from posters on street quality paper to prints on 100% cotton art paper. [4] He said, 'I'm trying to get away from posters. To get your head in that space you've got to gear up into a whole different ballgame.' [5]

Martin's father, Dr Henry Sharp, died 23 January, two days after Martin's 42nd birthday. His wife, Dorothy told Martin that his father had left him nothing. His mother was furious but Martin was okay with that but bothered by the speed of the burial, 'He was very swiftly put in the ground. I understood why we couldn't love each other – it was because I wasn't the child of Henry and Dorothy, I was the child of my mother. I think because a Dad is a Dad, love is still there but it couldn't happen on this worldly level to the degree that it should have. When he died all the love that was inherent in my father was freed and it could flow on. His spirit came to me. He came as soon as he could. It was great. It couldn't be better. You can't lose your family. You never really lose your father. It's impossible. At his funeral the next day - I was smiling!' [6]

After his father's passing, Martin made a resolute effort to take care of his stepmother Dorothy. Cousin Roslyn helped. She explained, 'Martin felt an obligation to keep an eye on Dorothy. He would regularly ring me up. (He loved talking on the phone.) If he had to take Dorothy out for lunch he would ask me to come along as a conversationalist.' This continued for the next 15 years. [7]

Henry was born in 1908 in the Old Candelo Hospital, 22k south-west of Bega NSW. Martin's grandmother Elizabeth (Bessie) was born in Bega in 1886.

In March, Martin crammed his grandfather Stuart Ritchie's trunk with Luna Park documents and took a trip to Bermagui, on the coast from Bega. It was mostly a study trip, family history was a convenient sideline. Martin's focus was to oppose the proposed demolition of Coney Island to make way for a new roller coaster ride. It was also to conceptualise his next exhibition – titled *Luna Images* - to be held at Ivan Dougherty Gallery Paddington in August, 'I went to Bermy to filter through the Luna Park material, these events that are caused by plotting, not caring for kids, carelessness, living a human life – the way of the world.' [8]

Martin spent a week on the south coast, a short drive from several dairy farm holdings once owned by the Sharp-Ritchie side of his family. At the turn of the century Martin's great-grandfather's brother, William Ritchie (1840-1896) held oyster leases and ran cattle a 10-minute drive south of Bermagui in an area known as the Murrah. Slightly further south Martin's great-grandfather, Henry Lucas St George Ritchie (1843-1905), had a farm/gold mine in Tanja. Martin checked out both areas. There was no visible trace of his ancestry - or of anything else really, other than farms, paddocks and wonderful waterways.

Martin went for occasional swims at the beach and he met the locals, like sharkmesher and a former abalone diver Allan Broadhurst. Allan described their meeting, 'Martin seemed really interested in what we were doing. In my case, I was a fisherman but he's an international artist. I would struggle to come up to his level. He didn't let that enter the equation. Instead he came down to mine where I was the champion and he wasn't. He talked about fishing as a teenager, Port Hacking that's for sure. He had early childhood memories of enjoying the solitude of recreational fishing.' [9] While this conversation took place, Allan's little daughter Kate got her crayons out, sketched the face of Luna Park and presented it to Martin. Along with other child art, he hung it with the other *Luna Images* in the August exhibition.

On his return, Martin watched the Frank Moorhouse TV drama, *Who Killed Baby Azaria?* And he looked for Ghost Train fire parallels in the Lionel Jeffries film *The Amazing Mr Blunden*. Martin then checked the Michael Barker documents, re-read his correspondence with the Barker family and pondered the meaning of the sacred blue kingfisher. Then he sorted Luna Park news articles, material from the Inquest, letters and child art. From these he made big collages that he asked Fergus to deliver to Acme Framing St Peters. Martin designed their business card.

Jo's health was deteriorating. She could no longer manage her self-contained Elizabeth Bay apartment, the sale of which provided her with a comfortable budget to renovate upstairs in Wirian where she could have her own rooms. Even though Street of Dreams was broke, Martin spent big on these renovations. Of course, the renovation money came from Jo whereas Street of Dreams was Martin's problem. Again he asked the Australian Film Commission (AFC) for support. AFC sent a representative who watched the film and declined. He also approached

AVCO Finance for a second mortgage. AVCO extracted a lot of financial information and also said no. [10]

Meanwhile, Wirian was going a bit mad. Someone called Philip moved in and started dealing speed. He only lasted three days before Martin ejected angrily. The cycle of Wirian inners-and-outers and callers seemed just as fast: Philippe Mora, Richard Liney, Margaret Fink, Robert Wolfgramm, Jonny Lewis, Tim Lewis, Peewee and Carla Wilson, Denny and Clare Burgess, Sky McCreadie, Steve Mackenzie, Isabelle Morse, Mad Robyn, Jeannie Lewis, George Gittoes, Toto Renshaw, Pilot Pete, Fix-It Bob, Clayton Simms, Marilyn Karet, Peter Royles, Richard Neville, Julie Clarke, Al Jones, Nico Flamer-Caldera, Yensoon Tsai, Les Bean, Harold the Kangaroo, Beth, Fergus, Sue, Marro, Robbie, Gary and Garry – were all there.

Some came with a purpose, like architect Alex Popov who drew the plans for Jo's renovation. Others were simply curious, like the well-known New York Pop and graffiti artist Keith Haring, who was in Australia to create temporary murals in Melbourne and for the Art Gallery of New South Wales. Haring sat quietly in the Inner Sanctum, reading, sketching and awaiting Martin. But Martin didn't show up. So Haring gave stickers and badges to everyone who sat with him and talked. He retreated a bit when Les strode through the house proclaiming, 'Get his autograph! He's famous! He's famous!'

Around this time, Tiny met New York glamour piece, Jan Alweiss – Miss Jan – who moved into the Olcott Hotel NY with him and his mother Tillie. Miss Jan couldn't abide living with Tillie and promptly moved out. Tiny and Miss Jan remained married for a decade but they didn't live together. Martin played a tape of Tiny explaining all this.

*

Meanwhile in Epping Sydney, with twenty-two thousand subscribers, Phil Ward's *Small Business Letter* had become Australia's most successful business newsletter and the cornerstone of his Australian Newsletter Publishers (ANP) enterprise. For a businessperson, Phil was a rare bird, not primarily motivated by money and business success. He poured his profits into the Free Lindy campaign.

Phil and Michael Chamberlain had studied theology together at the Seventh-day Adventist Church's training centre, Avondale College in Cooranbong NSW. When Lindy was pronounced guilty, Phil knew they were innocent and launched a private investigation into the case, which resulted in the publication of his book *Azaria, What the Jury Wasn't Told*.

Not only did Phil write that a dingo took the baby, he even said which one: Ding, the one that park ranger Ian Cawood and his wife Val treated as a wild pet. Notwithstanding the 'don't feed the dingoes' signs, Phil claimed the rangers broke their own rule and kept feeding them. In August 1980, there were drought conditions at the Rock and dingoes were frighteningly audacious. They were hungry enough to enter tents and attack at least two children prior to taking Azaria.

On the fatal August night – according to Phil - Ding broke into the Chamberlain tent, picked up baby Azaria, snapped her neck and carried her east to Anzac Flag Pole where he put her down because he heard commotion from the camping area. The noise Ding heard was the panicky start of the search. So Ding changed direction and headed for somewhere 'safe' – the Cawood residence. According to trackers Nipper Winmatti and Nui Miningerie, the dingo entered the Cawood property, but couldn't say what happened next because they were stopped at the Cawood fence. Shortly afterwards, Peter Elstrom, a young pilot from the city, spotted someone burying something in the Cawood backyard. Whatever it was, the wild life must have dug it up and consumed it before sunrise. This and more was in Phil Ward's book and Martin was convinced Phil was right. (In 1988 the book attracted a $500,00 defamation case, resulting in an out-of-court settlement to seven people.) [11]

Michael Chamberlain was less certain about Phil's theory. His views shifted back-and-forth over the years but in 1984 he said, 'I personally do not think that anyone was involved in the disposal of Azaria's body. However, that does not mean that I don't think there's been a cover-up of some kind'. [12]

Martin taped late night talkback radio programs about Azaria and collected the Chamberlain broadsheets, put aside for him by the Double Bay newsagent. Martin was fascinated how headlines were so easily manipulated, with shout-lines like '**LINDY GUILTY**' in big print and 'witness says' in small. 'Often people don't buy the paper – but they do read the broadsheets. Whilst the paper may cover itself editorially, broadsheets are unquestioned. In a few words a libel has been published – but I doubt ever prosecuted. This could be important evidence because it is before the judgment is handed down by the Courts.' [13]

Martin held the same exhalted opinion of Michael Chamberlain as he did Jenny Godson. These people were special, having walked the Valley of the Shadow of Death and come out the other side. Keen to connect, Martin found Michael Chamberlain's contact details and mailed him a copy of Tiny's *Keeping My Trouble to Myself* record. Michael agreed to visit Martin and was welcomed at Wirian by everyone except Sanderson - who skulked off. At the time, Sanderson was working for Haydn Keenan on the film *Pandemonium,* the tackiest Azaria film of all.

On arrival, Michael had that haunted-hunted look from having suffered too much media attention. He was jumpy, as if expecting a journalist to suddenly spring out from behind a clown. Michael had never been in a house like this before, one with its own film editing room and private toy museum. Clearly this was not another trap. So Michael settled down and asked Martin about the pieces from the funfair. The reply inevitably led to the events surrounding the Ghost Train fire and into Carl Jung's concept of synchronicity. Michael listened, in his thoughtful way, when Martin played the Gary Shearston song *Dingo*. He was shown all the Azaria articles, tapes of Free Lindy talkback radio, TV news videos, Martin's drawing of a dingo in the jaws of Luna Park as the cover art for Robert Wolfgramm's *Persecution Games* LP. Michael was nothing less than astounded. He didn't disagree with anything. He simply didn't comprehend Martin's motivations. Why the stack of 'Azaria' billboards? Why Tiny Tim posters adorning most walls, 500 Mickey Mouse figurines, blueprints of Jan Utzon's Sydney Opera House – why?

On his way out Michael walked past the LJ Hooker For Sale sign propped near the door - what was that about? Martin dropped the news that the place was on the market. 'Don't sell this house…' said Michael in an off-the-cuff manner.

'Did you hear that!' Martin stressed after Michael had gone. 'He told me not to sell the house!' Later that night, around midnight, after a short ceremony, Martin gathered together all live-in Wirianites and announced the house was off the market. The LJ Hooker For Sale sign was taken down, signed and dated by Martin - who arranged for Fergus to get it framed.

From Seventh-day Adventist minister Michael Chamberlain to former-Seventh-day Adventist minister the controversial Dr Desmond Ford, Martin drove to Macquarie University to hear Ford talk. Undeterred that the esteemed Biblical exegete had never heard of Tiny Tim and had no involvement in the Azaria case, Martin gave the Doctor of Theology a signed copy of *Keeping My Troubles to Myself*. [14] On his way out, Martin checked his big Tiny Tim painting that the university had commissioned almost a decade ago. It was hung in a stairwell. Martin wanted to touch it up.

Martin's *Luna Images* exhibition at Ivan Dougherty Gallery expressed his 'take' on the fate of the Park. It was all there. The changing face, starting with Rupert Brown 1935-1945, Arthur Barton late 60s-1973, Martin 1973-1981 and the 1982 fibreglass face. Anyone who took on the microscopic task of reading every word of newsprint would have gained a comprehensive summary of Martin's current metaphysical thought about the fire. Martin admitted his medium was too dense, 'It's a bit of a complicated exhibition to understand. It takes a lot of hard looking.' Abe Saffron's name, though small, was peppered throughout. The devil was in the detail. [15]

Phil Ward was back in the news, this time for being physically restrained by five policemen during a Chamberlain press conference. Admiring his pluck, Martin invited Phil to visit Wirian and when he did, Martin took him to see his *Luna Images* exhibition. Martin personally walked select guests around the exhibition room, talking about each piece, hoping they might grasp what he was trying to express. Sometimes he was a bit too optimistic. Impressing Patrick White was never easy - everybody knew that. Martin arranged a private showing for Patrick who brought Jim Sharman along. 'You're looking fantastic,' said Martin, opening the conversation. Patrick growled, 'Never say that to anyone, they might drop dead the next day. In fact, if you say that to them they usually do!' Martin handed him a copy of Phil's *Azaria, What the Jury Wasn't Told*. Patrick glanced at the cover, shoved it back and walked off, leaving Martin trailing him around the room. [16]

In the end, Martin was disappointed in the exhibition, 'People stayed away in droves. There weren't many Friends of Luna Park. I would have liked people to say, "Ted Hopkins' photographs of Luna Park are extraordinary". Or, "Arthur Barton's paintings are amazing" but it didn't get a critical response at that level. I'll have to accept the more esoteric feedback over the general public.' [17]

Meanwhile Luna Park management pressed on with their plan to demolish the Coney Island building. Friends of Luna Park had to act! Martin and Kingo strongly expressed their feelings to manager Hal Droga, who gave no satisfaction. Turning to the press was no better, the Sydney Morning Herald applauded the direction management was taking. In his book, *Luna Park, Just For Fun*, Friend of Luna Park, Sam Marshall described the drama, 'Plans for a massive Arrow Huss roller coaster running the full length of the Park are revealed. To fit it on the site, Coney Island would have to be demolished. Harbourside Amusements approaches the Museum of Applied Arts and Sciences to determine whether they will take the building. A report commissioned by the Department of Public Works on the importance of Coney Island recommends its retention'. [18] With the Department of Public Works onside, all was not lost.

In Sydney for his 1984 Australian tour, Eric Clapton decided to drop in on Wirian to look up his old friend. With no fanfare Martin introduced him to astonished friends, just 'This is Eric…' It wasn't an evening about past times, the difficult 70s. 'Patti Boyd' was off limits. Wine was forbidden. Instead, Eric sat through the film footage about Tiny after which Eric raised the matter of the dingo that had hit the news in England. Martin explained that the dingo did it. No body, no motive, no opportunity - Lindy is clearly innocent. Eric paid quiet attention and chain-smoked Rothmans cigarettes.

Knock knock. Peter Royles unexpectedly showed up carrying a new guitar. Not recognising Eric, Peter asked him, 'What do you do?'

'I'm in a band.'

'Then you'd know about guitars - what do you think of this one?' Peter thrust his new Takemine into Eric's hands, who played a few chords, handed it back, said it was fine and Peter went home.

Two nights later, Martin threw a grand party for Eric and his band. Everyone was there – OZ people, Yellow House people, Wirian people, media people, friends, Donald Duck Dunn (from Eric's band), Renee Geyer (Eric's support act) and so on. Les banged her drum, William took lots of photos, Brett Whiteley and Eric had a tête a tête that no one dared interrupt, Toto berated a young woman for no apparent reason, Wendy Whiteley confronted Yensoon – 'Who ARE you?' Peter Royles burst in - 'You didn't tell me that was Eric Clapton!' he accused Martin. Peter sang 'Wonderful Tonight' at Eric, which seemed to frighten him. And so the party progressed. Eric was long gone before it hit its rowdy climax. Later that week he and his band performed the Hordern Pavillion. Martin, Yensoon and a few friends were there.

Then 64-year old Harold 'the Kangaroo' Thornton moved in, with the words 'Greatest Genius' hand-painted on the back of his jacket. Harold made his mark in Amsterdam in the mid-70s where he painted the mural on the first Cannabis Café, even though he never smoked cannabis. His psychedelic pictures (Magic Realism) and his persona made him seem like an old acid-eater, even though he'd never dropped acid either. He was naturally, not chemically, eccentric.

Harold's greatest artwork was himself. Like Les, he painted his clothes, lilac suit-coat, even his little chapeau and its wooden doily. Sometimes he wore a chicken suit. He danced like an imp and he danced often. Notwithstanding their 30-year age difference, Les and Harold seemed fated to combine. Like Les, his songs followed no conventional musical structure. Now there were two of them coming last at Talent Quests!

To clear the end room for Luna Park research, the Dream Museum was temporarily moved out. Martin's working papers and files were moved in along with some eerie photos, menacing cartoons and two newly acquired comic books. Australian artist Trevor Weekes made pointed references to 'Mr Big' and the Ghost Train fire in an *Outcast* comic book published by Angus & Robertson in North Ryde. But the *Strange Days* comic was a puzzle. No one knew anything about its creator, British artist Brendan McCarthy, nor his Californian publisher, Eclipse Comics. One of McCarthy's segments featured a ship of fools, with the Luna Park face and towers as the ship's figurehead. Richard Walsh was involved in the publication of *Outcast*, which explains Luna Park coming to the fore. But – coming out of America - why would *Strange Days* care? [19]

Then Martin bought a photocopier and copied a lot of newspaper clippings and documents. While enlarging a picture 400% Martin noted the pixilated effect of blowing up newsprint. Enjoying himself, he worked over the best blow-ups with his Derwent coloured pencils. It gave him ideas for a portrait of his mother, a portrait based on the photo on display of Jo looking young and beautiful.

Martin spent time with Jo every day. Jeannie came to see her. As a little gift, she gave Jeannie a beautiful velvet cap with sequins and glass beads. Marilyn and Al Jones also kept her company. Yensoon became her part-time carer. Jo occasionally came downstairs. There would be an announcement before Martin assisted her passage down the stairs to the kitchen, where she would seat herself at the head of table and good-naturedly converse with Al, Marilyn, William – people like that. Les Bean would usually come up with something that put a smile on her face. Sometimes Russell brought her flowers. The kitchen often had lavish flower displays, provided by Russell's end-of-the-day flowers from his *Just for Love* (later, *Flower King*) business. [20]

The Wirian crowd was always shifting in or moving out. Marilyn moved out but continued working on the film. Fergus and William left too. Al moved into

William's under-the-house room. Dave Sanderson took a room in the upstairs servant's quarters and unexpectedly won a Daytime Emmy Award for Outstanding Individual Achievement in Children's Programming. It came from America in the mail. On receiving it, Dave raced upstairs to brag about it to Jo. Appalled Roslyn said, 'That crazy guy David Sanderson had come back from LA and won a film award. Jo was in bed. In exuberance he threw the award at her, it hit her in the ribs and broke her ribs!' [21]

Regular drop-ins included Peter Thompson who reckoned that he was a flight pilot, so everyone called him Pilot Pete. He played chess without rules. Any piece could move anywhere. One of Pilot Pete's musings was that Jesus drove a Citroen. Martin never had an easy time with Citroens. He bought a new Honda Civic that he kept for the rest of his life.

Straight from an asylum, Mad Robyn phoned Martin every night on the stroke of midnight. She seemed meek at first but could certainly turn forthright. Twice, she threatened to come around and torch the place if Martin didn't come to the phone straight away. Another time she introduced herself to a Wirian first-timer, announcing, 'I masturbated last night' where a simple 'hello' would have done. Julie, Richard, Kingo and others pled with Martin to monitor his houseguests. Julie feared Toto might do something dreadful. Richard thought the place was getting 'too mad'. Kingo couldn't stand the aggressive dogs, especially Mio the bull terrier who shredded a guinea pig on the lawn.

Some calm was restored when Garry Shead and his wife Judit Englert-Shead returned from Hungary. They had a commission to paint a 50-metre mural on eight panels of concrete on the Harris Street wall of the Dunbar Building of Sydney Technical College. [22] Garry and Judit were a friendly presence in the house, helping out, avoiding dramas, with Garry playing chess with Toto (and others) according to a conventional set of rules.

Said Garry, 'We came back from Hungary and moved from one place to another. I told Martin and he said, "Come and stay here". That's what we did.' Sometimes Martin and Garry sat up late and talked. 'The film was being made. He knew I was into esoteric/spiritual things - that was where we got this connection. Martin asked me for help (he probably asked many other people). I certainly had some definite ideas that Martin took on board. I'm quite aware that there were dark forces. I heard everything about Luna Park. I accept what Martin said. It's true! I just didn't want to go down that track too much' [23]

Martin barely ate. He smoked 60 cigarettes per day and drank endless cups of strong coffee. Judit kept him fed and Yensoon often switched the coffee to herbal teas. She also brewed up an ancient Chinese de-tox recipe that she regularly gave Martin. It smelled dreadful.

On the sixth anniversary of the Ghost Train fire, 9 June 1985, Martin attended a Requiem Mass for Jonathon Billings, Richard Carroll, Michael Johnson and Seamus Rahilly, the four Waverley College boys who died in the Ghost Train. It was held at St Mary Magdalene Catholic Church, Rose Bay. He came and went quietly and partook of the Eucharist.

Clayton Simms and Fix-It Bob from Bermagui, both came to Wirian for short stints as handymen. Mal was another Bermagui contact. He had done time in Long Bay Jail. There, he overheard a nasty group of inmates try to out-grose each other. The one that caught Mal's ear said that he'd 'torched the Park for Abe'. He sent word to Martin who set up a meeting. (24)

Martin was cooking up a lot of information in that end room, but no commercial press was interested in specifically linking Abe Saffron to the Ghost Train fire. They were probably worried about defamation and patently disinterested in synchronicity. *Rolling Stone* and the *National Times* said no, so Martin approached Fairfax journalists Max Suitch and Brian Toohey. They too declined. Everyone seemed indifferent to Martin's story then the Police took notice. This was most unexpected.

One night Mad Robyn had an angry confrontation with Pilot Pete. Claiming he had raped her, she picked up Martin's phone and called the Rose Bay Police. Two young cops came around. Martin ushered them into the Inner Sanctum to discuss the matter but Robyn suddenly lost all interest in the rape, took Pilot Pete to the kitchen and left Martin to explain. So Martin brought out his Luna Park files and showed them everything - testimonials, legal documents, witness statements, pictures of the Minotaur, Mr Sin cartoons, the *Strange Days* comic. The young cops couldn't believe they'd walked into all this! They felt Martin should make a formal presentation to Superintendent Ernie Shepard ('the Good Shepherd') of the NSW Police Internal Security Unit (ISU) near Central Station, which Martin was more than willing to do. He asked Bermagui-Mal to come along too.

'I was hanging out with the Freddy Owens crowd,' Mal began, 'and they were bragging about what they'd done. One said he'd chucked his girlfriend out of a first floor window...'.

Superintendent Ernie Shepard interrupted, "Hang on...I have a document about that case on my desk right now.' Just like that, Mal convinced them he wasn't making everything up. 'Go on.'

'Anyway this guy called Scar said, "I torched the Park for Abe".' (25)

Checking his files, the Good Shepherd said there were two 'Scars' currently in the New South Wales prison system and he produced mug shots. Malcolm picked one. Ernie Shepard promised to follow it up.

Although the *National Times* had told Martin they weren't interested in connecting Saffron to the Ghost Train fire, they ran a story that was almost as accusing. Journalist Patrick Howard linked six other fires to Saffron-linked properties in 1980-81, shortly after the Ghost Train fire. Like Luna Park, these buildings were part of the fringe entertainment industry, distantly connected to Saffron. The question of arson was raised in all cases. (26)

The next newspaper report was not so good. Headlined, 'Good Shepard Dumped', Shepard was removed from the case. The report read, 'The replacement of Superintendent Ernie Shepard as head of the NSW Police Internal Security Unit has surprised and angered many of his colleagues. The Sunday Telegraph has learned that Mr Shepard and his wife had received a number of death threats in recent weeks. During the 10-months he occupied the top ISU job – charged with rooting out corruption in the force – Shepard's unit has taken action against 19 police, the majority on charges of conspiracy to pervert the course of justice.' (27)

With the removal of the Good Shepard, the ISU investigation was over for Martin but the matter did not end there. Independent NSW MP John Hatton made a speech in State Parliament claiming that Saffron was the beneficial owner of the park. He reopened the Inquiry by raising questions 'of any relationship between one or more of the directors (of Harbourside) and Mr Abraham Saffron'. Those lingering suspicions simply would not go away. (28)

One evening John Barker came to Wirian in a fluster and told Martin about a death threat he'd received that afternoon. Martin got him to make an official statement, which read, 'At about a quarter past three today I was sitting at my desk at the Housing Commission. I get calls all day from people wanting to know how much they've got to pay off on their house. This one said, "Is that John Barker?" I said it was. Then a voice said, "Stop going to Martin Sharp's or you'll wind up like your brother". That's definitely what he said and he said it slowly, in an older voice. I remember him as being very articulate. Everything pronounced and punctuated. And then there was silence'. (29)

Who would do that? A serious hitman wouldn't mess around with phone calls. No, it was an insiders' threat, someone who knew Martin's relationship with Michael Barker. Who could it be? John said, 'I never felt truly threatened though our dear friend Martin was certainly very concerned in the light of the ghost train fire and Michael's death. (30)

Martin was very concerned indeed. Under the heading 'Luna Park – A Case of Arson' he issued the following statement which he photocopied and handed around. 'A threat was received yesterday afternoon (31 May 1985) as a telephone call to John Barker. It was received at approximately 3.00pm at his place of work. He was threatened that if he didn't stop coming to see me, that he'd "wind up like his brother". Michael Barker was working as a photographer with the Friends of Luna Park. He was killed in a hit-run accident on 21 November 1980. Very few people know anything about my relationship with John Barker and we believe that this threat came from someone who is in a position to imply that John's brother Michael had been murdered. Prior to this threatening phone call we had not thought of his death as anything but an accident. I have been studying the history of Luna Park with John Barker, who has carried on his brother's work in respect to Luna Park. Not as a photographer, but in other ways. John was among those who believed that the fire in the Ghost Train on 9 June 1979 was an act of arson. And that the perpetrators were commissioned by Abe Saffron, who is now in control of Luna Park through his solicitor David Baffsky and his cousins Hal and Colman Goldstein who – with no previous experience in funfairs – won the lease from the NSW Government.

'There was a perversion of justice in the intimidation of witnesses when the Police constructed a case which gave the illusion of the fire being caused by an electrical fault. There was a lot of haggling over the lease and Michael Edgley is only the front man. They have shown themselves – in my estimation – to be insincere in their running of the amusement park, which they obtained through criminal means. The evidence includes the testimonies of Mona Smith, Les Dowd, Peter Royles, Malcolm Mead, Jimmy Anderson (ed: a crime figure, not Jim Anderson from OZ) and others. Anderson suggests that the gang commissioned to start the fire were the Loners. Ringleaders, Redman and Animal were arrested soon afterwards and put away on charges of stabbing and rape. The remnants of the gang joined the Comacheros and were part of the split who formed the Banditos, which were involved in the Father's Day Massacre. The fact that John Barker has today been threatened implies that we are indeed onto something with this case'. [31]

Everything had built to a crescendo. Something had to give.

Martin retreated into himself. He drove around the streets of Double Bay checking out numberplates. Three days of this and Martin claimed to have 'solved' the case!

Abe Saffron had three cars.

Numberplates: ABE-111, ABE-222 and ABE 333.

Add it up = 666.

Martin also pointed out that 666 was the number of the free bus on a loop between Town Hall Station and the Art Gallery of New South Wales. Six-six-six indeed! Could anything be sillier? Some friends made fun of Martin.

'These things are deliberately chosen,' answered Martin. 'Pentacle necklaces, 666, $13, tattoos and when you see a personalised numberplate – someone chose that!' [32]

On 5 December, Abe Saffron was arrested at his home on one charge of 'conspiracy to defraud the Commonwealth' between 1969 and 1981 and 12 charges relating to false income tax declarations between 1975 and 1981. [33]

6.
TIDYING UP

Martin did the cover of Bop Til You Drop because of the show we did with Tiny Tim. Synchronicity and coincidence!
Peewee Wilson (Delltones)

'What are you working on Martin?' guests would ask. The answer was always 'tidying up'. Tidying up was Martin's process for distilling information into themes. It might be a simple task like putting cassettes back into cases or delving into diaries, poems, personal letters, Vincent's letters, old encyclopaedias or his own family history. Eventually some document would point to a core theme - and that's the path Martin would follow next.

And so the Luna Park documents got filed, the newspaper clippings catalogued, the Tiny Tim tapes numbered while the film progressed ever so slowly. Editors came and went, none more faithful than Marilyn, who spent a lot of time in the film editing room, the room where Martin now stored his growing collection of Tiny Tim memorabilia, latest 45rpm releases from America - like Tiny's rendition of the Mr Ed song from the TV show - and even a book about flowers titled 'Tiny Tim'.

Poems. Martin loved poems. Nine years before the fire, poet Laurie Duggan wrote, *Inside the amusement park scared and shattered, we clutch at gratuitous image discarded style...* when Martin discovered that he exclaimed, 'he was inspired by a visit to Luna Park!' But what could he mean? [1] Another riddle was the Bernard O'Dowd poem 'Australia' taught by Cheery Bell, the Cranbrook teacher cheeked-out by teenage-Martin in a high school painting - '*Last sea thing dredged by sailor Time from Space, Are you adrift Sargasso...?* [2] Closer to home was, 'The Meeting of the Waters' by Thomas Moore, a poem found amongst his father's papers. The lines, '*Sweet vale of Avoca...*' suggested a connection with his father's side of the family, 'Avoca' being the name of a former Sharp family house in Bega. (3)

The visiting 'Wirian kids' were growing older. Instead of having them playing in the Dream Museum, Martin would put them to use by asking them to tidy it up - creative play. This often meant setting the figurines in new scenarios, like placing Alice in Wonderland in a Smurf kingdom, putting Obelisk and Asterisk in a Star Wars setting, etc. (4)

Figurines continued to capture Martin's interest. He was pleased to complete his Beatle set. He was one short until Peter spotted the fourth in a junk shop, which he gave Martin. Martin sifted through his grandparents' cabinets, checking out heritage figures that he remembered from childhood. He found Grandmother Vega's frog orchestra that had been broken and professionally repaired. Martin scratched away at the reparation, returning the frog orchestra to its authentic broken self. 'I'm taking off the repair, I think that's more powerful', he explained. 'It's a bit of a rash move I know – especially that somebody paid the restorer a lot to do that'. (5)

Most of Martin's 60s friends had been making a living from their art for the past 20 years. Some even won awards. Those 60s opinion-makers had become an extremely successful group of comrades in arms. They had spent that decade protesting, challenging and arguing with the powers-that-be. They were now running the show. Eric Clapton, Germaine Greer, Barry Humphries and Robert Hughes, were bona fide stars.

Richard Walsh was director and publisher of Australian Consolidated Press (ACP). He oversaw *The Bulletin, Australian Women's Weekly, Cleo, Australian House & Garden, Wheels* and another 55 Packer-owned magazines. Richard Neville invented his own job, a 'futurist'. Evolving from his daytime TV appearances, Richard presented a half hour Channel Ten show - *Extra Dimensions* - about sustainability and human potential. Whenever Richard appeared onscreen he got enthusiastic Wirian support - as did Martin's cousin Andrew Sharp, who played the suave Dr Andrew Baxter in the prime time show, Young Doctors.

The filmmakers were impacting too. Albie Thoms' book *Polemics for a New Cinema* sealed his position as Australia's champion of underground film. (6) Philippe Mora was directing films, working with stars like Alan Arkin, Christopher Lee and Christopher Walken. (7) Peter Weir directed Robin Williams in *Dead Poets Society* and Harrison Ford in *Witness*. Bruce Beresford directed *The Fringe Dwellers* and Phillip Noyce directed *The Hitchhiker* TV series.

Kathy Lette was well on her way to something big. *Rocky Horror* star of stage and screen, Little Nell (Campbell) opened a fashionable nightclub in Manhattan. Her younger sister Cressida was acclaimed for her woodblock prints of landscapes, interiors and still life. Jeannie Lewis represented Australia in the Cervantes International Arts Festival, Mexico. Lin Utzon was gaining a huge reputation in Europe as a ceramicist. George Gittoes and his wife Gabrielle travelled to the Northern

Territory to make a series of documentary films. Roger Foley – Mr Fogg – successfully introduced creative Lightshows to the corporate and private world Australia-wide. Bruce Goold created prints for Mambo Graphics and fine art galleries.

Gary Shearston enjoyed Top 10 success in England with Cole Porter's 'I Get A Kick Out of You' (1984). Returning to Australia, he shocked friends by studying for the Anglican priesthood. He became the Rev Gary Shearston and ran a parish in rural New South Wales (with his forthcoming *Aussie Blue* CD under wraps). Tim Lewis managed a heritage-listed pub in the Rocks - the Hero of Waterloo. Trying for an alternative lifestyle, Greg and Suzie Weight bought an acreage near Glenorie, a rural suburb on the edge of Sydney. Greg was doing portraits of Australian artists. He also lectured in photography, as did William Yang and Jonny Lewis.

After leaving Wirian, William lost many of his negs in a house fire. Recovering from the loss, he researched his Australian-Chinese heritage (dating back to the 1890s) and developed his own style of storytelling in a theatre environment. [8] Jonny came up with something different too. Inspired by Pete Townshend's *Face the Face* record, he started capturing the faces of absolutely everyone who came through the door of his Bondi studio: Martin, Brett, William, Albie, Thelma Clune, Justin O'Brien, Peter Royles, James Ricketson, Michael Glasheen…

After completing the Harris Street Mural, Garry and Judit Shead moved into an apartment in Double Bay where Garry toyed with the idea of illustrating a children's story before settling on a better idea – portraiture. He painted a portrait of Toto for the Mahlab Art Prize and won it. Garry also fired a salvo in the direction of the Archibald Prize with his 1986 portrait of Martin. The following year he and Judit moved to Bundeena where Judit encouraged him to focus on his painting. She later returned to her own art, creating exquisite sculptures.

Even minor players were making the front pages, not always for the right reasons. Sallie-Anne Huckstepp was found murdered in Centennial Park on the same day that Lindy Chamberlain was released from prison. That evening, Martin watched a one-hour TV Special about Azaria and reminisced about Sallie-Anne. Around 11.00pm Les and Harold danced through the front door. Hellooo, we've arrived!

Hushed tones: 'Guys, this is what's happened to Sallie-Anne…'.

That steadied them down.

At Wirian, the cast had varied a bit. A recovering junkie called Antony moved in to dry out. He was a quiet young man who did a bit of gardening. One night he went back to old haunts, jacked up and died of 'accidental overdose'. Martin was convinced it was a hotshot. He loathed heroin. He called it 'Satanic'. William and Al were gone. Yensoon and Marilyn stayed off-and-on. Dave Sanderson re-connected with Peter Draffin, which brought Draff back. Les Bean and Harold had become the oddest couple in town. With some success, Harold entered his portrait of environmentalist Dr Bob Brown - *Dr Bob Brown and Green Old Time*

Waltz - in the Archibald Prize. Another contender was Les' portrait of Martin, which was not hung.

Old friends like Kingo, George, Richard, Tim, Marro, Jonny and Margaret dropped in regularly for a coffee and a chat. People like Sam Marshall and Sandy Gutman too. Lin Utzon stayed at Wirian when she was town. All were treated to Tiny's latest offering, 12-minutes of *Highway to Hell* which was exhausting to listen to. Every week or so, Tiny would phone Martin – reverse charges - from anywhere in the world. They'd talk for an hour or more and Martin would tape it. Much of Tiny's talk was what Martin called 'preaching'. The rest were sex fantasies, which were getting creepier.

Tiny talked like this, 'I've never tried this, but my fantasy would be – there's something called a Love Pillow – they hang from the ceiling and the woman straps her legs in there just like a swing. I'd like to have a woman hang from the ceiling and push her, you know, with the tongue while she's hanging'. [9]

Sometimes Tiny talked creepy but he didn't mention to his Australian friends that he was working on a B-grade horror film called *Blood Harvest* in which he played a harmless but creepy clown called Mervo. Maybe he was being Mervo, looping those schlock-horror film ideas into the conversation. Or maybe not. He startled people with too much sex information. More startling was Tiny's response when asked about his impact on Martin's religious beliefs. He said, 'I don't know that side of him'. [10] How could he not know that side of Martin? Everyone else did.

In the mid-80s the three most arresting graphic companies in Sydney were the Ink Group, Mambo Graphics and Ken Done Enterprises. With a staff of two in a small inner-Sydney office, Linda Langton and Jonathon Lee set up a greeting card publishing business they named the Ink Group. Within two and a half years they were flying. In 1984 the Ink Group had 130 employees and the pick of Sydney's artists, Ken Done amongst them. Linda approached Martin who didn't exactly refuse. He just never got around to saying yes. [11]

Located at the Rocks, the Ken Done Shop was a big hit with tourists. Ken and his wife Judy designed every type of fabric you could put in a bathroom or on a bed. Ken portrayed Australian capital cities like sunny Yuppie paradises on a leisurely weekend. He took a shine to Harold the Kangaroo and gave him an exhibition at his Moore Park Gallery. The art world had no idea what to do with Harold - maybe that's what he and Ken had in common? Colourfully-dressed, Harold would show up at art openings, make a splash, turn heads - but who the heck was he? Thanks to Ken Done Gallery in Surry Hills, Harold had an outlet for a time. [12]

And Mambo. Mambo Graphics was launched in 1984 in Alexandria Sydney by Dare Jennings and Andrew Rich. By the mid-80s teen fashion was about skatewear and Mambo was right on track. (Martin disliked their rival 'Natas' - in a mirror it read as 'Satan'.) Mambo's Farting Dog t-shirt (artist: Richard Allan) was an instant hit. There was a loose connection between Mambo, Regular Records and the band Mental As Anything - and all were friendly with Martin. Of course there was talk of a Martin Sharp Mambo top, which (again) didn't lead anywhere commercially. [13]

No one was more surprised than Peewee and Carla when the Delltones won a Gold record for their retro *Bop Til Ya Drop* album. 'I would have been happy if it just charted!' Peewee exclaimed, 'That's all we expected. It'd been 15 years since we'd released a record. Carla rang up K-Tel and they said, "it's bolted, it's pouring out of the store". For about two weeks you could not buy it. The cover definitely captured the feeling of it and it came about because of the show we did with Tiny Tim. Synchronicity and coincidence! Martin did our cover - and the first book that gave us a real lift into another lifestyle was the *Politics of Ecstasy* – Martin did that cover too!' [14] 'Synchronicity and coincidence' always found a sympathetic ear in Martin. For creating the cover image that contributed to the success of *Bop Til Ya Drop*, Peewee and Carla presented Martin with one of the plaques.

Notwithstanding an unmanageable private life, Brett Whiteley canvases were soaring in value and he won the Wynne Prize again. Importantly to Brett, he had credibility amongst the Rock fraternity. Dire Straits' live double album cover featured his multi-panelled masterpiece *Alchemy*. Dire Straits named the album after that painting, and guitarist Mark Knofler produced and played on Dylan's first gospel album, *Slow Train Coming*. So maybe it was 'Alchemy' that drew Dylan's attention to Brett's art? On his 1986 tour of Australia, Dylan agreed to a press conference in Brett's Riley Street Surry Hills studio. 'No wives man!' Brett urged Jonny Lewis when he invited him over the phone.

Jonny described that press conference, 'I drove Martin there. Michael Driscoll and Brett sat together, Mart and I sat next to each other. We arrived long before Dylan got there. There were a lot of eager people. The questions were crudely monitored. Martin had only one question for Dylan.' [15]

'I asked him, "What do you think about Tiny Tim?", said Martin. 'He answered, "What can you say about Tiny Tim?"' [16]

Jonny continued, 'Martin adored Dylan. He thought Dylan was extraordinary (like we all do) but he wasn't going to drop Tiny Tim. Brett was shameless in his pursuit of Dylan. Martin couldn't give a shit, really. I remember Brett jumping to his feet giving this mad rave about where did inspiration came from? Do you drag it down from the heavens? Dylan just looked at him very nonchalantly and said yes or no – a one word reply.' [17]

Next, Dylan played the Sydney Entertainment Centre with Tom Petty and the Heartbreakers. Starting with *In the Garden,* Dylan ended with *Knocking On Heaven's Door*, signaling his gospel phase was not quite over yet. Australian director Gillian Armstrong filmed the concert for an HBO Special on general VHS release. [18]

The morning after the concert, Jonny rang Brett who said, 'I can't talk man, I can't talk – Dylan's coming around to see the studio, ah gotta go, gotta go'. Jonny continued, 'I rang him back later, "How did it go?" Brett said Dylan went through what he had in the studio and said what thought of it. I remember Brett saying, "Man, he's got teeth like a horse!" Brett could be very funny.' [19]

Martin was under the impression that Brett and Dylan remained in touch after that meeting. He said, 'Dylan was very interested in painting - he'd ask, "How do you do that?" Brett wrote him a long letter on how to paint. That was probably the last thing Brett wrote. Someone should track it down - see that Dylan got the letter.' [20]

In March, Martin attended a 'paint for peace' paint-in along the covered walk-way to Sydney Opera House and painted Boofhead. Kingo, Garry and Judit, and many others painted too. Arriving with a bit of a fanfare, Harold and Les danced and painted simultaneously, which amazed the gathered crowd.

Back at Wirian, Martin re-painted his *Kold Komfort Kaffe* Nimrod poster on a big canvas and he organized his major works for his coming Progressive Retrospective exhibition to be held at Roslyn Oxley9 gallery in Paddington. Dave Rowe attended that show.

Dave had a music industry background with Polygram, BMG and Sony in mastering and production. He had a formidable personal archive of musicians he admired, among them Gary Glitter, Tom Waits, Elvis and Tiny, the latter being the reason why his flatmate Helen Theodore, suggested he should go to Oxley's. 'I went to see the exhibition,' said Dave. 'The weirdest thing I could never fathom - because I didn't know much about Martin at the time - was that he had the huge "For Sale" house sign in his exhibition. There was a lot I didn't know about Martin - but I could tell that he loved Tiny from the posters and the music in the exhibition. That was it for me!' [21]

The Oxley exhibition was a raucous affair. Martin dedicated it to his mother and first teacher, Jo. And it was opened by his second teacher, Justin O'Brien. The works were obscured by the massive crowd of people straining to see fragments of Luna Park, Laughing Clowns, popular memorabilia and a wide variety of Martin's paintings, collages, posters and film clips. Hippies, socialites, students, artists and bohemians attended. As fast as one wave of visitors got out, another surged in, all stuck limpet-like to the walls as they inched their way around the gallery. Arthur McIntyre from The Age enjoyed the show, he wrote Martin as, 'Beneath the flip-pant, seemingly loony, veneer of a lovable eccentric exists a man-child who, unlike Warhol and his factory clones, really cares about the purpose of his art beyond the degenerate function of cynical commercial exploitation.' [22]

Oxley's was a 'progressive retrospective', like all Martin's exhibitions. Martin exhibited 97 items – 17 contemporary paintings, 10 pictures from schooldays, 16 collage works, 31 prints and posters, 14 original poster artworks, seven 'objects', the Nimrod series of seven and Tiny Tim records for sale. It summarised Martin's past, pointed to future directions and reminded Sydney that the Martin Sharp name could fill a huge exhibition space twice-over and still spill onto the street. [23]

After 'Oxley', Martin started a painting that became *Pentecost*. He took the composition from his own collage in *Art Book* and repainted the Matisse and Magritte images in his own meticulous style, replacing the dark chair of the Matisse original with Vincent's chair. He also positioned Magritte's dove in the foreground – hence the title. (24)

Stephen Lawson printed it. He said, 'Martin was inspired by the Matisse *Red Room*, all the elements exactly there - the chair, table, rug, the positioning of the window. Martin would be refining that image all the time. The window for example in *Pentecost* eventually becomes Calvary, the hill with the cross on it. He kept that religious side of himself very discreet for a long while.' (25)

Jo Sharp was diagnosed with liver cancer and diabetes. She rarely got out of bed. Marilyn, Yensoon and Martin took time out to go upstairs, sit with her and talk. No more chats around the kitchen table, her room became her whole world. In her decline, Jo started 'seeing things' and Martin, who took hallucinations seriously, feared his mother had been possessed by the spirit - or the essence - of her disease. He wrote, 'I believe that the spirit which possessed my dear mother in these times was using her as a window.'

Jo didn't believe in the supernatural, yet she claimed to have been lifted to the ceiling by people in her room. Martin wrote, 'Jo (my mother) was not a person to hallucinate and, though highly imaginative, she was not a vocally spiritual person. Indeed, she would say, "The only thing up 'up there' are possums in the roof." (Which there were.)'

Yensoon wrote in her diary: 'Looking up at the ceiling with her right arm raised in the air, Mrs Sharp suddenly saw seven little Chinese men descend from the ceiling. They were three feet tall, all of them wearing Chinese coolie hats with a round brim. Their bodies were round, each of them wearing a different color: red, green, blue and yellow. The yellow little man seemed to be the leader. He gave Mrs Sharp a stern and icy cold look. As if a hole was bored into her heart and she shuddered. His subordinates were much more genial to her. They smiled at her and the blue little man touched her hand, murmuring words of comfort. She found that he had a slimy and soft body. The leader motioned his subordinates to lift Mrs Sharp up to the ceiling and then put her down onto the floor. She protested and ordered them to put her back to bed, but to no avail.

'In a trice, she found herself in a verdant park. The sun was setting. Although the surroundings were a joy to her eyes, no living things were visible, only the wind was sighing amidst the trees. It struck a note of desolation to her. She felt a sense of despair. The little blue man presented her with a blue silk flowing robe, which she happily put on because it was her favorite color. The moment she put it on the sun suddenly sank beyond the horizon and they lifted her up in the darkness, at which time she lost consciousness. Upon regaining consciousness she found herself to be in her own bed.' After this episode, Jo's condition declined rapidly.

As death approached, she lapsed into hypoglycemic comas. To bring her out of it, the doctors fed her barley sugar. There were several disturbing episodes during this period. In this state Jo would adopt two personalities - cheerful and cooperative or duplicitous. Martin wrote, 'She appeared possessed by an alien - hateful, intelligent, cruel, arrogant, despising help, physically strong. (My mother was very frail.) Palpably evil, the whole atmosphere of her room would change. It was most upsetting. Jo would have no memory of these experiences. Her doctor would sidestep the issue when I tried to talk about it. I thought it was very important to discuss but no doctor would. If I'd known more about exorcism I think I would have attempted to do it.' (26)

Jo Sharp was ambulanced to St Lukes Hospital where she spent her final weeks. The last thing Jo heard was Rev Allan Moyes radio broadcast, which closed with the Irish Blessing (May the road rise up to meet you). Jonny and Martin were present when she died. Her last words were, 'I've been talking to God for the last four hours…' Afterwards Martin said, 'I wanted her skeleton to put in a glass case with her walking stick – just a skeleton and a stoop. The years had stooped her. "The Artist's Mother." I really did want it. I couldn't get a clearance for it'. (27) After this Martin referred to himself as a 'childless orphan'. Robbie Tarling, a friend who knitted a pink Mickey Mouse jumper for Martin, responded, 'He's surrounded by his children but they're not his flesh and blood!' (28)

For all Martin's achievements, there remained only one more thing Jo wanted of him – a child. William Yang had confronted Martin with Jo's hopes - 'The child – isn't it?' Ruefully Martin admitted, 'I guess so, yes'. Jo had gone. Still no child. (29)

After Jo's death, Martin read his parents' love letters. Although his mother had told him that 'the marriage was all over on the honeymoon night…' Martin believed the letters showed otherwise. He played a lot of 30s and 40s music and allowed himself to drift into sadness. He also replayed the tape of Jo's funeral service in which Martin's childhood friend and neighbour, John Gregory-Roberts, delivered the eulogy before a rendition of Jo's special song, *Hello Young Lovers*. Martin wept. He read her diaries questioning, 'who is she writing for?' as he carefully noted comments about his childhood, OZ trials and bygone years. Ruminating over the past sparked in Martin an unlikely renewed interest in his Yellow House *Catalog*. He wanted Phil Ward to publish it. Phil, the business newsletter publisher from the Free Lindy campaign. Many publishers would have seized the opportunity, not Phil. He had no idea what Martin was talking about. Publisher Tom Thompson did.

As a 16-year old schoolkid, Tom would visit the Yellow House when he came to Sydney. A fulltime journalist in the mid-80s, with the assistance of his wife Elizabeth Butel, one of Tom's projects was packaging books for Penguin Publishing. Tom explained, 'Elizabeth was trying to do a book on Luna Park with Martin and

Kingo, but neither of them would ever get to the table with a contract because they all had their other things to do.'

A radio program called *Growing Up in the 60s* was Tom's next idea. He decided to publish the material as a slim 90-page book. Martin agreed to do the cover and pictures. Then Martin changed his mind, 'Tom, I can't do the cover, I'm caught up in (whatever painting he was doing)…'. Tom said, '…from his existing artwork Martin wanted me to choose anything relevant. I chose some pictures, paid him $200 - but I still had no cover. A friend of mine said "I'll do it in the style of Martin" – as a way of homaging him.'

Tom selected five pictures that had previously been published in OZ magazine and Craig McGregor's *People, Politics and Pop*. His idea of reproducing Martin's popular mid-60s Pop Art illustrations appealed to another author, who made the same request. Again, Martin said yes, providing he didn't need to draw anything new. [30]

Les moved out with Harold when she inherited enough money to buy a tiny flat in the back of Kings Cross. Then Yensoon moved on, leaving behind an all-male cast. Alcohol was taking its toll at Wirian and Martin - who never drank - was running out of patience with two or three drunks. Sometimes Wirian seemed like a Lonely Blokes Club. Sanderson became so morose that Martin kicked him out. Some guy called Paul was a regular visitor. Within the year he was charged with rape and sentenced to nine years jail in Risden Prison Tasmania. 'I can't throw him out,' Martin bleated, 'he looks like Vincent'.

Peter Royles didn't drink as much as before but he still had occasional breakouts. Peter had a creative force that seemed to push him to self-destruct out of sheer frustration. Recognising this, Martin wanted to get him into a studio and record an album but Martin could neither afford the time nor the expense. 'Martin loved me and hated me - didn't he?' questioned Peter, who continued drinking at the Bondi Pub less regularly. Peter wanted to dry out, get a driver's licence, buy a vehicle and move away. In exchange for painting the house, Martin bought Peter a Dormobile, which he parked outside Wirian in anticipation of passing his driving test. [31]

Then Peter Draffin moved in. He was AA (Alcoholics Anonymous), which meant he didn't drink at all - but on the rare occasion that he did, watch out. Things started well between Draff and Martin. At his best, Martin thought Draff was a gem. Richard Neville often popped in with daughters Lucy or Angelica. Richard was on the Speakers' Circuit and he'd call in after addressing some corporation about ethical business practices and environmental issues. He continually teased Martin with cheeky remarks about 'the regression of the Renaissance Man' and the 'Cosmic Crime-buster'.

Jo's Will: Martin poured through the trusts and accused the trustees of not acting in his best interests. Jo's estate was $1.7 million. According to Martin, $105,000 of that money was locked into a system that he couldn't unlock. Yes, he got his hands on some money from the brokers' trusts and sliced $750,000 off his mortgage, but what about the rest? Did the money go to beneficiaries like the Flying Doctor, Kings School Parramatta or even the Cat & Dogs Protection Association? He needed to know. [32]

Although Martin was telling friends he didn't plan to paint much more after *Pentecost*, the photocopier brought him back. Art - Martin reckoned - was the only way he could express his point of view. [33] He had continued to experiment with the photocopier ever since he'd bought it. He enlarged newsprint pictures, enlarged the enlargements, and kept going until he got what he wanted. He dubbed his process 'Art Journalism'. After a while he started colouring them, using crayon and linseed oil. Copying Martin's technique, Peter Royles did the same, with surprisingly good results.

Martin started a picture of the Ghost Train fire victims, hung in cruciform – four down, three across. He linked the number seven to the Willie Nelson/Ray Charles song *Seven Spanish Angels took Another Angel Home*. Like the Ghost Train fire, the Milperra bikie massacre was another example of seven plus one deaths.

Always keen to know what Martin was up to, the Sydney Morning Herald ran a story about Martin's toy collection, a sample of which generated interest in the Oxley9 exhibition. The SMH photographer snapped Martin in a striped Russian sailor's top, seated at the bottom of Wirian's central stairs. Beside him is a Kewpie doll and behind him, a painting of the Luna Park face by a 9-year old boy. The journalist was interested in all the Luna Park memorabilia that was saved from oblivion, Martin answered, 'They're not really mine, I'm just keeping them. They are part of the history of Australian comic art'. [34]

Further changes were afoot. Peter Royles passed his driving test, Draff consulted the i-Ching and assisted Martin with Luna Park research ('about bloody time!' said Martin). Paul became more irritating than usual Martin. And as if to fulfill Richard Neville's 'Cosmic Crimebuster' heckle, Martin wrote, 'I've worked out the government corruption angle. The dark forces got many of the politicians' children on heroin and then had them right in their pockets, having the ability to kill them by altering the doses. (Button's son dead, Unsworth's son dead… so it goes). To think that drugs wasn't even an election issue, the most important issue of all. Inflation = black money, that's the economic effect of heroin on a country.' [35]

The most surprising news of all was that Les was getting married. Aged 52, her prospective beau - Gareth - was a Cranbrook sports hero when Martin was at school. A veteran of three marriages, Gareth worked in advertising in Malaysia for 12 years. Martin picked out one of Jo's rings for Les and the wedding was held in a private ceremony in October. Martin was Best Man and Les' sister Penelope was the second witness. Harold was hopping mad. After this, Les Bean stopped being Les Bean. She didn't paint her clothes any more. She and Gareth moved to Coffs

Harbour where he had 28 acres of land. No longer a crazy eccentric, in time Les evolved into a successful businesswoman.

Martin gained two important assignments before the year was out. The artistic director of the 1982 Adelaide Festival, Gavin Henderson, returned to England where he took up the position of artistic director for the 1988 Brighton International Festival. Henderson had commissioned Martin's 1982 Adelaide Festival poster and wanted one for the Brighton Festival,. Since Jo's death, Martin had toyed with the idea of returning to England. When the Brighton Festival agreed to put Tiny on the bill that clinched it for Martin. He was going in May.

Martin's second major piece was a tapestry 3m x 6m in size, commissioned and donated to the State Library of New South Wales by Mr and Mrs Jim Bain. Martin created and editioned the print, after which four young weavers at the Victorian Tapestry Workshop spent six months weaving the design into an art object. The picture centred on the Sydney Harbour Bridge and the Opera House. The Southern Cross soars across the top and Luna Park is on fire. The tapestry was a summary document, comprising symbols from Martin's journey as a citizen of the country. He presented the blue groper, blue kingfisher, Captain Cook's Endeavour, 'the Moon is a harsh mistress', Uluru and the dingo. The tapestry is edged with the words from the Bernard O'Dowd poem, 'Australia'. Martin named it 'OZ?' [36]

Russell Sharp commissioned and sold Martin's posters when he wasn't being the Flower King. He said, 'I was living at Wirian at the time this was being created. I sat up all night while Martin cut it out. It was printed by Steven Lawson. There were only 87 in the edition. We each took a third and it sold out in three months @ $300 each'. [37]

7.
THE BRIGHTON CUT

When you meet people with Martin you don't know whether you are meeting someone off the street or somebody famous. He didn't differentiate.
Roslyn Sharp

Australia was very parochial, even in the late-80s. 'Making it' in Sydney might mean nothing in Perth, Brisbane or Melbourne and vice versa. Sydney lionised Brett Whiteley; Melbourne was all Howard Arkley. Sydney adored Margaret Olley; Melbourne had Mirka Mora. Until the advent of the worldwide web, very few – like cartoonist Michael Leunig – bridged the Sydney-Melbourne gap with ease.

Philippe Mora's younger brother ran the William Mora Gallery in Melbourne central. In 1988, William took an educated risk by exhibiting two artists from Bundeena, a waterfront village on the outskirts of southern Sydney where George Gittoes and Garry Shead had settled. They both had outback themes. George showed his Northern Territory collection. And Garry exhibited his *Outback Ballad* paintings dedicated to his father. Both were a great success.

RAW was a collective of Melbourne art students who shared an inner-city house and wore black. Having heard stories about the Yellow House, they bailed George up at his opening and questioned how they might turn their live-in collective into an art environment. Dave, Pasqual, Walter and others listened most attentively to his replies. [1] Moments like this must have impressed George that the Yellow House concept still had legs.

Artistic director for the Brighton International Festival, Gavin Henderson contacted Martin again, broadening his request from one poster to a 'Martin Sharp poster exhibition – the London Years'. This became a possibility, at least for a couple of months. Then Tiny declared an ultimatum: he would not perform in

Brighton unless the film was screened as well. Martin and Tiny had a standoff over this one. It was Martin who backed down. The film was more than enough work, a poster exhibition would be too much, especially as Henderson wanted Martin to pen a short piece as well. So it was all go! Go! Go! On the film.

To add to Martin's concerns, in April, Luna Park was closed 'for renovations and repairs'. The investment company changed its name from Prome Investments Pty Ltd to Luna Park Investments Pty Ltd, which sounded sinister and required whatever scant attention Martin could spare. There was Wirian to manage too. Clayton from Bermagui moved in and helped with maintenance, Al Jones came back and Peter Draffin was there too. Draff eschewed technology and believed the progress of humankind ended with the Industrial Revolution.

Draff lasted eight months. He said, 'I stayed there in 1988. Martin had someone working on the Tiny Tim film called Deanne (Judson) and I had this raving infatuation with Deanne. She didn't have one for me. I remember Martin working on the Brighton poster. That's one of his best posters I think.' [2] Draff confessed that his 'manic, drunken behaviour' was unacceptable though he was angered by the way Martin handled it. He wrote, 'No one gives Draffin the old carpet-out-from-under and stays mates!' [3] For a time, Martin and Draff went separate ways.

Martin, Marilyn, Paul Healy, John Barker, Sally Fitzpatrick and others worked tirelessly to complete the film in time. From a feature length, freeform documentary loved by friends, it needed to be structured enough to engage a generic audience at a public screening at a major arts festival. This edit was known as *The Brighton Cut*. [4] Some have thought it to be the finished product. It is not. Martin wrote, 'The Brighton Cut' will not be the final cut...more a trial...' [5]

Exhausted and cutting it fine, they only just met their deadline. Carrying the film, with no margin of time, Martin caught the Sydney-to-London flight but there was a delay. Martin explained, 'I was flying over with the film. It was meant to be shown that night in Brighton, We were going over Afghanistan or somewhere like that. I had a window seat. I always love the window seat to watch what's going on. All of a sudden I saw what looked like a big fire - it just went zzzzonk! - past the window and I knew I'd seen something happen. Then they said we had to go to Amsterdam where I was stuck when I was supposed to be showing the film.' [6]

On arrival, Martin was driven straight to the screening. There he met up with Aussie friends - Marilyn, Al, Nathan Waks, his wife Candice, Harold the Kangaroo and cousin Roslyn. Roslyn was living in London at the time. Martin invited her to photograph the event. She said, 'I was going to Brighton anyway because an old boyfriend was in the comedy section. It was fabulous but I kinda felt sorry for Martin that there weren't more people there. He introduced me to Richard Attenborough who was very warm towards Martin. They obviously were very fond of each other. Richard Attenborough hung around for the whole concert. I'm sure I would have met others too but when you meet people with Martin you don't know whether you are meeting someone off the street or somebody famous. He didn't differentiate in how he treated them.' Roslyn had a lengthy conversation with Tiny about moisturisers. [7]

Patron, Sir Richard Attenborough sat with Martin and watched Tiny's full marathon. Martin recalls him drawling out just one word to sum up Tiny's act - 'er-maaazing...'. [8] To the press Sir Richard enthused, 'They employ me to encourage people to give money to the festival, but I do like to see events when I can'. [9]

Tiny had arrived well before Martin, bringing his new wife Miss Jan. Just eight days before, Tiny had been in Dallas Texas headlining the third Mr Ed Musical Festival – 'Edstock' - organised by James (Bucks) Burnett. In 1984, 'Bucks' recorded Tiny singing the 'Mr Ed' song and he released it as a 45 rpm single. Bucks again took Tiny to a studio where they laid down the first takes for what would become Tiny's *Girl* album (1996). This happened the week before Brighton, [10]

For someone in terrible physical condition, Tiny certainly had boundless energy. Two boxes of Callard and Bowser butterscotch sweets were all he required to prepare him for his record-breaking romp through the history of popular song. After a quick prayer and a dash of makeup, Tiny hit the stage. Anchored by musical director Nathan Waks, Marvin Lewis (piano) and Al Jones (keyboards and piano accordion), the band just kept going and going...! One hundred and thirty-eight songs later, Tiny broke his own record and reestablished his World Non-Stop Singing Record for a Professional Singer. 'World Beater!' read the newspaper headlines.

Commenting on Tiny's endurance, his third wife Miss Sue said, 'Tiny had three times a normal person's energy. Even when he was old he had tremendous stamina. He could stay up for several nights in a row without affecting his performance too much. He was able to sleep sitting up in almost any kind of conveyance – whether it was a car or a plane or anything. He didn't have a lot of muscle strength but he was a big person and in some ways he could just go on and on like the Energiser Bunny. I suppose there was probably a lot of determination there to just keep going. I don't think he had much of a plan. He was just winging it, making it up as he went along. He was good at that kind of thing – thinking on his feet and figuring out how to get the audience interested and involved, and keeping them involved.' [11]

Brighton's *Evening Argus* wrote, 'Brighton Festival achieved a world record late last night when Tiny Tim sang for three hours, 11 minutes and 30 seconds without a pause. He smashed his own previous title which he gained nine years ago in Sydney with two hours and 15 minutes warbling the classics of the previous century. With a large and enthusiastic Zap Tent crowd cheering him on, he broke the three-hour barrier with All My Lovin', part of a Beatles selection and finished up with falsetto Tiptoe Through the Tulips and finally We'll Meet Again'. [12] After dueting with her husband on the closing song, Miss Jan herded Tiny back to their hotel and kept him to herself. 'She was difficult,' said Martin who was suffering with kidney stones during the festival.

In the end, Martin regretted that after such a big effort the film was not shown to advantage and that the marathon didn't really peak. Summing up he said, '*The Brighton Cut* was projected in a theatre. The light wasn't very strong in the projector. It was a bit of an uncomfortable night. The marathon lacked a bit of sparkle. We didn't have Adrian (Rawlins) there for the introduction to the marathon, so everyone noticed the difference between someone who could do an introduction for Tiny and someone who couldn't.' [13]

Other times Martin felt more positive, declaring it 'a great concert'. He had mixed feelings about the *Brighton Cut* of the film, but he was nonetheless pleased it had gone that far. 'The film needs a lot more work, though I would stand by what exists as the *Brighton Cut*. I had a great trip. I can't say it was a triumph, though TT's Marathon certainly was. IS.' [14] Reviewer Steven Puchalski wrote about the film, 'Although newcomers might be perplexed, it's all so unique and inspired that I couldn't stop smiling, as it captures his (Tiny's) humanity, hilarity, and belovedly twisted lifestyle. It's not difficult to imagine that Tiny Tim was an off-stage weirdo, but it's gratifying to see it chronicled for posterity, while realising he actually exceeded expectations.' [15]

And so, Tiny and Martin parted ways, Tiny returned to the States with Miss Jan and Martin spent a couple of months in London staying with Zandra Rhodes. [16] Having finished his stint with the Great American Circus, Tiny signed with Donnie Brooks for the '30 Years of Rock N Roll' tour. Donnie Brooks was an early 60s pop star with hits like *Doll's House, Mission Bell* and *Memphis*. He continued to accept all recording offers, which was the habit of a lifetime. The *Girl* album with Bucks was in abeyance and the film *Blood Harvest* was released to pathetic reviews. Critics praised Tiny's as Mervo the Clown as the only good thing in the film. Martin approached its producer Bill Rebane about brokering a distribution deal for the *Street of Dreams* film but Rebane couldn't generate interest. [17]

Meanwhile, in Sydney, Dave Rowe couldn't get enough of Tiny. He had attended the Oxley 'Progressive Retrospective' the previous year and loved Martin's Tiny Tim posters. When radio station 2-Double J played the Brighton marathon in its entirely, Dave taped it and wore the tapes out playing them. He wanted new copies. 'Ring Martin Sharp, he'll have it,' said Helen Theodore, the flat-mate who had told him to attend the Oxley9 exhibition.

'You can't just ring Martin Sharp!' Dave responded.

Apparently, you could and Dave did.

Martin invited him over.

Dave: 'I walked in – didn't get the tape, got a job!'

Dave Rowe's great-great-grandfather was Alfred Rowe, better known in the 1880s and 1890s as circus man, the Great Onzalo. Said Dave, 'Martin had written an article in *Quadrant* magazine (1977) and he mentions the Great Onzalo walking across what would become the Sydney Harbour Bridge. Martin states that, "they built the Harbour Bridge in his footsteps". Well lo and behold it turns out that it was my great-grandfather! (He went under the name of the Great Onzalo. His real surname was Rowe.) I would learn that Martin liked to synchronise all those connections.

'The second connection was that the same man, (the Great Onzalo) was the first to ever bring a gramophone to Australia. He imported one and charged a penny (or something) for people to have a listen in this tent. No one had ever seen one. It was like Sideshow Alley at the circus. Martin kept adding these up. I came to realise that connections mattered. I took him over some scrapbooks and things. I was so excited that he was as big a fan of Tiny as I was. I recall that day. He was so patient.' [18]

Having worked for Polygram, BMG and Sony, Dave could handle every production aspect of music - tape transfers, post-production, mastering, re-mastering, promotion and importantly, dealing with record companies, which is how he got to know Martin Fabinyi co-founder of Regular Records. The Regular Records label was initially created to manage the band Mental As Anything. It grew to include many acts like Kate Ceberano, Icehouse, The Reels, Austen Tayshus, and it was about to include Tiny Tim. As Martin's new assistant, the Brighton Marathon tapes were Dave's first task. Three hours-plus of Tiny's marathon was non-commercially viable from a record company's perspective, so Martin agreed they should produce an edited version, staying true to Tiny's marathon effort. Dave tightened it into one exciting hour. For a while it seemed this would be the product. Martin changed his mind at the last post. Said Dave, 'We edited all the best bits and made it one long marathon. We did a great edit. We had a nice smooth-flowing mini-marathon. We had the master ready to go into production and he left me a note, "Dave, let's release the whole tape". It suddenly went from one to three cassettes.'

Martin didn't want it cut back at all (except Tiny's final duet with Miss Jan for copyright reasons). He designed a black and white cover and Dave made it a commercially available 3-cassette pack. [19] 'I just felt the whole thing was too long to be commercially successful and Tiny agreed that the marathon would be too much in its entirety'. [20] Another idea was to release the Chameleon LP to CD, a project that would drag on for ages.

Clarifying his standing at Wirian Dave said, 'I was honoured that Martin asked me to work on this project, I went there to work on Tiny's music not for any other reason. A lot of people were doing what I was doing there. A stream of people worked on the Tiny tapes. He had set up a room, which we'd converted into an office. It was the room beside Martin's Inner Sanctum, which he loved because he could hear my edits all day long. What he didn't like was that whoever called in would hear what I was doing, hang out and chat. There's a lot of work that doesn't get done when you're continually interrupted.' [21]

In August George organised a Yellow House Reunion dinner at the Art Gallery of New South Wales. There was a proposal afoot for a reconstruction of the original rooms inside the gallery. 'A George Gittoes idea,' wrote Martin in a letter, 'Can't say I'm that keen – doing it once was hard enough.' Suddenly switching subjects in the next paragraph he added, 'The Tapestry looks great at the Library.' (22)

Hung for all Sydney-siders to enjoy, the *OZ?* tapestry overpowered the reception area at the State Library of New South Wales with its size, beauty and complexity. Through the windows, it could even be glimpsed by passing traffic. The prints too were a commercial success, which is more than can be said for the 3-cassette edition of the Brighton Marathon. Unable to get a record company's interest, Dave released it for Martin as a Street of Dreams production, which basically meant that Martin gave them away to friends.

'I'm trying to tidy up the house,' Martin continued the letter. 'Got a student called Jessica coming any moment. Something on The Bad Boys of Australian Art! The house is quiet at the moment - so much to tidy up and sort out it's almost overwhelming. (a) The film (b) Luna Park (c) Dream Museum (d) Mum's things (e) my Art (f) Tiny's Tapes (g) my life...'

The Brighton Cut behind him, Martin got back to tinkering with the film. He continued, 'The cutting room is being prepared for the next cut of the film, got Tiny's wedding footage in London at last. They hadn't forgotten me over there and it was great to see old pals again and new ones too. Zandra Rhodes was an absolute trooper & put me up, so I repainted her mural. Nicholas Roeg really adored Street of Dreams. Very encouraging. Didn't see Eric. Mick Jagger asked me to his party here.' In his brief attempt to launch a solo career without the Rolling Stones, Mick Jagger came to Sydney for a concert and gave Martin a fistful of free tickets, which Martin distributed among friends.

He continued, 'Tiny was great. I wish he could have come to London he would have loved it. His wife Jan came...we didn't really take to each other although I tried. They've separated now. Tiny says, "I've never known such peace!" Marriage still seems a million miles away for me – though my heart doesn't stop longing. I got flu and jetlag when I returned – I have just surfaced to "Tidy Up Before Art" mode. Palace of Art, Bricks of Boredom. Yensoon seems quite a lot happier and stronger. She been going to a Free Catholic Church & associated Lodge and loves Masonry, which she says comes from China. Draffin & daughter Christabel have just arrived.' (23)

Martin announced that Tiny was coming to Australia in May, so once again was all hands on deck. Martin had a stack of Tiny's live music from which to create a new release and he selected the 1983 recordings of *Highway to Hell*. Maybe Dave needed an assistant? Dave didn't think so. Martin got him one anyway.

Wendy Evans worked at Westpac Bank. Dave went there one day to cash a cheque. When Wendy saw the signature she exclaimed, 'I know Martin Sharp!' Back at Wirian, Dave checked with Martin, 'Do you know this Wendy Evans?'

He said, 'It doesn't ring a bell'. What she meant was that she knew his artwork. But because Dave had mentioned Wendy, the next time Martin went to the bank she opened with, 'I was talking to Dave about you…' and for some reason Martin drew some inference that there was a connection between Dave and her. 'Next minute she was employed!' said Dave. [24]

Like Dave, Wendy worked on the Tiny Tim tape transfers on-and-off for years. When things got rough between Dave and Martin, Wendy might take over. And when Wendy had other work, Dave would step back in. Dave and Wendy were quite different in their approach. Although not professionally trained, she did many hundreds of hours of safety masters, which to Martin were invaluable because he'd use them as listening copies.

Tiny was always optimistic about his new releases. Released in America, *I Saw Mr Presley Tiptoeing Through The Tulips* was a curious single that suggests Elvis might still be alive somewhere, at least that's what a few US journalists thought Tiny meant. Martin played it for a time, chuckled about it then shelved it among his ever-growing collection of Tiny Tim ephemera. His Australian release of Tiny's *Highway to Hell* seemed more appropriate, giving Martin a reason to reconnect with its musical director, Denny Burgess. Commenting on their 1983 sessions Denny wondered if that wrapped up his relationship with Martin, '…but then Martin rang us up and said, "That went really well, we'd love you to be Tiny's band when he comes back'. That's when we started to see Martin at various times.' [25] So Denny and his partner Clare became regulars at all Martin's events.

The murder of Lady Winifreda Ashton, widow of artist and former director of the Art Gallery of New South Wales (1937-1945) Will Ashton, captured Martin's interest for a time. A serial murderer had killed six elderly women in the Mosman area. When the police tracked down 'Granny Killer' John Wayne Glover, it was revealed that he lived next door to Barbara Thiering, wife of the Chaplain of Cranbrook School when Martin was there. Thiering's book *Jesus the Man* didn't impress Martin at all. He couldn't see anything other than fiction in what she called the 'pecher' method of Biblical interpretation, a code that defied all logic. 'I think it's rubbish,' said Martin. He didn't want the book in the house. [26]

John Godson's widow, Jenny – who reverted to her family name Poidevin – had remained close to Martin after the tragic loss of her husband and sons, Damien (6) and Craig (4). She spent hours with Martin going over the evidence and concurred that the Ghost Train fire had been deliberately lit. In February, she told *New Idea* magazine, 'I believe that - because the people who did it are evil, motivated by greed - there is an evil essence in there. Nine years ago I wouldn't have conceived I could think anything like this, it would have all been foreign to me. But after my own experiences and my reading, I believe there is evil in the universe which has the power to control people and situations.' The magazine featured a picture of Martin holding up the photograph of the minotaur beside her two boys. The magazine's headline was, 'The Luna Park Tragedy…a link with the occult?' [27]

George, Greg, and as many of the original Yellow House people as they could attract, started conducting regular meetings with an aim to persuade the Art Gallery of New South Wales into holding a Yellow House Retrospective exhibition some time in the future. With Tiny only a couple of months away from arriving, Martin wasn't particularly engaged in the Yellow House revival group. He attended no more Yellow House strategy meetings than necessary but Albie ensured that Martin received all circulars and was kept right up-to-date.

In April, Tiny returned to Australia. Martin always marked Tiny's arrival with the release of a new record. The original idea was a 45rpm single, with *Highway To Hell* as side A and either *Mickey Mouse, Forever Miss Dixie* or *Last Mile of the Way* on side B. In the end, with the support of Regular Records, they released a cassette single (cassingle) with *I Love Rock N Roll* on side B. Martin did the cover art, which was also printed as a promotional t-shirt. [28]

Tiny's *Highway To Hell* was perhaps the last-ever cassingle released on the Regular label. Never achieving the universal acceptance of vinyl records, in the 80s cassingles became popular thanks largely to the Walkman and car audio players. The CD format of the future would mark a big change in the music industry. Significantly it resurrected the back catalogue of every major artist, as the buying public updated their music collections to this new format.

The MTV film clip was another 80s phenomenon. MTV (Music Television) was an American cable TV show guided by 'video jockeys'. Every music release required an accompanying film clip. Martin sought the assistance of filmmaker Michael Glasheen to address this new challenge. Michael captured the pace of the music by filming the Sydney to Newcastle motorway as the 'highway' (...to Hell). It was screened on MTV and gradually tricked up into the version currently on youtube, with Tiny singing and AC/DC visuals on the power chords. [29]

Arriving in Australia to the usual Wirian reception, Tiny performed RSL Clubs and Martin organised a gig at the former Kinsela's club, renamed Kakadu, where Tiny sang a mini-marathon which included *Tiptoe, Whole World In His Hands, Mame, Wabash Cannonball, Amazing Grace, Heartbreak Hotel, Somewhere My Love, Loverly Bunch of Coconuts, Roll Out The Barrel*, and a couple of Aussie tunes - *Waltzing Matilda* and *Tie Me Kangaroo Down Sport*. The Doug Anthony All Stars played the late-night show; Tiny played the late-late night show.

To launch the *Highway To Hell* cassingle, Martin organized a private function at Wirian. The place was packed with friends, artists and celebrities, including Garry, Judit and Gria Shead, Denny & Clare, Draff, Harold the Kangaroo, Ros Oxley, Roslyn Sharp, Al Jones, Clayton Simms, Toto Renshaw, Craig McGregor and radio personalities Danno and James Valentine. Channel 10's *Good Morning Australia* was there filming. Martin and Tiny were innundated with at least 70 well-wishers before Tiny returned to the States and took up where he'd left off with the Donnie Brooks' 30 Years of Rock and Roll tour. Before leaving he told

Martin to clean the house up and to either marry Yensoon or terminate. It was Tiny's most understated Australian tour. Everyone was still drained from Brighton.

Before the year was out, there were two more new releases for Martin's friends to enjoy, Gary Shearston's 'Aussie Blue' CD and the Tiny *Marathon* triple-cassette pack. The *Highway To Hell,* Glasheen/Sharp video was aired on MTV and Martin started working on an album cover for Regular Records' celebration of 10 years in the business. Martin's 3-piece Boofhead band image was used for two LP records (*Greatest Hits* and *Hits That Missed*), the video and the boxed set. Tiny's *Highway to Hell* was track 4 on *Hits That Missed*. Production was credited to Martin Sharp and Al Jones. [30]

Over the years, Martin had mostly kept the details of his love life under wraps. He opened up to friends but didn't want these matters widely discussed. Not that he minded for himself, he said, 'but out of respect for the women involved'. Martin always expressed affection for past loves. His exes mostly stayed in touch for years after the romance was over. and maintained good relationships after relations ended. Martin wrote long letters to Eija Vehka-aho who lived in Europe, he supported Cressida Campbell's exhibitions and Victoria Cobden was invited to the Tiny Tim shows, Eric Clapton's party, opening nights and everything else Martin came up with. His tryst with Yensoon was a private matter. William knew the details, not many others did. As a muse, Martin painted Yensoon at least twice. A huge black on white portrait was hung beside the front door. He also painted her nude, which he kept out of sight upstairs. He later destroyed that picture.

Now, and for the next seven years, 48-year old Martin would fall in and out of love like a teenager. The average age of his sweethearts was early-20s and they were mostly platonic muses. After Tiny left the country, Martin told everyone that he was keen on Emma Walker. It started when one of Martin's friends, writer Edda Walker was dying of cancer at the Sacred Heart hospice. Edda asked friends to bring something beautiful to her room and Martin brought his picture *Pentecost*. That's how he met her daughter Emma, an aspiring young artist who came to live at Wirian. He wanted to marry her but wanted to follow Tiny's counsel and remain chaste. About sex, Martin said, 'If you don't scratch it, it doesn't itch'. [31]

Martin developed a fascination for paintings of young women. His first subject in this series came after he photocopied a photograph of his mother as a young girl, he blew it up and over-painted it. Since her death, Jo's room remained untouched. Everything was as it was when she was alive – her books, pictures, 1941 diary, comb – everything. Martin's portrait was a beautiful tribute, after which he cast around for more subjects. He was interested in the beauty expressed in that first blush of youth. 'I'd like to do for young girls, what Justin did for young boys', said Martin, who Justin had painted as a 15-year old high school student. Justin's portrait of Martin always had pride of place on the Inner Sanctum end wall.

Martin added, 'I still want to paint great nudes. I'm trying to work out if it's a temptation or a genuine artistic urge. Possibly both.' [32]

8.
THIS IS NOT THE YELLOW HOUSE

The Yellow House Gallery was never recognized by the art establishment because it was too difficult to categorise, too difficult to market and too subversive to ever be accepted.
George Gittoes

'Although it was not recorded in any conventional history, the Yellow House remained strong in the oral history of artists,' wrote art critic Joanna Mendelssohn. 'Even before its demise it had taken on a legendary quality, and its stature grew in the telling. Many of the younger artists who came there found it an important impetus to their creative life. Most who worked there found that, although intense, the experience of working in a communal way, and keeping their individuality as well as losing it, was worth the pain'. [1]

In the early 70s, 57-59 Macleay Street Potts Point wasn't the only performance art space in town. They were popping up everywhere. Now-forgotten places like the Workshop in William Street, the House of New World in West Ryde and the like. The difference was that the Yellow House was run by artists, those other venues were run by hippies, who were creative rather than artistic.

Eighteen years later, the Yellow House artists were still friends. There had been many small get-togethers, but 1990 marked their 20th anniversary. There was a pervasive feeling that they could link arms, come up with an idea and 'put the band back together'. After all, the key players were still around, still talking to each other and in good artistic shape. Could they expand the Yellow House idea from something ephemeral, regional and generational into filling a significant gap in the history of Australian art? In the early-70s, hippie art was everywhere. Yet it left not a trace in the late-80s art textbooks.

George did a head count – most people liked the idea, but not everyone. Musician Nic Lyon, thought once was enough. He reckoned, 'We'd had a bellyful of it all!' Although Nic didn't involve himself, George ensured his name was listed in the Catalogue along with the others. [2] A few others had moved on too, especially Brett. The main thing was that there was a core of interested participants and no opposition to the idea of putting a proposition to the Art Gallery of New South Wales, which they did.

Antony (Tony) Bond, Director Curatorial at the Art Gallery of New South Wales (AGNSW) in 1990, recalled the occasion, 'A small Yellow House delegation came to see me. George Gittoes, Greg Weight and Peter Wright came to see if I would be interested in doing this exhibition at the Gallery. They came first without Martin.

'I thought it was well worth doing, partly because of the anniversary but also because it was related to Sydney with a sort of international connection as well. I assumed they were trying to establish whether I was up for it and what the terms might be. They said, "We'd like to do an exhibition of the Yellow House" and I said, "What could that possibly be?" I don't think they were quite sure what it might be either but we workshopped it. We did a lot of workshopping before we came up with the concept of what it finally was.

'I could not have shaped it as an exhibition myself and I don't think they wanted me to. If we were not sure how we were going to work, there was the possibility of making an exhibition of all the works that had been shown at the Yellow House. That wouldn't have given a sense of what the Yellow House really was - but constructing the rooms would give us a sense of what the environment was. I thought we had to reinvent the whole thing and make it as engaging as possible.' [3]

It wasn't exactly a cold call. Greg was documenting art works at the gallery and George knew him from living in Bundeena when Tony was Curator for the Wollongong City Gallery. And Tony knew Peter Wright as a Hill End artist.

They did well to call on Tony. Not every curator was suited to handling their spontaneous, non-bureaucratic, freewheeling, charismatic, post-hippie, *laissez faire* approach to gallery art. You can't just throw together a major show at AGNSW at short notice. These things take time - sometimes years - in planning, negotiating and booking the space. But you can't do it, if you don't try.

Tony was charmed, fascinated and hooked. He just needed to get them to understand one small point: a show like this would not command a big budget because the gallery had no provisions for impromptu shows. The team agreed to call for sponsors and Tony would scrape together whatever funding he could. 'It was at relatively short notice,' he said. 'I just called in a few favours. Edmund Capon (Director 1978-2011) thought it was one of my crazed adventures I think!'

The meeting went well.

They said they'd bring Martin next time.

'He didn't do a lot of talking,' said Tony, 'he sat there with that look on his face'. Martin said very little because he had other priorities. There was a crisis at Luna Park. The park was shut and there was a serious plan to demolish it and hand the place to developers.

The key players name-checked those involved in the previous cartel, Harbourside Amusements. What Martin and others regarded as the 'Abe Saffron team' had certainly not given up. The next 12 months saw plans floated for restaurants, nightclubs, cinemas, cafes, a 200-room hotel, a 1200 space car park and an office block over Coney Island. Martin and Kingo joined architect Sam Marshall and other protesters to figure out a counter plan. Gearing up for more action, Friends of Luna Park, with fresh supporters, organised a public rally to mark the 10th anniversary of the Ghost Train fire. Performers included Gary Shearston, Ignatius Jones, the Castanet Club, Terry Serio and the Hummingbirds.

Martin feared the Yellow House retrospective would distract him from what he saw as more urgent matters. He said, 'I had to put aside the film for a while. I had to put aside Luna Park. I was worried the Yellow House was like a red herring to get me off those things.' Before the year was out, Martin and Premier Nick Greiner were guests on the *Vizard* TV show. Martin and the Premier had a backstage chat where Martin felt a satisfactory arrangement was reached about the Park. The following morning Martin received an official letter from Greiner saying the leaseholders had nine months to fulfill their current obligations and to re-open by 1 June 1990. [4]

Either way, the 20th anniversary of the Yellow House was neither here nor there to Martin but the date did coincide with something that was of major importance to him, the 100th anniversary of Vincent's death - 29 July 1890. Martin turned his attention back to Vincent's letters.

Looking deeper he concluded, 'Studying for the Yellow House show, the centenary of Vincent's death became very strong - I couldn't do anything else! The one thing that gave me the go-ahead with the Yellow House show was a letter I found in which Vincent said, "Jesus Christ is the greatest artist" and I thought that was an amazing statement coming from the greatest painter. That was the main part of the show. I did a few paintings myself but they were by-the-by. I couldn't repeat myself. I wasn't interested in reconstructing anything myself. George was – and he had an absolutely valid reason – inspiration. I was not inspired to recreate.' [5]

George and Greg formed the nucleus of the Yellow House Artists committee. Tony and the artists felt they should reconstruct elements of the Yellow House at its best. Martin disagreed. He felt they should commemorate Vincent's death. Tony said the space could accommodate both. The Yellow House committee could manage the entrance, the walk-in and the central area. And Martin could have the big back room where he could do whatever he liked.

Tony described their discussion, 'Martin did raise the Van Gogh anniversary. He did suggest, "Why don't we organize a Vincent van Gogh exhibition to coincide with it?" I explained that was a little bit far-fetched. That would have taken 4-5 years. You can't just do it instantly. "...but if you want to commemorate it yourself, that's fine...". Martin basically got a free rein in that respect.' [6]

The artists formed sub-groups and stayed in touch through circulars and meetings, which became a semi-regular event. They sometimes met at the gallery, sometimes at Wirian and sometimes at the Hero of Waterloo, a pub in the Rocks managed by Tim Lewis who had played a tiny role in the original Yellow House. 'I certainly wasn't involved like the others. I certainly was not a prime player,' he clarified. Back in Yellow House days Tim was in his 3rd year as an art student at East Sydney Tech. Jonny Lewis had invited him to meet Martin. Martin handed Tim a brush and got him to paint two Magritte figures in the *Magritte Room* after which he never stopped asking Tim to paint.

In 1973, Tim painted *Art Exhibition* alongside Martin in Jo's house in Cranbrook Lane. Tim worked with the team at Luna Park, lived at Wirian in the mid-70s and managed the place when Martin went to London and Paris. Martin and Tim knew each other well and, in 1988, here was Tim serving drinks to the Yellow House committee at the Hero of Waterloo pub, tenanted by his family. [7]

Other meetings were frequently held in Tony's office at AGNSW. 'It was usually three people at any one time,' said Tony: often Greg, not Albie, sometimes Roger, never Brett, not Kingo ('I don't think he was a meetings person.') and always George. 'George was taking the running quite a lot. What Martin didn't want to do - George would do that,' Tony explained. 'Having separate meetings with other people - doing the rooms for example - George would pull that together. It needed to be as collaborative as possible - but the way things go, somebody's got to have that sort of chutzpah.' [8] Martin felt the same way, 'George was the boss of the Yellow House exhibition at the Art Gallery of New South Wales because he was the only one prepared to take it on!' [9]

Key committee members were Peter Kingston, Dick Weight, Arthur Karvan, Albie Thoms, Roger Foley, Bruce Goold, Mick Glasheen and Frank Elgar. Everyone missed the presence of Jonny who was in Paris working with French master printer Pierre Gassman. Bruce held up Jonny's portrait to include him in the group magazine photo. [10]

Decisions, decisions. Should they snap-freeze the best of the Yellow House or keep it open-ended? Martin wanted it open-ended, which was not going to work in the gallery. Security issues would be a nightmare. Tony didn't need to say a word. George disagreed with Martin and everyone on the committee agreed with George. An open house 70s-style 'happening' was a thing of the past. The consensus voted: 'This is OUR show!' [11]

Said Tony, 'We got a kind of game plan, which was essentially to construct it around the rooms but Martin was quite keen to open it up and to have as many people as possible who had shown there or been involved. I said, "I'll leave that to you Martin". We left that end space relatively free so he could literally curate whatever.'

'The idea was to recreate the rooms of the Yellow House. The rooms were quite tightly managed and I was working with the people who initially worked on the rooms. I didn't see the originals so I didn't know how they looked then but Greg had some good photographs of the rooms. I suppose the question was – *do we make it an exact replica of what it was or do we try and fix it up a bit?* That proposition had never really been asked in the past because normally when you're creating something you're selecting, you're not re-making. But with a show like this - actually reconstructing the environment - my instinct is not to do it at all really, but if we're going to do it then maybe we make it as good as we can in the space.

'The original was very atmospheric. We could not have all that atmosphere. For example, we could not have impromptu musical performances within the space. So we would try to make the best of it. We worked through the floor plans and to my amazement (because there was clearly quite a lot of competitiveness) we actually came to an agreed distribution of space where we would build the walls and where the rooms would be constructed within the Project Gallery on the ground floor of the gallery.' [12]

The Statement of Intent was drafted by Albie, listing dates (July-October 1990), aims, room installations, supervising artists, performances, AGNSW role, curator's role, artists' roles and a budget of $225,000. [13] Albie suggested lifting the artists' personal fees from $20,000 to $30,000, given that they were individually responsible for so many things – locating artworks, painting walls, loan documentation, helping to install props, supervising installations, assisting in preparation of the catalogue, assisting in fund raising and assisting in publicity.

Greg had taken all the best photographs of the Yellow House in its prime. These shots were used as primary references for reconstructions. His picture of the Stone Room was the Catalogue cover, with spreads throughout capturing the ambience. [14] Joanna Mendelsson was invited to write the introduction to the Catalogue and Tony wrote the preface (but he omitted to give himself a by-line). [15]

'This is not like curating a normal exhibition,' Tony explained. 'Normally an exhibition would be my conception. I would design the show. I would invite artists to participate and I would polish it as well as I possibly could to give the public the best experience of that work. But in this case I was listening, trying to manage this team. Martin on the other hand wasn't really fussed about the team and I wasn't there to try and manage Martin.' [16]

'For me to put the Yellow House into the Art Gallery of NSW is like putting the Loch Ness Monster in a zoo!' Martin erupted. He wasn't prepared to drop all cooperation but he certainly complained a lot. Martin admitted that at one stage he got 'abusive' with the Gallery. 'How can you put the Yellow House in an art gallery?' Martin mocked, 'The Yellow House was a joke on art galleries!' [17]

Martin's refused to have anything to do with Administration. His terms and conditions included working nights - sometimes he didn't arrive before midnight. Tony accommodated Martin with special security arrangements allowing him to work (and smoke) in the Gallery until the early hours of the morning. Mostly he came on his own but once the word got around that Martin was there, other people started turning up. Some came to keep him company, others brought one of their own pieces to hang. Martin never questioned whether or not it hung in the original Yellow House. Martin never questioned anything.

'He wouldn't say no to anybody,' said Tony. 'Anybody who rocked up with a picture under their arm – Martin took it in. This made the registration process and security (documenting everything that entered the building) very difficult. It's a miracle we didn't have major problems with works being mislaid or works not being documented. It could have been a nightmare because I didn't have a registration-person on all the time. What was Martin doing at 3.00am? I have no idea. Nobody complained to me.

'Martin was interested in opening it up to all the players, which I think was appropriate in the circumstances. From a curatorial or a museum point of view, it was pretty unusual. We did have a consultation with a couple of the others whether or not I should be in there editing. I wouldn't have known where to start! My intuition was, "Either I curate it or Martin does. And I don't think it's going to work if I try to edit what Martin's doing." I can't remember Martin doing much by way of editing, he just sort of fitted it all in. In the end, the rooms worked well and the kind of chaos of Martin's curated room captured some of the spirit of the time. There were a lot of works there at one point, an awful lot of works.' [18]

The centerpiece of Martin's open door policy was the constant presence of Harold the Kangaroo – who never had anything to do with the original Yellow House, he was in Amsterdam at the time. Martin arranged for Harold to set up his easel and paint his psychedelic fairground art tableaux within the show. Harold, in multi-coloured clothes, crazy chapeau and silly little beard, hammed up his role. Whereas the actual Yellow House artists were more retiring by nature, Harold chatted to everyone. Without missing a paint stroke, he told passing young women they were beautiful and danced like an imp as required. Said Martin, 'Harold was a great contributor. He was there every day throughout the whole show with his hat out for money. He was the exhibit I'm sure they hated most, but the people loved him.' [19]

Another performance piece was an upright piano that came from Roger Foley. In the 1930s, one of Roger's aunts had traveled the world as a concert pianist. 'She actually met Adolf Hitler…' said Roger, '…but that's another story. I put the piano that I inherited from her in the middle of the exhibition and Martin wrote a little sign that said, 'Please Play Me'. Every kid that went past had a bit of fun. That added a sense of liveliness and fun.' [20]

The commemorate Vincent, Martin had to conceptualise something new. He needed an assistant: Tim Lewis! Tim - now working in a horrible Surry Hills pub because the lease held by his family at the *Hero of Waterloo* had expired, jumped at the chance. 'I find painting lonely in a way,' said Martin, 'that's why I enjoy working with Tim – we share a bit. Vincent said artists should work together – not necessarily on the same picture – but they can work together on similar things.' [21]

'I wanted to get back to painting,' Tim said, 'then out of the blue Martin rang. He asked me to help him with the Yellow House recreation at the Art Gallery of NSW. Do you want to come and help us?' YEAH!! [22]

Tim moved back to living and working at Wirian. He worked alongside Martin on a collage inspired by Vincent's letters after which they painted a series that included Martin's copies of Vincent's Dr Gachet, The Artist on the Road to Tarascon, Self Portrait and others – all in lurid colours.

There was plenty of media coverage in the lead-up to the exhibition. George often spoke for the group, chatting to Philip Adams on ABC radio like old mates. Others were also interviewed, including a reluctant Martin who talked up the show. Privately he may have complained, but publicly he didn't break ranks. In June, he told the Good Weekend magazine, 'The Yellow House was the best thing I've been involved with'. [23]

The Winter edition of *Art and Australia* magazine featured the splendidly illustrated, 'Yellow House, a Brief History' again by Joanna Mendelsohn. It published four of Greg's photos, Martin's 1969 picture of Vincent's Chair, George's 1970 *Self Portrait* and Brett's rarely seen 1970 *Portrait of Martin Sharp in the lyrebird tradition*. [24] FMG magazine ran a feature in which Albie explained the original ideas that inspired the place, 'Van Gogh had the idea – a community of artists in the south in the sun. Martin Sharp had the place – an old art gallery in Sydney's Kings Cross within two Victorian houses that could be used as studios, residences and exhibition spaces. It was called the Yellow House.' [25]

The *Australian magazine* too ran an article. 'Viva Vincent' by Berwyn Lewis featured seven of Martin's pictures, Vincent's self portrait by Tim, Brett's portrait of Martin and a current photo of George in a yellow jacket reconstructing his Puppet Theatre inside the AGNSW. Some hefty claims were being made. Nikki Barraclough credited Albie's launch of the Ginger Meggs Memorial School of Arts as the start of the 'later revival of Australian film'. [26] Jonny told the Australian magazine that the ideas for Nimbin and the Aquarius Festival came out of the Yellow House. [27] Art investment writers joined in too. *Australian Business* magazine featured the Yellow House artists in their investment section called 'Collectibles'. Maybe they were all right. [28]

The opening – at last! - at the end of July. Emblazoned across the entrance was a Roger Foley light show with the words, "This is NOT the Yellow House" in the style of Magritte. 'It set the right tone. Roger stressed, 'One of my installations was a projector installation on the front of the building. With very powerful projectors I wrote across the top of the entrance to the Art Gallery of NSW... It wasn't the Yellow House! The gallery had white walls and the Yellow House didn't know white walls!' (29) That established, visitors were ready for a highly innovative exhibition.

The opening night was another occasion where 'everyone' was there – artists, art students, poets, musicians, critics, journalists, socialites, art bureaucrats and people who were simply curious – basically what Nic Lyon described as 'a gathering of the clan'. Significantly a lot of visitors brought along their teenagers. After all this time their kids got a handle of what their parents had been telling them about over the years! Tony Bond described the spectacle, 'The opening night – there was a lot of spontaneity about that. An amazing crowd! There was an incredible atmosphere and there were a lot of people who hadn't seen the gallery, dressed up to the nines – performing really!' (30)

After speeches, there was music. Martin wanted his Fijian friend Robert Wolfgramm to sing his song *Emmaus*. Robert lived in Melbourne and no longer performed. Anyway, George, Greg, Roger, Albie – none of them - had heard of him. (31) Gary Shearston sang songs from his latest CD, 'Aussie Blue'. *Crafty Old Captain* was one high point. And Jeannie Lewis sang *Gary's Song* from her 1973 hit album, 'Free Fall Through Featherless Flight'. After this and some speeches, visitors walked through the Entrance Hall where Martin's *Catalog* was displayed in a glass cabinet. Then they swarmed into the rooms.

They saw: the Cloud Room painted after Magritte, with stage for performances, a display from Martin's *Artoons* and some of his *Incredible Shrinking Exhibition*. The Bonsai Room 'presented by Brett Whiteley'. The Stone Room by Peter Kingston with a tribute to George Greenough. The Magritte Room displaying works by Magritte, Martin, Bruce Goold and others. Mary in the Bathroom, a mannequin installation by Tim Burns. Spookyland, an ultra-violet environment with artworks by Peter Wright. The Fogg Capsule, a lightshow environment by Roger Foley (aka Ellis D Fogg). The Black Room featuring white sculptures by Judy Sale and Tim Burns. The Infinity Room, a photographic display by Greg Weight. The Puppet Theatre by George Gittoes. The Whaam Wall and Fur Tunnel by Albie Thoms. Corridor displays were by Antoinette Starkiewicz, Franklin Johnson, 'Hop, Liney, Hobby and Paolozzi'. Martin curated his own space up the back, featuring the Vincent-themed pictures he had worked on with Tim as well as other works. (32)

Films screened were: *The Yellow House Filmmakers' Cinema* by Albie Thoms, David Perry & Aggie Read, Garry Shead, Peter Kingston, Mick Glasheen, Chris McCullough & David Lourie, Bruce Petty & Peter Weir, A&C Cantrill and George Greenough. *Yellow House Cinematheque* mixed classical and avant-garde works with primitive cinema. *Yellow House Associated Films* by Paul Cox, Antoinette Starkiewicz & George Gittoes, Jim Sharman, Albie Thoms, Tim Burns, Albert Falzon & George Greenough. And a preview screening of Martin's film, *Street of Dreams –Brighton Cut*. (33)

Artists officially included in the Catalogue of Works for this incarnation of the Yellow House were: Tim Burns, Magdalene (Marie) Briebauer, Roger Foley (Ellis D Fogg), Juno Gemes, George Gittoes, Joyce Gittoes, Mick Glasheen, Bruce Goold, Franklin Johnson, Peter Kingston, Jon Lewis, Tim Lewis, Vivienne Pengilly, Peter Powditch, Julia Sale, Martin Sharp, Antoinette Starkiewicz, Albie Thoms, Greg Weight, Richard Weight, Brett Whiteley and Peter Wright. [34]

Adrian Rawlins came up from Melbourne for the spectacle. He expounded the significance of the Yellow House in his public address and afterwards to anyone who would listen. Roger filmed Adrian inside the reconstructed Stone Room talking with authority and flair. Here's just a sample, 'Absurd as it seemed at the time, this claim that Martin was genuinely responding to Vincent van Gogh's vision was in fact true. And in the Yellow House we found people prepared to create the most beautiful art for no reward. They did these great rooms and these true surrealist and romantic works in three dimensions, in four dimensions even. And they never had one thought of reward. The psychedelia of the late-60s was a reflection of a social movement which really had begun in 1848-1850 when European nations threw off traditional monarchies and embraced a truly democratic view of human potential. We saw in the poetry of Walt Whitman, various movements like the Chartists and the Suffragettes, where people really thought what we now call "People Power". Martin Sharp's involvement was to a romantic and transcendental love, which he saw manifesting in the work of Vincent van Gogh and in artists like Tiny Tim, the most cosmic artist we'd ever seen. All of that fructified in the Yellow House. Martin's art, Martin's posters - genuine psychedelia which he'd done in England in 1966-67 - still stand as the greatest expression of Psychedelic Art that was ever created.' [35]

The Yellow House exhibition generated quite a bit of momentum. It appealed to a younger audience too. Jason Whalley's high school band performed a cover of *Tales of Brave Ulysses* in 1990 when no one else was playing it. Recalling those days, the singer of Frenzel Rhomb said, 'I had only heard the Yellow House being talked of in reverent, hushed tones and had a vague idea that it was basically some squat in Kings Cross populated by a bunch of old hippies where anyone could walk off the street and paint a wall. It wasn't until seeing the Yellow House retrospective in 1990 that I realised I was right - but also completely wrong. As a 17-year old kid the concepts they were exploring and the psychedelic art blew my mind. The idea of this loose collection of artists doing whatever the hell they wanted in a shared communal space was both inspiring and exciting.' [36]

Aside from magazine articles, television coverage and radio interviews, it spawned two more Yellow House exhibitions - the Josef Lebovic Gallery (1990) and the other at Michael Nagy Gallery Potts Point (1999).

Josef Lebovic had built his gallery business up from scratch. He started with one of the first stands in the Paddington Market Bazaar and quickly graduated to buying Picasso prints in London and reselling at a tidy profit. Twenty years later, he'd bought-and-sold his way up to owning a smart gallery in Paddington that specialised in quality prints. Josef knew all about the 60s-70s art scene in Sydney and London. Some of the artists counted him as a friend. Unlike the AGNSW, Josef's Yellow House exhibition had pieces for sale. He was disappointed that Martin was not more commercially-minded.

'The reason Brett sells and Martin doesn't,' Josef explained, 'is that Brett publishes books of all his posters and prints. Each poster is dated and the editions are numbered, so collectors know exactly what they've got. But nobody knows how many posters Martin has done and nobody knows when he did them.' (Another three decades would pass before Michael Organ of the University of Wollongong would attempt a definitive listing of Martin Sharp posters/prints.) [37]

And so in August-September, concurrent with the AGNSW exhibition, Josef's exhibition included works by George Gittoes, Bruce Goold, Franklin Johnson, Peter Kingston, Garry Shead, Martin Sharp, Antoinette Starkiewicz , Greg Weight, Richard Weight, Brett Whiteley and Peter Wright. The featurepiece for Lebovic's ad was Martin's *Vincent* print of the collage that he gave Jeannie (all those years ago). [38]

Praise did not come from all quarters. Some felt that Martin had moved from appropriation to straight copying. He didn't care. Martin replied that he never created a new image when one was already doing that job. Still, he didn't count his contribution a total success, 'I don't think the paintings succeeded. None of the pictures are really finished. The criticism is exactly what Vincent did, whenever he wanted to make a spiritual point he went outside his own work. He painted copies of Millet's paintings, Delacroix' paintings. I'm not really a painter, I'm an occasional painter. Vincent was a painter, that was it - nothing else – (and a writer). Sometimes I paint but realise that to paint properly it's something like being a musician, you've got to do it all the time. I can bring out an image and sometimes I can paint them well but it's an enormous effort. I try to copy, but Tim can DO it!' [39]

The Yellow House retrospective enhanced the legend of every artist involved. They were all proud of the achievement. Said Greg, 'I think the *Retrospective* was timely - 20 years after the Yellow House itself and 100 years after Vincent's death. Those two anniversaries and the re-creation attracted huge attendances and, in a way, it proved the popularity of the place. It proved the synergy that the artists had, which was quite unique because we had a very constructive relationship. There was camaraderie among the group that encouraged the furthering of ideas. The thing is, the same group doesn't live forever – the Beatles were only five years I think. The individuals can't sustain, can't tolerate each other - or something. But the period of time that the Yellow House existed, those that were there really did cooperate with each other. That I think was the strength of it.' [40]

Tony was pleased too. Another of what Edmund Capon called his 'crazed adventures' had proven right. He said, 'I don't think anybody had any anticipation of it being a success. I was always told "it's a kind of niche really - it was a moment" - but I thought it might actually be quite popular because so many people had talked about the Yellow House during the time I'd been in Australia.' [41] In its long history of exhibitions, the Yellow House retrospective was the best-attended contemporary show held at the Art Gallery of New South Wales to 1990.

9.
COURAGE MY FRIEND

I never imagined that you could paint a picture longer than an hour or two. Martin taught me that art takes as long as it takes.
Joel Tarling [1]

Abalone Diver (The Lost Hokusai) was Martin and Tim's next picture. The possibility of Art Exhibition 2 was on the cards. Martin explained his tight artistic relationship with Tim, 'I'm the producer – if you like – Tim's the performer. I found the image, I've got the canvas, I've got the prints, I've got the studio, I've got the place to allow the picture to grow in – and a wonderful painter who's patient and humble enough to work on another person's image - which is a great thing I have with Tim after Art Exhibition. We'll both sign it.' [1]

Eternity was their next canvas, commissioned by Remo Giuffré. His 'general store' - named after himself - was located on the corner of Oxford and Crown Streets Paddington. It had a big street presence. It stocked a range of 'unique and thoughtful' items from Westclox fob watches and sleep masks to the type of t-shirts students - not skateboarders - might wear. Describing himself as a 'creative strategist' Remo was inspired by Arthur Stace's 'Eternity' motif. And who better to depict that than Martin Sharp? Remo commissioned a traffic-stopping 5-metre Eternity picture for his shop window, inside was a range of Eternity t-shirts, postcards and prints. [2]

Tim and Martin both worked on the *Eternity* canvas, Tim painted the blue background, Martin painted the yellow calligraphy. To make the blue background seamless, Tim overpainted the 'Eternity' motif, later to bring 'Eternity' back to the foreground. He said, 'I did layers of blue washes in that painting. As a result you get this luminosity coming through. It has a depth. In order to do these washes, you can't leave traces of the yellow. Sometimes I painted over the whole lot. One day, Martin came down from upstairs and the "Eternity" had gone. He totally freaked out. He related it to Patrick White's death, (30 September 1990). He was very superstitious about things like that. The next day it was all fine.' [3]

Early in the year Tim's sister, Sally Swinn, introduced Martin to 29-year old Paiwan Phongsitthisak with the possibly of employing her as a housekeeper at Wirian. Usually known as Pai, she was also nicknamed Pepsi. Her best friend was 'Tiny'. Martin said, 'Tiny is doing a Pepsi Cola commercial and her name is Tiny. Of course I notice! Names and coincidences are starting to emerge. I can see a similar pattern with the Luna Park Fire.' [4]

Pai was born in a small village on the border of the Mekong River, Laos. This once-great river was fished-out and Pai was raised poor. She wanted to earn money to raise her 5-year old son whom she had adopted to her brother. She met an American who took her to Bangkok. Pai worked as a dancer and a German guy brought her to Australia. 'I suspect there was a drug connection,' said Martin, 'possibly because he was shot'. In Sydney, Pai worked at the Birds of Paradise Club, Kellett Street, Kings Cross. One night, 42-year old real estate agent, David Smedley took a real shine to her. Smedley was dangerously possessive. He stalked her. Said Martin, 'He was violent towards her and made her do things sexually which she found extremely unpleasant. He actually said, "If she doesn't toe the line she's got to go back to Thailand because I've got the power over her visa".' [5]

To distance herself, Pai rented an apartment near Centennial Park but Smedley moved in, she couldn't get away from him. Late one night, Pai rang Martin in a distressed state. Smedley had been hitting her again. Martin hastened to the rescue. He located her near a phone box, drove her to Wirian and gave her a spare bedroom to sleep in overnight while Smedley jealously awaited her return. [6] Gria Shead became one of Pai's Wirian friends, she elaborated, 'It was a horrific time. She'd been beaten by that cretin, she was terrified. She said, "He's really dangerous, I've got to get away from him." So we told Martin. "Could Pai stay with me?" (I was living at Wirian.) He said she could. That was good, that was hopeful, that she could get away from this man. So she did move in.' [7]

Al Jones had formed a band, Al & the Gators, and he vacated the room under the house. It was convenient that Pai should take over his room. Meanwhile, Wirian was its usual hive of activity. Martin gave Ken Done some Tiny Tim music and phoned Michael Chamberlain for advice about whether or not to sell Wirian. He then began a small picture – about the size of a record cover - that he called a 'study' for his big canvas, *Artist on the Road to Tarascon*. [8] Willy De La Vega kept Martin company late into the night. Dave Rowe worked on the music. A singer called Patricia came and went. Greg and Suzie Weight broke up so Greg moved in and started cataloguing Martin's works. Gria carved linocuts in the Dream Museum. Pai told Gria about the dark side of Smedley. Gria said, 'I helped her get a

Restraining Order. I was only 17! I'd never done anything like that before but she was in danger. And sure enough she really was'. (9)

Tim urged Martin to keep Pai's situation at arm's length. Recalling his days managing the pub in the Rocks, Tim said, 'That guy used to come down to the Hero of Waterloo and say frightening things to me. I had a bargirl working for me and he'd get really threatening because he fancied her. I was scared of him!' (10)

Martin's relationship with Cranbrook School fluctuated with changing headmasters. He was annoyed that they weren't paying their contribution to the jointly-owned fence, yet with some reticence Martin took a talk for the Art Department. He said, 'I've gone back and talked about Tiny Tim once - but I'm not too hot at giving talks otherwise I wouldn't probably wouldn't paint. Some artists are good at talking, I'm not particularly'. (11) Martin always had time for students, as evidenced when Year 12 student, Joel Tarling, spent a week doing Work Experience at Wirian. Joel said, 'There was something really lovely about Paiwan being there. She cooked amazing Asian food, the kind that Martin liked. She kept Martin well fed, the house clean and everything was ticking over.'

What was work experience at Wirian like? Many students did it. Day one - Joel 'just moped around the house and weeded the driveway'. Day two - Martin checked Joel's sketchbook. They selected a picture and Martin set him up to paint it. Later that afternoon Joel thought he'd finished. Martin took a look and told him he'd only just begun. Joel worked that image for the rest of his stay - a little improvement here, a little improvement there. He explained, 'After a couple of hours painting, I thought I'd be done but Martin kept saying I could do more. He got me painting it for the remaining four days. I never imagined that you could paint a picture longer than an hour or two. He taught me that art takes as long as it takes. Dave Rowe was in the same room as me, the Dream Museum room, doing the Tiny Tim *Rock* album. I was working under Arthur Barton's *Loona Park* restoration. I now look back and think, "I am so lucky to be working in the shadow of that!" Martin gave me a book every night. I tried to like the *Coles Funny Picture Book* but it didn't connect with me. The next evening he gave me the *Robert Crumb 1967 Sketchbook*. I started drawing that night in bed and it changed the way that I drew. When my work experience teacher called to check on me, she was over the moon. I'd never seen her giddy like a schoolgirl. She couldn't believe that she was going into that house. I got an Honourable Mention certificate for Work Experience.' (12)

While watching Tim breathe life into the Lost Hokusai canvas, once again Martin contemplated the meaning of the picture, 'The arrangement of those shells represents a third eye - this rock-like creature on the bottom of the sea. I was gradually working it out and then I thought, "That's Hokusai! The figure is the muse. He's living underwater." which signifies one world. The diver has come down from another world, taken this part of himself and is representing it above the water. The abalone is a symbol of female generative organs, also a symbol of unrequited love, because it's a uni-valve shell not a bi-valve shell (bi-valve is requited love and uni-valve is unrequited love). And then I realised this is an oriental equivalent of Botticelli's Birth Of Venus!' (13)

And Tiny? He had been recording an album in Burns, a small township outside Nashville USA. It's where you'd operate if you couldn't afford Music City and where Gordon Stinson ran his NGT record label and recorded Tiny's impressive Leave Me Satisfied album. Tiny had an ill-timed business argument with Stinson. It was over a $1000 cheque that was paid into Tiny's mother's account and bounced, so Tiny refused to promote anything until Stinson made this right. For the first time in a long time, a Tiny Tim single hit the Top 100 charts, entering at No 88 with a bullet. It was Leave Me Satisfied/I Wanna Get Crazy with You. Stinson was a small man with a big belt buckle, just your basic Good Ole Boy. He lived in a trailer on his property and the house was the studio and had gone to a lot of trouble to get this album 'right'. On national TV, he arranged for Country music legend Buck Owens to join Tiny on a performance of Tiger By the Tail, the song Owens made famous. (14)

Without Tiny's cooperation and promotional value, the single was dead in the water. Instead of rewriting the cheque, Stinson pulled the record and no one could buy it. It was just another Might-Have-Been moment for Tiny. 'How often does a Tiny Tim record hit the charts!' said a disappointed Stinson. This left Stinson with a lot of unsold records, a promotional video and a heap of merchandising material. Stinson knew of Martin. He was hoping to sell Martin a 50% share of this failed venture for $100,000. Martin didn't have that much disposal cash but he checked out the offer and half-wished he could proceed.

Martin was a popular subject for magazine writers. There was a constant trickle of offers. He had repeated offers to 'do a book' to which he was completely amenable if it was about Tiny (which no publisher wanted). Martin was also offered a contract for a book about Luna Park. He declined. (15) An autobiography? He declined that too. Tom Thompson and Elizabeth Butel had previously tried to interest Martin in having his OZ drawings published in a book format. Nice meetings, no product.

In 1989 Tom became publisher of literature at Angus & Robertson, which strengthened his negotiating position. Said Tom, 'Elizabeth and I went to Wirian every month for about three years mostly to get a book out of Martin. I then got to be publisher at Angus & Robertson and thought, "I'm equipped financially, I'll start all over again with him". And so we went to Wirian at another level. I made two packages for Martin to try and get him to the party. We offered him a contract with A&R to do the *OZ Book*. He wouldn't do it.' (16)

Martin had converted the Dream Museum room into a second workspace (for Dave, Gria and others). The heart of the collection was moved elsewhere and representatives of the Powerhouse Museum came to Wirian and checked it out. Said Martin, 'The Powerhouse Museum had a lot of ideas. All these little things represent something for everyone who goes into it. The Yellow House was like that, there was a doorway into it for everyone - no matter where they came from, no matter what their age - it had a point of access. The Dream Museum is like that. I think the Dream Museum should go to Luna Park. That's what it was collected for initially.' [17]

Around this time Martin encountered Abe Saffron in person for the first and only time. Martin had softened his position on Saffron's involvement in the Fire. He felt others were implicated too, perhaps even more so. [18] Martin came face-to-face with Saffron in a restaurant called DB's at Double Bay. Martin had an arranged lunch date with Karen Robson ('a brilliant show business lawyer') and Martin Fabinyi. He said, 'Walking towards this place looking for Fabinyi, I notice this person looking at me, smiling. I turned around to save us a spot and he – Abe Saffron – is sitting right in the middle of this restaurant where I was supposed to meet Fabinyi. I was taken aback. I walked in with Karen ("We've got to meet Fabinyi here anyway…"), shook his hand and said, "Hi, how are you?" It was a strange meeting, quite good-natured in its way. What was I to do? Keep walking? Go somewhere else? It could have been set up of course – couldn't it? Or was it just chance? The thing was – it was as if Saffron was expecting me'. [19]

The Luna Park Trust people visited Martin too, checking out the pieces he had purchased or salvaged from the Auction. They planned an exhibition before the year was out, while also reconsidering the status of the Park, which was torn between restoration and development. A third player entered the ring. Representatives of the Eora Aboriginal tribe asked the Government to build a $300 million cultural centre on the Luna Park site. Martin was never going to disagree with them.

Then came the heartbreaking news that Eric Clapton's son, Conor, died after falling 49 storeys from an open window in a New York hotel. The accident happened during a visit from the housekeeper who had opened the window in order to clean it when Conor wasn't in the room. She was unable to stop the boy from playfully darting past her. Martin expressed immense grief about the pain his friend and former flatmate was going through.

Martin had met Marianne Faithfull in the late-60s. She was with Mick Jagger when he and Richard Neville called on Mick's house to raise money for OZ maga-zine. Marianne became friends with Martin's girlfriend Victoria Cobden when she accompanied Mick to Australia to film Ned Kelly in 1970. They remained in loose contact ever since. To celebrate Marianne's Blazing Away tour, Martin held a huge Wirian soirée in her honour. All Martin's friends were invited, the OZ crowd, the Yellow House people, Tiny Tim people - new friends and old. It was a big night at Wirian. Wine, music and cake. After this, Marianne and Martin frequently chatted on the phone. She sent him demos of her newest recordings. He gave her a print of Eternity, which she hung in the bedroom of her Paris apartment.

Martin had always painted portraits. Fictional ones in high school, real ones now. He had painted Chica Lowe, Polly Seidler, his mother, the victims of the Ghost Train fire. He now began a series of pictures of young girls. Amber Mackenzie was an art student. She shared a studio space alongside Luke Sciberras at the National Art School and agreed to sit for Martin. All the preparatory drawings were done upstairs in his verandah studio off his bedroom. The picture didn't come downstairs until Martin captured the essence of what he was after.

Amber described Martin's process, 'He ran off a lot of Polaroids. He just wanted my face. He was quite specific about my hair. There was a point where it could have been a nude. He asked politely, would that be comfortable for me? There was nothing weird about it. He was an utter gentleman, I said no. In that first session, I could feel he was seeking what he was trying to do. He found it in the second session and clicked in. That was quite relaxing for me because I could feel his artistic tension and I sorta felt a bit responsible for it. He started painting Minyo Weight around the same time. Minyo's portrait was more Botticelli and mine was Modigliani.' [20]

Occasional visitor, Ian Reid (owner of the Yellow House premises in the 1970s) summed up his thoughts, 'I think Martin's muse was nubile young women, best stated in that beautiful painting he did of the young woman in the Hokusai pool. *Abalone Diver* - I thought - moved towards his essence.' [21]

While painting Amber and Minyo, Martin continued working quite steadily on *On the Road to Tarascon* (later named *Courage My Friend*). Paiwan cooked beautiful Asian food. Willy de la Vega visited often. Distinguished artist, Judy Cassab painted Martin for the Archibald Prize. And Emelia Gypsy Fire wanted Draff to ghost her kiss-and-tell account about her alleged tryst with Bob Dylan. Richard Neville was simply fascinated.

Good news for Coney Island. In August came a serious proposal for a 3-stage development of Luna Park – stage one, refurbishment as an amusement park, scheduled for completion September 1993 at a cost of $18.4 million. Heritage items like the Face and Coney Island to be fully restored. The Palais de Danse to become a reception venue. The Crystal Palace to house a café, restaurant and a nightclub. A nightclub? Would alcohol be served on the premises? Martin wasn't pleased and immediately got on the phone to Kingo about that!

8 November, a gloomy Friday night.

Paul Healy finishes his work and leaves Wirian.

Gria goes out.

Tim goes out.

He says goodbye to Paiwan, in so doing he is the last Wirian person to see her alive.

The film *Performance* is on TV.

Martin returns home after attending a roast for John Singleton, says, 'Then I come home to a real roast!'

He plays a tape about Weary Dunlop and works on a commission called, *Fragments of a Funfair.*

Willy de la Vega drops in. They talk about Luna Park and Weary Dunlop. 'Willy understands why I love Weary,' said Martin, 'it's a bit naff but it's sincere'.

Around 3.00am the dogs bark.

Maybe Gria or Pai coming home?

Martin and Willy smell something.

They run to the room under the house.

Martin yells. 'Grab the fire extinguisher!'

They run past the ringing phone, 'Hi – this is a call for Tim Lewis from America…'.

'Not now!'

Flames at Pai's window.

Martin bursts in, extinguishes the flames.

Can't breathe. Can't see.

Then he does see.

Two people lying on the floor.

Pai, uttering her last gasp.

The other – a male - stands up.

It's Smedley, almost unrecognisable, clothes and hair burned off, skin translucent.

'Don't worry,' he says, 'Everything'll be all right'.

'You monster!' Martin cries.

He rings for an ambulance.

Four times, he rings for an ambulance…

'…and the next thing we see is him, walking the drive, covered in ash – pale blue, maybe a little jockstrap on – like an Indian monk – bald, completely unrecognisable, except the voice is the same. And calm. He's in a trance. He'd gone down, knocked her out and poured petrol over them both.'

Three fire engines arrive but Martin and Willy have already extinguished the fire.

Two ambulances and Police.

A policeman enters Pai's room and says, 'We've got a Code 4 here'.

Some guy with a video camera from Channel 9 arrives.

Smedley walks to the Wirian gate.

'Where are you going?'

'I'm leaving'.

Willy insists, 'You've got to stay'.

Smedley crosses Victoria Road, leans on a telegraph pole, 'but he had no skin, no clothes, all burned off'.

Smedley died 2.00pm the following afternoon. [22]

Journalist Mark Riley reported, 'A 29-year old Thai woman who was burned to death in an apparent murder-suicide on Saturday dreamed of saving enough money to bring her young son from her small village to live with her, according to her employer. The woman was a housekeeper for the artist Martin Sharp and lived in a downstairs flat at his Bellevue Hill mansion. She and her former defacto husband Mr David Smedley, whom she left two weeks ago, died in a fire at Mr Sharp's house soon after 3.00am on Saturday.' [23]

The following weekend, Father James (Jim) of Christ Church St Lawrence Broadway, conducted a Catholic-Anglican-Buddhist mass at Wirian. Around 50 people attended.

The *Luna Park – Fragments of a Funfair* exhibition was held between December-February in Sydney's Hyde Park Barracks. Most of the North Sydney councillors were present at the opening. Its 148 exhibits centred on photographs by Ted Hopkins and works by Arthur Barton. Greg Weight and Peter Kingston were well represented and Martin exhibited his *Fragments of a Funfair* print. [24]

Some of guests knew Pai and their reflections overshadowed the 'Just For Fun' celebration for which the organisers had hoped. Adding to the gloom, Martin toppled the second 'F' in his *Fragments of a Funfair* print, It now read: *Fragments of an Unfair*.

*

At the close January 1992 Martin took a trip to Bermagui with Richard Neville and Julie Clarke. The Nevilles did a house swap with a couple on a picturesque property called Umbi Gumbi on Lake Cuttagee. While there, Martin unsuccessfully tried to quit smoking.

Tim 'held the fort' at Wirian during Martin's brief absence. Jonny moved in and so did jack-of-all-trades Terry Stanton. Tim was surprised that Martin took a break. 'When I lived with him at Wirian – he might go out once a week, maybe once every two weeks,' said Tim. 'He might go to an opening or something like that. Other than that he'd rarely leave that living area where he had the big table. People would come to him.' [25]

Martin returned in time to attend the opening of Kingo's 'Cartoon Boxes, Paintings, Etchings, Chess Sets and Snakes and Ladders' exhibition at Australian Galleries. Martin and Brett were photographed together for the social pages, perhaps for the last time. Brett told Martin he had a dream in which Satan said to him, 'If you're kind to anyone, I'll kill you'. [26]

Martin and Tiny discussed another tour of Australia. This was to be the only time Martin brought Tiny out without a promoter, footing the bill himself. Martin had money on previous tours and Tiny was $short. This time it was the other way around, Tiny had contracts for two well-paying ads – Pepsi Cola and Budweiser Beer. Martin's finances had always been a bit borderline but previous tour expenses could usually be balanced by the arrival of a *Tales of Brave Ulysses* royalty cheque. This time, a bit more than that was at stake.

Tiny's tour coincided with Martin's exhibition at Australian Galleries. So did Bob Dylan's tour. In March, Dylan was playing Sydney the day after Tiny was due to arrive. Martin bought tickets for himself, Emma and Tiny. The plan was to orchestrate a backstage meeting between Tiny and Dylan after the concert, held at Sydney's State Theatre. Tim's Bob Dylan *Self Portrait* picture was hung in the foyer. It was so precise that the audience might have mistaken it for a blow-up of the actual album cover. Did Dylan see it? Maybe. As for the Tiny Tim-Bob Dylan meeting? That didn't happen. Tiny postponed his arrival date by three days because of commitments for the Budweiser ad.

In Sydney, it was all go. Martin asked Denny to put together a hard rocking band to back Tiny's Rock medley. Martin wanted a Vaudeville-type band as well, but switched to a Country band when Chris Löfvén, bass player and manager of the Prickles, applied to be Tiny's support. Chris and singer Steve Fasan called on Wirian and explained their intent. Dave said, 'A country band - we need one of those!' So they were in.

Dave got the media onside, *The Sydney Morning Herald, Drum Media, On The Street, Steve Vizard Show, The World Tonight* and Ray Martin's *Midday Show* where Tiny appeared with Chad Morgan. 'Everybody wanted him. Tiny Tim has left an amazingly good trail over the past nine years he's been here. There wasn't a bad word about the guy.'

Back at Wirian the core team comprised Dave, Terry, Tim and work experience student Blazey Best. Pitt Street tailor, Tony Bechini made Tiny's suits and Miss Scheherazade kept his heart aflutter.

Said Dave, 'I truly think Martin tried to stay out of it as much as he could, rather than cause confusion. Martin has to get a credit because he brought Tiny out, but as far as everything running smoothly is concerned it has been Terry Stanton, Blazey Best and myself. Tim's always been there to help. He's very talented computer-wise. My observation is that Tiny has to make decisions, which he doesn't want to make, so you have a recipe for disaster when Martin leaves the decision-making to Tiny. Martin himself can find it difficult to make business decisions. He's shy in that sort of way. They both need damn good organisers. The pair of them should be millionaires - they certainly deserve to be. The pair of them are a couple of angels, they really are.' [27]

Tiny was in Sydney when *Sharp On Paper* opened at Australian Galleries. The show was packed to the walls with smokers spilling on the street, where Martin joined them. The 90 pictures on exhibit included the Elvis collage, portraits of Amber and Minyo, *Film Script*, the Luna Park Crucifix, *Fragments of an Unfair* and a range of works dating back to 1965. Also on sale was Tiny's Brighton Marathon triple cassette and the *Highway to Hell/I Love Rock N Roll* cassingle. Tiny struggled through the crowd to reach the microphone where he sang four songs including a poignant song for artists about 'being careful' when painting... *That Mother of Mine*.

After that Martin and Tiny went to Rich Studios where they recorded *Eve of Destruction* and *Rebel Yell*. The band was Denny (bass), John Botica (guitar), Claude Woodward (keyboards) and Col Burgess (drums). Said Denny, 'We didn't do any rehearsals, we just listened to the recordings of Bon Jovi and followed Tiny – Tiny would just say, "Do you know such-and-such gentlemen?" And off he'd go.' [28]

Martin was using his prints/posters as a form of currency. That's how he paid musicians and others. Martin offered to create a poster for Denny's stage band (Burgess Brothers) but somehow – with regret - Denny didn't get around to taking up the offer. Martin even paid his dentist with a print! But Tiny was someone Martin couldn't pay with art. He only wanted cash. Martin didn't have the money and hoped this tour would be 'like two artists working together' which was not in Tiny's thinking. Notwithstanding that over the years Martin had spent a couple of million dollars on Tiny, especially on the film, Tiny's management expected payment in full. For the first time, Martin's entourage saw an uneasy relationship between the two, with Martin asking friends and banks for loans that were hardly forthcoming. Good relations between Tiny and Martin never broke down. But it came close.

Tiny turned 60 on 12 April and to celebrate, Martin organized a big gig and a midnight after-party at the Paddington RSL Club which held 1000. They were just short of filling it. Martin pulled out all stops to make it memorable – Denny's Rock ensemble, the Prickles, an Ellis D Fogg lightshow, film crew and the birthday cake from the well-loved Paddington cake shop, *Sweet Art*. Roger wanted to project onto the stage, so everything had to be white, white sets and white stage clothes. Roger filmed the show independently of Martin. [29]

The Prickles first, then Denny's band. Then Tiny. It was another sensational night. *Highway to Hell* ran for a solid 8 minutes. The dance floor was going nuts! Someone called 'Miss Josephine' climbed onstage, grabbed Tiny and kissed him. Denny recalls that two Hoodoo Gurus – Brad Shepherd and Dave Fawlkner - were impressed. They brought Tiny out a year later. [30]

After the show, Martin and Tiny returned to Martin's Honda Civic to find that someone had broken a window and stolen Tiny's ukulele and Martin's tape recording gear. Hoping to prick the thief's conscience, because the thief may not have known they had taken Tiny Tim's uke, Terry Stanton wrote a press release and the newspapers ran the story. Martin organised the purchase of a new 'Martin' (brand) uke. The stolen uke was later found amongst the rubbish at the back of the club. Tiny and Martin went to the Festival Studios with Denny, Col, John, Claude and Miss Blazey (backup vocals) and recorded *You Give Love a Bad Name* and *Rock N Roll Medley* into the early hours of the morning. Later, more recordings - Tiny and the Prickles recorded seven Country tracks which included *I'll Never Get Married*

Again, The Banjo Pickers' Wife and *Courage My Friend*. Said Chris Löfvén, '*Courage My Friend* was probably best of the lot. Monica from the Prickles and Blazey were doing the harmonies. Steve Coburn helped Martin mix it.' (31)

Martin was in the studio by night and Australian Galleries by day. He was at the gallery when former abalone diver Allan Broadhurst walked in. On seeing the *Lost Hokusai* picture Allan blurted, 'Shit! That's an abalone diver!' Martin overheard, invited him back to Wirian and gave him a print - signed, 'to Allan, the fisherman'. Allan told Martin, 'Women were known to be the best divers in many countries, not just Japan. So that's absolutely true to form. It was early days of harvest because this is not very deep. She's bringing the catch up for the person in the boat. She hasn't got a bag so she's just one-at-a-time. It's a wonderful way of presenting it'. (32) Before leaving, Allan sat through Tiny's extended version of *Eve of Destruction*.

Once again, Dave was supposed to create a commercially viable product but he feared that no one was going to give it airplay. 'Twenty-five minutes of it is too long especially in an industry where we live by the 3-minute song!' (33) Guitarist John Botica was surprised too, 'If *Eve of Destruction* had been edited down it may well have been a hit. There was a really powerful four minutes to be extracted from that track. I'm certain it would have been an absolute worldwide radio sensation! But obviously, that was not the producer's thinking.' (34)

Advisers were usually frank with Martin but when it came to editing Tiny, he seldom backed down. Said Dave, 'I think I'm pretty hard-hitting when I speak to Martin, I hope I am. I won't lie to him. He says, "Tiny's such a handful". Tiny - like any artist - would be guided. It's simply that Martin lets him be a handful. Martin is brilliant, but not in the PR department.' (35)

*

Even as his reputation soared, Brett Whiteley could not control his drug habit. On the night of 15 June, Brett checked into a motel in Thirroul, south of Sydney. Coincidently publisher Tom Thompson and Garry Shead were meeting in Austinmer, a kilometre away, discussing flipping Brett's Lawrence diptych, so that Garry's image would this time grace the cover of DH Lawrence's Kangaroo. Brett had already agreed. Garry was still not entirely happy about 'flipping the diptych'... Brett was found dead in the morning. Cause of death was 'due to self-administered substances'. Cressida gave Martin the bad news.

Art students made pilgrimages to Lavender Bay, sitting and drinking near the waterfront outside the Whiteley house, on the stretch of land later known as 'Wendy's Garden'. Brett was richly mourned, not always sympathetically, with many students suggesting an artist of such calibre had no right to squander himself on smack. Poet Robert Adamson eulogised him in his book Black Water and told the Sydney Review, 'our greatest artist is dead'. Michael Leunig wrote a poem about 'Burke and Wills and Whiteley too...' called Deepest Blue, Martin read it to guests while sketching a picture of the Little Prince against a blinding sky which he titled Thirroul. [36]

Brett was cremated in a private ceremony. Martin placed the bonsai-ed Morton Bay fig (from the Yellow House) on top of the coffin. He said, 'He was too much of a star, with all the pressures of stardom on him, which gets in the way of your work. He was trapped into the art gallery scene. He was the darling of the Art Gallery of NSW and all that sort of stuff. It was no good for him. I miss him in art. He brought many subjects to attention, which had never been brought into art in a contemporary way. Lyrebirds, Bex signs, all sorts of things no one was dealing with at all. I couldn't deal with the heroin side of it. I just didn't like that. He was very generous when he was free of it. He was wonderful.' [37]

Shortly after, Luna Park's $25 million the restoration was given the green light by the North Sydney Council with a view to opening as early as September 1993. The Luna Park Committee agreed in principle that a memorial to the victims of the Ghost Train fire should be built in the new Luna Park. Martin had strong views about the Memorial, above all it should not be seen as tokenistic.

Back home, Tim Lewis and Bernadette Trella got married and Martin was Best Man. The formal ceremony was held in Blackburn Gardens, across New Head Head Road and handy to Wirian where the after-party was held. Lots of friends gathered to celebrate – Greg, Sue, Dick, Willy, Marro, Marilyn, Mike (Bernadette's brother), Terry, Tim's daughter Tilly, Sky and Dave. He was out of sorts because Tiny's new management had turned down the release of the *Eve of Destruction* and Martin turned down the release a *Best Of* compilation.

One evening, Martin, Marilyn, Greg, Willy and Sky sat around the kitchen table while Martin read from a section titled 'Moronic Geniuses' in the *Encyclopaedia of Aberrations*, a book that Draff had brought to his attention. The section on Blind Tom – an idiot savant – fascinated Martin. [38] He suggested someone should write a book about him, an option not taken up – not even by Draff. A year later, author Dierdre O'Connoll called on Wirian and Martin asked her to look up Blind Tom in the British Library, which she did and got hooked on the idea. Quite a few years in the making, it was she who wrote the book, *The Ballad of Blind Tom*. [39]

Haydn Keenan's film *Pandemonium* was televised before the year was out as was Geoffrey Robertson's *Trial of OZ*. Neither impacted on Martin, although the outrageously handsome Hugh Grant playing Richard Neville triggered Martin's sense of the absurd! He just kept painting, which is exactly what he said he would not be doing.

The *On the Road to Tarascon* picture was still the current epicentre of Martin's oevre. He reworked it over the next 15 years and painted it three more times, adding Mount Fuji before settling on the final image, He titled it *Courage My Friend,* named for Tiny, Vincent, Paiwan, Eric, Brett, Jenny Poidevin, troubled friends - but mostly for sometime Wirian resident Patricia, who gave Martin a copy of the Koran and *Imitation of Christ* by Thomas à Kempis before killing herself. [40]

10.
TINY TIPTOES OFF THE STAGE

Tiny didn't like to go to the hospital, see a doctor or anything like that. That was unfortunate.
Hal Stein (Tiny Tim's cousin)

At the start of 1993 Martin was hospitalised and put on a respirator. In that first week he said he didn't care whether he lived or died. He didn't want it known that he was doing a hospital stint but people found out anyway. He had lots of visitors – Jenny Kee, Danton Hughes, Cousin Katie, friends, helpers and pests. The colours of his deliriums fascinated Martin. He wrote about them in his ever-present notebook.

Luna Park Amusements Pty Ltd was formally given the go-ahead to develop and operate the Park. The Trust contributed some of its assets to the site and Whittingslow Amusement Group contributed rides and cash. While Martin was in hospital, the reconstructed face of Luna Park was lifted into position. The administrators were moving ahead promptly, which agitated Martin as - although the Memorial to the victims had been agreed to in principle – conceptually, it was unresolved. 'If you put that face up without a memorial there, you're just inviting trouble,' he said - even though he hardly breathe, let alone protest. [1]

Martin believed the Memorial – not the face - was the place to start restorations, 'I'm not going for the face at the moment. Without the Memorial it's like putting the Old God there again. They've got to have something beautiful because all those carnivals have got a dark side to them.' [2] He liked the proposal that Michael Leunig or Bruce Petty should design the Memorial.

Having lost 10 kilos, Martin was visibly frail. Although technically clear of emphysema, he still had a lung problem. 'Water on the lungs' was what doctors called it. Working at Wirian and 'holding the fort' with Marilyn, Dave Rowe summed up Martin's health, 'He hasn't declined, the major concern is there's been no major improvement. The lung is really crapped out because of 30 years of 100 smokes a day. He's in the process of having tests. They're going down into the stomach with tubes. That'll exhaust him unbelievably. There's been a stack of people going through and that's quite exhausting for him as well. Marilyn was a bit upset yesterday because she could see how tired he was. People were pouring in and he doesn't say no. We're going to tell them that there are no visitors until the tests are over. But he seemed really good, talking positively, talking about carrying on with things. It was good hearing him trying to run the ship from the bed.' [3]

Still, the doctors were reluctant to discharge Martin because they felt he was in no position to take care of himself. They kept him an extra week and told him to quit smoking as a matter of urgency. [4] 'Is Martin still smoking?' is what guests would ask. Sure, he was still smoking. Martin never minded smokers. His Inner Sanctum was always heavy with nicotine but smokers copped dark looks from Martin's protectors when they chuffed in his presence, 'Smoking helps you concentrate. I don't think my health is fantastically good but I don't think I can handle things without smoking cigarettes and drinking coffee.' [5]

To convalesce, Martin stayed with George in Bundeena, near Port Hacking. George had won the 1992 Blake Prize for his painting 'Religious Prayer' and after Martin's stay he would travel to Somalia to document the contribution of the Australian peacekeeping force. Garry and Judit Shead lived in Bundeena too, so Martin felt comfortable there and he surprised everyone by not hurrying home. After Bundeena, Martin went to *Happy Daze* in Blackheath where he stayed with Richard and Julie. He didn't smoke over this six-week period.

When he got back, Martin had Willy de la Vega and Terry Stanton for company. Willy had become increasingly religious, almost a monk. He quit smoking and only read 'scripture'. Martin read Scripture too, he also continued reading all 55 years of his mother's diaries. Like, Martin's birth entry, 21 January 1942: 'Having a baby is simple'. 22 January: 'I feel marvellous'. 8 February: 'Martin is a little devil'. Martin reminisced about the past - his father's return from the War when he was four, the breakdown of his parents' marriage, his Art Father Justin O'Brien, high school paintings which hung in his Inner Sanctum. He read through family papers, letters and documents. He even revisited his great-grandfather William Kopson's Fiji Diary from the 1870s. About Sitiveni Rabuka's 1987 coup he conceded, 'I can see his point of view'. [6]

Dave worked on the tape transfers, Marilyn worked on the film, Terry worked around the house, Willy worked on conspiracy theories and Kingo tried to reach a compromise with Martin in the negotiations concerning the Memorial. Meanwhile, Garry Shead won the 1993 Archibald Prize with his portrait of publisher Tom Thompson. George won the Wynne Prize for his work 'Open Cut'. And Roger Foley-Fogg produced a show on behalf of the artists of Australia, to show support for Paul Keating and the Labor Government in the forthcoming election. Throughout all this, Martin kept a low public profile but he did muster the energy to accompany Lin Utzon to the Sydney Opera House in April when she unveiled a bronze plaque in honour of her father Jorn. Recognition of Utzon's genius was an issue that ranked high on Martin's list of concerns, dating back to Art School days when the Sydney arts community was horrified that the NSW Minister for Public Works, Sir David Hughes, brought about Utzon's resignation. Martin lampooned Hughes in OZ.

Flames started appearing in Martin's pictures. He reworked *Pentecost* with flames. He was preparing it for entry in the 1994 Sulman Prize. Martin's printer, Stephen Lawson said, 'I did two versions of *Pentecost*. The original one didn't have the flames, and then the next version has got flames starting to come through.' [7]

As his health improved, Martin's interest in honouring the victims of the Ghost Train fire intensified. He became argumentative about the stance the Luna Park Reserve Trust was taking on the Memorial. Martin said it had to be on the very spot where the tragedy occurred and he brooked no disagreement. On 18 June he wrote to the Luna Park Reserve Trust withdrawing his support. The management quickly responded, disappointed to lose him. They wrote, 'From the Park's point of view it is a pity that we are not able to make use of your undoubted commitment and obvious talents. Let us hope that we are not for too long the poorer for it'. [8]

In this, Jenny Poidevin, wife and mother of three victims, added her voice to Martin's. To the Trust, she wrote: 'I sincerely acknowledge your need to commemorate on my behalf the memory of my late husband John and our sons Damien and Craig Godson. My feelings until now have been mixed, regarding an actual memoriam. Upon meeting with you some months previous I was forced to accept whether or not this memoriam was really what I wanted for them. I am sure now that this is what I would like for my family. It has been an extremely painful and difficult decision to make. I have no problem with the proposed redevelopment of Luna Park, I only hope and pray it is beyond the corrupting powers that previously pervaded its atmosphere. And what's more, extremely safe, allowing future families to enjoy the new Luna Park to its utmost. If my memoriam is to be considered I would feel it be placed on the original Ghost Train site. For me this would be more meaningful. I would be open-minded in this regard. I know life goes on in this regard and change is inevitable, please accept my best wishes in regard to the reopening of Luna Park, as I have previously presented my ideas for a memoriam please accept this as my wishes. I am more than happy to discuss any future possibilities. Yours sincerely Mrs Jennifer Godson née Poidevin.' Martin added, 'If they try to hedge on this, I'll be out of the place quick-smart!' [9]

Then Martin got sick again and returned to St Vincent's Hospital. Marilyn was placed in charge of Wirian. Helpers came-and-went and Martin was again overrun with visitors to his bedside. Shortly after his release Martin got back to battling his nicotine addiction, strengthening up and creating a poster for Tiny's *Rock* CD. He had to get well and get ready - Tiny was booked for another Australian tour.

A lot had been happening in the world of Tiny Tim. The song that made him famous, *Tiptoe Through the Tulips*, was re-released on a compilation LP called *Dumb Ditties*. For the first time in a long time, fans without an original copy could actually play Tiny's hit song. Next, *God Bless Tiny Tim* was re-released in Japan in CD format. Out of circulation since 1968, the album was released with its original cover and Japanese liner notes inside. Some interesting obscurities also popped up. Dave tracked down four songs by Tiny Tim & the Band recorded amongst Bob Dylan's Basement Tapes. He also tracked Tiny's contribution to the 1969 Beatles for-fans-only *Christmas Record*, another rarity. [10]

Nineteen ninety-three was the year that Cream was inducted into the Rock and Roll Hall of Fame, in Cleveland Ohio. The band performed at their induction ceremony. In his speech Eric said that the rehearsal held the day before was the first time they had played together in 25 years. The performance sparked rumours of a reunion, which did not take place in the 90s due to solo projects and family-first commitments. Importantly, the induction established that they could still sound good as Cream, and that they could co-exist in the same room.

Days before coming to Australia and right out of the blue, Tiny picked up the phone and reconciled with his old friend, Bucks Burnett. Bucks – you may recall – produced Tiny's *Mr Ed* single in 1984. He and Tiny started the *Girl* CD in 1988. Then Bucks and Tiny argued about Miss Stephanie Bohm and parted company because – as Bucks puts it, 'his unrequited love for Miss Stephanie was too great to allow him to work with me'. [11] In August, Tiny and Bucks sorted out their differences. Work on the album resumed.

With the *Girl* CD back on track, as the re-energised president of the Tiny Tim fan club, Bucks started a newsletter called the *Tiny Tim Times*. It offered updates on the latest releases, concerts, appearances and fan club news - a club that was surprisingly successful. It even included a few famous names, like former Sex Pistols' singer John Lydon, and David Cassidy (from the Partridge Family). [12] Martin signed up too. He liked the idea of the newsletter and the club, describing it as, 'small but genuine'. He and Bucks remained in touch.

Yes, Tiny was coming, but negotiations with Australian promoter John Kannis (manager of the Hoodoo Gurus) took a backwards step. Kannis would only pay a business class flight and Tiny insisted on first class. 'So we had to cop the difference,' said Martin. 'Luckily a cheque came through for *Tales of Brave Ulysses* – a cliffhanger. It just zipped in, in time.' [13]

Angry about Martin cutting it fine again with the dollars, Dave was getting emphatic, 'We have run out of money Martin, stop spending!' [14] Health issues. Money problems. Martin hit a new low. 'Maybe I blew it,' he said in despair. Wirian may have to be sold - it was back to this again - talk about Cranbrook School buying it or putting Wirian on the open market. Even the economic rationalists among Martin's friends didn't like those options, believing that selling the house 'would kill him'. [15]

The finances of Tiny's tour were underpinned by Hoodoo Guru concerts in Adelaide, Melbourne, Canberra, Newcastle and Sydney - hard rocking venues - the idea of which Tiny found unsettling. The Hoodoo Gurus were a Pop-Rock band with punk sass. Tiny was used to genteel audiences of a couple of hundred - not a couple of thousand plus mosh pit. *Tiptoe Through the Tulips* was a hit way before this crowd was born, they mightn't know Tiny Tim at all. As their Special Guest, Hoodoo Gurus' singer Dave Fawlkner planned to introduce Tiny, who would then play his 15-30 minute set before the Gurus took the stage. There was talk of the band backing Tiny for a couple of Rock songs. Martin surmised, 'They're fans of Tiny, of a sort. Dave Fawlkner said *Highway to Hell* was their favourite song.' [16]

Then, shortly before slipping into Australia, Tiny broke the habit of a lifetime, quit living in New York City and did an overnight flit to Des Moines. The New York mobsters had always kept an eye on Tiny's career. Starting with Frank Sinatra, then Caesar's Palace, through to present times, the mob was always in the background somewhere. (Maybe that's how it was in the American entertainment industry!) Tiny's career had been taken over by a former police officer Mr Connolly and Tiny was genuinely scared of him. Enter Stephen Plym, an entertainment agent in Des Moines Iowa. Plym had booked Tiny on-and-off since 1971. On his own admission, when he first saw Tiny perform, he described him as a 'national joke' [17] but this time around the wheel, Tiny was doing it tough, Plym saw an opportunity and offered to manage him. All Tiny had to do was slip quietly out of the Olcott Hotel and check into the Savery Hotel Des Moines, which he did. Having ditched his New York agents Tiny now found himself travelling without his customary management support. Dave Rowe stepped up as Australian tour manager.

Tiny arrived on Halloween, Martin noted that this was a quiet Halloween year, 'it didn't have much Satanic stuff on television. This year though it was on a blue moon'. [18] Said Dave, 'When Tiny arrived he was impressed we'd got the *Rock* album out. But when he found tracks that went for 30 minutes he said, "No radio station is going to play this!" Tiny suggested that it'd be best if Martin edited it down - but that was never going to happen.' [19] They were creating Art, not music. By now, everyone was getting the message that Martin never edited Tiny, who he thought perfect in 'his purest form'.

The Regular Records Christmas party was held at Iona, a 19th Century heritage-listed mansion on the Paddington side of Sydney's Kings Cross. Mental As Anything launched their *Chemical Travel* album, Dog Trumpet launched their *Strange Brew* single (with its Martin Sharp cover), Relic of Mary Lou launched their *Monster* EP and Tiny launched his *Rock* album in the new digital CD format. [20] The Iona event went off with a bang. Tiny sang and the bands strutted their stuff, climaxing with Reg Mombassa's backdrop unfastening itself from the back wall, floating down like a parachute and draping over the drummer. Everything else went to plan.

A lot of record industry people attended. Social pages photographer Robert Rosen was there too. And a new face, Satoshi Kinoshita who lived between Sydney and Tokyo. Dave described him as 'a mad Tiny Tim fan, a photographer in Japan. He comes to Sydney often. In his own right, he's a music producer'. [21] Satoshi saw potential for Tiny's music in Japan, as evidenced by the success of the Japanese re-release of the *God Bless* CD. Martin, Dave and Satoshi held several think-tank meetings about releasing the *Chameleon* album in Japan, which in time – (a long time) – paid off.

The *Rock* CD was an extraordinary burst of sound. Some tracks seemed never-ending, which accounts for the album's mixed reception. Some people hated it. Others thought it brilliant. Shortly before his death (4 December 1993), Frank Zappa announced that he wanted to release it on his own label. [22]

All the gigs went well. At the sold-out Newcastle venue Dave Rowe introduced Tiny because Dave Fawlkner didn't arrive on time. Dave Rowe was surprised by the excitement, 'I could barely get the intro out, they were just chanting-chanting-chanting, Tiny Tim! Tiny Tim! Tiny Tim! The Hoodoos gave him his 15-minutes and they loved it. Of course the mixer from the Hoodoo Gurus made that ukulele sound like a bass guitar! Every show Tiny was scared as hell to go out and every show he came off unscathed. He got a massive reception in Melbourne. He was so over-the-moon, he said to me, "I can't believe it! I can't believe it!" That's the way it went all the way through.' [23]

Talk about guts! Tiny was a diabetic 61-year old with a little uke, playing to a thousand or two drunken Aussie head-bangers. He was terrified at Selinas Coogee. Beer cans zinged around the room. 'They threw Tiny in the middle...!' Martin complained, '...with just his ukulele. Tiny described it "like being armed with a slingshot in the desert" - going out to face this antagonistic vibe'. [24] Dave saw it differently. To get the audience onside, Tiny decided to give away his *Highway to Hell* cassingles by throwing them into the crowd. 'This is HIS idea!' Dave stressed, 'Well, I'm sorry - in a pub environment if you want to start a missile throwing session throw a missile! It wasn't just at him. They were throwing things everywhere.'

If Martin was short of money before the start of this tour, his scant resources dried up until the money simply ran out. 'Martin wasn't paying me,' Dave explained, 'I ended up leaving because I had rent to pay. I had to get work - which Martin didn't understand. I said, "I can't believe you took this on when you knew you didn't have the money!" His solution was "just live here" (Wirian) - but I didn't want to.' [25]

Running out of dough didn't keep Martin from recording Tiny. He recorded *That's What I Want for Christmas* and *What a Friend We Have in Jesus* on mini-disk, which set up a Christmas theme and so *Tiny Tim's Christmas Album* started taking shape. Three days after the mini-disk session, Martin took Tiny to Rich Studios and recorded *People Are Strange, Satisfaction, I Am I Said* and *Rainbow on the River.* Peter Jensen – the English master from Scots College who used to drop in back in the early 80s - videoed it all for Martin because Pete was the only person Martin knew who could work the equipment. Later they recorded *Rudolph the Red-Nosed Reindeer.* [26]

Frances Greening (aka Angelica Tremblay) was a gospel singer and missionary who had returned to Sydney after working in Africa. One evening she decided to go to a pub because she'd never been in one before. That's where she met Peter Royles who told her about his wonderful artist friend. (She later changed her name from Frances Angelica Greening to Angelica Frances Tremblay, Tremblay being her married name.)

She said, 'I thought, "I've never been in a pub in my life" and there was one at Coogee. I saw men bashing each other up, so I went across the road to the chemist to buy some Band-Aids and I started fixing everybody up. Then I met Peter Royles. He was next to this really big guy who was a boxer. Peter was smoking a cigarette and putting it out on this guy's arm. He'd just hassle people. He said to me, "I want you to meet someone real famous – Martin Sharp". After a couple of months Peter said, "Martin needs a Gospel singer". I went to the studio. Tom Kazaz was the producer. He said he needed some vocals on the *Christmas Album* so I did it and met Martin. Then I went back to his house. I'd never seen art like it before.' Martin asked her to sing backup vocals on four tracks - *White Christmas, Silent Night, O Come All Ye Faithful* and *Mission Bell.* [27]

Two days before heading home, Tiny played the Rose, Shamrock & Thistle pub (known as the Three Weeds) in Rozelle. Denny's Rock ensemble backed Tiny, Dog Trumpet was his support act and Triple-J radio host Maynard was emcee. After the show, Tiny went back to Martin's kitchen and, just like old times, he pulled out his uke and sang to a few friends until 3.00am. Next day, he flew back to the States, back to Mr Plym.

With Tiny back in America, Martin focused on (1) Tiny's *Christmas Album*, (2) a possible Pop album and (3) lobbying for a Memorial at Luna Park. Guests came-and-went, including some of the old crew like Mad Robyn and Pilot Pete. The more respected guests included, Sandy Gutman (Austen Tayshus) and Lin Utzon. Martin threw a party in Lin's honour. Guests included Opera House advocates and politicians. The building was approaching its 25th anniversary with no clear plan to reconcile with Jorn Utzon beyond symbolic gestures. Martin was pushing for Utzon to receive a belated honour for his masterpiece. He accompanied Lin when she presented her father's scale model of the main hall to the Sydney Opera House Trust, its governing body. [28]

Meanwhile, the Tiny Tim news from America was bleak. After an initial burst of celebrity appearances like baseball matches, the Iowa Variety Club Telethon and TV interviews, Tiny had done the rounds in-and-around Des Moines and Plym could no longer afford his keep him at the Savery Hotel. Too frightened to return to New York, Tiny moved to Hotel Fort, a historic 11-storey building in need of renovation. Tiny's room was not much bigger than his double bed. The view from his window was a brick wall. Through Bucks and his newsletter, quite a few supporters got to hear about Tiny's plight and Martin was one of them. For the lead article of the January 1994 issue of the *Tiny Tim Times*, Martin wrote, 'Somehow we have all got to pull together to give Tiny our best support. I don't know how we can do this; perhaps we should hold a convention or develop some effective network'. (29)

Enter: two new players - English experimental musician and outsider artist, David Tibet, and deejay Ernie Clark who would soon run the official Tiny Tim website. Bucks and Tibet worked together on a new Tiny Tim release, *Songs of An Impotent Troubadour*. Through Bucks, Martin got to know Tibet with whom he discussed releasing recordings internationally or at least in England. While this was going on, Martin – via Dave Rowe – was in the early stages of discussing a Japanese release of *Chameleon* with Satoshi. So even though Tiny had struck a career-low, ideas for five new CDs, plus website, were being mooted by supporters.

In the end it wasn't Bucks, Martin, Ernie, Tibet and certainly not Plym, who rescued Tiny. Tiny found his own way to issue a cry for help. Ever a reader of the *National Enquirer*, Tiny called up the magazine. They sent over a journalist who ran a small feature about Tiny's dire circumstances along with a sad photograph. Plym was furious, 'Who's gonna want to book you now?' he barked. Heiress, Sue Gardner read that article. She had a teenage crush on Tiny in 1968 and reminisced, '*God Bless Tiny Tim* was the first album I ever bought. I remember trying to figure out whether I wanted to marry Paul McCartney, Paul Simon or Tiny. I guess I finally settled on Tiny!' (30)

Miss Sue contacted Tiny in his hotel and along with Dennis her fiancé they looked him up. They caught Tiny in full flight, talking, talking, talking late into the night. On the drive home, Miss Sue speculated that Tiny might sing at their wedding. Dennis reckoned it should be the other way around - Dennis should sing at Tiny and Miss Sue's wedding! That's how quickly Tiny and Miss Sue bonded. (31)

The main obstruction to Tiny re-partnering was the question of divorce, always a complicated subject in terms of Tiny's religious beliefs. There were health issues too. Miss Sue had delicate health and not in a strong position to take on an invalid. She did it anyway, despite a specialist explaining that Tiny was in the early stages of heart failure as a result of untreated diabetes.

In the summer of 1994, Tiny recorded *Prisoner of Love: A Tribute to Russ Conway*. Recorded in Tampa Florida, the band called Clang was under the baton of Paul Reller, Associate Professor of Music at the University of South Florida. Tiny has always aspired to record tribute albums of all the great songsters, he and Mar-tin even had a title, 'Twentieth Century Suite'. Tiny regarded this Russ Columbo tribute as his best album, 'Believe me, this is the greatest recording I have ever done, including *Tiptoe Through the Tulips*'. (32)

Within the month Tiny officially filed for divorce from Miss Jan, leaving him free to marry Miss Sue. It wasn't the only wedding announcement: Denny Burgess and Clare Barrett wed at St Patrick's Church at the Rocks Sydney. Martin and Frances (Angelica) were amongst the guests. Martin gave Denny and Clare an *Eternity* print as a wedding present and Clare was surprised how religious he seemed. She remarked, 'When he came to our wedding it seemed that he had a really strong Catholic faith. I found it so surprising that such an unconventional person had such a strong conventional religious belief.' [33]

Then the Bucks Burnett-Dave Tibet project *Songs of an Impotent Troubadour* sold a surprising 1500 copies on release. Wow. This was an unexpected boost. [34]

Tiny and Miss Sue tied the knot at Immaculate Heart of Saint Mary Church 18 August 1995. After the wedding, Tiny moved partly into Miss Sue's Minneapolis suburban home. Conscious of not taking advantage of his partner's financial situation, Tiny insisted on generating his own income. Within three days he was back on the road, within two months of the marriage, he was diagnosed with congestive heart failure. He refused to be admitted to hospital and never missed a performance. In the first 12 months of marriage Tiny was on the road 300 days. No matter how exhausted he was, off he'd go – to the next gig, anywhere in America and sometimes overseas.

A new album came about after Pink Bob heard one of Tiny's songs on a radio show. He didn't know much about Tiny but loved what he heard. Pink Bob researched 20 years of Tiny's music before approaching him to record on his Ponk label. The *I Love Me* CD was a combination of new recordings and rare singles. Songs include, *Another Brick in the Wall, She Left Me With the Herpes* and a rerelease of *I Saw Mr Presley Tip-toeing Through the Tulips*. [35] This CD was followed by *Tiny Tim Live in Chicago* for Bughouse Records, with a cover featuring the pink and lime green lettering of Elvis's 1956 album and with *Are You Lonesome Tonight* as the opening track. [36]

Then Tiny returned to Miss Sue, who lived in Minneapolis. Tiny was unlike everyone in his suburb except neighbour Johnny Pineapple who had a Hawaiian band and also played uke. One night, Johnny videoed Tiny talking about the history of recorded music for hours. He drank lots of beer and walked Johnny and his young son through past forgotten names of chart-toppers. Martin was sent a copy of this video titled *Musical History Tour*. It inspired Martin to consider cutting the film back to its original 1979 marathon. [37]

Tiny's last appearance in England was 16 December 1995. Organised by David Tibet, he released the concert under the title *Live in London*. [38] Said David, '*Live in London* is a recording of the show he did at Union Chapel which I've released, and that was the only time I saw him live and that was just a phenomenal show. Absolutely amazing.' [39]

In a short space of 18 months – from Mr Plym to Miss Sue – Tiny had a big upward shift in popularity. It wasn't chart-topping stuff, more a lift in credibility.

The ukulele was making a comeback and over the years Tiny had more than paid his dues. For a time he was seen as the godfather of the uke craze. There were uke festivals all over America, England and Australia and Tiny was hailed as one of the original ukulele troubadours, the performer who knew 10,000 songs and was still strumming. Tiny knew exactly who Arthur Godfrey was. Everyone else had to look him up.

In September, Tiny was the headline act at the Ukulele Expo held in Montague Massachusetts. He was accompanied by his friend, Mark Mitchell. Tiny seemed tired but he got through a one-hour video interview without incident. Then he walked to the mike, opened his mouth to sing, collapsed, fell off the stage and banged his head on the floor. Screams, pandemonium. Mark pushed through the crowd and comforted Tiny who was terrified of needles and even more frightened of being cut by the doctors. [40] This was all filmed and screened on the evening News. 'Felled like a tree,' is how Martin described him.

The doctors said Tiny's heart was functioning at around 40%. Because of his poor physical condition, heart surgery out of the question. They gave him a year to live if he took things easy. Tiny remained in hospital for eight weeks, during which time daughter Tulip visited and informed him he had four grandchildren and that she was a convert to the Jehovah's Witness faith. [41] Tiny begged her forgiveness for having been an absent father.

Discharged to Miss Sue's care, after a month of rest at home Tiny got restless, singing around the house, always wearing a tie even when dressed in his pyjamas. 'A man must always wear a tie!' he proclaimed. Miss Sue described those sessions, 'He always felt that he had to give God the first-fruits of his voice. So he never would sing his romantic songs unless he'd sung one hymn. Sometimes he'd say, "I want to sing a song for you but I can't yet because I haven't sung to the Lord" and he'd sing *Praise the Lord the King of Heaven* one way through and then he'd sing the other song.'

He performed a couple of songs at a small gig and that went fine, which gave him more confidence than it should have. Then his mother-in-law asked him to play at the Minneapolis Women's Association, which he accepted. Miss Sue felt that was asking for trouble. They turned up, were ushered to their table and waited. The house band had little intention of giving up the stage until interval when everyone rushed outside for a smoke or a toilet stop until Tiny approached the mike, which caused everyone to rush back. When he started singing *Tiptoe Through the Tulips*, Miss Sue knew something was wrong. She rushed to his side onstage. Big Tiny leaned on little Miss Sue and slowly slid to the ground. He was pronounced dead three hours later. [42]

The *Christmas Album* had been released one week before Tiny died. Martin and Tiny had their last phone chat just two days earlier. On 4 December 1996 the Basilica of Saint Mary Minneapolis held the Christian burial rite.

In Sydney the press got straight onto Martin. The headline read, 'Bound for Heaven, my Amazing Friend – Martin remembers Tiny Tim'. The article ran alongside *The Guardian* obituary. There were a lot of Obituaries in the worldwide press. [43]

About Tiny's passing, Martin stated, 'It's been a huge effort but it's been worth every bit of it'. He added, 'Tiny is more alive than ever!' [44]

11.
THE GOSPEL ACCORDING TO MARTIN

There was a good deal of chaos at Wirian,
A kind of cosmic circus in which Martin acted as ringmaster.
Robert Tilley

Tiny's death did not diminish Martin's enthusiasm one skerrick. In some ways, it fired him up. It certainly reaffirmed the connections amongst the 'Tiny Tim people' worldwide, especially Bucks Burnett in Texas, David Tibet in London, webmaster Ernie Clark in Michigan and Martin & Dave in Sydney.

David Tibet collaborated with Bucks on Tiny's CD Songs From An Impotent Troubadour CD. And he collaborated with Martin on the UK release of Tiny's Christmas Album. Martin and Bucks did a swap: Martin designed the CD cover for Bucks' band The Volares, swapping original artwork for a 1970 Parker Bros Tiny Tim's Game of Beautiful Things. It was a win-win. Martin got a rare piece of Tiny Tim memorabilia and Bucks got a Martin Sharp album cover. Bucks was rapt, 'How the hell could I afford to hire Martin!' [1]

Two days after Tiny's passing Martin told the press that Tiny was 'Heaven-bound' adding, 'I thank God for bringing us together'. [2] Tiny was the crux, the cornerstone, of Martin's religious thought. In the wake of Tiny's passing, Martin reaffirmed his conviction that he was sent by God into the world of show business that 'wouldn't let him in'. [3]

'We knew the man - and now he's going to become a myth. I think it's a heroic life. You couldn't script a more perfect death. He died doing it 100 per cent. Tiny never stopped being famous. There are headline obituaries here, in America, in England. He was famous for being a failure! I think he was the King of American

Music but they couldn't admit it. Tiny is such a modern artist that I don't think a lot of people can understand him. He was too strange for them. Once they realised he was for real, they couldn't handle it, they were frightened by him. American show business didn't like what he was on about so they turfed him out. I understood him as an artist. That was my advantage. It doesn't seem as if he's died to me. Not at all. It's like the spirit is still here. He's so present still - in the singing. I'm doing a big tidy-up at the moment, getting all the files in order - Tiny's musical estate for his exiles here'. [4]

Joel Tarling had spent a week doing high school work experience at Wirian back in 1991. After this, he called in and maintained the relationship. Describing Wirian circa 1997, Joel said, 'Wirian was a collage of people all mixed in and I was part of that. Martin wanted a Greg Weight, a Garry Shead, a Willy de la Vega and a Joel-Nobody there as well. Finding that contact was something Martin did really well - drawing odd connections. Then the Bible started to dominate more and more.

'I saw things silently - more critical and in a different way. I felt Willy de la Vega and Wendy were a dangerous mixture for Martin because they were 'oh wow', 'amazing' - in awe of everything. Willy de la Vega would dive straight into the Bible and bring up a conspiracy theory!' [5]

Religion was another of Martin's collages. There was no consistent pattern of opinion amongst his friends.

Richard Neville affirmed the existence of a God on the Great Debate TV show. Richard and Julie were recovering from a car crash in Majorca. She suffered a fractured sternum, which has plagued her ever after. Richard too suffered a fractured sternum and several broken ribs. In his 1996 book *Out Of My Mind* Richard tastes every fruit the New Age had on offer. [6]

Yensoon was Taoist.
Jenny Kee was Buddhist.
Toto was a high-ranking Freemason.
Willy de la Vega attended Canon Jim Glennon's Healing Ministry at St Andrews Cathedral in the city. [7]
Garry Shead had alchemical sympathies. [8]
George Gittoes was a mystic. [9]
Roger Foley concluded, 'all beliefs are true'. [10]
Stephen Darmody moved in and out of religious circles.
Jesus Adam – the name speaks for itself.
Victoria Cobden had Seventh-day Adventist sympathies and loved Lindy Chamberlain's book.
Angelica attended an Anglican church in Auburn and a Baptist church in Sans Souci.
Rev Gary Shearston was an Anglican priest serving in the Diocese of the Riverina.

University (Melbourne) with a doctorate in Sociology.
Father Austin Day of Christ Church of St Lawrence was in regular contact with Martin – visiting him in hospital - as did Father James Murray, the Anglican priest a regular Sydney Morning Herald columnist. Martin read *Jews for Jesus* handouts
and had meetings with Jehovah's Witnesses when they called.

Susan Jensen, Martin's former assistant, came as close as anyone in understanding Martin's faith when she said, 'I think all denominations have something to offer and everyone needs to feel part of a community, so I don't think any denomination is "right" or "wrong". The thing that matters is that people who call themselves Christians truly love Jesus and try to follow his example'. [11]

Former owner of the Yellow House premises, Ian Reid, was unimpressed. He said, 'Martin was very obsessed in certain ways. He was looking at a little bit of the cosmos but the cosmos is very extensive. There was no point in telling Martin anything like that. Martin was well and truly tracked. My move was towards the East.' [12]

While broadly tolerant of unorthodox, idiosyncratic and even eccentric variations of Christianity, Martin did not approve of unchristian and anti-Christian thinking. He openly criticised Neville Wran and Richard Walsh for their atheism.

Somehow their atheism didn't count against other friends like Jeannie and Mic. 'I never challenged him on his Christian beliefs, I just avoided it,' said Mic, who never felt distanced from Martin. [13] Although unashamedly atheist, Martin saw Jeannie as a type of medium, someone who 'brought things through'. [14] This had her completely baffled. Jeannie often dropped in to see Martin but neither party allowed religion to cast a shadow over the friendship. Said Jeannie, 'He went on about his religious stuff and I didn't necessarily disagree or agree'. [15]

Friends have puzzled about Martin's form of Christianity because it didn't fit conventional constructs, yet it was painfully conventional in other ways. For example, he partook of the Eucharist in Anglican and Catholic churches and was a fundamentalist in the sense that he took Bible texts at face value. (He played tapes of Bible readings or had someone read to him while he painted late into the night.) On one hand Martin was a Bible literalist. On the other, he was selective. He certainly didn't accept the section where God asks Abraham to sacrifice his son Isaac (ie. Genesis Ch 22). Martin dismissed that passage, 'God would never do that!' [16]

Martin also enjoyed listening to conventional hymns, some of which even Christians felt were past the use-by date. Tiny's hymns were always top of the list - *Put Your Hand In The Hand, When The Roll Is Called Up Yonder, When The Saints Go Marching In* and *He's Got the Whole World in His Hands*. Tiny's *Christmas Album* offered a different flavour of hymns. Visitors trapped in the Inner Sanctum were treated to *O Come All Ye Faithful, Hark The Herald Angels Sing, O Little Town of Bethlehem, Amazing Grace, Throw Out the Lifeline, What A Friend We Have In Jesus* and *Silent Night.*

Even with Tiny, Martin took the bits he liked and passed on the rest. Tiny did the Rosary, Martin didn't. Tiny prayed earnestly in public, Martin didn't. Tiny prayed novenas, Martin didn't. Recalling Tiny in prayer (see the inside photo of the *Impotent Troubadour* CD), David Tibet said, 'I remember him doing the Rosary, he was invoking every single saint and saying little prayers to them. He also did Samael and Asrael – the angels of death. I said, "Tiny, it's very considerate of you to do the angels of death, but I don't think it's strictly called for by Christian orthodoxy, let's just stick with the main ones according to Christian belief – like Gabriel and Michael".' [17] David described Tiny as 'a weird type of Catholic'. Martin was Protestant in the sense that he did not invoke intermediaries.

Sometimes it became tricky to pick which religious line Martin might follow next. He didn't like people who dressed in black, yet Willy wore nothing but black. He picked and chose Popes he liked/disliked and brought Biblical characters to life in his day-to-day interactions. John Singleton, Martin described as the 'thief on the cross' – meaning that Singo would make a last-minute repentance. [18] The 'synagogue of Satan' in the Book of Revelation chapter 2, was a clear reference to Abe Saffron. And Vincent– of course – might as well have been Saint Vincent. Martin was offended by writers who questioned Vincent's sanity, insisting that he was 'patently sane' and pointing to his *Letters* as proof.

Jesus was Martin's No 1, Tiny made sure of that. Martin said, 'Tiny keeps referring one on. He doesn't let the buck stop with him'. [19] It was unclear what status Martin accorded to Jesus. A great teacher? A god or 'Very God of Very God, begotten not made'? (as stated in the Nicene Creed, which was familiar to him from school). Martin said, 'Truth is a characteristic of great leadership and Jesus always told the truth – that's what he based his teachings on, an expression of truth.' [20]

Maybe spurred on by the newly released Christmas Album, Martin began playing a lot of hymns – Little Richard (I Want Jesus to Walk With Me), Elvis (His Hand in Mine) as well as Tiny. Martin also enjoyed lesser-known gospel recordings. Robert Wolfgramm's song 'Emmaus' about two friends talking while walking down a road - then 'another joined in, they could not recognise…' reminded Martin of his late night musings with select friends, trying to get to grips with some religious obscurity. He was referencing the Gospel of Matthew 18:20, 'Where two or three are gathered together in my name, there I am with them'. [21]

When Robert sent Martin a transcript of his sermon 'The King's King of Kings' Martin was deeply impressed. Connecting Elvis - 'the King' - with Jesus, the 'King of Kings' was Martin's thinking exactly. Wolfgramm pointed out, 'Elvis won only three Grammys in his lifetime and they were all for his gospel albums – albums that his record company did not want recorded.' He pointed out that Elvis' favourite Scripture was the passage about love taken from 1 Corinthians 13. Wolfgramm said, 'This is what the King's King of Kings is all about – love. Thank you

Elvis for being a living testimony to our only hope'. Sixteen years later, Martin placed the transcript of Wolfgramm's sermon in the display cabinet of his last exhibition, 'Graceland'. [22]

Rev Gary Shearston's spiritual songs affected Martin too. Songs like, 'The Holy Spirit of Redemptive Love' from Gary's Aussie Blue CD (1989). Gary's decision to enter the Anglican priesthood was not welcomed amongst all his peers. 'Some friends of mine threw their hands up in horror when they learned I was going into the church. But I think you've put the thing in perspective. It's an instinctive feeling for a compassionate outreach to the underprivileged, the underdog, the people who are castigated in our society because they want to live a simple life, those who are suffering in any way, because our whole human condition is under a fair weight of suffering, especially in the present times. Given the climate of the times I have been a great admirer of the Catholic theologian Hans Kung'. [23]

Gary referenced Kung in a song, ('But as Mr Kung said, no peace will be had, til there's peace between all world religions…'). Martin liked that. He also pondered Gary's Aboriginal spiritual song, 'Baiame', about the Great Builder of All Things, the Great Spirit. [24]

Then Martin got a new gospel CD called *Straight Over the Moon* by Frances Greening (Angelica). Frances/Angelica was a back-up singer on Tiny's *Christmas album*, which is how she and Martin connected. 'Firstly, I want to thank Jesus for changing my life…' she wrote in her cover lines, 'Martin Sharp, this is your miracle'. Martin sometimes played her CD to guests on full volume when the Inner Sanctum was a waiting-for-Martin room. It was the last thing they expected to hear. [25]

Then – with plenty of encouragement from Willy – Martin started spotting pagan jewellery and imagery: pentacles, torcs, skulls, anything horned, the two-fingered 'Rock On' sign at concerts and No 13. These were deemed 'Satanic' even though Martin kept a large statue of a red Mephistopheles around the house (and you can't get much more Satanic than that!). He explained, 'One of the heaviest pieces in the Dream Museum is Mephistopheles. It doesn't matter how the Devil is portrayed, it's still a manifestation isn't it? Whether it's conscious or unconscious, it's still a manifestation.' [26] 'The Devil has a place. He's one of the characters. You don't avoid him.' [27]

Into this patchwork of religious thought came Robert Tilley who had studied these things. His qualifications were a BA, MA and a BD in philosophy and theology, all from the University of Sydney. At the time of meeting Martin, Robert was writing his PhD thesis. He was also writing an account of the Ghost Train fire titled 'Funhouse', subtitled 'Luna Park and the Ghost Train Fire and Martin Sharp'. [28] Robert explained, 'I used to meet with Martin before I moved into Wirian. I made a number of tapes with him where I got him to talk about the religious aspect of Luna Park. I used the tapes in the latter part of Funhouse when I discuss Martin's reading of the events that night'. [29]

Describing his own religious background, Robert said, 'I wasn't raised a Protestant/Calvinist in fact my parents were not particularly religious. However, for whatever reason, from a very young age I became a Calvinist on my own bat, but in my teens and early-20s I was more the hippy. I became a Catholic because I realised that Jesus Christ founded a visible Church with St Peter at its head and the only Church to answer this description is the Catholic Church'. [30] Robert moved into Paiwan's former quarters underneath Wirian. Being a lecturer in Biblical Studies at the Catholic Institute of Sydney, University of Notre Dame (Sydney) and a lecturer in theology and the arts for Catholic Adult Education, Robert added a scholarly voice to the discussions.

Martin had no systematic theology, which intrigued Robert, who came to the following conclusions, all of which he discussed with Martin, 'Martin very much saw himself in the role of the shaman. For a number of reasons, which I actually confronted Martin about and which he did not take issue with, Martin saw himself as a kind of Hermes-like figure (you might say that Hermes is the patron saint of those who think of themselves as "bridges" between worlds). That a good deal of chaos at Wirian was a means of rendering the borders between worlds permeable. A kind of cosmic circus in which Martin acted as the ringmaster.

'Martin found it difficult to submit himself to the teaching authority of the Church (any church for that matter) because he thought he knew better because he had experienced many things of a supernatural nature, especially at Wirian. He used dope as a means of creating this chaos and to aiding his shaman-like activities, as he did lack of sleep, drama, poor diet, incredibly strong coffee, mad people, and so on and so forth. Of course, he felt that all of this revolved around and devolved upon the events of the fire at Luna Park and the synchronicity served to confirm it for him.

'It is exactly this dimension to Martin that others do not get, cannot understand, indeed feel fearful of. And yet I would argue that it is exactly this dimension that tells the most about Martin; about the trajectory of his life; about his art; about his fascination with Tiny Tim; Luna Park; the way he ran Wirian; his manic episodes; his secrecy; his dabbling with people of many different and even strange religious and so-called spiritual backgrounds.' [31]

Willy reinvented himself and become what Martin called an 'Urban Monk'. He walked everywhere, wore black t-shirts, long black socks and black thongs and read nothing but Scripture, which stretched to include the Early Church Fathers, the Nag Hammadi library and forgotten gospels like the Gospel of Thomas and the Bible (naturally). That was what he read for several years. Robert and Willy's table discussions were wide-ranging. They might include subjects like the Council of Nicea, the stigmata or Willy's belief that the Papacy was 'full of Masons'. [32]. All this was quite interesting for Martin but challenging for a young woman caller Harmonie Downes who was flat out simply coming to grips with Tiny Tim!

Harmonie was a hippie child from Mullumbimby NSW. She had grown up in communes in northern NSW and came to Sydney to finish her education. She enrolled in Randwick TAFE and decided to call on Wirian because her mother knew people who knew Martin. With Luna Park memorabilia in the hall, posters, Popeye, Mickey Mouse, Kewpie dolls, Snugglepot & Cuddlepie, the Dream Museum, a room full of Tiny Tim memorabilia - and all the rest - Wirian was unlike any home Harmonie had ever seen. Despite a 35-year age difference, she fell in love with Martin. By May, Martin made it known that she was carrying his child and that they were 'on the edge of getting married'. [33]

This improbable marriage added a dimension that Martin had never encountered before. There was no wife to voice an opinion. He shared his finances with no one. Whether he could afford it or not, Martin hired recording studios, concert halls, framers, printers, film editors and – whether he knew how to use it or not – he kept buying state-of-the-art technology. People who knew how to use that equipment were on his payroll. Having a wife and child would require him to be a different type of 'Martin' and Wirian a different type of house. He'd had no constraints in his previous relationships. The birth of a son, due in October, would require a reordering of Martin's priorities. He worried about it, tried to think of a name and sought advice from friends.

Greg, Tim, Draff, Roger, Brett, all of them – they all had children. Not Martin. Not yet. It was the fulfilment of his mother Jo's hopes. [34] Several were critical of the age difference but Martin was way ahead of them. He visited Harmonie's family, who gave their consent to the union.

In the late 90s, social media was in its infancy. Google, Facebook, Twitter and YouTube had yet to be fully established. Most people had just switched from fax machines to email. Although he was well set up, Martin didn't even know how to use that. He often asked guests to check his emails. A hundred or so might come up and he'd dictate answers to some. Burning CDs had become a simple process that overtook the slower process of copying to cassette. Apple had released a range of film editing software that superseded the old-style cutting methods. Wirian's film editing room was equipped with all latest technologies. Visitors, students, nephews, callers would assist Martin with his computers.

Martin delegated the tape transfers to Dave and Wendy, and the film was sometimes being worked on by Marilyn or sometimes by young students who Martin would oversee though he would seldom get involved. He might ask an assistant to get onto a search engine and look someone up, like – say – Henry Burr, the Canadian singer Tiny had often referenced. Burr was a legend in his time but before search engines, getting information about him required a big effort. Other times Martin would ask someone to get onto Google Images and find – say - Georgio De Chirico's 1914 painting *The Song of Love*. Twenty or more images might come up. After studying the colours, Martin would pick one and ask for a printed copy.

Lots of callers dropped in, like Richard Neville – wearing a tie. Richard had ideas for a new book, which he discussed with Martin before heading home. Richard had co-established the Australian Futures Foundation with English businessman Oliver Freeman. He continued to write for the press, made regular media appearances and was on the speaking circuit. His 1991 novel *Playing Around* had gained scant attention. [35] In that same year Geoffrey Robertson fared better having written the TV drama *The Trials of OZ*. It was nominated for a BAFTA award. [36] Perhaps this inspired Richard to write his account of his London years.

Richard's new book *Hippie Hippie Shake* was the kind of memoir everyone liked, except those who were in it. It was self-critical, modest but indiscreet. On his own admission, Richard didn't allow the truth to overwhelm a good story. [37]

'I didn't like it much' said Martin, after scanning the book. 'I don't think Richard understood the 60s. I'm still living the 60s. He is too in a way, but obviously one trip wasn't enough'. Martin was offended by several sections including the claim that he slept with Richard's girlfriend Louise as payback for Richard sleeping with Martin's girlfriend Anou. 'Not true!' Martin exclaimed, ultimately blaming himself for not objecting sooner. He admitted that Richard gave him ample time to read it and make corrections. 'I could have changed it', he said. 'Richard gave me the opportunity but I was too sick at the time.' [38]

There are at least three different covers to Richard's book but Martin's was the most popular. Martin said, 'They put a lot of pressure to get a cover out of me. I had done a cover for Richard but he didn't like it. Then Marilyn suggested the Jimi Hendrix picture.' And that solved the problem. [39]

Sadly, Richard's older sister Jill died of uterine cancer in June. As *Hippie Hippie Shake* points out, Jill gave the travelling hippies - Martin and Richard – a toehold in London. Her house was where London OZ was conceived. Her contacts became Richard's contacts. Vale Jill Neville. [40]

Another death that rocked Martin was that of Lady Diana Spencer. He had always admired her. On 31 August, Diana was fatally injured in a car crash in the Pont de l'Alma road tunnel in Paris. Her funeral was one of the United Kingdom's most watched programs. Millions more watched it around the world, including Martin.'The St Alma Tunnel where Diana died - or Ayers Rock where Azaria died - these are sacred sites,' Martin concluded,. 'Diana was a great leader in her way, especially when she did that *Panorama* interview'. [41]

Panorama was an hour long 1995 BBC interview in which Princess Diana spoke frankly of Prince Charles' extra-marital affairs, questioned his suitability to be King and said the monarchy was in desperate need of modernisation. She was frank about her depression, bulimia and she admitted her affair with James Hewitt. Martin admired her honesty, 'She called them into line and put her own head on the block. I think it's very interesting to have a family that has been there for so long and who have seen so many politicians come and go. They certainly do very beautiful religious services'. [42]

Death often comes in multiples. Anou Kissler, Martin's first girlfriend and inspiration for *Tales of Brave Ulysses*, died too. She died of an aneurysm and Martin attended her funeral. And then came the terrible news of Martin and Harmonie's stillborn son. For the last month of her pregnancy Harmonie moved from Wirian to her father's home in Burringbar, north of Mullumbimby NSW where she planned a home birth. Leaving the care of Wirian in Cousin Roslyn's capable hands, Martin travelled north to welcome his son into the world.

One morning Harmonie felt stomach had gone cold and she felt no movement. She and Martin rushed to Lismore Base Hospital where no heartbeat could be detected. Born 14 October, their stillborn son was named Marcello (Cello). The distraught couple broke down in tears. Martin was overwhelmed by a deep sense of failure.

Richard and Julie, and George Gittoes rushed to Lismore. Three days later Cello was buried in Mullumbimby Cemetery. George painted the word 'Eternity' in copperplate writing on the tiny blue coffin. Afterwards, Martin stayed in Bundeena with George and his family. George took him boating to childhood haunts around Port Hacking, which affected Martin deeply. He then returned to Wirian where he immediately took sick again and took more time out to recuperate. Martin was open about the circumstances surrounding Cello's death, to friends he said, 'Ask any questions you like'. Not many did. [43]

In September 1998, Martin's *Street of Dreams* film was televised on late night TV, which gave the film a sense of work-in-progress completion. The ABC screened the *Brighton Cut*. In this form the film later found its way onto youtube, even though Martin, Marilyn and others continued working on it. [44]

Miss Sue circulated her *Memories of My Husband* as a private publication. In this she suggests Tiny had a physical ailment from childhood that accounted for some of his behaviour. 'There is nothing wrong with Tiny!' Martin affirmed, as offended as when other writers questioned Vincent's sanity. [45]

In early 1998 Lin Utzon came to Sydney and stayed at Wirian. Martin arranged a kitchen table meeting between Lin and the chairperson of the Sydney Opera House Trust Joe Skrzynski. Skrzynski assured her that the Opera House Trust was sincere in wanting a rapprochement between her father Jorn and Sydney Opera House Trust. On her return to Europe, Lin discussed it with her father who was open to the idea.

Crediting Martin with providing the convivial environment that allowed the discussion to take place, writer Joyce Morgan describes the events that unfolded, 'Skrzynski and Sydney architect Richard Johnson flew to Denmark to meet Utzon. In collaboration with his architect son Jan Utzon and Johnson, Joern Utzon developed a set of design principles to guide the building's future. He also redesigned the Opera House's reception hall, to be renamed the Utzon Room, and designed a large tapestry to hang within it. Lin oversaw the tapestry's installation, and Martin was with her for its unveiling. Indeed he accompanied her to every milestone involving the architect and the Opera House.

'In the wake of the reconciliation, the world appeared to rediscover Jorn Utzon. He was awarded architecture's top honour, the Pritzker Prize, in 2003. Although he never saw his completed masterpiece, when Utzon died in 2008 his building was hailed by British architecture critic Deyan Sudjic as having "transformed the world's view not just of Sydney, but of Australia". Lin regards the meeting around Wirian's kitchen table as pivotal: "That first meeting with me and Joe Skrzynski and Martin ... was when everything started cooking."[46]

Bad news: Macleay Street Developments revealed its plans to pull down the Yellow House building to make way for a modern development. Worse news: in 1999 Yellow House painter, printmaker and sculptor Peter Wright died of cancer in Bathurst Hospital NSW. Peter and his wife Mandy lived in the Hill End artistic community in the Bathurst region. He was a good friend to all Yellow House artists, delivering the eulogy at Brett's funeral in 1992. Peter's work was well represented at the Yellow House Retrospective at the Art Gallery of New South Wales.

In August 1999, Barry Stern Gallery, Glenmore Road Paddington, held the official launch of Martin's 1992 drawing 'Thirroul'. Also on exhibit was a range of Martin's recent – and not so recent – works, including *Art Galaxy*, with Boofhead showing a drawing book to Rodin's Thinker. Hokusai's 'Great Wave' features on the picture with Vincent's Starry Starry Night swirling to the fore, along with the Southern Cross. Jim Anderson created a book of cut and paste collages he had made from the photographs he had taken of the crowd and of Martin's works from that opening. He titled it *Jim Anderson presents From Where to Eternity a Suite of Paper Collage Portraits provoked by Martin Sharp*. After the demise of London OZ in 1973, Jim spent 20 creative years in the alternative town of Bolinas California and was finally back in Sydney to renew old friendships and ease himself back into an Australian world. Not necessarily easy after such a long time away.

Jim mused later, 'That first collection of collages began my small career as a paparazzo taking quick shots of people at the openings, often taking photographs of the artist's work separately, in order for them to be collaged behind the faces and bodies. It made for greater emphasis on the artwork. I gave him a copy of the book and he liked it. I'd see Martin from time-to-time at Richard's place or at parties. Although I loved the idea of someone living in a big mansion rather than just a big house, I found the wonderful magnet that was Wirian also contained elements of the dark and the spooky. I certainly went there enough to get a good feeling for the important thing it meant to Martin.' [47]

After his Art School studies, 23-year old Luke Sciberras moved into Wirian. He started doing handyman jobs until he grew into the role of Martin's assistant. One of his ventures was to assist in the organising of a revisiting of the Yellow House at the Michael Nagy Gallery. The *Yellow House Now* was opened by Richard Neville and featured 37 works. The artists represented were Roger Foley, Juno Gemes,

George Gittoes, Mick Glasheen, Bruce Goold, Peter Kingston, Jon Lewis, Tim Lewis, Garry Shead, Antoinette Starkiewicz, Albie Thoms, Dick Weight, Greg Weight, Peter Wright and Martin, who exhibited *Thirroul* and *Art Galaxy*. With an asking price of $37,500, the most striking work was *Portrait of Van Gogh/Mickey Mouse* by Brett Whiteley and Martin Sharp. [48]

Fourteen years later, Martin's *Art Galaxy* would become the cover for Mic Conway's National Junk Band CD titled, 'Diagonally Parked in a Parallel Universe'. [49] But in 1999 it was his brother Jim and the Backsliders band who asked Martin if they could use his Pentecost picture on their *Poverty Deluxe* CD. There are two versions of Pentecost, the first is a reworking of Martin's Art Book collage. The second is enveloped in flames. Jim chose the latter. [50]

Then the *Disraeli Gears* cover made a comeback. It was the cover of Cream's 1997 *Those Were The Days* 4-CD boxed set, which included both Sharp/Clapton songs, *Tales of Brave Ulysses* and *Anyone for Tennis*.

12.
WORLD'S GREATEST EDITOR

Suddenly I felt a powerful call from the Lord to write 'Eternity'.
I had a piece of chalk in my pocket and I bent down and wrote it.
Arthur Stace

Martin reckoned Arthur Stace was the world's greatest editor because he edited everything down to one word: Eternity.

Arthur Stace was born in an inner city Sydney slum in 1884. Both parents, both brothers and both sisters were drunks. His sisters also ran brothels and, like their brothers, spent a lot of time in jail. With no one sober enough to take care of him, little Arthur slept on canvas bags under the house and stole food or picked out garbage scraps. At the age of 12 he became a State ward and by the age of 14 he worked his first job. He spent his first pay cheque on booze and did his first jail stint at 15.

In his 20s he moved to Surry Hills, a seedy suburb at the time. His job was to carry liquor from the pubs to the brothels, especially his sister's brothel. He was also employed as a 'cockatoo' (lookout man) working for two-up schools and housebreakers. During World War 1 Arthur joined the Australian Imperial Forces, 19th Battalion, 5th brigade. Serving as a stretcher-bearer in France, Arthur came home gassed and partially blinded in one eye. He went straight back to old haunts, took to drinking with a vengeance and become a derelict alcoholic.

In 1930 he appeared in a Court House on Broadway (near Central Station). He was struck by the magistrate's words, 'Don't you know I have the power to put you in Long Bay Jail or the power to set you free?'

'Yes sir,' Arthur acquiesced, the word 'power' sticking in his mind. Power was what he needed to quit drinking.

Outside the Court House a group was heading to St Barnabas' Church. The church offered a free cup of tea and something to eat to all who sat through Archdeacon Hammond's sermon for an hour or so. There were about 300 attendees. Seated next to a well-known criminal, Arthur pointed to six spruce-looking men sitting down the front and asked, 'Who are they?' 'I reckon they'd be Christians', the crim replied. Arthur made an on-the-spot decision, 'Well look at them and look at us, I reckon I'm having a go at what they've got'. He quit drinking, cleaned up and got a job. In time he even got a wife, Pearl. They lived in Bulwarra Road Pyrmont.

Some months later, Arthur attended a sermon by evangelist Reverend John Ridley in the Burton Street Baptist Church at Darlinghurst. The preacher thundered, 'I wish I could shout "Eternity" through the streets of Sydney!' 'Eternity, eternity', Arthur kept repeating the word. He said, 'Suddenly I began crying and I felt a powerful call from the Lord to write "Eternity". I had a piece of chalk in my pocket and I bent down there and wrote it'. His usual scrawl was indecipherable but this one word – and only this word - came out in a beautiful copperplate hand. He said, 'I've tried and tried, but "Eternity" is the only word that comes out in copperplate'.

It is estimated that Arthur chalked 'Eternity' half a million times over the next 35 years. Several mornings a week, always before dawn, he wrote the word on Sydney pavements and entrances to railway stations from the city to Parramatta. Commuters would see the freshly written word but they'd never see the writer. Who could it be? The mystery was solved 24 years later when Arthur knelt to write on the pavement and Rev Lisle Thompson - who preached at the church where Arthur worked as a cleaner - saw him do it. In 1956 Thompson wrote a tract about Arthur's early life and *Sunday Telegraph* journalist, Tom Farrell, tracked Arthur down and interviewed him. Five years later a photographer cornered Arthur and asked to take a few pictures of him. He took four snaps of the little man in a suit and grey felt hat chalking 'Eternity' then ran out of film. He asked Arthur to stay put while he got more. When he returned Arthur was gone. [1]

As a child, Martin spotted Eternity in Cranbrook Road. It grabbed his interest, 'I'd never seen anything written on the pavement before!' [2] By the time Arthur Stace died in 1967 he had inspired a lot more people than he knew. In the early-60s Garry Shead used the Eternity motif in a cartoon published in the Bulletin, someone wrote a song about Mr Eternity for a university revue and poet Douglas Stewart provided a fitting epitaph in his poem 'Arthur Stace' - 'That shy mysterious poet Arthur Stace, whose work was just one single mighty stroke...'. [3]

Martin started appropriating "Eternity" too. The word appeared in major works like *Film Script, Portrait of Tiny Tim* and *Eternity Haymarket*. He didn't know much about the story of the man behind the word, no one did. Everything that was known was gleaned from a few newspaper articles until author Keith Dunstan included a chapter on Stace in his book about unconventional Australians like Bea Miles, King O'Malley, Percy Grainger, Justus Jorgenson and Stace. Said Martin, 'Keith Dunstan's book *Ratbags* (1979) brought me in touch with the story behind it. I knew it was a guy called Arthur Stace. Ross Campbell found a poem about him.

'Arthur Stace is part of folklore. I feel these are very much a part of Sydney – Boofhead, Arthur Stace, Ginger Meggs. Pop Art gave them a chance to gradu ate – go into Art and keep them alive. And it turned out well with Mr Eternity. Someone sang a song about him at a university revue called *First No Pinky*, which must have been 1961 (which I did some work for). It was a great song about Mr Eternity. That would be the first resurfacing. Arthur Stace has certainly been honoured in aluminium in the replica of his calligraphy at Sydney Square by the architect Ridley Smith - who was named after the Reverend Ridley, the preacher who inspired him.' [4]

Remo Giuffré brought Eternity to Sydney's attention in 1990 when he commissioned Martin to paint the storefront picture for his *Remo* shop, from which he made prints and Eternity t-shirts. Mambo t-shirts, Billabong t-shirts, Ken Done t-shirts, now there was Remo, turning Eternity into streetwear. Eternity seemed to inspire lots of creative ideas. Conductor of the Tokyo String Quartet, Richard Gill, sported his Eternity t-shirt for a media photograph. Musician Dennis Aubrey was given one by his sister, which inspired him to write his 'Eternity' song. Author Maggie Hamilton wrote a kids book titled *Mister Eternity*. [5] The film *Eternity* - written and directed by Lawrence Johnston - was screened at Paddington's Academy Twin theatre. [6] Australian composer Jonathon Mills combined with novelist and poet Dorothy Porter to create an opera based on Arthur Stace's life. In 2008, director Julien Temple made that opera into a film titled *The Eternity Man*. [7] Martin launched artist David Lever's exhibition of 27 works, *Eternity: A Tribute to Arthur Stace* held at Macquarie University Library. And the Eternity Gallery was opened in the National Museum of Australia Canberra. The Museum published an A4-size book featuring a rare Arthur Stace original *Eternity* cover image written in white chalk on black cardboard, 450 x 180mm. It appears to be the only remaining original copy of his work. [8]

The Millennium New Year celebrations were a coordinated series of fireworks and events televised from major cities around the world, celebrating the end of the second millennium and the beginning of the third. Kiribati was the first land to see the millennium. Auckland was the first industrial nation to do so. Then Sydney where revellers hit midnight long before the great cities of Asia, Africa, Europe or the Americas. Celebrations were televised to two billion people around the world who watched a firework display climaxed by a spectacular fireball that temporarily hid the Harbour Bridge from view. When the smoke cleared Arthur Stace's distinctive 'Eternity' was seen 18 metres tall, right there on the Bridge. 'Let's Keep It For Eternity' responded one newspaper headline. [9]

Everyone recognised this as a big nod to Martin, though he never claimed credit, which was typical of Martin. When asked whether the idea was his, Martin deferred to the creative director Ignatius Jones and then Remo. [10] Said Roslyn, 'Martin often asked me to come over on New Years Eve. I spent New Years Eve 2000 at Wirian. I took three people over there, walked in and there was an Anglican Archbishop having tea with Martin. *Eternity?* He talked about it in the third person, he never pumped his own work up.' [11]

Just when it seemed 'Eternity' couldn't get any bigger, the eyes of the world – 3.6 billion people - again turned to the harbour city at the Opening Ceremony of Sydney's 2000 Olympic Games in mid-September. There was a prelude, welcome, anthem, a segment called Deep Sea Dreaming, The Awakening, Nature, Tin Symphony (about European settlement) and a celebration of muliculturalism directed by Lex Marinos, with Jenny Kee. As this piece peaked, performers from the other segments came out and joined the dancers, which climaxed with a huge representation of the Sydney Harbour Bridge composed of sparklers set off in the middle of the stadium with 'Eternity' again shown in the centre of the Bridge.

This was followed by Governor-General Sir William Deane's opening address. Deane was a Patron of Reconciliation Australia and also Patron of the Australian Indigenous Doctors Association. Martin admired that speech, 'Sir William Deane put the Aboriginal cause into a spiritual context and that is what I liked. He could bring the spiritual into the political. He gave meaning to that job, which I don't remember in anyone else fulfilling the role. He was unique.' [12]

The Opening Ceremony concluded when former Australian Olympic champion Herb Elliott ran the Olympic Flame into the stadium. Former Australian women Olympic champions and medalists, Betty Cuthbert, Raelene Boyle, Dawn Fraser, Shirley Strickland, Shane Gould and Debbie Flintoff-King brought the Flame through the stadium, handing it to Cathy Freeman who climbed the long set of stairs towards a circular pool of water. She walked into the middle of the water and ignited the cauldron around her feet in a ring of fire. The cauldron then rose out from the water, above her head and was transported up a long waterfall, where it reached its final resting place, high above the stadium.

Martin was transfixed! He bought the photographic book *Catherine: Intimate Portrait of a Champion* and left it on his table where guests could pick it up and read the inspirational quotes 'that give her strength and focus'. [13] Martin admired her, 'Cathy Freeman is very special. I like the way she runs and I like the way she talks.' [14]

Indigenous Australian issues had been on Martin's mind. The 60s folk movement - especially Gary, Jeannie and Black Allen Murawalla - alerted thinking Australians about pro-Indigenous issues. [15] He praised Paul Keating's 'Redfern Speech' adding, 'Some Aboriginal leaders have been great – Eddie Mabo'. Martin loved the secular mysticism of Jimmy Little's *Messenger* CD - covers of alternative and classic Australian Rock songs from the 80s. As a teenager, Martin attended Jimmy Little's performances at the Sydney Stadium. He said, 'Jimmy Little kept himself completely modern. He is the Aussie King really – certainly as big as Slim Dusty, if not bigger - a broader artist and deeper'. (16)

Broad enough to offer compromise as a solution to the indigenous concerns that bothered Martin. Jimmy Little said, 'In blunt terms it means: we've survived without you so we can do it again. We've got the space. We've got the land. This is the hard cold facts - Black Australians are going to say to White Australians, "You've done it overnight while we were sleeping, you've built on the land. We don't want to push you away, we want you here, but compensation comes into play: a compromise".' (17)

Eddie Mabo, Paul Keating, Sir William Deane, Cathy Freeman, Jimmy Little, all these coalesced and changed Martin from a quiet sympathiser to an art activist on indigenous rights. A milestone was reached in the process of reconciliation when 250,000 people turned out for the Walk for Reconciliation across Sydney's Harbour Bridge, making it the largest political demonstration ever to be held in Australian history. Martin took part in it. He explained, 'The first thing to work out is the situation with the original inhabitants. I think a lot of prejudice is formed by guilt not by reality. Guilt and shame is the "best" reason for not talking'. (18) At times he gave away money he didn't have. 'Just paying the rent,' he'd say.

Actor David Gulpilil was a Yolngu man from Arnhem Land. Gulpilil played didge and clap-sticks on Tiny's *Chameleon* album. Martin knew him since then, but they'd met before that. Gulpilil's first acting role was in the Nicolas Roeg survival film *Walkabout* (1971) set in the outback. Roeg had co-directed *Performance* with Donald Cammell the previous year. Gulpilil's next film was Philippe Mora's *Mad Dog Morgan* (1976), which was released the same year as *Storm Boy* in which he played Fingerbone Bill, which earned him an AACTA Award for Best Actor. In the 1980s and 90s he had played major roles in eight feature films including *The Last Wave, Croc Dundee* and *Crocodile Dundee 2*. In 2000-2001 he was work-ing on *The Tracker*. Sometimes with fellow actor Jack Thompson for company, Gulpilil would call on Wirian where he was always welcome to stay when he was in Sydney. When Martin enthused about his glorious acting career, Gulpilil re-plied, 'Yeah, but I haven't got a house'. It needled Martin that this prince of actors didn't have a regular dwelling place in his own country. Martin decided to paint Gulpilil's portrait.

Based on a Polaroid taken by Jonny, Martin sketched Gulpilil's face onto a 180 x 120 cm canvas on which Martin developed the portrait. Like most of Martin's pictures, it went through several transmutations - the eye was moved slightly more left, the green changed to blue, etc, until it settled into a basic image that Martin would overpaint then overpaint some more. 'The Thousand Dollar Bill', was so named because Gulpilil joked about his face appearing on Australia's banknotes - like the indigenous preacher, inventor and writer David Unaipon, the face of the $50 note. Fifty dollars wasn't big enough for Martin who made a $1000 'banknote' as a way of honouring this great actor who didn't even have a house. [19]

Martin also began a work based on a cartoon originally published in an 1888 issue of the *Bulletin* magazine. 'A Curiosity in Her Own Country' started as a straight take of Phil May's cartoon and over the next decade it gradually evolved into a nativity scene that Martin circulated as a Christmas card and eventually a contender for the 2011 Blake Prize.

Martin wasn't the only one who suffered from kidney stones, Dave did too. After a severe bout, Dave absented himself for several months. When he came back several projects needed completing with some urgency because technology had taken another turn. The buying public no longer required anything in physical format to listen to music. Cyber-space meant buying music online and downloading it. Listeners didn't even need to purchase a whole album, individual tracks could be bought for around $1.50 each (at a time when CDs cost around $30). Dave knew all about that, so did Satoshi. To release *Chameleon*, Satoshi began negotiating with Japanese company, Zero Communications. The success of the Japanese release of *God Bless Tiny Tim* proved there was a market for Tiny in Japan and Zero saw that niche. To make *Chameleon* product-ready, the original LP needed remastering. Welcome back Dave.

While Dave was away, he did some useful work for BMG Records who launched their 'Legendary' series with a 3-CD pack of Harry Belafonte's hits. Dave explained, 'We had big change in the industry. A lot of knowledgeable people, the old timers, were being turfed out and replaced with young blond-haired kids. The guy that had been doing the *Legendary* was one of the old knowledge people. I got a call from some young kid saying, did I know Harry Belafonte? Of course, I know Harry Belafonte! "Would you be able to complete this…?"' Of course Dave could, because he also knew the difference between the artist's hits and their B-sides, which was a bit of a fog to the young up-and-comers. Cover lines were another mystery because, in updating, the record companies had dispensed with the original album covers. Here Dave again proved invaluable because (after Glenn A Baker) he had one of the most comprehensive record collections in the country, therefore having the original cover lines at his disposal.

The *Legendary Belafonte* did really well so they asked Dave to take over the whole series. His job was to create 3-CD 'Best-Of' Legendary packages for artists like Hank Snow, Perry Como, Della Reece and Eartha Kitt. His involvement continued over the course of the next five years, a period when Dave also worked for Martin. Martin enjoyed the musical trip down memory lane. Said Dave, 'Martin was very impressed with the *Legendary* series. I made sure I gave him one, whenever a new one was released.' [20]

'Maybe there's stirring of the spirit,' wrote Martin, 'Dave Rowe has got involved again which is great. The film is being developed, taking it right back to the original rushes, eg. the whole of Miss Natasha....then making a long film containing everything that is interesting, which most of it is. I really feel Tiny brought a completely new dimension to The Performer. It's amazing how alive he sounds on his tapes. Art is the only way to go. Wouldn't it be a sad world if someone somewhere didn't acknowledge Tiny Tim'. [21]

Since the early-60s, Martin had been a popular personality for magazine interviews. His accompanying photo-portraits usually depicted him with whatever picture he was working on in the background, but the interview subject matter didn't show much variation. Journalists usually started with OZ, then Swinging London, how he met Eric, the 'written on a serviette' story about *Tales of Brave Ulysses*, followed by Tiny Tim, Luna Park, and usually including something about Martin being 'reclusive'. No one was immune from Martin's ire when misquoted, not even Australia's most respected journalists. Martin often complained that they 'made up' their quotes. That was probably because they usually jotted down on a pad what they thought Martin said instead of using exact quotes. After they'd left he would sit with Dave – or one of the Wirian crew – and analyse what that journo was 'really' up to. Dave described Martin as 'constantly suspicious', which was true, especially around journalists from the Murdoch and Packer press. [22]

With students, he was the exact opposite, as 16-year old Electra Foley – Roger's daughter – found out when doing her high school art assignment. Martin couldn't have been more cooperative. The picture she chose for her art essay was *Ginger in Japan* originally a collage using the images of Japanese 19th Century artist Hiro-shige and Australian cartoonist of the 1930s, Jimmy Bancks the creator of Ginger Meggs. From the collage came the picture, with Tim again painting alongside Martin. The picture was completed in 1996 and part of the Albie Thoms collec-tion. Electra wrote, 'Sharp's works are generally about reconciliation and peace between cultures. *Ginger in Japan* could be seen as reconciliation as Ginger Meggs is regarded as "the average Australian boy" and Hiroshige was a well-known highly respected Japanese Artist'. [23]

Martin wrote back and thanked her, 'Dear Electra, you have written some excellent words'. With the letter, Martin enclosed a photocopy of the Biblical passage, 1 John Chapter 4, 'Beloved, believe not every spirit but try the spirits whether they are of God; because many false prophets are gone out into the world. Hereby know ye the Spirit of God: Every spirit that confesseth that Jesus Christ is come in the flesh is of God: And every spirit that confesseth not that Jesus Christ is come in the flesh is not of God'. That page was addressed 'Dear Fogg and Electra'.

Electra asked lots of questions giving Martin the opportunity to explain his earlier Ginger Meggs poster (for the Nimrod Theatre) in which Ginger is wearing the politically incorrect blackface. He wrote, 'in about 1976 I found some old Ginger Meggs Annuals (of collected strips) and there was a story of Ginger and his school friends at the School Concert. Ginger was going to perform the poem "If" by Rudyard Kipling. One of his rivals, Eddie Coogan, lured him over to a hole in the wall and squirted ink all over his face. Determined to perform, Ginger took advantage of his black face and went on stage to sing "Mammy" and "Sonny Boy", two hit songs of Al Jolson who was the singing star of the 20s. He sang in the costume of a negro-minstrel.

'The Actor's Benevolent Fund asked me for a postcard design. I suggested Ginger Meggs sings "Mammy" at the School Concert. Here he has a dark blue face. There was a Chinese person on the committee of the Actor's B Fund who thought I was poking fun at negroes…of course this wasn't the case but in these days of political correctness and hyper-sensitivity to such matters I solved the problem by painting Ginger's face white like a clown and retitling the picture "Bring On The Clowns". [24]

Greg Weight was another productive Wirian resident during this period. He photographed and catalogued Martin's pictures and produced commercial work - like the *1997 Australian Yoga Calendar*. He also wrote magazine articles and photographed artists George Gittoes, Peter Kingston, Cressida Campbell, Garry Shead and other artists for *Australian Artist* magazine. [25] Greg played a weekly game of tennis with Garry at the tennis centre at Cooper Park Woollahra. Other friends joined them too, like Luke Sciberras who was fresh out of art school.

'I met Luke through Dad,' said Gria Shead, who later married him. 'Dad said, "You should learn tennis" so I went down there, played a game and Luke was there. (He'd been assisting Dad or Greg.) We still joke that it was like an Arranged Marriage. I wasn't with anyone at the time and Dad said, "you should meet this guy". I thought, "Oh god no, I don't want to meet any of your friends thanks – I'm not getting set up". And so Luke and I met. We got on straight away. That was at Cooper Park.' [26]

Gria and Luke had a mutual friend in Martin because they had both lived at Wirian before meeting each other. Gria lived there for most of 1990 and Terry Stanton had invited Luke to visit Wirian after speaking to him on the phone. So Luke had camped at Wirian on-and-off. At the time of meeting Luke was living at Palm Beach.

The relationship started in 1997. Gria said, 'We got together one night after tennis. We visited Martin afterwards and Martin asked us to stay. We both moved in briefly but we didn't moved stuff in, we camped there, in Jo's flat. We got the Royal Suite - but only briefly, possibly because Luke was doing work for Martin at that time - cleaning, housekeeping kind of stuff, also in the studio. Martin would ask Luke to sort out papers or put the prints away in drawers or organise the library.'

Gria and Luke's daughter Stella was born in 2000. Martin was her godfather. At this time they were living with Gria's mother Merle in Vaucluse. Luke was employed by Martin as his artist's assistant, 'which got us through that initial couple of years' said Gria. 'I was painting the whole time but painting seriously by the time Stella was about 18 months old. Luke was working for Martin for about a year, then he got a studio at Kingo's for about a year.' [27]

Adrian Rawlins died in September, aged 62. That poet, raconteur and scamp, died of cancer. Martin did the black-and-white poster for a celebration of Adrian's life held at Paddo Markets Church Hall. Titled: 'Mr Fogg's Music Hall Proudly Present Adrian – the Cabaret', acts included Jeannie Lewis, Jim Anderson, Austen Tayshus, Edwina Blush, Kavisha Mazella, Al Jones and Nic Lyon. The meaning of the 1994 statue of Adrian in Brunswick Street Fitzroy Melbourne changed from a celebration to a memorial.

Shortly after Adrian's passing, Arkie Whiteley – an accomplished actor, living between Sydney and London – went to hospital in Sydney and discovered she had cancer in both lungs and her liver. The doctors did not initially detect the primary cancer in her adrenal gland. Arkie had an operation, underwent chemotherapy treatment and married her intended, Jim Elliott. Two weeks later, a week before Christmas 2001, she died in their Palm Beach house aged just 37. The sweet little Yellow House girl who came up with the name Spookyland for Peter Wright's room was gone. [28]

'Death...' said Martin ruefully, '...I have known death'.

Towards the close of the same year a developer was told to redraft an application to demolish the rear of the Yellow House in Macleay Street. David Katon of architects Burnley Katon Halliday said there was an application to demolish the rear of the 1890s Queen Anne terrace house to make way for a four-storey building. The terrace was subject to heritage protection and a local law preserving cheap accommodation. South Sydney Council gave the architects six weeks to supply additional information about their proposed development. [29]

13.
TELFORD, TRAVEL AND THE TINY TIM STAGE SHOW

Performers want to be loved. I'm sure Tiny was like that.
Mic Conway

The film editing room was brimming with memorabilia and tapes. It was like watching a museum grow. Rare singles, figurines of Tiny, books like Rudy Vallee's biography and pictures - some just photocopies taped to the wall – awaiting their moment. Miss Sue (Sue Khaury) sent Martin a dozen Tiny Tim Head Knockers (wobble-head) figurines. He kept some and gave away the others. [1] She also sent him video news footage of Tiny's onstage heart attack, death and funeral. That too was studied and filed in the film editing room.

Elsewhere in America, some guy had Tiny's handwritten 1963 Diary for sale. Martin and Dave hummed and hawed about that. How would they know it was genuine? The vendor mailed them photocopied samples and Martin set Dave a $3000 limit. Martin's ailing stepmother Dorothy had paid off the mortgage over Wirian, which gave Martin some much needed financial breathing space. [2]

Pilot Pete still called, though not allowed inside. He'd talk at the door, put the bite on Martin and off he'd go $50 richer. Peter Royles moved to Goulburn and quit drinking. Dave Sanderson was on medication. Mad Robyn had killed herself. Roger Foley visited occasionally, as did Sue Weight, Richard Neville, Mika (Lin Utzon's son) and many many many many more.

One evening Margaret Fink called in with a t-shirt on which she wanted Martin to write 'Eternity' in texta. A friend had died and the Eternity t-shirt was her burial gown. Friends brought food, frogs and crucifix orchids. Martin was also given two mightily aggressive chickens. If the French doors were left open, the chickens wandered into the Inner Sanctum and attacked. Guests had no guarantee of protection.

Martin loved the soundtrack of *The Tracker*, played tapes of Bible readings and edged his portrait of David Gulpilil with the colours of the Aboriginal flag. He didn't go out much, though he faithfully attended friends' art show openings. He bought a woodblock at Cressida Campbell's exhibition at the Rex Irwin Gallery and gave it to Dorothy as thanks for her support. Martin occasionally strolled to the Double Bay newsagency. Sometimes he bought a fabulous book from the bookshop. When given a choice of Double Bay eateries, Martin favoured *Arte e Cucino*, the venue for Garry's *Erotic Muse* book launch. Martin sometimes ran into Garry there, dining with poet Rudy Kaufman or owner of Australian Galleries Paddington, Stuart Purves.

In March, Garry and Judit made the *Sydney Morning Herald* front page when their 50-metre Harris Street mural was listed for demolition to make way for a development. Stuart Purves thought the developers were a bunch of philistines. He told the press, 'If you found a very early Picasso on the side of a building, would you pull it down? If it was an exhibition of ours, and if it was on canvas, the panels would be worth $60,000-$100,000 each!' [3]

A young Asian girl – Chaudry - was Wirian's cleaner now. Terry was the live-in handyman. Luke didn't live at Wirian but continued as Martin's assistant, sometimes his personal secretary. Robert Tilly lived outside downstairs and Willy lived inside upstairs. Robert and Willy sometimes bickered over topics like 'healing as a true gift of the Spirit'. In the film editing room, Wendy worked on the tape transfers until Dave came back, which he always did.

In 2002, Michael Wilkinson sold his Melbourne-based publishing house, Information Australia, to UK conglomerate Crown Content, a listed company that owned golf courses, gymnasiums and a publishing wing in England. As a condition of sale, Michael signed a restraint clause, meaning he couldn't compete in the publishing market for two years. The upside was that he was paid a lot of money. The restraint clause clipped his publishing wings, so he mused outside his regular comfort zone. Buying Melbourne's Comedy Theatre was an interesting option.

The Comedy Theatre is in Exhibition Street, in Melbourne's theatre district. Built in 1928, it seats 1000 people and is a perfect setting for nostalgic music. If he bought it, Michael wondered what he might stage there? More than 25 years had passed since he had interviewed Tiny for the *Melbourne Sun*. He was a cadet journalist then. 'Miss Vicky's gone and the tulips have faded,' wrote Michael in a 1975 piece titled, 'Tim's Just a Tiny Bit Broke'. Might a Tiny Tim stage show work? The foyer gloriously decorated with Martin Sharp pictures would be a helluva drawcard! [4]

Information Australia's flagship titles were the *Margaret Gee Media Guide* and *Australia's Who's Who*. It had also published Michael Chamberlain's book, *Beyond Azariah*, [5] which made Martin pleasantly disposed towards Michael when they met. Michael said he was confident the Marinner Group would sell him the theatre. They came to an 'in principle' agreement to move forward with a show. 'I enjoyed talking to Michael very much,' said Martin, 'We'll take this as a serious project'. [6] After he left Martin played Tiny singing 'Michael Row the Boat Ashore'.

Michael booked flights to America for himself and an assistant who interviewed Tiny's friends and family – cousins Bernie and Hal; daughter Tulip; producer of *God Bless Tiny Tim*, Richard Perry; the friend who was with Tiny the night of his first heart attack, Mark Mitchell; Tiny's webmaster, Ernie Clark; David Tibet, who released the *Christmas Album* from London, and Miss Sue who was totally obliging. After meeting her, Michael saw the show as a love story, with Tiny's 'Sue songs' as the finale – *Have You Seen My Little Sue? Sioux City Sue, If You Knew Suzie*.

Michael returned to Melbourne leaving Martin to contemplate stage design and who should play Tiny? Said Martin, 'The essence of theatre is making a few pots of paint, a bit of glitter, some lights, a few people and some music – turn into magic. This show could play Broadway, no worries. Melbourne's Comedy - that's the perfect theatre. If Michael's got it, let's go for that. Finding the right person to play Tiny is the essential thing. If you could get someone to talk like him, that would be something. Pure Tiny dialogue. I would have a person miming the singing with Tiny's voice, and once you've got Tiny onstage, you could have girls singing with him – you could have all sorts of things – but you should start with one person. You could do it in a theatrical way. You could start with the song *Welcome to My Dream*.' [7]

Michael wanted Barry Humphries to take the role. Michael knew Barry's writer, Paul Taylor, who felt the nostalgic songs would appeal to Barry.

'I know Barry - he won't do it,' snapped Martin. Martin wanted Mic Conway. Mic came over for a discussion but had doubts about taking the role, especially singing falsetto.

'The sound person can fix that.'

'I doubt it.'

'You might be able to direct it?'

'I would not be able to direct it', Mic replied (who thought Paul Capsis should play Tiny). 'I'm happy to collaborate with anyone who's writing it or not do anything at all. I'm happy to be whatever. I think you should do the set though.' [8]

Mic came up with the following draft, followed by two Acts:

Tiny Tim Show Fantasy

Outside the theatre, TINY and in smaller lettering 'A Beautiful Dreamer'. The generous foyer is an extravaganza of Martin's Tiny Tim images. Posters like Paddo, Opera House, Kinselas and Rock are on display as well as the portrait held by Macquarie University and Film Script. The music is from the Chameleon, Keeping My Troubles to Myself and Wonderful World of Romance CDs, which are for sale. Having taken all this in, theatre goers might stroll to one of the bars to sip and chat.

The prelim music stops, house lights are dimmed and the curtains part, revealing the inside of a huge circus tent arching over the entire stage. Within that tent is a two-storey stage evoking a Gnostic duality. Tiny's personality is torn between Heaven and Earth (not Hell). The stage props and imagery point to the conflict that is about to take place between Earthly Tiny – his lower self – and Heavenly Tiny – his higher self. Being already in heaven, Heavenly Tiny Tim is innocence and romance and not at all ambitious.. Earthly Tiny is ambitious and scared of sinning. The opening song, Welcome to My Dream, invites the audience into his world.

The stage show idea was an exciting idea for at least six months. The taped interviews with Tiny's cousins and friends gave Martin new depths to explore. 'Martin seems really nice,' Miss Tulip purred, 'I haven't really talked to him and I feel awful because he seems like such a nice person. He sends me books and things about my Dad and I feel bad because I never send anything back to him.' [11] Contact between Tiny Tim people in America and Australia was strong. Martin wanted to fly Tulip to Sydney and put her up at Wirian. Richard Perry offered to arrange an introduction to Tiny's first manager, Mo Ostin, if the Aussies would return to LA where he was recording *Great American Songbook Vol 1* with Rod Stewart.

Then the Marinner Group backed off on the sale of the Comedy Theatre. The deal fell over. Without the theatre, the show was just a might-have-been. Michael cancelled his LA flight. Martin did the overseas travelling instead. He had fallen in love with an Irish Rose that he nicknamed 'Min' (after Ginger Meggs' girlfriend). He wanted to marry her. He started playing Irish music, like John McCormack or the Fureys. Min didn't particularly like those artists, so he switched to Gram Parsons and Emmy Lou Harris. Martin held a big Wirian birthday bash for Min, attended by all Martin's short-notice crowd – Kingo, Roslyn, Russell, Philip, Greg, Denny & Clare, Tim & Bernadette, Alistair, Nathan, Dave, Jon, Victoria, etc. Happy birthday Min.

Then came another gathering, a family reunion from his mother's side - where Martin had only second cousins, no firsts. He explained, 'The Ritchie family branched out into the Hudson family and the Hoskins family, which goes into the Ashton and the Loveridge family. They were early successful railway people – builders, Scottish engineers. They had a family reunion and I went, which was great.'

Andrew Hudson now ran Telford as an Anglican Youthworks Conference Centre. He asked Martin to contribute a piece for their little magazine. Triggered by memories of George sailing him around Port Hacking when he was convalescing with the Gittoes' family in Bundeena, Martin wrote a 1000-word recollection. He titled it 'Memories of Telford'. Visions of his lost innocence came flooding back.

'George took me down there after I'd been sick. He knew the places,' Martin explained. 'I had a great experience with George. We got stuck in the sand bank in the houseboat. It was absolutely calm and we had to wait for the tide to come in. George had a rest and I got up on the reef and fed the fish, throwing bread in the water and seeing them swim up and take it on the sand bank. Suddenly the beauty of the place overwhelmed me. It said, "Martin where have you been? So good to see you again!" Suddenly it wasn't the house that had got me there but the place itself was my sacred site, the whole of the Port Hacking River, every young thing I had learned there.' (12)

Martin's written account starts with his childhood visits and friendship with the caretaker's kids, Ian and Jan Skinner. Martin reminisced about sharing a cigarette with Jan and nearly holding her hand. He wrote that the Skinner family home evoked a sense of love that his family lacked. They lost it when his parents headed for divorce. (13)

Rev Gary Shearston came to Sydney from Tenterfield to attend a different Anglican conference, one in the city. Gary did his Anglican stuff by day and spent his evenings with Martin. The Anglican clergy seemed oblivious that in Gary they had someone who got Aussie Folk music onto the music charts. The folk community were just as indifferent. Being a Christian priest did Gary's singing career no good. One problem was that he talked like an Anglican priest. He said things like, 'We need to remember the fanaticism that has occurred - and continues to occur in our own faith - and give thanks for the fact that in the middle of all this, the great theological minds of all these faith-backgrounds are continuing to dialogue and talk together and try and further understanding and appreciation of each other.' That's how he talked. (14)

Not everyone had forgotten Gary though. One evening, Celtic musician Carrl Myriad called on Wirian to arrange a concert to promote Gary's new CD, *Only Love Survives*. Carrl and Martin last saw each other 40 years ago, when Carrl had performed at the Yellow House in a duo called Carrl & Janie, (ie. Janie Conway, Mic and Jim's sister.) Carrl had the Druidic Awen symbol stuck on the headstock of his guitar, which at first didn't suit Willy. The meeting was strained until Gary arrived. Then it became perfect.

Gary and Carrl played a medley of Irish songs while Martin got out his brushes and daubed an updated version of his high school picture, *The Toff*. They switched to Scottish songs. Martin requested *Flower of Scotland*. They peaked when Carrl started strumming *Dingo* and Gary joined on vocals. 'Dingo, there's a hunter coming, run dingo run…'. Carrl understood *Dingo* as being about bushrangers, Martin read it as being about Azaria. It was joyous evening and a concert was booked with Carrl's band – the Ragged Band – as Gary's support and backing band. 'I'll do the poster!' Martin enthused, which he would have done had he not taken sick. (15)

This burst of interest in all things Irish reminded Martin that he was a double-Ritchie from both the Scottish and Irish sides of his family. The Irish Ritchies fascinated Martin. They hailed from County Tyrone, Northern Ireland. He wanted to see it for himself, meet Min's parents and do his courting in a traditional manner. At the end of July, Martin left for Ireland, England and Europe. It was meant as a two months trip but it took four. Robert, Marilyn, Terry and Luke 'held the fort' and Dave faithfully turned up five days a week to work on a new concept – Tiny's *Pop* album. Recorded in Sydney on Tiny's previous tour, the songs included *Rainbow on the River, My Girl, Satisfaction, House of the Rising Sun* and *I Am I Said*.

In Ireland, it didn't work out between Martin and Min, so Martin looked up old friends instead. He stayed with Marianne Faithfull before heading for Stockholm where his 60s girlfriend, assistant and inspiration, model Eija Vehka-aho put him up. Martin also looked up Lin Utzon and husband Count Hugues de Montalembert on the Spanish isle of Majorca. Then he returned to London where Peter Ledeboer of Big O Posters threw a big 'welcome back' party and discussed further reproductions. Simple ideas, like a pack of 10 Martin Sharp 60s posters-as-postcards to be sold at the Liverpool Biennial Festival of Contemporary Art and also the Tate. For the 2004 Biennial, the curator wanted to exhibit an exhibition of Martin's posters in a big space and Martin was as keen as his health permitted. (Unlike most bienalles, the Liverpool Biennial calls itself 'biennial' not 'bienialle'.)

Martin also stayed with Eric Clapton and wife Melia at Hurtwood Edge. While there, Martin's health started running down. Sometimes he was too sick to leave his bed, Melia brought him hot drinks and bowls of soup. So did Eric when he wasn't rehearsing for a memorial concert to be held at the Royal Albert Hall to celebrate Beatle George Harrison's music. George died in November 2001, his widow Olivia and son Dhani organised the concert with Eric co-directing and performing. Artists included Beatles Paul and Ringo, Monty Python, Tom Petty and the Heartbreakers, Billy Preston and other name acts. [16]

Shortly before coming home Martin attended *Concert for George* (later released to DVD). Paul McCartney recognised him, 'I'd forgotten how tall he was!' Martin chuckled. About Eric he said, 'I thought he was in his prime – magnificent, gone from strength to strength – his playing, singing, his organising of the concert, giving directions. He's made a wonderful marriage lately – children – living a very straight life and running that anti-addiction place. Remarkable, I think.' [17]

As a romantic quest, the trip was hardly a triumph. But it did remind Martin's London friends that his London art years were a 60s phenomenon worth celebrating. Said Dave, 'Martin told us about the trip but it was all about HER. You would have thought nothing else had happened other than that girl. But he stayed with Eric because he got sick and he did say to me that Eric had really looked after him. Marianne as well, I think.' [18]

While Martin was gone the Yellow House premises was converted from low-cost accommodation into up-market residential apartments. Restored by Philip Bartlett and Dr Ron White, two apartments in the rear of the building had an asking price of $825,000 each. Martin's Yellow House mural *Phantoma* was relocated to the foyer where could be seen by people strolling the pavement. At street level, the restaurant was named *Yellow*. None of the original Yellow House artists complained that it was they who had given the premises the provenance on which the developers $traded. [19]

Back home, apart from another bout of kidney stones, it was business as usual for Martin. The band Cold Chisel asked him to do the cover of their live *Ringside* CD. He liked that kind of commission because he liked the guys. [20] Indigenous-Australian, Kay Cook, moved into Wirian. Philippe looked Martin up while in the country. Harmonie visited when she came to Sydney. One of Martin's regular outings was taking his stepmother Dorothy to dinner. Although she didn't understand Martin's artistic vision, sometimes she helped financially, which was much appreciated. Roslyn often joined those luncheons. [21]

Dave divided his working life between Wirian and the Legendary Series. Dave prepared the Lou Reed and Hank Snow compilations for the Australian market. His work impressed BMG headquarters enough to hire him to compile the international release of *Legendary Jim Reeves*. He said, 'BMG-UK contacted me because I was doing those others for Australia. Would I be interested in helping them out with a project about Jim Reeves? They were in the process of releasing all the original albums to CD and needed to know all the information, cover lines, everything. That took me away from Wirian and there were times I'd explain my situation, "I've got to live Martin, I've got to earn my money".' [22]

And Richard Neville often popped in. Richard the Futurist was on the speaker's circuit. 'Steel workers last night,' he bemoaned. 'Advertising people today. It's an invention, my life. I am impudent enough to put the word "futurist" on my business card and I try to help people engage the future. I don't see that as any different to when I was publishing OZ. OZ magazine was essentially about social change and being alert to the signals of that change. I'm still looking for those signals of change.'

Don't see it as any different to publishing OZ???

Go on…!

'I'm just a futurist who wears bright shirts and jumps up and down a bit. When I go to a conference, I might be addressing franchise holders, advertising groups, TAFE students or people on local councils. At the end of the day these people have got to improve their material wellbeing so they can bring up their children and pay their mortgage. So how to you address that reality at the same time as catering to an idealistic impulse? You can't cost-cut your way to a sustainable future. Some of the older corporate heavies that I get to meet ask, "Is it too late for me to get stoned?" They're really expressing a recognition of their own existential vacuum. They've been so busy making the loot that their inner life was wasting away. What's that John Lennon line? "Life is what happens to you while you're busy making other plans".' [23]

Willy openly scoffs Richard's new book, *Footprints for the Future*. 'We don't need any more books! There are too many books already!' Martin was more concerned about Hippie Hippie Shake that he found plain indiscreet. [24] Richard was trying to sell *Hippie Hippie Shake* as a film concept, which is what Willy and Martin were worried about. There really wasn't much to complain about in *Footprints of the Future*. It was a grab-bag of facts, stats and thought-provoking Nevillisms like, 'Future pleasures will colonise the whole body, expand into cyberspace, download from a storehouse of digitized sensations and draw on a range of fleshy electro accessories which stimulate every nerve. The tyranny of the genitals is over!' [25]

Marianne Faithfull contacted Martin to let him know she wanted to catch up when she toured Australia in February 2003. Bob Dylan was in Sydney at the same time. Upon arrival Marianne spotted the billboards announcing Dylan's concert, so she organised to catch up with him through his road manager and was given tickets for herself, her boyfriend Francois Ravand, Martin and Dave for the Sydney Entertainment Centre concert on 17 February.

Said Dave, 'Marianne was to meet up with Dylan before the concert and from memory we needed to be at the back stage of the Entertainment Centre around 7.00pm. Marianne and Francois met up at Wirian prior to the meet-up time and Francois drove us there. Marianne went in on her own to meet up with Dylan. Francois, Martin and I went to grab some dinner before the show. We met up with Marianne just before show time and we had great seats.

'The show was amazing with Dylan in fine form. Whilst we and the packed Entertainment Centre were cheering for the encore we were interrupted by a torch shining down on us and at first I thought it was security and Martin had lit up a smoke or something, as he was prone to do anytime, anywhere. It was in fact Dylan's road manager asking us to come with him to the back stage area where we were all escorted up to the side stage area in time to see Dylan's encores of *Blowin' In The Wind* and *All Along The Watchtower*. Marianne was truly in awe and dutifully stood out in front of us on the stage to watch. As Dylan and band walked off stage after the encore, Marianne raced over to Dylan with us in tow. He gave her a hug, shook my hand while Martin stood back. In reflection, Martin's mood the following couple of days, he either regretted not coming over to speak to Dylan or he truly thought Dylan would recognise him and acknowledge him!' [26]

*

When cousin Sandy Sharp came up with the idea of a group exhibition of Sharps, Martin took to it instantly. Called '4 Sharps On A Flat Wall' the four exhibiting Sharps were cousins Martin, Roslyn, Sandy and Sandy's wife Yoli Salmona Sharp. Musician/cousin Kate Reid (Sandy's sister) composed a piece in the key of E Minor (four sharps). So it was really '5 Sharps'. Martin loved being part of a family, 'It's amazing how all these threads come together because it was like a tidal wave of Sharps!' (27)

Sandy was a program classifier for ABC television and photographer, Roslyn worked as a commercial photographer and radiographer, and Yoli had moved from fashion design to painting. 'All our fathers were doctors,' Sandy told the press. 'Martin's father was a Macquarie Street dermatologist, Sandy and Kate's father was a heart surgeon and Roslyn's was a radiologist.' Sandy felt it was their unconventional mothers who brought creativity into their lives.

One day Sandy said to Yoli, 'If ever I die before having an exhibition of photographs, would you organise an exhibition?' She replied, 'Why don't you do it now and have a group show?'

Roslyn joked, 'We weren't sure if we wanted Martin in the show and he asked to be in'.

Martin said, 'They were a bit tentative about asking me because they thought I might say no. I said yes. It's nice working with family.'

Sandy and Roslyn's photographs were well represented, as were Yoli's paintings. Martin exhibited cells from Sarah Weybourne's Scrapbook that he had collaged in 1974 for the film *Picnic at Hanging Rock*. ('God is Love'). The exhibition was held at The Depot Gallery, Waterloo, Sydney. (28)

There was a new CD project at Wirian too. While flicking through Arthur Rackman's illustrations for *Cinderella* (1919), Martin found a silhouette image of a King that resembled Tiny wearing a crown. Martin had the image blown up poster-size and came up with the thought that 'Elvis was the King, Tiny was the King-for-a-Day'. This became the concept behind the unfinished *King For a Day* CD. (29)

Said Dave, 'In that house there were many compilations and projects that we were going to do that never surfaced. *King for a Day* was one that Martin was really keen on. Martin took 'king' to mean Jesus but the project never saw the light of day.' (30)

Greg Weight won the 2003 Australian Photographic Portrait Prize with 'Railway Blues' a portrait of Jim Conway, in a wheelchair, on the railway track, harmonica in hand, ready-for-music.

At the New Theatre Newtown, towards the close of 2003, Jeannie launched *Southheart*, her new double CD. Inside, she thanked Martin, 'for constant creative pointers and poetry'. (31) Martin was present at the launch but Dave wasn't. Despite having worked with Jeannie on the mastering, Dave copped another kidney stone, which put him out of circulation for quite a while. Wendy left too, so all of a sudden the film editing room had no one working in it. No more *King for a Day*, no more film. Maybe it was time for change, the Liverpool Biennal and Big O Posters, got Martin mulling over his past. Ginger Baker, Jack Bruce and Eric were back on speaking terms and they were speaking about Cream.

'London' simply would not go away. *Art Monthly Australia* featured Philippe Mora's article 'Culture Shock: Australians in London in the Sixties' about his Pheasantry days. Philippe wrote, 'My role in all of this as a young artist was not particularly important, but I was a witness and a participant, and I had a productive time'. He looked back on living with Martin and Eric at the Pheasantry, George Harrison dropping in, exhibitions at Clytie Jessop's gallery in Kings Road Chelsea, meeting Peter Sellars – a real trip down memory lane with some previously unpublished photos. [32]

With OZ magazine celebrating its 40th anniversary, Nick Waterlow, curator Ivan Dougherty Gallery, put together an exhibition called *Larrikins in London* featuring people with an Aussie creative presence in London in the 60s. Waterlow made a generous list of creative Aussies in London, comprising a Who's Who that stretched the definition of 'Australian' to the max. For example, he included John Lennon because John wrote a song called *God Save OZ*. [33] And Yoko too, because she wrote *Do The OZ*. David Hockney because he drew nude full frontal sketches of the naughty OZ trio Richard, Jim and Felix. And Felix, because he worked with the Aussies.

The Larrikins were: Phillip Adams, Jim Anderson, Bruce Beresford, Ace Bourke, Clem Browne, Caroline Coon, Tom Cowan, Cream, John Crittle, Felix Dennis, Kerry Dundas, The Easybeats, Louise Ferrier, Andrew Fisher, Nicholas Garland, Juno Gemes, Germaine Greer, Barbara Hanrahan, Rolf Harris, David Hockney, Laurence Hope, Danne Emerson Hughes, Robert Hughes, Barry Humphries, Clive James, Clytie Jessop, Bronwyn Stevens Jones, Jenny Kee, Vern Lambert, Colin Lanceley, Kay Lanceley, John Lennon, Freya Matthews, Master's Apprentices, Mike Molloy, Philippe Mora, Lewis Morley, John Mortimer, Jill Neville, Richard Neville, Mike Newman, Sidney Nolan, Jane Norris, Jane Oehr, Yoko Ono, Michael Ramsden, John Rendall, Geoffrey Robertson, Marsha Rowe, Normie Rowe, Lilian Roxon, The Seekers, Martin Sharp, Garry Shead, Peter Smalley, Albie Thoms, Noel Tovey, The Twilights, Richard Walsh, Robert Whitaker, Brett and Wendy Whiteley.

Clive James' closing footnote in the accompanying booklet read, 'Dear Nick Waterlow – I am definitely not interested in being included in the Larrikin exhibition, which I think is a thoroughly bad idea.' [34]

14.
CHANGING DIMENSIONS

For some time I had been thinking about a reunion of Cream and given the fact that we were all still capable of playing together, I thought it would be fitting to pay tribute to ourselves while we still could.
Eric Clapton

With 2003-2004 came a surge of interest in Martin's late-60s art, partly because his return to London had stoked old sparks and partly – maybe mostly – because Cream was reforming after 25 years apart. The cover of their Martin-designed second album *Disraeli Gears* came up again and again: book cover, CD cover, 4-CD boxed set, DVD and eventually a print. [1]

Swinging London! Big O Posters wanted to reissue Sharp product in London and Liverpool. The 2004 Liverpool Biennial wanted to exhibit his London years. A TV camera crew was sent from BBC in England to Australia to interview him about that period. [2] And Belgian radio personality, Johann Rai, flew to Sydney and interviewed Martin about – yep - those London years. In each retelling, Martin never lost his spontaneity, making it sound fresh each time. [3]

At last, Martin conceded what he'd previously tried not to admit - that *Disraeli Gears* was indisputably his best-known work. He likened it to the way the image of *Demoiselles d'Avignon* flashes to mind whenever Picasso's name gets mentioned. [4]

As usual, Martin was more interested in his current works than in revisiting his past. Either way, he was certainly not in any shape to catch a flight if required in Liverpool or London. Health issues were in the background of everything that happened to Martin over the next two years, indeed for the rest of his life. He hadn't even kept his Medicare card up-to-date, and he needed it when he suffered a perennial abscess. Richard helped out with the forms and got him a new card. That abscess required a brief stint at the Prince of Wales Hospital where the doctor insisted Martin quit smoking, which he did for a time. 'I felt it gave me up. I was dedicated to it or it was dedicated to me, I just didn't need to smoke any more'. [5]

Martin spent New Year's Day 2004 sketching a 'toon for the front page of the next morning's *Sydney Morning Herald*. The city councillors wanted to disguise their smelly cross-city tunnel with a work of art. That was their news peg. The editor commissioned Martin and two other artists to contribute whimsical or satirical impressions. Martin drew a b/w chimneystack with the word 'Eternity' wrapped around it and named it *Smokestack Eternity*. He faxed it to the editor, who faxed back that he wanted it coloured. Martin simply made 'Eternity' yellow and that was that. [6]

Like Cranbrook School, there was always a new hassle with Luna Park. Martin wrangled with the committee and, to their credit, they didn't write him off and he didn't write them off. Martin returned all the memorabilia rescued from the tip after the 1981 auction and sold back the items he'd bought, like the Joy Wheel and the Turkey Trot. [7] There was a general agreement that a memorial should be placed on the site and Martin submitted the Eternity motif as his contribution. He said, 'I felt right at the beginning - eternity was there. Just set a plaque into Eternity. Eternity would be the best one.' Martin had originally favoured a green park, 'Maybe seven years ago, I thought the park should become gardens, I still think that's more valuable than an amusement park.' [8]

Six weeks later a dutiful-looking memorial was dedicated on the site. Set against a red wall, the plaque read, 'This building stands on the site of the Ghost Train, destroyed by fire on the night of Saturday 9 June 1979 with the loss of seven lives. John Godson, Damien Godson, Craig Godson, Richard Carroll, Michael Johnson, Jonathan Billings and Seamus Rahilly. They are remembered.' A more attractive memorial was dedicated in August 2007. The sculpture was located in Art Barton Park, near Cliff Street Milsons Point and designed by Peter Kingston and Michael Leunig. It read, 'To all those who take refuge in this place to make a small commitment to the protection of children as they play.'

Martin continued his concerns about indigenous Australians. He played a cassette of 'Aboriginal Prophets', watched a DVD that celebrated the life and ministry of Auntie Ella Gordon and read a biography of Pemulwuy, the leader of the Eora people who lived in the area occupied by the city of Sydney. [9] Martin conferred with Kay Cook on indigenous issues arising from the book and he reworked Gulpilil's portrait. (Gulpilil was the subject of the winner of the 2004 Archibald Prize, Craig Ruddy.)

There was also a surge of interest coming from England, Martin was asked to write about those years. He muttered, 'I'm trying to get together something for the Biennal in Liverpool next year – that's 2004…' As usual, he spent a long time ordering his thoughts. A two-page letter might take three days to complete. He'd write a bit, paint a bit, smoke a bit and come back to the writing.

Martin began this account with a false memory. For some misguided reason he thought late-50s boy-singer Laurie London hailed from Liverpool. (Laurie London came from Bethnal Green, East London.) Martin got an assistant to track Laurie London on Google Images. He printed off his picture and taped it to the wall. Martin started this memoir with, 'The first time I ever heard of Liverpool was in 1958 when Laurie London, a 13-year old black kid from Liverpool, had a hit with *He's Got the Whole World in His Hands*. I'd like to do a multi-media exhibition tracing my interest in Liverpool from Laurie London. Five years later the Beatles erupt out of Liverpool, break the domination of America on the popular music scene. The Beatles had something to do with Tiny being in England – that show at the Albert Hall was for a big charity called Cornerstone, like a showbiz charity gala night, and boy it was packed!' (10)

Martin surely must have foreseen that the Liverpool exhibition was never going to come off. The original curator wanted a Martin Sharp show only, no Tiny. Then the curator's marriage fell apart and so did he. Someone else took over, someone with even less interest in Tiny.

3 April - Harold the Kangaroo died. And Les? She was doing well running her own cleaning business. She was no longer known as Les Bean.

In August Gary Shearston's CD launch concert was held at Almost Acoustic, a folk music venue in Rozelle - the concert planned with Carrl Myriad, the one for which Martin had intended to do a poster. Martin was looking forward to attending. Instead he did well to stay home. He woke up feeling strange. It was a sensation he had previously experienced but on a lesser scale. There were other people in the house but none within earshot. Should he call for help? Or, should he ring 000? He thought not. He feared a worse attack if he moved. He didn't want to go downstairs, open the door and let the ambos in.

Instead he went back to sleep, woke up and felt okay. Next morning, he saw a GP. Roslyn explained, 'Martin got dropped off at Dr Hansen in Oxford Street, who must have done an ECG and told him he had to go straight to St Vincent's Hospital. He'd a small heart attack.' (11) Martin picked up the story, 'I went down to Emergency but it had moved. That's when I felt really bad - it was hard to get back up the hill to find Emergency. In Emergency they have a great big room, beds all around, anything and everything comes in the door. It's a fascinating place, all sorts of drama going on. They all rush. You're suddenly very impressed. One of the nurses said, "It's good you came here, this is God's own hospital". Someone else said, "Your heart rate's gone through the roof. This is going to hurt when we inject this into your heart." Then I went up to some ward upstairs. It was a new kind of social life made up of patients in extremis, doctors, nurses, tea-ladies, wardsmen - a whole other world. I was their guest.

'They do an exploratory. You're not unconscious. They stick a machine up your groin, going up an artery to your heart and they pump stuff in that they can film – quite a bizarre experience. They can see the state of your heart arteries. Then they decide what they're going to do. If you're lucky they put in a stent. Apparently I needed more attention than that. The Registrar said, "We've got to do a triple by-pass. We cut you open here, put you on this heart/lung machine while we operate on your heart…"

'He told me it would take 12 hours. I wasn't feeling up to going through that sort of operation. I said, "Oh? I think I'll go home," and his face looked so sad – sad that all he had to offer was being rejected. They let me stay for a few days to think about it. My cousin Philip (ie. Dr Philip Sharp) who's a surgeon, said it was a good operation and I should seriously consider going through with it. There was a lovely Chinese doctor with a long plait, very attractive. She was the one who talked me into it.

'The operation pushes you right to the edge of existence. On one level I thought I might go – pass away – or whatever it's called. I thought I might change dimension. You shift into a space with a different set of priorities. I didn't worry about the work or leaving a big mess behind - it's not the problem of the dying or the sick. I didn't have any ego or ambition towards finishing because I'd done what I could. I'd done my best. I thought it's not my concern any more. Then I slowly started to come back to life and I groaned inwardly because I thought, "Oh god, I've got to get back to all those problems again". I'm glad I'm back but at the time I wasn't so pleased. It's very uncomfortable and you really want to get away from the discomfort.

'They have to do it all in one go. It's very intrusive. They take arteries out of your leg, your breastbone - spliced into your heart. You are disconnected from your heart and lungs and put onto a machine. That's when they said you might have some dreams, surreal experiences. They said, "You might see things" so I thought, "Oh? I'll keep my eyes open if anything crops up". And I did. I took some notes. I did a few little sketches. I did a drawing for one of the nurses.' (12)

Roslyn added, 'Martin wrote extensively about how he felt about the heart attack. He was very interested because he had terrible hallucinations, which is a common occurrence with people who've had triple by-passes.' [13] Martin always took hallucinations seriously.

Martin eased back into Wirian. He seemed weak but well. He quit smoking again and proudly showed off the 18-inch cut on his left leg. George's film *Soundtrack to War* was televised and well received. Greg's *Portrait of George* was hung in the National Portrait Gallery Canberra. Garry and Luke dropped in with baguettes, camembert and conversation. And Martin's fisherman friend, Allan Broadhurst came to Sydney from Bermagui and presented Martin with a tiny abalone shell that Martin wanted embedded into the bottom of his *Abalone Diver* picture frame.

They got chatting about heart attacks. (Allan had one shortly before Martin.) Martin drained every detail of the subject, which was certainly not what Allan had expected. He expected something about Art. Allan said, 'It's amazing how people from such diverse fields suddenly find something in common through calamity. "Let's talk heart attacks - what sort of tablets are you on?"' (14)

Since Tiny's passing there had been a worldwide surge of interest in the ukulele instrument. It seemed that every community had its own uke-group - Newcastle had its Ukestra, the Blue MUGS were the Blue Mountains Uke Group, Mandurah had Manuleles, Melbourne had their Ukulele Kollective, etc. Such groups were peppered all over Australia, England and America. Greg Weight and Carol Ruff ran Gallery East, East Clovelly, exhibiting many fine artists. With 'Coral Reef' as her charming stage name, Carol was a uke player too. She and Greg decided on a uke-themed exhibition with ukuleles painted by 50 artists including Martin, Greg, Mic, Garry, Reg Mombassa, Bruce Goold, etc.

It was a welcome success. Along with Phil Donnison and Cazzbo Johns, Mic and Jim Conway performed on an outside stage, joined by uke virtuoso Azo Bell. Carol performed a few songs too. There was a festive air. The crowd spilled onto the road and blocked traffic. The Police eased everyone back to the pavement. Kate Ceberano, The Sandman, H G Nelson were there too. Martin was expected. His painted uke was hung (with tulips) and he had posed for publicity shorts with Greg and Carol. So where was he tonight?

Later in the evening Kingo announced that Martin had suffered a stroke and was back in hospital. It had happened at midnight the previous Saturday night, after Martin had taken leave of a party. He was walking up the driveway and attempted to say something to the people with him, but the words didn't come out right. Martin surmised that they probably thought he was alcohol-affected and offered to drive him home. They saw no improvement in him when he got out of the car, so they took him straight to St Vincent's Hospital. Martin said, 'I could understand what they were saying, but what I thought I was going to say and what I actually said were not combining. And I understood that when people look at you like you're a bit weird, you know that they're thinking things aren't right.' Martin had had a small stroke which he felt was related to his triple bypass operation, 'some little clots drifting around inside get stuck somewhere. It was like having a slightly defective video machine in one's brain - sticking and picking up the correct speed again.' (15)

The doctors asked a few questions. Martin got his name right and correctly stated that he lived in Wirian with the Cranbrook School next door. But for his address he wrote, '3 Coyagbictricovyn'. They checked him in immediately. He said, 'They put me on this strong de-coagulant which worked pretty fast.' (16) Roslyn explained, 'He was one of the first patients to be given the clot-dissolving drug that you have to give within three hours of a stroke. He was given it and he made a complete recovery.' (17) With a window view, Martin was okay about this hospital stint. He hated the food first time around, this time he looked forward to meals. He stayed in his room, read a John La Carré novel and sketched.

When he got home, Martin felt slightly impaired – not that anyone noticed. 'I think I'm a little bit disabled, sometimes when I walk I veer to the left a bit.' (18) Martin painted a bit and watched TV a lot. He watched the new Azaria film, with Miranda Otto as Lindy and Craig McLachlan as Michael. He watched tennis and he always watched the news. His music of choice was Archie Roach and Ruby Hunter's Opera House concert. In the film editing room, Wendy was gone and there was no sign of Dave. Marilyn was back as Martin's assistant, followed by Sam Reid, a cousin's son. Sam won the 2003 Justin O'Brien Art Prize in his final Cranbrook year.

Chaudry, Steven Darmody and Robert Tilley were around the house. Martin was back to eating at *Arte e Cucino* with Kay and Luke and a wall was constructed outside the kitchen window just beyond the *porte cochère*. It was built to accommodate a 'thank you' by Lin Utzon. First the wall was erected. Next the ceramic tiles arrived from Europe. Then they then had to wait for Lin to return to affix the tiles. Willy was living there at the time, Lin's wall was built shortly before he lost faith in the Healing Ministry. Canon Glennon – the healer - died 11 June 2005.

Robert explained, 'Willy was involved in Canon Jim Glennon's healing ministry. Glennon's brand of healing was akin to a kind of Christian Science/New Age idea that if one believed one was well then one would become well. He lost his faith in that ministry not because of Glennon's death (which I think was related to his asthma, but he was old). It was because a couple of people who had cancer and were involved in the ministry showed what appeared to be great faith but nevertheless died. Willy later joined his older brother José who was and is a very big developer of real estate programs. Willy and José are based in Argentina.' [19]

*

Thirteen years after their induction into the Rock n Roll Hall of Fame, Eric decided to reunite Cream because – as Martin explained, 'They're one of the bands that can – because they're all still living!' [20] Jack gave everyone a scare when he underwent liver transplant surgery the previous year. That crisis behind him, he was back on bass. In his autobiography Eric wrote, 'For some time I had been thinking about a reunion of Cream. It had been almost forty years since the creation of the band, and given the fact that we were all still capable of playing together, I thought it would be fitting to pay tribute to ourselves while we still could. I was also very aware that I had always been the reluctant one on this score so, cap in hand, I made some delicate enquiries as to whether Jack and Ginger would be interested.' [21]

Would Martin be attending the Cream reunion concert? 'If my health's good enough I'd love to go. It's great that they're getting back together again. It's really going to be something because they're very comfortable in the Albert Hall – it's their venue. I saw Tiny there – so there's a bit of an echo.' [22]

Cream booked three weeks of rehearsals. If the rehearsals went badly, they would cancel. The opposite happened, it came together so quickly that they didn't need the whole three weeks. Their four Albert Hall concerts sold out within two hours. Fans came from America and Japan, some paying over $2000 on eBay to see the band. Later Cream played Madison Square Garden, which is when Ginger and Jack got back to arguing just like old times.

The concert was released as a double-CD and a double-DVD. Caps, t-shirts, limited edition screen posters and other merchandise were sold at venues and online, many of them featured Martin's images. A biography of the band was published in 2005, acknowledging Martin's valued contribution. [23]

Having gloriously survived – or endured – the revival, Ginger and Jack weren't required to play together again. The type of thing they argued about was – say - the rhythmic phrasing of a song. They didn't have to do that any more, they could just reminisce to camera crews about the good times. They didn't even need to be in the same room to do that.

British TV documentary series *Classic Albums* created the *Disraeli Gears Story* for MTV and DVD formats. *Tales of Brave Ulysses* appeared twice on that DVD. The filmmakers interviewed a wide group of contributors - the band members of course, and others like lyricist/poet Pete Brown. They flew a film crew to Australia to interview Martin. In his Inner Sanctum, seated in front of his paintings of Hendrix, Gulpilil, and a print of *Disraeli Gears*, Martin retold his story for the camera. Martin and Eric's accounts were later spliced together.

'I was at the Speakeasy one night, just hanging out,' said Eric. 'I was dating this girl Charlotte Martin, a very beautiful French lady and I think she knew Martin. She introduced me to him. We started talking and we hit it off. He was a designer and an artist. He painted and drew pictures for a magazine called OZ. Martin had written these lyrics on this sheet of paper and Jack found a way to sing them over this riff.'

Martin teased, '*Strange Brew* was the A-side. I was a bit disappointed *Tales of Brave Ulysses* was on the B-side!' As for the cover Martin dismissed it as '…quite simple really. I'm glad they liked it'. [24]

A box of Martin's newly printed Big O postcards arrived from London. Martin was mostly pleased but not totally. Unhappily one of the cards was a poster he did for Cream. Martin ripped it up calling it 'the ugliest thing I've ever done!' The rest was fine. [25]

Again from London, Felix Dennis launched a poetry and pictures magazine, *The Illustrated Ape*, in which he featured eight of Martin's images, mostly as full-page illustrations. Martin shared cover lines with John Lennon, David Hockney, WB Yeats and Rudyard Kipling. [26] He painted a big red heart for the cover of Felix's *Lives and Rhymes* poetry CD that came with the magazine. [27] Felix, that bearded scamp from London OZ trials, had reinvented himself first as a hugely successful businessman and now as a poet. With a publishing empire worth $750 million, who was going to argue? Felix arrived at poetry readings in a helicopter and served only the finest wines. His tour was called 'And Did I Mention the Free Wine?'

Martin must have been flavour of the month because, writing for the London *Guardian*, even Robert Hughes had a piece of Martin, 'Where is Martin Sharp whose weird drawings used briefly to lighten the images of the long-defunct OZ magazine? (Answer: back in Australia, an acid casualty, still said to be pursuing his 20-year fantasy of making a film about the justly forgotten entertainer, Tiny Tim with his greasy ringlets and stupid little plastic ukulele, wherever he may now be).' [28] Martin chuckled about Hughes over the phone to Richard. 'I don't think he ever forgave me for beating him in Chess!' Martin laughed.

As part of the 2005 Queen's Birthday Honours, Martin was awarded the Order of Australia medal. The Old Establishment guys didn't nominate Martin - it was Luke. Disinclined to accept, Martin told the press, 'When the letter came, my postie could tell what it was. He insisted I take it. He's a wonderful postie so I felt I should.' [29]

Privately he explained his hesitation, 'I'd always thought it was wrong for artists to have Orders of Australia or knighthoods. Bureaucrats can't really judge those things. They give it - not for the things I consider most important I guess - just the things you'd do normally. Maybe for not dying! I said to the postie, "I don't know if I should take it". Anyway, the postie said, "You've got to take it for your grandfather". The Order of Australia is most commonly presented to artists and writers. There's three different degrees - this is the least honourable of the honours. I think they gave it to me for the Yellow House. Pop Art was one of the things mentioned - and maybe for encouraging young artists. Now I've got to encourage young artists!' [30]

In September, Martin attended the launch of Margaret Olley's new biography at the Art Gallery of New South Wales – *Far From A Still Life* by Meg Stewart. Barry Humphries launched it. Martin parked along Mrs Macquarie's Chair Road, a short walk from the gallery. He arrived exhausted. One of his lungs was playing up. The two Richards – Neville and Walsh - stayed in touch with Martin during this period of ill health.

Abe Saffron too was on the decline. Ritchie Walsh wrote an article in which he affirmed, 'there are two Abe Saffrons'. Ritchie depicted Abe One as the notorious owner of strip joints and other dubious enterprises. Abe Two, he wrote, was a part-time philanthropist, which is how Abe would like to be remembered. Martin read it to guests. As for Richard Neville? Martin chuckled when he told Martin that he'd figured out that he was descended from Shakespeare. 'Richard likes Shakespeare,' laughed Martin. 'When we were in Asia he used to recite Shakespeare to all these bewildered children!' [31]

Martin visited Braidwood NSW where he stayed with an old school friend, also called Martin. They were trying to save a church and – unusually for Martin – he made a public speech for the cause. [32] Martin turned his attention to church art. Religious themes combined with Indigenous themes in his new pictures, like the cross Martin painted in the colours of the Aboriginal flag. It was one of the few sculptures Martin ever made. Steve Darmody did the carpentry. He said, 'I had an idea of doing the Aboriginal colours on the cross – a bit like a Mondrian.' [33] Father Ted Kennedy was the priest of Redfern, some of the Aboriginal ladies from his church took Martin's cross to Rome at the beatification of Mary McKillop. Did they remain at the Vatican? Martin didn't know, 'I don't know what happened to those crosses. I'm sure they're doing okay. Vincent said, "A good picture does good wherever it is" – I love that line.' [34]

Built in 1885, St Saviour's Anglican Church Redfern was an innovative church, keen on community outreach. Cartoonist Reg Lynch organised an art exhibition there and contacted Martin. Martin agreed to lend his big Eternity canvas as a centrepiece. The newspaper reported, 'St Saviours Church is open for prayer and meditation during the week and no doubt many people will find Martin Sharp's painting an inspiration'. [35]

In America, Ernie Clark kept interest in Tiny alive via his website. He attracted filmmakers who were interested in making a biopic. Ernie was initially asked to write it, before being switched to 'adviser to the writer'. Jeff Goldblum was reported to have an interest in playing Tiny. (Then he wasn't.) Casting around for someone else, some thought John Turturro would be perfect.

The film project remained in the air for most of the year, with Ernie and Martin swapping ideas over the phone. One of the things Martin told Ernie was that it peeved him that Tiny was not inducted into the Rock N Roll Hall of Fame nor ever likely to be. Ernie thought the Ukulele Hall of Fame seemed more realistic and worked that front. After all, when people thought 'uke', sooner or later they thought 'Tiny'. Ukulele magazines featured articles about the type of uke he played and how unusual the instrument was in the 60s and 70s. Tiny was given a good spread in a recent book, *The Ukulele, A Visual History* by Jim Beloff. [36] All this revitalisation of Tiny stimulated Martin, 'I must get something out,' he said, 'not as a response to the movie but as a duty'. [37]

At this stage, the most efficient way of 'getting something out' was Satoshi's idea. On behalf of Martin, he entered into negotiations with Japanese company, Zero Communications. The initial interest was in releasing the *Chameleon* CD only. (Satoshi had his own online company too, Mojo Associates Fine Art, from which he sold a range of Martin's prints and posters.) Before the year was out, Zero compiled a limited edition 7-track demo of selections from *Chameleon, Wonderful World of Romance* and the *Pop* Album. The planned release date for the three albums was to coincide with the 10th Anniversary of Tiny's passing. [38]

*

Martin was precisely three days older than Roger Foley (Ellis D Fogg). And Luke approached Roger with a plan, 'Foggy - you've got to have a *When I'm 64* party!' Not keen at first, Roger softened when Luke suggested a combined Martin-Roger birthday event. Martin was happy to share his birthday with Roger but he didn't want to do the inviting because he feared leaving anybody out. Luke wasn't sure whom to invite either, so Roger stepped in and said, 'I know who your real friends are Martin... I'll take the flak!' Martin said, 'O good Foggy, I'll leave it up to you'.

For the venue, Roger suggested the old harbourmasters' cottage at Green Point, which was ideal. Along with his wife Francesca, Roger invited Jeannie Lewis, Tim Lewis, Albie Thoms, Louise Ferrier, Richard Neville, Peter Kingston, Luke Sciberras and Jim Anderson, who photographed the occasion. Roger said, 'We had a great party. A lot of the people who are Martin's friends influenced my life from an early age.' [39]

More than 30 years after opening the main building, Queen Elizabeth II returned to the Sydney Opera House to open a new colonnade addition. Martin was there with Lin and Jan Utzon (architect Jorn Utzon's children). He was 'very impressed' with the Queen who said it was fitting that the world-famous structure was now being considered for world heritage listing. Jan Utzon told the Opera House crowd that his 88-year old architect father who designed the building was disappointed he was unable to attend but sent his warmest regards. His father was pleased to have reconciled the differences over the building and to have the opportunity to work on it again, 'He (Jorn Utzon) is too old by now to take the long flight to Australia. But he lives and breathes the Opera House and as its creator he just has to close his eyes to see it. He also wishes to thank the many people who have supported him over the years, notably the famous Sydney architect Harry Seidler, who sadly passed away a few days ago'. [40]

Wednesday 10 May 2006: fire destroyed St Barnabas Church Ultimo. Built in 1859, St Barnabas' Anglican Church was famous as the church where Arthur Stace converted to the Christian faith. The landmark church burned down in less than three hours. Firefighters were called at 3.30am but could do nothing to save it. [41]

Greg Weight married artist Carol Ruff in Central Australia and Martin took the trip to Alice Springs and was Best Man. While in the centre, Martin visited the grave of the pioneer of indigenous art, Albert Namatjira. Greg and Carol also took Martin to Hermannsberg Lutheran Mission where Namatjira started to paint seriously at the age of 32 in 1934.

In September-November, Martin and Kingo held a joint installation at the Art Gallery of New South Wales. Titled, *Notes from the River Caves*, it was a collaborative cupboard of curiosities, a mini-museum of Luna Park memorabilia and other kitsch collectibles. It featured Kingo's England V Australia chess set (ie. Dame Edna, Ned Kelly, Norman Gunston, etc) V the Royal Family + corgis. Martin's pictures include some of his earliest works as well as *Abalone Diver, Miss World, Al Jolson, Swanee/Ginge, Donovan* and *Snow Job*.

As her health deteriorated, Martin's stepmother Dorothy moved from her Neutral Bay home to Lulworth in Elizabeth Bay. During this time Martin often consulted Roslyn. She said, 'It started with phone calls to talk about Dorothy before she died and when she went into Lulworth and it all centred about how he should care for her.' After Dorothy died, celebrity chef, Kylie Kwong cooked at the wake. For this kindness, Martin gave her the *Courage My Friend* print. [42] Dorothy left an unacceptable will that would entangle Martin in legal matters over the next two years.

Abe Saffron was also fading. Speaking in her role as a radiographer, Roslyn said, 'I started x-raying Abe Saffron at St Vincent's when he was really sick. I took his chest x-ray the day before he died. I told Martin.' [43] Abe Saffron died 15 September 2006.

In October the City of Sydney held its *Art & About* festivities, with displays of art and photography at Customs House, Circular Quay, many galleries and various locations. Especially interesting this year was 'The Face of Sydney' theme. Martin's face of Gulpilil was commissioned for street banners, posters, invitations, newspaper ads as well cover of the *Art & About* booklet, of which thousands were printed. The original portrait was also on display. [44]

Marianne Faithfull and Martin stayed in regular touch over the phone. He described the conversations as 'very loving'. One night Marianne phoned in a state of high anxiety. Test results showed she had breast cancer and her response was to undergo surgery. The press didn't know yet, only Martin and a few close friends. She spoke to Martin at length about her fears. She wasn't ready to 'change dimension' (as Martin put it) yet. Marianne got through the surgery and made a complete recovery. When she was ready, she went public and told the press about her ordeal, 'I didn't realise how many true friends I had. I feel so lucky and loved.' [45]

She sent Martin a demo copy of her newest CD *Before the Poison*. Someone else sent Martin a copy of Bob Dylan's 'Theme Time Radio Hour' a one-hour radio program in which Dylan introduced a selection of obscure and not-so-obscure songs. Dylan called this selection 'Flowers' and it got sent to Martin because Dylan selected *Tiptoe* as one of the featured songs. It came too late…Martin was through liking Dylan. In his Memoirs Dylan wrote about his Greenwich Village period and described one venue as full of 'Tiny Tim-type people', which Martin interpreted as a sneer. He said Dylan was 'mean-spirited' and stopped listening to him. [46]

After an intense career as a public sculptor, Tom Bass was holding a retrospective exhibition and the *Daily Telegraph* revisited the famous OZ cover where a youthful Martin, Richard and Ritchie supposedly pissed into Bass's water feature. To help publicise the exhibition they agreed to reprise the shot with Bass in the foreground, which was how Martin, Richard and Ritchie understood it would appear. But the editor cut Bass out of the picture and turned into an OZ story instead. Martin was furious, 'I was upset for Tom. He was a witness in our favour in the trial, so when we got called to help him with some publicity, we agreed to do it. We were publicising his exhibition.' [47]

Albie's films were screened, as was Tiny's marathon at Martin's next exhibition at Ivan Dougherty Gallery. The catalog was an impressive booklet with an introduction by Richard and an interview by curator Nick Waterlow. Martin exhibited his earliest pictures from childhood and high school days and brought viewers right up to date. New works included *The Toff 2, Abalone Diver, Babylon the Great is Fallen* and *Reprise of Giorgio de Chirico's Song of Love*. The face in the latter would gradually evolve into Elvis over the succeeding years. Titled 'Love Me Tender' in this exhibition and it was finally retitled 'Graceland'. [48]

15.
HIPPIE HIPPIE SHOCK

Martin: I'm in 55 scenes and none of them happened.
Richard: But Mart, it reads well…

In November 2004, Aboriginal Palm Island resident Cameron Doomadgee was allegedly causing a public nuisance and died within one hour of being picked up by the Police. He had a ruptured liver, which suggests that he copped a severe beating. The autopsy report did not state cause of death and a riot erupted when this was made public. The local courthouse, police station and police barracks were burned down. Eighteen local police and their families were forced to flee and barricade themselves in the hospital. Eighty police from Townsville and Cairns were flown in to restore order.

In response to the riot, the Premier of Queensland, Peter Beattie, established the Palm Island Select Committee to investigate the issues. In December 2006 the Director of Public Prosecution (DPP) announced that no charges would be laid against an arresting officer whose punches were thought to be the cause of death.

Four weeks after that verdict, Bwgcolman woman, Maggie Walsh and teenage daughter Lorraine, left Palm Island and arrived in Sydney. On Gulpilil's recommendation, they came to Wirian. Lorraine stayed a short time, Maggie stayed longer. Maggie was born in Townsville in 1964. She was separated from her mother from the age of two when her mother was sent away to work. Maggie was raised by her mother's friends, they were women sent to Palm Island, away from their homes and families.

Maggie played guitar, sang and wrote poetry that she recited with conviction. She wrote about things she knew, like clubs, pokies and domestic issues. Maggie soon got to know other Indigenous Australians from The Block in Redfern. Some came to Wirian to visit her. Martin got to know them too. Sometimes he gave them money. Martin had a soft spot for Redfern. As a founding Member of the Australian Labor Party (ALP) in 1891, Martin's great-grandfather William Henry Sharp won the Seat of Redfern, which he held for three years on a Labor-Protectionist platform. [1]

Sticking with Indigenous themes, Martin's kept reworking Phil May's *A Curiosity in Her Own Country* (*The Bulletin*, 1888). May's black-and-white cartoon depicts an Indigenous mother and her child dressed in European-style clothes and seated in a city street. They are surrounded by rudely staring well-dressed onlookers, including a Chinese man. Martin titled this curious and troubling nativity scene *What Next?* This slowly evolving picture would re-emerge three years later in a blaze of colour as the cover of Sydney Morning Herald's *Spectrum* magazine (2009) and as a Christmas card sent to friends. Martin added a wild Starry Starry night sky, spinning prisms and halos on the Aboriginal Madonna-and-child. [2]

Martin was low on energy. Painting was okay because everything was set up in the Inner Sanctum and he only had to pick up a brush. He could do that while talking to visitors. The film and the *King for a Day* CD required more energy, and Martin took a break from them. He daubed a few canvasses, took short walks, drank herbal drinks and smoked the occasional cigar because he had quit cigarettes.

Late one morning a package arrived from Zero Communications Japan. It was packs of three new Tiny Tim CD releases – about to be made available in selected stores and via the Internet. Martin and Dave had battled to negotiate a CD release of *Chameleon* for ages and Satoshi made it happen. Not just *Chameleon*, but *Wonderful World of Romance* too, with bonus tracks. The third was a new concept called *Stardust*. Its 26 tracks were a mixture of studio recordings, informal mini-disk recordings and a track sung in Luna Park's Floating Palace, 12 January 1979, the day of the marathon. Smartly packaged, each CD included a 16-page booklet in which Martin retold his story - from *Tales of Brave Ulysses* to Tiny's performance at an Australian worker's club - via the Royal Albert Hall. Martin's art was well represented in the booklets – *Hokusai's Wave, Boofhead Thinker, Eternity*, the *Chameleon* poster as well as a profile of Tiny wearing a crown, appropriated from Arthur Rackman. [3] Martin described Tiny as, 'The one singer who is all singers, the Spirit of Popular music made flesh'. [4]

The CDs sounded livelier because Dave remastered the original disks and in some instances, changed the mix. For example, he restored Gulpilil's clapping sticks and didge on the *Stayin' Alive* track. They were inaudible on the record. Dave and Satoshi were happy with all that but Martin wanted to do even more production work on *Chameleon*. He wanted to delay release and when he couldn't do that, he talked about it as if it was just a demo. Of course it was much more than that. *Chameleon* was the Tiny Tim record that Martin's friends had genuinely enjoyed, unlike the Brighton tapes that nobody played. (5)

After a year as Martin's assistant, Luke became a father. Said Gria, 'We were living in a tiny 2-bedroom flat with a baby. One of the rooms had been Luke's studio but when we had Stella there was no more studio. Two weeks before I had Stella I had my first show at Eva Breuer Gallery (Woollahra). I was painting until I gave birth. Luke's career took off the moment Stella was born so he had to have a studio. It was a tiny little section of Kingo's house where Luke was able to go and paint.' (6)

Later, Luke and Gria moved to Hill End, near Bathurst NSW, a former gold mining town that was a haven for artists ever since Russell Drysdale and Donald Friend discovered its charm in the 1940s. Hill End was home to several of Martin's creative collaborators in uni days - Peter Doring, the late Peter Wright, Mandy Wright and John Firth-Smith. Said Luke, 'I didn't move to Hill End to be surrounded by other artists or because of the town's reputation with previous artists. I moved here because I fell in love with the community'. (7)

Gria said, 'We bought Hill End together because Sydney rent was going out of control. We'd go back and forth because the place in Hill End had no running water and no toilet. We built it over years. Stella had to go to daycare in order for me to paint, so we straddled between the two places. We weren't staying in Wirian but Luke was still doing a bit of work for Martin here and there.' After 12 years together, Gria and Luke broke up. She moved to Woollahra and Luke continued to divide his time between Hill End and Sydney. (8)

Eric Clapton and his band returned to Australia for another tour and Eric called on Martin as part of his 2-day Sydney stopover. It was a quiet affair. Robert Tilley swept the verandah and Angelica snapped photos while Eric and Martin chatted like a couple of battle worn veterans. Peter Royles travelled from Goulburn – probably a six hour round trip - to play his rendition of *Wonderful Tonight* to Eric and get his autograph. Puzzled, Eric asked Martin, 'Why would anybody do that?' ('Because you're Eric Clapton' was the answer, I guess.) Eric was pleasant to everyone and everyone was calm, unlike his 1985 visit.

The royalty cheques from *Tales of Brave Ulysses* never missed a beat, as each new generation learned to enjoy Cream. But Dorothy's Will came as a shock, not just to Martin, but his friends and cousins too, with whom he openly discussed these matters. 'She's been got at' was the going phrase when it became known that Cranbrook School and St Paul's College were left bequests of $300,000 each. There were genuine grounds to suggest that Dorothy had been unduly influenced because the lawyer who drew up her Will was also the lawyer for Cranbrook School. Martin started procedures to contest the Will. It was a protracted legal struggle, putting Martin under considerable financial stress when he was physically at his weakest.

Said Roslyn, 'Dorothy paid off the mortgage in exchange that Martin would not get anything else. Martin told me she said that but he didn't think she would give everything away. Martin fought tooth and nail to get the Will drawn back at great expense. He fought it for the moral obligation. I went to the mediation court with him. I can't say what happened in there but he carved it back two Wills.' [9]

Judit Shead died nine months after being diagnosed with a virulent form of pancreatic cancer. Terrible.

Judit and Garry lived in Wirian while painting the Harris Street mural in the mid-80s. They moved to Bundeena where Judit helped Garry focus on his art. It paid off. Garry had become one of the nation's most respected figurative artists. Martin attended the opening of a combined Garry & Judit exhibition at Australian Galleries, commemorating Judit by featuring her beautiful sculptures and Garry's moving tributes. [10]

Back when Garry and Judit lived in Wirian, no major newspaper would touch Martin's theories about Abe Saffron and Luna Park. It was a surprise to all when the *Sydney Morning Herald* front-page featured an interview with Abe Saffron's niece, Anne Buckingham, who confirmed that her uncle was behind the Ghost Train fire. 'I don't think people were meant to be killed,' she told the news reporter. [11] The same writer followed her previous story in The (Sydney) Magazine. This article linked Saffron to the disappearance of Juanita Nielsen and reaffirmed the claim that Abe was the secret owner of Luna Park at the time of the fire.

In the years leading to his death, Abe Saffron had fought hard to clean up his shady reputation. He successfully won a defamation case against a Gold Coast newspaper that published a crossword clue: 'Sydney Underworld figure nicknamed Mr Sin' with Saffron as its answer. That didn't deter the *Sydney Morning Herald* running the headline, 'The sordid legacy of Abe "Mr Sin" Saffron'. [12]

Gentle Satan was the titled of Abe's son's biography about his father. That's quite a title, coming from someone trying to clear his father's name. Alan Saffron's tone was candid. He linked the murder of Juanita Nielson to one of his father's associates (Big Jim) - nothing to do with Abe - and admitted owning over 100 machines at Luna Park at the time of the fire, but denied that his father had anything to do with subsequent events. He wrote, 'Any suggestion my father was involved in the tragic fire had already been contradicted by the police and fire department reports at the time. Sadly, on 25 May 2007, after my father's death, *The Sydney Morning Herald* revisited these horrible events with front-page headlines based on allegations from my cousin Anne Buckingham who accused my father of being behind the tragedy. She provided no corroborating facts and later recanted the story, saying it was taken out of context.' [13]

Anne Buckingham got people talking about the Ghost Train fire again. Interviewed on ABC Radio, Martin moderated his position about Saffron. He laid the ultimate blame on the city of Sydney itself, 'Look at the organisations that have been tested by it. Government – fail. Law courts – fail. Police – fail. Church

– they're still not talking to me about the fire. It couldn't have happened unless the city had been in a position to have it happen – meaning there was enough corruption and enough control of Police – enough to make it appear that it was kids mucking up, not big businessmen!' [14]

Roslyn had more to do with Saffron than anyone else in Martin's crowd. When she photographed him, her Sharp surname must have connected her to Martin in his mind? On one occasion, Roslyn attended a venue accompanied by another cousin, Andrew. There were only six tables in the room. One had a card 'reserved for Sharp' and beside it 'reserved for Saffron'. Did Saffron not notice?

Roslyn said, 'I met Abe Saffron about five times because I became friendly with Christine Knight, a character in the Cross. And I was photographing "characters" in the Cross. She would get a box of French champagne every week from Abe. She lived in Darling Point and when I was visiting to photograph her, Abe rang up when I was there and she put Abe on the phone. She said, "Tell him to come over and meet you."

'I met him again when we did this fantastic little film of the community centre and Edwin Duff - the Be-Bop jazz singer - interviewed Abe Saffron. He had worked for Abe for years as a singer. There was some fantastic footage. I'd been hassling the Community Centre to get all the rushes transcribed digitally because it was only on videotape and would deteriorate. We had a small screening of it at the Mansions Hotel. Abe came to that and I photographed him with Mandy Sayers. He was an old man then. Martin told me to watch out if anyone knew I was related to him. He said I could be at risk and he didn't want to put me at risk.' [15]

Richard's *Hippie Hippie Shake* had received mixed reviews – many critics loved it. The *Independent on Sunday* called it 'the perfect Sixties book'. The *Book Depository* described it as a 'hilarious, colourful and provocative memoir'. The *Sunday Times* reckoned it was 'utterly unputdownable'.

Jenny Diski, *London Review of Books*, wrote, '*Hippie Hippie Shake* (what a title, for goodness sake) includes a multitude of photographs of Richard Neville in his twenties, but none of him in middle age; the writing, too, tells of his adventures then, even his hesitations, but there's no sense of having moved on intellectually or emotionally, of the man reassessing the boy. The present is barely referred to beyond the fact that he lives back in Australia and has a wife and two children. Of course, what he's up to and thinking now isn't necessarily any of our business, and he may have actually intended to write a book that merely described the events that brought him to the dock of the Old Bailey rather than a thoroughgoing analysis of the period, but the time warped effect contributes to the slightness of the enterprise. A lot of grand thoughts were rolling around – counter-culture, revolution, alternative reality – but when all is said and done in Neville's recollection, it appears it was little more than a hiatus, an overextended gap year between school and real life.' [16]

Richard was reputed to have sold the film rights for a six-figure sum. A film company put $A32 million into it and hired first class young British actors. Sienna Miller played Louise and Cillian Murphy played Richard. Martin and others depicted in the film were unsettled that their lives were being sensationalised to suit whatever the screenwriter wanted the plot to do. The draft script also offended them because they saw themselves as artists not hippies, whereas the film was a thumbnail sketch of clichéd hippie behaviour. Scriptwriter Lee Hall (known for *Billy Elliot*) did whatever he liked with the personal lives of the characters. Germaine was portrayed as a joint-smoking nymphomaniac and Martin had sex with people he never had sex with. [17]

'They call it dramatic licence! I was involved in 55 scenes in this film and none of them happened!' Martin protested.'

'But Mart, it reads well,' Richard replied. [18]

Germaine was not happy. She slammed Richard as 'one of the least talented people of the London scene in the 60s' and described his book as a 'continuing search of the fame and fortune that continue to elude him'. She disapproved of the actress chosen to portray her - Emma Booth. [19]

Not as blunt as Germaine, Martin too was genuinely nervous about who was going to play him. The film people told him he was being 'difficult' but he swears he wasn't. Martin, and others, didn't want to sell out their identities at any price. Max Minghella was the young actor picked to play Martin. Born in 1985, Minghella made his debut in *Bee Season* (2005) before starring in *Art School Confidentia*l in 2006, which drew reasonable reviews. Nice guy, rising star, but it was inconceivable that he knew the 60s in depth. 'It's a theft of one's life,' Martin told the press, 'and it's a very uncomfortable feeling.' [20]

Philippe didn't like it either. From his Los Angeles home he wrote, 'if real names are being used, why not keep it factual? The script I read is a clichéd attack on artists and hippies.' More dissatisfaction arose when it was noted that (1) the film was funded by General Electric and (2) Australian actors were not used to play the Australians. Philippe continued, 'I don't think you can be against the war on terror, as Richard has continued to write, then go and sell your life story to General Electric'. [21]

To assuage the tension, film director Beeban Kidron flew to Sydney for meetings with Louise Ferrier, Jenny Kee, Jim Anderson and Martin. Martin accepted no money from the film company and came to no agreement, even though they would have written him a $25,000 cheque on the spot for a 'yes'. On her return to London, Kidron amended the script once again not to anyone's complete satisfaction. So it was amended again until it began to resemble a sieve patched with Band-Aids. The film was eventually shot in 2009. Director Kidron and husband-writer Lee Hall, left during post-production, citing artistic differences with the producers.

Martin felt he'd been trashed. He scoffed the clichéd hippie content, 'Obviously you can't be at a love-in if you're working hard.' [22] Talking to Felix Dennis on the phone, Martin complained, 'No research - not even based on Richard's book!' He told Felix that he hated being treated like a Chess piece in the film. 'In life, all you've got is your name!' [23]

Once Felix got involved, that was the end of the film. Felix, who started out as a London OZ street-seller, was on Britain's rich list. (No 64 – something like that.) He agreed with Martin, Philippe and Germaine. His net worth of $750 million ensured that he had the legal clout to ensure the film was dead in the water if that's what he wanted.

OZ was about personal freedoms and social consciousness. Felix 'got' that. He was a philanthropist, he was good to friends and he poured profits into planting one million trees on 20.000 acres of forest. The world was a better place for having Felix Dennis. When Judge Argyle pronounced Felix 'less intelligent' than his cohorts in the OZ trials, that old fogey could not see beyond Felix's long hair and beard. Dennis Publishing made Felix wealthy enough to proudly indulge whatever he wanted. He made no bones about his libertine ways, drug use and penchant for fine wines. And he said no to the film.

Another film was released around this time, one about the art of Luna Park, exactly the angle that suited the artists. *The Art of Fun* was a 45-minute documentary film about the Park funded by the North Sydney Heritage Centre/Stanton Library and directed, written and produced by Helen McGrath and Cris Parker. *The Art of Fun* explores the people who created the Park and features interviews with artists Martin, Kingo and Leigh Hobbs all of whom celebrated Arthur Barton's legacy. [24]

Jason Holman spent his first night at Wirian at the start of December. Martin went out that night, so Jason accompanied Maggie to a karaoke night at the Redfern RSL. As a 5th form schoolboy, Jason was seated in the carriage that was about enter the Ghost Train, but was stopped when the fire was detected. The four Waverley College boys who died - Richard Carroll, Michael Johnson, Jonathan Billings and Seamus Rahilly – were his schoolmates. They were in the carriage before Jason, the one that was not stopped. Jason shared his story with Martin and in his capacity as a film director, Jason was hoping to convey his version of events at some point. Martin was eager to help and he appreciated Jason's positive energy.

After all these years, Robert Tilley still lived downstairs at Wirian. Never quite in sync, Martin and Robert continued their discussions on religion. Pope Benedict XVI was an unpopular Pope. Robert defended him by writing a book titled *Benedict XVI and the Search for Truth*. It was the first thematic and popular overview in English of the theology of Pope Benedict. Martin brushed that project aside. [25]

Robert Wolfgramm was another 'religious Robert' who called in. Martin had enjoyed his gospel songs over the years. He was appointed a member of the translation team for the *New Fijian Translation* (NFT) Bible project. Martin was so impressed: an actual Bible translator! [26] Not only that, Robert Wolfgramm came with information about someone who sang hymns non-stop for 30 hours straight. Regrettably, he told Martin, *The Guinness Book of Records* didn't acknowledge him. 'Like Tiny,' sighed Martin, mindful that neither of Tiny's 'Non-stop Singing Records (for a professional singer)' had been listed.

Robert Wolfgramm describes an encounter with Martin, 'I was sitting in the kitchen with him having a lunchtime coffee (with Marilyn in the background) and I asked him what he believed. He smiled and ah, grinned, and ah, "Believe, yeah, ah, (still grinning) - Lord I believe, help thou mine unbelief - is that how it goes?" I said yes and realised he was a person of genuine faith, because only people like that admit that belief and unbelief lie side-by-side. Pious hypocrites preach the myth of singularity. None of us are consistent. We all mute certain beliefs. We hide back-stage what we don't want to make front-stage.

'The other occasion that stands out in my conversations with Martin (they always came back to religion by the way) was when I asked him where he stood in relation to Tiny. He rambled a bit then said smiling, ah, grinning, ah, yeah, 'He must increase, I must decrease'. I was in awe that he should think like that - but summing up their relationship like that was deep and insightful.

'Martin's faith was like his house - chock-full of symbols. An array of collectible beliefs discarded from every religious tradition he came across, all thrown in there together, rooms cluttered with art and artefacts, belief and unbelief side-by-side, wow, it was jaw-dropping. A logician's nightmare - the enemy of religious rationalism. You couldn't talk religion, spirituality, faith, belief with Martin in anything like a straight line. He had Escherian loops that led everywhere. That was Martin's faith right there; a fundamentalist today, a mystic tomorrow. Existentialism in the morning - Jehovah's Witnesses in the afternoon - Zoroastrianism in the evening - and a smoke after dinner - without ever becoming any of these. What I loved about him was you could change the channel anytime you liked and he was still with you.' [27]

In mid-2006 David Gulpilil was in trouble with the law. He was charged with carrying an offensive weapon and found not guilty as his machete was deemed to be of cultural use. Gulpilil did not fare so well in March 2007 when a Darwin magistrate imposed a 12-month domestic violence order on him and told him to stay away from his wife when drinking. In December 2007 Gulpilil was hospitalised in Sydney and was in poor shape.

One night (perhaps with Maggie's assistance) Gulpilil absconded from hospital and showed up at Wirian still wearing the tag around his wrist. Maggie and a friend brought him over because he wanted to show Martin his latest short film *Crocodile Dreaming*. Jack Thompson was there too. Gulpilil was introspective that night. He sat in an armchair, watched the film quietly and occasionally pointed things out to Martin. Everyone fussed over him, even Jack. [28]

Over the years, Martin met a few of Tiny's family: mother Tillie in New York, second wife Miss Jan in London, and he had some email contact with Tiny's cousin Hal Stein and wife Sherry who announced that they were visiting Sydney for a stopover on their around-the-world cruise. Their ship, MS Statendam, moored at Circular Quay across the harbour from Luna Park, which Hal noted as the venue for Tiny's 1979 marathon. He and Sherry visited the Opera House, admired the harbour and called on Wirian.

Martin wanted the visit to be perfect. He described it as a visit from a member of the Royal Family of Popular Song. Being an only child, Hal was the closest that Tiny (or 'Herbie' to Hal) came to having a brother. They were playmates and confidants during the 30s and 40s when they lived in the same apartment block in Washington Heights NY. They attended the same school. Then Herbie became Tiny Tim and Hal became promotional manager for Radio WKTU. 'He got a better position than you!' is how Tiny's mother ribbed him on camera in 1981. [29]

Hal knew Herbie better than anyone – it was the 'Tiny Tim' persona that had him proudly bemused. And Sherry was amazed to find herself in a living museum to her husband's cousin! They couldn't look anywhere without seeing something of Tiny: records, his ukulele, the Tiny Tim game, a Wobblehead figurine, a painting of Tiny by a friend, a figurine of Tiny by Kingo, photos by William, press clippings, 1000 cassette tapes, Martin's ever-evolving *Film Script* painting and posters of Tiny at Luna Park, Paddo, Opera House, Kinsela's, Brighton and the *Rock* CD poster. Martin loaded Hal and Sherry up with all the best prints, which must have been awkward to carry while touring, but worth it when they got home to Bensalem Pennsylvania.

Martin screened the film footage on two iMac 21.5 computers – one showed the unedited marathon, the other the Brighton Cut. Wendy was Martin's assistant at the time. She organised a smoked salmon platter for lunch and took snapshots. Robert Tilley popped in and out - and Martin played lots of Tiny Tim music, including *Courage My Friend,* outtakes from *Chameleon* and Wirian kitchen recordings. Martin gave Hal and Sherry a full Tiny Tim experience. Privately, Sherry whispered, 'This is good for Hal. He never forgets Tiny's birthday'. [30]

Meanwhile, life progressed quietly at Wirian. Quite a few handyman jobs required attention. The gate was hung at last but the plumbing was deteriorating. One evening the downstairs toilet wouldn't stop flushing. Water spilled under the doorway until the entire hallway was under an inch of water. Everything had to be lifted off the floor and everyone in Wirian helped. Carpets, pictures, toys, anything made of paper or cardboard…an emergency that could not be fixed until morning. Martin stabilised the situation and went to bed instead of staying awake all night like old times. He frequently took afternoon naps too. He went walking when he remembered his doctor's orders, and started-and-stopped smoking according to his moods, sometimes quitting for weeks at a time.

Someone sent Martin a 1991 bootleg recording of Tiny performing at Hollywood High School. Half the set was about America (*California Here I Come, America the Beautiful, God Bless America, Yankee Doodle Dandy, I'm Coming Back to California*). Martin felt the song selection contained an important message. Another CD that caught Martin's interest was *The Last Ghost Train Home* by Perry Keyes, which John Barker brought it to his attention. Martin read a whole lot into that Perry said he never meant. Yet he was pleased that Martin had found a deeper meaning in his song, affirming that the essence of a song can be negotiable, according to performer, audience and circumstance. [31]

The Australian Songwriters Association (ASA) is a national organization founded in Melbourne in 1979. It holds an Awards Night every year, rewarding the best songwriters in their category and saluting some of Australia's best songwriters. In 2007 Brian Cadd was inducted into the Hall of Fame, in 2008 – the year Martin attended - it was the Angels. Held at the spacious West Ashfield Leagues Club, the evening was organised by events manager, Clare Burgess.

Said Clare, 'We always play a category winning song, but if the person's not there to perform it, we do something interesting on stage instead. This time we thought, why don't we have someone create a 3-minute painting on stage? We rang Martin to ask if he knew somebody who would do it? He didn't but said he'd like to come to the awards.' [32]

Martin was seated at Glenn A Baker's table. Accompanying him were Wendy, Angelica and Maggie. The evening was attended by pioneers of Aussie Rock - Little Pattie, Dinah Lee, Lonnie Lee - the writer of *I've Been Everywhere*, Geoff Mack, was present too. [33]

Maggie went to the Smokers' Room during intermission. She got everybody's attention by reciting an impressive stream of poems – which seemed like song lyrics, given the context of the night. Having stunned that audience, Maggie rejoined her table and heard Martin's name mentioned from the stage. It was Denny - acknowledging Martin's international contribution to Australian songwriting through co-writing *Tales of Brave Ulysses*. Said Denny, 'It was such an honour to have him come along!' Martin reciprocated by donating a poster as an auction item. [34]

When working directly under Director Curatorial Tony Bond, Wayne Tunnicliffe had expressed interest in the Art Gallery of New South Wales running a major Pop Art exhibition, featuring international artists as well as Australian content. To run a major exhibition, art galleries require a long lead-time, perhaps five years. In 2008 Tunnicliffe was promoted into a position where he could influence the decision to run a Pop exhibition for the general public, so plans were laid for the future event.

Tony Bond explained, 'It had been around as something Wayne wanted to do for 4-5 years I suppose. Wayne was very committed to doing an Australian component. If you were going to have Rauschenburg and Johns you probably need to look at Annandale Realists for example. That Australian component was very much Wayne's idea. The closest thing to Pop (as such) would be Martin - in terms of image in the public's mind and his interest in popular culture. It's something that Wayne was inevitably left to do.' [35]

The *Pop to Popism* exhibition was held for three months at the Gallery at the close of 2014. The banners featured Martin's 'Blowing in the Mind' Dylan poster, alongside Andy Warhol, Keith Haring, David Hockney and Roy Lichtenstein. But 2008 was when all the groundwork was being laid.

16.
POVERTY DELUX

Martin, God put you here for us to look at these things and contemplate the spiritual and sinister dimensions, and to not be blind to them and unconcerned.
Rachel Kohn

Dorothy's Will was the catastrophe that ruled Martin's life until April 2010 and beyond. In contesting the Will, the legal fees drained his finances to breaking point. Cranbrook School was among the beneficiaries, which was particularly galling, given that Martin was bullied and beaten in his student days and later pressured from the school as a neighbour.

The school honoured Martin while the Will was being contested, which made him uneasy, 'I was suspicious when they made me Old Boy of the Year at Cranbrook. It was completely unlikely, so I was suspicious of it. That was when my stepmother's Will was being brought down in favour of the school to a large degree, so it's like I've got to look like a sap because I was so very unlikely to be an Old Boy of the Year. I had been nominated by someone who is a nice person and it was a bone fide nomination but I can't stand that official level at school. They have come to tolerate me because I've endured. It's been a long hard haul to get an artist in there!' [1]

Said Roslyn, 'Martin was in a bit of a slump. He didn't know how he was going to work his future. Dorothy's Will - where he expected he was going to get his father's inheritance – really shook him. It definitely took years off his life. He became an expert on the law. He looked for things that people would have given up on a long time before. Like anything he got into, he really delved deeply – religion, Aborigines, law, health, crime, Abe Saffron....!' [2]

Roslyn accompanied Martin to court when the verdict was delivered. She described it as a 'moral victory'. He called it a 'pyrrhic victory'. The magistrate ruled in favour of going back two Wills. Cousins were now included as beneficiaries. Contesting this verdict would have meant mustering the energy for another battle, re-structuring his finances and cancelling a major retrospective exhibition at Sydney Museum.

Said Roslyn, 'He was incredibly short of money, that's when I became more involved. He kept asking me to come over and was very concerned with what he should do with everything he had and trying to work out what was the best thing. He pealed back two Wills which meant all the cousins got an inheritance from Dorothy which they didn't get from the last Will she wrote. Martin did not benefit financially from that at all, he did it for a moral reason. He was passing a kidney stone at the time. He could hardly walk when he left, he was in so much pain.' [3]

Said Martin, 'I initially thought I could beat these lawyers over my stepmother's Will and then you realise that you can't unless you want to re-mortgage Wirian. I thought it was probably wiser to hang onto the house, get on with the show and luckily I did have that exhibition (Sydney Museum Retrospective) because I wouldn't have won anyway if I'd put that extra attention in. I did a lot of work on it – three years worth, studying law and lawyers.' [4]

Although Dorothy had no children of her own, she gave $20,000-$50,000 to 20 members of her extended family which allowed for a bequest for the writing of a Sharp family history, a gift to the emerging generation, the children of Martin's cousins. (5) Reading the accounts of each of his 15 cousins' lives gave Martin a sense of family, 'The effect of our family was like a bomb exploding and we – my cousins and me - were the shrapnel of this powerful collision. And we spun off further. Now we're trying to swim backwards and pick up some of the pieces from the explosion.' [6]

Speculatively, Martin and his cousins may well be descendents of passionate slave abolitionist, Granville Sharp (1735-1813). If so, the painting titled 'The Sharp Family' by Johan Zoffany in London's National Portrait Gallery features 13 of Martin's antecedents. Knowing none of this when growing up, Martin was filling in the gaps, 'No one ever said to me, "you come from a great family who did all these things". I only found out when this family history was written. It gave me a sense of my own history'. [7]

*

Go back to the mid-60s when Martin placed an ad: 'Wanted Nude Model for a Martin Sharp collage'. A girl called Linda applied, did the shoot, got paid $40, got taken to lunch and that was that.

Not quite.

Linda became a lawyer and married Roland Gumbert, another lawyer. They lived in Oxford Falls, raised a family and after living in Sydney for 40 years they decided to move to a country town. They saw an ad for an early-19th Century homestead for sale in Goulburn NSW. Two days later they won the bidding, bought the property but what to do the place? They weren't farmers. They didn't want to run a bed and breakfast place. And - although the place seemed to suit a gallery - they didn't have a background in the arts.

'Maybe we should speak to Martin Sharp about how to open a fine art gallery,' Linda surmised, remembering the photo shoot. Too shy to phone, Linda wrote him, '...you wouldn't remember me but we're starting a gallery...' etc. Martin rang back and said, 'I remember you really well and still have the photos – come over'. And that's how South Hill Gallery started.

South Hill Gallery is a big homestead with a barn, shearing shed and heritage-listed chookyard. The homestead spills into a 4-room gallery, one of which the Gumberts turned into a museum celebrating Martin's art. With the Gulpilil street banners as the curtains, posters and prints hang on all walls, OZ magazines are on display and another glass cabinet is full of Martin's badges, postcards, illustrated books, LP and CD covers, letters and lots of Tiny Tim stuff. [8]

Martin accepted the Gumbert's request to become Gallery's patron. He reckoned it was a great role – 'you don't have to do anything' although Martin contributed a good deal more than just lending his name. He drew the gallery's logo, contributed museum items, signed beautiful fulsome autographs and encouraged other Yellow Housers to support the gallery too. In time, Dick Weight, Reg Mombassa, Max Cullen, Jon Lewis, Roger Foley, William Yang and Jim Anderson would exhibit in the gallery. Sandy Gutman would perform there as Austen Tayshus. Peter Royles – an original Yellow Houser who lived in Goulburn - was resident muso at the Yellow House get-togethers, which essentially comprised the Class of '72 - Tim Lewis, Jon Lewis, Roger Foley, Greg Weight, Michael Bell, Michael Glasheen, Garry Shead and others.

After spending six months traveling through the atolls of Kiribati, Jon presented 46 photographic images portraying the vibrant culture of these islands being devastated by storm surges and freakish waves. In October 2010 Martin launched Jon's exhibition *Portraits from the Edge, Kiribati* at the South Hill Gallery. Gary Shearston sang and Jon responded with a generous speech. He summed up the experience, 'There was a Yellow House feel to it'. Guests suggested that if anywhere had continued the Yellow House spirit, it was this place. On his return Martin checked straight into hospital where he was admitted for pneumonia. Horrified this happened immediately after his opening, Jon said, 'Martin was ill again and I hope it wasn't because of me wanting his endorsement! The day, as I recall, was cold.' [9]

Martin saw the upside, 'Pneumonia had a silver lining - being able to keep people away a bit, not go out and stuff like that. I'd rather just stay here and get on with my work because either it's worth something or it's not worth anything. And when you're not feeling good it doesn't seem that it's worth anything.' (10)

Justin Martell was a young filmmaker from Connecticut USA who contacted Martin because he wanted to write a biography of Tiny Tim. He was young – too young to remember Tiny during the 60s. Who was this guy? He came out of nowhere. There had always been a regular string of writers trying to get to Martin by feigning interest in Tiny. Was Justin just one of those? Dave checked, but webmaster Ernie Clark didn't know him, neither did Bucks Burnett. Dave couldn't find out much either, except that Justin was in his early-20s, had never met Tiny and claimed to be fascinated by everything he'd heard.

Over the next six months everyone hemmed and hawed whenever Justin's project was mentioned, then suddenly it was all go. Justin convinced Martin that he wanted to write a proper biography, not just a quickie. Martin agreed to a taped telephone interview and, in a moment of excitement, he even wanted to fly Justin to Sydney, put him up in Wirian and grant him access to the tapes, press clippings, the lot. Justin interviewed Martin and Dave. Writing the bio was a long project, his book *Eternbal Troubadour, the Improbable Life of Tiny Tim* was published in 2016. Along with the author's mother, the bio was dedicated to Martin and Ernie, neither of whom lived to see the final product. (11)

While Martin's health held out, life at Wirian continued much as before. Robert Tilley lived downstairs and continued lecturing at tertiary institutions. Terry Stanton and Stephen Darmody lived in the house and helped fix the place up. Martin attending opening nights, continued his own projects and bought a few more books. A facsimile edition of Vincent van Gogh's handwritten letters (in French) of 485 hand-numbered copies was for sale ($300) in a secondhand bookshop in Hornsby. Martin got someone to buy it for him. 'It brings you one step closer to the artist,' he explained. Maggie moved into Jack Thompson's Gearins Hotel Katoomba for six weeks before coming back. Wendy also left around this time and Dave came back and compiled what he and Martin dubbed Tiny's *New York Apartment Tapes*. Martin said, 'I'm just progressing with Tiny. I keep holding these things together, growing them. It's good *Chameleon* got out. Satoshi did his best but it was quite painful getting the CDs out. I don't think they've gone out far enough!' The royalty statement from Zero Records listed sales as: *Chameleon* - 418, *Wonderful World of Romance* – 352 and *Stardust* - 374. (12)

Julien Temple's *The Eternity Man* is a one-hour film/opera about Arthur Stace. Composed in 2004 it was released to DVD and general viewing five years later. Poet, Dorothy Porter's libretto was set to music and played by a grand 25-piece orchestra, which evoked the opposite of Stace's humble background. (13) Martin disliked opera as the chosen medium, 'I didn't see Arthur as an operatic character,' he said. 'I don't think that's the form for him. There's something to be said for a popular song as opposed to operatic. I think (actor) Christa Hughes was very good but I don't think they've actually "got" Arthur. It was a quite dramatic piece but it didn't have a Christian viewpoint - although it showed a lot of stuff from Luna Park.' [14]

Martin had his own opportunity to make a statement when a retrospective exhibition of his pictures was held at the Museum of Sydney in the heart of the city. There were at least 120 works displayed in chronological order from left to right. A grand piano was in the room for anyone to play and the Tiny Tim film was on constant screening. It came across as a kinetic art piece and, as such, was well received. Former Premier Neville Wran launched the show, giving a summary his involvement in the first trial of OZ. Wran's wife, businesswoman, Jill Hickson also made a speech. And Maggie recited some poems. Then it was all on. Like all Martin's openings, 'everyone' was there - scrunched against the walls, checking out pictures and posters from his earliest to his most recent. Martin sat quietly near the entrance, sipping wine and chatting to a queue of guests waiting to shake his hand and tell him how much they'd enjoyed his work.

Sydney Morning Herald reviewer, John Macdonald wrote about it, 'With the current show, Ace Bourke is credited as the exhibition coordinator, but can anybody coordinate Sharp? The show gives the impression it is largely self-curated – a rambling visual autobiography on shocking blue walls that takes us from the artist's days at Cranbrook, through the swinging 60s in Sydney and London and finally to the seclusion of the family home in Bellevue Hill where all Sharp's fondest obsessions have been incubated'. [15]

After the grand opening, Martin attended the exhibition as often as he could, usually sitting in the outside coffee shop area and greeting people on their way in. Martin reckoned, 'The Sydney Museum exhibition did a lot of good. I guess it did the trick – did the job. I almost cancelled. The people there were excellent. They weren't scared of any images. They were very supportive. There was enough there to baffle most people. My framer was a great help. I didn't have a bean at the time. I was hoping to get some money in from the settlement of the estate but they held that off for as long as they good.' [16]

A terrible November day: Nick Waterlow and daughter 37-year old Cloe Heuston were found dead of multiple stab wounds in her Randwick home. Waterlow had curated *Larrikins of London* and helped research Martin's Museum of Sydney exhibition. In a bid to repair their fractured relationship, Chloe invited her brother Anthony to a dinner at her house. Their father Nick was there too, as well as Chloe's three children. The meal had barely started when Anthony, a paranoid schizophrenic with a history of violent behaviour, took a carving knife from the kitchen and killed his father and sister. He then walked out of the front door and along Clovelly Road, his shirt covered with blood. Anthony was on the run for three weeks. In 2011 he was found not guilty of murder by reason of mental illness. Martin kept the press clippings and pinned a picture of Nick on his noticeboard. [17]

'How'd you like to spend Christmas on Christmas Island?' were the words to one of the songs on *Christmas in the Heart*, a Dylan album of hymns, carols and popular Christmas songs. News: December 2010, 48 asylum-seekers died off the coast in what became known as the 'Christmas Island boat disaster' when the boat they were in smashed against nearby cliffs. Martin saw Dylan's song as a pointer to that event. Although Martin had gone right off Dylan, Dylan's earnest rendition of *Little Town of Bethlehem* brought him back, though not enough to buy tickets when Dylan came out in 2011. Asked if he'd be going to the concert, Martin replied, 'This time he can come and see me'. [18]

Martin was interested in other singers too. One day he reckoned he had 'cracked' the mystery of Susan Boyle, a star contestant on the TV show Britain's Got Talent. He said, 'Susan Boyle was a major encouragement. She's like the voice of the Magdalene in the modern world. I wouldn't have thought of that if I hadn't been through all the experiences of Luna Park, the boys and the Magdalene Church. Her name is Susan Magdalene Boyle – a saint's name. I pricked up my ears at that. Through the name comes the connection. Initially Magdalene becomes the first disciple, the first Christian, though she's not generally attributed to that position. I've got Susan Boyle's first CD. I bought it at the Post Office and began to listen to it. Also there was a very good interview where she comes out with a statement that her sister was trying to stop her going in the singing competition, "you'll ruin the reputation of the family…" and "you'll bring disgrace on us all…!" Anyway, through hearing that her name is Magdalene and how serious she is about her faith, I started to listen to the album and – to me, at any rate – I felt that album was like Magdalene was speaking through her in the present day. She was telling her story from the inside, using the language of popular song, songs you wouldn't expect. I didn't think of it until I realised her name was Magdalene and then I started to listen to it.

'When she made that performance, which went round the world like a tidal wave of some sort – I watched it and was very impressed. And the back story - the courage she had, the promise to her mother to make something of her singing, and the battle with her sister and others trying to stop her from making a fool of herself. She made terrible mistakes, she couldn't find the venue, she was late, she fell over when she got there and it was only by the skin of her teeth that she managed to get out there and sing. Something happened as soon as she opened her mouth and sang those first lines. I read in that Joseph Campbell book "where the world turns" – she turned the world when she opened her mouth. And out of nowhere! Incredible! *I Dreamed a Dream* – she dreamed a dream!'

'Susan Boyle was stopped from singing *Perfect Day* to the Pope and the Queen. It was the first time the Pope had had an official tour of England for 600 years or something. She was going to sing that (and maybe *St Francis' Prayer* was the other song she was going to sing). She was ready to go with it and Lou Reed was attributed to stopping her. I listened to it in the light that she was going to sing it to the Pope and the Queen: "You're going to reap just what you sow…" for everyone, even the Queen! Apparently she was devastated that permission was refused her to sing *Perfect Day*. Maybe the protocol stopped her singing it to them - Lou Reed might have been the excuse. I think she sang *I Dreamed a Dream* for the Queen and the Pope. I thought she was very courageous. And through Luna Park comes the connection to the Magdalene Church Rose Bay where they had the Memorial Mass for the four boys in the fire. It's the only Magdalene Church in Sydney. It's a rare name. So it's a powerful, more romantic presence in the Christian story. [19]

After 40 years in Walker Lane Paddington, Clive Evatt closed the Hogarth Galleries and consigned its contents for auction. He opened the gallery in 1972 and after 40 years he and his wife no longer had the energy to oversee day-to-day operations. Among the pictures being auctioned was Martin's *Eternity Haymarket*. The Australian newspaper photographed Martin touching up the original. [20]

Rachel Kohn did a radio interview with Martin titled 'The Spiritual Vision of Martin Sharp'. She handled the interview sensitively, which encouraged Martin to open up on pet subjects. About Luna Park he said, 'I loved Luna Park but it was a Moloch Temple disguised as a funfair. You can expand it to include Hollywood and Las Vegas and places like this. The Beast rules these places. You see it for instance in the roulette wheels which are central to casinos. The numbers of the roulette wheel add up to 666, the number of the Beast in the Book of Revelation. These patterns are there.'

About Tiny, 'He wasn't a churchgoing person but he certainly kept the Bible very handy. He taught me a lot about religion. He did teach me about Christianity. I wondered why he had such a great attitude even though he was dropped from the peak of show business. I wondered where his good cheer came from. He was quoting scriptures often.'

And about Aboriginal matters, 'I think God put Aboriginal people here first - for a reason. It makes sense to me but we should try to understand what that reason is and treat them with the respect they deserve.' To which Rachel Kohn replied, 'Well Martin, I think God put you here for a reason – for us to look at these things and contemplate the spiritual and all the sinister dimensions, the underbelly of Sydney and to not be blind to them and not be unconcerned about them'. [21]

*

At the start of 2011, Marianne Faithfull slipped quietly in-and-out of Australia with no concerts and no media. She came for a holiday during the course of which she shared the demo tracks of her forthcoming album 'Horses and High Heels' with Martin. The song titled *Eternity* is one of her own compositions. Martin's *Remo Eternity* print hung in her Paris apartment and although she never dedicated the song to Martin and he never claimed it, his print was surely an inspiration behind the song.

Robert Tilley was still living at Wirian as well as Steve Darmody. Maggie was around. Shane (from Broome) and Lisa his assistant took photos of Maggie for screen tests and they also photographed Martin painting *Curiosity in Her Own Country*. Richard got Martin to sign a small stack of OZ prints for a forthcoming exhibition. Willy de la Vega still called in, so did his niece Chi. Louise Ferrier and Albie Thoms called in too, reminiscing the Museum of Sydney exhibition, for which Martin had sometimes turned to them for advice. Garry and his new partner Rose called in with gozlemé. Marilyn was handling Martin's bookkeeping. Harmonie's sister Anna stayed at Wirian with her friend Heidi. It was not unusual to find indigenous people from The Block in the Inner Sanctum, often sitting silently. Carol Barossa from South America was in-and-out, cleaning, helping, bringing drinks. Dave worked on *The Kitchen Tapes* – tapes of Tiny singing in the Wirian kitchen circa 1974. He reckoned he could hear Martin straining for breath after the shortest exertion. There was a new Tiny Tim release, a CD called *I've Never Seen A Straight Banana*. [22] With Tiny's new music playing in the background, Martin happily remarked that the place was running like an internal Yellow House.

Martin always had an ever-changing group of confidants. Up to the mid-90s it was always the late night drop-in crowd. This changed when Martin started getting sick. There were no more all night sessions, in fact Martin often had an afternoon kip, leaving guests alone in his Inner Sanctum to flick through some book left on the table, like a history of Steinway pianos because Martin had been approached to paint one. He didn't do it because they wanted something that resembled *Disraeli Gears* whereas he had something else in mind.

Richard and Martin talked through plans for the future of Wirian, which seemed to be a 'museum' of sorts. When Martin stopped eating, Richard asked Dave to keep him informed, 'But I don't live there…!' Dave complained. Richard often visited Wirian, invariably with interesting gossip. Like, having had supper with Geoffrey Robertson whom he described as 'getting pompous, like a high court judge'. He also told Martin about Julian Assange. He reckoned he was great on technology but unable to handle the public sex stuff. After getting Martin to sign a Mick Jagger OZ print, Richard offered to go out and get some food. Martin reluctantly considered eating fried prawns. When Richard returned, he settled in with Martin and watched all three hours and 38 minutes of Prince William's wedding to Kate Middleton.

Martin's health declined even further. He stopped accepting calls, and visitors were kept away. Russell organised a Japanese girl to work as his cleaner and when that didn't work out he got him Andrea (Andy) Warrell who had worked for their Aunt Elizabeth. Roslyn said, 'Martin was impossible to look after. One cleaner got sacked because he didn't like the noise of a vacuum cleaner. But Andy is very strong-minded, she organises people's lives but she has to do it her way. Martin and her would argue all the time about how things were done. She was working out a strategy to keep him fed.' (23)

Despite declining health, Martin continued producing new works, like the poster for *World AIDS Day*, which became a t-shirt produced by Josef Lebovic Gallery. He also encouraged young artists. One afternoon three Year 12 Cranbrook students - Steven, George and Joe (the son of Todd Hunter, bass player for the band Dragon) - called in to show Martin their visual diaries. Martin stopped what he was doing and gave them as much time as they needed.

OZ that Never Was

Mojo is a popular music magazine published monthly in the United Kingdom with a circulation of around 75,000 and available from all newsagencies. The periodical features Classic Rock acts and regularly includes CDs that tie in with a magazine article or theme. In covering the 60s phenomenon, the editors decided to run a feature about the underground 60s press. They contacted Richard and proposed an OZ magazine insert inside the regular magazine. This was to be a 16-page 'Best Of' centrepiece combined with new material.

Jim Anderson and Richard met in Martin's Inner Sanctum where OZ to create one final OZ, with Martin on hand to assist. 'I'm keeping out of it', said Martin, who had other things on his mind. He'd been invited to participate in a panel discussion for artist Robert Crumb's Australian tour, though he didn't feel well enough to accept. (The tour was cancelled.) Jim had other things on his mind too. He was moving his current Redfern exhibition to South Hill Gallery. Richard was enthusiastic. He and Jim covered the table with blank pages, which they proceeded to fill up with ideas. Felix wouldn't (or 'couldn't') be involved but gave them permission for them to publish his poems. Martin contributed *A Curiosity in her Own Country* and his 'Give us this day our daily bread' b/w anti-pokies OZ-toon of money pouring from a one-armed bandit into a punter's gullet.

After working all afternoon, Martin got testy with Jim, so he and Richard withdrew. Jim said, 'When we were doing mini-OZ/Mojo and Martin was ill. We decided we'd go to my place where we'd work for the rest of the day.' (24) Richard and Julie were staying in Bondi at the time, where Richard planned to work an all-nighter. Jim did the same. They finished around midnight.

Richard and Julie hurried home with some urgency because the lead story on the TV News was 100kph winds in Blackheath, which did a lot of damage, but Happy Daze was okay. Trees and branches were down everywhere, so Richard loaded up his vehicle and delivered a load of ironbark to Wirian so that Martin could light the fire in the Inner Sanctum. When mini-OZ hadn't been published by November, Richard checked with the editors who said they'd postponed it until May of the following year. But it never happened. Martin didn't care. Said Dave, 'Martin wasn't keen on the project in the first place. It was like he was be-ing pushed into doing something he didn't want to do and you couldn't do that with Martin.' (25)

Getting Martin to sign anything was always easy, except contracts. He autographed everything put in front of him, the Yellow House *Catalog*, Tiny Tim records, posters, old copies of Peter Draffin's *Pop*, and Craig Macgregor's *People, Politics and Pop*. One afternoon Martin signed a stack of prints for Richard. He just sat, smoked and signed as Richard placed each one in front of him and replaced it with another. With contracts though, Martin was cautious. One day he said, 'You should never take a publisher's advance – because then you've got to deliver the book!' With contracts Martin usually had the same objection, the subsidiary rights – the add-ons.

There were always plenty of offers. Like a well-respected Rock journalist who approached Martin with an offer to release a boxed set of Tiny Tim CDs, but the small print included a promotional documentary. Martin reckoned the boxed set was the 'bait' - the doco was what they really wanted, 'but they don't realise the amount of disruption the presence of a film crew causes to one's work'. [26] Martin was always wary of feigned interest in Tiny as a way of getting to him.

Blue Pie Records is a multi-national digital music company with a presence in Australia, USA, UK, Ireland, China and Canada. Dave had been negotiating Tiny's music with Damien from Blue Pie and Damien had been coming over in the evenings and cooking meals for Martin. The original agreement was straightforward, then Martin gained the impression that Blue Pie was getting a stranglehold on Tiny from all his material, plus they were negotiating with Justin Martell to publish the Tiny Tim biography. 'Does Justin know that Blue Pie has never pub-lished a book before?' Martin questioned. However, Dave's negotiations meant Martin would get a few cents off each track whereas at the moment, he was getting zip. Martin wanted to revert to the original agreement, which was the Chameleon album only. He felt the add-ons in the contract had grown with time - Disraeli Gears t-shirt rights, 10 more points like that. Plus he was unhappy with the ac-companying booklet because he felt the writer had gleaned the information about both Tiny and Martin from nothing more than Wikipedia. Dave's great disap-pointment, after a lot of hard work putting together an online digital-download distribution deal, Martin pulled the plug on the Blue Pie deal.

Dave was incensed, 'Martin didn't want to go ahead with it. He was trying to pull out of this but we'd already struck a deal. We'd agreed to do the download. The project was ready to roll. So to appease Martin, Damien said, "Let's call it *Chameleon* but we'll change the track listing so it's not the original album. We'll put *I Love Rock N Roll* on it as well." So we changed the track listing and released it. It's set up in Martin's account. At least we got it out on iTunes!' Phew. [27]

One July night, Jason Holman whizzed Martin to hospital with a problem with his right side. Not pneumonia, not a stroke, not the lungs, not the heart – this time Martin was diagnosed with dehydration and malnutrition. Dehydration and malnutrition are sicknesses caused by neglect. Friends were concerned. They started discussing some sort of system to keep Martin fed.

Then came news of two deaths. Following a long illness, Martin's *Disraeli Gears* collaborator, photographer Robert Whitaker, died in England. Margaret Olley was closer to home. Greg was the last of Martin's friends to see her. He was photographing her latest canvases for her next show. As he was loading the last painting into his car, she stopped him and said, 'Not that one. I want to do a bit more on it. Come back tomorrow at 2.00.' Next morning Greg received a phone call to say that she had died during the night. Greg hurried to her house and recorded her workspace before anything was moved. (Greg's 'Photographic Studies from the Studio of Margaret Olley' was exhibited at Australian Galleries in 2012.)

Knowing Martin had the facilities and an assistant (Dave) who could change recording formats, a friend of Margaret's, Philippa Drynan, called in with an ABC radio interview with Margaret, snippets of which she wanted extracted to play at her funeral service. [28] Martin and Dave helped Philippa choose the segments and Dave did the transfer. Martin suggested her saying, 'I'd liked to be remembered for helping people'. Margaret Olley's private funeral was held at Northern Suburbs Cemetery.

Sixty years after Justin O'Brien won the inaugural the Blake Prize, Martin's picture *Stranger in her Own Country* (renamed 'Madonna') was short-listed among the finalists for the Blake. Sadly, the judges' decision marked the triumph of conceptual art over Art. It ruined the hope of Martin winning on the anniversary of his art teacher's triumph. Instead, the winner was Khaled Sabsabi whose work was a 90-minute video presentation on three TV monitors, showing a group of Sufi Muslims practicing communal chants and prayers.

Sydney Morning Herald art critic John McDonald wrote, 'Around 1999 the prize went to a crypt and was reborn the following year as an award for "spiritual" rather than "religious" art. At this point the floodgates were thrown open. Soon the prize was full of dumb abstracts, dull landscapes, oblique photos, aimless videos and every other permutation of contemporary art'. [29] When Rachel Kohn featured art critic McDonald on her radio program he reiterated his thoughts that the Blake was no longer 'religious art', just art that the artist had decided to vaguely label as 'spiritual'. When asked which pieces deserved to be there, Martin's picture was the first that he named.

Martin's health continued to decline. Then his dog, Imelda, died, 'the only one who cared for me when I was sick' said Martin. He painted, re-read *The Territorial Imperative* by Robert Ardrey, because there were tensions in the Wirian kitchen, where Martin was feeling banished by his own tenants. By October Martin's health got worse and he was trying to keep quiet about it. He stopped smoking, this time for keeps. Russell stepped in and told guests that Martin wasn't well enough to take visitors. Angelica started helping in an official capacity. Roslyn made more frequent visits. She was on a high because her 'Breakfast at Sweethearts' photo (from her Kings Cross series) was blown up on the big screen at a Cold Chisel concert. Martin was pleased for her. He liked the boys from Cold Chisel.

By November, Martin ill health was common knowledge. There was no 'keeping it quiet'. Radio presenter Philip Adams talked about it on his radio program. In the same week Martin returned to hospital. Again he said he was 'okay' – whatever that meant. So he came home briefly, then went back for another fortnight. 'I took him to a lot of doctors and tests in those first six months', said Angelica. [30]

When Martin came back he was put on an oxygen mask and he could no longer go upstairs. A four-poster single bed was moved into the Inner Sanctum in the corner where the sound system used to be. Metal supports were installed in the downstairs toilet and Angelica, Roslyn, Gria and Fairlie Kingston were rostered to take care of Martin. [31]

17.
STAYIN' ALIVE

Tiny was a major inspiration to Martin and everyone thought that was really funny. But I thought no, the substance was Tiny - and it always was.
Dave Rowe

Martin was on a leash. He could go no further than the length of the oxygen tube that tethered him in his Inner Sanctum where he spent most of his time anyway. Martin had a form of blood cancer known as myeloma, which develops in white blood cells. Symptoms include bone pain, frequent infections, excessive thirst, nausea and weight loss. Although the recovery rate was higher than it had ever been, myeloma was not considered curable. [1]

Said Roslyn, 'It's a precursor to leukaemia - nothing to do with smoking. It was terrible. White blood cells stop infections and the red blood cells take the oxygen around. The oxygen being taken around Martin's body was compromised by emphysema and a bad heart. So the blood was not doing its job. That's why Martin had to have blood transfusions.' [2]

Every Wednesday, until he could no longer leave his bed, Martin was wheeled into St Vincent's Hospital where he would undergo a full blood transfusion. He often invited friends along for company. Tim was one, 'Martin was always glad to see me. I went there during his illness and this lovely lady walked down the driveway and said, "Who are you?" It was Lin Utzon. I was in tears. I said, "I'm Tim". She said, "He's having a transfusion in the hospital, come with me". So I went with her.' [3]

Martin would not engage professional healthcare. He preferred the assistance of friends and family who worked out a roster between themselves. That's how Martin wanted things to run. Angelica was rostered three days per week but was also on 24-hour call. She lived with husband Davy Alan in the Sydney suburb of Moorebank, a full 45-minute drive from Wirian, so Angelica had a big job. She also wheeled Martin around in his wheelchair when he went out, which was less and less.

'Angelica looked after him three days a week,' said Roslyn. 'She would come in the afternoon and stay until she was picked up. Angelica would also come if there was a special appointment that no one could take Martin to when he became sick. She would do the extra things and then at the end of his life she stayed more. Martin had his public life and he had his private life. He didn't have to put on a show with Angelica and I'm glad he had that comfort. Andrea would come in two days, look after him and clean the house. Fairlie Kingston would come in and Gria Shead would come in as well. I would do Sundays.' [4]

Other help came from Jubilee the cleaner, Ella Walker (Roma's daughter, ie. Martin's nanny when he was four) and lots of other friends, some of whom would bring food, sit around, talk or read to him. Luke was one of those. Jonny too. Sometimes Steve Darmody took over. Neighbour, Dr John Gregory Roberts was another regular. He had attended Cranbrook School with Martin and took Martin out to dinner once a month. When Martin could no longer go out, he brought the meals to Martin. [5]

Visitors came and went. They were vetted by Martin's respective 'gatekeepers' but at the start of his bedridden phase they called in unannounced, as they had always done. As Martin's mobility became restricted, certain 'friends' started helping themselves to items around the house, ('Oh, I lent Martin that, etc,') necessitating the closing of certain rooms.

Wirian was seeping around the edges. Tighter management was required, so Roslyn and cousin Sandy Sharp stepped in. 'Crazy things were happening,' said Roslyn. (Like a rumour that went around that Wirian was on the market. Cranbrook School picked up on it. Their lawyer contacted Martin's lawyer only to find it was untrue.) Roslyn continued, 'Some weird texts were going around offering Wirian for sale for $9 million. That's when we had to say, "enough's enough!" Martin asked me to do the Power of Attorney (POA). I said, "No, I reckon you should use Sandy and Marilyn…" because Marilyn had done his books and Sandy would be absolutely loyal to Martin. I took on his Guardianship. That was all set up 18 months before Martin died.' Martin's Will was dated 20 September 2012.

'Martin had the added anxiety about worrying about money on his deathbed. He was getting the interest of his stepmother's estate while he was alive - and it was a lot of money (after he died that went to Cranbrook and St Paul's College). I said, "How come you have no money Martin?" It turned out that they hadn't been sending the income. I said, "I'll ring up Hugh Massie…" (Hugh Massie was an executor of Dorothy's estate and would have been horrified.) Martin agreed with that. All I had to do was email Hugh Massie and say, "Hugh, if there's any money send it immediately".' [6]

Projecting into his own future, Martin's thoughts went straight to the Wirian. 'You think, "My god, how much am I going to get finished before Rookwood Cemetery?" Wirian is quite difficult to maintain, just to keep it good and let it hopefully flow on. It's a great old house. It's done some interesting things in its time. You don't know what happens in the future – the attitudes of the school or whatever. I see Wirian as quite a scholastic place in its way. But I realise what a controversial subject Tiny is and Luna Park. Boy! [7] I've felt at times - when I've seen it clearly - that the Wirian is the work of art, the whole place and all its ingredients make sense.' [8]

In the past, Martin had often projected that Wirian might be a Tiny Tim/Luna Park university. But before the year was out, it was Martin himself who received the honour. The University of Sydney conferred on him an honorary doctorate, making him Dr Martin Ritchie Sharp OA, Doctor of Visual Arts. At the graduation ceremony held in the Great Hall, the Chancellor Her Excellency Professor Marie Bashir (Governor of New South Wales) conferred the degree.

The opening words of the citation read, 'Chancellor, it gives me great pleasure to commend Martin Sharp to you for admission to the degree of Doctor of Visual Arts. As an artist, cartoonist, songwriter and film-maker he has distinguished himself through his outstanding contribution to the visual arts and his creative achievement in Australian and international culture since the early 60s and he is hailed as Australia's foremost Pop artist.' Clothed in a professorial hat and gown, Martin eased himself out of his wheelchair to accept the degree. [9]

Martin's condition worsened and he was readmitted to hospital. (He was admitted a total of 97 times.) His plight caught the attention of the Governor-General of Australia. With a film crew trailing her, Governor-General Quentin Bryce visited St Vincent's Hospital. There a Sister of Charity informed her that Martin was a patient. She had always wanted to meet Martin. This was organised and the meeting photographed. Lying in his bed and breathing from his oxygen unit, Martin showed Quentin Bryce a Hokusai sketchbook.

Christmas can be a tough time for people requiring healthcare, often with only emergency staff on deck. Australians party, cook BBQ prawns, sip wine, attend family gatherings and bestow gifts on eager grandkids. Most medics go on holiday. So Christmas Day was tough on Martin, who needed help. This alerted Roslyn and Angelica to the seriousness of looking after him at all times.

In January Roslyn wrote, 'Martin has been very sick but is making slow progress. It has been very difficult not having medical help available over the Christmas break. His medical people are around again now. Martin is still not answering the phone but he does listen to his messages when he's up to it. It has been a rough time having him so sick but he is a joy in so many ways to look after as he is determined to get better.' [10]

Martin turned 70 in January. The Aboriginal flag flying above St Vincent's Hospital was Martin's gift to them. He also gave a print of *Pentecost* to the West-mead Children's Hospital. In February, Martin wrote, 'As I sit here at my table in my studio at Wirian surrounded by the pieces of my life, in this physical feebleness at the beginning of my seventieth year I wonder about the mystery of life… not for the first time, and probably not the last, but there will be a last time. It is not too far away. I am feeble in my body so I very much live in this room, a tube brings me oxygen. My friends bring me food. In these words I hold on to life. I am not ready to leave. I have things to do before I go, God willing! 5.00am.' (11)

A segment on the ABC television program, the *7.30 Report*, left no doubt about the gravity of Martin's condition. He was skinnier than anyone had ever seen him, breathing through his oxygen machine and he appeared frightened. Martin was filmed lying in his bed in his Inner Sanctum with Garry sketching him in the style of Dr Gachet's drawing of Vincent on his deathbed. Garry had often sketched Martin but never like this. Having decided to paint Martin's portrait again (he did so in 1986) Garry entered his *Martin Sharp and His Magic Theatre* in the Archibald Prize. It was a picture of a white-bearded Martin with piercing eyes, Luna Park glowing in the background and figurines to the fore: Ginger Meggs, Popeye, Mo (Roy Rene), Jiminy Cricket, Mickey Mouse, Tiny Tim and Eadweard Muybridge's little running men.

Said Garry, 'I drew Martin when I decided to do the painting. When I heard that he was sick, I thought I needed to be there to see him. I didn't think he was going to last that long and the painting just flowed out. I did some studies and when I came back everything fell into place. Greg took a lot of photos I was able to use.' (12)

The Governor of New South Wales Marie Bashir saw that program and was startled by Martin's condition since she had last seen him. 'What can we do to help this national treasure?' she questioned. Bashir wanted to ensure Martin was getting the best health care, especially when told of the neglect that he experienced around Christmas. She organized a banquet at Government House for Martin and his retinue: Martin, Roslyn, their Aunt Elizabeth, Fairlie and Peter Kingston, Garry and Gria Shead, Luke Sciberras, Lin and Mika Utzon, Lucy Neville, Julie Clark, Angelica, Jenny Poidevin, Maggie Walsh, Lois Cook and King Des (Barnes), allegedly Edward VIII's illegitimate son. Angelica took a lot of photos and made a splendid album recording the occasion. Before dashing off to meet-and-greet the Israel ambassador, Bashir discussed Martin's estate with him, especially with regard to the future of continuing Wirian as an art place. (13)

When it got out that Martin was so ill he was inundated with phone calls. People just kept dropping in. Many were turned away because he didn't have the energy for them but some long-term friends got through. Dr Pepper (David Pepperall) visited from Melbourne. Victoria Cobden made contact. Martin tried to reach out too, to Miss Tulip, Michael Chamberlain and others.

Beating back bad health, Martin continued taking on new projects. With Natalie Pratt and Kingo's assistance, he started a boxed set of prints – the *Schoolbook*

Series - based on the portraits he painted as a schoolboy. The boxes were to be individually covered with extracts from his school reports. Martin entered the *Gulpilil* portrait in the Archibald Prize. It was named among the finalists, as was Garry's portrait of Martin. Then Martin started a new picture – a big one - the 'Hendrix' picture - an image he'd previously painted twice as a poster-print. One image had Jimi playing left-handed, the second had him playing right-handed. Hendrix was a left-handed guitarist who played an upside-down right-handed guitar, which Martin found difficult to grasp.

'What type of guitar is that?' Martin asked. Answer: a Fender Stratocaster. 'What it's like upside down?' Martin acquired a small figurine of the instrument, about four inches in size, which he referred to as a check point. Roslyn saw the new *Hendrix* picture develop, 'Hendrix was a photo of the painting that he'd already done, he was painting over the top of it but it didn't look right. He didn't finish it. The paint did not work on photographic paper.' [14]

Martin had always punctuated conversations with music – whatever caught his ear - and always Tiny of course. Although he didn't play much music any more, he enjoyed Paul McCartney's new studio album, the cheekily titled *Kisses on the Bottom*. 'Like Tiny...' Martin reflected. The record comprised a dozen good-natured covers of traditional hits that read like a set-list from one of Tiny's marathons. Songs like *Ac-Cent-Tchu-ate the Positive, Sit Right Down and Write Myself a Letter, Always, Bye Bye Blackbird*, etc. [15]

Although Dave Rowe had given Martin a copy of *Elvis 30 #1 Hits*, Martin didn't play many Elvis songs. He wasn't playing much Tiny either. 'I haven't done anything for Tiny,' Martin rued, 'I had to put down that load'. Dave added, 'Martin would listen to those rambling Tiny Tim tapes while he painted. Maybe it was a bit crazy but he needed it for inspiration. People write off the Tiny connection with Martin but I think it's more relevant than anyone could possibly know. He needed that. The substance was Tiny and it always was. He would quote Tiny when I'd arrive in the morning, "Dave, listen to this bit..." and you'd sit there thinking, "Why is he playing this?"' [16]

Tiny was definitely the heart of the matter. Martin explained the importance of Tiny to Lin Utzon and Roslyn too. Roslyn said, 'Tiny and Luna Park were the two major things he talked about. He explained how Luna Park was about good/evil/religion and the moral compass of the city. He was quite lonely then. There weren't a lot of people dropping in.'

Friends were no longer sure where they would find Martin. Was he in bed or in hospital? Said Roslyn, 'He was so patient in hospital. Everybody loved looking after him because he was so polite and he didn't push his weight around. When he was going to hospital every six weeks or so, I'd say to the head nurse, "I know your beds are full but he will improve very quickly if he is put next to a window". He hated the food but towards the end he was loving the food.' [17] Located with an outside view, Martin sketched what he saw from his window, some of which were his last prints.

The honour that moved Martin most was conferred by the National Art School (East Sydney Tech) where he had studied in the early-60s, along with the old gang. It was where he met Peter Powditch, Jenny Kee, Garry Shead and so many others, sometimes not even at art school – but where the art students hung out. Martin described picking up the award, 'I reckon it was one of the greatest nights of my life! They were so good to me, I felt very at home, I felt very moved. I spoke about being at my old alma mater. I stood up to do it with my oxygen machine. I was pretty feeble but I was moved to tears by the citation and the atmosphere. I started off saying, "I left school, I didn't know what to do but it was Justin O'Brien my art teacher who told me Why don't you go to the National Art School? So I did. And here I am…" - and it went from there…' [18]

At one memorable Wirian gathering, everyone sat around a spread laid out on a table on the back porch. (The oxygen man was present to ensure that Martin had a long enough line-extension.) Steven, Angelica and Maggie sat with Martin outside while Natalie was computerising Martin's pictures inside. Cousin Katie's son Rupert Reid called in and sparked Martin up. As writer and director, Rupert was a finalist in the Tropfest short film festival for his short film *Boo* – a sardonic comment about death. Greg gave Martin a smaller oxygen inhaler and Martin presented a possum skin cloak to Maggie. There is great significance around the making and wearing of possum skin cloaks, which Martin understood when he honoured Maggie that afternoon. She responded by reciting her poems from memory. Then she got out her book and kept reciting. Martin happily exclaimed. 'This is exactly what Wirian is about!'

One of Angelica's hospital patients had given her a photograph depicting Henry Lawson (or someone playing him) drunkenly holding forth at Speaker's Corner at Sydney's Domain. It was a picture no one had seen before and Martin wanted to verify its authenticity. If genuine, he wanted to make an official release via the Mitchell Library. The Library had recently taken down Martin's *Tapestry* for cleaning, with plans to re-hang it two floors down.

After a long illness, art critic and fellow 'Larrikin of London', Robert Hughes died in New York in August. His best selling books include *The Shock of the New* (1980), *The Fatal Shore* (1986) and *Goya* (2006). Martin and Richard used to frequent Vadim's coffee lounge in the early-60s where Robert held court to admirers who clung on his every word. While between digs, Martin lived with him briefly in London. He laughingly recalled his mother meeting Robert and telling him, 'I can't understand a word you are saying. You are far too clever for me'. [19]

Albie Thoms died too. Albie - the pioneer underground filmmaker and cornerstone of the original Yellow House. The years had passed but his colleagues' high esteem remained unchanged. Said Tim, 'Everyone loved Albie. Jonny took a great shot of Martin and Albie standing outside the Mitchell Library arm-in-arm. They went there for a function and they were both dying of cancer. They had a wake for Albie at Paddington Town Hall. He was a very good writer. He wrote the book shortly before he died. His last thing was to write his book, *My Generation*'. (20)

Albie's memoir gave an inside look at the period when he and his peers were at the epicentre of Sydney's creative happenings. In his Foreword, he wrote, 'This is an account of the Counter-Culture in Sydney in the Sixties as I experienced it. Beginning in 1960 at Sydney University, where some of its ideas first emerged, it ends in 1972 with the election of the Whitlam government, pledged to deliver much of its program. In between are the efforts of a diverse group of people, most of whom had some sort of contact with one another, though they rarely acted in unison. They were, however, united in their opposition to censorship, conscription, cultural conservatism, racism, sexual discrimination and Australia's role in the Vietnam War.' (21)

Jeannie was another strong 60s voice. She released her *So U Want Blood* album to CD and gave Martin a copy to enjoy - he did the 'So U Want Blood' poster for her 1983 show. Since then, Jeannie had never stopped looking Martin up. Sometimes she'd sing to him. Other times they'd talk, 'One day when he was sick, Kingo brought over a DVD of James Michener who wrote a book about Hokusai. I knew nothing about Michener but we watched the interview. The day we were there Martin had bought the eight books of Hokusai's drawings and he showed us that. I came home so inspired so I wrote him a letter. I said, "Even when you're not well you give me inspiration when I come to see you!"' (22)

In February 2013 the Damien Minton Gallery in Redfern, held an Eternity-themed exhibition with Martin's big painting as its crowning glory. Enthroned in his wheelchair with his oxygen pack, Martin was wheeled in by Angelica. Guests queued to say hi and to be photographed with him. Martin told those people how well he felt and that – at last – he was on good terms with the school.

Held annually in Katoomba NSW, the Blue Mountains Music Festival marked OZ Magazine's 50th Anniversary by having Richie Walsh and Richard Neville interviewed as one of the featured acts. Martin's health made it inconceivable that he should accompany them. Anyway, he didn't feel Richie and Richard needed him. They were a self-contained lively 2-person act. They didn't even need the ABC interviewer – they bounced ideas off each other and knew all the feed lines. Richard had sold his OZ files to Yale University for a good price. As for the general public, as if too much OZ was barely enough, *The Australian* newspaper commemorated its 50th anniversary with a celebratory 3-part article spread over four days. (23)

Afterwards, Richard checked out the other acts. He was terribly impressed by Arlo Guthrie playing the Big Tent. 'How long has this been going on?' he asked. *The Blue Mountains Music Festival was in its 19th year and only 15 minutes drive from Happy Daze. How could Richard ask such a question?* Whispers were spreading that Richard was suffering from Alzheimer's Disease. Martin would have none of it. 'What's Alzheimer's!' he snapped, as if it was all fiction. (24)

When the documentary *The Sharp Edge - The Art of Martin Sharp* was televised on ABC-TV's Artscape program. Martin reckoned it was like watching one's own obituary – 'it almost killed me!' he exclaimed. Directed by Rebecca Baillie, a regular producer of *Australian Story* and the *7.30 Report*, the documentary followed Martin's artistic journey through the eyes of friends Julie Clarke, Richard Neville, Jenny Kee and Peter Kingston. Martin was not pleased. He felt they had been edited the wrong way. He was also annoyed to see himself portrayed as a smoker, having not smoked for eight months. Martin believed the program was scheduled for screening two months earlier and that they expected him to be dead when they screened it. [25]

Angelica overheard all this, 'I had a lot of feedback about *The Sharp Edge*. They said, "Why did they make it like an obituary?" We thought it was going to be about Martin's art but it's not, it's all about Martin's friends. He's been very brave. He doesn't smoke. He can't have smoke around him. In his spirit he's a lot better. He's had some very tough days. It's been hard for me, because I had to be there, just to be a support. The hardest part for me was watching how hard Martin struggled. People didn't understand that. People would get really mad at me at times because when someone is really sick, they can't handle talking to people. More questioning, more turning up, it exhausted him. It's just that he couldn't cope with it as well as fighting his body. People would understand in some respect. If you say "Please, not today" you're not offending them, it's just saying, "I've got to fight for my life right now".' [26]

In his room, Martin re-stoked his interest in the Kopson side of his family – the Fijian connection – and Angelica assisted him to source his family documents. He also read the Bobbie Hardy book, *Their Work Was Australian: The History of the Hudson Family*, which linked to the railroad side of his family. [27] He also enjoyed flicking through old copies of the *National Geographic* magazine, where he found pictures of wild prehistoric men and saw a parallel between them and the Minotaur photo of the boys at Luna Park.

Gary Shearston suffered a stroke at the end of June. Knowing it was his time to say goodbye Gary's attempted to contact Martin. But Martin didn't answer the phone that night because, as Angelica put it, 'Martin had his own battles'. [28] By the time Martin found the strength to return the call, Gary was gone. Said Garry Shead, 'Martin told me he received a message but didn't answer the phone. He must have picked it up the next day. It was Gary Shearston saying, 'I'd just love to talk to you Martin' and then he died that night.' [29]

The Yellow House premises in Macleay Street had been earmarked for development for several years. Downstairs was a smart restaurant called *Yellow* which was the venue chosen for a Yellow House Reunion, a gathering of the remaining troops and a celebration of their past. Martin sat hunched in a corner, sometimes struggling for breath as he called each Yellow House artist by name and awarded each person a certificate from the 'Ginger Meggs School of Arts' – they each accepted their certificate from Martin - George, Kingo, Peter Royles (who filmed the whole thing)...and so on. Certificates were inscribed with a personal message - 'friendship' being included alongside artistic achievements.

Martin struggled through that speech, reminding everyone that the Yellow House premises had always been an art-place. He name-checked Russell Drysdale, John Coburn, Terry and Thelma Clune. He commended George's *Yellow House Jalalabad* project. Martin closed with special mention to departed Yellow House friends like Peter Wright and Albie Thoms. He lifted his glass of short black coffee and proposed a toast. Before leaving, Martin autographed a brick on the outside of the building. In texta pen he wrote, 'This is a brick – 28.7.13' which the new owners have endeavoured to preserve. Using Marcel Duchamp logic, in signing the building, Martin declared the building a Found Object art piece and he claimed it. [30]

Returning to his Inner Sanctum, Martin worked on his enlarged version of De Chirico's *Song of Love*, a picture he'd developed with Tim Lewis in 1973 and never stopped working on. It had been exhibited several times as a work-in-progress, most notably in the Ivan Dougherty Gallery exhibition in 2006. [31] In his darkened room, with a shaft of light striking the picture, Martin scratched away at the hair on the picture that he would soon retitle 'Gracelands' and – with Peter filming him – Martin told the camera that the face was redolent of Elvis. Said Roslyn, 'He was changing the De Chirico one to make the face look more like Elvis. His last picture was for the Elvis show.' [32]

Held at Damien Minton Gallery Redfern, the 'Gracelands' exhibition was the last that Martin would attend. Like the Eternity exhibition, guests queued to talk to him as he sat confined to his wheelchair. The 'Elvis' billboard collage was exhibited and Martin sought Robert Wolfgramm's permission to reproduce a long extract from his sermon 'The King's King of Kings' in his explanatory letter to contributing artists. It was about Elvis's favourite Scripture, 1 Corinthians 13, about love. [33] In the display cabinet, Martin exhibited a framed transcript of the sermon alongside Robert's *Refugee* CD.

Many friends called to see Martin at home. Pop people like Peewee and Carla, Denny & Clare too. Martin suggested to Denny and Clare that they release his Tiny Tim tapes – particularly the talking tapes - through their Regal Records. Denny recalled, 'Martin would tape everything Tiny did, even his talks. Martin specifically said that he wanted us to take the Tiny Tim tapes so we could get them all out. We said we'd do that. He was also talking about all the dialogue he had on tape. I was thinking - "Hmm, that'll take a while…"'

Clare picked up the thread, 'He called us in to talk about that a couple of weeks before he died. He said he couldn't rest easy knowing they're not out there. We emailed back after that meeting and said "You can put it out on Regal Records if you want to and we'll see what we can do about editing them down". He was happy with that.' It was later suggested that Martin's entire collection of 1000 Tiny Tim tapes should be donated to the Smithsonian Institute, which has 19 museums and galleries across America. [34]

For her final year school Art project, Mic Conway and Roey Cook's daughter Tango chose to paint a 4-panel tribute to four artists: Martin, Reg Mombassa, Greg Weight and herself. Mic said, 'At that time Jeannie was having much more contact with Martin than me, so I said to Jeannie, "How do you feel about us going down, having fun with Martin, me singing to Martin, you singing with me as well and Tango doing drawings?" So that's what we did. Martin really enjoyed us coming around. Sometimes he was in bed and sometimes sitting up. The Cranbrook headmaster came over a couple of times when I was there. Martin was certainly happy to have this headmaster guy in there. Martin gave me and Tango a print (*Art Galaxy*). When I looked at it I asked him, "Can we use it on the CD?' He said, "Certainly, I'd love you to."' [35]

Jeannie explained too, 'Tango wanted to do a drawing so Mic and I came over and sang. (I'd already been singing there.) Mic and I did *Over the Rainbow, Singing in the Rain, Cheek to Cheek*, even Tiny Tim songs like *The Old Front Porch*. Even if I didn't know them to play I'd still sing them. Some of the songs from God Bless, or even The Second Album - *Down Virginia Way* and of course *Street of Dreams*.' [36]

And the Cranbrook headmaster, Nicholas Samson was another regular caller. Said Roslyn, 'Martin felt terribly responsible for what happened to Wirian right up to the end. He tried to do another deal with Cranbrook, they put a proposal and he didn't accept it. So he was resolving his issues with Cranbrook, maybe for pragmatic reasons to save Wirian but they couldn't come up with a deal that suited him. The headmaster was constantly dropping in. Martin wanted him there. I think he gave Martin comfort. I remember he would come over Sundays. When they first got to know each other their relationship was quite formal but they did get very close.' [37]

Martin was asked to judge the 2012 and 2013 Cranbrook art awards. 'He also created a sculpture for the school to be placed in the Chapel. It was his gift of love and the last piece of art that he did,' said Angelica. [38]

Wirian was in shutdown for the last two months of Martin's life. Joni Nelson, who had a regional radio program in Sydney's inner west decided to call Martin right out of the blue. She said, 'I decided I would try to get in touch with Martin Sharp. I found his phone number in the White Pages and just rang him up. He answered and I was nervous as hell. I thanked him for his work and we chatted about Tiny for a while. "He was one of Elvis' generation, a great performer," Martin said. "I'm still working with him." Eventually I told Martin I'd love to organise a screening of *Street of Dreams*, which I had just seen for the first time that day, and asked him if he'd like to come and introduce it. He seemed receptive but hesitant - and asked me to put it all in an email. "At least we have goodwill," he said. He died a few weeks later.' [39]

Martin's health continued its downward spiral. Said Roslyn, 'The cardiologist registrar said, "Martin, when you've had these attacks – there's not much we can do. You can see the chemicals aren't really bringing it back. There's not much hope." So he knew and he thanked them. Martin had a bit of cry in hospital about his parents and life being so short. Also that he didn't show enough love to people and stuff like that.

'He talked extensively about Luna Park, Tiny Tim and Wirian. He was very sentimental about keeping things, even a spider's web. There's some graffiti on the wall near the patio saying "do not remove" and it's a spider's web. Towards the end of his life he moved into a different way of making posters - a photographic image on art paper. Natalie Pratt was working very closely with him and she was his last printer. She's very loyal to Martin and he was very fond of her. A lot of the last prints – like the *Schoolbook Series* that he was doing that he never finished - the painting has been photographed and he's reproduced it on photographic paper rather than on silk screens. Then he would put his stamp on it to make it individual. He was moving into the digital age. He wanted to learn how to work an iPad. Martin wasn't interested in his emails but he liked Google.' [40]

Martine kept a visual diary of drawings and notes to the end. He also contributed to Carol Ruff's bi-annual Ukulele Exhibition, which he could no longer attend.

Moana Olson of the Pinjarra tribe saw Martin four days before he died. He asked her represent the Aboriginal Nations at his funeral by carrying the Aboriginal Cross that he had painted. Said Angelica, 'The last thing Martin asked me to do the week before he died was send out Christmas Cards that were his drawings he gifted Cranbrook School to print and send them out to all his friends.' [41]

Many friends found it tricky getting past Martin's gatekeepers to say goodbye but Garry wangled a brief moment. 'The week before he died he really didn't want to be visited but I went in,' said Garry who stayed overnight in the eastern suburbs every week to play tennis with Greg, 'I'd sleep over then I'd spend the morning going to Martin, every Thursday. So I thought, "I'll just draw a little drawing" – I did a drawing of Vincent and Martin with angels wings sitting together.

'I had some sunflowers. I went there and was told, "You can't go in". I said, "I'll just put them on the end of his bed" and said "bye". He saw me, yes. I didn't wait for him to look at it - I just went.

'That was it.' [42]

That was it indeed, bringing this story to a close with the sad conclusion with which all biographies end.

18.
WHY MARTIN MATTERS

Martin was at a crossroad - whether to go to New York. He would have mixed in well there. But he chose to come back here and his life took a different turn. It would have been very different if he'd gone to New York. We're very glad he came back here.
Peter Kingston

When Cream reunited in 2005 it became abundantly clear to everyone, including a reluctant Martin, that *Disraeli Gears* was his best-known work. Before 1967 no one was doing concept covers. Pre-1966 covers belonged to Marketing Departments. They'd find a promotional mug shot of the singer's face, or if it was a band, they'd line them up and someone would go click. That's how album covers were done: Beatles, Elvis, Beach Boys, Bob Dylan, Pink Floyd, The Who, Rolling Stones…click.

Then Eric asked Martin to do a cover for Cream. What he expected, we don't know. Maybe he wasn't sure himself. However, he'd seen Martin's posters, OZ artwork and paintings at the Pheasantry. Maybe Eric sensed the era of photo-covers was over (at least for a time). Maybe that's why he asked Martin…?

After *Disraeli Gears* the **concept cover** was unleashed. Some artists built a career out of it - Hipgnosis for example. Three of the best-known album cover artists were part of Martin's crowd. Matí Klarwein designed Santana's *Abraxas* and Miles Davis' *Bitches Brew* (both 1970). It was his wife Sophie who invited Martin to accompany her to a Salvadore & Gala Dalí soirée (and what a soirée that was!). Bob Seidemann designed the *Blind Faith* cover (1969) and Jerry Garcia's first solo album, *Garcia* (1972). When the Pheasantry got busted and the place was full of cops, Seidemann was the guy knocking to get in when everyone else was trying to get out. Most notorious of all was Bob Whitaker's *Butcher's Cover*, which is the Beatles 'meat' cover that was withdrawn in America. Whitaker was Martin's flatmate for a time and court-photographer to the Beatles. He and Martin did the *Beatles Calendar* together. It was Whitaker who did the Eric, Jack & Ginger photo shoot that Martin snipped up, combined with Albrecht Dürer wings and other images to create *Disraeli Gears*.

What would the cover have been without Martin? A Bob Whitaker photograph seems logical. Therefore, it would have been a band portrait of sorts. Cavorting on Ben Nevis if they wanted to look friendly - though Cream was a progressive blues band and serious musos liked to look surly, as if to enhance their musicianship by looking the opposite of smiley Pop stars. Martin's luminous colours made the cover an acid trip not a music lesson. And he made Cream look like artists not Rock stars.

Martin simply cut up the work of a 'famous' photographer, splashed a pink wash over the faces, overwhelmed the image with cut-ups and created what had never been done before and copied ever after. Where did he get that confidence? The sheer confidence of – not just Martin, all those larrikins in Sydney and London – was staggering. Even as 20-year olds, Martin, Richard Neville and Ritchie Walsh handled an obscenity trial in the Court of Criminal Appeal with aplomb. They chipped the Stipendiary Magistrate in the OZ magazines leading to the verdict and conducted themselves as if they regarded the whole matter as rather silly. Back in suburbia, everyone else's parents were hassling their teenagers for growing long hair. Yet here was a tribe of slightly older peer leaders who were way…way…beyond that!

Martin regarded his Psychedelic and Pop Art of that period as part of the flavour of the times. Art about Pop Music was everywhere. British Pop artist Peter Blake did the Beatles' *Sgt Peppers* and Richard Hamilton did their *White Album*. Normally, high art thumbed its nose at popular culture but during this brief late-60s hiatus the two art forms were forced to face off. It was enthralling to see the two styles complement each other until someone invented Baroque Rock and rendered the coupling absurd.

In his book *Cross-Overs – Art into Pop, Pop into Art*, John Walker writes, 'As art forms develop through time it becomes harder and harder to find something new to say; consequently there is a tendency to renew old art forms by appropriating material from other media and by recycling the art of the past. Transposing an image or idea from one context to another is often sufficient to alter its meaning or significance, or to recharge its shock value.' [1]

The word 'appropriation' has often been used to categorise Martin's art. He reckoned he didn't know what the word meant, but if it was a way of legitimising his *Art Book-Art Exhibition* period, he was pleased enough. Martin described the art world of the time as a car park with an empty space. He reckoned he slipped into that spot with his 1972 *Art Book*, which were cut-outs of classic paintings, with characters intermingling in each others' pictures. It was art about art. Martin depicted a Degas ballerina lilting through Vincent's cornfield, Lichtenstein's 'Whaam!' was set against Mondrian, Munch's nude was in Vincent's *Late Night Café* sitting on the pool table...

Martin said the first surfacing of that idea was Magritte's *Ready Made Bouquet* (1956), which is a figure in a black coat and bowler hat on which the artist has superimposed a glorious female figure from Botticelli's 15th Century painting *The Allegory of Spring*. The Botticelli image was cut-out and stuck on and what Martin called 'in its purest form'. Martin also said that *Art Book* was been deeply influenced by popular song. Other than Hamilton's Bing Crosby against a De Chirico streetscape, it's difficult to know what Martin meant. Did he see in his own montages a collage of song that would later become Tiny's marathons?

London publishers Mathews Miller Dunbar, published *Art Book* and Martin returned to Australia carrying those themes. In 1973 he decided to paint some of those pictures on canvas, and so – with Tim Lewis as his co-artist – they created *Art Exhibition,* a concept he never lost. Through the maze of film, posters and music that became Martin's life, it may be difficult to see that fine thread in Martin's later pictures, but *Pentecost* came out of *Art Book*, as did the concept of his final picture, De Chirico's *Song of Love* that he retitled *Gracelands*. And the Dream Museum - what was that if not an intermingling of different worlds? *Eternity* too, popping up in Haymarket, with Tiny, on the road to Tarascon, in 'Australia' (*Federation Tapestry*). Martin would say, 'I never create a new image when one already exists doing that job'.

Martin also impacted on some of Sydney's most significant buildings. The current face of **Luna Park**, since 1982, is a fibreglass mould of his 1973-1981 face, so in a distorted way, Martin's face still serves as the gateway. We probably wouldn't have Coney Island if not for the efforts of Martin, Kingo, Sam Marshall and other Friends of Luna Park. If not for the whole tribe of them, many valuable pieces of Arthur Barton's art would not have been preserved. First - they attended the auction, second - they bought everything they could afford, third – they rescued the pieces that didn't sell from the tip, fourth – they stored them, fifth – they restored them until they finally got them back into the Park. And the Memorial? Who knows if there would have been any memorial if the Friends - with the support of Jenny Poidevin - had not insisted?

After the Ghost Train fire, Martin pieced together a theory that Abe Saffron had deliberately orchestrated the conflagration as a way of getting control of the place and turning it into a development. Six children and one adult died, which no one wanted to happen. Martin reasoned his case from synchronicity rather than from empirical evidence, which made some people think his ideas were quite loopy. The years pass. Nobody ever records this period about Luna Park without tabling Martin's case, whether they agree with it or not. They laughed then but they're not laughing now.

Martin also impacted on the **Sydney Opera House** saga. In 1965 Jorn Utzon withdrew as Chief Architect and even though the Utzon name has always been synonymous with the Opera House in the minds of Sydneysiders, his name was omitted from speeches at official functions. For an architect deserving of the highest praise, the insult could not have been more palpable. Martin always backed Utzon. He had the Opera House blueprints framed and hanging in his hall. Along with Jorn's daughter Lin, Martin played a crucial role in affecting reconciliation between the architect and the Opera House committee. Utzon may not have travelled to see his masterpiece but his son and daughter did and he graciously accepted the committee's efforts to make peace and give him the credit that is his due.

Martin seldom claimed credit himself but in the Millennium New Year celebrations and Olympic Games 2000, the **Sydney Harbour Bridge** was ablaze with the word 'Eternity' for a worldwide audience of 3.6 billion. Asked whether this was his input, Martin usually credited Ignatius Jones, Remo Giuffré and Arthur Stace, even though everyone else associated the 'Eternity' revival with Martin. He used it to great effect in the *Haymarket* poster for the public rally that resulted in Paddy's Market's building facade being preserved. Another 'Eternity' features in Martin's big portrait of Tiny held by Macquarie University. 'Eternity' just kept going and going – at least three films, several books, lots of poems and songs, and often featured on the billboards outside Protestant churches.

Another building associated with Martin was 59 Macleay Street Potts Point, which became the **Yellow House**. It went through many phases and many changes but never lost its provenance as the site where Martin and crew created an exciting live-in art gallery that Sydneysiders have never forgotten. The effect of the Yellow House on one repeat visitor was that it taught him that you could live in Art, which he has attempted to do ever since. The Yellow House was always a Martin Sharp place. Maybe that's what he was acknowledging when he signed the building in 2013. After he left in 1972, Martin left his pictures, which is why it always seemed like a Martin Sharp place even after he was gone.

Given enough time, most of Martin's fascinations came good, even the little running men. Eaweard Muybridge is known for using multiple cameras to capture stop-motion photographs and is credited with being a pioneer of motion pictures. In 2015, a film was made about him directed by Canadian actor, writer and director Kyle Rideout with Michael Eklund (*Smallville, Bates Motel, Dirk Gentley's Holistic Detective Agency...*) taking the role of Muybridge.

Even the Dream Museum lives on. Surely the **Toy Museum** in Leura in the Blue Mountains was inspired by Martin and Richard Liney's Dream Museum?

Hokusai has gone from strength to strength too. In August 2017, the claim was made that Hokusai's 'Great Wave' is the most reproduced artwork in history. It's on t-shirts, canvas shoes, socks, laptop cases. It is also used in advertising and as a reference in films. *Hokusai's Wave* is also a pictogram or what is known as an emoji used on iPhones. It certainly did not enjoy that status when Martin started appropriating it.

Even Martin's most contentious subject found a comfortable place in music history. That Tiny had never been given a boxed set annoyed Martin for years. Ten years after Tiny's passing Rhino Entertainment, a division of Warner Bros, released the 3-CD boxed set of Tiny's complete Reprise recordings. And in 2000, Richard Perry released Tiny's inspirational Royal Albert Hall concert to CD. Nothing is obscure any more, thanks to the Internet. Tiny is there for everyone who wants him. The worldwide web has ensured that everyone, anywhere, can track Martin's pictures. His strike rate on Instagram exceeds many great Australian artists. Martin gets 700 hits to their seven. Like Toulouse-Lautrec, Martin's best-known works are his posters.

The building Martin treasured most was **Wirian**, his family home. Its status was described by the *Sydney Morning Herald* in these words: 'The dying wish of Australia's greatest Pop artist, Martin Sharp, was that his grand heritage home Wirian in Bellevue Hill be preserved and used for exhibiting and continuing his work. And he asked the Cranbrook school to stop using his name for its annual art prize, saying his permission was never sought or granted. His estate was valued at $11.25 million including $2.1 million of art, furniture and personal effects, most of which are inside Wirian. He envisaged the property to be a place for education in his work and that of other artists.' [2]

Martin protected important buildings, important ideas and he made people feel good about space and colour. After Martin's passing, many artists painted tribute pictures to their friend and mentor. South Hill Gallery's celebration of Martin in their 2014 *Art for Mart* exhibition was a flood of pictures from Martin's peers and admirers. Roger's lightbox creation *Abraxas Redux* and Philippe's portrait of Martin with Vincent certainly stood out.

Sitting in his lounge room where the walls feature five big Martin Sharp posters, Lex Marinos described his feelings when Martin died. Lex reminisced, 'I was writing to Richard Walsh at the time Martin died - I was working with Richard on a book – I wrote: "whatever it is you're feeling today, I'm sitting here writing this in what is the happiest room in the house". We've been in this house 30 or something years now. We've had deaths, weddings, births, anniversaries, all in there and it's just the happiest room in the house. Every morning I walk into it and I turn around and look at all these posters and think – WOW - I just feel good. I'm eternally in Martin's debt for that!' [3]

Martin matters to me for all the above and some personal reasons too - things he taught us. I say 'us' because my family and I were present at many – perhaps most – of the events recorded in this book. The list of my personal indebtedness is too long and too inconsequential to readers for me to include, though early one Thursday morning in April 1983, Martin took me to an electrical store in Bondi where he checked out Aiwa handheld cassette recorders. He bought one for himself and suggested I follow suit, 'You're going to need it…' he said.

That purchase changed my life forever. It changed the way I wrote and made this biography possible.

NOTES

CHAPTER 1

(1) Inquiry into the fire and deaths at Luna Park, NSW Coroner's Court, 3 September 1979, p. 1082-1086.

(2) Tina Shakeshaft, Police statement, North Sydney Police Station, 10 June 1979.

(3) Trevor Dinsmore, Police statement, North Sydney Police Station, 10 June 1979.

(4) Robert Baikie, sworn statement to the Coroner, 21 August 1979.

(5) Leslie Dowd, statement given to John Bracey (private detective) and Grahame Gambie (journalist).

(6) Robert Tilley, Funhouse: Luna Park and the Ghost Train Fire: A Secret History, unpublished, see end of Chapter 3.

(7) Martin Sharp, interview 3 March 1984.

(8) Peter Kingston, interview 24 October 2114.

(9) Martin Sharp, interview 3 March 1984.

(10) Martin Sharp, interview 18 August 1983.

(11) Duncan McNab, pp. 1-20, 77, The Usual Suspect, the Life of Abe Saffron, Pan Macmillan Australia, 2005.

(12) Ibid, pp. 82-84.

(13) Roger Foley-Fogg, interview 23 October 2014.

(14) Sam Everingham, Madam Lash, p. 71, Allen & Unwin, 2010, 288 pp.

(15) Jonny Lewis and Roger Foley, interview 26 July 2014.

(16) Duncan McNab, pp. 137-139.

(17) Martin Sharp, interview 3 March 1984.

(18) Sam Marshall, Luna Park, Just for Fun, p. 117-120, Luna Park Reserve Trust 1995.

(19) Report on Luna Park Sydney, Australia, 1980. Section titled, 'History of the Friends of Luna Park'.

(20) Registration of the company Harbourside Amusement Park Pty under the NSW Companies Act.

(21) Martin Sharp, interview 3 March 1984.

(22) Martin Sharp, interview 3 March 1984.

(23) Maurice Spatt, taped statement to Russell Sharp, 31 May 1981.

(24) Sam Marshall, Luna Park, Just for Fun, p. 125.

(25) Auction Catalog, called 'Auction Souvenir, Sun/Mon May 31/June 1', 28 pages, printed on a duplicating machine by Geoff K Gray Pty Ltd, 1981.

(26) Martin Sharp, interview 11 December 1983.

(27) Martin Sharp, interview 7 November 1983.

(28) Peter Kingston, interview 24 October 2114.

(29) Jon Lewis, Facebook message, 28 July 2015.

(30) Martin Sharp, interview 7 March 1984.

(31) John Barker, Facebook message, 5 May 2115.

(32) Mal Ramage, interview 8 February 2116.

(33) Susan Jensen, Facebook message June 2115.

(34) Ian Reid, interview 13 February 2116.

(35) Martin Sharp, interview 27 May 2005.

(36) Richard Neville, article, 'An Enfant Terrible Turns 20', Sydney Morning Herald, Good Weekend, 9 April 1983.

(37) Martin Sharp, interview 7 November 1983.

(38) Martin Sharp, interview 7 March 1984.

(39) Street of Dreams, film (as screened by ABC Television).

(40) Martin Sharp, interview 1 February 1983.

(41) These are the full credits for contributors to Street of Dreams, the Brighton Cut (1988). Produced and directed by Martin Sharp. Executive Producer: Jo Sharp. Co-Producer: Deanne Judson. Supervising Editor: Paul Healy. Assistant Editor: Marilyn Karet. Musical Director: Nathan Waks. Associate Producers: Elizabeth Knight, Hadyn Keenan, Marilyn Karet. Assistant to the Producers: Marsha Bennett, Russell Sharp. Camera: Geoff Burton, Russell Boyd, Tom Cowan, George Gittoes, Mike Edols, Mike Molloy, Simon Smith, Peter Levy, David Sanderson, Michael Glasheen. Camera Assistants: Marsha Ansara, Fergus Lindsay, Jan Kenny, John Brock. Lighting Directors: Brian Bansgrove, Roger Foley, Paul Moyes. Extra Special Lighting: Michael Glasheen, David Lourie, James Ricketson, George Greenough. Recording Engineers: Jeff Doring, Bill Hicks, Rob Hicks, Mark Lewis, Laurie Fitzgerald, David Glasser, Richard Merryman, Nick Swift, Barry Wolfison, Ted Robinson, Grant Roberts, Peter Hammond. Editors: Michael Balson, John Scott, Chris Cordeaux. Editing Assistants: Pam Barnetta, Mitzi Goldman, Helen Martin, Claire O'Brien. Sound Editors: Sally Fitzpatrick, Ashley Grenville, Malcolm B Smith, Jodi Rose, Sarah-Jane Campbell. Sound Mixing: Peter Fenton, Martin Oswin. Palais Design at Luna Park: Richard Liney, Tim Lewis. Wardrobe: Melody Cooper, Les Bean. Tailor: Tony Bonnici. Make-Up Artists: Edwina Archer, Melody Cooper, David Lucas, Richard Lucas. Research: Alison Lockwood, Chris Connolly, Amy Wells. Marathon Musicians: John Harding (violin), Dave Donovan (electric guitar), Dave Ellis (bass), Jeff Oakes (sax), Doug Gallagher (drums),

Tony Ansell (electric piano), Peter Haslem (trombone). Additional Musicians: Tommy and Phil Emmanuel (guitars), Nathan Waks (piano, cello), Alistair Jones (piano), Mike Kenny (electric piano), Eric Thompson (trumpet), David Gulpilil (didgeridoo). Song Marathon Continuity: Linda Ray, Still Photographers: William Yang, Jon Lewis, Robert McFarlane. Production Assistants: Albert Peck, Doris Ricona, Andrew Sharp, Jannie Higginson. Production Secretaries: Wilma Schinella, Alison Gentle. American Crew: Director Mike Edols. Associate Producers: Sussan Ray, Raymond Brazil. Gaffers: Karl Shumann, Mark Peterson. Sound Recordists: Helen Kaplan, Silvi Thomrad, Larry Hoff. Title Animation: Michael Glasheen.

(42) Martin Sharp interview 13 April 1983.

(43) In 2006 (approx.) Dave Rowe transferred the Marathon to CD format but it has never been commercially available to the public.

(44) Mic Conway, interview 24 January 2015.

(45) Lex Marinos, interview 27 May 2115.

(46) Jeannie Lewis, interview 7 May 2115.

(47) The picture Couples (created in 1979) was purchased by Patrick White, a bequest to the Art Gallery of New South Wales.

(48) Sam Marshall, Luna Park, Just for Fun, p. 130-131.

CHAPTER 2

(1) Martin Sharp, interview 6 September 1982.

(2) Ken Done, interview 23 May 1990.

(3) Richie Walsh, author's diary notes, 19 December 2005.

(4) Richard Neville and Julie Clarke, The Life and Crimes of Charles Sobhraj, Jonathon Cape 1979.

(5) For a sample of his wide-ranging subject matter see Richard Neville, Out of my Mind, Penguin Books, 1996.

(6) Max Skeen, interview 24 February 2016.

(7) Jim Anderson, 12 May 2115.

(8) Philippe Mora, email 1 September 2016.

(9) For Albie Thoms see, Polemics for a New Cinema, 427p, Wild & Woolley, 1978. For Roger Foley-Fogg see, Maggie Tabberer, Maggie, pp. 160-161, 164-165, 209, 275. Allen and Unwin 1998.

(10) Amber Tarling, interview 20 February 2016. Zoë Lake, 23 February 2016.

(11) Electra Foley, Ginger in Japan, Sceggs Darlinghurst Year 9 Visual Arts Assignment, 2001.

(12) Roslyn Sharp, email 28 September 2016. Also see, William Yang, Sydney Diary, pp. 24-27, James Fraser Publishers, 1984.

(13) Martin Sharp, interview 29 November 2009.

(14) See: www.environment.nsw.gov.au

(15) Martin Sharp, interview 29 December 1990.

(16) Martin Sharp, interview 16 October 2003.

(17) Martin Sharp, interview 27 May, 2005.

(18) Born in 1960, to Ruth and Ross Campbell, Cressida Campbell studied at East Sydney Technical College in 1978-1979. Having developed an interest in woodblock printing, in 1980 she left Australia to study at the Yoshida Hanga Academy in Tokyo. Cressida is Little Nell's the youngest sister.

(19) Kathy Lette, quoted in Living in the 70s by Alison Pressley, p.123, Random House Australia, 2002.

(20) John Dale, Huckstepp – A Dangerous Life, pp. 135-136, Allen & Unwin, 2000.

(21) William Yang, interview 5 August 1983.

(22) Martin Sharp, interview 5 August 1983.

(23) William Yang, interview 5 August 1983.

(24) Martin Sharp, interview 5 August 1983.

(25) Melody Cooper, email 5 July 2115.

(26) William Yang, interview 5 August 1983.

(27) Martin Sharp, interview 5 August 1983.

(28) Melody Cooper, email 5 July 2115.

(29) Russell Sharp, interview 5 June, 2115. And Stephen Lawson, interview 10 June 2115.

(30) Roslyn Sharp, interview 1 April 2016.

(31) Russell Sharp, interview 5 June, 2115. Russell assisted Martin in creating the finished artwork for the Chameleon cover using a photograph of Tiny Tim taken by William Yang.

(32) The Chameleon sessions were released on LP record in 1982. Rereleased to CD in 2006, the tracks St Louis Blues, Dancing in the Street and Tiny Bubbles were included on the CD, and Stayin' Alive was remixed to include David Gulpilil on didgeridoo.

(33) Martin Sharp, interview 13 April 1983.

(34) William Yang and Martin Sharp, interview 5 August 1983.

(35) Tiny Tim, interview 24 August 1982.

(36) Martin Sharp, interview 5 August 1983.

(37) Mal Ramage, interview 8 February 2016.

CHAPTER 3

(1) Martin Sharp, interview 6 September 1982.

(2) Stephen Lawson, interview 10 June 2015.

(3) Martin Sharp, interview 6 January 2006.

(4) 'William Sharp (Australian politician)' see Wikipedia, and Martin Sharp, interview 1 February 1983.

(5) Dave Rowe, interview 8 May 2015.

(6) Martin Sharp, interview 1 February 1983.

(7) Dingo is the title song on the 1974 album released on the Charisma label. We Want Freedom (The Charter of Aboriginal Rights) appears on the 1964 album Songs of Our Time. See also Gary Shearston, interview 1 November 2001.

(8) Martin Sharp, interview 6 January 1991.

(9) Tiny Tim, Live at the Royal Albert Hall was released to CD by Rhino Records (a division of Warner) in 2000.

(10) Albert Goldman, Elvis, Viking Books, 1981. See also, New York Times, 28 April 1968.

(11) Albert Goldman, letter to Martin Sharp dated 7 February 1982.

(12) Albert Goldman, letter to Martin Sharp dated 20 April 1982. See also, Albert Goldman, Ladies and Gentlemen – Lenny Bruce!! pp. 448, 457, 498, Random House, 1974.

(13) Martin Sharp, interview 6 September 1982.

(14) Lowell Tarling, diary notes, 27 August 1982.

(15) Tiny Tim, interview 24 August 1982.

(16) Lowell Tarling, 'The Great Pretender', Southern Flyer, September 1982.

(17) Martin Sharp, interview 1 February 1983.

(18) Martin Sharp, interview 25 February 2002.

(19) Martin Sharp, interview 6 September 1982.

(20) Martin Sharp, interview 1 February 1983.

(21) Mic Conway, interview 24 January 2115.

(22) John Singleton, Martin Sharp and Tiny Tim, taped conversation at Eliza's Restaurant Double Bay, 26 August 1982.

(23) Roslyn Sharp, interview 1 April 2116.

(24) Tiny Tim, interview 24 August 1982.

(25) Martin Sharp and Tiny Tim, interviewed on ABC Radio by Tony Bowral, 1982.

(26) The Olcott Hotel is located in New York City's Upper West Side, close to the Dakota Hotel. It was Tiny's home for the next 12 years. His mother Tillie lived with him until her passing in 1986.

(27) Bucks Burnett, Facebook 2016.

(28) Michael Duffy, 'At Home with Clive Evatt', Sydney Morning Herald, 15 April 2012.

(29) Peter Kingston, interview 7 October 2010. Kingo did the Marquette and a tradesperson from Lithgow took the design and created the sculptures.

(30) Martin Sharp interview 7 July 1984.

(31) Russell Sharp, interview 5 June 2115.

(32) Roslyn Sharp, interview 1 April 2116.

(33) Martin Sharp, interview 13 May 1983.

(34) Letter from Martin Sharp to Lowell Tarling, 30 July 1984.

(35) Martin Sharp, Cartoons, p. 40, 47, Scripts Pty Ltd, 1966.

CHAPTER 4

(1) Martin Sharp interview 5 July 1984.

(2) Martin Sharp interview 18 August 1983.

(3) Martin Sharp interview 6 September 1982.

(4) Martin Sharp interview 1 February 1983.

(5) Tiny Tim, Keeping My Troubles to Myself, 45 rpm mini-album. A Noive and Voive Production for Street of Dreams 1983. Kinselas poster, see James Anfuso, Rockin Australia – 50 Years of Concert Posters 1957-2007, Volume 3, page 1916, Starman Books, Tuart Hill WA, 2014.

(6) Martin Sharp interview 14 November 1984.

(7) Toto Renshaw and Peter Royles at Wirian, 16 April 1983.

(8) Martin Sharp interview 13 April 1983.

(9) Martin Sharp interview 5 August 1983.

(10) Peter Royles, statement recorded by Martin Sharp, 27 July 1983.

(11) William Yang, Sydney Diary, James Fraser Publishing, 1984, page 129.

(12) Martin Sharp interview 5 August 1983.

(13) Martin Sharp letter to Lowell Tarling, 30 July 1984.

(14) Ludvig Nordstrom, William Kopson's Diary, 144 pages, translation by GM Lindergren, published by Alb Boniers Boktryckeri, Stockholm, 1933. See also, Martin Sharp interview 11 April 1993.

(15) Stephen Lawson interview 10 June 2015. See also, Stephen Lawson, Martin Sharp Works on Paper, 38 pages, published by Stephen Lawson 2010.

(16) Roslyn Sharp, interview 23 April 2011.

(17) Tiny Tim, Peter Royles and guests ('room' tape), 21 August 1983.

(18) Les Bean, interview 3 September 1983.

(19) Neil Hollander expelling Les Bean from the Wentworthville Leagues Club, (taped) 3 September 1983.

(20) Tiny Tim plays the Castanet Club, Newcastle, (tape) 4 September 1983. See also, Joyce Morgan, 'Tiny on Love, Sex and Sin', Newcastle Herald, 5 September 1983.

(21) Tiny Tim plays Kinselas Sydney (tape), 1 September 1983.

(22) The musicians were: Denny Burgess (bass), Di Pritchard (guitar), Mac Lancaster (keyboards), Colin Burgess (drums). Musical producer: Al Jones. Recorded at Sun Studios Sydney, 7 October 1983.

(23) Denny Burgess interview 28 July 2115.

(24) Kate Fitzpatrick, 'Tiny Tim, What's That Secret You're Keeping?', The Good Weekend, Sydney Morning Herald, 3 September 1983.

(25) Justin Martell and Alanna Wray McDonald, pp. 258-260, Eternal Troubadour, the Improbably Life of Tiny Tim, Jawbone Press, 2116. See also, Truth, 14 September 1985.

(26) Martin Sharp interview 7 November 1983.

(27) Gary Shearston, Dingo from the album of the same name, Charisma Records, 1977.

(28) Robert Wolfgramm and Lowell Tarling, Persecution Games LP, Galilee Records 1985.

CHAPTER 5

(1) Martin's 'Syd Fest '84' colour poster was also the cover of the festival's program and their A4 handbill. The second poster resembled Martin's Catalog. It was a full page in Sydney Morning Herald, 7 December 1983.

(2) POL magazine, January 1984, for sale on p.42 for $20. This issue featured a 'summary' collage of Martin's past two years. Pages 57-58 were a double-page Jonny Lewis collage of Martin, Albie, Toto, Cressida, Jo, Brett, Kingo, William, Richard, Yensoon – and Jonny himself.

(3) See Michael Organ, University of Wollongong online. 'Martin Sharp posters 1982-1983': (1) Adelaide Festival, (2) The Arias, (3) Art Sale for Land Rights, (4) Festival of Sydney, (5) Circus OZ, (6) Tiny Paddo Masquerade, (7-8) Cold Chisel Circus Animals – two posters, (9) Tiny Tim – The Chameleon, (10) Tiny Tim Eternal Troubadour Opera House, (11) Jeannie Lewis, So You Want Blood, (12) Sydney Opera House is Ten, (13) Music Week, (14) Maureen Turquoise, Sydney Textile Fashion Show, (15) Tiny Tim Kinselas.

(4) Stephen Lawson interview 10 June 2115.

(5) Martin Sharp interview 11 December 1983.

(6) Martin Sharp interview 12 February 2011.

(7) Roslyn Sharp interview 1 April 2016.

(8) Martin Sharp interview 3 March 1984.

(9) Allan Broadhurst interview 25 May 2014.

(10) Martin Sharp, letter to Lowell Tarling, 30 July 1984.

(11) Phil Ward, Azaria! What the Jury Were Not Told, 192 pp, published by PCW 1984. See also Lowell Tarling, Azaria's Rock, Rolling Stone magazine (Aust), April 1984 pages 70-77, 87-88. In October, Martin bought the John Bryson book Evil Angels, on which the film was based.

(12) Michael Chamberlain, telephone conversation with author, 15 May 1984.

(13) Martin Sharp, letter to Lowell Tarling, 4-7 May 1984.

(14) Tape of Dr Des Ford's sermon at Macquarie University, 25 February 1984.

(15) Martin Sharp interview 23 August 1983. Exhibition catalog, The Face of Sydney, 24p, Sydney College of Advanced Education, 1984.

(16) Patrick White quoted by Martin Sharp, 23 August 1983.

(17) Martin Sharp interview 23 August 1983.

(18) Sam Marshall, Luna Park: Just for Fun p. 131.

(19) Strange Days comic, written by written by Peter Milligan, art by Brendan McCarthy and Brett Ewins, Eclipse Comics, California, 1984. Also, Outcast pages 17-18, Vol 1 No 1, Angus & Robertson, North Ryde, 1980.

(20) Jeannie Lewis interview 7 May 2015.

(21) Roslyn Sharp interview 1 April 2116.

(22) Garry Shead and Judit Englert-Shead, The Mural, The Meaning, NSW TAFE Information Services Division, 47pp, April 1985.

(23) Garry Shead interview 13 February 2115.

(24) Lowell Tarling diary notes, 13 January 1985.

(25) Malcolm Mead, statement 1 June 1985.

(26) Patrick Howard, 'The Case of the Unexplained Fires', The National Times, 28 June-4 July 1985. The six properties are: The Creole Disco – Bondi Beach, 148 Brighton Boulvarde – Bondi, 194 Victoria Street – Kings Cross, The Peak Restaurant – Bondi Junction, The Venus Room – Kings Cross and Fonzies Amusement Arcade – Darlinghurst.

(27) 'The Good Shepard Dumped', Sunday Telegraph 1 September 1985.

(28) Sun Herald, Sunday 13 October, Luna Park Enquiry re-opened.

(29) John Barker, statement 31 May 1985.

(30) John Barker, Facebook message, September 12, 2012.

(31) Martin Sharp, statement 1 June 1985.

(32) Lowell Tarling, diary notes.

(33) Duncan McNab, The Usual Suspect, the Life of Abe Saffron, pp. 245-248.

CHAPTER 6

(1) Laurie Duggan, The New Australian Poetry p. 277. Also, Martin Sharp interview 29 January 1985.

(2) Bernard O'Dowd, 'Australia' p.187, Poetry in Australia Volume 1, From the Ballads to Brennan, Angus & Robertson 1964. Martin Sharp, interview 11 April 1993.

(3) Thomas Moore, The Meeting of the Waters.

(4) Amber Mackenzie, interview 20 February 2016.

(5) Martin Sharp, interview 5 July 1984.

(6) Albie Thoms, Polemics for a New Cinema, 426pp, Wild & Woolley 1978.

(7) Philippe Mora, films 1976-1987 – Mad Dog Morgan (1976), The Beast Within (1982), The Return of Captain Invincible (1983), A Breed Apart (1984), Howling II (1985), Death of a Soldier (1986), Howling III (1987).

(8) William Yang, Starting Again, 122pp, William Heinemann, 1989.

(9) Tiny Tim, interview 6 September 1983.

(10) Tiny Tim, interview 30 August 1983.

(11) Linda Langton, interview 9 October 1987.

(12) Ken Done, interview 23 May 1990.

(13) Dare Jennings, interview 17 December 1991.

(14) Peewee and Carla Wilson, interview 14 February 1984. See also, Timothy Leary, The Politics of Ecstasy, 302pp, Paladin 1970.

(15) Jonny Lewis, interview 8 June 2016.

(16) Martin Sharp, interview 11 November 1992.

(17) Jonny Lewis, interview 8 June 2016.

(18) Gillian Armstrong, concert video of Bob Dylan's True Confessions tour. Screened as an HBO special.

(19) Jonny Lewis, interview 8 June 2016.

(20) Martin Sharp, interview 11 November 1992.

(21) Dave Rowe, interview 8 May 2015.

(22) Arthur McIntyre, 'Man-Child Sharp - a force for good', The Age, 13 September 1986.

(23) Roslyn Oxley9 catalogue for 'Sharp Art Show'.

(24) Martin Sharp, Art Book, p. 31, Mathews Miller Dunbar, 1972. Martin incorporates 'Red Room' by Matisse, 'Bird in Flight' by Magritte and Vincent van Gogh's 'Chair with Pipe'.

(25) Stephen Lawson, interview 10 June 2015.

(26) Louis Whitely Strieber, Transformation: The Breakthrough, Beech Tree Books, New York, 1988. Strieber uses Jo Sharp as a case study about the shattering effects of an assault from the unknown. He quotes directly from Martin and Yensoon's written notes.

(27) Martin Sharp, interview 3 March 2011.

(28) Martin Sharp and Robbie Tarling, diary notes (Lowell Tarling) 26 March 1987.

(29) William Yang and Martin Sharp, interview 5 August 1983.

(30) Tom Thompson, interview 8 July 2015. See also, Tom Thompson, Growing Up in the 60s, 88pp, Kangaroo Press, 1986. And, Lowell Tarling, 1967, This Is It! 214pp, Generation Books 1990.

(31) Peter Royles, 7 November 2014. And, Lowell Tarling, 1987 diary notes.

(32) Martin Sharp, diary notes (Lowell Tarling) January-February 1987.

(33) Martin Sharp, diary notes (Lowell Tarling) 22 May 1987.

(34) James Cockington and Caroline Taylor, 'A Collective Obsession', Sydney Morning Herald, 4 June 1987.

(35) Martin Sharp, letter to Lowell Tarling, 14 July 1987.

(36) Hugh Anderson, Australia to OZ? The making of the tapestry, 24 pp, Red Rooster Press 1996.

(37) Russell Sharp, Facebook 26 September 2015.

CHAPTER 7

(1) Lowell Tarling, diary notes 10 March 1988.

(2) Peter Draffin, interview Peter Draffin, 20 March 2015.

(3) Peter Draffin, letter to Lowell Tarling 12 January 1989.

(4) Street of Dreams, film, see in its entirety on youtube.

(5) Martin Sharp, letter to Lowell Tarling, 7 August 1988.

(6) Martin Sharp, interview 29 November 2004.

(7) Roslyn Sharp, interview 1 April 2016.

(8) Martin Sharp, interview 29 November 2004.

(9) Susan Young, 'World Beater!' Evening Argus, 28 May 1988.

(10) Bucks Burnett, liner notes Girl CD, Rounder Records 1996.

(11) Sue Khaury, interview 1 April 2002.

(12) Susan Young, 'World Beater!' Evening Argus, 28 May 1988.

(13) Martin Sharp, interview 29 November 2004.

(14) Martin Sharp, letter to Lowell Tarling, 8 October 1988.

(15) Steven Puchalski, ShockCin@aol.com.

(16) Martin Sharp, interview 29 November 2004.

(17) Justin Martell & Alanna Wray McDonald, Eternal Troubadour, the Improbable Life of Tiny Tim, p. 381, Jawbone Press, 2016.

(18) Dave Rowe, interview 8 May 2015. See also, Martin Sharp, 'Notes from the River Caves, p. 34, Quadrant magazine, February 1977. And, Mark St Leon, Circus in Australia, p.112,

Greenhouse Publications 1983. Lilian Roxon, 'Sawdust, Greasepaint, Sideshows & Spruikers', Australia Album, 96p, Sungravure Sydney, 1974.

(19) Tiny Tim, World Non-Stop Singing Record, Brighton 1988, Street of Dreams, 1989.

(20) Dave Rowe, interview 8 May 2015.

(21) Dave Rowe, interview 21 August 1992.

(22) Martin Sharp, letter to Lowell Tarling, 7 August 1988.

(23) Martin Sharp, letter to Lowell Tarling, 8 October 1988.

(24) Dave Rowe, interview 8 May 2015.

(25) Denny and Clare Burgess, interview 28 July 2115.

(26) Martin Sharp, interview 24 January 1994.

(27) 'The Luna Park Fire Tragedy…a link with the occult?' New Idea, 11 February 1989.

(28) Tiny Tim, Highway to Hell/I Love Rock and Roll, cassingle, Regular Records 1989.

(29) Tiny Tim, Highway to Hell, youtube. Production: Martin Sharp and Michael Glasheen.

(30) Regular Records 1979-1989, the Boxed Set, two LP records and one DVD, four variations of Martin's Boofhead Band as cover images for each of the two LPs, the video and the box itself.

(31) Lowell Tarling, diary notes 1989.

(32) Martin Sharp, letter to Lowell Tarling, 8 October 1988.

CHAPTER 8

(1) Joanna Mendelsshon, 'The Yellow House, A Brief History', Art and Australia, Winter 1990, page 568-575.

(2) Nic Lyon, interview 16 August 2015.

(3) Tony Bond, interview 12 June 2015.

(4) Sam Marshall, Luna Park – Just for Fun, p. 132-143.

(5) Martin Sharp, interview 29 December 1990. See Vincent van Gogh letter to Emile Bernard, 27 June 1888.

(6) Tony Bond, interview 12 June 2015.

(7) Letter dated 31 October 1988, from Albie Thoms to Roger Foley.

(8) Tony Bond, interview 12 June 2015.

(9) Martin Sharp, interview 29 December 1990.

(10) Berwyn Lewis, 'Viva Vincent', The Australian magazine, 14-15 July 1990 p 42. FMG magazine, June-July 1990.

(11) Lowell Tarling, diary notes 24 January 1990.

(12) Tony Bond, interview 12 June 2015.

(13) Albie Thoms Productions, circular letter dated 6 February 1989. To Yellow House artists.

(14) Greg Weight, a series of 18 b/w postcards published by Aggie Read, printed by Southwood Press Sydney, 1971.

(15) The Yellow House 1970-1972 catalogue, 56pp, Art Gallery of New South Wales.

(16) Tony Bond, interview 12 June 2015.

(17) Martin Sharp, interview 14 October 2006.

(18) Tony Bond, interview 12 June 2015.

(19) Martin Sharp, interview 29 December 1990.

(20) Roger Foley, interview 11 February 2014.

(21) Martin Sharp, interview 29 December 1990.

(22) Tim Lewis, interview 2 June 2013.

(23) Martin Sharp, quoted by Nikki Barraclough in 'Curious Yellow', Good Weekend 30 June 1990.

(24) Joanna Mendelsshon, 'The Yellow House, A Brief History', Art and Australia, Winter 1990, page 568-575.

(25) Albie Thoms, quoted in FMG magazine, June-July 1990.

(26) Nikki Barraclough, 'Curious Yellow', Good Weekend, 30 June 1990.

(27) Jonny Lewis, quoted by Berwyn Lewis, 'Viva Vincent', The Australian magazine, 14-15 July 1990.

(28) Collectibles, The Yellow House, Australian Business, 3 October 1990.

(29) Roger Foley, interview 11 February 2014.

(30) Tony Bond, interview 12 June 2015.

(31) Martin Sharp, interview 25 July 1990. The song 'Emmaus' appears on Robert Wolfgramm's CD titled Refugee, Galilee Records 1979.

(32) Albie Thoms Productions, circular letter dated 6 February 1989. To Yellow House artists.

(33) Yellow House Film Program July 25-September 21 1990. 8p. Published by the Public Programmes Department of the Art Gallery of New South Wales.

(34) The Yellow House 1970-1974, pp. 48-49, published by the Art Gallery of New South Wales.

(35) Adrian Rawlins, filmed by Roger Foley inside the reconstructed Stone Room, 1990.

(36) Jason Whalley, Facebook statement, 10 March 2015.

(37) Josef Lebovic, interview 23 July 1991. See also Brett Whiteley, Graphics, 72pp, (38) The Ginger Meggs School of Arts (The Yellow House) flyer, 8pp, Josef Lebovic Gallery, 1990. Art Gallery of Western Australia 1986.

(39) Martin Sharp, interview 29 December 1990.

(40) Greg Weight, interview 24 November 2014.

(41) Tony Bond, interview 12 June 2015.

CHAPTER 9

(1) Martin Sharp, interview 16 January 1991.

(2) http://remogiuffre.com/post/100398132342/general-thinker

(3) Tim Lewis, interview 2 June 2013.

(4) Martin Sharp, interview 15 November 1991.

(5) Martin Sharp, interview 15 November 1991.

(6) Martin Sharp, police statement, 9 November 1991.

(7) Gria Shead, interview 19 January 2017.

(8) Property of Robbie Tarling, purchased from Josef Lebovic Gallery. The three versions of Courage My Friend are on p.32, 'Martin Sharp, Work on Paper', by Stephen Lawson, 2005.

(9) Gria Shead, interview 19 January 2017.

(10) Tim Lewis, interview 2 June 2013.

(11) Martin Sharp, interview 5 January 1991.

(12) Joel Tarling, interview 11 June 2016.

(13) Martin Sharp, interview 16 January 1991.

(14) Gordon Stintson, interview 21 October 1991. See also Tiny Tim, 45 rpm single, Leave Me Satisfied/I Wanna Get Crazy With You, released on NGT Records, 1993.

(15) Sam Marshall, Luna Park, Just for Fun, was first published in 1995 and well received as a concise history that summarised its creation, the artists and the highlights, 152pp, Luna Park Reserve Trust. In 2004 it was condensed into an attractive (40p) volume, again, well received.

(16) Tom Thompson, interview 8 July 2015. Letter to Martin Sharp from Tom Thompson, ETT Imprint, 8 June 1995.

(17) Martin Sharp, interview 5 January 1991.

(18) Martin Sharp, interview 11 November 1992.

(19) Martin Sharp, interview 6 January 1992.

(20) Amber Mackenzie, interview 20 February 2016.

(21) Ian Reid, interview 13 February 2016.

(22) Martin Sharp, interview 15 November 1991.

(23) Mark Riley, 'Jilted Lover Ends Mother's Dream of Seeing her Son', Sydney Morning Herald, 11 November 1991. Also, John McNamee, 'Woman Dies in Blaze', Sunday Telegraph 10 November 1991.

(24) Catalogue, Luna Park, Fragments of a Funfair, 8p, Historic Houses Trust of New South Wales.

(25) Tim Lewis, interview 2 June 2013.

(26) Martin Sharp, interview 11 November 1992.

(27) Dave Rowe, interview 15 April 1992.

(28) Denny Burgess, interview 11 July 2015.

(29) Tiny Tim's 60th Birthday Party produced by Martin Sharp
https://youtu.be/pW1404dWLZ0)

(30) Denny Burgess, interview 11 July 2015.

(31) Chris Löfvén, interview 25 June 2005.

(32) Allan Broadhurst, interview 25 May 2014.

(33) Dave Rowe, interview 15 April 1992.

(34) John Botica, Facebook, 11 March 2017.

(35) Dave Rowe, interview 15 April 1992.

(36) Robert Adamson, 'Creon's Dream' pp.69-77, Black Water, Brandl & Schlesinger, 1999. Whiteley, An Unauthorised Life, by Margot Hilton and Graeme Blundell, p.265, Macmillan, 1996. Martin Sharp, 'Thirroul' drawing 1992.

(37) Martin Sharp, interview 18 January 1994.

(38) 'Moronic Genius', pp. 339-341, Encyclopaedia of Aberrations, 1920.

(39) Dierdre O'Connoll, The Ballad of Blind Tom, p.10, Overlook Duckworth, 2009.

(40) Martin Sharp, interview 2 November 1992.

CHAPTER 10

(1) Martin Sharp, interview 11 November 1992.

(2) Martin Sharp, interview 11 November 1992.

(3) Dave Rowe, phone 29 January 1992.

(4) Lowell Tarling, diary notes 24 January 1992.

(5) Martin Sharp, interview 16 January 1991.

(6) Ludvig Nordstrom, William Kopson's Diary, 144 pages, translation by GM Lindergren, published by Alb Boniers Boktryckeri, Stockholm, 1933.

(7) Stephen Lawson, interview June 2015.

(8) Martin Sharp, letter to the Luna Park Reserve Trust, 18 June 1993. General manager Chris Mangin, letter to Martin Sharp, 25 June 1993.

(9) Jenny Poidevin, letter to Luna Park Reserve Trust, read by Martin Sharp, interview 11 November 1992.

(10) Tiny Tim, Bob Dylan and the Band, Down In The Basement, released to CD in 1996. And, the Beatles 1968 Christmas Record.

(11) James 'Bucks' Burnett, cover lines, Tiny Tim with Brave Combo, Girl CD, 1996.

(12) Justin Martell and Alanna Wray McDonald, Eternal Troubadour, the Improbably Life of Tiny Tim, p. 447.

(13) Martin Sharp, interview 2 November 1993.

(14) Dave Rowe, interview 8 May 2015.

(15) Lowell Tarling, diary notes 2 November 1993.

(16) Martin Sharp, interview, 2 November 1993.

(17) Vivien Kooper and Stephen Plym, Tiny Tim and Mr Plym, p.27, Edee Rose Publishing 2004.

(18) Martin Sharp, interview, 2 November 1993.

(19) Dave Rowe, interview, 8 May 2015.

(20) Tiny Tim, Rock, Regular Records 1993.

(21) Dave Rowe, interview 8 May 2015.

(22) John Botica, Facebook message 30 August 2016.

(23) Dave Rowe, interview, 8 May 2015.

(24) Martin Sharp, interview 18 January 1994.

(25) Dave Rowe, interview, 8 May 2015.

(26) Tiny Tim, Tiny Tim's Christmas Album, released from England on the Durtro label, 1995. Also Tiny Tim's Pop Album, which has never been released. Tracks are: Satisfaction, St Louis Blues, Rainbow On the River, Caravan, Mission Bell, My Girl, House of the Rising Sun, People R Strange, Those Were the Days, I Am I Said, Without You, Egotesticle (with Nitocris).

(27) Angelica Tremblay, interview 23 April 2013.

(28) Joyce Morgan, The Life and Times of Martin Sharp, Allen & Unwin 2017. Also Philip Drew, The Masterpiece, Jorn Utzon – A Secret Life, 574pp, Hardie Grant Books, 1999.

(29) Martin Sharp, Tiny Tim Times, front page, January 1994.

(30) Sue Khaury, interview 30 March 2002.

(31) Sue Khaury, Memories of My Husband, Tiny Tim, p. 3, unpublished 1998.

(32) Tiny Tim, Prisoner of Love, Ponk Media 1995.

(33) Clare Burgess, interview 11 July 2015.

(34) Tiny Tim, Songs of an Impotent Troubadour, Durtro label 1995.

(35) Tiny Tim, I Love Me, Ponk Media 1995.

(36) Tiny Tim, Live in Chicago, Bughouse Records 1995.

(37) Tiny Tim, Tiny's Musical History Tour, unreleased 5 CDs, transferred from three VHS vidoes by Ernie Clark, USA.

(38) Tiny Tim, Live in London, Durtro, 1997.

(39) David Tibet, interview 7 April 2002.

(40) Mark Mitchell, interview 30 March 2002.

(41) Nicole Siverman & Jim Nelson, 'Tiny Tim's Desperate Plea to Daughter: Please Forgive Me', National Enquirer.

(42) Sue Khaury, interview 30 March 2002.

(43) Martin Sharp, 'My Friend Tiny Tim', Daily Telegraph, 3 December 1996.

(44) Martin Sharp, interview 3 December 1996.

CHAPTER 11

(1) James 'Big Bucks' Burnett, Facebook message, 12 March 2015.

(2) Martin Sharp, interview 24 January 1997.

(3) Martin Sharp, 'Bound for Heaven – My Amazing Friend', Sydney Morning Herald, 3 December 1996.

(4) Martin Sharp, interview 24 January 1997.

(5) Joel Tarling, interview 11 June 2016.

(6) Sydney Morning Herald, 4 June 1996. See also Richard Neville, Out Of My Mind, 216pp, Penguin Books 1995.

(7) Canon Jim Glennon founded the St Andrews Cathedral's Healing Ministry in 1960.

(8) One book that strongly influenced Garry 60s-70s was Authoritative Occultism by HA Wallis, a 40-page book published by Garry Shead. See Garry Shead, interview, 13 February 2015.

(9) George Gittoes, Blood Mystic, 400pp, Pan Macmillan Australia, 2016.

(10) Roger Foley, email 11 May 2017.

(11) Susan Jensen, email, 11 July 2015.

(12) Ian Reid, interview 13 February 2016.

(13) Mic Conway, interview 24 January 2015.

(14) Martin Sharp, interview 3 March 1984.

(15) Jeannie Lewis, interview, 7 May 2015.

(16) Lowell Tarling, diary notes.

(17) David Tibet, interview 7 April 2002.

(18) Martin Sharp, interview 29 December 1990.

(19) Martin Sharp, interview 1 February 1983.

(20) Martin Sharp, interview 17 April 2002.

(21) Robert Wolfgramm, Refugee CD, Galilee Records, 1979.

(22) Robert Wolfgramm, 'The King's King of Kings', a sermon preached in Frankston Seventh-day Adventist Church. A transcript was sent to Martin.

(23) Gary Shearston, interview 1 November 2001.

(24) Gary Shearston, Baiame (The Greatest Stone on Earth), Anthology, Rouseabout Records, 2007.

(25) Frances Greening (Angelica Tremblay), Straight Over the Moon CD, 1997.

(26) Martin Sharp, interview 3 March 1984.

(27) Martin Sharp, interview, 5 January 1991.

(28) Robert Tilley, Funhouse, an unpublished manuscript.

(29) Robert Tilley, email 3 February 2015.

(30) Robert Tilley, email 16 March 2017.

(31) Robert Tilley, email 2 July 2015.

(32) Lowell Tarling, diary notes, 24 January 1997.

(33) Martin Sharp, telephone conversation, Lowell Tarling, diary notes, 16 May 1997.

(34) Martin Sharp interview with William Yang and Lowell Tarling, 5 August 1983.

(35) Richard Neville, Playing Around, Arrow Books, 1991.

(36) Geoffrey Robertson, The Trials of OZ, a video-taped BBC television drama shown in the UK, 9 November 1991.

(37) Richard Neville, Hippie Hippie Shake, 376pp, William Heinemann 1995.

(38) Martin Sharp, interview 16 May 1995.

(39) Martin Sharp, interview 22 October 2003.

(40) David Leitch, Obituary: Jill Neville, The Independent, 12 June 1997.

(41) Martin Sharp interview, 30 January 2003.

(42) Martin Sharp, interview 17 April 2002.

(43) Lowell Tarling, diary notes 8 November 1997.

(44) Street of Dreams, see www.youtube.com/watch?v=pzvbDL-ilZQ

(45) Susan Khaury, Memories of My Husband, Tiny Tim, an unpublished manuscript, 1998.

(46) Joyce Morgan, Martin Sharp: His Life and Times, p. 254-256, Allen & Unwin 2017.

(47) Jim Anderson, interview 12 May 2015. Also Jim Anderson, email, 19 May 2017.

(48) Catalogue, 'Yellow House Now', Michael Nagy Fine Art, 1999.

(49) Mic Conway's National Junk Band, Diagonally Parked in a Parallel Universe CD, 2014.

(50) The Backsliders, Poverty Deluxe CD, Shock Records, 1999.

CHAPTER 12

(1) Keith Dunstan, Ratbags, p. 177-183, Golden Press 1979.

(2) Martin Sharp, interview 5 January 1991.

(3) Douglas Stewart, poem, Arthur Stace.

(4) Martin Sharp, interview 5 January 1991.

(5) Maggie Hamilton, Mister Eternity, 234pp, Scholastic Press, 1997.

(6) Eternity, produced with the assistance of the Australian Film Commission, the NSW Film and Television Office and Film Victoria, 1994.

(7) The Eternity Man, a film by Julien Temple, made for Channel 4 and the Australian Broadcasting Commission, Madman 2008.

(8) Marion Stell (editor), Eternity, Stories from the emotional heart of Australia, 124pp, National Museum of Australia, 2001.

(9) Mark Skelsey, Daily Telegraph, 6 January 2000.

(10) Martin Sharp, interview 7 January 2004.

(11) Roslyn Sharp, interview 1 April 2016.

(12) Martin Sharp, interview 17 April 2002.

(13) Basquali, Catherine, Intimate Portrait of a Champion, Pan Macmillan 2000.

(14) Martin Sharp, interview 17 April 2002.

(15) Jeannie Lewis, interview 7 May 2015. Gary Shearston, interview 1 November 2001.

(16) Martin Sharp, interview 16 October 2003.

(17) Jimmy Little, interview 1 November 1999.

(18) Martin Sharp, interview 17 April 2002.

(19) Lowell Tarling, diary notes.

(20) Dave Rowe, interview 1 August 2002.

(21) Martin Sharp, letter to Lowell Tarling, 2 August 2000.

(22) Dave Rowe, interview 8 May 2015.

(23) Electra Foley, Ginger in Japan, SCEGGS Darlinghurst Year 9 Visual Arts Assignment, 2001.

(24) Martin Sharp, letter to Electra Foley, 31 December 2001/1 January 2002.

(25) Greg Weight, May 1993, 'George Gittoes' Industrial Revolution', Australian Artist. Also, 'Kangaroo! Garry Shead's Tribute to DH Lawrence', August 1993.

(26) Gria Shead, interview 19 January 2017.

(27) Gria Shead, interview 19 January 2017.

(28) Janet Hawley, Arkie Whiteley, Obituaries Australia.

(29) Sunday Telegraph, 3 December 2000.

CHAPTER 13

(1) NECA Head Knockers figurine, *Susan Khaury, under license.

(2) Roslyn Sharp, interview 1 April 2016.

(3) Richard Macey, 'Back to the wall in fight to rescue artist's salvation; Sydney Morning Herald, 6 March 2002.

(4) Michael Wilkinson, 'Tim's Just a Tiny Bit Broke, The Melbourne Sun, 26 June 1976.

(5) Michael Chamberlain with Lowell Tarling, Beyond Azariah, 214pp, Information Australia, 1999.

(6) Martin Sharp, interview 25 February 2002.
(7) Martin Sharp, interview 25 February 2002.
(8) Mic Conway, 6 May 2002.
(9) Mic Conway, 6 May 2002.
(10) Songs: Welcome To My Dream (God Bless Tiny Tim), Legend In My Time (3 May 1976), Tiptoe Through The Tulips (God Bless), Stay Down Here Where You Belong (God Bless), Mr Phonograph (Luna Park Marathon 1979), O Gee I'm Glad I'm A Boy (Live at the Albert Hall), Original song: mother expressing disgust, People Are Strange (Stardust), Satisfaction (Stardust), The Great Pretender (Chameleon), Street of Dreams (Chameleon), Deep Tongue (… in a vault somewhere), Original song: The Tightrope of Desire, On The Old Front Porch (God Bless), Great Balls of Fire (Tiny Tim's 2nd Album), Religious Medley (Christmas Album), That Wonderful Mother of Mine (Wonderful World of Romance) Daddy Daddy, What Is Heaven Like (God Bless), The Other Side (God Bless), Beautiful Dreamer (3 May 1975), She's Just Laughing At Me (Tiny Tim's 2nd Album), Have You Seen My Little Sue (Tiny Tim's 2nd Album), I Got You Babe (Live at the Royal Albert Hall), Beautiful Dreamer (3 May 1975), Tiptoe Through The Tulips (God Bless), Stayin' Alive (Chameleon).
(11) Tulip Stewart (Miss Tulip), interview 2 April 2002.
(12) Martin Sharp, interview 6 May 2002.
(13) Martin Sharp, Memories of Telford, a special interest publication, 2002.
(14) Gary Shearston, interview 1 November 2001.
(15) The concert was held at Almost Acoustic, Rozelle, 14 August 2004.
(16) Dave Rowe, interview 8 May 2015.
(17) Martin Sharp, interview 19 March 2005.
(18) Dave Rowe, interview 1 August 2002.
(19) Domain, Sydney Morning Herald, 2-3 August 2003.
(20) Dave Rowe, interview 8 May 2015.
(21) Roslyn Sharp, interview 1 April 2016.
(22) Dave Rowe, interview 8 May 2015.
(23) Richard Neville, interview 21 February 2003.
(24) Lowell Tarling, diary notes, 24 February 2003.
(25) Richard Neville, Footprints of the Future, p. 55, Richmond Ventures, 2002.
(26) Dave Rowe, interview 23 July 2017.
(27) Martin Sharp, interview 5 April 2011.
(28) Susan Wyndham, 'Family Hang-Ups', Sydney Morning Herald, 1-2 March 2003.
(29) Arthur Rackman, Cinderella, p.82, Exeter Books, 1987.
(30) Dave Rowe, interview 8 May 2015.
(31) Jeannie Lewis, Southheart, 2 CD, Sole Music, 2002.
(32) Philippe Mora, Art Monthly, p 8-12, Dec-Feb 2003.
(33) John Lennon, Wonsaponatime CD, track 8 - God Save OZ.
(34) Larrikins in London, curator Nick Waterlow, 120pp, CFOA-UNSW, 2003.

CHAPTER 14

(1) John Platt, 161pp, Schirmer Trade Books; Disraeli Gears CD; Cream, Those Were The Days 4-CD boxed set; Classic Albums DVD.

(2) Disraeli Gears, Classic Albums DVD, Rajon Vision, 2006.

(3) Martin Sharp interview, Johann Rai, 19 March 2005.

(4) Lowell Tarling, diary notes 28 September 2005.

(5) Martin Sharp, interview 8 June 2005.

(6) Jonathon Pearlman, 'The Building that is really a Smokestack', Sydney Morning Herald, 2 January 2004.

(7) Martin Sharp, interview 30 January 2003.

(8) Martin Sharp, interview 7 January 2004.

(9) Eric Wilmott, Pemulwuy – The Rainbow Warrior, 310pp, Weldon, 1987.

(10) Martin Sharp, interview 31 July 2003.

(11) Roslyn Sharp, interview 1 April 2016.

(12) Martin Sharp, interview 18 June 2005.

(13) Roslyn Sharp, interview 1 April 2016.

(14) Allan Broadhurst, interview 25 May 2014.

(15) Martin Sharp, interview 18 June 2005.

(16) Martin Sharp, interview 18 June 2005.

(17) Roslyn Sharp, interview 1 April 2016. Professor Tom Borody suggests this was probably TPA (Tissue Plasminogen Activator) with a trade name of Alteplase.

(18) Martin Sharp, interview 18 June 2005.

(19) Robert Tilley, email 16 March 2017.

(20) Martin Sharp, interview 19 March 2005.

(21) Eric Clapton, The Autobiography, p. 324-325, Century London 2007.

(22) Martin Sharp, interview 19 March 2005.

(23) Dave Thompson, Cream, The World's First Supergroup, p. 256-257, Virgin 2005.

(24) Martin Sharp and Eric Clapton, Disraeli Gears, Classic Albums DVD, Rajon Vision, 2006.

(25) Lowell Tarling, diary notes 17 July 2005.

(26) The Illustrated Ape, Issue 21, Dennis Publishing, 2005.

(27) Felix Dennis, Lives and Rhymes poetry CD, Dennis Publishing, 2005.

(28) Robert Hughes, The Guardian, 7 March 2005.

(29) Matthew Thompson, 'Pop Art Master Accepts Postie's Advice', Sydney Morning Herald, 13 June 2005.

(30) Martin Sharp, interview 18 June 2005.

(31) Lowell Tarling, diary notes, 7 October 2005.

(32) Lowell Tarling, diary notes, 12 November 2005.

(33) The Everlasting World of Martin Sharp, p. 25, Ivan Dougherty Gallery 2006.

(34) Martin Sharp, interview 16 January 2011.

(35) 'Eternity finds its home in Redfern', South Sydney Herald, front page, November 2005.

(36) Jim Beloff, The Ukulele, A Visual History, 'Tiny Tim', pp. 70-72, Miller Freeman Books, 1997.

(37) Lowell Tarling, diary notes, 1 January 2006.

(38) Martin Sharp presents "Eternal Troubadour" Tiny Tim, the tracks were: Street of Dreams, Song Without a Name, Wonderful World of Romance, Love You Funny Thing, Memories of France, Satisfaction, I Am I Said. Zero 2006.

(39) Roger Foley, interview 11 February 2014.

(40) David Braithwaite, Sydney Morning Herald, 13 March 2006.

(41) James Phelps, 'Historic Church is lost for all Eternity', Daily Telegraph 10 May 2006.

(42) Geraldine Harris, 'Favourite Things', The Good Weekend, 6 October 2007.

(43) Roslyn Sharp, interview 1 April 2016.

(44) Art & About, 28pp, City of Sydney.

(45) Marianne Faithfull, 'Marianne Faithfull makes full recovery from breast cancer', Daily Mail, 6 November 2006.

(46) Bob Dylan, Chronicles Volume One, pp.11-15, Simon & Schuster, 2004.

(47) Martin Sharp, interview 8 November 2006. Elizabeth Fortescue, 'Now the Truth Behind Oz's Standing Joke', Daily Telegraph, 3 November 2006.

(48) John MacDonald, 'A The Sharp End of Satire', Sydney Morning Herald, 16-17 December 2006. The Everlasting World of Martin Sharp, 30p, Ivan Dougherty Gallery 2006.

CHAPTER 15

(1) Martin Sharp, interview 6 January 2006.

(2) Spectrum (cover), Sydney Morning Herald, 24-25 October 2009.

(3) See Tiny Tim, Wonderful World of Romance CD and Cinderella illustrated by Arthur Rackman.

(4) The three CDs are: Chameleon, Wonderful World of Romance and Stardust, Zero Communications 2006. Martin Sharp, inside cover lines.

(5) Dave Rowe, interview 8 May 2015.

(6) Gria Shead, interview 19 January 2017.

(7) Luke Scriberras, quoted by Peter Adams, Ore What! p 163, Lettuce Spray Productions 2010.

(8) Gria Shead, interview 19 January 2017.

(9) Roslyn Sharp, interview 1 April 2016.

(10) Judit and Garry Shead, A Creative Collaboration, 48pp, Australian Galleries, 2007.

(11) Kate McClymont, 'Niece Links Saffron to seven deaths', Sydney Morning Herald, 26-27 May 2007.

(12) Kate McClymont, 'King of the X', Sydney Morning Herald, pp. 46-49, The (Sydney) Magazine, June 2007.

(13) Alan Saffron, Gentle Satan, 166pp, Penguin 2008.

(14) Martin Sharp, interview 11 November 1992.

(15) Roslyn Sharp, interview 1 April 2016.

(16) Jenny Diski, 'Whatever happened to Ed Victor', London Review of Books, Vol 17 No 13, 6 July 1995.

(17) Paola Totaro, 'Hippie Hippie Shock: Hollywood deflowers the pioneers of Oz', Sydney Morning Herald, 17-18 November 2007.

(18) Lowell Tarling, diary notes, 20 September 2007.

(19) Barbara McMahon, 'Film to lay bare Greer's hippy days', The Guardian, 1 July 2007.

(20) Paola Totaro, 'Hippie Horror! The wizards of OZ face trial by film', The Age, 17 November 2007.

(21) Philippe Mora, quoted in Paola Totaro, 'Hippie Hippie Shock: Hollywood deflowers the pioneers of Oz', Sydney Morning Herald, 17-18 November 2007.

(22) Martin Sharp, interview 19 March 2005.

(23) Lowell Tarling, diary notes, 2 December 2006.

(24) Helen McGrath and Cris Parker, The Art of Fun, a 45-minute documentary, the Stanton Library and North Sydney Heritage Centre, 2009.

(25) Robert Tilley, Benedict XVI and the Search for Truth, Sydney: St Pauls Pr, 2007.

(26) Nai Vola Tabu Salavata, NFT Parallel Bible, commissioned by Ambassador Sir James Michael Ah Koy, 2009.

(27) Robert Wolfgramm, email 20 May 2017.

(28) Lowell Tarling, diary notes, 8 December 2007.

(29) Street of Dreams, film (as screened by ABC Television).

(30) Lowell Tarling, diary notes, 21 December 2007.

(31) Perry Keyes, interview 9 May 2015.

(32) Clare Burgess, interview 11 July 2015.

(33) Lowell Tarling, diary notes, Thursday 28 October 2008.

(34) Denny Burgess, interview 11 July 2015.

(35) Tony Bond, interview 12 June 2015.

CHAPTER 16

(1) Martin Sharp, interview 18 May 2013.

(2) Roslyn Sharp, interview 1 April 2016.

(3) Roslyn Sharp, interview 1 April 2016.

(4) Martin Sharp, interview 8 November 2006.

(5) Sharp family document, 423 pp, unpublished 2013.

(6) Martin Sharp, interview 12 February 2011.

(7) Martin Sharp, interview 12 February 2011.

(8) Nigel Featherstone, 'An Icon Reborn', Canberra Times, 5 March 2011. Also, Leigh Bottrell, 'Their Home is where the Art is', Goulburn Post, 29 June 2011.

(9) Jon Lewis, email 14 July 2016.

(10) Martin Sharp, interview 16 January 2011.

(11) Justin Martell and Alanna Wray McDonald, Eternal Troubadour, the Improbable Life of Tiny Tim, pp. 478.

(12) Martin Sharp, interview 16 January 2011.

(13) The Eternity Man, a film by Julien Temple, made for Channel 4 and the Australian Broadcasting Commission, Madman 2008.

(14) Martin Sharp, interview 16 January 2011.

(15) John MacDonald, 'Sydney's Master of Familiarities', Sydney Morning Herald, 6-7 February 2010.

(16) Martin Sharp, interview 8 November 2006.

(17) Footnote.

(18) Lowell Tarling, diary notes, 3 March 2011.

(19) Martin Sharp, interview 8 November 2006.

(20) Michaela Boland, 'Gallery Owner courts new incarnation for his treasures', The Australian, 14 December 2010.

(21) Rachel Kohn, 'The Spiritual Vision of Martin Sharp', 26 December 2010, ABC Radio National.

(22) Tiny Tim, I've Never Seen a Straight Banana CD.

(23) Roslyn Sharp, interview 1 April 2016.

(24) Jim Anderson, interview 12 May 2015.

(25) Dave Rowe, interview 8 May 2115.

(26) Lowell Tarling, diary notes, 2 April 2003.

(27) Lowell Tarling, diary notes, 19 July 2011.

(28) Marius Benson, A Conversation with Margaret Olley, The World Today, ABC Radio, 27 July 2011.

(29) John McDonald, 'The 60th Blake Prize Exhibition', Sydney Morning Herald, 1 October 2011.

(30) Angelica Tremblay, Facebook message, 8 February 2-17.

(31) Lowell Tarling, diary notes, 24 December 2011.

CHAPTER 17

(1) See Myeloma, Wikipedia.

(2) Roslyn Sharp, email 12 January 2012.

(3) Tim Lewis, interview 2 June 2014.

(4) Roslyn Sharp, 12 January 2012 and interview 1 April 2016.

(5) Mal Ramage, interview 8 February 2016.

(6) Roslyn Sharp, interview 1 April 2016.

(7) Martin Sharp, interview 8 November 2006.

(8) Martin Sharp, interview 18 May 2013.

(9) Honorary Awards, the University of Sydney, http://sydney.edu.au/arms/archives/history/HonSharp.

(10) Roslyn Sharp, email 12 January 2012.

(11) Martin Sharp, notebook entry, February 2012.

(12) Garry Shead, interview 13 February 2015.

(13) Lowell Tarling, diary notes 23 February 2012.
(14) Roslyn Sharp, interview 1 April 2016.
(15) Lowell Tarling, diary notes, 18 May 2012.
(16) Dave Rowe, interview 8 May 2015.
(17) Roslyn Sharp, interview 1 April 2016.
(18) Martin Sharp, interview 18 May 2013.
(19) 'Robert Hughes Made High Art Accessible', The Australian, 7 August 2012.
(20) Tim Lewis, interview 2 June 2014.
(21) Albie Thoms, Foreword, My Generation, 480pp, Media21 Publishing, 2012.
(22) Jeannie Lewis, interview 7 May 2015. James A Michener, The Hokusai Sketchbooks, Charles E. Tuttle, 1959.
(23) 'OZ – Fifty Years Ago, a maverick magazine changed the way we see the world'. Helen Trinca, 'The Sum of OZ', Weekend Australian, 23-24 March 2013. Richard Walsh, 'Wizards of Satire put OZ on the map', The Australian 25 March 2013. 'OZ era's feminist offspring', Helen Trinca, The Australian, 26 March 2013.
(24) Lowell Tarling, diary notes 17 March 2013.
(25) Lowell Tarling, diary notes, 17 April 2013.
(26) Angelica Tremblay, interview 23 April 2013.
(27) Bobbie Hardy, Their Work was Australian, The Story of the Hudson Family, Hudson Family, 1970.
(28) Angelica Tremblay, Lowell Tarling, diary notes July 2013.
(29) Garry Shead, interview 13 February 2015.
(30) Peter Royles, Yellow House Reunion film, 28 July 2013.
(31) The Everlasting World of Martin Sharp, p 15, Ivan Dougherty Gallery 2006.
(32) Roslyn Sharp, interview 1 April 2016.
(33) Damien Minton, May 2013, an invitation to artists to contribute to the Gracelands exhibition.
(34) Denny and Clare Burgess, interview 11 July 2015.
(35) Mic Conway, interview 24 January 2015.
(36) Jeannie Lewis, interview 7 May 2015.
(37) Roslyn Sharp, interview 1 April 2016.
(38) Angelica Tremblay, FB 30 October 2014.
(39) Joni Rush, FB 18 January 2017.
(40) Roslyn Sharp, interview 1 April 2016.
(41) Angelica Tremblay, FB 21 February 2016.
(42) Garry Shead, interview 13 February 2015.

CHAPTER 18

(1) John Walker, Cross-Overs – Art into Pop, Pop into Art, p.12, Comedia Methuen, 1987.
(2) Louise Hall and Lucy Macken, 'Artist tells school hands off my estate', Sydney Morning Herald, 31 October 2015.

(3) Lex Marinos, interview 25 May 2015.

BIBLIOGRAPHY

Aiton, Doug & Lane, Terry, The First Century, Information Australia 2000.

Anderson, Jim, Lampoon, Dennis Publishing, 2011.

Anfuso, James, Rockin Australia – 50 Years of Concert Posters 1957-2007, Starman Books, Tuart Hill WA, 2014.

Auction Catalog, called 'Auction Souvenir, Sun/Mon May 31/June 1', 28 pages, printed on a duplicating machine by Geoff K Gray Pty Ltd, 1981.

Baker, Ginger, Hellraiser, John Blake Publishing 2010.

Baker, Glenn A, The Beatles Down Under, Magnum Imprint 1996.

Baldwin, Neil, Man Ray – American Artist, Da Capo Press 2001.

Basquali, M, Catherine: Intimate Portrait of a Champion, Pan Macmillan 2000.

Beloff, Jim, The Ukulele, A Visual History, Miller Freeman Books, 1997.

Bonython, Kym, Modern Australian Painting 1975-1980, Rigby Ltd 1980.

Bourke, Antony, and Rendell, John, A Lion Called Christian, Bantam Press 1971, expanded and updated 2009.

Bruce, Jack, Composing Himself, Jawbone Press, 2010.

Buck, Paul, Performance, A biography of the classic sixties film, Omnibus Press 2012.

Bungey, Darlene, John Olsen, An Artist's Life, ABC Books, 2014.

Catalogue, Luna Park - Fragments of a Funfair, 8p, Historic Houses Trust of New South Wales.

Chamberlain, Michael, with Lowell Tarling, Beyond Azariah, 214pp, Information Australia, 1999.

Child, AC, Cranbrook – The First Fifty Years (1918-1968), Waite & Bull, 1968.

Clapton, Eric, The Autobiography, Century London, 2007.

Coombs, Anne, Sex and Anarchy, The Life and Death of the Sydney Push, Penguin Books 1996.

Dale, John, Huckstepp – A Dangerous Life, Allen & Unwin, 2000.

Dennis, Felix, Lives and Rhymes, Dennis Publishing, 2005.a

De Saint-Exupéry, Antoine, The Little Prince p. 82, Harcourt Inc, 1941.

Draffin, Peter, Pop, Scripts Pty Ltd, 1967.

Drew, Philip, The Masterpiece, Jorn Utzon – A Secret Life, 574pp, Hardie Grant Books, 1999.

Dunstan, Keith, Ratbags, Golden Press 1979.

Dutton, Geoffrey, The Innovators, MacMillan 1986.

Dylan, Bob, Chronicles Volume One, pp.11-15, Simon & Schuster, 2004.

Errico, Angie, author of Rock Album Covers, Octopus 1979.

Everingham, Sam, Madam Lash, Allen & Unwin, 2010, 288 pp.

Foley, Electra, Ginger in Japan, Sceggs Darlinghurst, Year 9 Visual Arts Assignment, 2001.

Fountain, Nigel, Underground – the London Alternative Press 1966-1974, Routledge, 1988.

Goldman, Albert, Elvis, Viking Books, 1981.

Graham, Bill, My Life Inside Rock and Out, Da Capo Press, 1992.

Jonathon Green, Days in the Life – Voices from the English Underground 1961-1971, Heinemann, 1988.

Greer, Germaine, The Female Eunuch, Granada Publishing, 1970.

Hamilton, Maggie, Mister Eternity, 234pp, Scholastic Press, 1997.

Hardy, Bobbie, Their Work Was Australian, The Story of the Hudson Family, Hudson Family, 1970.

Hewison, Robert, Too Much, Art and Society in the Sixties, Oxford University Press, 1987.

J Hillier, Hokusai, Phaidon Press, 1955.

Hilton, Margot and Graeme Blundell, Whiteley, An Unauthorised Life, Pan MacMillan, 1996.

Howell, Georgina, In Vogue, Sixty years of celebrities and fashion from British Vogue, Penguin Books 1975.

Hughes, Robert, Heaven and Hell in Western Art, Weidenfeld & Nicolson, 1968.

Humphries, Barry, Neglected Poems and Other Creatures, Angus & Robertson, 1991.

Carl Jung, Synchronicity – An Acausal Connecting Principle, Routledge and Kegan Paul, 1972.

Kee, Jenny, A Big Life, Penguin 2006.

Kennedy, Brian, A Passion to Oppose, John Anderson, Philosopher, Melbourne University Press 1995.

Khaury, Susan, Memories of My Husband, Tiny Tim, an unpublished manuscript, 1998.

Lanceley, Colin, Colin Lanceley, Craftsman House 1987.

Lawson, Stephen, Martin Sharp Works on Paper, 38 pages, published by Stephen Lawson 2010.

Leary, Timothy, The Politics of Ecstasy, Paladin 1970.

Lewisohn, Mark, The Complete Beatles Recording Sessions, Hamlyn 1988.

Litvinoff, Emmanuel, Journey Through a Small Planet, Penguin, 1972.

Marinos, Lex, Blood and Circuses, An Irresponsible Memoir, Allen & Unwin, 2014.

Marshall, Sam, Luna Park – Just for Fun, Luna Park Reserve Trust, 1995.

Martell Justin, with Alanna Wray McDonald, Eternal Troubadour, the Improbable Life of Tiny Tim, Jawbone Press 2016.

McGregor, Craig, People, Politics and Pop, Ure Smith, 1968.

McNab, Duncan, The Usual Suspect, the Life of Abe Saffron, MacMillan 2005.

Mendelsshon, Joanna, 'The Yellow House, A Brief History', Art and Australia, Winter 1990.

Meyrick, Julian, See How It Runs, Nimrod and the New Wave, Currency Press, 2002.

Michener, James A, The Hokusai Sketchbooks, Charles E. Tuttle, 1959.

Milligan, Peter, Strange Days comic, Eclipse Comics, California, 1984.

Mora, Mirka, Wicked But Virtuous, My Life, Viking, 2000.

Morgan, Joyce, The Life and Times of Martin Sharp, Allen & Unwin 2017.

Muybridge, Eadweard, The Human Figure in Motion, Bonanza Books NY, 1989.

Neville, Richard, Hippie Hippie Shake, Wm Heinemann Australia 1995.

Neville, Richard and Clarke, Julie, The Life and Crimes of Charles Sobhraj, Jonathon Cape Ltd, 1979.

Neville, Richard, Out of my Mind, Penguin Books, 1996.

Neville, Richard, Playing Around, Arrow Books, 1991.

Neville, Richard, Playpower, Jonathon Cape, 1970.

Nordstrom, Ludvig, William Kopson's Diary, 144 pages, translation by GM Lindergren, published by Alb Boniers Boktryckeri, Stockholm, 1933.

O'Connell, Dierdre, The Ballad of Blind Tom, Overlook Duckworth, 2009.

Organ, Michael, Sixties Sharp - the pop & psychedelic art of Martin Sharp, online.

Palmer, Tony, The Trials of Oz, Blond & Briggs, 1971.

Pressley, Alison, Living in the 70s, Random House Australia, 2002.

Rackman, Arthur, Cinderella, p.82, Exeter Books, 1987.

Report on Luna Park Sydney, Australia, 1980.

Rhodes, Zandra, The Art of Zandra Rhodes, Jonathon Cape, 1984.

Rice, Brian & Evans, Tony, The English Sunrise, 80pp, Mathews Miller & Dunbar, 1972.

Roland, Betty, The Eye of the Beholder, Hale & Ironmonger 1984.

Roxon, Lilian, 'Sawdust, Greasepaint , Sideshows & Spruikers', Australia Album, 96p, Sungravure Sydney, 1974.

Scaduto, Anthony, Bob Dylan, Abacus, 1972, p.236, 239.

Sharp, Martin, Art Book, Mathews Miller Dunbar, London 1972.

Sharp, Martin, Cartoons, Scripts Pty Ltd 1966.

Sharp, Martin, Catalog, Reid Books, 1971.

Sharp, Martin, exhibition catalog, The Face of Sydney, 24p, 1984.

Sharp, Martin, 'Notes from the River Caves', Quadrant magazine, February 1977.

Sharp, Martin, Twice Upon A Time, unpublished, 1966.

Shead, Garry and Englert-Shead, Judit, The Mural, The Meaning, NSW TAFE Information Services Division, 47pp, 1985.

Shead, Garry and Englert-Shead, Judit, A Creative Collaboration, 48pp, Australian Galleries, 2007.

Stell, Marion, (editor), Eternity, Stories from the emotional heart of Australia, 124pp, National Museum of Australia, 2001.

Strieber, Louis Whitely, Transformation: The Breakthrough, Beech Tree Books, New York, 1988.

St Leon, Mark, Circus in Australia, Greenhouse Publications 1983.

Stewart, Meg, Margaret Olley, Far From a Still Life, Random House, 2005.

Tabberer, Maggie, Maggie, Allen & Unwin, 1998.

Tarling, Lowell, 1967, This Is It! 214pp, Generation Books 1990.

Thompson, Tom, Growing Up in the 60s, 88pp, Kangaroo Press, 1986.

Thoms, Albie, My Generation, Media21 Publishing, 2012.

Thoms, Albie, Polemics for a New Cinema, 427p, Wild & Woolley, 1978.

Tilley, Robert, Benedict XVI and the Search for Truth, Sydney: St Pauls Pr, 2007.

Tilley, Robert, Funhouse: Luna Park and the Ghost Train Fire: A Secret History, unpublished.

Tiny Tim, Beautiful Thoughts, 1969 JP Torcher.

Townshend, Pete, Who I Am, Harper Collins 2012.

Van Gogh, Vincent, The Complete Letters of Vincent van Gogh, in 3 volumes, Thames & Hudson, 1958.

John Walker, Art Since Pop, Thames and Hudson, 1975.

John Walker, Cross-Overs – Art into Pop, Pop into Art, p.12, Comedia Menthuen, 1987.

Wallace, Christine, Greer – Untamed Shrew, Macmillan 1997.

Ward, Phil, Azaria! What the Jury Were Not Told, 192 pp, published by PCW 1984.

Waterlow, Nick, The Everlasting World of Martin Sharp, 30p, Ivan Dougherty Gallery 2006.

Waterlow, Nick, Larrikins in London, 120pp, CFOA-University of New South Wales, 2003.

Bob Whitaker, Bob, The Unseen Beatles, Conran Octopus 1991.

Whiteley, Brett, Another Way of Looking at Vincent Van Gogh, Richard Griffin Publisher, 1983.

Weight, Greg, a series of 18 b/w Yellow House postcards published by Aggie Read, printed by Southwood Press Sydney, 1971.

Wilmott, Eric, Pemulwuy – The Rainbow Warrior, 310pp, Weldon, 1987.

Yang, William, Starting Again, 122pp, William Heinemann, 1989.

Yang, William, Sydney Diary, James Fraser Publishing, 1984.

The Yellow House 1970-1972, published by Art Gallery of New South Wales, 1990.

INDEX

A

Abalone Diver – 335, 394, 396, 397, 404, 450, 457-458.
Abbey Road Studios – 113.
Abeles, Peter – 232.
Aboriginal Tent Embassy – 184, 186.
Abraxas – 101, 119, 157, 166, 216, 253, 256-257.
Abraxas (album) – 177.
AC/DC – 350, 381.
Acme Framing – 353.
Adams, Phillip - 32, 389, 446, 481
Adamson, Robert – 404.
The Adventures of Barry McKenzie – 55, 176.
Ahearn, David – 164.
Aims, Pleasure – 320.
Ain't Misbehaving – 155.
Alchemy – 60.
Ali, Muhammad – *33, 212, 220, 240.*
Ali, Tariq – *118.*
Alice in Wonderland – 212, 340, 364.
Alice Springs – 341, 456.
All My Lovin' – 376.
Allan, Richard – 366.
Allen, Johnny – 378, 386.
Allen, Peter – 326.
Alweiss, Jan (Miss Jan) – 354, 376-379.
Amédée Joubert & Son – 81.
Amphlett, Patricia (Little Pattie) – 54.
Anderson, Colin – 72.
Anderson, Jim – 121, 123, 131-132, 146-147, 169-171, 181, 194, 325, 426, 436-437, 446, 456, 464, 478.
Anderson,, 'Big'Jim – 314, 362.
Anderson, John – 34.
Anderson, Kevin – 312.
Andrews Sisters – 26.
Anglican Press – 50.
Angry Penguins – 36.
Animal Crackers – 175.
Another Way of Looking at Vincent Van Gogh – 142.
Ansell, Tony – 238.
Anyone for Tennis – 101-104, 327.
Apmira, Art Sale for Land Rights – 335.
Arcadia Amusements & Vending – 317.
Are You Lonesome Tonight – 347, 349, 414.
Apple Boutique – 98.
Aquarius Festival – 156, 184, 194, 389.
Are You Experienced – 96.
Argyle, Michael – 147, 171.
Arkin, Alan – 364.
Armstrong, Gillian – 367.
Armstrong, Louis – 26, 34.
Arp, Jean – 128.
Art Book – 109, 128-129, 173-174, 177-178, 181, 187-188, 199-200.
Art Exhibition (Sharp Art Exhibition) – 109, 128, 140, 186, 188, 190-191.
Art for Mart's Sake – 68, 187.
Art Gallery of New South Wales – 32, 83, 327, 362.
Art Galaxy – 326-327, 491.

Art of Australia, The – 103.
Art Since Pop – 200.
Arts Lab – 135-136, 146.
Artoons – 128-129, 323, 390.
Ashton, Will – 380.
Ashton, Wilfreda – 380.
Atherden, Geoff – 42.
Arty Wild Oat – 41-43, 47.
Atlantic Studios – 89, 99, 103.
Attenborough, Richard – 375-376.
Aussie Blue – 365, 382, 390, 421.
Australia (poem) – 25, 76, 196.
Australian Amusements – 317, 357.
Australia Council – 185-186.
Australian, The – 61.
Australian Broadcasting Corporation (ABC) – 19, 32, 45, 47, 67, 105, 150, 161, 230.
Australian Chamber Orchestra – 236.
Australian Film Commission – 221, 323, 331, 339, 353.
The Australian Londoner/The London Australian – 76.
Avalon, Frankie – 34.
Azaria, What the Jury Wasn't Told – 354, 357.

B

Babyface – 236.
Babylon the Great is Fallen (Revelation 18 v2) – 226.
Bacon, Francis – 112, 142.
Backsliders – 427.
Baffsky, David – 319, 362.
Baikie, Robert – 312.
Baker, Ginger – 88-89, 94, 96-99, 104, 108, 114, 116, 122, 126, 137, 445, 352-353, 494.
Baker, Karen – 97-98.
Barbie (doll) – 340.
Bardot, Brigitte – 107.
Barker College – 19, 28, 38,
Barker, John – 319, 361-362, 375, 468.
Barker, Michael – 237, 258, 318-320. Barnes, Jimmy – 326.
Barraclough, Nikki – 389.
Barrett, Denis – 341.
Barrett, Syd – 80, 99, 171,
Barton, Arthur – 24-25, 191-192, 206, 216-217, 317, 326, 344, 356-357, 396, 401, 448, 465, 495.
Bashir, Marie – 483, 485.
Basic Wage Dream, The - 69.
Bass, Tom – 63, 457-458.

Baudelaire, Charles – 73.
Baume, Eric – 50.
Bazaar – 81.
Beardsley, Aubrey – 83.
Beast Within, The – 325.
Beatles - 27, 54, 57-60, 69, 72, 81-83, 94, 107, 113, 131, 150, 171.
Beatles Calendar – 77, 82-83.
Bechini, Tony – 337, 402.
Beck, Jeff – 99.
Bee, John – 150, 167.
Begin the Beguine – 203.
Belafonte, Harry – 26, 34, 53, 314, 433.
Bell, Cheery – 25, 363.
Bell, John – 38, 135, 185, 325.
Beresford, Bruce – 42, 55, 120, 138, 205, 364, 446.
Berlin, Irving - 143.
Best, Blazey – 402-404.
Bhagwan Shree Rajneesh – 224.
Bhaktivedanta Swami Prabhupada – 224.
Bianchi, Vittorio – 134, 323.
Biba's Boutique – 79.
Bible My Mother Left For Me, The – 338, 343.
Big Dipper – 228-229, 247-251,
Big O Posters – 84-85, 92, 95-96, 102, 108, 128, 173, 177, 442, 445, 447.
Bill Haley & the Comets – 26-27.
Billings, Jonathon – 254, 359, 448, 465.
Bilu, Asher – 60.
Billy Blue – 323.
Billy Thorpe & the Aztecs – 54.
Binkie's Burgers – 48-49, 80.
Binns, Vivienne – 154,
Birth of Venus – 190,
Bitches Brew – 177,
Black Room – 390.
Blackman, Barbara – 60,
Blackman, Charles – 60,
Blake, Peter – 40, 84, 93.
Blake Prize – 13, 20,
Blaxland, Gregory – 340.
Blind Faith - 115, 126, 169.
Blind Tom – 405.
Bliss – 142, 144, 167.
Blonde-Headed Stompie Wompie Real Gone Surfer Guy – 54.
Blonde On Blonde – 79.
Blood Harvest – 366, 377.
Blue Groper – 15, 200,
Blue Skies – 143,
Blush, Edwina – 436.
Bohm, Stephanie – 409.
Bond, Antony (Tony) – 384-388, 390, 393.

Bond, Grahame – 176.
Bonnard, Pierre – 128.
Bono, Sonny – 117.
Bonython Galleries – 190, 205.
Bonzai Room – 390, 405.
Bonzo Dog Doo-Dah Band – 130, 169.
Boofhead – 10, 76, 195, 200, 218, 227, 340, 382, 426, 430, 460.
Bop Til Ya Drop – 347, 363, 367.
Botica, John – 403-404.
Borges, Jorge Luis - 127.
Borobudur – 191-192, 255.
Botticelli, Sandro – 128-129, 190, 397, 399, 495.
Bourke, Anthony (Ace) – 132, 446, 474.
Bowie, David – 131.
Bowlly, Al – 116-117, 150.
Boy George – 339.
Boyd, Arthur – 36, 39, 60, 122, 340.
Boyd, Jamie - 122.
Boyd, Pattie – 357.
Boyd, Russell – 244.
Brando, Marlon – 26.
Braund, Michael – 325.
Bravo Pour le Clown – 215.
Brennan, Christopher – 133.
Brennan, Richard – 42.
Bresslau, Erica, née Sharp – 14, 22, 204.
Brett, Chrissie – 159.
Brian Poole & the Tremeloes – 54, 58.
Briebauer, Magdalene (Marie) – 391.
Brighton Cut (Street of Dreams film) – 374-375. 377, 379, 390, 425, 467.
Brighton International Festival – 373-379, 382, 402.
Brissenden, RF – 65,
British Broadcasting Corporation (BBC) – 78, 80,
Broadhurst, Allan – 53, 404, 450.
Broadhurst, Kate – 353.
Brodziak, Ken – 57,
Broken Hearted – 71,
Brooks, Donnie – 377, 381.
Brother Can You Spare a Dime? – 116-117, 202, 239.
Brown, Bruce – 54.
Brown, Mike – 39, 79.
Brown, Pete – 89, 98, 102,
Brown, Peter (Charlie) – 28, 32, 35, 68, 125, 137, 140, 144, 348.
Brown, Rupert – 356.
Browne, Clem – 446.
Bruce, Jack – 88-89, 90, 96, 98-99, 102, 111, 122, 445, 452-453.

Bruce, Janet – 96,
Bruce, Lenny – 336.
Bryce, Quentin - 483.
Bubba Free John – 224,
Buddha – 192, 255-256,
Buddhism – 224,
Budinger, Vicki (Miss Vicki) – 126, 174, 199, 218-219, 243, 333.
The Building of Loona Park – 326, 344, 396.
The Bulletin – 39, 41, 44,
Burgess, Clare – 354, 414, 468, 490.
Burgess, Col – 350, 403.
Burgess, Denny – 350, 354, 380-381, 402-403, 412, 414, 468, 490.
Burnett, James 'Bucks' – 339, 376-377, 409, 413-414, 417, 473.
Burns, Tim – 158, 164, 167, 390-391.
Burns, Tommy - 33,
Burr, Henry – 220, 236, 423.
Burrows, Sally – 339.
Butel, Elizabeth – 370, 397.

C

Caesar's Palace – 127.
CaféAu Go Go – 99.
Cahill, Tony – 122.
Calwell, Arthur – 30.
Cameron, Sue – 220.
Cammell, Donald – 112-113, 130, 176, 432.
Campbell, Cressida – 229, 235, 328-330, 364, 382, 404, 435,438.
Campbell, Laura (Little Nell) – 143, 146, 155, 163, 172, 177, 194, 229, 325, 327.
Canberra Times – 49.
Cannes Film Festival – 200.
Can't Buy Me Love – 57.
Capon, Edmund – 384, 393.
Cappy, Joe - 221.
Capsis, Paul – 439.
Captain Marvel – 227.
Captain Matchbox Whoopee Band – 163.
Carlos, Michael – 215.
Carroll, Judy – 71.
Carroll, Richard – 254.
Cartoons – 16, 76, 87.
Cash, Johnny – 34.
Catalog – 19, 24, 29, 45, 143, 157-158, 161.
Caton, Michael – 176.
Cell Block Theatre – 165.
Central Station – 205.
Ceberano, Kate – 378, 451.
Cezanne, Paul – 128.

Chamberlain, Azaria – 341-342, 351, 353-357, 365, 424, 438, 441, 452.
Chamberlain, Lindy – 341-342, 354-357, 365, 370, 418, 452.
Chamberlain, Michael – 354-56, 365, 395, 418, 438, 485.
Chameleon – 235, 239-241, 330-331, 334, 337, 339, 349, 378, 411, 413, 432-433, 439, 455, 460-461, 467, 473, 479.
Chaplin, Charles – 227.
Charles II – 90.
Charles, Ray – 335, 372.
Checker, Chubby – 34, 53, 314.
Chelsea Arts Club – 81.
Chelsea Hotel – 142.
Chevron Hotel – 69, 138-139, 148.
Children of God – 224.
Christesen, Clem – 65.
Christie, Lou – 131.
A Christmas Carol – 200.
Christo – 155.
Circus Animals – 321.
Circus OZ – 321, 334-335.
City Lights Books – 46,
Clapton, Conor – 398.
Clapton, Eric – 87-94, 96-107, 110-117, 120-123, 126-130, 158, 171, 184, 200, 224, 326, 338, 357, 364, 379, 382, 398, 405, 409, 434, 442, 445-447, 452-453, 455, 461, 493-494.
Clark, Ernie – 413, 417, 439, 455, 473.
Clark, John – 71.
Clark, Terry – 137, 140.
Clarke, Julie – 167, 204, 230, 324-325, 328, 344, 354, 401, 489.
Clarke, Rolley – 324-325.
Clay's Books – 134.
Cleo - 193, 230.
A Clockwork Orange – 138.
Cloud Room – 390.
Clune Gallery – 37, 48, 68, 72, 75, 79-80, 125, 128, 135-137.
Clune, Frank – 135.
Clune, Terry – 135, 490.
Clune, Thelma – 135, 365, 490.
Cocksucker Blues – 211.
Cocker, Joe - 130.
Cobden, Richard – 188-189, 196, 209,
Cobden, Victoria – 209, 223, 226, 244, 319, 328, 342, 382, 398, 418, 485.
Coburn, John – 490.
Coburn, Kristin – 335.
Coburn, Steve – 404.
Cold Chisel – 321, 334-335, 345, 443, 481.
Cole, Nat King – 26.
Coleman, Jonathon – 314, 337.

Collins, Judy – 86.
Collingwood, Lyn – 38.
Columbo, Russ – 220, 413.
Comedy Theatre (Melbourne) – 438-440.
Company Caine (Co-Caine) – 155.
The Complete Letters of Vincent Van Gogh – 87, 109-110, 121, 135, 223, 363, 389, 420, 473.
Concert in Fairyland – 175.
Conway, Janie – 163, 341.
Conway, Jim – 335, 337-338, 441, 445, 491.
Conway, Mic – 163-164, 321, 334-335, 337-338, 419, 437, 439, 441, 451, 491.
Conway, Tango – 491.
Conyngham, Peter – 336-337.
Cook, Kay – 443, 448, 452.
Coon, Caroline – 446.
Cooper, Melody – 229-230, 233-235, 237-238, 242, 244, 246, 328-330.
Cooper, Robyn – 47.
Cordeaux, Chris – 246, 325, 338.
Cosmopolitan Hotel – 237, 336-337.
Country Life – 116, 120.
Country Queen – 240, 331.
Couples – 321.
Country Radio – 155.
Courage My Friend (painting) – 394, 399, 405.
Courage My Friend (song) - 394, 404.
Cowan, Tom – 244, 446.
Coward, Noel – 62.
Cox, Paul – 390.
Craddock, Crash – 314.
Crafty Old Captain – 390.
Cramphorn, Rex – 329.
Cranbrook School – 6, 12-13, 17-28, 37, 68, 77, 105, 140, 143, 145, 187, 207-208, 211, 226, 326-327, 347, 363, 372, 396, 409, 448, 451-452, 461, 470, 474, 483, 491-492, 497.
Cream – 87-90, 92-104, 108, 110-113, 116, 122, 173, 409, 427, 445-447, 452-453, 461, 493-494.
Cream (poster) – 108.
Cream - The World's First Supergroup – 97,
Crittle, John – 446.
Crocker, Barry – 55.
Crosby, Bing – 11, 15, 116, 143, 199-120,
Crossroads – 104.
Crosthwaite, Roger – 337.
Crothall, Ross – 39,
Crowe, Russell – 326.
Crows Over the Cornfield – 196.
The Crucifixion (song) – 215, 254.

Crumb, Robert - 103, 107, 143, 157, 170, 396, 478.
Cullen, William Portus – 64.
Cumming, Bernard – 227.

D

Daily Mirror – 12, 78,
Daily Planet – 247,
Daily Telegraph - 42, 80, 145, 337, 361, 429, 457.
Dale, John – 328.
Daley, Bob – 167.
Dalí, Gala – 178-179,
Dalí, Salvadore – 118, 128, 179-181, 285
Dalton, Gabrielle – 325.
Daltrey, Roger – 179.
Dame Everage, Edna – 31, 76, 227.
Damien Minton Gallery – 488, 490.
Dancing in the Street – 239, 331.
Dantalian's Chariot – 99.
Darling! – 76.
Darling Do You Love Me? – 112.
Darmody, Stephen – 418, 452, 455, 473, 477, 483.
Davis, Miles – 175, 177.
De Chirico, Giorgio – 128, 174, 189, 190, 199, 423, 458, 490, 495.
De La Vega, Willy – 222, 344, 395, 399-400, 407, 418, 476-477.
De Saint-Exupéry, Antoine – 137.
Dead Poets Society – 364.
Dean, James – 26.
Dean, William – 431-432.
Dean-Butcher, Peter – 338.
Deep Night – 239, 331.
Degas, Edgar – 128.
Degenerate Art Show (aka Crucifixion Show) – 138.
Dellasandro, Joe – 180.
Delltones – 347-349, 363, 367.
Demoiselles d'Avignon – 126, 189.
Dennis, Clarence (CJ) – 191.
Dennis, Felix – 95, 106, 121, 123, 131, 146, 156, 169-171, 194 446, 453-454, 465, 478.
Dennis Publishing – 194.
Derek & the Dominos – 171.
Devo – 237.
Diagonally Parked in a Parallel Universe – 427.
Dietetic Baby – 331.
Diamond, Neil – 202.
Dickens, Charles – 200.

Dickinson, John Nodes – 64.
Digger – 247.
Dignam, Arthur – 38.
Ding A Ding Day – 39, 45, 67, 76, 163,
Dingo – 186, 335, 351, 441.
Dinsmore, Trevor – 312.
Dire Straits – 367.
Dirty Mac, The – 120,
Disraeli Gears – 89-90, 93, 96-98, 101, 108, 177, 427, 447, 453, 477, 479-480, 493-494.
Do the OZ – 171, 446.
Do You Love Me? – 102.
Dobell, William – 36, 133.
Dog Trumpet – 410.
Doll's House – 377.
Done, Judy – 324.
Done, Ken – 323-324, 395.
Donegan, Lonnie – 27.
Donovan – 84-85, 95, 114, 175, 224.
Donovan, Dave - 238.
Don't Be Cruel – 26.
Don't Leave Me Here Standing All Alone – 125.
Don't Pass Me By – 113.
Doring, Geoff – 32.
Douglas, Kirk – 28.
Dowd, Leslie – 312, 362.
Down Under – 349.
Downes, Harmonie – 422-423, 425, 443, 477.
Dr Gachet – 389, 485.
Dr Strange – 227.
Draffin, Christabel – 326, 379.
Draffin, Peter – 76-77, 85-87, 92, 105, 365, 372, 375, 379.
Dream Museum – 195, 212, 227.
Dream Museum – 326-328, 340, 348, 359, 364, 379, 396-398, 421, 491, 495-496.
Driscoll, Michael – 185, 367.
Droga, Hal – 357.
Drooker, Eric - 202.
Drummond, Pat – 185.
Drysdale, Russell – 36, 489.
Duchamp, Marcel – 128.
Duggan, Laurie – 363.
Duke of Edinburgh – 118.
Dundas, Douglas – 44.
Dundas, Kerry – 446.
Dunlop, Weary – 399.
Dunn, Donald (Duck) – 357.
Dunstan, Keith – 197, 429-430.
Dusty, Slim – 321.
Dutton, Geoff – 37, 57, 63, 65.
Dylan, Bob – 72-73, 77, 79, 83-85, 117, 130-131, 150, 156, 211, 216, 316, 346, 367-368, 399, 409, 446, 457, 469, 493.

E

Eastman, Linda – 96.
Easybeats – 446.
Edgley, Michael – 317
Edols, Mike – 244, 320.
Edison, Thomas Alva – 237, 242.
El Alamein Fountain – 134, 156.
El Greco (Doménikos Theotokópoulos) – 28.
El Rocco – 134-135.
Edgley, Michael – 317.
Elgar, Frank – 385.
Ellis, Bob – 38, 42, 55.
Ellis, Dave – 238.
Elstrom, Peter – 355.
Elvis Calling from Heaven – 346-347.
Emerson, Francesca – 456.
Emmaus – 390, 420.
Endless Summer, The – 55.
Englert-Shead, Judit – 325, 359, 365, 368, 381, 407, 438, 462.
English Sunrise, The – 174.
Epstein, Brian – 57-61, 150.
Ernst, Max – 94-95, 113, 128.
Errico, Angie – 97.
Ertegun, Ahmet – 89.
Essex, David – 177, 20.,
Eternity – 45, 72, 119, 197, 224, 226, 237, 394-395, 398, 414, 425-426, 328-331, 437, 448, 455, 460, 473, 476, 490, 495-496.
Etting, Ruth – 116.
Evans, Wendy – 379-380, 418, 423, 438, 445, 452, 467-468, 473.
Evatt, Clive – 327,339-340, 476.
Evatt, Elizabeth – 339-340, 476.
Evatt, Herbert Vere – 339.
Eve of Destruction – 404.
Evening Standard – 80.
Eviston, Gina – 47-48.
Ewbank, John – 186.
Expatriotism – 124.
Exploding Galaxy – 99.
Extra Dimensions – 364.

F

Fabinyi, Martin – 378, 398.
Fabulous Furry Freak Brothers – 131.
Faithfull, Marianne – 326, 398, 440, 444, 457, 476.
Fall Girl – 78.
Family – 126.
Fancy Our Meeting – 128, 195.

Fasan, Steve – 402.
Fatty Finn – 246,
Fawkner, Dave – 403, 410-411.
Female Eunuch, The – 110, 151, 168.
Feldman, Marty – 164.
Ferlinghetti, Lawrence – 46.
Ferrier, Louise – 48, 67, 70, 75, 77, 79-80, 84, 92, 95, 104, 117, 119, 127, 168-169, 184, 198, 200, 426, 446, 456, 464, 477.
Ferrier, Noel – 176, 483.
Fields WC – 344.
Film Script (also *Song of Songs*) - 188, 222, 225, 233-234,
Fink, Leon – 181-182, 193, 213, 217, 227-228, 231-232, 235, 247, 249, 254, 312.
Fink, Margaret, née Elliott – 35, 182, 193, 225, 235, 344, 354, 437.
Finks Circus – 321.
First No Pinky – 72, 75, 154, 430.
Firth-Smith, John – 42-43, 71, 216, 241, 325.
Fisher, Andrew – 446.
Fisher, Meredith (Meme) née Millear – 22.
Fisher, Peter – 79.
Fitzgerald, Ella - 26.
Fitzgerald, Sally – 325.
Fitzgerald, Tom – 65.
Fitzpatrick, Kate – 40, 233, 350.
Fix-It Bob – 354, 360.
Flamer-Caldera, Nico – 338, 350.
Flamingo Park – 184, 229, 323.
Fleischmann, Arthur – 7.
Fogg Capsule – 390.
Foley, Electra – 326, 434.
Foley, Roger (Ellis D Fogg) – 71-72, 76, 124-125, 134, 139-140, 151, 154-155, 164-167, 184, 189, 205, 234, 314-315, 326, 352, 365, 386, 388-391, 407, 418, 426, 434, 437, 456, 472.
Fonda, Jane – 130.
The Fool (Simon Posthuma, Marijke Koger and Barry Finch) – 98.
For All My Little Friends – 199.
For Your Love – 88.
Ford, Desmond – 356.
Ford, Harrison – 364.
Forever Miss Dixie – 338, 343, 381.
Fox, James – 94, 113.
Fragments of a Funfair – 401-402.
Francesca, Piero Della – 128.
Free – 130.
Free Fall Through Featherless Flight – 205, 390.
Freedom Ride – 137.
Freels, Larry – 317.

Freeman, Cathy – 431-432.
Freeman, Oliver – 424.
Freudenstein, George – 160,
Fresh Cream – 87-89,
Freud, Lucien - 91
Friend, Donald - 7, 133,
Friends of Luna Park – 316, 317-318, 321, 357, 361, 385, 495.
Fringe Dwellers – 364.
Fromm, Erich – 157,
Fuller, Lyn – 167,Festival of Sydney – 235,
Funhouse – 421.

G

Gaden, John – 38, 233-234.
Gallagher, Doug – 238.
Ganpatsingh, Hazel – 117.
Garland, Judy – 34, 81.
Garland, Nicholas – 446.
Gas Lash – 49, 69, 80, 137.
Gassman, Pierre – 386.
Gaughin, Paul - 28, 128, 174.
Geldof, Bob – 326.
Gemes, Judy (Juno) – 169, 391, 466.
Geoff K Gray Auctioneer – 317.
George, Sir Arthur – 317, 330.
Gernreich, Rudi – 134.
Gerry & the Pacemakers – 54.
Get Folked – 64, 76.
Geyer, Renee – 357.
Ghost Train – 202, 213, 215-218, 229, 248-249, 250-258, 312, 318-321, 323, 328, 341, 346, 350-351, 353, 355, 358-362, 372, 380, 385, 392, 405, 421, 448, 462, 465, 468, 495.
Glasheen, Mick – 47-48, 55, 71, 79, 142, 146.
Giffen, Robyn – 340, 354, 359-362, 412, 437.
Gilliam, Terry – 68.
Ginger Baker's Airforce – 108, 137.
Ginger Meggs – 10, 205, 212, 227, 430, 435, 440, 485.
Ginger Meggs in Japan – 321, 334.
Ginger Meggs Memorial School of Arts – 146, 389, 490.
Ginsberg, Allen – 46, 155, 159.
Girl – 376-377, 409.
Gittoes, Gabrielle (Dalton) – 325, 364.
Gittoes, George – 125, 136, 140-141, 151, 153, 160, 163, 167, 184, 195, 204, 241, 244, 325-326, 364, 365, 374, 379, 381, 383-386, 389-392, 407, 418, 425, 427, 435, 440-442, 446, 450, 490.

Gittoes, Joyce – 153, 391.
Gittoes, Naomi – 326.
Giuffré, Remo – 394, 430-431, 496.
Glasheen, Michael (Mick) – 325, 365, 381-382, 386, 390-391, 427, 472.
Glennon, Jim – 418, 452.
Glitter and Be Gay – 253.
Glover, John – 380.
Go-Set – 247.
God Bless Tiny Tim – 104, 117, 321.
God Save OZ – 171, 466.
God Save the Queen (Sex Pistols song) – 201.
Godson, Craig – 254, 380, 408, 448.
Godson, Damien – 254, 380, 408, 448.
Godson, Jenny (Poidevin) – 355, 380, 405, 408, 485, 495.
Godson, John – 254, 408, 448.
Goin' Down – 348.
Goldman, Albert – 336.
Golding, John Ivor – 345.
Goldstein, Colman – 317, 362.
Goldstein, Harold – 317, 362.
Goofy – 344.
Goold, Bruce – 144, 151, 154-156, 159, 167, 184, 365, 386, 390-392, 427, 451.
Gordon, Lee – 26-27, 34, 53, 314.
Gorton, John – 124.
Gould, Bob – 35.
Goya, Francisco – 128.
Graham, Bill – 83, 100.
Granny Takes A Trip – 81, 94, 121, 171,
Grant, Hugh – 405.
Grateful Dead – 107.
Gray, Vivean – 208.
The Great Pretender – 239.
The Great Society Blows Another Mind – 103.
Great White Wonder (bootleg) – 131.
Greenough, George – 153, 160, 164, 176, 390.
Greer, Germaine – 35, 38, 65, 75, 95, 102, 110, 112, 120, 151, 165, 168-169, 182, 186, 200, 324-325, 364, 446.
Gregory-Roberts, John – 370, 483.
Greig, Julian (Jewellion the Mime) – 145, 155, 160.
Greiner, Nick – 385.
Gresch, Rick – 126.
Griffin, Rick – 83.
Grock – 227.
Grose, Peter – 41-42, 47-48, 50-51, 61.
Growing Up in the 60s – 371.

GTK-TV (Get to Know) – 150, 161.
Guard, Dominic – 208,
Gulpilil, David – 6, 239, 326, 331, 432, 438, 448, 453, 457, 459-460, 466, 472, 480.
Gumbert, Linda – 471-472.
Gumbert, Roland – 471-472.
Gunston, Norman – 208, 227.
Guru Maharaji – 224.
Gutman, Sandy (Austen Tayshus) – 342, 366, 378, 412, 436, 472.
Gwynn, Nell – 90-91.
Gye, Hal – 195.
Gypsy Fire (Emelia) –399.

H

Hair – 134.
Halligan & Wilton (architects) – 326.
Hamilton, Richard – 107, 128, 199.
Handke, Peter – 191, 196.
Hanrahan, Peter – 446.
Hapsash and the Coloured Coat – 121.
Happy Daze – 324-325, 328, 407, 478, 488.
Hara Krishna Temple – 134, 224.
Harbourside Amusements P/L – 317, 333.
Harcourt Brace & Jovanovich – 194.
Hard Day's Night, A – 57.
Harding, John – 238.
Haring, Keith – 84, 326, 354, 469.
Harrigan, John – 53.
Harris, Chester – 165.
Harris, Max – 65.
Harris, Rolf – 446.
Harrison, George – 57, 61, 82, 98, 113-114, 224, 443.
Harrison, Patti – 82.
Hartley, Ian – 165.
Haslem, Peter – 238.
Hawkins, Gordon – 66.
Hayden-Guest, Anthony – 112.
Haymarket – 226.
Haynes, Jim – 135.
Haywood, Chris – 196.
He's Got the Whole World in His Hands – 27, 243.
Healy, Paul -325, 375, 399.
Heartbreak Hotel – 26.
Heaven and Hell in Western Art – 103, 110.
Heaven Is My Home – 200, 320.
Hedges, Noni – 341.
Heide (Heide Museum of Modern Art) – 36, 59.

Hello Hello – 212.
Helpmann, Robert – 165.
Henderson, Brian – 32, 40, 70.
Henderson, Don – 69, 185.
Henderson, Gavin – 373-375.
Henderson, Marion – 185.
Henderson, Jane, née Massy-Greene – 22.
Hendrix (painting) – 96, 108, 166.
Hendrix, Jimi – 90, 96, 104, 156, 175.
Herbst, Peter – 65.
Hero of Waterloo – 364, 386, 389, 396.
Heseltine, Harry – 66.
Hesse, Herman – 157, 160.
Hester, Joy – 60.
Hicks, Bill – 244.
Hickson, Jill (Wran) – 231.
Highway to Hell – 350, 366, 379-382, 402-403, 410-411.
Hipgnosis – 107.
Hillier, Joseph – 180, 335.
Hippie Hippie Shake (book) – 67, 77, 424, 444, 463.
Hippy Hippy Shake (film) – 444, 464-465.
Hippy Hippy Shake (song) – 34.
Hobbs, Leigh – 206, 213, 235, 465.
Hobby, Karen – 167.
Hockney, David – 84, 446, 453, 469.
Hoffman, Abbie – 104.
Hogarth Galleries – 222, 323, 325, 339, 476.
Hokusai – 128, 151, 173, 179-180, 335, 394, 396, 399, 404, 426, 460, 484, 489, 496.
The Hokusai Sketchbooks – 201, 484, 488.
Hokusai's Wave – 113, 119, 153-154, 197, 200, 226, 426, 460, 496.
Holbein, Hans – 128.
Holdsworth Galleries – 140.
Hollander, Bill – 337.
Hollander, Neil – 348-349.
Hollingsworth, Keith – 23, 35, 71.
Holly, Buddy – 126.
Holman, Jason – 365, 479
Holmes, Darryl – 321.
Home (band) – 224.
Honi Soit – 39, 41-42, 47, 61, 76.
Hoodoo Gurus – 403, 409-411.
Hooton, Harry – 35.
Hope, Laurence – 446.
Hopkins, Livingstone (Hop) – 10, 157.
Hopkins, Ted – 213, 231, 318, 358, 401.
Hopper Dennis – 225.
Horler, Ken – 135, 185, 205.
Horn, Clayton – 46.
Houdini – 227.

Howard, Patrick – 360.
How Great Thou Art – 345.
Howl – 46, 64, 155.
Hubert's Flea Circus – 100, 219.
Huckstepp, Sallie-Anne – 325, 328, 365.
Hudson, Andrew – 440.
Hughes, Danne Emerson – 103, 446.
Hughes, Danton – 406.
Hughes, David – 408.
Hughes, Davis – 70-71.
Hughes, Robert (Bob) – 35, 42, 47, 55, 65, 75, 80, 103, 110, 119, 122, 135, 171, 200, 325, 365, 406, 446, 454, 487.
The Hukilau – 239.
The Human Figure in Motion – 108.
Hummingbirds – 384.
Humphries, Barry – 31, 49, 52, 55, 57, 75, 120, 325, 364, 439, 446, 454.
Hurtwood Edge – 120, 171.
Hyde Park (London) – 85, 123.
Hyde Park (Sydney) – 205.
Hynde, Chrissie – 173.

I

I Am the Walrus – 114.
IBC Studios – 98.
I Got You Babe – 117, 202, 335.
I Saw Mr Presley Tip-toeing Through the Tulips – 180, 414.
I Was Rolled by the Stones – 69, 76.
Icecaps Are Melting, The – 119, 253.
Ignatz Paints His World – 321.
The Illustrated Ape – 453.
I'm So Glad – 92.
In The Garden – 367.
In Bed with the English – 95.
In Shoppe – 148.
In the Presence of the Lord – 126.
Infinity Room – 390.
Ink Group – 366.
Inoki, Antonio – 220-221, 240.
Incredible OZ Band – 156.
Incredible Shrinking Exhibition – 133, 138-139, 141, 143, 390.
Ingres, Jean-Auguste-Dominique – 128.
Innermost Limits of Pure Fun – 153.
International Socialist Congress – 334-335.
International Year of the Child 1979 – 248, 255.
INXS – 339.

Ivan Dougherty Gallery – 351, 353, 356, 446, 458, 490.
I've Got a Loverly Bunch of Coconuts – 16.
I've Got a Tiger by the Tail – 397.
I Wanna Get Crazy With You – 397.
In His Own Write – 57.
International Times (IT) – 83, 124, 135.
Isle of Wight Festival – 130, 174.

J

Jackson, Linda – 184, 229.
Jackson, Michael - 339.
Jagger, Mick – 69, 85, 91, 94, 108, 112-114, 118, 147, 189, 226, 379, 398, 477.
James, Clive – 446.
James, Nikki – 188-190.
Jamieson, Laura – 108.
Jarratt, John – 208.
Jarry, Alfred – 51.
James, Clive – 35, 38, 65.
James, Francis – 50, 64-65.
The Jazz Singer – 202, 221.
Jefferson Airplane - 107
Jennings, Dare – 366.
Jensen, Peter – 334, 412.
Jensen, Susan – 223, 225, 229, 231, 319, 328, 419.
Jessop, Clytie - 111, 129, 446.
Jesus Adam – 224, 418.
Jesus Christ – 118, 138, 226, 254, 257, 320, 359, 380, 385, 419-422, 434, 445.
Jewish News – 61.
Jimi Hendrix Experience – 96.
Jiminy Cricket – 212.
Jimmy & the Boys – 323, 344.
John, Elton – 130, 323.
John Mayall's Bluesbreakers – 88, 94,
Johnny Carson Show – 174.
Johnson, Franklin – 151, 167, 390-392.
Johnson, Jack – 33.
Johnson, Keith – 72.
Johnson, Michael – 254, 359, 448, 465.
Johnson, Stephen – 321.
Jolson, Al – 15, 116, 197, 202, 221, 243,
Jonathon Cape publishers – 123.
Jones, Alistair (Al) – 239, 321, 325, 330, 328, 334, 343, 350, 354, 358, 375, 381-382, 395, 436.
Jones, Brian – 85, 114, 211.
Jones, Gillian – 155.

Jones, Ignatius – 385, 431, 496.
Jorgensen, Justus – 156.
Jorgensen, Sebastian (Seb) – 156-157, 160, 163-165, 166, 186, 234,
Joubert Studios – 81.
Jovic, Slavka – 167.
Judson, Deanne – 375.
Juke – 247.
Julian Ashton Art School – 7.
Juillet, Patric – 159.
Juillet's Restaurant – 155, 159, 315.
Jumping Jack Flash – 91, 129, 147.
Jung, Carl – 119, 201, 223.
Just For Fun – 192, 216.
Just For Love (also the Flower King) – 341, 358.

K

Kaleidoscope – 167.
Kaiser, Ann – 47.
Kangaroo – 404.
Kannis, John -409.
Karet, Marilyn – 246, 320, 325, 328, 345, 350, 354, 358, 363, 365, 369, 375, 405, 407-408, 425, 442, 452, 466, 478, 483.
Karvan, Arthur – 158, 166-167, 386.
Karvan, Claudia – 326.
Kaspar – 172, 191, 195-197, 205, 207, 214, 324.
Kaufman, Irving – 220.
Kay Kyser – 15.
Kaye, Danny – 16.
Kazaz, Tom – 412.
Keating, Paul – 408, 431-432.
Kee, Jenny – 32, 53, 58-59, 69, 75, 79, 84-85, 87, 119, 122, 169, 184, 224, 229, 324, 406, 418, 431, 446, 464, 487.
Keenan, Haydn – 241, 244, 246, 315, 331, 348, 355, 405.
Keeping My Troubles to Myself – 338, 343, 348, 355-356, 439,529.
Kelly, Anne – 189.
Kenny, Mike – 238.
Kerr, John – 66.
Kevans, Denis – 215.
Keyes, Perry – 468.
Khaury, Butros – 99-100.
Khaury-Gardner, Sue (Miss Sue) – 413-415, 425, 437, 439.
Khaury, Tillie – 100, 320, 354, 466.
Khaury, Tulip – 199, 218, 415, 439-440, 485.
Kidron, Beeban – 464.

Kincaid, Hilton – 313.
King, BB – 101,
King, Bill – 112,
King, George – 100,
Kinoshita, Satoshi – 411, 413, 433, 455, 460, 473.
Kirk Gallery – 234, 237.
Kissler, Anou – 33, 47-48, 50, 58-60, 67, 72, 77, 85-86, 104.
Kings Cross Whisper – 49, 135.
Kingston, Fairlie – 481, 483.
Kingston, Peter (Kingo) – 19, 47-48, 55, 71, 79, 119, 138, 140, 142, 145-146, 153, 167, 176, 204, 213, 216-217, 227-227, 235, 247-248, 252, 254, 257-258, 312, 316, 318, 325, 340, 344, 347, 357, 359, 366, 368, 371, 385-386, 390-392, 399, 401, 407, 427, 435-129, 436, 44, 451, 456, 461-465, 467, 485, 488-490, 493, 495.
Kinoshita, Satoshi – 411, 413, 433, 455, 460, 473.
Kinselas – 323, 344, 348-349, 439.
Kiss – 319.
Kissler, Anou – 425.
Klarwein, Matí – 107, 177.
Klarwein, Sophie – 177-178.
Klippel, Robert – 49, 135.
Knight, Elizabeth – 244.
Knockin' On Heaven's Door – 367.
Kogarah High School – 205.
Kohn, Rachel – 470, 476.
Kold Komfort Kaffee – 231, 238, 334, 368.
Koltai, Christine – 165.
Kopson, William (great-grandfather) – 347, 407, 489.
Koulson, Miss – 4, 12.
Kray Brothers – 90, 129, 147-148.
Krauss, Sigi – 129-130, 138, 174.
Krazy 4 You – 321.
Krazy Kat – 227.
Krishna – 255.
Krishnamurti – 224.
Kubrick, Stanley – 138.
Kung, Hans – 114.

L

L'Amour – 180.
Lady Chatterley's Lover – 35, 46, 66, 146.
Lady Diana – 212.
Lagerfeld, Karl – 180.
Laine, Frankie – 62.
Laing, RD -112.

Lambert, Anne-Louise – 208.
Lanceley, Colin – 39-40, 43, 59-60, 75, 189, 446.
Lanceley, Kay – 446.
Landa, Paul – 66.
Langton, Linda – 356.
Lansell, Ross – 161.
Lascaris, Manoly – 323.
The Last Mile of the Way – 338, 340, 343, 381.
The Last Wave – 225.
Lathouris, Nicholas – 214.
Laugh-In (Rowan and Martin's Laugh-In) – 175.
Laurel, Stan – 238.
Lawrence, DH – 404.
Lawson, Henry – 487.
Lawson, Peter – 48.
Lawson, Stephen – 330, 347, 352, 369, 373, 408.
Lawson, William – 340.
Lear, Amanda – 178.
Leary, Timothy – 104, 119, 170.
Leave Me Satisfied – 397.
Lebovic, Josef – 391-392, 478.
Led Zeppelin – 123.
Ledeboer, Peter – 84, 442.
Lee, Brenda – 34.
Lee, Christopher – 364.
Legalise Cannabis – 85.
Legalise Pot Rally, Hyde Park - 85, 123.
Lennon, Cynthia – 87.
Lennon, John – 57, 59, 61, 82, 87, 98, 113-114, 118, 120, 130, 171, 339, 443, 446.
Leonard, Roma (Nursy) – 5, 12-13, 72, 483.
Les Bean – 237-238, 344, 348, 350, 354, 358, 365, 372, 449.
Lette, Kathy – 328, 365.
Leunig, Michael – 195, 374, 404, 406, 448.
Leurella – 339-340, 496.
Lewis, Berwyn – 389.
Lewis, Jeannie - 67, 137, 152, 155, 166, 184- 186, 201, 205, 213-216, 225, 236, 242, 246, 252-254, 321, 335, 343, 351, 354, 358, 364, 390, 392, 419, 431, 436, 445, 456, 488, 491.
Lewis, Jon (Jonny) – 142, 144-146, 148, 153-154, 157-158, 161, 167, 184, 187, 204, 213, 216, 231, 235, 315, 318, 325, 329-330, 347, 350, 354, 36 5-367, 370, 386, 389, 391, 401, 427, 432, 440, 446, 472, 483, 487.
Lewis, Marvin – 238, 240, 242, 376.

Lewis, Tilly – 326, 379, 405.
Lewis, Tim – 17, 68, 148, 151, 167, 187-194, 196, 197, 203-204, 209-210, 213, 223, 226, 230-231, 235, 241, 255, 316, 321, 325, 327, 347, 354, 365-366, 386, 389, 391-392, 394-396, 400-401, 405, 423, 427, 434, 456, 490, 495.
Lewis, Tom – 213.
Lichtenstein, Roy – 56, 84, 128, 157.
Lieberson, Sandy – 176-177, 201.
The Life and Crimes of Charles Sobhraj –324.
Lindsay, Fergus – 350, 353-354, 356, 358.
Lindsay, Joan – 207.
Lindsay, Lionel – 36.
Lindsay, Norman – 43.
Liney, Richard – 188, 191, 193, 197, 199, 203, 209, 211-212, 216, 226, 235, 241, 316, 327-328, 340, 348, 390, 496.
Liney, Sharon – 191, 209, 230, 327-328.
Lisztomania – 177.
Little, Jimmy – 431-432.
Little Richard – 419.
Little Nemo – 118, 227.
The Little Prince (Le Petit Prince) – 137, 143, 157, 197, 200,
Litvinoff, Barnet – 91.
Litvinoff, David – 90-91, 112, 129, 147-149, 156, 158, 161, 167, 185, 189, 211, 315.
Litvinoff, Emanuel – 91.
Live Give Love – 95.
Liverpool Biennial Festival of Contemporary Art – 445, 447-449.
Living Daylights – 194-196, 204.
Lloyd, Owen (Bird Man of Kings Cross) – 134.
Locke, Gerald – 64-65.
London, Laurie – 27, 58, 449.
Lonely Troubadour – 238, 245.
Lozano, Carlos – 178.
Lorca, Federico – 127.
The Lost Hokusai (Abalone Diver) – 179, 180, 208, 228.
Love Machine – 68.
Love Me Do – 54.
Löfvén, Chris – 402, 404.
Lourie, David – 390.
Lovin' Spoonful – 89.
Lowe Chica – 7, 399.
Lowndes, Graham – 205.
Lowrie, David – 246.
Lucas, Bill – 345.
Luckock, Elizabeth (Lizzy), née Millear – 22.
Luna, Donyale – 114.

Luna Images – 353, 356.
Luna Park – 24, 39-40, 58, 71, 181-182, 189, 191-194, 200, 202-207, 211-213, 215-217, 221, 223, 226-229, 235, 242, 246-258, 312-313, 315-321, 325, 329-330, 333-334, 336, 339-342, 344, 346, 349, 351, 353, 356-363, 368, 370, 372-373, 375, 379-380, 385-386. 395, 397-402, 405-406, 408, 412, 421-423, 434, 448, 456, 460, 462, 465, 467, 474-476, 484-486, 489, 492, 495.
Luna Park Amusements – 406.
Luna Park Holdings P/L – 181.
Luna Park Report – 316-319.
Luna Park Song – 321, 334.
Lust for Life (film) – 28.
Lust for Life (book) – 28, 109.
Lydon, John – 408.
Lynn, Elwyn – 66, 227.
Lyon, Nic – 144, 155, 155, 160, 163, 167, 184, 384, 390, 436.
The Lyre Bird – Tiny Tim – 221.

M

Mabo, Eddie – 431-432.
Macallum, Mungo – 35, 42, 61, 66.
Macfarlane, Robert – 241.
Macquarie University – 197.
Mad – 31.
Mad Dog Morgan – 225, 325.
Mad Hatter – 340.
Mad Max – 323, 345.
Madame Tussaud's – 58.
Madden, Nikki – 163.
Madison Square Garden – 237.
Madonna – 339.
Magic Theatre OZ – 119, 121-123, 143.
Magritte, René – 99, 107, 109-110, 118, 128-129, 135, 141, 146, 151, 153-154, 157, 167, 173, 178, 181, 188, 190, 369, 386, 389-390, 497.
Maharishi Mahesh Yogi – 224.
Maher, Vickii – 58-59.
Mallard, Garry – 205.
Malley, Ern – 36.
Mambo – 330, 365-367, 430.
Man Ray – 109, 128, 177-178.
Mandrake the Magician – 227.
Mantegna, Andrea – 128.
Marceau, Marcel – 155.
Marinetti – 146, 290.
Marinos, Lex – 172, 196, 214, 216, 321, 337, 431, 497.
Markstein, Ted – 48, 138, 148, 153, 158, 167, 241.
Marriner Group – 440.
Marsh, Berys – 196.
Marshall, Sam – 192, 216, 248, 250, 316-317, 321, 357, 366, 385, 495.
Martell, Justin – 473, 479.
Martin, Charlotte – 87-88, 110, 113, 123, 453.
Massy-Greene, David – 22.
Massy-Greene, Elizabeth (nee Sharp, aunt) – 8.
Massy-Greene, Kate – 22.
Massy-Greene, Roger – 22.
Master's Apprentices – 350, 446.
Mathews, Miller & Dunbar publishers – 174.
Matthews, Freja – 111, 114, 446.
Matisse, Henri – 128, 179, 188.
May, Phil – 10, 433.
May, Professor – 66.
Mayall, John – 88.
Mavis Bramston Show – 49.
Mayne, Robert – 42.
Max's – 104.
Max – the Birdman – Ernst – 94-95, 113.
McAuley, James – 65.
McCarthy, Brendan – 358.
McCartney, Paul – 57, 59, 61, 82, 113, 413, 442, 486.
McClean, Don – 346.
McCreadie, Sky – 326, 354.
McCullough, Chris – 390.
McDonald, Garry – 208, 225.
McGregor, Craig – 48, 64, 77, 105, 371, 381.
McGregor Screenprints – 330, 347.
McGuinness, Paddy – 35.
McKenzie, Steve – 354.
McKeon, Phillip (aka Phillip Arts) – 165.
McLaren, Malcolm – 173.
McNab, Duncan – 313-314.
McNicoll, Penny – 42.
McPherson, Lennie - 70, 314-315.
McTell, Ralph – 175.
Mead, Mal – 360, 362.
Meanjin – 65, 77.
Meher Baba – 150, 224.
Melbourne Museum of Modern Art and Design – 40.
Melly, George – 121, 168, 174.
Melody Burlesque – 320.
Memories of My Husband – 425.
Men at Work – 349.
Mendelsson, Joanna – 383, 387, 389.
Mental As Anything – 316, 367, 378, 410.

Menzies, Robert – 30, 36, 50, 124.
Mercury, Freddy – 172.
Merioola artists – 7, 13, 189.
Meyrick, Julian – 185.
Michael Nagy Gallery – 391, 426.
Michener, James – 201.
Mickey Mouse – 11, 127-128, 137, 160, 169-170, 172, 195-196, 200, 212, 218, 227, 238-239, 344, 356, 370, 381, 423, 485.
Mickey Mouse Club March – 239,
Mike Walsh Show – 324.
Miles Twins – 178-179,
Millear, Katherine, née Sharp (aunt) – 8.
Millear, Katherine (Margie) – 22.
Miller, Sienna – 464.
Mingella, Max – 464.
Miningerie, Nui – 355.
Minstrel Boy – 130.
Miss Australia – 210.
Miss Natasha – 241.
Missing Links – 58.
Mission Bell – 377, 412.
Mitchell, Guy – 16.
Mitchell, Joni – 175.
Mitchell, Mark – 415, 439.
Mitchell, Mitch – 120.
Mo – 225, 227.
Moby Grape – 107.
Modigliani, Amadeo – 399.
Moermann, Joseph – 248.
Moody Blues – 130.
Molloy, Mike – 446.
Molnar, George – 35.
Mombassa, Reg – 326, 410, 451, 472, 491.
Mondrian, Piet – 128.
Monet, Claude – 128.
Money, Zoot – 99.
Montsalvat – 156.
The Moon is a Harsh Mistress – 205, 254.
Moore, Thomas – 363.
Moorhouse, Frank – 353.
Mora, Georges – 60, 67.
Mora, Mirka – 60, 67, 102.
Mora, Philippe – 60, 102, 107, 112, 114-116, 118-120, 122-123, 127, 129, 135, 138, 151, 159, 171-172, 176, 186, 200, 225, 325, 344, 354, 364, 374, 432, 443, 446, 464-465, 497.
Mora, William – 374.
Morgan, Joyce – 425-426.
Morley, Lewis – 446.
Morrison, Alastair (Afferbeck Lauder) – 30.
Morrissey, Paul – 180.
Morse, Helen – 208.
Morse, Isabelle – 354.
Mortimer, John – 147, 446.
Moscoso, Victor – 83, 109.
Moth – 155, 167.
Mouse, Stanley – 83.
Mr Ed – 339, 376.
Mr Jiggs – 227.
Mr Tambourine Man (poster) – 83-84, 110.
Mr Tambourine Man (song) – 72.
Muggeridge, Malcolm – 103.
Muktananda – 224, 251.
Munch, Edvard – 128, 157, 178.
Munro, H – 65.
Murao, Shigeyoshi (Shig) – 46.
Murawalla, Black Allen – 67-68, 185-186, 431.
Murdoch, Rupert – 61.
Murphy, Cillian – 466.
Murphy, Lionel – 66.
Murray, Bill – 236.
Murray-Smith, Stephen – 65.
Museum of Sydney – 132.
Muybridge, Eadweard – 107-108, 118, 125, 143, 157.
My Canary Has Circles Under His Eyes – 163.
My Generation (book) – 146.
My Song – 239, 331.
My Way – 239, 336.
Myriad, Carrl – 163, 441, 449.

N

Nancy – 10,
Nation Review – 204, 247, 314.
National Art School (East Sydney Tech) – 32-33, 36, 39-40, 43-44, 49, 58, 167, 187,
National Gallery Canberra – 190,
National Institute of Dramatic Art (NIDA) – 231,
Nelson, Joni – 491.
Nelson, Sandra – 134, 315.
Neruda, Pablo – 214-215,
Neville, Jill – 75, 78-80, 84, 92, 424, 446.
Neville, Judy – 78,
Neville, Richard – 32-33, 37, 41-44, 47-48, 50-52, 54-56, 58-59, 62, 63-67, 69-70, 73, 75-80, 82, 84, 87, 92, 95, 102-104, 110-111, 115-119, 121-123, 127, 131, 146-147, 156, 168-171, 184, 188, 194-195, 198, 200, 204, 224, 229-231, 237, 252, 320, 324-325,

328-329, 344, 364, 371-372, 398-399, 401, 405, 418-419, 424, 426, 437, 443, 446, 454, 456, 463, 474, 485, 488-489, 496.
New Ensemble Circus – 321.
New York Times – 114,
News of the World – 85,
Newport Arms – 54,
Nimrod (posters) – 323, 330, 334, 368, 434.
Nimrod 10 – 334.
Nimrod Theatre – 135, 185-186, 191, 195, 205, 225, 231, 235, 238, 241,
Nixon, Richard – 118,
Noddy – 340.
Noffs, Ted – 134,
Noive & Voive Records – 330.
Nolan, Sidney – 36, 40, 60, 446.
North Shore – 73,
North Sydney Swimming Pool – 258, 319.
Norton, Michael – 246,
Norton, Rosaleen – 135,
Nowra, Louis – 321.
Noyce, Phillip – 140, 205, 364.
Nuclear Disarmament Party – 334.
Nye, Alan – 73.

O

Oakes, Geoff – 238.
The Observer – 80.
O'Brien, Justin – 7, 12-13, 19-21, 24-25, 28-29, 32, 68, 109, 187.
O'Brien, Richard – 112.
Ochs, Phil – 215, 254.
Octopus's Garden – 113.
Odetta – 105.
O'Dowd, Bernard – 25, 363, 373.
O'Grady, John (Nino Culotta) – 31.
O'Keefe, Johnny – 26, 58, 347.
Olcott Hotel – 339, 356, 410.
Old Pacific Sea, The – 55.
Old Shep – 26.
Oldham, Andrew Loog – 69.
Olley, Margaret – 7, 454, 480.
Olsen, John – 37, 40, 49, 60, 64, 66, 133, 135.
On Stage OZ – 76.
On The Good Ship Lollipop – 175.
On the Road to Tarascon – 13, 87, 109, 128, 160, 202, 395, 399, 405,495.
Ono, Yoko – 118, 171, 446.
Orbison, Roy – 314.
Organ, Michael - 108, 128, 392.
Ormsby-Gore, Alice – 123.
Orpheus and Eurydice – 202-203, 221.

Oswald, Lee Harvey – 118.
Outcast – 358.
Owens, Buck – 398.
Oxley, Ros – 368-369, 372, 377, 381.
OZ (Australia) – 41, 43-44, 46-52, 54-58, 60, 61-73, 75-80, 82, 94, 103-104, 115, 119, 122-124, 135, 182, 186, 323-324.
OZ (London) – 78, 80, 85, 92, 95, 102-105, 107-108, 110-111, 113, 117-118-119, 121-123, 126, 129, 131-132, 135, 143, 146-147, 156-157, 165, 168-171, 177-178, 181, 185, 194, 200, 225-226, 229.
OZ Guide to Sydney's Underworld – 70.*OZ Newsletter* – 123.
OZ? (tapestry) – 25, 319, 373, 379, 495.

P

Packer, Frank - 32.
PACT Folk- 163, 186.
Page, Jimmy – 123.
Paint Your Own Gallery – 137, 139, 141.
Paladin Granada publishers – 119.
Pallenburg, Anita – 113.
Palmer, Tony – 171.
Pandemonium – 355, 405.
Paolozzi, Eduardo – 112, 159, 390.
Pappalardi, Felix – 89, 99.
Paradise Club – 134.
Paris Theatre Company - 233, 244.
Parnell, Jim – 338.
Parra, Angel – 214.
Peanuts – 157.
Peck, Albert – 191, 203-204, 209-211, 218, 229-230, 237, 246, 325,3 28-330, 333, 336.
Pengally, Vivienne – 151, 391.
Penguin Books – 46, 66, 91.
Pentecost – 128, 188, 369, 372, 383, 408, 427, 484, 495.
People, Politics and Pop – 77, 105.
Pepperall, David (Dr Pepper) – 247.
Perceval, John – 60.
Perceval, Mary – 60,.
Performance - 94, 112-113, 122, 129, 146, 171, 176, 178, 201, 207, 211, 399.
Perry, David – 71, 390.
Perry, Richard – 117, 335, 338, 439-440, 497.
Persecution Games – 347, 351, 356.
Peter, Paul and Mary - 34, 100.
Petit, Philippe – 194.
Petty, Bruce – 61, 249, 390, 406.
The Phantom – 157, 227.
The Pheasantry – 90-92, 94-97, 99, 102, 107,

109-112, 114, 116, 119-128, 136-137, 171, 173, 177.
Philadelphia Museum of Modern Art – 178.
Phongsittisak, Paiwan – 395-403, 405,
Piaf – 321.
Picasso, Pablo – 36, 126, 128, 178, 189-190.
Picasso's – 81.
Piccolo Bar – 132, 323, 330.
Picnic at Hanging Rock – 207-209, 341, 445.
Pilcher, Norman – 84-85, 114-116.
Pineapple, Johnny – 414.
Pink Bob – 414.
Pink Floyd – 80, 99, 107, 125, 164.
Pink Pussycat – 134.
Pinniger, Gretel (Madam Lash) – 165, 184, 315, 323.
Pinocchio – 10, 212.
Pinter, Harold – 345.
Pitney, Gene – 34.
Plant a Flower Child – 102, 201.
Playboy – 50, 249.
Playboy Press – 219.
Play Power – 110, 119, 123.
Playing Around – 424.
Plunkett, Brad – 90.
Plym, Stephen – 410, 412-414.
Pointer Sisters – 335.
Polemics for a New Cinema – 364.
Politics of Ecstasy, The – 119, 367.
Poor Little Rich Girl – 62.
Pop (novel) – 76-77, 85, 105.
Pop Into Popism – 84.
Pope Paul VI – 118.
Popeye – 212, 227.
Popov, Alex – 47, 354.
Portrait of Tiny Tim – 197.
Poverty Deluxe – 427.
Powditch, Peter – 32, 49, 53, 151, 159, 187, 391, 487.
Pratt, Natalie – 485, 487, 492.
Presley, Elvis – 26, 34, 117, 131, 240, 331, 336, 342, 345-347, 368, 380, 402, 414, 420-421, 445, 458, 486, 490-491, 493.
Pressed Rat and Warthog – 104.
Pretenders – 173.
Prickles – 402-404.
Primavera – 129.
Prince Charles – 212, 344, 424.
Princess Diana – 344, 424.
Princess Eugenie – 326.
Princess Margaret – 131,
Prisoner of Love – 413.

Private School – 77.
The Procurer – 91.
The Projectionist – 224.
Prome Investments P/L – 375.
Proud, Philip (Pip) – 135,
Pruniers in the Park Restaurant – 231.
Punch and Judy – 227.
Puppet Theatre – 389-390.
Purves, Stuart – 438.

R

Rai, Jonathon – 447.
Rainey, Michael – 91.
Rahilly, Seamus – 254, 359, 448, 465.
Ramage, Mal – 144-145, 148, 155, 162, 166-167, 319.
Ramsden, Michael - 129, 138, 159, 235, 446.
Ratbags – 197.
Rawlins, Adrian - 61, 124-125, 150, 152, 155- 156, 184, 224, 237, 242, 244, 337, 344, 377, 391, 436.
Ray, Johnny – 16, 26.
Ray Price Jazz Quintet – 137.
Rebel Without a Cause – 26.
Read, Aggy – 48, 71, 124, 140, 142, 167, 390.
Ready Made Bouquet – 129.
Rebane, Bill – 377.
Rebel Yell – 403.
Reed, John – 59-60.
Reed, Sunday – 59-60.
Refugee – 347, 490.
Regency Entertainment – 233.
Regular Records – 323, 367, 378, 381-382, 410.
Reid, Barrett – 60.
Reid, Catherine (Katie, née Sharp) – 22, 106, 163, 319. 345, 406, 444-445.
Reid, Ian – 136, 141, 145, 149, 152-153, 156- 157, 159, 162-163, 166-167, 319, 399, 419.
Reid, Jamie – 201.
Reid, Rupert – 487.
Reid, Sam – 452.
Reller, Paul – 413.
Rendall, John – 132.
Rene, Roy (Mo McCackie) – 225.
Renshaw, Anthony (Toto) – 329-330, 345, 354, 357, 359, 365, 381, 418.
Renshaw, Jack – 329.

Reprise Records – 100, 199.
Restivo, Johnny – 34.
Reuben Tice Memorial Band – 156.
Revolver – 82.
Revue of the Absurd – 49, 51.
Rhodes, Zandra – 159, 167, 177, 200-201, 326, 377, 379.
Rich, Buddy – 26.
Rich, Andrew – 366.
Richard, Cliff – 27.
Richards, Keith – 69, 85, 108, 114, 120, 130.
Richmond, Harry – 236.
Ricketson, James – 365.
Riley, Bridget – 76, 83.
Rip It Up – 26.
Rising of the Tide – 253,
Ritchie Bros – 5, 21, 36,
Ritchie, Harold – 37.
Ritchie, Henry Lucas St George – 353.
Ritchie, James (great-paternal grandfather) – 5.
Ritchie, Stuart (maternal grandfather) – 6-7, 10, 14, 21, 23, 36, 62, 74, 209, 326-328, 323, 341, 353, 454.
Ritchie, Vega (Vee) née Kopson (maternal grandmother) – 5, 11, 13, 105, 191, 209-210, 326-327, 347, 364.
Ritchie, William – 353.
Roadknight, Margret – 185, 214.
Roberts, Rachel – 208.
Robertson, Geoffrey – 147, 405, 424, 446, 477.
Robinson, Ted – 235.
Robson, Karen – 398.
Rock – 409, 411,
Rock Album Covers – 97.
Rock Around the Clock – 26.
Rock Island Line – 27.
Rock and Roll Circus – 120.
Rocky Horror Show – 112, 172, 176, 194, 321, 364.
Roeg, Nick – 112, 379, 432.
Rolling Stone – 247.
Rolling Stones – 58, 69, 78, 85, 117, 120, 188-189, 211.
Rosemary's Baby – 339.
Rosen, Robert – 410.
Roslyn Oxley Gallery – 368-369, 372, 377.
Rousseau, Douanier – 117.
The Roving Kind – 16.
Rowe, Alfred (The Great Onzalo) – 194, 377-378.
Rowe, Dave – 334, 368, 377-378, 395-396, 407, 410-411, 413, 433, 446, 482, 486.
Rowe, Marsha – 446.
Roxon, Lilian – 103-104.
Royal Albert Hall – 16, 33, 116-117, 122, 130, 174, 176, 333, 335-336, 338, 442, 449, 452-453, 460.
Royal Easter Show (Sydney) – 24, 192.
Royal George Hotel – 34.
Royles, Peter – 156, 160, 167, 184, 216, 329, 345-346, 348-350, 354, 357, 362, 364-365, 371-372, 412, 437, 461, 472, 490.
Rubin, Jerry - 104,.
Rubin, Victor – 188, 328, 338.
Rudy Komon Gallery – 40.
Ruff, Carol – 446, 492.
Rule Brittania- 175.
Rushdie, Salmon – 325.
Rushton, Ernest – 42.
Russell, Ken – 177.
Rydell, Bobby – 34, 53, 314.

S

Sad Sack – 212,
Saffron, Abe – 53, 313-316,329, 356, 360, 361, 385, 398, 420, 454, 457, 462-463, 470. 495.
Saffron, Doreen – 314.
Sagan, Carl – 87, 118.
Sale, Julia – 151, 153, 390.
Samson, Nicholas – 491.
Sanderson, David – 208, 355, 359, 365, 371, 437.
Sangster, John – 135.
Santa Claus – 23, 227.
Santana, Carlos – 177.
Save Luna Park (poster) -321.
Sciberras, Luke – 399, 426, 435-436, 438, 442, 450, 452, 454, 456, 461, 483, 485.
Scripts P/L – 76.
See How it Runs – 185.
See You Later Alligator – 26.
Seideman, Bob - 107, 115, 126, 169.
Seidler, Harry – 50, 213.
Seidler, Polly – 398.
The Seizer – 255.
Self Portrait (album) – 130, 150.
Self Portrait (painting) – 94.
Self Portrait (Tim Lewis exhibition) – 204, 401.
The Sentimental Bloke – 191, 195, 227, 245.

Serio, Terry – 384.
Seurat, Georges – 128.
Seven Sermons to the Dead – 119.
Seventeen Minutes to Four – 68.
Sex! (poster) – 95.
SEX (punk clothes shop) – 173.
Sex Pistols – 173, 201.
Seymour Centre – 214.
Signac, Paul – 127.
Sgt Pepper's Lonely Hearts Club Band – 93, 96, 321.
Shakeshaft, Tina – 312.
Shannon, Del - 34.
Sharman, Jim – 76, 112, 140, 166-167, 172, 225, 356, 390.
Sharman, Jimmy – 24, 356, 390.
Sharp Alan (uncle) – 8, 22, 73.
Sharp, Alexander (Sandy) – 22, 106, 176, 444-445, 483.
Sharp, Andrew – 22, 106, 176, 196, 209, 330, 364, 463.
Sharp, Barbara (née Davies) – 52-53.
Sharp, Dorothy, née Muller (stepmother) – 23, 35, 62, 105, 125, 186, 238, 352, 437-438, 443, 457, 461-462, 470-471, 483.
Sharp, Edith (Dinks), née Lycett – 14, 52-53, 204.
Sharp, Elizabeth (Bessie) – 8, 22, 37, 53, 62, 125, 191, 204, 352.
Sharp, Frank (uncle) – 8, 12, 14, 22, 37, 204.
Sharp, Henry Ritchie (father) – 4-14, 17, 22-23, 35, 37-38, 52, 62-63, 71, 73, 105, 115, 125, 128, 186, 327, 344, 352, 363-364, 407, 445, 470.
Sharp, Joan (Jo) née Ritchie (mother) – 5-16, 20-21, 23, 26-27, 35, 52-53, 58, 62, 65, 71-72, 74, 105, 113, 125, 158, 166, 183, 187, 189- 190, 204, 210, 218, 222, 256, 327, 331, 344, 350, 352, 358, 369-370, 382, 399, 407, 440, 487.
Sharp, Marcello (Cello) – 425.
Sharp Martin and his Silver Scissors – 130.
Sharp, Phillip – 14, 22, 204, 450.
Sharp, Roslyn (Rozzie) – 14, 22, 106, 204, 330, 339, 341, 345, 348, 352, 359, 368, 374-376, 381, 425, 431, 440, 443-445, 449-450, 457, 462-463, 470-471, 477, 480-486, 490-492.
Sharp, Russell – 10, 18-19, 23, 27, 30, 34, 38, 51, 66, 133, 170, 173, 321, 329, 413, 511, 541-542.
Sharp, Walter Ramsay (paternal grandfather) – 8, 13, 17-18, 22, 37.
Sharp, William Henry (great-grandfather) – 27, 153.
Shaw, Artie – 26.
Shea Stadium – 82.
Shead Garry – 30, 33, 36-45, 47-48, 55, 67, 71, 73, 77, 79, 105, 120, 125, 146, 163, 176, 184, 186, 205-206, 216-217, 227, 235, 241, 247, 249-250, 325, 344, 359, 365, 368, 374, 381, 390, 392, 404, 407, 418, 427, 429, 435, 438, 446, 450-451, 462, 472, 477, 485-487, 489.
Shead, Gria – 216, 326, 381, 395, 397, 399-400, 435-436, 461, 481, 483, 485.
Shead, Meryl – 216, 435.
Shearston, Gary – 67, 69-70, 183, 186, 335, 341, 352-355, 365, 382, 385, 390, 418, 421, 441, 449, 472, 489.
Shepherd Brad – 403.
Shepherd, Cybill – 220.
Shepard, Ernie – 360-361.
Sheraton Hotel – 60.
She's A New Kind of Old Fashioned Girl – 240.
Shrimpton, Jean – 108, 114, 188, 190.
Sideshow in Burlesco – 334.
Signal Driver – 234, 321.
Simmonds, Anita – 341.
Simmonds, Peter – 341.
Simms, Clayton – 162, 354, 360, 381.
Sinatra, Frank – 314.
Singleton, John – 32, 323, 333, 337-338, 400, 520.
Skeen, Max – 325.
Skinner, Ian – 14-15.
Skinner, Ida – 14.
Skinner, Jan – 14-15.
Skipper, Marcus – 156-157.
Skrzynski, Joe – 425-426.
Slessor, Kenneth – 133.
Slim Dusty Band – 239.
Slow Train Coming – 316, 367.
Small One, The – 11.
Smart, Jeffrey – 340.
Smartiples – 119, 125.
Smedley, David – 395, 400-401.
Smilde, Roelof – 35.
Smith, Mona – 362.
Snow Job – 342, 457.
Snugglepot and Cuddlepie – 227.
Soapbox Circus – 321.
Sobhraj, Charles – 229, 231.
Social Deviants – 99.

So You Want Blood – 335, 488.
Solanas, Valerie – 327.
Solomon, David – 61.
Song of the Disembraining – 51.
Song of Love – 190.
Song Without A Name – 239, 331.
Songs of an Impotent Troubadour – 413-414, 417, 420.
South Hill Gallery – 472.
Southern Cross – 197, 200,
Southern Cross Hotel (Melbourne) – 61,
Southern Cross Hotel (Edgecliff) – 221,
Spatt, Maurice - 213, 228, 247, 252, 317.
Spatt, Nathan – 181, 213, 227, 231, 236, 247.
Speakeasy Club – 87-88, 127, 198, 453.
Spears, Steve – 225.
Spectator – 80.
Spencer Davis Group – 126.
Spookyland – 390, 436.
Spoonful – 92, 104.
St Barnabas Church – 197, 429, 456.
St John, Colette – 144, 188, 204.
St John, Edward – 66.
St Louis Blues – 239, 321.
St Mary Magdalene Church – 360, 475.
St Paul's College – 37.
Stables Theatre – 321.
Stace, Arthur – 197, 223, 394, 428-431, 456, 473, 496.
Stanton, Terry – 401-403, 407, 435, 473.
Starkiewicz, Antionette – 158, 390-392, 427.
Starr, Ringo – 57, 61, 113, 130, 177, 201, 335.
Starry Night – 180, 194, 197, 202, 226, 240.
Stayin' Alive - 239, 244, 331, 460.
Steele, Jackie – 70.
Steele, Tommy – 58.
Stein, Hal – 326, 406, 467.
Stein, Harry – 218.
Stein, Sherry – 326, 467.
Steve Paul's Scene (The Scene) - 100, 116, 177, 219.
Stevenson, Pamela – 176.
Stewart, Rod – 335, 440.
Stigwood, Robert – 99, 114.
Stinson, Gordon – 397.
Strachan, David – 38.
Stone, Judy – 114.
Stone, Sandy – 31, 52.
Strange Brew – 89-90, 104.
Stanshall, Viv – 169.
Stewart, Douglas – 429.
Storrier, Tim – 340.
Street of Dreams (film) – 239, 321, 331, 348, 353, 377, 390, 425.

Street of Dreams (song) – 337, 491.
Street of Dreams Productions – 321, 330, 334, 337, 353, 379.
Street, Philip Whistler – 64.
Stone Room – 387, 390-391.
Straight Over the Moon – 421.
Strange Days – 358, 360.
Strauss, Lucinda – 348.
Subterranean Imitation Realists (also known as the Annandale Imitation Realists) – 39-40, 60.
Sue-Ellen – 158, 167.
Summer in the City – 89.
Sunshine City – 146, 185.
Sunshine of Your Love – 89, 104.
Sunshine Superman (poster) – 84, 95.
Superman – 10, 194.
Surf City – 53-54.
Sun (band) – 155.
Sun Myong Moon – 224.
Sunbury Music Festival – 184.
Suitch, Max – 360.
Sutinen, Asco (Axel) – 164-165.
Swastika – 176, 200.
Sweet Art – 403.
Sweet Shop – 108.
Sweeten, Jimmy – 315.
Sydney Diary – 346.
Sydney Festival – 324.
Sydney Harbour Bridge – 19, 41, 140, 194.
Sydney Morning Herald – 17, 39, 41, 67, 76- 77, 139, 241.
Sydney Opera House – 70-71, 186, 191, 193, 202, 225, 235, 248, 316, 336-338, 351, 356, 368, 373, 408, 412, 425-426, 439, 452, 456, 467, 496.
Sydney Push – 34-35, 46, 51, 67-68, 78, 137, 151, 169, 182.
Sydney Showground – 188.
Sydney Stadium – 26-27, 33-34, 58, 73. Sydney String Quartet – 236.
Sydney Symphony Orchestra – 236.
Sydney Textile Museum – 347.
Sydney Town – 70.
Sydney University Revue (Dramatic Society) – 38, 51, 185.
Sylvia & the Synthetics – 323.
Synchronicity: An Acausal Connecting Principle – 201,.

T

Tabberer, Maggie – 205, 306.
Tales of Brave Ulysses – 86-90, 104, 184, 237, 391, 402, 409, 425, 427, 434, 453, 460-461, 468.

Tanner, Les – 39.
Tarling, Amber (McKenzie) – 326, 399, 402.
Tarling, Joel – 394, 396, 418.
Tarling, Zoë (Lake) – 326.
Tate Gallery – 36-37, 142.
Tatlock Miller, Harry – 7.
Taylor, Derek – 59.
Taylor, Elizabeth – 130.
Tears of Steel & the Clowning Calaveras – 205, 213-214, 225, 235-236, 246, 252-253, 351.
Teather, Steven – 246, 328-329.
Telford – 5, 14-15, 33, 105, 440-441.
Temple, Julien – 330, 473.
Toff, The – 25.
Thames & Hudson – 200.
Tharunka – 41-43, 47, 51, 76.
That'll Be the Day (film) – 177, 201.
There'll Always be an England – 175.
Thiering, Barbara – 380.
Thompson, Dave – 97.
Thompson, Eric (Boof) – 238.
Thompson, Jack – 326, 432, 466, 473.
Thompson, Peter (Pilot Pete) – 354, 359-360, 412, 437.
Thompson, Tom – 347, 370-371, 397, 404, 407.
Thoms, Albie - 39, 42, 46, 49, 51-52, 55, 71- 72, 120, 122, 124, 135-136, 140-150, 154-156, 160, 161-163, 165-167, 176, 185-186, 205, 207, 234,325, 364-365, 381, 386-387.
Thomson, Brian – 167.
Thornton, Harold (the Kangaroo) – 354, 358, 366, 388,449.
Those Were the Days – 427.
Three Gaoled Filthy Paper – 77.
Three Little Fishies – 15.
Thriller – 339.
Throb – 350.
Tibet, David – 413-414, 417, 420, 439.
Tiger Tim – 227.
Tilley, Robert – 417, 421-422, 438, 442, 452, 461, 465, 467, 477.
Times, The – 80.
Til Time Brings Change – 205.
Tintin – 340.
Tiny Bubbles – 331.
Tiny Tim (Herbert Khaury) – 16, 92, 99-102, 104, 107, 116-119, 126-127, 130-131, 138, 143-144, 150, 157, 174-177, 181, 197-203, 207-208, 210-212, 218-226, 228, 230, 233- 245, 247, 250, 257, 316, 320-321, 323, 326-327, 330-340, 343-45, 347-351, 354-357, 366-368, 371, 373-382, 386, 391, 395-398, 401-406, 409-423, 425, 429, 432-434, 434-440, 442, 445, 449-452, 454-455, 457-458, 460-461, 466-468, 472-474, 476-477, 479, 482, 484-486, 490-492, 495-497.
Tiny Tim's Christmas Album – 411-412, 415, 417, 419-421, 439.
Tiny Tim's Second Album – 126, 174, 335, 491.
Tiny Tim Times – 408.
Tipperary – 239.
Tiptoe Through the Tulips – 100, 104, 117, 237, 252, 333, 350, 376, 381, 409-410, 413, 415, 457.
Toad – 104.
Togima Leasing P/L – 315.
Tommy – 177.
Tom Petty & the Heartbreakers – 367.
Toohey, Brian – 360.
Townshend, Pete – 90, 177, 201, 224, 365.
Tracey, Dick – 70.
Traintime – 104.
Treasure, Brian – 317.
Trella, Bernadette – 405, 440.
Tremblay, Angelica (Frances Greening) – 226, 412, 414, 418, 421, 461, 468, 480-485, 487-489, 491-492.
Trials of OZ (book) – 171.
Trials of OZ (film) – 171.
Trials of OZ (off-Broadway production) – 171.
Trouble in Molopolis – 122, 171, 176.
True Records – 240.
Tsai, Yensoon – 346, 348, 350, 354, 357-359, 365, 369, 371, 379, 382, 418.
Twist, The – 34.
Tucker, Albert – 36, 40, 60.
Tully – 124-125, 135, 150, 224.
Tunnicliffe, Wayne – 468-469.
Turner, Joseph – 81.
Turquoise, Maureen – 347.
Twice Upon a Time - 87, 102.
Twiggy – 108, 114.
Two Innocents Abroad, the Adventures of Martin and Richard – 76.
Two Innocents Abroad, Part 2 – 76.

U

Ubu Films – 71, 124, 140.
UFO Club – 80, 99, 103.
Uluru (Ayers Rock) – 200, 341, 373, 424.
University of New South Wales – 37, 41, 43, 137.
University of New South Wales Revue – 72, 74.
University of New South Wales Roundhouse - 42, 152.
University of Sydney – 34, 38-39, 41, 43, 137, 140, 145, 151, 158, 185, 232.
University of Wollongong – 108, 128.
The Unexpected Answer (Whaam) – 157, 190.
The Unseen Beatles – 59, 82, 97.
Untitled Red Painting – 37, 142.
Ure Smith Publisher – 77.
Utamaro – 180.
Utzon, Jan – 425, 456.
Utzon, Jorn – 70-71, 191, 193, 351, 356, 408, 412, 425-426, 456, 496.
Utzon, Lin – 326, 351, 364, 367, 408, 412, 425, 437, 442, 452, 456, 482, 485-486.
Utzon, Mika – 437, 485.

V

Vadim, Roger – 130.
Vadim's Restaurant – 33, 35, 40, 47, 58.
Vallee, Rudy – 117, 220, 321.
Van Gogh, Theo – 110, 181,.
Van Gogh, Vincent – 13, 28, 87, 107, 109-110, 118, 121, 128, 135-137, 140, 142, 152, 157, 161, 181, 200-201, 219, 223, 226, 240,
Van Gogh-Bonger, Johanna – 110.
Van Rijn, Rembrandt – 151.
Van Wieringen, Ian – 42-43.
Vaude Villians – 335.
Vehka Aho, Eija – 83, 110, 382, 442.
Velvet Underground – 107.
Venetian Twins – 334.
Vermeer, Johannes – 128.
The Very Best of Cream – 104.
Victoria and Albert Museum – 180.
Village Theatre – 99.
Van Gogh, Vincent – 342, 344, 351, 363, 369, 371, 385, 389-392, 405, 420, 425-426, 455, 473, 485, 492, 495, 497.
Vincent van Gogh (collage) – 152, 201, 342, 344, 351, 389.
Visions – 233, 321.

Vizard – 485, 402.
Visions of Johanna – 79.
Vogue – 177.
The Volares – 417.
Voorman, Klaus – 82.
Voss – 36.

W

Wahroonga Lady and Her Naked Lunch – 73.
Wake In Fright – 183.
Waks, Candice – 375.
Waks, Nathan – 236-239, 240, 242, 325, 337, 375-376, 440.
Walken, Christopher – 364.
Walker, John – 200.
Walker, Kath (Oodgeroo Nunnuccal) – 335.
Waller, Fats – 155.
Walsh, Janthia – 69.
Walsh, Maggie – 459-460, 485, 488.
Walsh, Richard (Ritchie) – 19, 28, 37-38, 41-42, 44, 47-48, 50-52, 55-56, 63, 65-66, 73, 76, 95, 102-103, 105, 115, 123-125, 194, 204, 324, 358, 364, 419, 446, 454, 488, 495.
Walsh, Sue, (née Phillips) – 103.
Ward, Phil – 354-357, 370.
Warhol, Andy – 56, 84, 104, 107, 128, 145, 180-181, 195, 327, 368, 469.
Warwick Electronics – 90.
Waterlow, Nick – 446, 458, 474.
Waters, Darcy – 35.
Watters Gallery – 73, 154.
Watts, Charlie – 130, 189.
Waverley College – 254, 359, 465.
Waymouth, Nigel - 121, 127, 296.
Weaver, Jackie – 208.
Webster, John – 134.
Weekes, Trevor – 358.
Weight, Alex – 326.
Weight, Greg – 32, 58, 67-68, 72-73, 75, 88, 125, 133, 139-140, 145, 148-154, 158, 164, 167, 184, 186-187, 204-205, 318, 325-326, 365, 381, 384-387, 389-392, 395, 401, 405, 418, 423, 427, 435, 440, 445, 450-451, 456, 472, 480, 485, 491-492.
Weight, Minyo – 326, 399, 402.
Weight, Osha – 326.
Weight, Richard (Dicky) – 140-141, 144-145, 150-151, 162, 165, 167, 186, 386, 405, 427, 472.
Weight, Suzie (née Cuthbert) – 87-88, 184, 326, 365, 395.

Weir, Peter – 140, 176, 205, 207-208, 225, 364, 390.
Well All Right – 126.
We'll Meet Again – 376.
Welles, Orson – 10.
Wentworth, William Charles – 340.
Westwood, Vivienne – 173,.
We've Been Told Jesus Is Coming Soon – 224.
Whalley, Jason – 391.
Wheels of Fire – 97-99, 101, 103-104, 112, 124.
Wherrett, Richard – 185, 191, 195-196, 235.
Whild, James – 248.
While My Guitar Gently Weeps – 113.
Whistler, James – 128.
Whitaker, Robert (Bob) – 59-61, 75, 77, 80-83, 87, 91-92, 95-97, 103, 110, 112, 120, 446, 480, 493-494.
Whitborne, Tim – 112.
White Album, The (actually titled *The Beatles*) – 107, 113.
White, Patrick, 36, 234, 321, 323, 356-357, 395.
Whiteley, Arkie – 151, 158, 251, 326, 436.
Whiteley, Brett – 32, 36-37, 142, 149-151, 154, 158-159, 167, 176, 184, 186, 188-189, 211, 216, 251, 323, 325, 333, 338, 340, 357, 365, 367-368, 374, 384, 386, 389-392, 401, 404-405, 423, 426-427, 446.
Whiteley, Wendy – 142, 158, 167, 251, 357, 404, 446.
White Room – 104.
Whiter Shade of Pale, A – 86.
Whitlam, Gough – 183, 186, 434, 488.
Whittingslow Amusement Group – 406.
Who, The – 90, 130, 177.
Wighton, Rosemary – 65.
Wild Life in Suburbia – 31.
Wild One (song) – 26.
The Wild One (film) – 26.
Wilde, Oscar – 81.
Wilkinson, Michael – 438-440.
Williams, Carl – 126.
Williams, Esther – 27.
Williams, Fred – 60.
Williams, Robin – 364.
Wills, David – 131, 170.
Wilson, Carla – 354, 367.
Wilson, Gahan – 249.
Wilson, Peewee – 347, 354, 363, 367.
Wind in the Willows – 321.
Winmatti, Nipper – 355.

Winwood, Steve – 126.
Wirian, 3 Victoria Road, Bellevue Hill – 4-8, 18, 26, 35, 105, 133, 166, 187, 191, 203-204, 207, 209-215, 218-226, 229-231, 236-237, 240, 246-247, 252, 315, 317-319, 323, 325-328, 330-331, 336, 338-339, 345-351, 353-361, 364-366, 368, 371-373, 375, 378-379, 381-382, 386, 389, 395-402, 404-405, 407-409, 411, 417-418, 421-423, 425-426, 431-432, 434-435, 437-438, 440-441, 443-445, 450-451, 459-462, 465-467, 477-478, 480, 483-485, 487, 491-492, 497.
Witzig, Paul – 54, 176.
Wolfgramm, Robert – 347, 351, 354, 356, 418, 420-421, 465-466.
Wonderful World of Romance – 240, 334, 349, 439, 460, 473.
Wood, Sue – 42.
Woodward, Claude – 403.
Word Flashed Around the Arms, The – 54-55, 64.
Worker's Club Newcastle – 198-199.
World Non-Stop Singing Marathon – 220-221, 234, 236-238, 240-246, 376.
World Trade Centre P/L – 181.
Wran, Jill (Hickson) – 351, 474.
Wran, Neville – 66, 217, 231-232, 246, 248, 255, 417, 419, 474.
Wran Marcia, Wran – 417.
Wright, Mandy – 251, 461.
Wright, Peter – 142, 144, 151, 155, 167, 251, 315, 385, 390-392, 426-427, 436, 461, 490.

#

Yang, William – 207, 209-211, 230, 237, 239, 246, 325, 328, 330-331, 335, 339, 343, 345-346, 350, 357-359, 365, 370, 382, 467, 472.
Yardbirds – 88.
Yarrow, Peter – 100.
Yellow House Catalogue – 166.
Yellow House – 19, 24, 28, 45, 72, 121, 128, 135-136, 139-177, 184, 186-190, 198, 207, 216, 224, 230, 234, 247, 314-315, 319, 323-325, 337, 340, 348, 357, 370, 374, 398-399, 405, 419, 426, 436, 441-443, 448, 454, 472, 477, 479, 487, 489-490, 496.
Yellow House Retrospective (AGNSW) – 45, 153, 379. 381, 383-395.

Yesterday and Today ('the Butcher Cover') – 82.
Young Mo – 225, 334.

Z

Zappa, Frank - 104.
Zero Communications – 126, 148, 153, 166.

www.ingramcontent.com/pod-product-compliance
Lightning Source LLC
Chambersburg PA
CBHW030329240426
43661CB00052B/1570